Best Broadcasts of 1938-39

Best Broadcasts

of 1938-39

Selected and Edited by

MAX WYLIE

Director of Script and Continuity,
Columbia Broadcasting System;
Lecturer, New York University
Radio Workshop

WITH A FOREWORD BY

NEVILLE MILLER

President, National Association
of Broadcasters

New York WHITTLESEY HOUSE *London*

MCGRAW-HILL BOOK COMPANY, INC.

PUBLISHED BY WHITTLESEY HOUSE
A division of the McGraw-Hill Book Company, Inc.

Printed in the United States of America by the Maple Press Co., York, Pa.

Preface

IT IS indeed ironical that fifteen years of scheduled broadcasting have left so little behind them in the way of permanent record. The first dignified and respectable anthology of radio material appeared only a few months ago. It was a collection of fourteen dramas produced by the Columbia Workshop, selected and edited for publication by Douglas Coulter, Associate Director of Broadcasts of the Columbia Broadcasting System. This book was carefully prepared, and it truthfully represents the best efforts of one of America's outstanding radio institutions. It is distinguished also for its unusual readability and great variety of mood, and it is not likely to be surpassed in its special class for many years. The book is concerned with the presentation of dramatic material only.

In compiling the *Best Broadcasts of* 1938–39, it has been my intention to offer to the public for the first time a collection of superior programs representing all the major subdivisions in which the written word and the spoken word express themselves over the air. It will perhaps be charged that the classifications into which this volume falls are arbitrarily arrived at. This is partly true. The circumstance springs from the inescapable fact that what I consider to be the significant piece and the significant department might be considered by some other critic to be without significance. In this regard the book will have to speak for itself. Beyond saying that I believe this effort to be a true cross section of radio enterprise as we know it today, I shall bring no other defense to the selections that make it up.

The preparation of this work was a matter of sixteen months of reading. It was, of course, impossible to read or to hear every show originating in this country during the period covered by the book, but over six thousand individual properties were examined. Thirty-two have been reprinted. The experience was a considerable chore because it was necessary to eat so much stale popcorn before finding a prize. But the findings compensated for the search, and if the following pages bring to the reader the conviction that I hold myself—that there is much in radio that deserves to be perpetuated in print—that in itself will be sufficient reward for anything this collection may have cost in lost week ends and lonely nights.

The scarcity of the good radio script is something that is known and understood by most professional broadcasters, but laymen so frequently ask why radio plays aren't better than they are that the question may as well be answered here quickly and simply. Radio scripts aren't written by the best writers. That is why they aren't better than they are. There is a great deal of bad writing in American radio (as there is in radio all over the world), but this fact reflects neither shame upon nor lack of interest in the industry, for radio is in the business of pleasing multitudes a great part of the time, and multitudes prefer the banal and the inferior to the beautiful and the superior. The great mass of mankind is not congenitally appreciative; the average person is not discriminating. Good things bore him or embarass him because he cannot comprehend them. He cannot grow into a preferred acceptance of excellence without a corresponding growth in himself, and this kind of growth happens usually through application and study. Few are sufficiently searching and critical to discover for themselves those things of enduring value.

This argument is not offered in defense of broadcast policies. I do not believe that the existing policies in network broadcasting require much defense, and I say this because radio policy derives from the will of the listener and never from the caprice of executives. Executives merely put into operation the code of prohibitions and preferences created by public interest.

I have stated, however, that in radio much time is spent in transmitting banal entertainment, and no group would be quicker to acknowledge this fact than the broadcasters themselves. Now—if radio felt that its public responsibility had been discharged with the satisfying of all the poor taste in America, then it would be and should be subject to censure. I do not need to point out to the reader that this is not true or to enumerate the many fine things to be heard daily in every part of the country. At the same time there is a persistent complaint that the literature of radio is pretty junky and that somebody ought to do something about it. Since this is precisely the problem to which I devote all my time and energy, I should like to state a simple, ineluctable fact that the detractors of radio have not bothered to notice. If these critics of radio literature would stop rifling at radio and, instead, send a load of bird shot into the general region of the entire literary migration, they would bring down a couple of trophies worth stuffing for a more unhurried study.

The over-all view will, of course, reveal that most radio literature is tripe. But here is an item that is hard to get around: the over-all view of *any* field of writing will reveal that most of its literature is tripe. A hundred and seventy-four plays were produced in Greater New York last year. Most of them failed; most of them were tripe. Most movies are tripe; most novels are tripe; most stories are tripe. So is most poetry. This is not alarming. Or if it is, literature has been in an alarming state since Josephus.

Although I believe this to be true, it would be the rankest sort of tergiversation to excuse radio's literary delinquency on the grounds that others were equally delinquent, and I haven't any intention of doing so. Radio is quite as aware of the problem of the good script as is the publisher of fiction, the director of motion pictures, or the producer of plays. We all want the same thing: the best possible property; we all accept the same thing: the best obtainable.

But radio does have script problems peculiar to itself. The problem of impermanence is one. The problem of money is another. The problem of delivering regularly and quickly is still another. And a fourth—which is gradually disappearing—is this unfortunate and undeserved stigma: radio does not as yet enjoy a respectable place in the personal opinion of a large proportion of America's first-class writers. Many writers whose services have been hopefully invited by radio people have turned down the invitation cuttingly and with scorn. Most of this response is due to their own ignorance of what is going on in the business; some of it is due to fear; and a little of it, to their disinclination to work for less money than they are in the habit of getting and, at the same time, to work in a medium they consider unfamiliar.

I have sympathy with some of the reservations that certain writers feel in regard to radio. If a writer is writing solely to make money and if he is making a great deal, one can understand his not wanting to be bothered with radio writing. Similarly, if a writer is writing for the purpose of creating a great body of work and of enjoying the attendant prestige that this will someday afford him, one can understand this attitude, too. Such a writer's radio work will die with the program's sign-off. The impermanence of the work and the anonymity of the writer represent two of the greatest handicaps of radio in attracting established writers to the industry. A third handicap is the demand of radio for frequent and uninterrupted output. To work any writer beyond his capacity for normal output is certain to emasculate his powers. All writers are in a sense wells of inventiveness, and their creative flow is in most cases measurable, predictable, and constant. To force this flow beyond its natural rate of production adulterates it. Sludge comes up, not oil.

Alexander Woollcott has been writing every day for thirty years, but radio drained him dry, and he had to take time out to refill. In Mr. Woollcott's defense—not that he needs any—it should be added that it took radio nearly three years to empty him. Channing Pollock, "dean of American playwrights," undertook a weekly one-hour original. It nearly killed him. "It's over half of a full-length play," he said. "It takes me six months to write a play." There you have it. These two men, both of front-rank prominence in their respective fields, both of them craftsmen with the most exacting habits of work, were finally pinioned by radio, the most regular and voracious consumer of material in the world's history of entertainment. Woollcott and Pollock are in no way exceptions. Both of them have fine contributions to make in radio. They have already done so—Woollcott especially—and will again. But they can't turn it on forever and at will. Nobody can. Radio has to wait for the good thing.

I hope this book will do something toward removing from the darkness of anonymity a few names that have every right to be known. I hope it will also do something toward preserving written material that has every right to be preserved long after its last syllable has been pronounced by an actor. I should like to say here, too, that radio today is sufficiently flexible to take the work of the best workmen whenever they can find time to write for us. This means that the true craftsman can ignore the enervating insistence of dead lines; that he can work according to his own humor; that he can work in his own time. After all, it is the writer who matters most, for it is he who provides functions for all the others who make up a show. None can have existence without him. He alone creates; the rest are translators, interpreters, transmitters, imitators; surely something less than inventors. Most acting is a domestic science; little of it is creative. Acting can exist only after something else already living, and acting is important only in so far as it reveals the meaning in the material it activates. As all broadcasters know, to wait for good material is a chancy assignment, but even so, such attendance has had its gratifications, and I have set them down here as I have found them.

Waiting for the good thing has brought to the American radio audience much that is rich and beautiful, much that is exciting, and much that deserves equal rank with the best of present-day work in any field. Radio has delivered fine work by Wilbur Daniel Steele, Maxwell Anderson, Carl Sandburg, William Saroyan, Dorothy Parker, J. P. Marquand, Stephen Vincent Benét, William Rose Benét, Lord Dunsany, Albert Maltz, William March, Percival Wilde, Edwin Granberry, Carl Carmer, Marc Connelly, T. S. Stribling, Paul Green, Zora Neal Hurston, DuBose Heyward, Hendrick Van Loon, Hamlin Garland, Robert Frost, Phil Stong, Ernest Hemingway, James Gould Cozzens, Hilaire Belloc, Eric Knight, Pare Lorentz, T. S. Eliot, Sutton Vane, Frank O'Connor, Richard Connell, Stanley Young, Mary Ellen Chase, Evelyn Waugh, and a great many more I can't remember. I hope that this list will indicate to some extent the exploratory enterprise of the industry as well as the conscientiousness with which the pursuit of good material is being prosecuted. This pursuit will continue as long as radio enterprise endures.

There are other aspects and other values to be mentioned. The service rendered by American broadcasters is so regular and so varied that most listeners are spoiled by its excellence. In America, radio actually amounts to the most hopeful symbol of democracy on earth today. It is human, newsy, informative, and disciplined; it is codified but not regimented; it is robust but not stiff. It is, in short, the great parabolic reflector of the needs and emotions of a great people, and it will change exactly and immediately with changes in these needs and emotions. Vague people in lofty offices don't run American radio. It is run by its listening public. That is its guarantee of service; that is its promise of improvement; that is its degree of permanence.

As I write these few pages of introduction, something of the pandemic power of the industry is carried to my ears by a portable set that sits under a striped umbrella thirty yards down the beach on a lonely scree of scrub and sand dune somewhere south of Cape Cod. Yesterday morning for many hours the stretched voice of Hitler bruised the atmosphere with another broadside of his inane insanities and insane inanities. This morning the voice is an English voice, composed, tired, almost perfunctory. Is it war we hear declared or the momentary postponement of war? Whatever the news may be, it is shooting into every state in this nation simultaneously with its reception here, and it is revealing honestly and continuosly the truth of what is happening. The technique in news coverage of the Czechoslovakian crisis over a year ago will not only be duplicated but improved upon with the coming of a new international upheaval, and the American public will receive, hour by hour, more accurate reports of world affairs than any people in the world.

The arrangement of the programs reprinted in this anthology has sought to departmentalize material, *sui generis,* whenever such grouping seemed sensible and appropriate, but generally no great emphasis has been placed upon sequence. The book contains properties of every sort, and the order in which they have been set down has been determined by reasons of variety and of contrast in theme, length, and mood. There is one conspicuous omission in this collection. There is no Charlie McCarthy sketch. I very much wanted to include the "Oliver Twist" spot—probably the funniest single piece of nonsense of the past year—but it was impossible to clear the material. A few other properties—mainly local educational programs of merit—could not be incorporated because of page restrictions. However, the book represents American radio in its widest ranges, and I hope it will bring enjoyment to the lay reader.

I trust, too, that educators whose energies are being used in this same medium will find something here that is instructive. Perhaps the now famous quotation of President Robert M. Hutchins of the University of Chicago will become obsolete. Two years ago before the National Conference on Educational Broadcasting he said, "The trouble with educational broadcasting is that the programs are no good." The statement was disputed by very few. In a dozen words he had completely expressed an opinion entertained by over a hundred million listeners. Many of the programs are still no good. Some aren't so bad as they were, and a few are excellent. The educational field is still the most expansive unexplored territory of radio, and, through cooperation between professional broadcasters and America's teachers, it will be in this field that radio's next great advances will be made. I hope it will soon be possible to tell Mr. Hutchins that the condition of educational broadcasting is not a chronic headache but merely a momentary migraine.

MAX WYLIE.

Contents

CONTENTS

xiv

Foreword

THE collection of broadcasts here presented will bring forcibly to the lay reader an acceptance of the known but neglected fact that in its daily service to the public radio is constantly producing material not only amazing in its scope but rich and various in its literature. Max Wylie's selection of the *Best Broadcasts of* 1938–39 is a timely, sensible, and truthful representation of the industry's output in the range of its interests and the quality of its workmanship.

Every accepted type and form of broadcast has been included from the best talk to the best variety program, and each appears in its uncut "as broadcast" version. In length these vary from a few minutes to a full hour. But it is the sharp juxtaposition of contrasting themes that compels and sustains the reader's interest. One moves from the elucidating remarks of Raymond Gram Swing on the post-Munich situation to the curling metaphors of MacLeish's poetry; from an eye-witness description of the rescue of the *Squalus* survivors to the jostling nonsense of Fred Allen's Town Hall. The book is by turns sober and exciting, fanciful and realistic, an authentic reflection of the mood and purpose of contemporary broadcasting in America.

That there is so much good writing in radio today will surprise many of the readers of this volume. That it has here been set down permanently for the pleasure of the average reader and for the critical attention of the student of the techniques of the industry is one of the happiest contributions in many years to the health of broadcast enterprise. I feel confident that the anthology of broadcasts will establish itself as a regular annual collection and take its proper place beside its cousins of the stage and the short story. During the past twenty years radio has delivered to America's loud-speakers many hundreds of superior properties that are now forever lost to the public. With the appearance of the *Best Broadcasts of* 1938–39 there is assurance that the good things of radio have found and will continue to find the perpetuation they rightly merit. As one impartially concerned with the freedom of the medium, the improvement of its skills, and the health of its future, the present volume is to me both gratifying and prophetic.

NEVILLE MILLER,
President, National Association
of Broadcasters.

Best Broadcasts of 1938-39

BEST SHORT STORY ADAPTATION
(COMEDY)

Surprise for the Boys

by HERBERT LEWIS

Adapted for radio by VICTOR SMITH

"SURPRISE for the Boys" has been selected for reprinting not only for the comic excellence of the story itself but for the strong evidence of technical mastery in every scene of the adaptation. The basic idea of the story is simple; a dour and colorless convict, awaiting execution at Sing Sing, cheats the chair by telling his executioners that he has just swallowed a small cylinder of fulminate of mercury which will blow up the entire jail the instant an electric current passes through his body.

The comedy situations created by the author (Herbert Lewis, in *Esquire Magazine*) were considerable; but for successful conversion to radio the task of performing the complete story in dialogue, of keeping clearly before the listener the identity of fast scenes as they shift back and forth between the death house and the city room of a newspaper, of alternating scenes described and scenes dramatized, of maintaining suspense and of steadily accelerating pace—this task has also been considerable. From the point of view of broadcasting, the brilliance with which this has been effected marks the adapter, Victor Smith, as an extremely competent professional in this field.

"Surprise for the Boys" was heard over station WOR and the Mutual Network on Sunday, March 6, 1938, from 8:00 to 8:30 P.M. It was the first in a series of short story adaptations conceived, arranged, and presented by the Radio Division of the WPA Federal Theatre Project under the personal supervision of Leslie Evan Roberts, director of the Federal Theatre Radio Division in New York.

3

Surprise for the Boys*

(Open cold on mike)

SOUND.—*Jiggling of telephone hook.*

FALLOW.—(*Impatiently*) Hello! Hello! Hello! . . . operator!

OPERATOR.—(*On filtered mike*) This is the operator.

DIRECTION.—*All following speeches except Fallow's on filtered mike until otherwise indicated.*

FALLOW.—I've been cut off, operator. I was talkin' to the Journal city desk.

OPERATOR.—(*Formally*) I will try to get your party. . . .

SOUND.—*Clicking of plugging in and out.*

OPERATOR.—Here is your party.

FALLOW.—Hello! Hello . . . Brady! This is Fallow again. I was cut off.

BRADY.—You weren't cut off, Fallow. I hung up. I told you we don't want it. . . . We can't use it.

FALLOW.—What do you mean you don't want it? Am I your state prison correspondent or ain't I?

BRADY.—Of course you are, Fallow. . . . Sure you are. You can shoot the story in to the day side tomorrow.

FALLOW.—Oh, so it's the run-around. The day city desk tells me to give it to you at night, and now you tell me to give it to them tomorrow. Well, it won't be news tomorrow. The guy's dyin' right now.

BRADY.—But I tell you the story's not worth . . .

FALLOW.—Listen, Brady. . . . I been your state prison man for 23 years, and I never once missed phonin' in a burnin'. Not once.

* Copyright, 1938, by *Esquire Magazine.*

4

BRADY.—I know, Fallow . . . but even as an execution this one doesn't rate. Besides, we're already protected. A.P. is covering.

FALLOW.—I *know* A.P.'s covering. *I'm* A.P. up here. I'm A.P., U.P., I.N.S., N.A.N.A., and the Jewish Telegraphic Agency. I'm even Nippon Dempo when there's a good Jap angle.

BRADY.—Then you'll be supplying the story anyway . . . as part of the regular service. Why should we pay you when we're paying A.P. and *they're* paying you?

FALLOW.—How do you expect me to make both ends meet if you don't give me a break on burnings? I got a wife and three kids. I don't expect to phone in a Damon Runyon story. I just wanna make my usual five slugs. What the devil's the newspaper business coming to if a guy can't make five slugs out of a burning any more?

BRADY.—If you want the truth, Fallow, the yarn's not worth five. . . . It's a piece of tripe.

FALLOW.—It *ain't* a piece of tripe. The guy's a human being, ain't he? Is that a nice way to talk about a human being?

BRADY.—Any murder that was worth only two paragraphs when it was fresh is *still* a piece of tripe, for my money.

FALLOW.—Say. . . . This guy got *more* than two paragraphs the day he killed his landlord in Chemicville. It was a *big* story up there.

BRADY.—Well . . . it was just an item to us. Forget it.

FALLOW.—You talk like I was tryin' to sell you a stink bomb. Everybody who knows me knows Pete Fallow doesn't do business that way. This story's got a lot of swell angles. F'rinstance, the guy . . .

BRADY.—Wait a minute! Did you have these phone charges reversed?

FALLOW.—What do you think I am, a millionaire? I got a wife and . . .

BRADY.—Never mind. . . . I've got to show something for these phone charges. . . . Give the story to Stewart on rewrite . . . and make it snappy!

5

FALLOW.—O.K., O.K., I'll make it snappy. Just switch me over.

SOUND.—*Clicking of telephone receiver . . . circuit plugged in.*

OPERATOR.—Yes, please?

BRADY.—Operator, transfer this call to Stewart on the rewrite desk.

OPERATOR.—Thank you.

SOUND.—*Buzz of ringing . . . click of lifted receiver.*

STEWART.—Hello.

FALLOW.—Stew?

STEWART.—Right. Who's this?

FALLOW.—Fallow.

STEWART.—Hi. How's the wife and kids?

FALLOW.—All doing nicely.

STEWART.—What's on your mind?

FALLOW.—I'm callin' from the state prison. Execution. Ready?

STEWART.—Go ahead. Shoot.

FALLOW.—Say, Stew, don't tell Brady, but just between you and me this is the biggest hunk o' limburger I ever phoned in in my 23 years as state prison correspondent. All I want is a couple o' paragraphs so I can make my fin. Honest, I don't know what the execution business is comin' to when they burn guys like this. I've wracked my brains, but I can't find a spot o' color in this, and if you know me you know this is the first time *that* ever happened.

STEWART.—Come on. . . . Let's have it. What's the yarn?

FALLOW.—The guy's name is Waldemar Kossciuhowicz.

STEWART.—Whoa! Take it easy! Spell it out.

FALLOW.—Sure, I know I gotta spell it. What a name! You can't even get a good American name in the papers any more these days. Why don't these guys go back where they came from? Kossciuhowicz. It's pronounced just like I'm saying it . . . Koss-kee-hoe-itz . . . with the accent on the hoe. The Waldemar is with a doubleyou,

6

and then comes the Kossciuhowicz . . . K for Karpis, O for Ossining, double S for Sing Sing, C for Capone . . .

STEWART.—Say, what are you tryin' to give me, a build-up?

FALLOW.—All right, Stew, all right. I ain't tryin' to build it up, honest. Spell it any way you like. . . . It don't make no difference. Anyway, everybody up here calls him Kosky. . . . It makes things a lot easier.

STEWART.—I can imagine it would.

FALLOW.—Twenty-nine years old. First-degree murder, Chemicville, last September.

STEWART.—Chemicville? Never heard of it.

FALLOW.—Why, Chemicville is the biggest village in the state.

STEWART.—No foolin'!

FALLOW.—Kosky killed the landlord with an ice pick. He claimed the landlord dispossessed his old lady, and as a result she froze to death. No defense. Unmarried. No woman in the case at all . . . not even a wife. No appeal. And so help me, Stew, Kosky didn't even ask for executive clemency.

STEWART.—Must be a queer duck.

FALLOW.—You oughta see Kosky. A big lump of a guy who ain't said two words since they showed him into the death house last winter. In all my three decays up here I never see a mug with less interest. Why, I bet you ain't even got his murder in the clips. Think o' that.

STEWART.—I am thinkin' . . . and wonderin' where the story's comin' from. You're not much help, Fallow.

FALLOW.—I'm givin' you all I've got. The only visitor he ever had was his sister. She came here this mornin' to say good-by, but the guards tell me they didn't even talk . . . only held hands for a couple of minutes, and that's all. That shows what a state prison man you've got in me, Stew. Tell this to Brady. Another reporter would o' tried to build this story up . . . F'rinstance, Kosky worked in a chemical factory, and there could be an angle to that. . . . You know, killin' the landlord with chemicals, maybe . . . but with me the truth is the truth. I got a reputation to hold up, Stew.

STEWART.—Sure . . . oh, sure.

FALLOW.—I'll tell you something. Why, they din't even have to shave Kosky's head for the hot seat electrode, 'cause he turned out to be bald in just the right place.

STEWART.—Is that right?

FALLOW.—Sure, and I'll tell you something else you won't believe . . . but it's true, take my word for it. . . . Kosky didn't even have a last supper.

STEWART.—Well, well.

FALLOW.—That shows what I'm up against these days. A couple o' years ago a last supper was always good for five slugs with any sheet in the country. But today not only don't some sheets not want last suppers no more, but guys like Kosky come along who don't even eat 'em. What a man!

STEWART.—One of those guys who can take it or leave it alone.

FALLOW.—The guard asks him what he wants for last supper. "You can have everything and anything," he tells Kosky, "but I recommend the roast turkey with chestnut dressing and cranberry sauce, 'cause that's what the others usually take." And do you know what Kosky said?

STEWART.—I'll bite.

FALLOW.—He says, "Just bring me some bread and butter." After that they ask him if he wants to see the chaplain in private and he shakes his head, no. Well, Stew, in just about 3 minutes Kosky will be on the hot seat. I guess it won't make no difference to him and the rest of us, 'cause the guy's been dead from the neck up for a long, long time. I bet he wouldn't even make a Monday feature. I'm discouraged, Stew. Well, I guess I'll hang up now and call back with the flash when he burns.

STEWART.—Wait a minute, Fallow. . . . We're not very busy here. . . . You might as well keep the line open.

FALLOW.—O.K. Say . . . if you want, just to pass the time, I'll give you a blow-by-blow account o' this burning.

STEWART.—Sure, go ahead.

FALLOW.—There ain't a single newspaperman except me up here. I'm phonin' as usual from the seat of honor which took

8

me 20 years to wangle. You remember, Stew, I showed it to you the time you was up here . . . the seat by the glass window that looks into the execution chamber.

STEWART.—Sure . . . I remember.

FALLOW.—On big executions Warden Roth shuts the window and don't let me use the phone at my elbow, on account of some of the other boys might claim special privileges. But on small burnings like this he don't give a damn. The window's open a little, and I can look right in and down on the oak electric chair fitted with that screwy plush headrest . . . but on account of the window is heavily glazed none of the bigwig politicians in the witness stand can see me. In fact, nobody except the warden knows I'm up here lookin' down on what's goin' on.

STEWART.—Who's viewin' the festivities?

FALLOW.—Oh, the warden didn't have no trouble roundin' up 10 witnesses for this burning, as small as it is. Steve Blathery, the biggest and crookedest politician in Anatomie County is among those present, as usual, with a bunch of his ward heelers. Blathery likes watchin' 'em burn. Father McCauley is standin' on the rubber mat in the center o' the concrete floor. The warden's standin' in the corner lookin' tired. Burnings always make him sick. Dr. Sugar and Dr. Blint are in the other corner with their deathoscopes. Four or five guards are scattered around the room.

STEWART.—Just a nice, happy, domestic scene. And what about the honored guest?

FALLOW.—Here he comes. . . . Here comes Kosky now. This is hot. He's comin' through the death house door, and do you know what the sign on that door says?

STEWART.—All right . . . I'll bite again.

FALLOW.—It says . . . *silence*. Ain't that a pay-off? As if you need a sign to keep Kosky quiet. Two guards are escortin' him in . . . one in front and one in back . . . and he's comin' very quiet. There won't be no trouble with Kosky at all, Stew. Take my word for it. Say, are you still listenin'?

STEWART.—Sure, I'm listenin' . . . but I ain't heard nothin' startlin' yet.

9

FALLOW.—Well, it'll all be over in about 2 minutes. Pettigrew, the executioner, has stepped away from the control board. . . . That's at the far wall. . . . And now he's dustin' off the hot seat. You oughta see Kosky glide over to that seat! There won't be no trouble . . . no trouble at all, Stew. He's walkin' like in a dream. . . . He's practically tiptoein' those last couple o' steps to the hot seat like he was scared o' disturbin' his own last thoughts. Father McCauley starts comin' over to him, but Kosky shakes his head and waves the priest away. A funny lunkhead Kosky is, Stew.

STEWART.—I'll take your word for it.

FALLOW.—You oughta see 'im. . . . He's smilin' . . . a happy smile, like he was glad the fatal moment has come. Pettigrew has just pushed Kosky down onto the hot seat, and Kosky acts a little scared when old Pet touches him. But he sits down all right without makin' no demonstration. Old Pet has stepped back, and I can see the two guards fastenin' the leg electrodes on poor Kosky. The headrest'll be on him in another minute. You know, Stew, I actually feel sorry for Kosky.

STEWART.—Goin' soft in your old age.

FALLOW.—No kiddin', I do. . . . He's so helpless. Just a big hunk o' flesh and bones without no brains. Why do guys who can't afford good lawyers go around killin' people? Well, no use feelin' sorry for him now. Old Pet is walkin' over to put the black mask on Kosky's face, and in just one more . . . Holy Smokes! *Holy Smokes!* Stew! *Stew!* STEW!

STEWART.—Whatsa matta? What's breakin'?

FALLOW.—Stew, for Pete's sake . . . stop the presses! Have Brady listen in on the extension! Get ready to replate! Holy Smokes! What a story! *And I got it exclusive!*

(*Fade out*)

DIRECTION.—*From this point only Fallow's speeches on filtered mike until otherwise indicated.*

(*Fade in*)

BRADY.—Hello! Hello! *Hello* . . . Fallow?

FALLOW.—Yeah . . . this is Fallow. Who's this?

BRADY.—This is Brady. What's the matter? What's happened!

FALLOW.—Plenty! You know that guy, Kosky . . . the one they were going to burn? Well, he swallowed dynamite!

BRADY.—*What!* Kosky . . . swallowed . . . dynamite! What do you mean? Are you nuts? How can a man swallow dynamite?

FALLOW.—In a cylinder . . . and it wasn't exactly dynamite . . . it was fulminate of mercury.

BRADY.—Fulminate of mercury, you say. *Fulminate of mercury!*

FALLOW.—That's a powerful explosive, ain't it?

BRADY.—Wow! Is that a powerful explosive! It's the most powerful they make. Oh, boy, what a yarn! Fallow, if you're horsing us up, I'll have you deported. Now hang right on this wire.

FALLOW.—O.K. You know me, chief.

BRADY.—Boy!

BOY.—Yes, Mr. Brady.

BRADY.—Run into the composing room. . . . Tell Ted to be ready to make over page one. Boy!

BOY.—Right here, Mr. Brady.

BRADY.—Get the managing editor. Tell him to hurry in here. Tell him a guy on the electric chair has swallowed a cylinder of double dynamite.

BOY.—Gee, whiz!

BRADY.—Tell him the guy has just told the warden if they turn on the juice he's gonna *explode* and blow everybody to hell. (*Fade out*)

DIRECTION.—*All following speeches except Fallow's on filtered mike until otherwise indicated.*
(*Fade in*)

FALLOW.—Hello! Hello . . . Stew? This is Fallow.

STEWART.—O.K., kid, shoot.

FALLOW.—Lemme catch my breath. Now, in the first place, yell over and tell Brady I'll give you this exclusive for 100 fish. Not a penny less. If he tries to bargain I'll hang up and call the opposition. . . .

STEWART.—Now, don't do anything rash, Fallow. Wait a second. . . . I'll ask him. He's right here. O.K. He says it's O.K.

FALLOW.—Well, well, that's fast work! Tell him he better not double-cross me. Now listen, Stew, and take down every word. Clamp on your earphones tight. . . . Everything is runnin' smooth in the execution chamber. The witnesses are sittin' quiet. Father McCauley is movin' his lips in prayer. And old Pet walks over to put the black mask on Kosky's face. Suddenly Kosky raises his right hand very slow and looks at the warden. . . . Then he says . . .

(*Fade out*)

DIRECTION.—*Filtered mike out entirely until further indicated.*

(*Fade in*)

KOSKY.—Pardon me for troubling you, warden, but I've got to say a few words.

WARDEN.—All right, say what you want . . . but make it snappy.

KOSKY.—Warden, you think I'm just a hunky with no brains. Well, you are wrong. I happen to be Dr. Waldemar Kossciuhowicz, Bachelor of Science from the famous University of Lodz. And I also happen, like everybody else who graduates from the famous University of Lodz, to be an expert chemist and engineer.

WARDEN.—(*Impatiently*) Well?

KOSKY.—(*Unperturbed*) Now, what I want to say is that just before coming into the death chamber I have swallowed a sealed cylinder. This cylinder contains fulminate of mercury . . . the most powerful explosive in the world . . . ten times more terrific than TNT. And it contains *enough* fulminate of mercury to blow up me and you and everybody else *in* this room and *near* this room for 300 yards around. The cylinder is the size of my thumb and is cleverly built with a detonating cap so that any sudden or violent *muscular* movement will cause the necessary spark to explode it. *Like, for instance*, the muscular spasm caused by electro-

cution. *So*, everybody please sit or stand exactly where
you are, because if anybody makes the slightest move I'm
going to hiccup and knock the walls down!
(*Fade out . . . fade in*)

FALLOW.—That is what Kosky says, Stew, word for word, and
then he shuts his mouth very slow, and a terrible silence
falls over the death chamber that is broken only by one o'
the ward heelers fallin' on the floor in a dead faint. Kosky
just sits there on the hot seat, grinnin' very funny, with the
bald spot on the top of his head shinin' like a moon on the
water. Old Pet, the mask in his hand, stands a few feet
away, his mouth wide open and his eyes glassy. All the
witnesses hunch up in their seats. The guards stand with
their big beefy hands straight down at their sides. Dr.
Sugar blinks his eyes, and Dr. Blint bites his lips. The
warden turns pale and grim, and Father McCauley stops
prayin' and just stands there, his hands clasped over his
chest. Finally the warden says . . .
(*Fade out . . . fade in huskily*)

WARDEN.—You can't get away with this Kosky. Do you think
we're all crazy fools?

SOUND.—*Ad lib murmurs in background . . . suddenly cease.*

KOSKY.—No, I don't think you are crazy, warden. I think
you are all very smart men . . . and that's why I know
you know I'm not lying.

WARDEN.—Kosky, you picked the wrong warden to pull this
trick on. Because when I was a youngster I worked in a
construction camp . . . and I happened to be the powder
monkey. So I know everything that there is to know about
explosives. And I know that what you claim won't work,
even if you did do it, and anyway I think you're lying.

KOSKY.—That's a matter of opinion, warden, and every man is
entitled to his opinion. So if you think I'm lying, or I won't
blow up, if I'm *not* lying, go right ahead and electrocute me.
I'll let Mr. Pettigrew move around for that, though I'm
warning you nobody else make the slightest move or you'll
find out soon enough I'm not lying. The second Mr. Pettigrew pulls the switch you'll all know who was right and who
was wrong. Or rather . . . you won't.

13

WARDEN.—I know all about fulminate of mercury. It's what we use in detonating caps to explode dynamite. It's a powerful explosive. *But* . . . it's absolutely harmless unless a spark hits it, and how are you gonna create a spark in the middle of your stomach? Now tell me that.

KOSKY.—Very simple, warden. There's a tiny coil inside the cylinder that is held in place by a little rod. Now any harsh muscular movement will jolt that rod and unspring the coil . . . against a little contraption that works like a cigarette lighter.

BLATHERY.—(*Off, panicky*) Cigarette lighter! (*Shrieks*)

VOICE.—(*Off*) Be a man, Blathery. We're all in the same boat.

WARDEN.—I guess you expect us to believe the cigarette lighter gadget will create the spark to set off the explosive . . . in the middle of your stomach . . . where there isn't any air.

KOSKY.—Oh, there's air, all right. It's a sealed cylinder, and there's enough air inside to feed the spark. The watchmaker who made the cylinder for me tested it and it worked fine.

WARDEN.—I guess they teach watchmaking, too, at the University of Lodz.

KOSKY.—I should say they do. That's one of their best courses.

WARDEN.—And you swallowed that big cylinder containing the explosive and the coil and the rod and the little cigarette lighter all at once down your own throat. Ha! Tell me another.

KOSKY.—Well, it wasn't very big. Not for me, anyway, because over at the University of Lodz we don't play baseball or football or anything like that, but we do have a lot of fun practicing sword swallowing. Anyway, I doused the cylinder in a lot of butter and it went down quite easily.

GUARD.—Holy Smokes! That's right! He did use a lot of butter. All he ordered for lunch was bread and butter, and I brought it to him. Only he didn't eat any of the bread.

KOSKY.—Come here, warden. Why, you can feel it. Here. . . . Feel. . . .

BLATHERY.—(*Off, shrilly*) Let me out of here!

14

VOICE.—(*Off*) That's Blathery again.

KOSKY.—(*Shouting*) Shut up! Yelling like that puts me right on the edge of blowing. (*Laughs hollowly*)
(*Fade out*)

DIRECTION.—*Fallow only on filter until further note.*
(*Fade in*)

FALLOW.—And listen, Stew, when Kosky starts to laugh you oughta see everybody duck. He's laughin' now.

SOUND.—*Faint laughter in background.*

FALLOW.—Long, loud peals of laughter. . . . Only he's managin' not to shakes his sides too much . . . I *hope*.

STEWART.—Wait a second, Fallow. . . . Brady wants the wire.

BRADY.—Hello, Fallow. . . . Now you stay right where you are because . . .

FALLOW.—Hold on now, Brady. . . . I'm not hangin' around here much longer. I don't mind sayin' I'm gettin' the jitters.

BRADY.—What! You don't mean to tell me you're scared. What kind of a newspaperman are you to be scared at a time like this? Am *I* scared? Is Stewart scared? Are you yellow, man?

FALLOW.—You don't have to worry about the walls falling on top of you.

BRADY.—What if they do fall on you? You'll be dying with your boots on, won't you? Is there a more glorious way of dying than with your boots on?

FALLOW.—I can think of quite a few.

BRADY.—Well, I have no time to argue about that now. I'll send the check to your wife if anything happens.

FALLOW.—I'll haunt you if you don't.

BRADY.—Is that a nice thing to say? Did I ever go back on my word? Now look, Fallow. You gotta keep Kosky in the death chamber for a couple of minutes. I want a personal interview. I want pictures. Find out who made the cylinder. Where did he get the idea of doing this? Find out if he's in love.

15

FALLOW.—That's a big order. What do you want for dessert?

BRADY.—Don't think we're letting you down on our road. I've got the wires burning. We're looking up all the clips and all the encyclopedias on explosives. We're contacting the head of the Bureau of Combustibles. We're getting in touch with the research head of the American Explosives Company. We're looking up all we can find about the University of Lodz. I never heard of it before. Now you yell right down to Kosky and tell him you want that interview.

FALLOW.—I won't do it, Brady, I tell you, I won't do it.

BRADY.—What do you mean you won't do it? Do it! What do you think we're paying you $50 for?

FALLOW.—A hundred, Brady. What are you tryin' to do, gyp me?

BRADY.—All right, hundred, then. I made a mistake. A slip of the tongue.

FALLOW.—(*Excitedly*) Hold on, Brady! Get this! Kosky's getting off the hot seat!

BRADY.—(*Sputtering*) What! He's getting off the hot seat!

FALLOW.—Yes! He's unstrapping the leg electrodes! He's standing up! Brady . . . did you hear me?

BRADY.—(*Bellowing*) Did I hear you! Wow! Hang on! (*Off*) Stop the presses! Another replate! (*On mike*) Are you there, Fallow?

FALLOW.—Right with you.

BRADY.—Hold on. I'll have you switched over to Stewart. Operator, put this call on Stewart's phone.
(*Fade out*)

DIRECTION.—*Stewart only on filter.*

FALLOW.—Hello, Stew? Fallow again. Plenty has happened since I spoke to you. How far did I get?

STEWART.—You said Kosky was laughing.

FALLOW.—That's right. Then he stops laughin' and just looks around, and everybody is quiet again. Now get this picture:

Warden Roth shoves his jaw forward a full 2 inches and glares at Kosky. . . .
(*Fade out*)

DIRECTION.—*Filtered mike out entirely until further indicated.*
(*Fade in*)

WARDEN.—This is a good gag, Kosky, and I'm glad to see you're enjoying yourself so much at our expense. (*Pause*) Go on with the execution, Mr. Pettigrew.

PETTIGREW.—Yes, sir . . . in my opinion, warden, this man is bluffing. In all my experience I never heard of such a fantastic thing.

WARDEN.—You two guards . . . stand one on each side of him.

KOSKY.—Excuse me, but I have heard that the black mask is optional. Is that so?

WARDEN.—(*Incensed*) Yes! Never mind the mask! Hurry it up!

KOSKY.—You see . . . you see, I don't want the mask, because when I blow up I want my eyes to pop out like machine gun bullets. (*Chuckles, subsides*)

WARDEN.—All right, Pettigrew, hurry up over to the control board and thud that switch!

SOUND.—*Slow footsteps.*
(*Fade out*) . . . (*fade in*)

FALLOW.—Then, so help me, Stew, Kosky starts puffin' out his cheeks. I never seen anything like this before in my life! He puffs 'em out so far he looks like the world's biggest bomb achin' to explode to everybody present . . . me included. That cinches it. Steve Blathery is off his bench in one record-breakin' broad jump. . . .
(*Quick fade*)

DIRECTION.—*Filtered mike out entirely.*

BLATHERY.—No! No! For God's sake don't pull the switch. He'll blow up! I *know* it! The man's mad, and he's tellin' the truth!

WARDEN.—Blathery! Keep away from that control board! Get back, I say, or I'll . . .

17

SOUND.—*Heavy scuffling . . . thud of bodies striking floor . . . low moans.*

FIRST GUARD.—This is a nice mess, Blathery. . . You've knocked the warden out.

BLATHERY.—I didn't mean to. . . . He tackled me.

SECOND GUARD.—His head must have hit the concrete. He's out cold.

FIRST GUARD.—Dr. Blint, will you see what you can do?

BLINT.—This is unheard of, preposterous, ridiculous. We must go on with the electrocution.

BLATHERY.—Dr. Blint! Let me remind you I'm the political head of this county. And let me tell you . . . all of you . . . that you owe your jobs to me . . . and that if a single one of you don't do what I order, you won't have jobs tomorrow. . . .

KOSKY.—(*Pointedly*) If you are here to *have* jobs tomorrow . . . (*Fade out*) . . . (*fade in*)

DIRECTION.—*Following speeches Fallow only on filter.*

FALLOW.—It was Kosky pipin' up, Stew, which is his first remarks in many minutes, and everybody just keeps quiet and looks at him. Then, very slow but very sure, Kosky bends over and starts unstrappin' his leg electrodes, and not one of the guards makes the slightest move to stop him. He works as if he has all the time in the world, and finally he gets 'em off and wiggles off the hot seat and stands up like a lazy man wakin' up in the mornin! . . . Hey! Get this! *Flash!* Kosky just hotfooted out of the death chamber! He escaped. And he took Steve Blathery with him as hostage!

STEWART.—Great stuff! Wait a minute. . . . Here's Brady . . . wants to talk to you.

BRADY.—Hello, Fallow? This is Brady. I just spoke to Dr. Fullerton, head of the American Explosive Company. He says a man can't explode.

FALLOW.—No?

BRADY.—No. At least he said it never has been done before. I told him Kosky invented a new kind of deadly machine. He says he'd like to see it. I told him we haven't got time to arrange it. . . . Wait a minute. Hold on, Fallow.

BOY.—Mr. Brady, here's a report I was told to give to you.

BRADY.—Wow! One of the boys just got hold of Chief Bentley of the Bureau of Combustibles. Bentley says even if all the fulminate of mercury in the world exploded inside a man's stomach it wouldn't do much damage because the body would smother the explosion. Yeah, Fallow . . . Bentley says the fulminate of mercury would only "pothole." Kosky might be a mess on the floor, but nobody would get hurt. He never could knock the walls down. . . . He couldn't even shake the walls.

(*Fade out . . . fade in*)

STEWART.—*Stewart only on filter.*

FALLOW.—Hello, Stew? Fallow.

STEWART.—Say, did Kosky get away?

FALLOW.—Yeah, he's gone. And it looks like he won't come back. Here's the picture. Kosky gets off the hot seat and walks over and grabs Blathery by the scruff of the neck. You ought to see Blathery squirm. It did my heart good. The warden is out cold, so he ain't no use at all, and all the others are standin' there, 'cause Blathery holds the power o'life and death over their jobs, and they darn well know it. Then Kosky says in a very gentle voice . . .

(*Fade out . . . fade in*)

DIRECTION.—*Filter out.*

KOSKY.—Mr. Blathery . . . you're my friend, aren't you?

BLATHERY.—Why, Kosky! Kosky! Of course, I'm your friend! You know that.

KOSKY.—Well, that's fine. Because you and I are going for a little walk together right this minute, and if you come gently and do what I tell you I won't harm a hair on your head. However—however, if you act the slightest bit as if you weren't going to do exactly what I tell you, or if any of the men in this room try to follow us, or if anybody gives an alarm so that people outside start shooting at me, I am afraid I am going to develop a sudden, severe attack of stomach cramps. And you know what that means.

BLATHERY.—Kosky, you can't do that to me! You can't! Why I'm the boss of Anatomie County. Let me go, Kosky, and I'll get a reprieve! You won't even have to stay in jail. I'll give you a job at the social club . . . anything you want.

KOSKY.—Get moving.

BLATHERY.—You heard what he said, boys. And all I can say is that if anybody gives Kosky the slightest cause to explode he might as well leave Anatomie County, but even that won't do any good, because my six brothers will trail the skunk to the ends of the earth and catch up with him some day. Good-by, boys, and just remember that, if anything happens to me!

KOSKY.—Come on, and stop beefing.

FALLOW.—(*On filter*) And then . . . let me tell you, Stew . . . Kosky gives him a soft little shove, and both of them march out the door marked . . . *silence.* That's exactly what we've been having for the last three minutes . . . silence . . . except for the warden. He's layin' on the floor comin' to an' moanin' . . .
(*Fade in regular mike simultaneously with fade off filter*) but everybody is so scared to move that not even the doctors have gone over to see how he is, Stew. I bet the perspiration in the death house is enough to float one o' those pocket battleships. *Flash!* Stop the presses!

STEWART.—(*On filter*) What's happened now, Fallow?

FALLOW.—Here comes Blathery back alone. Kosky stole his pants! Whoopee! Who'd ever thought Steve Blathery wears green and purple underclothes?

SOUND.—*Crowd murmurs rising to hubbub, sustained behind.*

FALLOW.—Can you hear that racket? Everybody's yellin' and excited, Stew, and I can't get very clear what happened. The warden is sittin' up and rubbin' his neck. *Flash!* Kosky escaped in an auto! He made Blathery walk him out o' the prison. He made Blathery smile nice every time they passed anybody. He walked Blathery half a block outside the prison. A car was waitin' down the block with a woman at the wheel. Kosky got in, made Blathery remove his pants . . . yip-ee! and then without a word he an' the dame sped away in the car. Blathery is yellin' now for

20

somebody to lend him a pair of pants, but nobody seems willin' to do it. What a man! What a night! The warden looks like he's gonna sock Blathery in the jaw. Wow! Ouch! He did! Blathery don't need pants now. . . . They'll have to get him a stretcher. Oh, my heart!

(*Fade out . . . fade in*)

DIRECTION.—*Fallow on filter.*

BRADY.—Fallow? This is Brady.

FALLOW.—Oh, hello, Brady. . . . How did you like the yarn?

BRADY.—How do you like this? The office boy just looked up the University of Lodz in the encyclopedia. It doesn't say anything about them teaching chemistry there or watchmaking or sword swallowing. But it does say this: "The University of Lodz is famous for its courses in advanced psychology."

ANNOUNCER.—You have just heard the first of a series of dramatizations of short stories from contemporary magazines by the Federal Theatre Radio Division. Tonight's program was based on the story, "Surprise for the Boys," by Herbert Lewis, which appeared originally in the magazine, *Esquire.* It was adapted for radio by Victor E. Smith and produced under the direction of Ashley Buck.

This was a presentation of the Federal Theatre Radio Division, a project of the Works Progress Administration, in association with the Mutual Network.

In addition to the usual facilities of the Mutual Network, this program came to you as an international exchange feature over the coast-to-coast network of the Canadian Broadcasting Corporation.

BEST SHORT STORY ADAPTATION
(SERIOUS)

A Trip to Czardis

by EDWIN GRANBERRY

Adapted for radio by ELIZABETH *and* JAMES HART

DETERMINING the best broadcast in the classification of serious short story adaptations presented one of the severest problems met with in the preparation of this anthology. The short story adaptation is one of radio's most common dramatic types, and it has been estimated with reasonable accuracy that over thirty thousand programs for this division alone are broadcast every year. Four hundred and fifty were examined for this book. Many fine pieces were rejected as candidates for inclusion and the final choice was arrived at only by making the criteria of qualification so severe as to render ineligible, on one claim or another, most of the disputed properties. In the final judgment the following factors were taken into account:

1. Literary merit of the original.
2. Difficulty of the adaptation problem.
3. Artistic integrity of the adapter's inventions.
4. Adherence to the pattern, mood, and intention of the original.
5. Recognition and use of expansible suggestion.
6. Playing power.

In the degree to which each story adaptation met these tests, it was given its independent rating. "A Trip to Czardis" was deficient in no category. The original story is the work of Edwin Granberry, published in *Forum* in 1932. The piece was adapted by Elizabeth and James Hart for the Columbia Workshop and has been printed in its broadcast version in the anthology, *Columbia Workshop*

Plays, the first important collection of radio dramatic material ever to be published.*

The story as Granberry has told it is a superb piece of writing, intensely moving, economically wrought. Its mood fastens itself upon the reader in the first few paragraphs, and it moves unpretentiously and quietly to its agonizing conclusion by a series of half disclosures and submerged revelations and by dark but meaningful overtones. One becomes entirely acquainted with the Cameron family and does so seemingly without ever being told very much about them.

There is very little dialogue in the original and practically none at all of which the adapter can make use. The laconic snatches of talk that Granberry has given, the embarrassed taciturnity of the uncle, the natural reticences of the older child, and the diffidence and docility of the younger—these place an urgency of the most exacting sort upon the adapter. He must reveal no more than the author has, and at the same time he must keep his characters talking for thirty minutes.

The adaptation succeeded in doing this. The invented conversations that are given to the cast are exactly right for each character in mood, in content, and in duration. The use of the flash back to recapture the flavor of Czardis on a happier day is a piece of creative discernment that few writers in the craft can handle and that none can surpass. Yet this exists in the original only as the briefest whisper. Plausible inventions of this kind and masterful reconstructions of full personalities from fragmentary suggestion are possible only to those radio writers with a true gift of perception and sympathy. No discriminating reader, familiar with both the original and its radio adaptation, can believe other than that the finished script is precisely what the author of the story would have given us had he fashioned the piece for the broadcast medium.

* *Columbia Workshop Plays*, edited by Douglas Coulter, Associate Director of Broadcasts for CBS, was published by Whittlesey House, August, 1939.

A Trip to Czardis[*]

MUSIC.—*Open melody, fading into*

SOUND.—*The subdued sounds of daybreak in the Florida scrub. Now a distant cock crow. Presently the far-off howling of a dog. Close at hand, the sad call of mourning doves, drawn out, repeated, subsiding through*

ANNOUNCER.—A trip to Czardis!

SOUND.—*Weary footfalls mounting steep stairs; they cross a creaking, bare floor and fade into the heavy breathing, the meaningless mumbles and sighs of sleeping children.*

MAMMA.—(*A taut compassion in her voice*) Sleepin' and dreamin' . . . still full of their baby concerns. Hit ain't in my heart to waken 'em. Hit ain't in my heart to . . . oh, Lord, I'm fearful. I don't know iffen I'm actin' right or not, Lord.

SOUND.—*The mourning doves call softly at the window.*

MAMMA.—Our Father which art in heaven, Hallowed be thy name. Thy kingdom come. Thy will be done on earth as it is in heaven . . . (*Breaks off sobbing*)

JIM.—(*Startled from sleep*) Mamma! Mamma!

MAMMA.—(*Reassuringly*) Nothin's wrong, Jim. Don't be scairt.

JIM.—Mamma, you ain't cryin'?

MAMMA.—No, Jim.

JIM.—You're a-prayin'?

MAMMA.—Yes, I were prayin'. Hit'll be day soon. You better be risin' up. Your Uncle Holly'll be along directly.

JIM.—(*With growing excitement*) Hit's really come. The day. The day we're goin' to Czardis in the wagon to see papa.

* "A Trip to Czardis," dramatic version, copyright, 1939, by Elizabeth and James Hart; original story, copyright, 1932, by *Forum Magazine*.

MAMMA.—(*Dully*) Hit's come, all right.

JIM.—Seems like I jest cain't believe yet we're goin' . . .

MAMMA.—(*Cutting in*) There ain't time fur talk now, Jim. You best bestir yourself. And waken up Dan'l too.

SOUND.—*Receding footfalls on floor boards.*

MAMMA.—(*Voice more distant*) Put on the clean things I washed out fur you so you'll look decent and be a credit to your raisin'.

SOUND.—*Footfalls descending stairs; fade-out. Mourning doves call briefly.*

JIM.—Wake up, Dan'l. Wake up!

DAN'L.—(*Whimpering in his sleep*) Leave me be. Make 'em leave me be. Jim! . . . Jim!

JIM.—(*Patient, kind*) Don't be feared, Dan'l. Ain't nobody a-botherin' you.

DAN'L.—Hit's dark. I cain't see, Jim.

JIM.—Ain't e'er a soul here but me and you. See, I got my arm around you. Open up your eyes now.

DAN'L.—(*Wakes, still frightened*) Oh . . . oh, I were dreamin'.

JIM.—What dreamin' were you havin'?

DAN'L.—Hit's gone right out of my head. But it were fearful, Jim, fearful, what I dreamed.

JIM.—The day's come, Dan'l.

DAN'L.—What, Jim?

JIM.—The day. Hit's here right now. The day we been waitin' fur to come. You'll recollect it all in a minute.

DAN'L.—I recollect. Hit's the day we're goin' in the wagon to see papa.

JIM.—We're goin' all the way this time, right on to Czardis, where papa is. I never see sech a place as Czardis. Papa takened me one time he were going to market. You were too little then, and he were feared you'd get tuckered. You started up whimperin' jest as we drove off, and papa jumped outen the wagon and run back and told you, "Don't take on, Dan'l. Soon's you get to be six, I'll bring you, too, and we'll have us a right fine time." (*Fading*) Hit were terrible long ago that papa takened me, but I can see it all plain, just like it was happenin' now.

MUSIC.—*Fade in merry-go-round.*

SOUND.—*Babble of many voices. Cries of market vendors:* "'*Taters! Sweet 'taters! Pick 'em up, gents. Pick 'em up! Grapefruit, oranges, and lemons! Grapefruit, oranges, and lemons! Floridy's finest, ladies! Floridy's finest! Fresh, fresh fish! Fresh, fresh fish! Red snapper! Red snapper! Right out of the gulf, folks! Right out of the gulf!*"

JIM.—(*Cutting in and over*) You mean I can sure enough ride on 'em?

MUSIC.—*Merry-go-round slows and stops.*

PAPA.—That's jest what I do mean, young 'un. Which do you favor? How about this red colt? Here, I'll h'ist you on his back. Mind you holt on tight now.

MUSIC.—*Merry-go-round up loud.*

SOUND.—*Laughter and squeals of children.*

MUSIC.—*Merry-go-round gradually fades **out**.*

SOUND.—*Crowd in background.*

PAPA.—Well, son, were it a good ride?

JIM.—Papa, hit were like nothin' else in the world, a-ridin' the horses that make music.

PAPA.—I'm happy it pleasured you, son.

JIM.—Are they always in Czardis?

PAPA.—Only jest on market day. Likely the feller that owns 'em figgers there'll always be a parcel of young 'uns a-comin' along with their mas and pas, and iffen the mas and pas ain't downright mean they can spare a nickel to give the young 'uns a treat.

SOUND.—*Vendors' cries up momentarily, then fade into background.*

JIM.—Oh, look, papa. Over yonder on top of that big buildin'. They got a gold ball stickin' up in the air!

PAPA.—That's the courthouse. I calculate that ball must be 20, 25 foot round the middle. Awful purty, catchin' the sun the way it does.

JIM.—Is it bigger round'n our well?

PAPA.—Oh, it's a sight bigger'n the well.

VENDOR.—(*Fading in*) Lemonade! Ice-cold lemonade! Here you are. Ice-cold lemonade!

PAPA.—Reckon you could stand wettin' your whistle, eh, Jim? Here, mister, let's have a couple of them lemonades.

VENDOR.—Mighty hot day. . . . Here you are.

PAPA.—I thank you. . . . Well, how do it go down, son?

JIM.—Hit's colder'n the spring water in the hollow. I never knew there could be somethin' so cold. I can feel it a-freezin' my teeth together.

VENDOR.—That's the ice makes it so cold.

JIM.—I ain't never had ice.

VENDOR.—Here, young feller, I'll put a little piece in your glass, so's you can eat it.

SOUND.—*Tinkle of ice.*

JIM.—I sure thank you.

SOUND.—*Crowd noises and vendors' cries intrude briefly. Gabble of flock of turkeys, fading shortly.*

PAPA.—Don't them turkeys look plump 'n' tasty? Now, iffen I jest weren't so scarce of money, I'd certain take one home to your mamma. Hit's a long time since I were able to shoot her a wild one.

JIM.—I never see so many things to eat in my life! Oh, look, papa, look comin'. What's all them?

PAPA.—Them's balloons.

JIM.—Balloons. They're somethin' like a big soap bubble, only with the same color all over. Jest look at 'em a-bobbin' and swayin' like as if they was tryin' to get away.

PAPA.—Hit's the gas in 'em makes 'em pull that-a-way.

27

JIM.—Gas?

PAPA.—Somethin' in 'em that makes 'em go up in the air iffen you let go the string.

JIM.—(*Wistfully*) I reckon they cost a heap of money.

PAPA.—(*Laughs*) Hit's a good thing you don't come often to town, young squirrel, lessen your papa wouldn't have a cent to his name. I expect we can get you a balloon, though. Hey! you . . .

JIM.—(*Solemnly*) Oh, papa, I won't forget today all the other days I live, papa.

SOUND.—*The crowd, the vendors' cries grow louder, then fade into silence. After a moment a cock crows . . . the doves stir.*

JIM.—(*Dreamily*) I never see anything like it. You jest can't pitcher it, Dan'l, till you been there.

DAN'L.—I recollect the water tower.

JIM.—Not in your own right. Hit's by me tellin' it you see it in your mind.

DAN'L.—And lemonade with ice in it . . . and balloons of every kind of color . . .

JIM.—(*Cutting in*) That, too, I seen and told to you.

DAN'L.—(*Incredulous*) Then I never seen any of it at all?

JIM.—Hit's me were there. I let you play like, but hit's me went to Czardis. You weren't olden enough.

DAN'L.—I'm six now, ain't I, Jim?

JIM.—Well . . . and you're a-goin' today.

DAN'L.—But it's mamma and Uncle Holly that's takin' me.

JIM.—Papa would of done it iffen he'd stayed here. Anyways, hit's much the same. We're goin to see him.

DAN'L.—Do papa live in Czardis now?

JIM.—I don't rightly know. He went there a long time back, but . . .

MAMMA.—(*Off, cutting in*) Jim! Dan'l!

28

Jim.—Yes, mamma?

Mamma.—(*Off*) Are you a-gettin' your clothes on? Breakfast is 'most fixed.

Jim.—Yes, ma'am. (*To Dan'l*) Come on, pile outen that bed.

Sound.—*Bare feet on floor boards . . . mourning doves up.*

Dan'l.—(*Shiveringly*) Oh-h . . . the cold aches me!

Jim.—Skin into your britches quick, while I'm a-holdin' 'em. There. Stay still now, and I'll get that shirt over your head. (*Soothingly*) You won't be shiverin' long, Dan'l. Hit's goin' to be fair. Mournin' doves startin' a'ready. The sun'll bake you warm.

Dan'l.—Is it sunshiny in Czardis?

Jim.—Hit's past believin', Dan'l. And when it shines on that gold ball that's perched on the courthouse . . .

Dan'l.—The one that's bigger'n our well?

Jim.—Hit's 25 foot round the mid. . .

Mamma.—(*Off; cuts in*) Come eat now, you young 'uns!

Jim.—(*Calling*) Yes, ma'am, we're a-comin'.

Sound.—*Double footfalls gropingly descend a stairway . . . continue through next speeches.*

Jim.—Catch a holt of my hand. These stairs is mighty dark.

Dan'l.—Mornin', mamma!

Mamma.—Mornin', boys. (*A pause*) You look right neat. But your hands could be a mite cleaner. There's a bucket of fresh water yonder and some soap. Look careful you don't drip none on your clothes.

Sound.—*Splashing of water continues through next two speeches.*

Dan'l.—Might I could touch the gold ball, Jim?

Jim.—Not lessen you was to get you the tallest ladder in Floridy and climb up to the courthouse roof. Then you'd need you another ladder to . . .

Mamma.—Draw up, boys, and get to eatin'. Dan'l, you look half froze. Best set close to the stove.

29

SOUND.—*Scraping of chairs on floor.*

MAMMA.—(*Sternly*) Ain't you forgot somethin', Jim?

JIM.—Huh? . . . Oh! . . . (*In a rapid singsong*) We give thanks, Lord, fur the food that Thou has provided and that we're a-goin' to eat. Amen.

MAMMA.—I don't want never again to see you tearin' into your rations before you're said a blessin' for 'em.

JIM.—(*Meekly*) I didn't study to do it, mamma. It's jest that I was thinkin' about us goin' to see papa in Czardis till I forgot.

MAMMA.—All right; go ahead and eat now, so's you'll be ready when your Uncle Holly comes.

DAN'L.—(*In a confidential undertone to Jim*) Will Uncle Holly buy us lemonade in Czardis?

JIM.—It ain't decided yet. He ain't spoke.

DAN'L.—Mebbe papa . . .

JIM.—Likely papa will. Mebbe somethin' better'n lemonade.

DAN'L.—What would it be?

JIM.—It might could be ice-cream cones.

DAN'L.—(*Rapturously*) Ice-cream cones? Oh, Jim!

SOUND.—*Knock on light door.*

JIM.—(*Warningly*) Hush! There's Uncle Holly now.

SOUND.—*Door opens.*

MAMMA.—Mornin', Holly.

HOLLY.—Mornin', Mary. Mornin', young 'uns.

SOUND.—*Door slams shut.*

DAN'L.—(*With shrill eagerness*) Can I sit up in front with you, Uncle Holly?

HOLLY.—I'll have to study about that, Dan'l. (*To mamma, in a low, disapproving voice*) You fixed on takin' them still?

MAMMA.—(*Quietly*) I am.

HOLLY.—I reckon you know, Mary, hit's not my nature to meddle in other folks' doin's, but I can't he'p thinkin' you're dead wrong to take 'em. It'd be different if they were older.

JIM.—(*Breaks in protestingly*) Uncle Holly! I'm ten years now, and papa takened me when I wasn't hardly older'n Dan'l.

MAMMA.—Hush, Jim. (*Still very quiet but with complete finality*) He asked to see them, Holly. Nobody but God Almighty ought to tell a soul what it can or can't have.

HOLLY.—God knows I don't grudge him the sight of 'em. I were only thinkin' iffen they were my sons . . .

MAMMA.—They are Jim's sons, Holly. (*Abruptly*) It's time I were hitchin' the wagon. You can he'p me if you've a mind to. (*Fading*) Boys, come out soon's you finish. Don't tarry.

SOUND.—*Door opens and closes.*

DAN'L.—That were mighty mean of Uncle Holly.

JIM.—(*Slowly*) Uncle Holly ain't got a mean bone to his body. I can't figger why he didn't want us, lessen he were feared we'd fret papa while he's ailin'.

DAN'L.—Is papa ailin?

JIM.—Not bad. But the doctor don't like too many folks a-visitin' him. He must be a sight better now, though, or mamma wouldn't be takin' us. (*A pause*) You haven't et your corn pone.

DAN'L.—I'm savin' it to take to papa.

JIM.—Papa don't crave e'er ol' corn pone.

DAN'L.—Mebbe he would want to have my whistle . . . the one that were in the Crackerjack box Uncle Holly brung me.

JIM.—That ain't a whistle fur a man, Dan'l. Papa'd jest laugh at a puny, squeakin' trick like that.

SOUND.—*Chair pushed back.*

JIM.—Iffen you've et enough, we'd best go out. Mamma'll be riled if we keep 'em waitin'.

DAN'L.—All right. (*Wistfully*) Seems like there must be somethin' I could take him.

SOUND.—*Opening and shutting of door; then sounds of horses near at hand . . . switching of tails . . . stamping . . . slobbering. Barnyard background.*

MAMMA.—Jim, where you off to?

JIM.—(*Off, breathlessly*) Jest a minute!

MAMMA.—Come back here. You hear me? (*Voice growing fainter as she pursues him*) Jim! (*Voice comes up stronger again*) Get down out of there! Are worms gnawin' you that you skin up a pomegranate tree at this hour? Don't I feed you enough?

JIM.—(*Timidly*) I were only . . .

MAMMA.—(*Cuts in, more quietly*) We ain't yet come to the shame of you and Dan'l huntin' your food offen the trees and grass. People passin' on the road and seein' you gnawin' will say that Jim Cameron's sons are starved, foragin' like cattle of the field.

JIM.—I were gettin' the pomegranates fur papa.

MAMMA.—Oh. . . . (*Gently*) I guess we won't take any, Jim. But I'm proud it come to you to take your papa somethin'.

JIM.—(*A bit reluctantly*) Well . . . hit were Dan'l it come to, mamma.

MAMMA.—It were a fine thought, and I'm right proud . . . though today we won't take anything.

JIM.—I guess there's better pomegranates in Czardis anyways.

MAMMA.—There's no better pomegranates in all Floridy than what's right above your head. Iffen pomegranates were needed (*a faint tremor in her voice*) we would take him his own.

JIM.—(*Anxiously*) Is papa feelin' too poorly to relish 'em?

MAMMA.—(*Hesitates*) Yes . . . I reckon he is. . . . You'd best got to know, Jim . . . papa won't be like you recollect him. He's been right sick . . . sicker'n I've let on to you till now. Dan'l were sech a baby when he seen him last that he won't take any notice likely . . . but you're older, son.

JIM.—(*Troubled*) Mamma . . .

32

MAMMA.—Papa will look pale, and he won't be as bright-mannered as you recollect. So don't labor him with questions. Speak when it behooves you, and let him see you are upright.

JIM.—Yes, mamma. (*With anxious eagerness*) He's mendin' now, though, ain't he? He's gettin' . . .

HOLLY.—(*Off, calling*) Sun's risin', Mary.

MAMMA.—(*Her voice receding as she walks away*) Come along. We got to get started.

SOUND.—*A horse whinnies. Stomping and the creaking and jingle of harness fade in.*

HOLLY.—Climb up in back of your ma, young 'uns. I've bedded it down with straw to spare your bones some.

DAN'L.—Ain't you drivin', Uncle Holly?

MAMMA.—Uncle Holly's goin' ahead of us in his own wagon. Get in, Dan'l.

JIM.—Why do we got to take two wagons? Can't we all ride together in Uncle Holly's?

DAN'L.—His horse goes faster'n ours.

HOLLY.—(*Brusquely*) Climb in, you pesky little varmints, before I toss you in.

SOUND.—*The scrape of shoe leather . . . the squeak of a spring.*

MAMMA.—(*Off*) What are you doin' back there, Holly?

HOLLY.—I were fixin' to put the top up. Could be you'd feel right glad to have it over you when we get to the highway.

MAMMA.—(*Off*) I thank you, but we're all right as we are.

DAN'L.—We don't never have the top up lessen rain's fallin'.

HOLLY.—(*Muttering*) There's things a shield'd be needed against more'n rain.

JIM.—What things, Uncle Holly?

HOLLY.—(*Embarrassed*) Uh . . . er . . . why the sun, young 'un. Hit's like to be a turrible hot day. You'll be plumb roasted time we get to Czardis.

DAN'L.—I like feelin' roasted.

MAMMA.—I been ridin' under the open sky all my life. So has the boys. I guess we won't change our ways today.

HOLLY.—(*Resignedly*) Iffen that's the way you feel, Mary, there's no more to be said. I'll go on now.

SOUND.—*Receding footfalls on clay road.*

HOLLY.—(*Off, calling back*) Do I be gettin' too far ahead, give a holler and I'll slow her down. Giddyap.

SOUND.—*Horse's hoofs, off, jog-trotting briskly away, continuing through next speeches.*

DAN'L.—(*Excitedly*) Betsy's a-trottin'! Hurry, mamma, hurry!

SOUND.—*A cluck to the horse . . . more hoofbeats come up . . . the pace quickens under the pattern of sound.*

MUSIC.—*Enters slowly. Joins and smothers the hoofbeats with an intensified variation of the opening melody. Sustained for a long interval. As it finally subsides, we hear*

SOUND.—*Hoofbeats, this time sharper and more staccato, as though falling on asphalt instead of clay. An old-fashioned auto horn sounds in the distance, and the wheezing noise of an ancient car comes up gradually.*

DAN'L.—(*Cutting in and over car noise*) Howdy! Yoo-hoo, Miz Fletcher!

SOUND.—*Roar of car passing, fading gradually into clop-clop of hoofbeats, which continue in background.*

DAN'L.—Jim! That were Fletcher's truck went by us!

JIM.—Sounded like it.

DAN'L.—Miz Fletcher were sittin' up on the front seat, and Clem were drivin' it. (*Disappointedly*) Wonder why they didn't holler back?

JIM.—Likely they didn't hear you. That ol' car makes sech a ruckus you couldn't hardly hear a wildcat was he to howl in your ear.

DAN'L.—(*Wistfully*) It do go fast, though.

JIM.—Not so turrible fast. Were we to try, we could give 'em a right good race in the wagon.

DAN'L.—(*Doubtfully*) Mebbe.

JIM.—And I bet Uncle Holly could beat the puddin' out of 'em with Betsy.

DAN'L.—(*Sighs*) Jest the same, I'd admire to ride in a truck sometime.

JIM.—Did I ride, I'd pick me somethin' spryer'n Fletcher's ol' car.

SOUND.—*"Beep-beep" of a modern motor horn and purr of auto passing at average speed; fades out quickly. Hoofbeats continue in background.*

JIM.—Now there goes somethin' like.

DAN'L.—Hit sure were travelin'. And weren't it a purty one!

JIM.—You'll see a heap jest as purty when we get to Czardis·

DAN'L.—I already seen more'n I ever did before.

JIM.—There do seem a plenty goin' our way, a heap of wagons too. Must be market day.

DAN'L.—(*In high excitement*) Oh, Jim! Then will I get to see the balloon man? And the horses that makes music?

JIM.—Iffen hit's market day, they'll be there.

DAN'L.—Mamma, is it market day today in Czardis? (*Mamma makes no reply*) Is it, mamma?

MAMMA.—You and Jim get your mind offen balloons and flyin' horses and sech. We've no business that'll take us to the market today, be they havin' it or not.

DAN'L.—(*Plaintively*) Aw, mamma!

MAMMA.—(*Sternly*) I don't want to hear you frettin', Dan'l, and I don't want to hear you tormentin' papa to take you, neither.

JIM.—(*Quickly*) We won't mamma. (*In a low tone to Dan'l*) Don't take on, Dan'l. There's a sight of things in Czardis besides the market.

DAN'L.—(*In an anxious whisper*) Papa'll buy us the ice-cream cones, won't he?

JIM.—You don't want to go askin' him fur 'em.

DAN'L.—(*Whimpering*) But you told me . . .

JIM.—(*Cuts in*) Hush up and have patience. We'll get somethin' sure. (*In an effort to distract*) Look! Ain't that old man Bennet a turnin' at the fork?

DAN'L.—Where?

JIM.—Right up there ahead of us . . . ridin' on that runty little black horse. We'll be passin' him in a second.

MAMMA.—(*Severely*) Don't neither of you call to him or wave. Sit up tall, and look straight ahead like I do.

SOUND.—*Hoofbeats come up and merge with those of a different tempo, which are gradually left behind.*

MAMMA.—You stay that way now. We're a-comin' into Czardis' and it ain't seemly for you to be lollin' all over the wagon, peerin' and hollerin' at everybody you see.

JIM.—But, mamma, should they call "howdy" to us first?

MAMMA.—(*Bitterly*) There's a small risk of that. You do like I say, anyways. (*Pause*)

DAN'L.—Ain't it mannerly to call "howdy" in Czardis? (*Mamma does not reply, and Dan'l speaks to Jim in a worried undertone*) Is mamma riled?

JIM.—Not truly, Dan'l. She jest . . . (*He hesitates*)

DAN'L.—Why does she keep rompin' on us fur?

JIM.—(*His growing bewilderment and apprehension escaping into his voice*) I don't rightly know. There's things this mornin' I jest cain't figger.

DAN'L.—(*After a pause*) Jim! Why you lookin' scairt?

JIM.—Why, I ain't! Whatever is there to be scairt of? (*Laughs*) I never see the like of you fur gettin' notions. Look, Dan'l . . . rearin' up there against the sky!

DAN'L.—(*Almost shouting*) Hit's the water tower!

JIM.—That's what it is.

DAN'L.—I knowed it right off. Hit's jest like you told, only it goes up higher. Hit's higher'n even the big pine to Palmetto Swamp!

36

JIM.—And yonder's the depot, where the trains come in from Jacksonville and sech.

SOUND.—*Small-town street noises . . . creaking of wagons . . . clatter of horses' hoofs . . . an occasional "whoa" . . . now and then an auto horn, the roar of a motor, and the hum of voices. All this is heard clearly for a moment, then fades into background.*

DAN'L.—Does all these folks live here, Jim?

JIM.—This here's Main Street. All the stores mostly is along here, and the movin' pitcher theayter.

DAN'L.—(*Breathlessly*) Where's that, Jim? Show me.

JIM.—It's down the block a piece . . . (*In dismay*) Mamma! Why's Uncle Holly turnin' off here?

MAMMA.—Because that's the way we're goin'.

JIM.—Cain't we keep along Main Street jest a little ways further? Dan'l ain't even . . .

SOUND.—*Street noises flare up, then fade. The hoofbeats are now falling on cobblestones.*

MAMMA.—(*Almost pleadingly*) Please, Jim! Don't fuss.

DAN'L.—I didn't get to see the movin' pitcher theayter.

JIM.—Mebbee we can see it goin' back.

DAN'L.—Jim! The gold ball!

JIM.—Why, so 'tis! That must be the courthouse, on'y we're seein' it sideways 'stead of straight on, or mebbee that's the back of it. I've got kind of muddle-minded with all this twistin' and turnin' we're doin'.

DAN'L.—What's the other big buildin'? The one with the wall all 'round it? Look, they got a bobbed-wire fence fixed on top of the wall! What's the sense of that? Ain't no bear nor wildcat could jump that high anyways, and they'd have a right hard time climbin' them slippery stones.

JIM.—'Tain't there to keep the beasts out. If I recollect right, this buildin' is . . .

DAN'L.—(*Cuts in*) I never see so many windows! And every one of 'em with rails acrost it.

JIM.—Them ain't rails. Them're bars, made outen iron. This is . . . (*He breaks off suddenly, then goes on in a shrill voice compounded of horror and incredulity*) Mamma! Uncle Holly's stopped here! He's hitchin' up Betsy to a tree!

MAMMA.—(*Her voice deep with compassion*) We come to where we were goin', Jim.

SOUND.—*Hoofbeats slowing to a walk, then stopping . . . creaking of wagon wheels . . . a weary puff from the horse.*

DAN'L.—Can we get out, mamma?

MAMMA.—In a second, son.

DAN'L.—Who's that man Uncle Holly's talkin' to at the gate? Is he a soldier? (*No one replies*) Mamma! Look at all the men peerin' out the windows.

HOLLY.—(*In a low voice*) Hit's all right, Mary. I talked to him, and he'll let us in this way. Like I thought, they's mostly gathered on the other side.

MAMMA.—Get out boys.

HOLLY.—Hold your arms out, and I'll lift you down.

DAN'L.—Why do they have those things acrost the windows, Uncle Holly? Jim says they're made outen iron.

JIM.—(*In a high, strained, unnatural voice, close to hysteria*) Hush up, Dan'l! Don't talk. Don't say nothin' more. We're goin' to see papa now, and he's sick. Talkin' makes him worse. He's turrible sick . . . turrible, turrible sick.

MUSIC.—*Tempestuous and somber. Sustained at length, then fading into*

SOUND.—*Footfalls of five people passing down stone corridor.*

GUARD.—Jest come along this way, Miz Cameron.

SOUND.—*Footfalls continue for a second, then halt . . . a key grating in lock . . . the clang of a steel door being shut and locked again.*

GUARD.—Right down the hall, ma'am, where the deputy's standin'. He's got the door open for you.

HOLLY.—Me 'n' the boys'll wait here a spell, Mary. You jest call us when you're ready.

38

JIM.—(*In a low voice*) Mamma . . .

MAMMA.—Wait here with your uncle, now. (*Huskily*) I'm right proud of you, son. (*A long pause*) We're here, Jim.

PAPA.—(*Agonized*) Mary! Mary!

MAN.—Mornin', Miz Cameron.

MAMMA.—Mornin', Reverend.

MAN.—I'll be comin' back, Jim. Good-by, ma'am; God bless you and he'p you.

MAMMA.—I thank you, Reverend.

SOUND.—*Slight creak of hinge . . . soft footfalls receding.*

PAPA.—Let me holt you to me, Mary, honey. Let me feel you to me again!

MAMMA.—(*Passionately*) Jim! Jim! I ain't never goin' to let loose of you. Ain't no one can make me. Ain't no one . . . (*Her voice breaks in a hard sob*)

PAPA.—(*Recovering*) This ain't the way fur me to act . . . makin' the misery worse fur you.

MAMMA.—There's no makin' worse what I'm feelin'.

PAPA.—(*Cuts in*) Young 'uns come?

MAMMA.—(*Controlling herself*) Like you asked. They're waitin' with Holly.

PAPA.—I thank you, Mary. I know it were cruel hard on you to bring 'em. Mebbe I shouldn't of asked it. But . . .

MAMMA.—Hit's your right to see 'em, Jim.

PAPA.—You ain't spoke to them?

MAMMA.—Only to tell 'em you were ailin' bad. I'll fetch 'em in now. (*Calls softly*) Holly! You can come along now.

PAPA.—(*Quickly*) Do they guess more'n you . . .

MAMMA.—Dan'l don't. He's too little. But Jim's right sharp and . . . (*Breaks off*) Step in, boys, and greet your papa.

SOUND.—*Creak of hinge. Brief, shuffling footsteps.*

PAPA.—Mornin', Holly. . . . Jim! Dan'l! Hit's a treat to see you, sons! It's a treat to my heart.

MAMMA.—(*Speaking after a silence*) Have your feet froze to the ground that you can't do nothin' but stand there gapin'? Seems like you'd want to give your papa a hug after not seein' him fur so long.

DAN'L.—(*Shyly*) Howdy, papa.

JIM.—Oh, papa . . .

PAPA.—(*Confused, tremulous laughter and broken endearments as first Jim, then Dan'l throw themselves into their father's arms*)

JIM.—(*His voice catching*) I'm turrible happy to see you, papa!

PAPA.—(*Jerkily*) Me, too, Jim! Me, too, young 'un! And Dan'l! I'm like to squeeze the breath outen you both, I'm that glad.

DAN'L.—We come all the way in the wagon, papa.

PAPA.—That were quite a trip fur you, young feller. You ain't done so much travelin' yet.

DAN'L.—I aimed to bring you my whistle, but Jim said it made too puny a sound fur a man.

PAPA.—Never mind, Dan'l. The thought you would want to bring it pleasures me more'n the finest whistle in the world.

MAMMA.—Jim, here, picked some pomegranates offen the tree to bring you, but . . .

PAPA.—Son, I'm mighty happy you recollected how I used to love them pomegranates. I thank you. I'm right proud of both of you and Dan'l.

HOLLY.—Jim . . . I hates to say it, and you too, Mary, but this feller outside says there ain't much more'n 10 minutes now. Iffen you want to get the young 'uns out, Mary . . .

JIM.—Do we got to go?

PAPA.—Yes, son.

MAMMA.—(*Uncontrollably*) Oh, Jim!

PAPA.—(*Gently*) Best go now, Mary. I want you should be on the road before . . .

40

JIM.—Can we come back soon, papa? Might we could come back next week?

PAPA.—Come over here, son, and you too, Dan'l. Papa wants to say somethin' fur you to hear.

DAN'L.—Papa, will you . . .

MAMMA.—(*Cutting in*) Dan'l! Listen while your papa's speakin'.

PAPA.—I want you should both grow up to be upright men. Take care of your mamma, and always do her biddin'.

JIM.—(*In a stifled voice*) Yes, papa.

PAPA.—Mind against anger catchin' you by the throat and blindin' your eyes. Anger and hate . . . don't never let them master you and drive you on. (*A pause*) I'm goin' to give you my watch, Jim. You're the oldest. I want you should keep it till you're a grown man. And, Dan'l, here is the chain. That's fur you.

HOLLY.—Come on, young 'uns. Come along with me.

DAN'L.—Ain't mamma . . .

HOLLY.—She'll follow after. Come along.

DAN'L.—(*Off, voice receding*) I thank you, papa.

PAPA.—(*Desperately*) Mary, honey! Mary, honey!

MUSIC.—*Surges up menacingly, fades, and continues under*

SOUND.—*The clang of steel doors . . . heavy feet marching along stone corridor, at first muffled and distant, then increasingly loud and close.*

MUSIC.—*Up again, over marching feet. Both music and sound increase in force . . . fade quickly.*

HOLLY.—You want I should walk to the wagon with you, Mary? There's a millin' throng out there.

MAMMA.—(*With still, cold hatred*) Black-hearted trash! May what they've come to peer at rot their eyes in their heads! We'll walk alone, Holly. You wait here.

SOUND.—*A door opens. Then rises the muffled roar of a great crowd.*

DAN'L.—(*Voice high with excitement*) Look yonder at them trees! Every one full of folks, perched up like squirrels!

JIM.—(*Shrill with shock and horror*) Mamma! They're a-peerin' over the wall here! They're . . .

MAMMA.—(*Fiercely*) Put your head up, son. Dan'l, catch a holt of my hand. Come along now, and don't waste one look at that swarm of carrion flies!

SOUND.—*Crowd noises up to a roar, long and terrifying. Abruptly they are cut off. A short pause.*

MUSIC.—*The opening theme holds softly for a time, then fades to the regular clop-clop of horses' hoofs.*

SOUND.—*Exactly as in earlier scenes, sustained for a full half minute, then fading into background.*

JIM.—Mamma?

MAMMA.—Yes, Jim.

JIM.—(*Chokingly*) Is papa . . . comin' home with Uncle Holly?

MAMMA.—Yes, son.

JIM.—(*Sobs*)

DAN'L.—We never got our ice-cream cones, did we, Jim?

JIM.—(*Sobs are louder, more convulsive*)

DAN'L.—Don't take on. We got somethin' better. We got a watch and chain, Jim.

JIM.—(*Through his weeping*) Dan'l . . . he don't know, mamma.

MAMMA.—No, son.

SOUND.—*The hoofbeats become more insistent under Jim's sobs.*

DAN'L.—(*With slow, happy wonder*) I never see sech a place as Czardis!

MUSIC.—*Welling up in quick climax.*

BEST ONE-ACT PLAY ADAPTATION

Blood of the Martyrs

A one-act play by PERCIVAL WILDE

Based on a short story by STEPHEN VINCENT BENÉT

Radio adaptation by DONALD MACFARLANE

IT IS indeed remarkable to find a play that has been through so many processes of change without having suffered losses in both meaning and playing power. The privilege of usurpation that the motion picture industry has given itself in matters of adaptation is of course well known and widely decried, and it is interesting to note in this connection that Hollywood's most artistic efforts have invariably been those in which the film translation has effected the closest possible parallel of the original that photography can devise. This derives, of course, from the inescapable rule that to outrage the structure of the play is to outrage the play. Radio has been far more accurate in its adaptations and interpretations of good plays and good stories and good books than the picture people have, and the probable reason is that in radio the responsibility for adaptation is fixed on only one or two people. "Blood of the Martyrs" survived its various transformations only because of this fact.

The play that follows—the most direct and powerful denunciation of totalitarianism that radio has thus far presented—was first a short story. It was the work of Stephen Vincent Benét and was published in *The Saturday Evening Post*. Structurally it was already furnished with the implements necessary for its conversion to a one-act play. The story impressed Percival Wilde with its force and dramatic tension, and he asked for permission to redo the piece as a play. The play was published in the September, 1937, issue of the *One Act Play Magazine* and was accompanied by a statement from Mr. Wilde that so thoroughly illuminates the problem met with that his remarks have been reproduced in full. What he has said applies with almost equal directness to the problem of the radio adapter. The radio adaptation of Mr. Wilde's play, based on Mr. Benét's story, has faithfully observed the ground rules of all adaptation: the adapter may do anything with any piece, whether poetry, prose, or drama, that truthfully translates to radio the import, the flavor, and the purpose of the original in its fullest possible integrity. Adaptation, in its simplest definition, is a transplantation from one medium to another of a series of sympathies and antipathies already established in the original. These are sacred, belonging to the first writer. They cannot be outraged, and they cannot be neglected.

Percival Wilde, with 117 one-act plays to his credit, can be trusted with the property of other writers. Donald Macfarlane, the radio adapter, has been equally scrupulous, and the result is a memorable radio play, authentically telling the same story that Mr. Benét wanted us to hear in the first place.

It was performed on the evening of December 7, 1938, over station WQXR in New York City.

Here is Mr. Wilde's statement.

Mr. Benét is a poet who has brought to his prose writing the spiritual and imaginative qualities that characterize his verse. His conception, in the short story which became the basis of the present play, may be stated concisely: if the scientist does not teach the objective truth as he knows it, there will be an end to continuity and to science. Many men have sought the truth, but have, in these horrible days, compromised with their consciences so that they might continue to work; but to the true scientist compromise is unthinkable. It is better for him to die at his post than to lend the weight of his authority to the spread of false beliefs, and this is both the tragedy and the triumph of Malzius: if there are enough men like him the world will eventually emerge from the quagmire of expedient creed into which the dictators have led it. "The blood of the martyrs," declared Tertullian, "is the seed of the Church." In these times the blood of the martyrs is the seed of liberalism and science and truth.

It is important and interesting, I think, to make clear what in the play is Mr. Benét's, and what is mine, though I have attempted, in adapting it for the stage, to work in the spirit which animated him. The original short story began in Malzius' cell. He is resting, "fairly well over his last beating," and the author tells us something of his past. He is brought before the General, under whom he has suffered, and the Dictator, whose "picture had presided over his beatings," and whom he now meets for the first time. He is given the choice between becoming president of the new National Academy and proving by scientific law "that certain races—our race in particular—are destined to rule the world"—and proving everything else the Dictator preaches —or of returning to "the process of rehabilitation." He knows that if he is beaten again he may give in; therefore he takes action so drastic that it leads to his instant death. He is hurried to the stake and is shot: "But Professor Malzius did not hear the three commands of the officer. He was thinking about the young men."

Here is a noble story, and one which should not be quickly forgotten. In making it into a play I could not artistically begin with the cell and then change the scene to the General's room, so I chose to place most of the action in the cell itself and have the Dictator and the General come there. In the story the desk, chairs, and the inkwell which is to figure so prominently in the action are naturally among the furnishings of the General's room; in the play the business of carrying them in is a logical change, and permits me to draw attention to the inkwell several times before it is used. Mr. Benét, with the same careful technique, refers to it three times before his climax.

It was necessary to make clear the initial situation, but the dramatist, unlike the prose writer, cannot relate what is in the mind of a character. I therefore attempted to invent a series of scenes which would lead, with ascending interest, to the point after the entrance of the Dictator where Mr. Benét's razor-keen dialogue first commences. The opening scene, with the voices of unseen speakers, is pure invention.* Malzius interrupts it—an essential part of the preliminary exposition—with a few lines spoken while he is "only partially awake." This is again invention, as is the long student scene which follows. It is necessary to make concrete and visible the background the poet had in mind but did not detail himself, and I have tried to carry out his thoughts by placing in the mouths of the characters, notably

* Omitted in the radio version.

Gregopoulos, many of the descriptive phrases which occur in the story. Wissotzski, Ellermann, Anton, Max and Elsa are invented; Bonnard, who according to the story, is a professor living in Paris, is made a student and is assigned important speeches, based, so far as possible, on the story. For this liberty I trust Mr. Benét will pardon me; and since he did not state what the students were plotting, I took it upon myself to rectify the omission.

The scene of the two troopers is pure invention, necessary both as a cover scene and as clarification. It is illuminated by a single speech of Malzius taken directly from the story.

The torture chamber and the scene which occurs in it are invented. It is indispensable to show the fate of the students. They must die, but if they die at the end of the scene, anticlimax will follow. The action, therefore, returns to the front scene, and the "muffled report of a volley" ten minutes later is an attempt not only to answer every question dealing with the students, but to punctuate effectively the point at which the main action is about to ascend to a higher plane of interest. For the General's long speeches and his colloquy with one of the prisoners I alone am to blame—but the General's allusion to Bonnard is essential preparation for the reference to Bonnard's protest which is to occur later. In his story the poet speaks frequently of Bonnard: "An excellent man in his field"; "deplorably like an actor, with his short gray beard, his pink cheeks and his impulsive enthusiasms"; "a fellow who signed protests." Since this material could not be used in the play, other preparational material had to be devised.

The following scenes with the Dictator and the General are ninety per cent Mr. Benét's, expressed, so far as possible, in his own words, descriptive matter being frequently transformed into dialogue. Mr. Benét states, for instance, "He paused again, seeing their faces before him." I allow Malzius to state that he is weak, "so when I speak of the young men I seem to see them," again drawing heavily on Mr. Benét's descriptions.

In the grandly conceived ending of the story Professor Malzius "was thinking about the young men." I, needing a visible scene, took the liberty of inventing the faces of the dead—and the cheering—and the sudden silence—and the lines which terminate the play. Having actually introduced the students, I could use them again—carrying a step farther Mr. Benét's thought that Malzius, without his glasses and dizzy on his way to execution, "could see them very plainly . . . all the men whom he had taught." Finally Malzius, studying the Dictator while in his presence, is reminded of a deranged woman Charcot showed in his clinic many years before and diagnoses an endocrine unbalance plus hysteria. It is logical to emphasize the latter and to bring down the curtain on an outburst in that vein.

What is good about the play, the lofty conception, the pervading spiritual quality, the thought that "the important thing was the truth" is Mr. Benét's. The working out in terms of theatre and the attempt to devise a scene sequence which cannot possibly rise to the high poetic level of the story are mine.

Blood of the Martyrs*

ANNOUNCER.—Tonight the Contemporary Theatre presents "Blood of the Martyrs" by Percival Wilde, based on a story by Stephen Vincent Benét.

The gesture of this play is a decided stand against a certain doctrine . . . not in any one land . . . but anywhere and everywhere. It may be noted in passing that the expression of opinion at variance with that of the party in power is treasonable, in the present year of grace, in the majority of European countries.

MUSIC.—*Up and under.*

NARRATOR.—As the curtain rises, we distinguish a man lying on a cot in a dungeon. His limbs are frail. His back, if he were standing, would be marked by an academic stoop. His front teeth have been broken, and some of them are missing. His eyes have been closed in sleep, but we find him just at the point of waking.

MALZIUS.—Gentlemen, do not beat me again. This body of mine cannot stand it. It is sixty-two years old, and its blood count is poor. You follow me? At your service, gentlemen: Malzius; Professor Gregor Malzius. Possibly you have heard the name. (*Yawns . . . chuckles*) Benedictus Dominus!

MUSIC.—*Up and under.*

NARRATOR.—In a secluded room in another part of the town is a group of graduate students and laboratory assistants, all devoted followers of the great scientist, Professor Malzius. They have not heard that their idol is in prison.

BONNARD.—(*Forty odd, a typical Frenchman*) Flemming saize
. . .

ELLERMANN.—(*In the thirties*) What is the difference what he
says?

BONNARD.—He saize, like Virchow, "Omnis nucleus e nucleo."
Like "Omnis cellula e cellula." W'at iss, iss not new. It iss
from somet'ing else. Zere iss ze chenetic continuity of
cells . . .

ELLERMANN.—But we have come here to learn what Malzius
says!

MAX.—Vivat!

ELSA.—Vivat Malzius!

WISSOTZSKI.—Malzius, the Bear! Ursus Major! Floreat! Vivat!

ELLERMANN.—You, Bonnard, from the Sorbonne, Paris; me,
Ellermann . . .

ANTON.—(*Interrupting*) Yes, we all know you travel three
hundred and eighteen miles when you visit the girl with the
yellow eyes!

ELLERMANN.—(*Nothing daunted*) There, Elsa, she travels further.

ELSA.—Gregopoulos comes from Athens.

GREGOPOULOS.—(*With a strong foreign accent but with fluency*)
Many years ago. Now I am naturalized.

MAX.—The best of the young men: Malzius always gets them!

ELSA.—And the young women, too!

WISSOTZSKI.—Me. You. Us.

MAX.—He says so himself.

ANTON.—The Bear: Malzius!

WISSOTZSKI.—Cellular phenomena: Malzius!

BONNARD.—'E woot explain ze last judgment in tairms of cellular
phenomena.

ANTON.—He would explain the present régime in terms of
cellular phenomena.

GREGOPOULOS.—That is easy: certain cells of the body rebel against the normal processes of nature and set up their own warlike state. Like the others, they, too, have a destiny: but we call it cancer.

ELLERMANN.—For God's sake, Gregopoulos!

GREGOPOULOS.—As I shall demonstrate in an essay, the new regime is a cancer, gnawing away all that is healthy in the nation.

WISSOTZSKI.—Cut it out before it destroys everything!

GREGOPOULOS.—Let the people know their danger!

ELSA.—That is what we learn from cellular phenomena!

GREGOPOULOS.—We must not wait long. This morning a band of hoodlums drove out Brémond. . . .

BONNARD.—No? Not really?

GREGOPOULOS.—You were not there, Bonnard, but we know, we others. They marched into the lecture room where Brémond was demonstrating. They smashed his slides. They spat on his prepared specimens. They scrawled, "Long live the state!" on the blackboard. They hooted Brémond from the platform.

ANTON.—They would never dare to do that to Malzius.

MAX.—You cannot be sure. . . .

ELSA.—But why? Why? Science is science! The truth is the truth!

WISSOTZSKI.—Not to the tyrant who has seized this nation by the throat!

ELLERMANN.—Hush, Wissotzski!

GREGOPOULOS.—Why should he not speak? To speak, that is the important thing. What Elsa says is right. Science is science. When I look through a lens into worlds too tiny for the unaided eye, I see truth; but when I look at the world about me, at the land which was ours and is now theirs, I see nothing but lies.

BONNARD.—W'at iss it to you? One gouvernement iss as goot as anozzer.

ELLERMANN.—Gregopoulos, you have no quarrel with any government. Hang out any flag they want. Stand at attention. Salute. Scream, "Hail! Hail! Long live the state!"

ELSA.—So long as the truth is the truth!

ANTON.—Will they leave their hands off Malzius?

GREGOPOULOS.—They should. The scientist is concerned with the eternal, not with transient political phenomena. . . .

ELLERMANN.—(*Horrified*) "Transient?" Gregopoulos, be careful!

GREGOPOULOS.—Transient I said, and transient I meant. Long after the Dictator is gone, the name of Malzius will be remembered.

ELLERMANN.—For God's sake!

GREGOPOULOS.—I ask you, which one is the glory of this country: Malzius, because of whom thousands who should be dead are alive, or the Dictator, because of whom thousands who should be alive are dead?

ELLERMANN.—Gregopoulos, this is treason!

ELSA.—Treason? Pfft!

WISSOTZSKI.—We had a meeting last night. . . .

ELLERMANN.—Don't tell me anything about it!

GREGOPOULOS.—Why not? Tell him everything about it.

WISSOTZSKI.—We were all there . . . except Bonnard. Max . . . Anton . . . Gregopoulos . . . Elsa. . . .

ELSA.—We must have freedom even under the new régime.

GREGOPOULOS.—To talk of a free world is a delusion. Men are not free in this world.

ANTON.—The world should be like a chemical formula: full of reason and logic.

GREGOPOULOS.—We will make it so! The cancer cries out for treatment!

ELSA.—In our first number we are publishing . . .
(*Fade out*)

ELLERMANN.—I will hear no more.

SOUND.—*Door slams. Pause.*

ANTON.—Is he safe?

ELSA.—Perfectly.

ANTON.—Will he tell?

ELSA.—Ellermann? Never!

WISSOTZSKI.—When our magazine comes out he'll shake his finger at us, but he'll read it.

BONNARD.—Go on. I shoot like to 'ear more.

GREGOPOULOS.—Bonnard, are you on our side?

BONNARD.—If I muss choos sides, yes; but I prefair not to choos. I find it amusant: ze passwairds; ze bar of musique you w'istle in answer. Like a game . . .

ELSA.—It is more than a game.

BONNARD.—It iss a shildish game of conspiracy! So stupide! So 'opeless! You come 'ere from efferyw'ere. You wear sheap clothes. You eat ze bad, starchy foot of ze poor restaurants. You haf seelly leetle lof affairs, an' you play shildish games of politics . . . instead of doing your wairk. W'at woot Malzius say?

ELSA.—Last night Malzius was with us!

BONNARD.—(*Thunderstruck*) No!

WISSOTZSKI.—He didn't want to come. . . .

BONNARD.—(*Raging*) You shoot not haf asked him!

ELSA.—We can trust him. . . .

BONNARD.—'E does not want to be trusted!

ELSA.—We have brought him our other problems. . . .

BONNARD.—So you muss bring 'im zese, also? Seelly leetle dogs, trotting to 'im wiss your stupide bones in ze mouth? Politics? Politics? Politics? For you . . . pair'aps! Only pair'aps! But for Malzius, neffer! For Malzius ze pure lof of science! Ze scientis' shoot be able to lif anyw'ere!

GREGOPOULOS.—Listen, Bonnard: we met, more than twenty of us. We planned . . .

ANTON.—(*Lowering his voice*) We planned . . .

MAX.—We must have freedom!

ELSA.—The people must be warned of the danger!

GREGOPOULOS.—We shall publish what we please!

BONNARD.—An' Malzius haird?

ANTON.—He sat there and laughed.

BONNARD.—I weesh zat I, too, coot laugh, but I cannot. Shildren shoot not play wiss fire! Tomorrow I leaf for Paris.

ELSA.—We are neither communists nor Fascists. But freedom . . .

GREGOPOULOS.—Intellectual freedom . . .

WISSOTZSKI.—We have a right to that!

ELSA.—We shall take the right!

MAX.—We planned . . .

ANTON—Very secretly we planned . . .

SOUND.—*Kick door.*

VOICE.—Open in the name of the state!

ALL.—(*Ad lib terrified whispers.*)
  It's the troopers!
  The troopers!
  They must have followed us!
  Be quiet! Say nothing! Be quiet!

SOUND.—*Door crashes open.*

VOICE.—Long live the state!

GREGOPOULOS.—What is it you want?

VOICE.—You are all under arrest.

ALL.—(*Ad libs*)

VOICE.—Long live the state!

MUSIC.—*Up and fade out.*

53

NARRATOR.—The scene changes to the prison in which Professor Malzius is confined.

SOUND.—*Opening of prison door. All metal.*
(*Fade in, as if echo of previous line*)

OTTO.—Long live the state!
(*Fade in*)

ROLF.—(*Who has been drinking*) Long live the state!

SOUND.—*Close door.*

OTTO.—He's asleep.

ROLF.—The pig dog! Pig dog Malzius!

OTTO.—(*Scornfully*) *Professor* Malzius.

ROLF.—Pig dog professor!

OTTO.—Who can't see a foot without his glasses!

ROLF.—I broke them once when I knocked him down. You wouldn't hardly believe it, Otto: he was like a woman. He didn't have no strength at all.

OTTO.—Broken glasses! Much he can see through them!

ROLF.—Lucky I was careful, like I always am, or I'd have cut my knuckles on them glasses.

OTTO.—You ought to know better than to hit a man wearing glasses.

ROLF.—(*Incredulously*) *Not* hit him?

OTTO.—Not hit him with your fist. Hit him with a club.

ROLF.—Nex' time I'll let him have it with the butt of my pistol!

OTTO.—We got to wake him up. The General is coming. (*Lowers voice*) They say maybe His Excellency is coming with the General.

ROLF.—What?

OTTO.—(*Lowering his voice still more*) The Dictator . . .

ROLF.—The Dictator coming to see Malzius? Never!

OTTO.—We got orders to wake him.

54

Rolf.—Let me do it, Otto. (*He expectorates*) Wake up, pig dog professor!

Otto.—(*Chuckling*) He didn't move.

Rolf.—They sleep good after one of our treatments. Best thing in the world for in-so-mon-i-a. (*He kicks him*) Wake up, Malzius!

Malzius.—(*Suddenly waking*) Long live the state!

Otto.—A hell of a lot you care about it!

Rolf.—Attention! Pig dog! Malzius, when I call you "pig dog" answer, "Present." . . . Pig dog!

Malzius.—Present.

Rolf.—Pig dog!

Malzius.—Present.

Rolf.—(*Delighted*) See? He learns quick!

Otto.—He better or we'll learn him.

Rolf.—Pig dog, what do you know about the traitors?

Malzius.—Nothing.

Rolf.—He don't know nothing. He says so himself, and he's a professor!

Otto.—What was they planning to do?

Rolf.—Tell us about them, and we won't hurt you . . . much.

Malzius.—In God's name, gentlemen, what sort of conspirator do you think I would make? A man of my age and habits? I am interested in cellular phenomena.

Rolf.—(*Laughing*) That's a good one! Say, Otto, I guess pig dog Malzius has seen lots of cellular phenomena right in this here cell! Ho! Ho! Ho! Ho!

Otto.—(*Laughing*) Cellular phenomena is right!

Rolf.—He's gonna see some more right now, the pig dog! Pig dog! He didn't say "Present." Watch me have a little fun with him.

Otto.—Not now.

55

ROLF.—Listen. This here's a new belt, and it's got a big heavy buckle, and I ain't a-goin' to hurt my knuckles. . . .

OTTO.—After the General is through with him; not now. The General is coming. . . . You know it as well as I do . . . and maybe His Excellency, too; and if you're not careful, the General may have a little fun himself . . . with you! The General is a great one for having fun. The General's got his own ideas about different kinds of fun. . . .

MUSIC.—*Up and under.*

NARRATOR.—The scene changes to the chapel of an old church now used for purposes of the state. A light falls only upon the pulpit, but in the shadows we discern various human forms that seldom move. One of them is a woman.

SOUND.—*Metal latch and door creak.*

VOICE.—Attention!

ALL.—Long live the state.

SOUND.—*Door creak . . . slam . . . latch.*
(*Fade in*)

GENERAL.—Long live the state.

SOUND.—*Feet ascending to pulpit.*

GENERAL.—Good afternoon, ladies and gentlemen. I beg your pardon: lady and gentlemen. Though you are fewer than you were when we met, nearly four months ago, it is a pleasure to see you again. You are doubtless surprised to note that I, a full general, am relieving the junior officer who has been in charge of your exercises during so many happy weeks, but we feel that we have already wasted too much time on you. I miss Ellerman . . . that promising young man who insisted he had attended none of your meetings.

ELSA.—Neither he had.

GENERAL.—Indeed? He was so stout in his denials . . . and in his protestations that you were all innocent . . . that we were particularly attentive to him. It is unfortunate that he succumbed to heart failure.

ELSA.—He was shot.

56

GENERAL.—You exaggerate, dear lady. It was heart failure, exactly as with our amusing little friend, Wissotzski: he used to hop about so comically while he was being beaten . . . and that charming young girl with the dark hair . . . I forget her name . . . and the tall man who limped . . . and the gentleman with the Greek name. . . .

ELSA.—Gregopoulos.

GENERAL.—That was it: Gregopoulos, author of a brilliant if unpublished essay entitled, "Man's Right to Freedom." Whether from heart failure or from some other cause, Gregopoulos is now thoroughly deceased. He is as dead as Miltiades. And there must be others that I have forgotten. Let me see: there were nearly two dozen of you in the beginning. Malzius is still alive: yes, we have him safe elsewhere. Bonnard has returned to Paris: how like a Frenchman! It appears that he was in the habit of calling daily at the French embassy, and they made representations immediately he was missed. We beat him and turned him loose. I may tell you this state secret because you will never tell it to anybody. Your dossier is about to be closed. Where was I? Since there are only four of you left . . . plus Malzius and Bonnard is six . . . and you were originally two dozen, there are a number to be accounted for. I cannot do it. My arithmetic is horrible. (*Pauses . . . speaks more sternly*) You planned, a handful of you, to overturn the state! Two dozen traitors against fifty million people! You deserve the worst, and you shall have it! At the outset we were patient with you. Your memories were faulty, and we endeavored to stimulate them with exercises . . . which became brisker only gradually. We got nothing out of you . . . except heroics . . . and the trouble with heroics is that they require an appreciative audience. Without one they are only damp squibs. Nevertheless you persisted. . . . Well, my patience is at an end. The Dictator is honoring us with a visit this afternoon, and he must not breathe the air which you pollute. You have information which he should like to possess: names; addresses. For a final ten minutes the officer in charge will question you urgently . . . most urgently. When the ten minutes expire . . . so will you! Lady and gentlemen . . . long live the state!

MUSIC.—*Up and fade out.*

OTTO.—Stand straighter, Malzius.

MALZIUS.—It is difficult.

ROLF.—Difficult?

MALZIUS.—The knee has been badly set . . . and there are two broken ribs.

OTTO.—Straighter!

ROLF.—I'll make him stand straighter!

MALZIUS.—(*Groans*)

ROLF.—There.

OTTO.—Careful, Rolf! (*To Malzius*) Put on your glasses, you old fool! The General is coming here.

ROLF.—Well, why don't you put them on?

MALZIUS.—The glasses—I cannot see them.

OTTO.—Here they are.

MALZIUS.—(*Putting them on*) There is a crack in the left lens.

VOICE.—(*Outside*) Attention!

OTTO.—Attention!

SOUND.—*Metal door opens.*

GENERAL.—Well, Professor?

MALZIUS.—(*Surprised*) Long live the state!

SOUND.—*Metal door closes.*

GENERAL.—Long live the state! (*As though looking Malzius over*) Hmmm . . . so . . . a well-trained animal, Rolf.

VOICE.—(*Outside*) Attention!

OTTO.—Attention!

SOUND.—*Door opens . . . marching feet come in.*

ALL.—Long live the state!

DICTATOR.—Long live the state!

SOUND.—*Door closes.*

58

DICTATOR.—Corporal!

CORPORAL.—Yes, Your Excellency.

DICTATOR.—Place the desk and chair here.

CORPORAL.—Yes, Your Excellency.

DICTATOR.—Be sure that pen and paper are there also . . . and . . . the ink, of course.

CORPORAL.—Yes, Your Excellency.

SOUND.—*Desk on floor, chair, paper, inkwell.*

GENERAL.—Careful. . . . You nearly spilled the ink.

DICTATOR.—Is this . . . Malzius?

GENERAL.—Yes, Your Excellency.

DICTATOR.—Tell the man to come closer. . . . Can he hear me? Is he deaf?

GENERAL.—No, Your Excellency. He is a little old, though perfectly healthy. . . . Are you not, Professor Malzius?

MALZIUS.—Yes, I am perfectly healthy. . . . I am very well treated here.

DICTATOR.—Come closer.

MALZIUS.—(*Speaking nervously, automatically*) I have been very well treated here, and the General has acted with the greatest consideration. But I am Professor Gregor Malzius . . . professor of biochemistry. For thirty years I have lectured at the university; I am a Fellow of the Royal Society, a corresponding member of the Academies of Sciences at Berlin, at Rome, at Boston, at Paris, and at Stockholm. I have received the Nottingham Medal, the Lamarck Medal, the Order of St. John of Portugal and the Nobel Prize. I think my blood count is low, but I have received a great many degrees, and my experiments on the migratory cells are not finished. I do not wish to complain of my treatment, but I must continue my experiments. (*He stops, like a clock that has run down*)

DICTATOR.—(*In a harsh, toneless voice*) Yes, Professor Malzius, there has been a regrettable error. In these days the nation demands the submission of every citizen. (*His voice rises and falls jerkily . . . his speech is that of a neurotic*) En-circled by jealous foes, our reborn land yet marches forward toward her magnificent destiny. We have overcome obstacles. It is because we have within us the will to conquer. Jealous and spiteful tongues in other countries have declared that it is our purpose to wipe out learning and science. That is not our intention. There has been a cleansing, but after the cleansing, the rebirth. We mean to move forward to the greatest science in the world: our own science, based on the enduring principles of our nationhood.

MALZIUS.—(*Hesitantly*) I was part of the cleansing? You did not mean to hurt me?

GENERAL.—Yes, Professor Malzius, you were part of the cleansing. Now that is over. His Excellency has spoken.

MALZIUS.—But I do not understand.

GENERAL.—(*In a slow, careful voice*) It is very simple. You are a distinguished man of science: you have received the Lamarck Medal and the Nobel Prize. That was a service to the state. You became, however, infected with the wrong political ideas. That was treachery to the state. You had, therefore, as decreed by His Excellency, to pass through a certain period of probation and rehabilitation. But that, we believe, is finished.

MALZIUS.—You do not wish to know the names of the young men any more? You do not want the addresses?

SOUND.—*Rifle volley . . .*

GENERAL.—The names and addresses are no longer of im-portance. The conspirators have been caught and executed. There is no longer opposition.

MALZIUS.—(*Mechanically*) There is no longer opposition . . . oh!

GENERAL.—In their testimony you were not even involved.

MALZIUS.—I was not even involved . . . yes.

GENERAL.—Now we come to the future. I will be frank. The new state is frank with its citizens.

DICTATOR.—(*As if in a dream*) It is so.

GENERAL.—There has been . . . let us say . . . a certain agitation in foreign countries regarding Professor Malzius. That means nothing, of course. Nevertheless, your acquaintance, Professor Bonnard, and others have meddled in matters that do not concern them.

MALZIUS.—(*Surprised*) They asked after me? It is true, my experiments were reaching a point . . .

DICTATOR.—(*Interrupting*) No foreign influence could turn us from our firm purpose. But it is our inflexible will to show our nation first in science and culture as we have already shown her first in manliness and statehood. For that reason you are here, Professor Malzius.

MALZIUS.—(*Trembling*) I do not understand. You will give me my laboratory back?

DICTATOR.—Yes.

MALZIUS.—My post at the university? My experiments?

DICTATOR.—It is the purpose of our régime to offer the fullest encouragement to our loyal sons of science.

MALZIUS.—First of all, I must go to a hospital. My blood count is poor. But that will not take long. (*His voice becomes impatient*) Then . . . my notebooks were burned, I suppose. That was silly, but we can start in again. I have a very good memory, an excellent memory. The theories are in my head, you know. I must have assistants, of course; little Gregopoulos was my best one. . . .

GENERAL.—(*Sternly*) The man Gregopoulos has been executed. You had best forget him.

MALZIUS.—Oh? Well, then, I must have someone else. You see, these are important experiments. There must be some young men . . . clever ones. They cannot all be dead. I will know them. The Bear always got the pick of the crop. (*He laughs a little nervously*) They used to call me "the Bear," you know. (*He stops abruptly*) You are not . . . you are not fooling me? (*He bursts into tears*)

SOUND.—*Cell door opens.*

MAN.—Long live the state!

DICTATOR.—Long live the state!

MAN.—Your Excellency, the parade of the Young Guard is ready to proceed now.

DICTATOR.—Very good . . . I will review them. (*Fading*) Leave everything here. I shall return.

SOUND.—*Footsteps march off. Cell door closes.*

GENERAL.—His Excellency forgives your unworthy suggestion. He knows you were overwrought.

MALZIUS.—(*Sobbing*) Yes . . .

GENERAL.—Come, come, we mustn't have our new president of the National Academy crying! It would look badly in the photographs.

MALZIUS.—(*Quickly*) President of the Academy? Oh, no! I mustn't be that! They make speeches; they have administrative work. I am a scientist; a teacher.

GENERAL.—I'm afraid you can't very well avoid it. Your induction will be quite a ceremony. His Excellency himself will preside. And you will speak on the glories of our science. It will be a magnificent answer to the petty and jealous criticisms of our neighbors. (*As Malzius is about to interrupt*) Oh, you needn't worry about the speech! It will be prepared; you will only have to read it. His Excellency thinks of everything.

MALZIUS.—Very well; and then may I go back to my work?

GENERAL.—(*Smiling*) Oh, don't worry about that! I'm only a simple soldier; I don't know about those things. But you'll have plenty of work.

MALZIUS.—(*Eagerly*) The more the better. I still have ten good years. (*He laughs*)

GENERAL.—Hmmm—let me look at you. . . . Well, well! The teeth must be attended to . . . at once. (*As if to himself*) And a rest, undoubtedly, before the photographs are taken. Milk. He should have milk. . . . You are not feeling sufficiently well, Professor Malzius?

MALZIUS.—I am very happy. I have been very well treated. I come of peasant stock, and I have a good constitution.

GENERAL.—Good. (*He pauses . . . speaks in a more official voice*) Of course, it is understood, Professor Malzius . . .

MALZIUS.—Yes? I beg your pardon, I was thinking of something else.

GENERAL.—It is understood, Professor Malzius, that your . . . er . . . rehabilitation in the service of the state is a permanent matter. Naturally you will be under observation, but even so there must be no mistakes.

MALZIUS.—(*Impatiently*) I am a scientist. What have I to do with politics? If you wish me to take oaths of loyalty, I will take as many as you wish.

GENERAL.—I am glad you take that attitude. I may say that I regret the unpleasant side of our interviews. I trust you bear me no ill will.

MALZIUS.—Why should I be angry? You were told to do one thing. Now you are told to do another. That is all.

GENERAL.—(*Stiffly*) It is not quite so simple as that. (*Puzzled*) And I'd have sworn you were one of the stiff-necked ones! (*Pauses*) Well, well, every man has his breaking point, I suppose. In a few moments you will receive the final commands of His Excellency. Tonight you will go to the capital and speak over the radio. You will have no difficulty there: the speech is written. But it will put a quietus on the activities of our friend, Bonnard, and the question that has been raised in the British Parliament. Then a few weeks of rest by the sea . . . and the dental work . . . and then, my dear president of the National Academy, you will be ready to undertake your new duties. I congratulate you and hope we shall meet often under pleasanter auspices.

VOICE.—Attention!

SOUND.—*Door opens.*

ALL.—Long live the state.

SOUND.—*Footsteps march in . . . stop on cue.*

DICTATOR.—Is it settled? Good. Gregor Malzius, I welcome you into the service of the new state. You have cast your errors aside and are part of our destiny.

MALZIUS.—Yes. I shall be able to do my work now.

DICTATOR.—(*Frowning*) You will not only be able to continue your invaluable researches but you will also be able . . .

and it will be part of your duty . . . to further our national ideals. Our reborn nation must rule the world for the world's good. There is a fire within us that is not in other peoples. Our civilization must be extended everywhere. The future wills it. It will furnish the subject of your first discourse as president of the Academy.

MALZIUS.—(*In a low voice*) But I am not a soldier. I am a biochemist. I have no experience in these matters you speak of.

DICTATOR.—You are a distinguished man of science. You will prove that our women must bear soldiers, our men abandon this nonsense of republics and democracies for trust in those born to rule them. You will prove by scientific law that certain races . . . our race in particular . . . are destined to rule the world. You will prove that we are destined to rule by the virtues of war and that war is part of our heritage.

MALZIUS.—But it is not like that. (*Expressions of alarm*) I mean in the laboratory one looks and watches. One waits for a long time. It is a long process, very long. And then, if the theory is not proved, one discards the theory. That is the way it is done. I probably do not explain it very well. But I am a biochemist: I do not know how to look for the virtues of one race as against another, and I can prove nothing about war, except that it kills. If I said anything else, the whole world would laugh at me.

DICTATOR.—No one in this nation would laugh at you.

MALZIUS.—But if they do not laugh at me when I am wrong then there is no science. (*He pauses . . . earnestly*) Do not misunderstand me. I have ten years of good work left. I want to get back to my laboratory. But you see, there are the young men . . . and if I am to teach the young men . . . (*He breaks off*) You must pardon me. The food that is given me here is deficient in proteins. My blood count is poor, and I am weak; so when I speak of the young men I seem to see them: the many who have passed through my classrooms. From all over the world they have come: Williams, the Englishman who died in the War; and little Gregopoulos. . . .

GENERAL.—(*warning him*) Hmmm. . . . !

MALZIUS.— . . . with the fox terrier eyes; and Indians and Persians and South Africans and Chinese. They go, and if

64

later on they die, that does not matter; but while they are
with me they must be given the truth. . . . Otherwise there
can be no continuity and no science.

DICTATOR.—(*Sharply*) I thought everything had been explained
to Professor Malzius.

MALZIUS.—Why, yes. I will sign any papers. I assure you I am
not interested in politics . . . a man like myself, imagine!
One state is as good as another. And I miss my tobacco . . .
I have not smoked in months. I should like to smoke. But
you see, one cannot be a scientist and tell lies. (*He pauses
. . . then speaks in a low voice*) What happens if I do not?

GENERAL.—(*Sternly*) Why, then, we shall resume our conversations, Professor Malzius.

MALZIUS.—(*Simply*) Then . . . I shall be beaten again?

GENERAL.—The process of rehabilitation is obviously not quite
complete, but perhaps in time . . .

MALZIUS.—(*Wearily*) It will not be necessary. I cannot be
beaten again. (*Pause . . . then in a clear, changed voice*)
Call in your other officers. There are papers for me to sign. I
should like all of them to witness.

GENERAL.—(*Surprised*) Why . . . why . . .

DICTATOR.—You will feel so much better, Professor Malzius. I
am so very glad you have given in.

MALZIUS.—Why, of course, I give in. Are you not the Dictator?
And besides, if I do not, I shall be beaten again . . . and I
cannot . . . you understand? . . . I cannot be beaten
again. (*He pauses, breathing hard*)

DICTATOR.—I am happy. I am very happy. Gentlemen . . . I
am glad you have come. We are receiving today into the
service of the state the president of the new National
Academy, our most distinguished scientist, the winner of
the Lamarck Medal and the Nobel Prize, Professor Gregor
Malzius.

ALL.—(*Slight applause*)

GENERAL.—(*In an undertone*) Take the pen. The inkwell is there,
Professor Malzius.

MALZIUS.—Is there plenty of ink in it?

GENERAL.—Plenty of ink. Now you may sign.

DICTATOR.—In the name of the state, I welcome you.

MALZIUS.—Ah yes . . . the ink . . . the ink. The state . . . the state. But science does not know about states. And you are a little man . . . a little unimportant man!

SOUND.—*Almost the sound of a blow; followed by the fall of a small, heavy object on the floor. Malzius has thrown the inkwell at the Dictator.*

ALL.—(*Ad libs continue*)
The inkwell!
He threw the inkwell!
In the Dictator's face!
Treason!
Look at His Excellency!
Covered with ink!
Face and uniform!
Treason!

GENERAL.—You dog of a traitor!

SOUND.—*Blow.*

MALZIUS.—(*Groan*)

ALL.—(*Ad libs continue*)

MALZIUS.—(*Hysterical laughing*)

DICTATOR.—Take that man out and shoot him at once!

ALL.—(*Ad libs . . . seizing prisoner*)

SOUND.—*Body blows.*

MALZIUS.—(*Board fade laughing*)

ALL.—(*Board fade back in with less struggle*)

NARRATOR.—Professor Malzius is seized by the soldiers. He is led out into the courtyard to be executed. And as he stumbles along in the hands of his captors, he seems to see the faces and hear the voices of the many, many students who have studied with him . . . and who have preceded him to death.

MALZIUS.—(*To himself*) A schoolboy covered with ink! An hysterical schoolboy, too! Such a man, such a face should not rule countries or young men! But you cannot kill the truth!

VOICES.—You cannot kill the truth!
You cannot kill the truth!

MUSIC.—*Up and under the following.*

ANTON.—Malzius, the Bear!

GREGOPOLOUS.—The pick of the crop!

MAX.—The best of the young men!

ELSA.—And the young women, too!

ANTON.—Malzius, the Bear!

WISSOTZSKI.—Ursus Major!

ELSA.—You cannot kill the truth!
(*Start Board fade*)

ANTON.—Vivat!

ELSA.—Malzius!

GREGOPOLOUS.—Malzius!

MUSIC.—*Out sure.*
(*Board cut and open full*)

OFFICER.—Make ready! Aim! Fire!

SOUND.—*Rifle volley.*

GENERAL.—(*Sententiously*) If bullets can kill, there died an enemy of the state!

DICTATOR.—But what . . . what (*his voice rises to a hysterical scream*) if bullets cannot kill?

MUSIC.—*Up and under narrator.*

NARRATOR.—The play is ended. The curtain slowly falls as the two fanatics face each other in silence.

MUSIC.—*Up and under . . . out on cue.*

ANNOUNCER.—You have just heard the première performance of the series entitled The Contemporary Theatre which comes to you as a presentation of the Federal Radio Theatre, a project of the Works Progress Administration. Tonight's play was Percival Wilde's "Blood of the Martyrs," based on a story by Stephen Vincent Benét. The plays in this series are adapted for radio and produced by Donald Macfarlane.

VOICE ONE.—*For your information!*

VOICE TWO.—Every week the Federal Theatre brings to your neighborhood new and vital plays . . . at neighborhood prices. For dates and locations, see your newspaper . . . or call Murray Hill 4-5903 . . . Murray Hill 4-5903.

ANNOUNCER.—On the stage . . . and on the air . . . The Federal Theatre is your theatre!*
(*Station signature*)

* The Federal Theatre Project was liquidated by Act of Congress, June 30, 1939.

Information Please

THIS WEEKLY broadcast stands out as a good-natured refutation of a theory long entertained by professional broadcasters: that in matters of form and content the more intelligent a broadcast is the fewer are its listeners. This anthology is no place to point out the basic fallacy in this reasoning, but the theory was sufficiently strong as recently as three years ago to allow such a solid and sensible idea as Information Please to go begging for over fifteen months.

In defense of all those broadcasters who reviewed and rejected the idea, it must be pointed out that the submitted treatments were much weaker than the shows that the radio audience has heard. Not only was this true but the original plan, although stating the necessity for a battery of experts, did not at first name the experts now performing. This fact is important in retrospect because after a year of continuous production there are few thoughtful people who would dispute the fact that the amazing success of this series depends largely upon the great versatility of the quartet that does so much of the work. Nowhere in radio is there a smoother, more complementary unit.

Credit for this broadcast belongs to Mr. Dan Golenpaul, originator of the idea and producer of the present series. The selection of Clifton Fadiman as master of ceremonies immediately brought forth one of the most engaging and resourceful personalities in radio today; the trio of experts, Mr. Adams, Mr. Kieran, and Mr. Levant, among them seem to have read everything ever written and to have remembered it well enough to quote it upon request.

F. P. A., whose "Conning Tower" has been the delivery room for many a bouncing masterpiece, is as conversant with the records of contemporary writers and entertainers as any other man in the country; Oscar Levant is musically all but unstumpable; and John Kieran, sports columnist of *The New York Times*, has become known the nation over as a walking and talking encyclopedia, seeming to possess what psychologists conveniently term "complete recall." All are witty, F. P. A. particularly so, and all are happily and hereditarily furnished with fine senses of humor.

The pivotal difference of the show from other quiz programs is in its open invitation to trip up authority. The sparring and the readiness, the incalculable and surprising knowledge of the participants continuously hold the audience through the light treatment of heavy subjects, the delightful badinage, and the occasional but inevitable collapses.

Usually Information Please does not present all its experts on the same program but seeks to vary the show by the inclusion of a guest or two, men and women recognized as outstanding in the professions with which their names are identified. A sample cross section heard in the past few months would find such names as Helen Wills, Rex Stout, William Lyon Phelps, Lillian Gish, Kathleen Norris, Deems Taylor, Bela Spewack, John Gunther, Gracie Allen, H. V. Kaltenborn, and many others equally scattered in their interests and occupations. The reprinted transcript is a show of this type. It has been selected not only because it is superior of its sort and representative of the series as a whole but because no show that included the musical contributions of Oscar Levant could be effectively reproduced in print. Mr. Levant yielded his place in this instance to Bernard Jaffe and Clarence Buddington Kelland. The broadcast was heard over NBC's Blue Network on April 14, 1939.

Information Please*

CROSS.—Information Please! Presented each week at this time by Canada Dry, famous the world over for its fine beverages. (*Cock crow*) Wake up, America! Time to stump the experts and enjoy a glass of refreshing Canada Dry Ginger Ale. Every week at this hour Canada Dry presents Information Please . . . 30 minutes of quizzing, with John Public supplying the questions and our panel of experts supplying the answers plus whatever else they feel like saying. Send us stickers. We set up a four-man board to answer them. You may submit from one to three original questions. For every question our quartet fails to answer the sender gets $10, with the compliments of Canada Dry. For every question we use, whether or not it is answered correctly, the sender gets $5. So you can make $15 if our experts miss out, which, human nature being what it is, they occasionally do. Our editorial staff may reword your question a trifle. Don't fret over it. Wherever there is a duplication of questions Information Please uses the one that was submitted first. All questions become the property of Information Please and should be addressed to Canada Dry, 1 Pershing Square, New York City.

And now may I present our master of ceremonies, Mr. Clifton Fadiman, literary critic of the *New Yorker* magazine? Mr. Fadiman.

MR. CLIFTON FADIMAN.—Good evening, ladies and gentlemen. Information Please is an ad lib program. We have fun doing it that way, and we hope you do, too. The rules are very simple, though the questions often aren't. The experts raise their hands if they know the answer or feel like guessing, and if they miss Canada Dry cheerfully pays out $10 to the sender plus $5 for the use of the question itself. Tonight our board consists of our reliable brace of veterans, Franklin

---

* The transcript of this broadcast, Information Please, is here reprinted by special permission of the J. M. Mathes Agency, Inc, and Canada Dry Ginger Ale, sponsors of Information Please.

71

P. Adams, creator of the famous humorous column, "The Conning Tower," which appears regularly in the *New York Post*, and the practically unstumpable John Kieran, sports expert, practical authority, bird fancier, and what have you. Our guests of honor this evening are Bernard Jaffe, author of *Crucibles*, *Outposts of Science*, and other works humanizing scientific knowledge, and the ever-popular Clarence Buddington Kelland, whose stories and novels have delighted millions.

A moment ago I referred to Mr. Kieran as a bird fancier, which leads me to believe that I had better settle the famous woodpecker controversy which has been agitating the nation . . . or should I say tearing up the dovecote . . . all during the last week. We had a question last week in which we asked the board to tell us something about the life expectancy of the woodpecker, the lion, the swan, and the tortoise and to arrange them in the proper order. Mr. Kieran said the woodpecker had the smallest life expectancy, then the lion, the swan, and then the tortoise. I questioned the information and promised to tell you this evening which was correct. According to *The World Almanac*, last paragraph, page 468 . . . don't bother to turn to it now . . . we were right in our listing. On the other hand, according to the National Association of the Audubon Society, woodpeckers may range from 10 years to 25 in their life expectancy, according to their size and probably according to the kind of life they've lived. I think we ought to accept the Audubon Society as our authority this evening, and therefore I am going to adjudicate the question in Mr. Kieran's favor. Or rather, if I may, in the favor of Information Please. So K.O. Kieran wins over *World Almanac*, thus bringing great credit to this remarkable program. I could go on . . . I have three or four cards of information . . . and further confuse you about the life expectancy of the woodpecker, the lion, the swan, and the tortoise, but that's enough for this evening. How do you feel, Mr. Kieran?

MR. JOHN KIERAN.—I feel a little better. (*Laughter*)

FADIMAN.—Very good. Very handsome of you. All right, let's see what you can do with this one. The first question has nothing to do with woodpeckers. It comes from Miss Elizabeth C. Bailey of Philadelphia, Pennsylvania, and, gentlemen, you've got to reach pretty far back to answer this one. I'm going to ask you to identify the following ads of yesteryear. When was yesteryear, Mr. Adams? I've always wanted to know just about when it was.

MR. FRANKLIN ADAMS.—Two years ago.

FADIMAN.—Information Please never fails. Now there is an ad, a slogan, which went: "See that hump?" Mr. Kelland?

MR. CLARENCE BUDDINGTON KELLAND.—Delong's hooks and eyes.

FADIMAN.—How did you happen to know that, Mr. Kelland?

KELLAND.—Just hanging around with the girls.

FADIMAN.—Now suppose you saw the ad in those days, when you were a small boy, Mr. Kelland . . . and a very cute little boy you must have been, Mr. Kelland, if I may say so . . . "Good morning, have you used . . . "?

KELLAND.—Pear Soap.

FADIMAN.—Mr. Kelland says Pear Soap, and that's quite correct. Don't forget to raise your hand. I know you're eager, Mr. Kelland, I know you're eager.

KELLAND.—You picked me with your eyes.

ADAMS.—He cannot choose but hear.

FADIMAN.—"Ask Dad. He knows." Mr. Jaffe.

MR. SAM JAFFE.—I think I remember that one. That was Sweet Caporal cigarettes.

FADIMAN.—But you couldn't have been a small boy.

JAFFE.—No, I was in my baby carriage, I think.

FADIMAN.—Long before that, Mr. Jaffe. You were hardly a threat in those days. "Have you a little fairy in your home?" Mr. Adams.

ADAMS.—Fairy Soap.

FADIMAN.—Fairy Soap. Four out of four. Very good indeed. The next question from Mr. John A. Schaff of Little Ferry, New Jersey, is based on familiar lines of poetry. They always seem very popular, that sort of question. John asks you to answer these queries: Who stood in Venice on the Bridge of

73

Sighs? It's a famous line of poetry, of course. "I stood in Venice on the Bridge of Sighs." But who was it? I'll go on with the line. "A palace and a prison on each hand." Mr. Adams, want to guess at that?

ADAMS.—'Tain't famous to me. "The Prisoner of Chillon."

FADIMAN.—You got the right author but the wrong character. It was "Childe Harold" in Byron's famous poem, "Childe Harold's Pilgrimage." That was pretty near, Mr. Adams, but not near enough for us. Our standards are high, aren't they, Mr. Adams? That's one wrong.

ADAMS.—I thought you said high.

FADIMAN.—What stood on the floor because it was too large for the shelf? Mr. Kelland?

KELLAND.—Grandfather's clock.

FADIMAN.—That's right. "Was too large for the shelf, so it stood ninety years on the floor." Who wrote it, Mr. Kelland? Do you know?

KELLAND.—I wouldn't know.

FADIMAN.—Do you know, Mr. Adams? I looked it up. I may as well tell you. I find it was written by a man named Henry Clay Work, who also wrote one of Mr. Adams' favorite songs. . . .

ADAMS.—"Marching through Georgia."

FADIMAN.—And another one, Mr. Adams?

ADAMS.—"Kingdom Comin'."

FADIMAN.—And another one? . . . "Father, Dear Father, Come Home with Me Now." He wrote all those famous poems. What stood on the shores of Gitchegoomie?

KELLAND.—Something out of "Hiawatha," but darned if I know what it is.

FADIMAN.—That's right, Mr. Kelland. That's quite right. You're doing very well. If you push it close as that, go ahead, Mr. Kelland; you've almost got it. I can almost read it in your eye.

KELLAND.—Canoe.

74

KIERAN.—No, it was somebody's lodge.

FADIMAN.—That's right. Who?

KIERAN.—The gal. Whatever her name was. Hiawatha's lady friend. Minne-ha-ha.

FADIMAN.—You gave us both her names. That's not quite correct, I think. It was the wigwam of Nokomis, who was the grandfather of Hiawatha. That's pretty good, though, Mr. Kieran.

KIERAN.—Grandfather? I thought it was an old lady.

FADIMAN.—I think Nokomis was the grandfather.

KIERAN.—Let's not quibble. I think you're thinking of his father. That was Papakewis.

FADIMAN.—Father, dear father, nokomis with me now, you mean. (*Laughter*) We got about half on that. What stood four to six? It's a cinch. As a matter of fact, it's in Mr. Kieran's department, more or less. Mr. Adams, all right.

ADAMS.—Casey's team.

FADIMAN.—The team itself couldn't stand four to six.

ADAMS.—The score. With one inning left to play.

FADIMAN.—That's right. Extremely rocky for the Mudville Nine.
"That day the score stood four to six,
With but an inning left to play."
Well, I think we'll have to call that wrong. We got about two and a half out of four. That means Mr. Schaff gets $10 plus $5 for the use of the question, courtesy of Canada Dry. The next one comes from Mr. W. G. McKenzie of Marion Station, Pennsylvania. It involves your knowledge of history. Who were the chief obstructionists to the aims and ambitions of the following? Let's get three out of four on this. Marc Antony? The one who finally destroyed Marc Antony's plan and ambition. Mr. Kelland?

KELLAND.—Octavius.

FADIMAN.—That's quite right. Octavian, the nephew of Julius Caesar, wasn't he? And at what battle was it that he won his great victory?

KELLAND.—Actium?

FADIMAN.—Actium is quite right, Mr. Kelland. Don't be reticent. You see, you know these things. You'll gain in self-confidence. Who was Boss Tweed's most famous antagonist? Mr. Kieran.

KIERAN.—A cartoonist named Nast was his most effective antagonist.

FADIMAN.—That's quite right. Thomas Nast, famous cartoonist. Napoleon the Third . . . his antagonist and the destroyer of his plans? Mr. Kieran.

KIERAN.—Bismarck.

FADIMAN.—Bismarck. And Helen Jacobs? Mr. Jaffe?

JAFFE.—Miss Wills.

FADIMAN.—That's quite right. Helen Wills Moody. Very good. You know a lot of other things besides chemistry, don't you, Mr. Jaffe?

JAFFE.—Sometimes.

FADIMAN.—All right. See what you can do with this one. That's four out of four. The next question, from Mr. F. C. Prensky of Brooklyn, New York, has to do with your knowledge of . . . well, I should say home science, more or less. What article in common use is suggested by the following material? If you put together mercury in a thin glass tube with a constriction in it, you get, Mr. Jaffe, what?

JAFFE.—A thermometer.

FADIMAN.—On the other hand, if you take a silver double glass wall and a vacuum and put those together, what do you get out of the merger?

JAFFE.—A Thermos bottle.

FADIMAN.—A Thermos bottle. The thing that you use to keep liquids lukewarm in the summer at picnics. (*Laughter*) And suppose you have a sheet of celluloid, some gelatine, and silver bromide. Put those together and what do you get?

JAFFE.—Photographic film.

FADIMAN.—Yes. Put them together, and you get the candid camera. Now sulphur dioxide and a compression pump put together. Any other volunteers beside Mr. Jaffe on this? Mr. Jaffe.

JAFFE.—Household electric refrigerator.

FADIMAN.—Yes. An ice cube manufacturer. Very good. Four out of four, Mr. Jaffe. Are your students listening in, Mr. Jaffe?

JAFFE.—I hope so.

FADIMAN.—You mean you hope so so far.

JAFFE.—I'll assign this for homework.

FADIMAN.—I hope you don't make any blunders on the next few questions, Mr. Jaffe. Keep tuned in, all students of Bernard Jaffe, keep tuned in. The next question, from Charlie White of Seattle, Washington. Mr. White just wants you to describe three famous boners in sports. Any sports. Mr. Kieran, start us off?

KIERAN.—Merkle made one of the most famous boners in sports in a game of the New York Giants. He was on base in 1909, playing the Chicago Cubs, and with the supposed winning hit made, he being on first, he ran to the clubhouse instead of touching second base, and the ball was recovered at second base . . . so they say! . . . and the game ended in a tie instead of the Giants winning. It had to be played off, and the Giants lost the play-off game and the pennant.

FADIMAN.—Would you call that perhaps the most famous boner in baseball?

ADAMS.—It was the most famous boner of 1908.

KIERAN.—Eight . . . right.

FADIMAN.—Did you have another boner on your mind, Mr. Adams? I know you had your hand up.

ADAMS.—Mr. Kieran just made one. (*Laughter*)

FADIMAN.—We'll add that to the list. All right, Mr. Kieran, another boner?

KIERAN.—Long John Anderson of the Yankees stole second base with the bases filled on the Old Hilltop ground.

FADIMAN.—You know, Mr. Kieran, you sound almost as if you were reading that. How do you know these things? That's two boners. Let's have another. Mr. Kelland?

KELLAND.—Riegels ran the wrong way with the ball in the Rose Bowl game.

FADIMAN.—That's right. Between what teams?

KELLAND.—California and somebody else.

FADIMAN.—Georgia Tech, I think it was. Did you see that boner made, Mr. Kelland?

KELLAND.—No, I read about it.

FADIMAN.—I've never believed in it, and here it is down on the card. That's quite right. Three boners out of three. Very good. Now let's see. So far the boys in the counting house have counted out only $10 to send to these sagacious questioners who have stumped our experts. We're doing pretty well, Mr. Adams, aren't we, don't you think? And now Canada Dry's own expert, Mr. Milton Cross, takes his trick at the microphone.

CROSS.—Thank you, Mr. Fadiman. Many people enjoy every day drinking a long, tall glass filled with sparkling ginger ale, for it's a most refreshing and delicious beverage. Pure and healthful, too, as proved by the fact that one of the first liquids prescribed for convalescents is ginger ale. So if you haven't tried it recently may we suggest you do. During the day, when you're busy and tired and want a pickup, while you're motoring, when it is hot and dusty, when your children come home from school and want some refreshment, any time, in fact, you'll find a glass of ginger ale is a tasty, tangy, and enjoyable drink. And when you ask for ginger ale order Canada Dry, for it's made with the most fastidious care, using only the finest ingredients, the purest water, and bottled under rigid sanitary conditions. Yes, ginger ale is a refreshing beverage, and Canada Dry is known as the champagne of ginger ale.

FADIMAN.—Very good. That message from Canada Dry was delivered by Mr. Cross. . . . I clocked it at 52 seconds. Now suppose we get to the second half of the program, with a question coming from Mr. Paul Grant of Cedar Rapids, Iowa. What did each of the following lose: Lucy Locket? Mr. Kelland?

KELLAND.—Her pocket.

FADIMAN.—Lucy Locket lost her pocket. Very good, Mr. Kelland. Who found it?

KELLAND.—Katie Fisher.

FADIMAN.—Yes. That's extra. Here's one that's harder. Belinda? Mr. Kieran?

KIERAN.—She lost a lock of hair.

FADIMAN.—Yes. What's the reference?

KIERAN.—"The Rape of the Lock" by Pope.

FADIMAN.—Very good. What century?

KIERAN.—Oh, shucks. Are you trying to pin me down?

FADIMAN.—Let's have the first two lines of "The Rape of the Lock," Mr. Kieran. Any chance of getting that out of you?

KIERAN.—I can't recall it, no.

FADIMAN.—"What dire offense from amorous causes springs?
      What mighty contests rise from trivial things?"
How true. Very good. Peter Schlemiel. Mr. Kieran again.

KIERAN.—His shadow.

FADIMAN.—What is the literary reference?

KIERAN.—It's a child's story, but I'm afraid I've sort of slowed down now. I don't remember who wrote it.

FADIMAN.—Most people would fall down on that. Not a very well-known writer. Adelbert von Chamisso, I think it was. A very hard name to pronounce. That's why it has not become very popular, perhaps. What did the organist lose? Mr. Adams.

ADAMS.—A chord.

FADIMAN.—Yes. What is the reference?

ADAMS.—Sullivan's "The Lost Chord."

FADIMAN.—"Seated one day at the organ." Four out of four on losses. Very good. The next one, from Mr. G. Simpson of Detroit, Michigan. Gentlemen, you of course know the difference between a gourmand and a gourmet. Mr. Kelland, do you know the difference?

KELLAND.—I fancy.

FADIMAN.—Very well, if you are gourmets you should be able to tell me what the following phrases used in cookery mean: *"au gratin."* Mr. Kieran.

79

KIERAN.—With cheese.

FADIMAN.—With cheese, or, more generally, with a brown crust of bread crumbs often made with butter or cheese. But "*au gratin*" and cheese are connected, there's no doubt. If you saw the word "Parmentière" after a dish, what would it mean to you? Mr. Kieran, apparently you eat out a good deal.

KIERAN.—Parmentière was, of course, a Frenchman. Yes, he's the man who introduced potatoes into France.

FADIMAN.—That's quite right. If you saw "Parmentière" after the name of a dish . . .

KIERAN.—There would be potatoes with it.

FADIMAN.—Yes. Made with potatoes. In Gaelic, known simply as spuds.

KIERAN.—From the French for *pomme de terre*.

FADIMAN.—Don't any of you other gentlemen eat?

ADAMS.—You're getting me awful hungry right now.

FADIMAN.—Let's get on to another question for you, Mr. Adams. Suppose you saw the word "jardiniere" after the name of a dish on a menu. Mr. Kelland.

KELLAND.—It means it's cooked in the flower pot.

FADIMAN.—No, I'm sorry. That wouldn't be right in terms of cookery, though possibly in terms of pottery. "Jardiniere" really means, I guess . . . Mr. Adams?

ADAMS.—With a lot of garden vegetables.

FADIMAN.—Now you might have guessed that from the word "jardiniere." *Jardin* . . . French for garden. A kind of vegetable dish. A mixture of vegetables served in soup or with beef. Thank you, Mr. Adams.

ADAMS.—Fifty-five cents.

FADIMAN.—No blue plate?

ADAMS.—On the blue plate.

FADIMAN.—Ever succeed, by the way, Mr. Adams . . . I know you had a campaign once going to have waiters give you the coffee after the meal. Any luck on that? How did you make out? Didn't you run a campaign once to have waiters give you the coffee after the meal instead of with?

ADAMS.—No, I wanted it with or not at all. It's useless. They won't do it.

FADIMAN.—How about, Mr. Adams, a menu on your favorite blue plate special in which you saw the word "*à l'anglaise*"? Mr. Kieran.

KIERAN.—It means English style.

FADIMAN.—Which means what?

KELLAND.—Tastes like mutton.

FADIMAN.—Thank you, Mr. Kelland. But more generally what would it mean, in the English style? You're all right. Mr. Kieran said roasted or broiled. In the simplest or plainest manner would be *à l'anglaise*. I think we got three out of four on that. Mr. L. Lytell of Brooklyn, New York, wants you to answer the following: What scientific discoveries do the following bring to mind: A broth of germs? Mr. Jaffe, have you your hand raised?

JAFFE.—Yes. I would say Pasteur.

FADIMAN.—Well, what did he do?

JAFFE.—Well, he was trying to find a connection between disease and microorganisms. . . . Wait a minute, it might refer to Spallanzani's attempt to . . .

FADIMAN.—I wish you had stuck to Pasteur.

JAFFE.—Well, I'll go back to Pasteur. He was trying to show that microorganisms would be killed when heated in a fluid.

FADIMAN.—Would be killed when heated in a fluid. . . .

JAFFE.—In other words, they couldn't resist high temperature.

FADIMAN.—Well, I think you're all right on Pasteur; and you're all right on germs or microorganisms, but I don't think you're quite precise in telling us what he attempts to prove. He was attempting to disprove the theory of spontaneous generation.

JAFFE.—That's why I mentioned Spallanzani, who did that really first.

FADIMAN.—Ah, that's clever of you, Mr. Jaffe. Very clever. Think I ought to let him get away with it, Mr. Adams?

ADAMS.—I would, on account of the kids. (*Laughter*)

FADIMAN.—All right. . . . Well, what Pasteur did was to cover one flask of broth and allow the other to be exposed to the air; and in the one that was exposed to the air, the germs developed, and not in the other. A case of too many germs spoiling the broth . . . as you were going to say, Mr. Jaffe, without the slightest doubt. . . . Now, suppose I give you the term "six teams of horses" . . . Would that mean anything in the history of science? . . . Mr. Jaffe.

JAFFE.—That was an incident where air was taken out of a large metal ball, and three teams of horses on each side tried to pull them apart.

FADIMAN.—Yeah . . . what did it prove?

JAFFE.—It proved that the air exerted a certain amount of pressure.

FADIMAN.—Yes . . a great deal. Once you created a vacuum between those two iron halves of . . .

JAFFE.—Hemispheres. . . .

FADIMAN.—Could you give me the name of the man who's responsible for this experiment?

JAFFE.—Uh . . .

FADIMAN.—You don't have to. Otto von Gerricha. By the way, do you know where you will find that experiment very beautifully recounted, Mr. Jaffe?

JAFFE.—In the Museum of Science and Industry.

FADIMAN.—Yes. And also in a book called *Crucibles* by Bernard Jaffe. You've forgotten it. (*Laughter*) Described the experiment at great length. Two out of two, so far. . . . Now, "hysterics and anesthetics"; "hysterics and anesthetics" . . . what would that bring to mind? If I just use those two words? . . . Mr. Kieran.

KIERAN.—That would bring laughing gas to mind . . . used as an anesthetic.

FADIMAN.—That's right. What's the effect of laughing gas . . . that is, the first time it was used?

KIERAN.—The first time it was used?

FADIMAN.—Yeah.

KIERAN.—I think it was inhaled by the inventor rather accidentally, and he began to laugh. . . .

FADIMAN.—Yes, I think the experiment is connected mainly with Sir Humphry Davy. . . . Yes, that's exactly . . . exactly right.

ADAMS.—With nitrous oxide . . . eh?

FADIMAN.—"Eh" is right. Nitrous oxide, Mr. Adams. . . . Now, the fourth and last is "sparkling water." That's a setup for a plug for our product.

ADAMS.—Canada Dry.

FADIMAN.—Yes, I know, Mr. Adams. Do you think I'd take advantage of a setup like that? Of course we would. . . . Now, Mr. Jaffe.

JAFFE.—Well, are you referring to the discovery of seltzer water by Priestley?

FADIMAN.—Yeah . . . yeah.

JAFFE.—That was back in the latter part of the eighteenth century.

KIERAN.—Yeah, a lot of funny things were happening then.

FADIMAN.—And Priestley did what?

JAFFE.—He bubbled carbon dioxide gas through water.

FADIMAN.—And found out what happened?

JAFFE.—That it had a very pleasant taste . . . like Canada Dry, I suppose.

FADIMAN.—Thank you very much, Mr. Jaffe, thank you very much. That's four out of four. Think we were pretty good on that. . . . The next question: from Ruth Malloy of Philadelphia, Pennsylvania. Please identify the following quotations, all beginning with the two words "Call me." The first one is, "Call me Ishmael." . . . "Call me Ishmael." Mr. Kieran.

KIERAN.—That's the opening phrase of *Moby Dick* by Hermann Melville.

FADIMAN.—Yes. And I should say one of the greatest opening phrases of any book that's ever been written.

KIERAN.—And the phrases that follow are equally good. . . .

FADIMAN.—Equally good. Thank you very much, Mr. Kieran. And, Mr. Melville . . . unhappily deceased . . . thanks to you, too. . . . "Call me what instrument you will." "Call me what instrument you will." . . . That's the toughest of the four.

ADAMS.—It's a line that Hamlet uses addressing Guildenstern. "Call me what instrument you will; Though you can fuss me; you cannot play upon me." You know. . . .

FADIMAN.—Yes, Mr. Adams, of course we do. . . . "Call me pet names, dearest." It is not from Shakespeare, Mr. Adams. "Call me pet names, dearest." . . . Yes, Mr. Adams.

ADAMS.—It's a song.

FADIMAN.—Yes, very good. Do you know how it goes on? "Call me pet names, dearest."

ADAMS.—"Call me . . .

FADIMAN.—That's right, that's right. . . .

ADAMS.— . . . a . . . and then the pet name is there, but . . .

FADIMAN.—A bird, a bird, Mr. Adams. "Call me a bird that flies to thy breast at one cherishing word." Very good. . . . "Ye call me Chief." . . . Mr. Adams.

ADAMS.—Spartacus to the Gladiators.

FADIMAN.—Very good. Do you care to recite it, Mr. Adams?

ADAMS.—I'd love to. (*Laughter*)

FADIMAN.—Go ahead.

ADAMS.—"And you do well to call me Chief,
    Who for four long years in the arena," et cetera.
    (*Laughter*)

FADIMAN.—That's perfect. It's 12 long years, but that's all right.

ADAMS.—Written by the Reverend Elijah Kellogg.

FADIMAN.—That's quite right. How did you know that, Mr. Adams?

ADAMS.—Because he lived in Casco Bay. (*Laughter*)

FADIMAN.—That seems perfectly clear to me. Uh . . . we're supposed to get four out of four on that; so we lose $10 to Miss Malloy of Philadelphia, plus $5 for the use of the question.

SOUND.—*Cash register.*

FADIMAN.—Thank you. . . . Now, the next question comes from Leroy Singer of this city. The following were slang terms during the last World War. Can you explain what each one means? The first . . . "a shavetail." That's pretty easy . . . Mr. Jaffe.

JAFFE.—A second louie.

FADIMAN.—A second louie. You say that with a little bitterness in your voice.

JAFFE.—I never did like it.

FADIMAN.—Never did like it, uh? "Goldfish." . . . "Goldfish." . . . Mr. Kelland.

KELLAND.—Canned rations.

FADIMAN.—Canned what?

KELLAND.—Rations.

FADIMAN.—Yes, but what particularly?

KELLAND.—Salmon.

FADIMAN.—Yes, salmon. Canned salmon. . . . "Peewee" "Peewee." . . . Mr. Kieran.

KIERAN.—"Peewee" was an aviation cadet before he got off the ground.

FADIMAN.—Yes. What's the word mean?

KIERAN.—A flightless bird.

FADIMAN.—The life expectancy, Mr. Adams and Mr. Kieran?

ADAMS.—Sixty-four and three-quarter years. . . .

FADIMAN.—I'm sure that's correct. (*Laughter*)

FADIMAN.—And "Reading your shirt" would mean what? . . . Mr. Kieran again.

KIERAN.—Looking for quaint little visitors. (*Laughter*)

FADIMAN.—How did they do it exactly?

KIERAN.—Took off their shirt and went through and picked them out and stepped on them.

JAFFE.—Well, sometimes . . .

FADIMAN.—Do you have a different method, Mr. Jaffe?

JAFFE.—Well, it was usually done at night, by candlelight.

KIERAN.—Yes, singeing. . . .

ADAMS.—A pretty trick.

FADIMAN.—Now we have time for only one more . . . or part of one more. The next from Mr. A. Singer of New Orleans, Louisiana. Quote a famous question asked of an old man. Question asked of an old man. . . . Mr. Adams.

ADAMS.—"Do you think at your age it is right?"

FADIMAN.—Very good.

ADAMS.—It was from "Father William" by . . .

FADIMAN.—All right. A question asked of a baby? Of a baby? . . . Mr. Adams.

ADAMS.—"Where did you come from, baby dear?"

FADIMAN.—Yes. How does it go on?

ADAMS.—"Out of the nowhere into the here."

FADIMAN.—Out of the Everywhere, I think.

ADAMS.—Everywhere. All right.

FADIMAN.—And I'm afraid that will be all we'll have time for tonight. That brings Canada Dry's losses up to $20. Now Mr. Cross has a word for you; then I'll tell you about our guests for next week.

CROSS.—When a man has done a job well, words of praise always ring happily on his ears. I am sure this is true of even the most modest author who appears on Information Please. And it is equally true in industries as in the arts. The creators of Canada Dry water quite frankly relish the praise that is constantly given their sparkling products. For ever since this delicious soda became available, people all over the country have been praising it most heartily. There is every reason for the popularity of sparkling Canada Dry water. It blends well, makes your favorite drink taste better, come to life, and stay lively for a good time. For actually, laboratory tests have proved that after a bottle has been opened this water will stay alive and sparkling for at least 24 hours in a refrigerator. So ask for Sparkling Canada Dry Water the next time you order club soda, and, incidentally, now you can purchase Information Please questions and answers in regular book form at your favorite book or department store.

FADIMAN.—Thank you. And may I remark, in passing, that the Indian Department has just called in to tell us that Nokomis is a grandmother and not a grandfather, which will be a surprise to everybody. (*Applause*) Thank you, Mr. Jaffe and Mr. Kelland, for your noble efforts this evening. Next week, Mr. Adams, Mr. Levant, Mr. Kieran will be with us again, and our guest of honor will be one of the ablest newspaper men of our day, the well-known author of *Mrs. Astor's Horse*, *The Night Club Era*, and *City Editor* . . . Stanley Walker, now editor of the *Philadelphia Evening Public Ledger*. To all you listeners we say, please send your questions along, and if you have a stumper to stump our board of experts, let's have it. There is $5 in it for you if we use the question and another 10 if we fail to answer it correctly. That means $15 in all if you win. Send your letters with questions to Information Please, 1 Pershing Square, New York City.

We the People

WE THE PEOPLE is a true cross section of American life. More than 900 persons have been brought to New York from every state in the union to participate in this program. All races and all ages have appeared on "We, the People," from a two-year-old youngster to a one-hundred-nineteen-year-old slave, from college presidents to down-and-outers. There have been Indian chiefs, an eye witness to the Chicago Fire, the first woman ever elected to Congress, a man who assisted the great Pasteur in the first inoculation against rabies, a man who escaped from Devil's Island, the man who brought us the Statue of Liberty, the soldier who carried the Armistice message, Casey Jones's fireman, the original "Ragtime Kid" in the shooting of Dan McGrew, the man who let himself be bitten by yellow fever mosquitoes for humanitarian purposes, the man who photographed the bombing of the *Panay* in China. Donald Budge, Tom Mooney, Cornelius Vanderbilt, Jr., and Mrs. Franklin D. Roosevelt have also been guests of this program. So have several hundred other people equally dissimilar.

It will be seen by any of those who do not happen to know this program that its great public appeal lies in the telling of the story of the affecting moments in people's lives, of important and obscure people alike. The show was conceived and originated by Phillips H. Lord and had its first performance October 4, 1936. Lord left the show two years later (September, 1938) and Gabriel Heatter took command as permanent master of ceremonies. Heatter's great value to the series lies in large part in his ability to put at their ease the people he presents, to relieve their nervousness by his calm and encouraging manner. He inspires great trust and confidence, and under his handling people who are flustered in the extreme when they first enter the studio have given very creditable performances on the air.

As a Phillips Lord production the show caught on from the start. After Lord's departure and with the advent of Gabriel Heatter (with the firm of Young and Rubicam producing), the material of the show was given a new direction. Young and Rubicam went after more newsworthy and significant stories and people. The show "hit" harder, took on a faster pace and wider interest. Today the audience has expanded to a more general and all-comprehensive following, including the discriminating listener.

On many radio shows musical cues are a matter of routine only. On We the People, conductor Mark Warnow has the problem of finding melodies exactly suited to the various situations and attitudes that bring Mr. and Mrs. Average American to the air. Several months ago, for example, a Mr. Al Mingolone, newsreel cameraman, went to Maine to photograph a balloon-jumping experiment. People in Maine were leaping into the air, supported by buoyant clusters of gas balloons of small diameter. They were jumping over barns and houses and enjoying it very much. Mingolone took a few pictures, then had himself tied into a bunch of the bags in order to take more pictures from the air. The sun came out after his take-off, expanding the gas in the balloons that held him aloft. He went on up, unable to disentangle himself enough to puncture any of the bags. Obviously he couldn't drop his camera without multiplying his confusion. He was blown all over New England. Finally a Catholic priest saw him, and, understanding his problem, brought him to earth again by piercing three or four balloons with a rifle. When Mingolone was presented over We the People, Mark Warnow thumbed through the catalogue of old numbers and came up with a melody that was perfectly right: "I'm Flying High but I've Got a Feeling I'm Falling."

Guests of the program, irrespective of the distances they have to travel, are well taken care of in New York. Fares are paid in advance, hotel reservations are made, and five dollars a day for expenses are provided.

89

In my personal opinion the most exciting and dramatic of all the presentations of this series was the story of Mr. X, a victim of amnesia. A reconstructed sketch of this unfortunate man's history was presented on the broadcast of January 17, 1939, and the man himself spoke on the show. In the broadcast four weeks later We the People brought the solution to this disturbing story. The identity of the man had been discovered through this program, he had been restored to his family, and he had completely recovered from the loss of memory that had tortured him for eight years. It is regrettable that print cannot record the overtone of courage and gratitude that Mr. Lawrence demonstrated when he told his own story on the night of February 14, 1939.

We the People*

FROM THE BROADCAST OF JANUARY 17

HEATTER.—On the afternoon of June 25, 1931 . . . to a hospital in Jackson, Mississippi . . . police brought a well-dressed man who had collapsed on a city street. For weeks he lay in a coma . . . hovering between life and death. Then one morning the patient regained consciousness, and Dr. Hunt of the hospital staff stood at his bedside . . . happy to see his patient coming back to life. . . .

DOCTOR.—(*Cheerful*) Well . . . you're feeling better this morning, aren't you!

MAN.—(*Weakly*) Yes . . . doctor.

DOCTOR.—That's fine. . . . Well, now, the first thing I'd like to know is your name. You see, there was no identification in your clothes. We'd like to get in touch with your relatives. Let them know you're all right.

MAN.—My name? Why, yes . . . it's . . . er . . . (*disturbed*) Why . . . I . . . I . . .

DOCTOR.—What is it? Is there something wrong?

MAN.—(*Struggling*) Doctor . . . that's funny. . . . I . . . I can't seem to remember. But . . . I know where I live. My address is . . . it's . . .

DOCTOR.—Yes?

MAN.—(*It hits him*) Doctor . . . I can't remember that either.

DOCTOR.—(*Concerned*) There, there, now take it easy. You're . . . you're sure you can't remember?

MAN.—(*Terrified*) No . . . doctor. I can't remember. But I must know my name! My name is . . . it's . . . it's . . . No doctor, I can't remember! I can't remember anything!

HEATTER.—For days the doctors in that hospital worked to help that man recall something about his former life. He couldn't remember a thing. Somewhere . . . somehow the link that bound him to the past had snapped. The days became weeks, and the weeks became years. Every agency, every possible source of information was exhausted . . . without discovering a single clue. The man became known as Mr. X. And tonight that man is here beside me. And being here means so much to him . . . his heart is so full of emotion . . . it may be difficult for him to speak to you. For he comes here with a heart-breaking appeal for help. WE THE PEOPLE presents the man known as Mr. X.

MR. X.—Today, I live at the Mississippi State Hospital in Jackson. Doctors there say I am about seventy years old. Physically I have changed little since I was found in 1931. I am almost bald, and what hair I have is gray. But my eyebrows are very heavy and black. My eyes are brown, and I wear glasses. I am 5 feet 7 inches tall and weigh 145 pounds. My doctor believes I was well educated. From the very first day, I have chosen books from the hospital library that would only be interesting to a well-read man. And I have read every newspaper and magazine I could, hoping to find some clue to my past. It is also evident that the care of flowers was either my profession or a hobby, because I can identify unusual plants by their botanical names. And I know a lot about making them grow. Also, I remember the rules of complicated card games like bridge, and I am sure I was once familiar with financial statements.

Gradually I have recalled several places where I have been . . . but I do not know when or with whom. I remember best Pensacola, Florida. I remember a man there who took me to the Osceola Club. He used to have a special brand of cigars, and I used to joke with him about it. My doctors have checked my description of Pensacola and have decided I was there about 30 years ago. I remember distinctly playing cards with some friends . . . a druggist and his wife . . . but I cannot recall their names.

The doctors at the Mississippi State Hospital have done everything in their power to help me discover who I am. . . . Now, after 8 years, it seems impossible, hopeless. I will be forever grateful to WE THE PEOPLE for giving me this last chance. I am an old man. There are only a few years left for me on this earth. Somehow . . . I must find out who I am, where I came from, whether I have loved ones who have given me up for dead. I can only pray with all my heart that someone listening in tonight will recognize something I have said about myself . . . or my voice.

I do not want to die nameless and alone. . . .

HEATTER.—Ladies and gentlemen . . . if you have any clue to the identity of Mr. X . . . no matter how insignificant it may seem . . . We the People asks that you let us know at once . . . *please.*

IDENTIFICATION OF MR. X ON BROADCAST OF FEBRUARY 14

HEATTER.—Four weeks ago tonight a man seventy years old stood before this microphone and made a dramatic appeal for help. For that man did not know his own name. Nor who he was. For eight heart-breaking, agonizing years he had lived in the Mississippi State Hospital. Unless he could find out who he was he would die there . . . friendless, alone, known only as Mr. X. Then he found help . . . help from WE THE PEOPLE. Telegrams, letters, telephone calls poured in from every part of America . . . a tidal wave of human sympathy, eager to help. Tonight he is no longer Mr. X. Tonight he is William Henry Lawrence of Birmingham, Alabama. And he is waiting at this minute in a radio studio in Birmingham. He and his sister, Mrs. J. P. Haley, who identified him. First . . . Mrs. Haley, who will tell you what happened when the family of Will Lawrence first realized their brother had joined the world of missing men. All right, Birmingham. (*Switchover*)

MRS. HALEY.—My brother, Will, was a single man, a traveling insurance salesman. He was often away from home for months at a time. On May 24, 1931, he left to go on one of his trips. During the first few months we got several letters. The last one was postmarked Jackson, Mississippi. In it Will said he was leaving Jackson. He did not say where he was going.

We did not hear from him again. At first we didn't worry, because Will had always been a poor letter writer. But as months passed without a word, our alarm grew. We notified police and missing persons bureaus. Every possible agency joined in the search. It was useless. Will had apparently vanished from the face of the earth. Month after month we prayed, hoped we would hear something, anything that would give us a clue. But after a year and a half we had to admit what seemed to be the terrible truth. Will was dead. Eight years passed. Time helped to soften our grief . . . a little. Then one day last week a neighbor telephoned. She said she had heard a Mr. X on this program, WE THE PEOPLE. Mr. X had said he was from Jackson, Mississippi, where Will was last heard from. The next day my son rushed into our house. He had pictures of Mr. X out of *Time* magazine and the *Memphis Commercial Appeal*. I looked at the pictures, and all the hope that had died in me years ago came surging back. The face in those pictures was not the face I remembered. . . . It was a face grown sad with grief and despair. But I knew Mr. X was my brother Will. My brother, Ben, and I hurried to the hospital in Jackson. As long as I live I shall never forget the hopes and fear that raced through my heart as we waited in the anteroom, praying we weren't wrong. Finally Dr. Donaldson, said, "This is Mr. X." It was Will. Ben and I rushed to him to take him in our arms. We were both crying with happiness. But Will just stood there. He did not know us. We showed him pictures of the family. We talked of old days. We could see him trying desperately to think back. It was useless. Ben and I were stunned. We could not stand the tragic suffering written on the face of our brother. Then Dr. Donaldson told us there was one last chance. We were a link connecting Will to the past. Under the influence of a mild drug, that link might be strengthened. We went to Will's room. Dr. Donaldson administered the drug . . . sodium amytol. We sat there waiting. Suddenly I saw Will turn his head and look at me. Recognition dawned on his face. He knew me. My happiness was so deep I could not speak. And as long as I live . . . I will never forget the look on my brother Ben's face as he clasped the hand of the brother we had loved and mourned as dead. My brother, Will, the man you knew as Mr. X, is here with me . . . waiting anxiously to speak to you. All right, Will.

WILL (MR. X).—Four weeks ago when I spoke on WE THE PEOPLE, I was a lonely unhappy old man. My life stretched ahead of me, a long, weary road. And I believed that broadcast was my last chance to find out who I was. Tonight my happiness is complete. I am back with my loved ones, and what is left of my life I shall spend rich in their love.

Tonight, from the bottom of my heart, I want to thank the thousands of people who tried to help me. I want every one of you to know your letters were each and every one a thread of hope. I am eternally grateful.

I remember now that fateful morning of May 24, 1931, when I left Birmingham to go to Jackson. I remember writing from Jackson, Mississippi. . . . I remember writing a letter to my nephew and going out of the hotel on an errand. I had money in my pocket. But when or how I lost my memory I cannot remember.

The doctors believe I was drugged and robbed.

But one day stands out in my memory, February 7, 1939, when suddenly a dark cloud lifted from my mind, and I saw my brother and sister bending over me. Suddenly . . . I knew who I was. Sixty-two years of my life came rushing back to me. The memories of my childhood, my family, and my friends.

It seems strange that I had to travel 1,000 miles to ask help . . . when all those years, my family lived less than 100 miles away. If it were not for WE THE PEOPLE I would still be in the Mississippi State Hospital . . . a nameless, lonely old man . . . an old man denied even his memories. Instead, the time that is left to me on this earth is filled with the promise of happiness. There are no words to tell what is my heart . . . but as long as I live . . . I will remember in my prayers . . . all those who helped me in my time of need.

BEST VARIETY SHOW

The Kate Smith Hour

ℓℓ

KATE (KATHRYN ELIZABETH) SMITH is unquestionably one of the world's great entertainers. Prior to her radio successes, she was starred in such hits as "Honeymoon Lane," "Flying High," and "Hit the Deck." Her professional debut took place a few years before her first important muscial show when she sang for American soldiers encamped near her Washington home. Since then she has been a top-flight vocalist and mistress of ceremonies in every channel of entertainment in which she has appeared.

Her great artistry as a popular singer was recognized by her present manager and director, Ted Collins, in the latter part of 1930. Under his able chaperonage she was introduced to radio's millions on the evening of May 1, 1931. The popularity she had enjoyed theretofore was multiplied overnight. In four years of radio (by the end of 1935) she was so much beloved by the American public that a short personal appearance broke the all-time attendance record at New York's vaudeville mecca, the Palace.

Aside from a thoroughly sound singing technique and a great natural radio voice (and there are many in radio who have this much), Kate Smith's phenomenal success is attributable to the two basic virtues of her character—simplicity and sincerity. She enjoys the amusing ballyhoo that has accompanied her career (Governor "Ma" Ferguson officially bestowed upon her a Texas Ranger's badge, and the Winnebago tribe of the Sioux Indians call her Hom'b-o-goo-win-go, meaning "Glory of the Morn"), but she is an unspoilable workman. She sings her songs pretty much as they are written, and she is very nearly the only singer in radio who does this. She doesn't slur, drag, jump, anticipate, or telescope the notes and phrases that make up

96

her songs, and she is one of the most industrious troupers known to the radio medium.

Besides the characteristics of sincerity and simplicity, she has subsidiary virtues that even her invisible audience are willing to ascribe to her—genuineness, humor, wholesomeness, and confidence—all of which can be heard in what she does, what she says, how she says it. A great fun-loving spirit seems to knit these qualities together. (In this connection it will be remembered that much of her stage attractiveness was explained by her skillful stomps and tap routines, quite an assignment for a girl who weighed 235 pounds.)

Under the direction of Ted Collins she has put together the best variety show in American radio. Her Christmas broadcast (December 22, 1938) was an excellent example of well-balanced variety entertainment, properly routined and programed.

The Kate Smith Hour*

MUSIC.—*"When the Moon Comes Over the Mountain."*

BARUCH.—Swans Down Cake Flour and Calumet Baking Powder . . . your two best baking friends . . . present the *Kate Smith Hour!*

MUSIC.—*Orchestra swells into "Along the Texas Trail." Fade on cue, but continue softly through following.*

TED COLLINS.—Good evening. This is Ted Collins inviting you in to our radio playhouse, where brilliantly lighted Christmas trees reflect the holiday spirit. Tonight our Kate Smith Christmas party features:

BARUCH.—The Kate Smith Singers.
Jack Miller's Band.
Abbott and Costello.
The Aldrich Family, starring Ezra Stone.
The Senior Chorus of the New York Institute for the Blind.
And that great lady of the theater . . . Miss Ethel Barrymore!

COLLINS.—And now the spotlight falls on your hostess . . . The Songbird of the South . . . Kate Smith!

MUSIC.—*Orchestra up.*

KATE SMITH.—Hello, everybody. Welcome to our big Christmas party. We're full of good cheer, and this first song by the boys and girls explains it . . . "I Never Felt Better."

MUSIC.—*"I Never Felt Better."* (*Orchestra and chorus*)

MUSIC.—*"Funny Little Snowman." Fade for*

COLLINS.—A new song makes its first air appearance as Kate Smith sings . . . "Funny Little Snowman."

* Reprinted by special permission of Ted Collins, authorized agent of the Kate Smith Hour, copyright, 1939.

Music.—(*Orchestra and Kate.*) *"Funny Little Snowman."* Follow by *"What Have You Got That Gets Me?"* Fade for

COLLINS.—The Songbird of the South puts this question to swing . . . "What Have You Got That Gets Me?"

Music.—*"What Have You Got That Gets Me?"*

Music.—*Aldrich theme. Fade for*

KATE.—The Aldrich Family, starring Ezra Stone and supported by Betty Field, Lea Penman, and Clyde Fillmore, is written for us each week by Clifford Goldsmith, whose current hit, "What a Life," is now playing at the Biltmore Theatre here in New York.

The scene opens in the Aldrich living room. Mr. Aldrich is enjoying the open fire. Mrs. Aldrich is wrapping packages.

MR. ALDRICH.—Well . . . it seems good to sit down here by this fire.

MRS. ALDRICH.—It seems good to sit down any place. The fruit cakes are all baked and wrapped.

HENRY.—(*Door opens*) Mother.

MRS. ALDRICH.—I thought you had gone to rehearse your play, Henry.

HENRY.—Do you think I ought to take Miss Stevens some kind of a present?

MRS. ALDRICH.—Who is Miss Stevens?

HENRY.—She's the one that's directing our play.

MR. ALDRICH.—Is Miss Stevens giving you anything?

HENRY.—I thought you shouldn't think about things like that, father.

MR. ALDRICH.—You shouldn't. And let us hope Miss Stevens doesn't either.

HENRY.—But don't you see, tonight is the night Miss Stevens decides whether Jimmy Bartlet or I get the leading part . . .

MRS. ALDRICH.—Then don't you think a present would look just a bit like bribery?

99

HENRY.—In what way? . . . It would just be a gesture of good will.

MR. ALDRICH.—If all you want to give her is a gesture, you have my permission to do so.

HENRY.—Isn't there anything around the house I could give her?

MRS. ALDRICH.—Such as what?

HENRY.—Well . . . how about a silver vegetable dish?

MR. ALDRICH.—Yes!

HENRY.—All right. . . . (*his voice fades*) . . . (*door closes*)

MRS. ALDRICH.—I wonder why it is, Sam, Christmas never seems the same.

MR. ALDRICH.—Christmas has changed. We don't even have as much snow as we used to.

MRS. ALDRICH.—And this is the first year since I can remember that we haven't been having a houseful of company.

HENRY.—(*Door opens*) Mother.

MRS. ALDRICH.—Henry! I thought you had gòne!

HENRY.—I just had an idea. Have you mailed that box of presents to Aunt Harriet yet?

MRS. ALDRICH.—No.

HENRY.—Couldn't I take some little thing out of that? Something she wouldn't even miss?

MRS. ALDRICH.—Do you think that would be very nice?

HENRY.—She'll only send you back most of it next year anyhow.

MR. ALDRICH.—Can you promise Miss Stevens would do as much?

MRS. ALDRICH.—Supposing you take Miss Stevens a fruit cake?

HENRY.—Why didn't we think of that before?

MRS. ALDRICH.—Be sure you take one of the pound cakes, dear. Are you listening?

HENRY.—(*Slightly off*) Yes, mother.

MRS. ALDRICH.—They are in the pantry on the second shelf. The 5-pound cakes are on the first shelf.

HENRY.—Yes, mother. Thank you, mother. Good-by. (*Door closes*)

MRS. ALDRICH.—I don't like to admit it, Sam, but I do hope Henry beats that awful Jimmy Bartlet out for the part.

MR. ALDRICH.—I never cared for Mr. Bartlet . . . always showing off his money.
(*Board fade on last two lines*)

SEVERAL VOICES.—*Ad libbing. Out of the hum comes*

MISS STEVENS.—(*A rather pleasing voice*) Quiet, everybody! Quiet, please! (*Voices die down*) We can't rehearse with everyone talking, you know. (*Voices fade*)

HENRY.—Good evening, Miss Stevens.

MISS STEVENS.—Good evening, Henry. Everybody backstage until I'm ready for you, please. (*She claps her hands*)

HENRY.—When are Jimmy Bartlet and I going to have our tryout, Miss Stevens?

MISS STEVENS.—Right away, Henry. And I hope that no matter how I decide, neither of you will feel there was anything personal about it.

HENRY.—Not so far as I'm concerned, Miss Stevens. Of course, Jimmy Bartlet may be a little jealous in the end. . . . Here's something I brought you.

MISS STEVENS.—Why, Henry!

HENRY.—It's just a . . . fruit cake.

MISS STEVENS.—It must be enormous.

HENRY.—It's only a pound one.

MISS STEVENS.—Now, Henry! . . . That must weigh at least 5 pounds!

HENRY.—Yeah? . . . Five pounds? . . . Hmm. . . .

JIM.—(*Approaching. His enunciation is perfect . . . and he probably wears glasses*) Good evening, Miss Stevens.

Miss Stevens.—Good evening, Jimmy Bartlet.

Jim.—Here is a gift I just happened to bring you.

Miss Stevens.—Jimmy!

Jim.—It's a fruit cake.

Henry.—About how much does it weigh?

Jim.—Three pounds.

Henry.—Three. . . . That's just a nice size . . . if you can't get a 5-pounder, of course.

Jim.—I bought it at Jones's Bakery.

Henry.—Oh . . . your mother didn't have time to bake it?

Jim.—My mother doesn't have to bake, I'll have you understand.

Henry.—I'll bet she doesn't know how to.

Jim.—My mother happens to be spending the holidays abroad. Where is your mother spending hers?

Henry.—She's sick of Europe. This year she's staying home.

Jim.—Would you excuse me while I speak to my chauffeur? (*Voice fades*)

Henry.—Imagine!

Miss Stevens.—After all, underneath, Jimmy is a very fine boy.

Henry.—Underneath. . . . Nice-looking fellow on the stage, too . . . provided he doesn't face you head on, of course. . . . But maybe you could have him play the part so that he keeps his back to the audience.

Miss Stevens.—Henry.

Henry.—I hope I don't seem to be running him down, Miss Stevens.

Miss Stevens.—No . . . no . . . not at all.

Henry.—Jimmy would look very good playing opposite Phoebe Anne . . . if Phoebe could just wear some slippers that didn't have any heels on them. . . . You know what I mean? So Jimmy wouldn't look so runty beside her?

Jim.—Who looks runty?

MISS STEVENS.—All right, boys. For the time being, Henry, you will read the lead and Jimmy can be Henry's uncle. On the stage, please.

JIM.—From the beginning?

MISS STEVENS.—From the beginning.

HENRY.—Yes, Miss Stevens.
(*The microphone remains with the two boys. We hear them mount the steps on the stage. Miss Stevens is slightly off*)
Could you stand over there, please, Jimmy?

JIMMY.—It seems to me this is where I would stand.

HENRY.—(*Patiently*) Miss Stevens, could you please ask Jimmy to stand over there?

MISS STEVENS.—Is there any particular reason, Henry?

HENRY.—He's right between me and the audience.

JIM.—But this is the natural place for me . . . or do you want me to stand some place that is contrary to my whole character?

HENRY.—Miss Stevens, would you mind asking Jimmy once more to stand over there? Or must I muss up his character?

JIM.—I'd like to see you dare to muss me.

HENRY.—Oh, you would, eh?

SOUND.—*A book drops to the floor.*

MISS STEVENS.—Boys!

HENRY.—I'll have him moved in just a minute, Miss Stevens!

MISS STEVENS.—Henry!

JIM.—Let go of me!

MR. ALDRICH.—Henry Aldrich!

HENRY.—Yes, father! . . . Are you here?

MR. ALDRICH.—I certainly am!

HENRY.—Did you want something, father?

MR. ALDRICH.—I do.

HENRY.—Yes, sir.

SOUND.—*Henry going down the steps and then walking.*

HENRY.—Is somebody in the family sick, father?

MR. ALDRICH.—Just come here, please.

HENRY.—Yes, father.

MR. ALDRICH.—(*Lowers voice slightly*) I want to ask you something. Did you take a fruit cake from the pantry shelf?

HENRY.—Yes, sir.

MR. ALDRICH.—Was it a 1-pound or a 5-pound cake?

HENRY.—I picked up . . . I suppose . . . you mean there's a 5-pound one missing?

MR. ALDRICH.—Will you please go to Miss Stevens and explain the circumstances and tell her you would like to have the cake back?

HENRY.—But I can't do that, father!

MR. ALDRICH.—Why not?

HENRY.—Well . . . she might have eaten it.

MR. ALDRICH.—The entire 5 pounds? Do you realize that your mother went to considerable trouble to bake that cake for a poor family that is going to have little else for Christmas?

HENRY.—But couldn't I at least wait until Miss Stevens has decided which of us is to get the leading part?

MR. ALDRICH.—Perhaps you would prefer that I ask her!

HENRY.—I'll ask her. . . . I'll ask her. . . . You wait here a minute. (*Walking*) Miss Stevens, could I . . . (*clears throat*) speak to you about something?

MISS STEVENS.—I'm busy right now, Henry.

JIM.—(*Approaching*) Miss Stevens, would you mind taking this?

MISS STEVENS.—What in the world is it, Jimmy?

JIM.—I asked the chauffeur to go and get you a larger cake.

MISS STEVENS.—You shouldn't have done that, Jimmy!

JIM.—It wasn't any trouble, I assure you. (*Voice fades*)

HENRY.—Could I say just one word, Miss Stevens?

MISS STEVENS.—Don't tell me you have one that is even larger, Henry.

HENRY.—No, ma'am. . . . It's a funny thing, but . . . when my mother baked that cake I gave you she made a little mistake.

MISS STEVENS.—I'm sure that no matter how she made it it will taste delicious.

HENRY.—But the trouble is . . .

MISS STEVENS.—Now don't apologize.

HENRY.—But when she baked it she accidently put some poison in it.

MISS STEVENS.—Henry!

HENRY.—It's deadly poison. And my father would like it back.

MR. ALDRICH.—I'm sorry, Henry, but did you explain that we want the cake for a poor family that won't be having anything else for Christmas?

MISS STEVENS.—With the poison?

MR. ALDRICH.—What poison?

HENRY.—In the cake.

MR. ALDRICH.—In what cake?

MISS STEVENS.—I see. . . . (*she almost laughs*) Won't you come with me, Henry? I left it in this back room. (*They are walking*)

HENRY.—My father doesn't always hear very well.

MISS STEVENS.—Isn't it lucky we didn't pass the cake around to everyone?

HENRY.—It certainly is.

MISS STEVENS.—Here we are. . . .

HENRY.—It's dark in here.

Miss Stevens.—Perhaps there's enough light coming in from the street lamp so we can see. . . . There it is. . . .

Henry.—Yes, Miss Stevens.

Miss Stevens.—Henry, do you mind my asking you something?

Henry.—What about?

Miss Stevens.—Would you be too disappointed if you didn't play the lead opposite Phoebe Anne?

Henry.—I see. . . . You're giving it to Jimmy Bartlet?

Miss Stevens.—I'm simply asking you, Henry.

Henry.—Yeah?

Miss Stevens.—Something tells me Jimmy Bartlet is a rather lonely boy . . . much more so than any of us might imagine.

Henry.—Lonely? . . . With a chauffeur in the family?

Miss Stevens.—Even with a chauffeur. I happen to know that on Christmas Day his mother and father will be in Europe . . . as they were last Christmas.

Henry.—Well . . . ?

Miss Stevens.—Would you like to come downstairs on Christmas morning in an enormous house . . . with no one to say Merry Christmas to you but a chauffeur and a butler and a housekeeper? . . . Don't you think he'd be just a bit happier that day if he knew that some place he had some friends who thought quite a bit of him?

Henry.—In spite of his looks?

Miss Stevens.—In spite of everything . . . even in spite of all his money. . . . What would you think, Henry . . . if we should give him the lead?

Henry.—Don't you think a little home-made fruit cake would cheer him up just as much? He said he'd never had any.

Miss Stevens.—I don't believe anything could mean quite so much to him as that part, Henry.

Henry.—I know. . . . But I'd planned on it quite a little myself, Miss Stevens.

JIM.—(*Approaching*) You aren't going to go on with the tryout, Miss Stevens?

HENRY.—The tryouts are all over.

JIM.—They're all over!

HENRY.—That's what I said, they're all over!

JIM.—I understand. . . . Then I'm out.

HENRY.—What do you mean, you're out? You poor dope. . . . You get the lead!

JIM.—I don't really, do I?

MISS STEVENS.—Didn't Henry say you did?

JIM.—I know . . . but . . .

HENRY.—I never did like the part.

MISS STEVENS.—Look out the window, boys. Under the street lamp . . . the snow is starting to fall. . . . Have you ever seen such large flakes?

MR. ALDRICH.—(*Off*) Henry!

HENRY.—I've got it, father! (*To Jim*) Listen, Funnyface, if you aren't doing anything else on Christmas why don't you come over to our house for dinner?

JIM.—I'd like very much to, only the help have instructions not to let me out of their sight.

HENRY.—How much help have you got?

JIM.—Three.

MR. ALDRICH.—(*Off*) Henry!

HENRY.—Well, bring them along!

JIM.—You don't mean it, do you?

HENRY.—Why not? We'll just set four more places! Coming, father!

MUSIC.—"*That's Silly.*" *Fade for*

KATE.—Well, everyone in Mopeyville is happy with Christmas cheer and fun tonight, for as Mopeyville goes . . . so go . . . *Bud Abbott and Lou Costello.*

Lou.—(*Sings*)
"Jingle bells, jingle bells, jingle all the day.
Three more days till Christmas, and then what bills to pay."

Bud.—Costello, you're certainly in a happy mood. I suppose you're all through with your Christmas shopping. Hey! What's that string tied around your finger for?

Lou.—That's to remind me to remind my wife to ask me if I forgot something she told me to remember.

Bud.—Which reminds me. I forgot to get my wife a nutcracker.

Lou.—What kind? Flat iron or rolling pin?

Bud.—Talk sense. What did you forget?

Lou.—A present for my Uncle Bumble Bee.

Bud.—What a name. Uncle Bumble Bee.

Lou.—Yeah. That's because everybody he touches gets stung. I'm gonna buy him a shaving brush and a razor.

Bud.—Has he got a mug?

Lou.—Oh, boy! You should see her.

Bud.—Well, all I need now is my Christmas turkey.

Lou.—Abbott, was I lucky! I got a turkey for running.

Bud.—Who did you beat?

Lou.—The butcher and two policemen.

Bud.—Costello, you'll end up by spending Christmas in the police station.

Lou.—Well, that's all right in a pinch. Hey, Abbott, come over to the house Christmas and eat some turkey.

Bud.—Why should I have to eat turkey on Christmas? Maybe I'd like chicken.

Lou.—I haven't got any chicken. I got turkey.

Bud.—Well, is that my fault? Why didn't you ask me what I'd like before you invited me over? If I want chicken, why should you force me to eat turkey?

Lou.—Who's forcing you to eat turkey? Don't eat it.

108

BUD.—I see. Now I shouldn't eat it. I should go hungry while you stuff yourself.

LOU.—Who wants you to go hungry? Aw, I'll go out and steal a chicken.

BUD.—And what happens to the turkey?

LOU.—I'll give it to the dog.

BUD.—That's fine. You feed the dog turkey and want me to eat chicken.

LOU.—Look, Abbott, what do you keep arguing for? Look at me. I'm congenial.

BUD.—Oh, now you're using an assumed name. Who are you to travel incognito?

LOU.—Who's traveling in magneto? I ain't using a consumed name. I use my own name. You can find it on my front door.

BUD.—Why should I look for your name? I know what it is.

LOU.—Then don't look for it.

BUD.—I see. I shouldn't look for your name. I should walk into somebody else's house by mistake and get shot for a burglar.

LOU.—Ah, I don't want you to get shot. I'm trying to tell you, you're welcome at my house. The door is always open for you.

BUD.—Now, you're going to leave the door open. You want me to sit in a draft and catch cold.

LOU.—Who wants you to catch cold! I'll close the door. I'll lock the door.

BUD.—And what am I supposed to do, crawl in the window?

LOU.—What do you mean, crawl in the window? I'll bring you into the house.

BUD.—Oh, you'll bring me in. What's the matter, don't you think I can walk? Do you expect me to come over inebriated?

LOU.—Who cares if you're inebriated? You don't have to be inebriated. You can wear anything you want. I just want you to have some nice young turkey.

Bud.—How do you know it's a young turkey? How can you tell a turkey's age?

Lou.—By the teeth.

Bud.—A turkey has no teeth.

Lou.—No, but I have.

Bud.—Is the turkey dressed?

Lou.—Did you ever see a turkey running around the streets without any clothes on? Certainly it's dressed. It has on a suit of feathers.

Bud.—If it has feathers on, then it isn't dressed.

Lou.—How do you like that? If it has feathers, it isn't dressed. Look; I'm talking about a turkey, not a fan dancer.

Bud.—So am I talking about a turkey, and if it has feathers on, it isn't dressed.

Lou.—Well, what do you want it to wear, a shirt waist and panties, or do you want me to take it to my tailor and say, "Make my turkey a cutaway suit, he's going out for Christmas dinner"?

Bud.—That's not necessary. I thought maybe the butcher dressed the turkey.

Lou.—That's ridiculous. Do you think the butcher has time to put clothes on animals?

Bud.—No.

Lou.—Do you think he says to his customers, "How would you like your turkey dressed, as Snow White or one of the Seven Dwarfs"?

Bud.—You don't understand. When I say, "Is the turkey dressed?" I don't mean, is the turkey dressed?

Lou.—No? What do you mean?

Bud.—I mean, is the turkey dressed?

Lou.—Ah, this thing is getting too complicated for me. I should a stole a hot dog.

Bud.—Then why did you steal the turkey in the first place?

Lou.—Who stole it in the first place? I had to try three places before I got it.

Bud.—Well, what I'm trying to find out is this: Did *you* pick its feathers?

Lou.—Did I pick its feathers! I never saw the turkey before. Do you think I know the style in turkey feathers? It picked its own feathers.

Bud.—That's impossible. It couldn't pick its own feathers.

Lou.—All right, then its mother chose them for it.

Bud.—Costello, when I say, "Pick its feathers," I don't mean pick its feathers.

Lou.—I know. You mean, pick its feathers. This thing gets sillier all the time.

Bud.—There's nothing silly about it. You've got to pick its feathers. They're good for quills.

Lou.—Well, who's got quills. I haven't been sick a day in 5 years.

Bud.—Costello, I'm trying to tell you that you can't cook that turkey with its feathers on.

Lou.—Are you kidding?

Bud.—Certainly not. You've got to pick the feathers.

Lou.—I'll let my wife pick them. She picks everything else I get.

Bud.—Does she pick your clothes?

Lou.—Only the pockets.

Bud.—That's fine. You get mad if your wife picks your pockets, but it's all right for you to steal a turkey. You don't care if the mama and papa turkey sit in their coop all day on Christmas and cry because you're having their baby turkey for dinner.

Lou.—I'm a bad boy.

Bud.—You *are* a bad boy.

Lou.—I'm the kind of boy my mother don't want me to associate with.

Bud.—You bet you are.

III

Lou.—I shouldn't be allowed to carve the turkey on Christmas.

Bud.—You won't be allowed. I'll carve the turkey. I'll hand out the portions.

Lou.—Then I'll probably end up with the wishbone.

Bud.—What's the matter with the wishbone? It's lucky.

Lou.—Yeah? Well, the turkey had it, and it didn't do *him* any good.

Bud.—Keep quiet while I figure out how I'll serve the turkey. Now, I'll take the two legs.

Lou.—Look, Abbott, I'd like to have one of the legs.

Bud.—Sure, the turkey only has two legs, and you want a leg. You're the most selfish person I've ever met.

Lou.—Oh, I'm a wanton.

Bud.—What do you mean, you're a wanton?

Lou.—I'm a wanton one of those turkey legs.

Bud.—Never mind that. I'll take the two legs. My wife will take the two wings. . . .

Lou.—Well, could I sit under the table and pick up the crumbs?

Bud.—I'll take care of your share later. Let me see. That's the two legs and wings, and your wife will take the white meat, your uncle the heart and liver.

Lou.—Look, Abbott, could I lick the plate? I gotta come out of this with something.

Bud.—Will you stop butting in! Now, that takes care of the legs, wings, white meat, heart, liver and oh, yes, your mother-in-law gets the neck and giblets, and you . . .

Lou.—Aw, never mind me, I'll sit on the fence and grab mine as it goes by!

Music.—*Chord. Then "Laugh and Call It Love" and fade for*

Collins.—Here's Kate with some rhythmic philosophy . . . "Laugh and Call It Love."

Music.—*"Laugh and Call It Love."*

112

KATE.—Ladies and gentlemen, have you ever been called up before the boss to explain something you have done? . . . It's kind of a ticklish proposition, isn't it? . . . Well, tonight . . . the situation is reversed. I have called on *my* boss tonight . . . *not* to put him on the carpet but to have him say a few well-chosen words in behalf of Christmas. . . . I am happy indeed to present the president of General Foods . . . my boss . . . Mr. Clarence Francis . . .

FRANCIS.—Thank you, Kate Smith! . . . Any time you need a job . . . let me know!

Ladies and gentlemen, I know we agree on one real reason for happiness, regardless of our own personal fortunes or misfortunes at this particular moment. . . . We are living in good old America. I say "good old America" advisedly, because the more we learn of war, strife, class hatreds, and misery in other parts of the world, the more certain we are that we are indeed fortunate in living here. I know you share this feeling. I am sure that down deep in your hearts you are thankful and therefore happy.

We all know, however, that there are far too many men and women unemployed. Theirs may be a bleak Christmas unless in each community those who are more fortunate do what they can to help. The parents can *"take it,"* but let us each think of the children.

Real Americans want to work. The best Christmas present to the unemployed would be jobs. Would that Santa could deliver one to each right now! Making jobs for all who would work is America's Job Number One! I feel happy because of many signs that industry, labor, and government intend to meet on common ground to start the wheels of industry whirling at a faster clip. I feel sure that, with the sympathy, understanding, and determination to provide more jobs, great progress will be made.

Thank goodness that our good neighbor, Canada, shares our ideals, principles, and determination. Canada, too, is a grand country.

On the prairies . . . in remote corners of our two countries, live millions of men and women who raise food for all our families . . . to them we send our greetings. Also to the merchants, our customers.

To our own family of 10,000 workers and to nearly 70,000 men and women who have intrusted their savings with us, your company extends its gratitude and wishes you a Merry Christmas.

To all others devoting their lives to feeding our two countries . . . the delivery boy, driver, wholesaler, warehouseman, supplier, factory worker, salesman, typist . . . to all friends of the Kate Smith Hour . . . General Foods says: A Merry Christmas and a New Year of peace, prosperity, and happiness. Keep the faith. . . . Carry on. There are better things in store for all! . . . Thank you!

MUSIC.—"*The Rosary.*" *Fade for*

COLLINS.—For her memory song this evening, Kate Smith sings "The Rosary."

MUSIC.—"*The Rosary.*" (*Orchestra and Kate*). *Segue into "Sweet Melody." Fade for*

COLLINS.—We pause for just a moment to tell you that you are listening to the Kate Smith Hour, brought to you by Calumet Baking Powder and Swans Down Cake Flour . . . your two best baking friends. We shall continue after station identification. This is the Columbia . . . Broadcasting System.

MUSIC.—"*Jingle Bells.*"

COLLINS.—Here we are back again to go on a sleigh ride with Ted Straeter and the Kate Smith Singers to the tune of "Jingle Bells."

MUSIC.—(*Orchestra and chorus*). "*Jingle Bells.*"
Applause . . .
Mood music. Fade for

KATE.—At this Christmas season I am happy to be able to bring you carols by one of the finest vocal organizations I have heard. I've brought this chorus of boys and girls . . . every member of which is blind . . . to my program tonight so you too may enjoy their glorious voices. The Senior Chorus of the New York Institute for the blind, under the direction of Mr. Noel Kempton, sing first . . . "Noel" and then "Lo, How a Rose E'er Blooming."

MUSIC.—"*Noel.*" "*Lo, How a Rose E'er Blooming.*"

KATE.—And now our Christmas play.

MUSIC.—*Mood music. Fade for*

KATE.—We are privileged in having with us to appear in this play one of the most famous names the theatre has ever known. A name made famous by the great dramatic talents of its bearer . . . Miss Ethel Barrymore.

MUSIC.—*Few bars of gay Spanish fiesta song. . . . "B." . . . . Fades for*

NARRATOR.—The very same late December sun that dances on the winter snows up north sprawls indolently at ease in the thick white dust of El Camino del Norte, Old Mexico. A lean and ancient woman has paused to rest in the cool dripping shade of a pepper tree. . . . She is suddenly awakened by the shrill voice of Pablo . . . aged ten . . . who stands with bare brown legs wide apart in the center of the road and bitterly addresses a small discouraged donkey.* . . .

PABLO.—(*In high indignation*) A donkey. A *donkey*, you call yourself, Estupido! A fine animal with four stout legs . . . a splendid tail to shoo off the flies . . . and a head stuck on the front to point the way you are going! Asi! And what use do you make of this most excellent equipment the good God has given you? *Nothing! Absolutely nothing!* You are a disgrace to all the donkeys of all Mexico! Of all the world . . . of all the . . .

WOMAN.—(*Just off*) Pablo . . . !

PABLO.—(*Automatically*) Si. . . . (*Sees the woman*) Oh . . . buenas dias, I did not know that . . .

WOMAN.—(*Coming in*) Whatever is the trouble, my son? What has the poor beast done that you should be so angry?

PABLO.—(*Exasperated*) But *nothing* . . . !

WOMAN.—Then why?

PABLO.—(*Bitterly*) And nothing is all he ever *wants* to do! Here it is . . . but two days until Christmas . . . when a load of wood could be sold in the village to buy gifts and a candle. But does that matter to him? *No!* He cares for nothing but nothing!

WOMAN.—(*Laughing*) Well . . . a donkey's a donkey, Pablo. They're all the same.

* Original sketch by Charles Tazewell.

PABLO.—But why should it be so? Of all beasts, why must a donkey be so . . . so stubborn?

WOMAN.—Stubborn? Oh, no, Pablo . . . that's wrong. . . .

PABLO.—But . .

WOMAN.—(*Quickly*) I know! Everyone says they are. They curse him and belabor his back with sticks and call him stupid. But that's only because they don't know the true facts.

PABLO.—The *true* facts?

WOMAN.—Si. It's really not stubbornness but pride that makes all small donkeys so . . . well, so aloof. No sun, wind, storm, pain or adversity can touch them. Their pride is a shield against all the discomforts man or the elements can offer.

PABLO.—But what has a donkey to be proud of?

WOMAN.—Oh . . . a great deal, Pablo! Bring your beast over here in the shade . . . and perhaps I can explain it to you. . . .

PABLO.—(*Clicking his tongue*) Tsch . . . tsch! Come along, Cupido. . . .

MUSIC.—*"C" cue xylophone . . . muted with hand so that the notes are dull and metallic. First four notes of "Silent Night" . . . the fourth note thrown up an octave so that the tune will not be recognized . . . these same four notes are repeated three times, representing the donkey's hoofbeats as he is led to the shade of the pepper tree.*

WOMAN.—(*During second sequence of four notes*) Listen! Do you hear that, Pablo? Only a small donkey can make that sound with his hooves as he walks on the stones. No other beast can do it. . . . Sit down . . . sit down, my son. . . .

PABLO.—Gracias . . . Gracias.

WOMAN.—Now . . . as I was saying . . . people are all wrong about donkeys, you see. . . . A very long time ago . . . a great honor came to one of them . . . an honor so great that it raised him and all his many descendants to an exalted place. A place that you or I or all the world might envy. Ever since then all small donkeys have been content to stand and drowse in the sun or shade . . . for they alone, of all other animals and men, have already fulfilled their destiny.

PABLO.—I . . . I don't quite understand.

WOMAN.—Well . . . once upon a time, as all stories must begin . . . there was a little donkey. He was fourteen unhappy years old . . . and he had worked for at least twice fourteen masters. . . .

MUSIC.—*"D" cue. Start xylophone very dim . . . first four notes of "Silent Night" . . . raising fourth note one octave. Put slight rest between third and fourth note to denote limp . . . continue until cued out.*

WOMAN.—*(Continuing)* He was battered and scarred . . . and presented a most disreputable appearance. His tail was naught but a piece of rope, unraveled at the end. One of his ears stood straight up like a cactus plant . . . while the other hung drooping like a wilted cabbage leaf. In his off hind leg was a decided limp.

PABLO.—What was his name?

WOMAN.—They called him Small One. His latest master was a woodcutter, who also owned four younger and therefore stronger donkeys. But Small One was the special charge and favorite of the woodcutter's son. It was the boy who saw that Small One always had dry straw for his bed . . . and that the load of wood to be carried to the town was not too heavy for Small One's aging back. But . . . one day the woodcutter called his son to him and said . . .

MUSIC.—*"E" cue. Xylophone, with violins.*

FATHER.—Son!

BOY.—*(Coming in)* Yes, father?

FATHER.—*(Ponderously)* I have a task for you to do in the town.

BOY.—A load of wood?

FATHER.—No. I wish you to take the old donkey . . . the one you call Small One . . . to a shop just inside the town gates. I have already spoken to the man. He will give you one piece of silver in exchange for the beast.

BOY.—(*Horrified*) You mean . . . you *don't* mean you're going to sell Small One?

FATHER.—(*Sternly*) He can no longer do his share of the work. Even carrying half the load of the other donkeys, his worn-out legs tremble, and his sides work like a bellows. . . .

BOY.—(*Eagerly*) But he'll be as strong as the others soon! You wait and see. Give him a few weeks and . . .

FATHER.—(*Breaking in*) An old donkey is of no use! One day soon he might drop dead on us up in the hills . . . a total loss. Better to take the piece of silver and say good riddance to the animal. You will start at once.

BOY.—(*Trying to keep back the tears*) Yes, father. . . .

FATHER.—The shop is the second on the left as you enter the town gates. . . .

BOY.—The second? But . . . but that's the tanner's!

FATHER.—And what of that? The Small One's hide is old . . . but it will make good leather nevertheless.

BOY.—But he's been faithful. . . . He's worked. . . . He's done his best! You can't sell him to the tanner to be killed.

FATHER.—(*Sternly*) Come, now. . . . I'll have no tears!

MUSIC.—*Xylophone begins same sequence of four notes . . . dim.*

FATHER.—(*Continuing*) No crying over a miserable donkey. Hurry . . . be off with you. And take care not to lose that piece of silver on the way home. . . .

MUSIC.—*"F" cue. Orchestra comes in, improvising on theme of four notes played by xylophone . . . hold for a few seconds . . . then fade down and out, leaving xylophone muted, continuing. . . .*

WOMAN.—(*Fading in*) . . . And so, Pablo, the small boy and the small donkey began their sorrowful journey toward the town. The boy was heartbroken . . . and cried for a while. Then he tried desperately to think of some way to save the life of his friend. The sound of the Small One's hooves on the road seemed to repeat, over and over again, "Going to the tanner's . . . going to the tanner's."

WOMAN.—Then . . . it suddenly came to the lad's mind that there was a horse market in the town . . . and if he could sell small one to some new and kind master, the little donkey would still live and the father would also have his piece of silver! It was early afternoon when the boy and Small One passed through the town gates and neared the market place. . . . As the padre says, "It was early afternoon . . . "

SOUND.—*Voices, shouts, cries, rumble of wheels, stamp of hooves, barking of dogs, the tinkling bell of a blind beggar, and all the other sounds of a busy market place fade in. These sounds come up full as the padre finishes. Take out xylophone back of sound.*

WOMAN.—As he came closer, he could hear the booming voice of the auctioneer as he cried, "Who'll bid 51 for this fine Arabian steed . . . whose sire is so famous that naught but kings have sat his back . . . going at 51 . . . 51 . . . sold!

MUSIC.—*Registers a second or two cue "G."*

WOMAN.—The small boy was stunned to think that such beautiful horses were selling for 50 and 60 pieces of silver. . . . If he could only get one piece of silver for his aged donkey . . . just one. . . . He approached the auctioneer, dragging Small One behind him. . . . He stopped a few feet from the stand. "Would you like to buy a fine donkey, sir?" he said. . . . "He is kind and gentle, and I know he can do twice as much work as those horses they're bidding 50 and 60. . . . "

SOUND.—*Loud laughter in the market place.*

WOMAN.—Time and again the boy went from person to person, trying to sell Small One. He could not face taking his wonderful donkey to the tanners . . . but they laughed at him. . . . Finally . . . the boy and the donkey left the market place!

MUSIC.—*Comes in . . . improvising on four-note theme, played by xylophone. Music dies out, leaving xylophone.*

WOMAN.—The hours were slipping by . . . and the boy knew he must soon start for home . . . and that he must have the piece of silver to give his father. He stopped people on the street. . . . He inquired from door to door . . . But no one desired to buy a small, tired donkey. The sun was sinking fast when he came at last back to the town gates and stood before the tanner's door. The boy's face was tear-streaked, and the Small One's head drooped so low that his limp ear nearly touched the ground. The boy said good-by to the little beast . . . asked his forgiveness for what he was about to do . . . and there was understanding in the little donkey's eyes. Then . . . as the boy lifted the latch of the tanner's door . . . a voice spoke to him. . . .

MUSIC.—*Xylophone, which has been repeating sequence of four notes through above, stops . . . the fourth note of the last sequence timed to come just after woman stops speaking. The violins come in on this final note . . . sustaining it for a few seconds to mark change of scene. As this last sustained note ends . . .*

VOICE.—(*Just off*) My son . . .

BOY.—Yes? . . . Yes, sir?

VOICE.—(Coming in) I have a great favor to ask of you. Are you the owner of that small donkey?

BOY.—Oh, yes, sir. . . .

VOICE.—I have a journey to make . . . and my wife is not well. I have need of a strong animal to carry her safely. . . . .

BOY.—Small One is very strong . . . and very trustworthy. . . .

VOICE.—Would you sell him to me?

BOY.—(*Eagerly*) Yes. Oh, yes, sir! For but one piece of silver. . . .

VOICE.—A very reasonable price for such a beautiful animal.

BOY.—He's . . . he's not very beautiful . . . but . . . but he's good.

VOICE.—I can see that. I'll be kind to him . . . I promise you that.

BOY.—Then he'll work hard to please you. . . .

VOICE.—Here is your piece of silver. Come, Small One . . . we've a long way to go. . . .

MUSIC.—*Xylophone starts repeating four notes.*

BOY.—Do you mind . . . do you mind if I go as far as the town gate? You see, Small One and I . . .

VOICE.—Of course. You want to say good-by to him. You can do that while I see my wife safely on his back. Here we are . . . easy, Small One!

MUSIC.—*Xylophone stops.*

BOY.—(*Trying to hold back the tears*) Good-by, Small One. . . . You must be very faithful. And . . . and it isn't forever, you know. . . . When I grow up . . . and earn many pieces of silver . . . I'll buy you back. . . . And you'll have a fine stable . . . and nothing to do at all but sleep and eat. Won't that be fine, Small One?

VOICE.—All right, my boy . . . we're ready to go. . . .

GUARD.—(*Off . . . coming in*) Wait, traveler! I must make out the record before you pass through the town gates! Who are you?

VOICE.—My name is Joseph.

GUARD.—Your wife?

VOICE.—They call her Mary.

GUARD.—Your destination?

VOICE.—Is Bethlehem.

GUARD.—Pass!

VOICE.—Come, Small One. (*Xylophone begins the same four notes . . . the last note, as before, raised an octave*) Good-by, son. . . .

BOY.—(*Crying*) Good-by . . . good-by, Small One. . . . Carry . . . carry her safe to Bethlehem. . . .

MUSIC.—*The xylophone continues . . . but with each repeat of the four-note sequence, the fourth note drops one tone lower until it is a true repetition of the first four notes of "Silent Night." When this is established, full orchestra picks it up and continues on into the song with chorus of voices back of it . . . dims for*

WOMAN.—And so, Pablo . . . the Small One traveled the weary miles to Bethlehem . . . and there in a stable . . . which became a king's stable . . . he saw a king born . . . a king of men . . . of centuries . . . of life . . . of death. The Small One's old, tired eyes saw the Wise Men and shepherds who came to pay homage to his master . . . and he heard the voices of angels . . . rejoicing . . . singing the same notes his hooves had rung out on the stones of the road. And it came to pass that those who had laughed at his ragged coat, his limping gait, and his drooping ear . . . they envied the Small One he was a part of a great miracle. . . . That was long, long ago, Pablo . . . but today, all little donkeys stand and dream . . . especially at Christmas time . . . dream of the Small One . . . the Small One of Bethlehem.

MUSIC.—*Orchestra and voices up full. Segue "Silent Night" (Orchestra, Kate, and Institute Chorus). On cue orchestra segue into "Along the Texas Trail" and fade under following.*

COLLINS.—This is Ted Collins, saying good night. Be with us again next Thursday at Kate Smith time to celebrate the passing of good old 1938. The Aldrich Family and Abbott and Costello will, as usual, take part in the festivities, and as I talk to you one of Hollywood's most beloved stars is en route to New York to join us. His name is Jean Hersholt. Until then . . .

KATE.—All of us at Swans Down and Calumet want to wish you a very merry Christmas. Thanks for listenin'. . . . And good night, folks!

MUSIC.—*Orchestra up to finish.*

Czech Crisis

by H. V. KALTENBORN

ℓℓℓ

HARVEST time in war-torn Spain. The year is 1936. Rebels are attacking the Loyalist city of Irun. A fierce battle is being fought on farm land just outside the city. Shells and bursting bombs dropped by planes wheeling overhead turn the once calm countryside into a holocaust.

Suddenly a tall man dashes out from behind an abandoned farmhouse and sprints for a haystack a hundred feet away. It is H. V. Kaltenborn, equipped with earphones and microphone, dragging a cable attached to the transmitter in near-by Hendaye. He makes the haystack in safety and from its vantage point gives Columbia Network listeners an on-the-scene account of Spain's civil war.

The incident is typical of Kaltenborn's entire life. Wanderlust has sent him all over the world. Resourcefulness and courage have given him many such scoops, both as newspaperman and radio reporter.

He has interviewed Mussolini and Hitler and was often in Soviet Russia in the 1920's, where he broadcast over Moscow's powerful Comintern station. Mahatma Gandhi personally told him about conditions in India. Kaltenborn was one of the few Americans able to get into General Chiang Kai-shek's headquarters for an interview. While in China, Kaltenborn was captured by bandits and held for ransom. They were on the point of thrusting him in front of a firing squad when the money arrived.

The Columbia news analyst's wanderings started when he was only nineteen, when he ran off and secretly enlisted to serve in the Spanish-American war. A cattle-boat trip to Europe followed, then a job with the *Brooklyn Daily Eagle* on his return.

At twenty-four, he decided that a college education was desirable and enrolled as a special student at Harvard. He won a Phi Beta Kappa key, the Boylston Prize for public speaking, and the Coolidge Prize for debating.

After graduation, Kaltenborn tutored Vincent Astor in Europe and aboard the latter's yacht in the West Indies. Then Kaltenborn returned to his *Eagle* desk. Working for the paper did not interfere with his traveling, however. Every summer he "shut up shop" and set out for new points on the globe—Hawaii, Japan, Brazil, Alaska, the Philippines.

Kaltenborn's radio career began eighteen years ago on April 21, 1921. Speaking from Newark, N. J., he addressed the Brooklyn Chamber of Commerce across the Hudson River. Two years later he was being heard regularly on the air. In 1928 he joined Columbia's news staff.

Unlike most other commentators, Kaltenborn never reads from a script. He speaks "ad lib" from scribbled notes. This habit stood him in good stead during the Czechoslovakian crisis last September. He would go on the air to translate a speech by Hitler as it came across the ocean from Berlin and shortly afterward return to the microphone to analyze what he had said. In addition to German, Kaltenborn speaks French and Spanish fluently.

Kaltenborn credits the simplicity of his home life for the energy that enabled him to work such long stretches without relief during the Czechoslovakian trouble and to carry on his many public activities. He is married to the Baroness Olga von Nordenflycht, daughter of a German Ambassador to Uruguay, whom he met on one of his European trips.

For many years prior to his outstanding performances during the Czechoslovakian crisis in 1938, H. V. Kaltenborn was an international figure of great prominence. But the merciless assignment that was given to him during the three tempestuous weeks during September, 1938, revealed for the first time the incredible resources that are his: resources in stamina, temper, in memory, perception, and intelligence. During the twenty days and twenty nights of perpetual uncertainty he was on the air as often as fourteen times within the same twenty-four hours, and the picture he presented to the American radio audience and to those foreign countries receiving his programs by short wave was, short of a general war itself, the most graphically sustained adventure radio listeners are ever likely to have.

Quite frankly, it is impossible to pick out the best of all these broadcasts, but I have selected a midafternoon report of September 20, 1938, not only for the reading interest it affords but for lack of being able to find anything superior to it. Mr. Kaltenborn's opening sentence refers to the reading of the Czechoslovakian reply to the proposal recommended by Great Britain and France. The reply reads as follows: "The Czechoslovak government has handed to the British and French Ministers in Prague a note in which the government expresses its point of view with regard to the proposal which has been interpreted to it by Great Britain and France. This point of view makes further negotiations possible in the spirit of conciliation which the Czechoslovak government has always shown." Mr. Kaltenborn picked up the broadcast at that point.

Czech Crisis*

KALTENBORN.—That was a highly dramatic conclusion to the talk of Maurice Hindus from Prague. It gave the world first news of the answer of the Czech government to the Franco-British proposals that it surrender Sudetenland to Germany. The answer is as I ventured to predict it would be when yesterday I said that the Czech government would naturally play for time; that it was not likely to give an unequivocal "yes" or "no" in reply to the proposals that had been made. As you heard the official communiqué read: "The point of view of the Czech government makes further negotiations possible in the spirit of conciliation which the Czech government has always shown."

In other words, the official communiqué does not reveal the text of the answer. And that is quite natural, for when governments communicate with one another upon important subjects, they do not immediately issue the texts of those communications unless they desire to accomplish a propaganda purpose by doing so. Where negotiations are to be carried on, in a spirit of amity and conciliation (which is the spirit the Czech government desires to emphasize), the communications are kept secret until they have reached the government to which they are addressed. Then both governments usually agree upon a simultaneous release. But we must remember that since we have not had any official statement as to the text of the original proposals— only probably 90 per cent accurate guesswork—it is only natural that the Czechoslovak government's official answer is not yet released.

However, we do not know now that it is not an acceptance of the proposal. Nor is it a rejection of the proposals. It is the expression of a willingness to discuss what must be done to preserve peace, an expression in which the Czech government emphasizes its desires for peace, its spirit of conciliation, demonstrated by the Czechoslovak government in all the negotiations that have been carried on so far.

* Copyright, 1938, by Random House, Inc.

126

Mr. Hindus gave you an extremely interesting account of the spirit of the Czechoslovak people, and that spirit, remember, is always tremendously important in a democratic government, where public opinion controls what a government can and must do.

Last night he pointed out to us that the Czech Government was definitely leaning toward acceptance. But the session last night was not final. And this morning the atmosphere and the situation have changed. One important point stressed by Mr. Hindus that has not previously been brought out in anything that I have seen from Prague is the part that the Czech army might play in this situation.

That army, as he told you, has been trained for 20 years. It was generally recognized as one of the most powerful, one of the best-equipped, one of the finest-spirited armies of all Europe. And that army, on which the Czech people at a great sacrifice have expended a billion dollars in the two decades in which they have built it up—that army representing also the Czech people, for it is an army that comes from the people—will not be willing to surrender. That explains the statement that was made to Mr. Hindus by one of the Czech observers, that if the Cabinet should be unwise enough to make complete acceptance of this proposal, that then there might be a military dictatorship in which the army itself would act to create a government that would resist the German demands.

In a few hours the whole temper and the character of the situation in Europe have once more changed. Reflect for just a moment as to the effect of that change on the projected meeting tomorrow of Prime Minister Chamberlain and Adolf Hitler at Godesberg. They will have before them a reply from the Czech government that is not direct acceptance. It is a reply that will require careful and delicate and patient negotiation. Knowing Adolf Hitler as I do, knowing his temper, knowing his spirit, knowing the attitude that he has shown, again and again, toward international problems, I am convinced that he personally cannot and will not enter such negotiations.

The chances are that the Godesberg meeting will be postponed, because certainly the time is not ripe for a final showdown between the French representatives and the British representatives.

127

Here is a cable from Berlin. It just came in and it bears out what I just told you. It is not often that a commentator has the good fortune to be confirmed when he has only just made his guess. But our Mr. Shirer in Berlin has just sent us word at this very moment that the special train scheduled to take the correspondents to Godesberg tonight will not leave. That is the immediate response from Germany to the answer that has come from Czechoslovakia. For these things are flashed instantaneously to the capitals of the world, and decisions are instantaneously made. So what I said a moment ago is true: the negotiations are postponed. We are now confronted by a situation that may break out in military action on the Czechoslovakian frontier any time.

I read to you a little while ago the headlines from the German press this morning. Those headlines show that Germany is emphasizing the idea that Czech military forces are attacking Germans; that they are conducting raids on German soil. Now I must say again that the American correspondents who have been at the front in Sudetenland again and again and who are there today have found no evidence of any such aggression on the part of the Czech soldiers. On the contrary, there are two points on which all the Americans agree: That aggression has come entirely from the Sudetens. Second, that the Czech police and the Czech soldiers have acted with remarkable restraint. It is well that we should heed this testimony from neutral American sources, because our country has been bombarded and will continue to be bombarded with propaganda of every type and kind. Public opinion in the United States should be based on the truth and not on propaganda.

One more dispatch, yes—the discussion that has been taken up by Adolf Hitler with representatives of Poland and Hungary. Now that is important, because it is clear today that there can be no settlement of the Sudeten problem without the corresponding settlement for that part of Czechoslovakia which is inhabited by the Poles, the so-called Teschen district adjoining Silesia where there are 100,000 Poles who have not been particularly happy under Czech rule. Also, there is that much more important part of Czechoslovakia lying contiguous to Hungary, taken from Hungary after the World War, and including 700,000 Hungarians. I am convinced that when we come to a final settlement of this problem, the Polish minority and the Hungarian minority will probably be taken care of on exactly the same basis as the German minority—that is, unless events get beyond control and war comes. If that happens, no one can tell what will come to pass. It is fortunate, though, that we have had this respite. It has given the world a chance to catch its second breath, so to speak. We were not hurried into an immediate crisis, because in France, in Britain, in Czechoslovakia, even in Germany, there is perhaps a heartfelt appreciation of what a war might mean. That justifies some hope that we may be able to continue along the painful path of negotiations toward final peace. Good afternoon.

BEST NEWS COMMENTARY
(PREPARED)

The Situation in Europe

by RAYMOND GRAM SWING

RAYMOND GRAM SWING is one of the most lucid intelligences in radio today. He is thoughtful, observing, and vigorous and probably more mature in his perceptions than any commentator in the industry. He is never sensational, never spectacular, rarely humorous. With every justification for being cynical, he has instead converted his store of findings into an intellectual library as complete and many-sided as can be found in the possession of any journalist of our day.

He began working in Europe as Berlin correspondent for the *Chicago Daily News* in 1913 and covered the World War until America broke with Germany. Immediately after the war he returned to Germany as foreign correspondent for the *New York Evening Post* and the *Philadelphia Public Ledger*. He served in this capacity for fifteen years. In 1934 he started broadcasting for the BBC and has been one of their commentators—more or less regularly—for the past five years. He was heard over the Canadian Network for two years, over CBS for one, and has been heard regularly over WOR for the past three. He has had an active quarter century of news gathering and news reporting; he has been on the scene when the thing happened; he has seen sellouts, betrayals, war and the threat of war, treaty rupture and territorial rape, treachery, collusion, and repudiation—in short, all of the amenities that make up international diplomacy as we know it today. But if his philosophy has sustained the disillusionment that such an experience would explain, it is not apparent in Mr. Swing's writing nor in his thinking. He is balanced, sober, and impartial.

He prepares his broadcasts with great care, taking as much as five hours in the writing of a fifteen-minute talk. All these talks are highly listenable and informative. That they never sound labored is explained principally by the fact that his thinking never is, either.

I have selected his broadcast of October 13, 1938, as the outstanding performance of the year for the division in which he is included. The very assignment he undertook was in itself staggering: he endeavored in fifteen minutes to clarify the most notorious international mess of the generation, and he did it. It is a superior piece of reportorial summation, and it is doubtful if there is in radio today any other personality who could equal it for clarity, interest, and simplicity.

The Situation in Europe*

pppppppppppppppppppppppppppppppppppppppppppppppppppppp

MR. RAYMOND GRAM SWING.—A month and a half ago I broke off my talks on world events to visit Europe. I knew that the momentum of crisis was very great, but I did not foresee that before I could return to America the crisis should have reached its breaking point and that grave decisions of an unalterable nature would have been taken.

Tonight I have a sense of the almost painful limitation of the time at my disposal and of my own mind in grasping the full measure of what has happened. Very great forces have been at work, far greater than the individuals who have seemed to shape them. The stage of the drama of Berchtesgaden, Godesberg, and Munich is too vast to be seen at a glance. It will be my temptation to simplify and so unintentionally falsify the story, but you will welcome simplification, because one *has* to try to understand what has happened and how it could have happened. I must confine my account of what has taken place to a few of the undeniable facts and leave out a great deal that belongs in the story.

Let us look first at results. Try to think back six months ago, when the crisis was first evident. If anyone had told you then that by tonight Czechoslovakia was to be deserted by its allies, dismembered at their request, that Germany in this short time was to be given mastery of Eastern Europe and so of the European continent, that France would voluntarily step down from being a first-class power to being shut up in Western Europe with only Britain and no further allies to secure it, if anyone had said this would happen at the point of the gun, in terms of an ultimatum, and would be accepted by Britain and France without the firing of a shot, you would have thought such a prophet was mad. You would have said that to achieve such a result, the statesmen of Britain and France would have to show great creative power, that they would have to devise a new way to lose a war without bloodshed, and, indeed, in *this* result, would have to lose two wars, for they have now lost the World War

* Reprinted by special permission of Raymond Gram Swing and station WOR. Copyright, 1938, by Raymond Gram Swing.

and the war that threatened over Hitler's demand that Czechoslovakia should be demobilized as a power factor in Eastern Europe. What I am trying to remind you of is that this result, six months ago, would have seemed wholly incredible. And then I must do my best to explain how this incredible thing has happened.

It would be convenient to be able to explain it all in terms of treachery. Well, I believe there has been some treachery, but that does not explain it. It would be convenient to explain it in terms of a victory for peace; how glad I would be if I could for a moment regard the peace that has been bought as either lasting or indeed anything but a peace of decaying morals and mounting tyranny. It would be convenient to say, simply, that the British and French leaders preferred to live under Hitler's domination than to beat him with the aid of Soviet Russia, which is, I think, an element in the story. But none of these key phrases is enough to explain what happened. I think one must start with the examination of air power.

Now Mr. Chamberlain decided to go to Berchtesgaden, on the urging of Premier Daladier of France, on the day that the British and French governments were officially informed that in event of war Italy would fight on the side of Germany. You may doubt whether Italy would in fact have fought. But if you had been responsible for the safety of Britain and France you would have had to believe it and act accordingly. If Italy came in, the British and French air forces in the west of Europe would not have been equal to the air forces against them. They might have been sure of beating Germany in a year or so by military action and blockade. But the price would have been the ruin of many British and French cities.

There was doubt, too, about the effectiveness of the Soviet air force. I believe the doubt was exaggerated. I am not in a position to know. All I say is that the decision to carve up Czechoslovakia and make a present of part of it to Germany, was due in the first place to a sense that the British and French air forces were inadequate to protect their home countries, and that the Soviet air force was not to be relied on. If the British and French leaders wanted to avoid the disaster of a war in which they were inferior in the air, they had to clear their consciences for making Czechoslovakia pay the price. And this they did, perhaps more reasonably than they have been given credit for doing.

133

At first they were not going in for dismemberment. They hoped for a solution in Czechoslovakia which would maintain that country's strategic frontier and give enough rights to the Sudeten Germans to satisfy them. But when the crisis reached the boiling point, they saw that in the Sudetenland the fury had gone too deep for compromise. Agitation, provocation, and racial hysteria had been pushed so far that it was impossible to appease these Germans. If they were kept within the Czech state they would be a permanent menace to its security. Furthermore, if war came, the help that could be given Czechoslovakia would not have saved it from fairly complete ruination. Even if Germany had been beaten in the end, there would not be much left of Czechoslovakia, and the men at the helm said to themselves, Czechoslovakia is ruined in any case, it must be dismembered in any case, so why fight a ruinous war about it? There is a risk in war, there is a risk in peace. It is hard to say which is greater, but if they are in any way comparable, we must choose the risk of peace. That, I think, is a fair presentation of the minds which chose the way to Berchtesgaden, Godesberg, and Munich.

But now let us look at other elements in the story. The Czechs were not consulted about their sacrifice. Nor was the true military position ever at the disposal of the Anglo-French conference where the decisions were made. Here is where I think the word "treachery" is not too strong. I was in Prague on September 21, the day when the Czechs submitted to the Anglo-French program calling for dismemberment. Czechoslovakia was ready to fight. It was ready to go through the war, even through ruination, if in the end it might live on its democratic life. But Benes on that day was told that he must accept the Anglo-French plan and that if he did not Britain would not support France in any war that ensued, and so France would consider Czechoslovakia the guilty party and would not fulfill its treaty obligations. These were the two threats that were used to club down President Benes.

He could not believe his ears. He could not believe that what he was being told was the true desire of the French Cabinet. He had reason to suspect Bonnet, the French foreign minister, and he did suspect him. He at once told Ossousky, the Czech minister in Paris, to go to Daladier and find out if what Bonnet was doing was the will of the French Cabinet. To get this word to Ossousky he could either telephone, in which case the Germans could hear the conversation, or send the message in code by telegraph. He telegraphed. Someone in the French post office held up that wire, and Ossousky did not receive it in time to go to Daladier. And Benes, without being able to make sure that he needed to, agreed to the Anglo-French demands.

Now the fact is that the French Cabinet and the British government had neither of them authorized that Benes should be threatened as he was. And when the French Cabinet was told what Bonnet had done, that he had exceeded his instructions, six ministers resigned, including Reynaud, Mondel, and Sarraut. And more will be heard of this phase of M. Bonnet's zeal for peace. There is, too, another charge against Bonnet. At the Anglo-French conversations in London, where the surrender to Germany was decided on, he had to give a report on France's military preparedness. General Gamelin, the French chief of staff, was not there to speak for himself. Bonnet spoke of weakness in the air, and that he could do truthfully enough. But he did not tell the truth about France's military preparedness. He implied that the French army, because of the new Siegfried line, would be unable to render any useful aid to the Czechs. But a few days later, when Gamelin did go to London, when the British and French were actually preparing for war after the Godesberg ultimatum, Gamelin astonished the British by saying that the French army was at the peak of its power, that the Siegfried line—and these are Gamelin's own words—was "so much marmalade," and he could be through it in four days!

There is going to be, I am sure, a great debate for many years as to who sold out Czechoslovakia and the Western democracies to the domination of Hitler. Was it Chamberlain and the British pro-Nazis, or was it the French? I happen to know that many months ago Chamberlain told American correspondents in an interview they were not allowed to use that he favored the dismemberment of Czechoslovakia. I am sure that he will be called the architect of this peace of Munich. But this needs to be said.

France was the country which had a treaty obligation to Czechoslovakia. France was the country whose power in Europe depended in part on the survival of Czechoslovakia. France did not have to consult Britain about its obligations to its Bohemian ally. It needed only to consult its own interests and its own conscience. If France had so wished, there need have been no surrender to Hitler, and Mr. Chamberlain, even though he was ready to submit to Hitler, would have had to follow the French lead.

There are many aspects of this peace of Munich which I should like to stress. I want to say with all possible emphasis that the people of Britain and France did not demand this peace. They were magnificent. God knows they did not want war, but they were ready for war after Godesberg, and they knew what it was to have been in a war to keep one man from dominating Europe. They looked into the coming horrors of that war grimly, silently, and unflinchingly. One could never have asked more from a nation than the British and French gave in those days of the crisis. When they were given peace, they rejoiced. Why not? Will ever any democracy throw out its rulers and insist on going to war? I think that is impossible. They had been told by their leaders they must face war, and they faced it. They were then told by their leaders they need not fight, that a peace had been made for them that was peace with honor. They believed it. But now they are beginning to see that something about it all is false and humiliating. They begin to see that they lost to Hitler because they were weak in armaments, and yet, in losing, they have made Hitler relatively still stronger.

If they are not to be humiliated again, they must redouble the effort to build armaments, and yet, if they do that, they repudiate the peace that they so desperately want to believe in. They will be preparing for a war that in the next crisis will not be averted. I cannot begin to tell you the perplexity and despair that reign in Paris and London. There will be war if Britain and France stand up to Germany. And it will be fought at far worse terms than if it had been fought this summer. Hitler has free now the divisions he needed to overrun Czechoslovakia. In a few months he will have ready another army recruited from his Austrian provinces. France and Britain have wrecked the Soviet pact, and in another crisis they cannot count on the Soviet air force or the vast Soviet armies. They have driven Poland, Rumania, Hungary, and Yugoslovia into the arms of Germany and Italy. But if there is not a war, they are junior partners of Nazi Germany, putting off the evil day when they themselves will be victims of German expansion. It is on a Europe in such a dilemma that the peace of Munich has dawned. Good evening!

BEST NEWS DRAMATIZATION

The March of Time

ᵉᵉᵉ

ESTABLISHING famous "firsts" usually ends in controversy, and no sensational claim is to be made for the March of Time beyond saying that *Time's* editors were among the very earliest of those who realized the opportunity radio offered. *Time* magazine had a popular quiz program on the air as early as 1924! It was conducted by editor Briton Hadden, and it ran for over two years. The exact date of its discontinuance is uncertain. In 1928 *Time* sent throughout the country daily releases called News-Casts and, the following year, supplemented these printed releases with electrical transcription dramas of five minutes' duration called NewsActing. The combination of these two made a fifteen-minute show, and it was during the electrical transcription period (1929) that the name March of Time was first used.

The program in its present form was conceived by Roy Larsen* in 1931, and in the eight years it has been heard since that time no major change has been made in the structural setup of the show. It was almost exactly right from the beginning.

The simplicity and clarity and excitement with which these broadcasts meet their American listeners are in contrast to the weekly preparation of the material that makes them up. To prepare a single program of the March of Time takes 1,000 man-hours of labor, 33 hours for each minute of broadcast time; 500 hours for news research, writing, and rewriting by Editor William D. Geer and his seven assistants; 40 hours of clerical work; 60 hours for music rehearsal; 400 for rehearsal of cast and sound crew.

The program has been flattered since its inception by attempts at imitation. No organization has ever succeeded

* Now president of Time, Inc.

in doing this, because there is no organization in radio today that is equipped to do such meticulous work and at the same time to draw on so many sources for the type of work that it does. All the news-gathering and news-checking facilities that are available to *Time* magazine, to *Life*, and to the March of Time movie are available also to the March of Time broadcast.

The March of Time is a weekly reenactment of memorable scenes from news of the world. Conceived in 1931, the March of Time became almost immediately radio's most popular, most-listened-to show, and when the editors of *Time* decided to take the program off the air after its first season popular demand compelled the Columbia Broadcasting System to keep the show on as a sustaining feature.

It takes an average of 72 people to prepare and produce the March of Time each week. Work for this Friday night feature starts on the Sunday morning preceding, when the editors and writers of the March of Time exercise their intuitive news sense and select preliminary news events to be converted into acts for the next show. Out of some twenty scripts prepared by Tuesday evening, ten or a dozen are selected for tryouts in Wednesday's rehearsal.

After the regular cast and sound crew rehearse a dozen sets during their three-hour rehearsal period on Wednesday, approximately seven acts survive. These are chosen particularly for their news importance but also from the production viewpoint of dramatic balance, diversity of content, and interest. Humorous spots are often included.

The regular March of Time actors are adept at impersonation and can simulate the voices of news figures so well that it is frequently difficult for listeners to believe they are not actually hearing the voices of these news figures. Each actor is particularly adept at about a half dozen voices (Stalin, Mussolini, Hitler, etc.). However, the regular actors are sometimes supplemented by other actors who possess specific talents and who are chosen from an available list of from 500 to 700 names. Here may be found almost any unusual requirement, from Swedes to Abyssinians. The list includes even the voices of gnomes and elves. Calls for the special voices needed each week are sent out on Tuesday night.

On Thursday, Howard Barlow, director of the March of Time musicians, studies the week's scripts, selects in conference with the March of Time editor and Messrs. Fickett and Spier of B.B.D. & O. (the advertising agency entrusted with the production of the March of Time) some music cues to be played during the broadcast. Each of these cues is from four to eight seconds long. Frequently original music especially adapted to certain acts in the broadcast is composed.

Every member of the cast wholeheartedly cooperates in rehearsing every simple phrase dozens of times until perfection is achieved. Thus, the March of Time provides vision through sound, and no explanation is necessary to identify the Japanese soldier, the apprehensive mother, the threatening gangster, etc. Sound effects are rehearsed over and over again for perfection. All creaks, wheezes, and squeaks must be technically accurate. Once when a California doctor revivified a dead dog, the sound crew went down onto the street, stopped a few dogs, listened to their heartbeats, and then duplicated the technically correct sounds.

Aiding in accuracy is a library of thirty-second recordings of over six hundred voices that may possibly be in the news. March of Time actors listen to the inflection and accent of these persons and are able to reproduce a startling duplication of them. If the voice is not in this special library, it may be on the sound track of a March of Time cinema reel, or March of Time actors can hear it in a newsreel theatre.

Official checker of March of Time is Harry Levin, upon whose shoulders falls the ultimate responsibility for complete accuracy for every news and historical fact. When the word "streptococci" (infectious germs) appeared in a medical sketch, Levin was not satisfied with consulting dictionaries. Dictionaries gave the final letter the value of a long "e," but a telephone checkup with physicians and hospitals indicated that in the profession the word was pronounced "strepto-cock-eye." The March of Time used the professional pronunciation.

The March of Time broadcast, already an established institution, has done more than any series in radio to bring before the American public accurate information in memorable and provocative style. It is preeminently the finest news broadcast in the world today. Its dramatic handling of last year's European distress was a vivid experience to all those who heard the series. I have selected the broadcast of September 16, 1938, as the best of them all.

The March of Time*

MUSIC.—*Fanfare.*

VAN.†—The March of Time!

MUSIC.—*Second fanfare.*

VAN.—Life!

VOICE.—The life of the world, its conflicts and achievements, its news and fun, its leaders and its common people.

MUSIC.—*March.*

VAN.—Tonight, hour after hour, by short-wave wireless through the ether and along the cables undersea, the news piles up from the capitals of Europe . . . world-shaking, momentous news that sends Britain's grave Prime Minister flying to Adolf Hitler and President Roosevelt hurrying back to Washington . . . the grim, portentous news that Sudeten Germans are in armed revolt, and behind every dispatch the mounting fear that the field-gray German regiments, mobilized and ready, may march into Czechoslovakia. All this week, day after day, and every hour of each day, the news poured in . . . and tomorrow and all next week news will come from London, from Paris, from Prague, from Berlin. And as the headlines record each flying fact and rumor, United States citizens watch and wait and try to understand.

VOICE OF TIME.—*Life*, the magazine of pictures, has one single and continuing purpose . . . to bring the events of our times and the people of our world before the eyes of its readers with the new impact and understanding that only pictures can give. Readers of *Life* have a keener comprehension of the crisis of this week, for they have seen France's impenetrable Maginot line and the amazing defenses of little Czechoslovakia, where lies Europe's destiny. They have gone with *Life* to look upon the faces of the people of

*Copyright, 1938, by Time, Inc.
† Cornelius VanVoorhies, the Voice of Time.

Europe . . . Poles and Slavs and Czechs and Prussians . . . faces proud and humble and fearless and frightened. They have eyewitnessed the setting of the stage of the great dramatic story that, in the critical weeks and months to come, will be found week after week *in pictures* in the pages of *Life.*

VAN.—Pictures . . . which add a new dimension to our understanding of the life of the world. And now, the March of Time!

VOICE OF TIME.—The second week of September, 1938.

VAN.—The most important week since mid-July of 1914 is drawing to a close. And the peoples, governments, and armies that make the destinies of nations this week again stand where stood those of a generation ago, in a week of crisis whose events led to a great world war. A week of crisis whose full significance was not known until four years later, in armistice and in a treaty of peace.

VAN.—"The allied and associated powers, being equally desirous that the war in which they were successively involved and which originated in the declaration of war by Austria-Hungary on July 28, 1914, should be replaced by a firm, just, and durable peace, have affixed their seals to this treaty, together with those of the German Empire and every component state."

NEW VOICE.—Article 81. Germany recognizes the complete independence of the Czecho-Slovak state, which will include the autonomous territory of the Ruthenians south of the Carpathians and the portion of Silesian territory known as the Sudeten area. German nationals habitually resident in any of these territories will obtain Czecho-Slovak nationality *ipso facto* and lose their German nationality.

MUSIC.—*Up and down.*

HITLER.—The shame of Versailles has only made more imperative the rise of the German people to fulfill their destiny.

VAN.—In a windowless cell of grim Landburg fortress, an emaciated, fanatic-eyed young man is writing a testament in fine German script. It is Adolf Hitler, in September, 1923.

HITLER.—German Austria must return to the mother country. But the final path of German empire lies not through Austria to the South nor France on the west but eastward, to Russia and the wheat fields of the Ukraine.

VAN.—Between Adolf Hitler and the east lies the Republic of Czechoslovakia. (*Music up and down*) The second week of September, 1938, Monday, the twelfth. In Russia, avowed objective of Adolf Hitler's eastward march of empire, in Czechoslovakia, number one obstacle in that line of march; in France, hereditary foe of Germany, pledged to prevent that march; in Great Britain, pledged to fight if France fights; in the United States, awestruck spectator of a theatre in which one spoken word may set off a war . . . the governments and peoples of the world are waiting to hear by radio a message of Adolf Hitler, speaking in his native tongue to people of his own race and mind.

MUSIC.—*Up and down. Big sieg heils out of music.*

HITLER.—Die Befestigungswerte in Westen werden noch vor Beginn des Winters fertig sein. Hinter dieser Front aus Stahl und Beton, steht das deutsche Volk in Waffen! (*Sieg heils*)

VAN.—"The fortifications in the West will be finished before the beginning of winter. Behind this wall of steel and concrete stand the German people . . . under arms."

HITLER.—Ich werde unter Keinen umständen der weiteren unterdrückung der deutschen Volksgenossen in der Tschecho-slovakei in entloser Rube zuzusehen! (*Sieg heils*)

VAN.—"I will tolerate no further oppression of German people in Czechoslovakia."

HITLER.—Sie werden mir auch am freudigsten zustimmen wenn ich vor dem ganzen deutschen Volk feststelle das wir nicht verdienten Deutschen zu sein wenn wir nicht bereit wären eine solche Haltung einzunehmen, und die daraus volgenden Konsequenzen so oder so zu tragen.

VAN.—"I say that we shall not deserve the name of Germans if we were not prepared to take this position, ready to bear whatever consequences may follow." (*Sieg heils up big into singing of "Deutschland über Alles"* . . . *carry singing under*)
In Nuremberg's Congress Hall and in every nation of the world has climaxed one of the most remarkable pieces of

oratory in modern times . . . the September 12 speech of Adolf Hitler. (*Up to finish with orchestra*) Balmoral Castle. The Scottish highlands. (*Piano register*)

It is evening in the summer residence of the British royal family. In the music room, Their Majesties, King George and Queen Elizabeth, and Princess Margaret Rose listen to Crown Princess Elizabeth at the piano. The King's equerry, Sir Arthur Erskine, enters, steps quietly to His Majesty's side. (*All sotto*)

EQUERRY.—I beg pardon, Your Majesty . . .

KING.—What is it, Sir Arthur?

EQUERRY.—I have very grave news, sire, from Mr. Chamberlain . . . regarding Czechoslovakia. Serious disorders have broken out as a result of Mr. Hitler's speech. The Czechs invoked martial law in the Sudeten provinces, and the Germans demand cancelation of the decree within 6 hours.

KING.—Six hours.

QUEEN.—What is it, dear?

KING.—An ultimatum to Czechoslovakia.

EQUERRY.—An ultimatum, yes, sire. Mr. Chamberlain and the defense ministers are making our defense plans on a war basis. (*Pause*)

KING.—Six hours. In that case, I had best return to London immediately.

EQUERRY.—Yes, Your Majesty.

MUSIC.

VAN.—By immemorial custom of the unwritten British Constitution there can be no mobilization, no declaration of war without the signature of Britain's King. (*Music up and down*)

Prague, Tuesday . . . the day of the German ultimatum, at the barracks of the first Czechoslovakian army corps.

C.O.—Attention! (*Sieg heils*) The first army corps is ordered to proceed immediately to the northern border for extraordinary defense duty. Headquarters of the first division will be at Boehmisch-Kermau. The third, fifth, and eighth regiments are assigned to patrol the Sudeten mountains westward. Be ready with full military equipment to march in one hour!

MUSIC.—*Up and down.*

VAN.—The German ultimatum has 4 hours to run. In Paris, capital of Czechoslovakia's ally, pledged to resist German aggression, hour after hour over the Paris radio station . . .

VOICE.—(*Filter*) Citizens of the French Republic! Attention! Municipal authorities have begun the distribution of sand throughout the city. Within a short time, heaps of sand will be found in every street. Citizens are urged to store the sand in the top rooms of their homes for use in sand bags and to fight fires started by bombs and shells in the event that Paris is bombarded. (*Music up and down*) Six hours have passed. The German ultimatum has expired. In Prague's Gragany castle, in his library, Czechoslovakia's baldish little President, Eduard Benes, sits at his desk, a microphone in front of him, a pitcher of water beside him. He looks inquiringly at an announcer.

ANNOUNCER.—Ten seconds, Mr. Benes.

BENES.—All right.

ANNOUNCER.—Ladies and gentlemen . . . the President of the Republic, Eduard Benes.

BENES.—My people, I know you are all waiting to know our answer to the demands of the German Sudeten party. Their ultimatum would have meant for us to abdicate the sovereignty of part of our nation and in effect turn it over to another state. (*Pause*) We have rejected it. I speak, not as one who orders your destinies but as your elected President . . . of Czechs, Slovaks, Germans, and all other nationalities in our democracy and nation of Czechoslovakia. Be calm, be considerate, keep your nerves steady. That is all your country requires of you. Then, God willing, your government can do what it is pledged to do . . . keep peace. not only for this country but for the whole world.

MUSIC.

SOUND.—*Marching feet.*

VAN.—One hour later Czech troops are on the march, for the German ultimatum has been rejected. From Prague to Cheb, from Pilsen to Vimperk, from Mor to Kraliky, Czech troops go to man their frontiers. The troops of Czechoslovakia's ally, France, 6,000,000 strong move up to the vast subterranean bulwark, the Maginot line. All through the night Belgian soldiers march toward Liége and the German border. (*Music up and down*) Wednesday morning, in London's dead-end Downing Street, outside Number Ten, official residence of Britain's Prime Minister, crowds linger, watch ambassadors of the world's powers come and go. American Ambassador, Joseph Kennedy, emerges, is stopped by a British correspondent.

BRITON.—Mr. Kennedy . . . Mr. Kennedy!

SOUND.—*Feet marching off.*

KENNEDY.—Say, what is that . . . a parade going on there?

BRITON.—It's the Scots guards, sir, marching up to their barracks.

KENNEDY.—Oh.

BRITON.—Mr. Kennedy, has the United States declared officially on the side of the allies?

KENNEDY.—Allies?

BRITON.—I mean to say Britain and France.

KENNEDY.—United States relations with Britain are as friendly as ever.
(*Fade in marching and drums*)

BRITON.—But what about President Roosevelt's statement that the United States was with us?

KENNEDY.—The President has explained that more fully to me personally. (*Begin band*) In no sense of the word is the United States taking sides in the present crisis.

BRITON.—Mr. Kennedy . . .

KENNEDY.—Say . . . that's "Tipperary" they're playing, isn't it?

BRITON.—Yes.

KENNEDY.—"Tipperary." I haven't heard that in 20 years.

Music.—*Up and down.*

Van.—In London, troops marching to the music of a song that sent them into battle 20 years ago. In Czechoslovakia, men march to a new song of conquest, as, from Sudeten farms and villages, Nazis, uniformed and in mufti, join bands converging on the towns along the German border, shouting the forbidden words of the "Horst Wessel Lied" as they march into the still-darkened streets. For it is 8 hours since the time limit on the Nazi ultimatum to the Czech government expired. (*Music up and down*) By noon on Wednesday, the quiet villages of the Eber district are a bedlam of wild disorder and violence. At Habersparirk, six gendarmes take refuge in the police station; and a mob of 50 grows to 1,000 outside. (*Wham*) Then, inside the building, the six trapped men hear the threatening sound of a timber forcing the massive door. (*Wham*)

Captain.—You'd better try the phone again, Lieutenant.

Lieutenant.—Yes, sir. (*Click*) Hello . . . hello . . . hello. . . . (*Wham*) It's no use, sir.

Captain.—There's nothing else to do . . . unless the troops arrive . . . (*Wham*)

Bartosch.—I could climb up to that window, sir. Speak to them through the bars.

Captain.—Too late for that. (*Wham*)

Bartosch.—Try it anyway. Here. Give me a hand.

Lieutenant.—Right. (*Grunt*) . . . (*wham*)

Bartosch.—All right. People of Eger . . . stop. . . . This will do you no good. . . . (*Wham*) You are only harming your own cause. . . . You will . . .

Sound.—*Shot . . . glass . . . groan . . . fall.*

Captain.—Bartosch! Are you hurt, Bartosch?

Bartosch.—Through the chest . . . I think so. . . . (*Wham*)

Lieutenant.—Here, tear his shirt. . . . We'll bandage him up.

Bartosch.—No . . . the door . . . watch the door. . . . (*Wham*)

147

CAPTAIN.—Better let him lie where he is. . . . He's out of the way here.

LIEUTENANT.—I'll try to stop the bleeding. (*Wham*)

BARTOSCH.—The door . . . the door (*Wham*). . . .

SOUND.—*Door splinters in . . . crowd.*

CAPTAIN.—Stop. . . . This man is hurt. . . . This . . . (*He is drowned out by great mob*)

MUSIC.

VAN.—War begins as a state of mind, is justified by an "incident." The incident may be the murder of an archduke or the sinking of a battleship; a quarrel with a customs official or the hanging of a political zealot. This week six Czech policemen are trapped and killed by a mob of Sudeten Germans in the town of Eger in Czechoslovakia. Czech police retaliate, fire indiscriminately upon every marching band of Nazis in the Eger district. And by Wednesday afternoon 2,000 Czech government troops are engaged in a civil war against 4,000 armed storm troops of the party of Adolf Hitler. (*Music up and down*)

In Geneva, in the cloakrooms and corridors of the great white League of Nations palace, the delegates gather in little knots, their faces grave and expectant with the foreboding of Hitler's march to the east. Slowly they file into the vaulted Assembly Chambers, still talking in swift, nervous questions; at last take their seats.

CZECH.—Monsieur le Président.

PRESIDENT.—The delegate from Czechoslovakia.

CZECH.—Gentlemen of the Assembly, word has just come from my country that a civil war is in progress. (*Pause*) Gentlemen, in my country, in the center of Praha, there stands a statue of Woodrow Wilson. It was on the faith and optimism of that man, coming into a Europe weary and half mad from 4 years of war, that the Republic of Czechoslovakia was founded. Europe today is not half so weary nor half so mad as it was in the days when these things were inspired. Gentlemen, is there not something left that united peaceful action can accomplish? (*Stir . . . pause*) Gentlemen, I don't want to make an appeal to you. I ask a simple question. (*Pause*) Very well. That is all, Monsieur le Président.

SWEDEN.—Monsieur le Président, there is very little more to be done here at this time. I suggest that the League Assembly now adjourn.

MUSIC.

VAN.—In Rome, Benito Mussolini mobilizes 140,000 men, begins recalling airplanes from Spain. At Invergorden the British fleet weighs anchor, sails out across the North Sea to hold maneuvers opposite German Heligoland. It is late Wednesday afternoon. (*Music up and down*) There has been no word in 12 hours from Berlin and Adolf Hitler; and in Washington, at the United States State Department, news hawks have been waiting since morning for an interview with Cordell Hull, are ushered into the presence of a grave and deadly serious Secretary of State.

HULL.—I'm sorry to have kept you waiting, gentlemen.

SOUND.—*Murmurs and ad libs.*

ONE.—Mr. Secretary, the situation in Europe is so acute, we feel it is proper to ask that you explain the attitude of the government . . . give the public your appraisal of the crisis.

HULL.—One person can appraise the situation as well as another, gentlemen.

THREE.—Is it true that you have discussed the situation with President Roosevelt?

HULL.—Whenever developments require it. I talk with the President every day.

ONE.—Mr. Secretary, will you tell us how many American nationals are in the danger zone?

HULL.—Yes, I can tell you that. There are 12,000 in France, almost 6,000 in Germany, and more than 5,000 in Czechoslovakia. Altogether, about 23,000.

TWO.—Are any arrangements being made to care for them in case of war?

HULL.—Our envoys already have their instructions. They have full discretion to deal with any emergency which would require evacuation of American nationals. In Prague and other posts, there are bombproof shelters, and American consular authorities have arranged facilities for our citizens.

SOUND.—*Door.*

AIDE.—(*Coming up*) Excuse me, Mr. Secretary. The President is calling from Rochester.

HULL.—You must excuse me, please, gentlemen. (*Sound of news hawks exiting*) Good morning. Good-by. (*Phone off hook*) Hello . . . hello, Mr. President. . . .

MUSIC.—*Up and down.*

VAN.—From Cordell Hull to Franklin Roosevelt goes word that three more Sudeten districts have been placed under martial law. Czechoslovakia has called out two more reserve classes to the colors . . . 140,000 men. And a few hours later, on the observation platform of a train, drawn up in the station at Rochester, Minnesota, home of the famed Mayo Clinic, stands Franklin Roosevelt, his hands gripping the railing in front of him:

F.D.R.—My friends . . . here I came as a father and not as President, and you treated me accordingly. I am going away knowing that you still will be pulling for that boy of mine. (*Pause*) I am not going back to my Hudson River home now but to Washington. For, as you know, conditions of affairs abroad are extremely serious. That is why I go back to the national capital, as President.

COUPLE OF VOICES OFFSTAGE.—Good-by, Mr. President . . . Good-by, Mr. Roosevelt . . . good-by. . . . (*Train starts chuffing . . . music sneak*) Good-by . . . good-by. . . .

SOUND.—*Train and music up and down.*

VAN.—It is late Wednesday night when the first official communiqué is flashed from Germany, and the world learns that Adolf Hitler has summoned an emergency meeting of his Council for War. In Nazi party headquarters in Munich, Chief General von Brauchitz, Reichswehr Chief of Staff Keitel, General Reichenau have been conferring with their Führer for 3 hours. An aide enters the council chamber.

AIDE.—A telegram, Führer . . . from London.

HITLER.—From London? Read it.

AIDE.—(*Reading*) In view of the increasingly critical situation, I propose to come over at once to see you with a view to trying to find a peaceful solution. I propose to come across by air and am ready to start tomorrow. Please indicate the earliest time you can see me and suggest a place of meeting. I should be grateful for a very early reply. Signed, Neville Chamberlain. (*Silence*)

AIDE.—(*Pause*) The English ambassador is waiting, Führer.

HITLER.—Tell His Excellency that I am very ready to meet with his Prime Minister. I suggest that he leave tomorrow morning. He will be able to see me at my home in Berchtesgaden in the early afternoon.

MUSIC.

SOUND.—*Plane idling under.*

VAN.—Early next morning, at London's Heston Airdrome, out from his car (*Crowd murmur under*) steps Great Britain's Prime Minister Neville Chamberlain, followed by two aides from the Foreign Office; pushes his way through an anxious, waiting crowd toward an airplane, ready, its motors idling.

SOUND.—*Motors nearer.*

BOBBY.—Stand back, please. . . . Stand back there. . . . This way, Mr. Chamberlain. . . .

COCKNEY.—Good luck, Mr. Chamberlain. . . .

ANOTHER.—God bless you, Mr. Chamberlain, sir. . . .

A THIRD.—Stand by Czechoslovakia!

CHAMBERLAIN.—All ready, Sir Horace? Strang? (*Ad lib yes, sirs*) Hop on in then. . . .

RADIO.—One moment, sir. . . . Could you just say a few words, Mr. Chamberlain . . . to our listeners?

CHAMBERLAIN.—Very well. I am going to see the German Chancellor because the situation seems to me . . . to be one in which discussions between him and me may have useful consequences. My policy has always been to try to ensure peace . . . and the Führer's ready acceptance of my suggestion encourages me to hope that my visit to him will not be without result.

RADIO.—Thank you, sir . . . thank you. . . .

CHAMBERLAIN.—Well, Halifax, I'll keep in touch with you through Neville Henderson. . . .

HALIFAX.—The very best of luck, Neville. . . .

CHAMBERLAIN.—I hope so. I sincerely hope so. Good-by . . . good-by. . . .

SOUND.—*Plane door shuts . . . motor gunning.*

VAN.—It is the first time that a British Prime Minister has left his island to confer with the head of a European state . . . since the World War. (*Plane begins take-off under*) For Neville Chamberlain, statesman and diplomat, son of a family of Britain's foremost statesmen, is off to confer with a one-time Austrian house painter, is off to Berchtesgaden, where Adolf Hitler conferred with little Kurt von Schussnigg, one week before the annexation of Austria.

SOUND.—*Plane off and fading. Music . . . rain under . . .*

VAN.—At five o'clock Thursday afternoon, up the winding mountain road from Berchtesgaden climbs a black limousine, through heavy rains on up to the Wackenfeld, Adolf Hitler's villa. Out steps Neville Chamberlain, his umbrella still tight-rolled, is greeted by a bareheaded Reichsführer, his hand upraised in the Nazi salute. Three hours later, Neville Chamberlain returns to his hotel, to proceed to London. And from the meeting that may determine the future course of European history comes just one official comment . . . from Britain's Prime Minister . . . Neville Chamberlain.

CHAMBERLAIN.—Yesterday afternoon I had a long talk with Herr Hitler. It was a frank talk, but it was a friendly one. Later on, perhaps in a few days, I am going to have another talk with Herr Hitler. This time he has told me that it is his intention to go halfway to meet me . . . in order to spare an old man another such long journey.

VAN.—One statement: noncommittal . . . and cryptic. And whether it means collapse of negotiations, plebiscite, or a decision to march is known this week to only two men.

But well does the world know that Neville Chamberlain has cut short his visit by 2 days; that Viscount Runciman, England's neutral negotiator, has left Czechoslovakia suddenly and unexpectedly; that in the Sudeten mountains 9 Sudeten Germans and 20 Czechs lie dead in civil strife. Historically neutral Switzerland has mined all frontier approaches against invasion, tripled her border guard; Rumania has met in council of war to reiterate her alliance with France and Britain; in Zagreb, Yugoslavia, mobs have stoned the Nazi consulate; Japan has reaffirmed the anti-Comintern pact, announced that she will fight beside Germany. And this afternoon comes news from Prague: that the Czechoslovakian government is moving methodically to crush the entire Sudeten German movement, has ordered the dissolution of the Sudeten party, disbandment of the party's storm troopers, seizure of their property, surrender of all arms and ammunition within 24 hours, and the arrest of their leader, Konrad Henlein, for high treason, on charges which may well mean for him the executioner's ax. Tonight, at nine forty-five Czechoslovakia's Foreign Minister Kemil Krofta announces officially that his government will not accept dismemberment, will not sanction a plebiscite, will resist any efforts to disrupt the Republic of Czechoslovakia with any means at its command. At week's end, in London, silent crowds pause to watch a single woman, on her knees in prayer at the base of the Cenotaph, memorial to Britain's dead in the World War; across the whole island the congregations of the Free Churches bow their heads to ask for peace. And by day and night, in a never-ending stream, the people of London file into Westminister Abbey to kneel and pray; and among them Annie Chamberlain, wife of Great Britain's Prime Minister; as this week from the pulpit speaks white-haired old Cosmo Gordon Lang, Archbishop of Canterbury, primate of all England . . .

LANG.—Almighty God, Father all-merciful, now in this hour of our greatest need look down on us with compassion. Guide Thy servant, our Prime Minister, that we may come out from the shadow of world sickness. Touch our hearts with Thy divine understanding, O Lord, and in Thy infinite mercy protect us in Thy grace, through Jesus Christ, our Lord. . . . Amen.

MUSIC CURTAIN.

VAN.—What will Hitler do? His pledged word of support to the Germans of Czechoslovakia has been given before the world. . . . How will he maintain it? And what of Neville Chamberlain, Britain's solemn, angular Prime Minister who swallowed pride and brushed aside precedent in a dramatic eleventh-hour bid for peace? Will he go down in history as a futile blunderer, or will he emerge as a great and grim figure whose dogged courage and British tenacity triumphed over the mystic-minded man of destiny who would give Germany her place in the sun? If England and France abandon their 20-year stand, what new realities must they face . . . of an insurgent Germany which they seem powerless to turn aside except by arms? Can England and France give up peacefully what Hitler demands? What decision will come to Adolf Hitler in the day or in the night . . . tomorrow . . . no man can tell.

But one thing is certain . . . that the crisis of this week's news is not the *end* but the *beginning* of one of the most tempestuous, news-packed eras any age has known! It will be an era of fast-moving events greater in the vast sweep of their influence than any events in history before them. And it will be an era that will be *seen* as no era has been seen before! For week after eventful week, *Life's* pages will make the 18 million men, women, and children who read *Life* each week *eyewitnesses* of the news of the world and the ways of the world's people. And, having *seen*, their knowledge of the world will be enriched and their understanding deepened. For they have discovered in *Life* a new kind of pictorial journalism, which satisfies that strangely compulsive modern desire to see and to know and to be informed. That is why *Life* is the most potent editorial force in America today. And that is why LIFE has the greatest readership ever brought together by one magazine. Tonight, people throughout the country are reading their copies of this week's new issue of *Life*, thinking about it, talking about it. Your copy is waiting at your nearest newsstand. *Life's* price is 10 cents.

VOICE.—Again next Friday night at this same hour . . . join *Life* on the air with the March of Time! This is the National Broadcasting Company.

BEST TALK

by JAN MASARYK

THIS, the most compelling and the most sincere of statements ever to be transmitted by radio, was delivered at four o'clock on the morning of September 23, 1938, from a small studio on the eighth floor of London's Broadcasting House. For sheer bravery, honesty, and simplicity, it is not likely to be equaled during the experience of those now living. Sanguine, patient, devoid of hysteria and suspicion; resolute in idealism and insistently trusting of the good will of neighboring democracies, Jan Masaryk's talk reached millions of American homes at a moment when the meaning of democracy suddenly held a vast and unexpected significance.

That Masaryk, the Czechoslovakian Minister to England, was not permitted to know what was happening in the surrounding darkness of English diplomacy, is probably the most ironical and affecting sentence in his speech. Yet it comes forth without rancor, ingenuously parenthesized as a necessary phase of a circumstance that is beyond him. But this very ingenuousness that characterizes his every phrase and paragraph does not bespeak the inexpert politician; it reveals unmistakably that rarest of all things in public life—the true social integrity.

His simplification of issues by honest utterance, his natural capacity for intimacy without sentimentalism, his candor and his optimism—these are the qualities that lift his sentences to the pantheon of the great speeches of history.

There are many in America who wept at this innocent, impromptu recital; there were many more, anticipating the sellout that reached the headlines of the newspapers of this nation only nine hours after Masaryk had finished, who were impotently ashamed.

Mr. Masaryk's talk has been likened by many to the great speech delivered at the time of his abdication by the present Duke of Windsor. This comparison is in many ways understandable and legitimate. The difference, of course, lies in the impulses that prompted them. Edward forsook his country for himself, and both his actions and his words were caught up in the ephemerality of romanticism. Masaryk stood for the principle and the selfless cause; what he has said will endure.

Best Talk*

MR. JAN MASARYK.—It is for me quite an unexpected pleasure
to visualize millions of the citizens of the great American
democracy listening to me. At the same time it is an unexpected responsibility, believe me. It has been a very long
day for me. It's four o'clock in the morning in London, and
I have not overslept myself lately.

Today my beloved little country ordered a general mobilization. We have definitely decided to resist aggression, and
I can tell you that this move was not made without the
knowledge of France and Great Britain. Quite the contrary.
In a very few words, the history of the last few weeks and
days has been about as follows. Lord Runciman came to
Prague as a mediator. We welcomed him. The Sudeten
Germans welcomed him and gave him on both sides all the
facilities to learn the real facts of the situation. Before he
was quite able to finish his task, Mr. Chamberlain, in a
definitely honest endeavor to save the peace of the world,
went to Berchtesgaden to discuss the fate of my country
with Herr Hitler. The visit of the French statesmen in
London followed, and my government was suddenly, without in any way having been consulted, faced with a plan
which meant, to say the least, a permanent crippling of my
country.

After terribly hard and tearful deliberation they accepted
this plan in full, *in toto*, as they say in Latin . . . and in full
confidence that this time France and England will not forsake us. And there the matter stands at the minute. Mr.
Chamberlain is again visiting Herr Hitler, and at this
moment he is being handed a memorandum containing
Mr. Hitler's considered and final opinion of the Sudeten-
German question. He will deliver it to us tomorrow. What
the memorandum contains I have no idea. Just as I have
no idea what the Anglo-French plan was till 24 hours after
it had been decided upon. I hope and pray that it will be

* Copyright, 1938, by the Columbia Broadcasting System, Inc.

acceptable to us and that neighborly relations will at last be established worthy of such proud peoples as the Germans on one side and the Czechoslovaks on the other.

My people have gone further in self-restraint, discipline, and international solidarity in these last few days than anyone could have expected, and I am more proud than I ever was to be a citizen of Czechoslovakia. We shall study Mr. Hitler's proposal with good will and that same conciliation which made us swallow many little pills and bitter pills in the last few days. But I solemnly declare that we shall not give in on the fundamental issues.

We believe in democracy, humanitarianism, freedom of religion and speech, and the importance of the individual. I personally insist upon reading the Bible and reading the poems by Heine. Whether Heine was a Jew or not does not interest me in the least. He's the author of *"Lorelei,"* the most beautiful German poem I know.

And now I want to tell you that my country has not been perfect always. We have made mistakes. We are young and inexperienced, but we are proud to be a democracy where a mistake can be acknowledged and where it can be rectified. But please know this . . . and I am speaking in a very serious mood tonight. Our German minority was treated better than any other in Europe, and if it would not have been for the shocking propaganda from across the border, we and our Sudeten Germans, among whom I have hundreds of personal friends, would have settled our differences with dignity and without bloodshed.

My father was buried just a year ago. My united nation is assembled around his simple village grave, firmly resolved to safeguard the principles he laid down for us, and we are convinced that truth, decency, freedom, and love will triumph in the end. We shall defend it to our last breath. I tell you, Americans, our powder is dry. As one who has spent many years in America, who knows and loves it, who earned his first dollar in New York City when he was nineteen years old; as one whose mother was an American, and as a citizen of a small country where St. Stanislaus and Jan Huss are our two native heroes and patrons, I greet you, brother democrats, and may God give us peace. May he replace hatred by love and deliver us from evil.

Good night to you all. There is one more thought I had in my head. I know there are many of my countrymen who are listening in at the moment, people who perhaps fought in the last war to allow Bohemia and Slovakia to be free. Will you majority allow me to speak to this minority in their own tongue and tell them something?

[Mr. Masaryk greeted his fellow compatriots in America in the Czechoslovakian language and said, "Truth must triumph and will triumph. I salute you, brother democrats."]

BEST ROUND TABLE DISCUSSION
(REHEARSED, AD LIBBED)

Crisis in Coal

From THE UNIVERSITY OF CHICAGO ROUND TABLE

eeeeeeeeeeeeeeeeeeeeeeeeeeeeeeeeeeeeeeeeeeeeeeeeee

THIS excellent weekly program has the distinction to be the oldest continuous educational series in the broadcasting industry. It delivers fifty-two shows a year and has done so uninterruptedly for nine years. Its triangular setup and method of operation are unique in educational radio. The sense of spontaneity and variety that it brings into American homes has popularized it, year by year; it has grown from an obscure Sunday afternoon spot heard over a single NBC outlet in Chicago to a nationwide influence heard over seventy-seven stations of the Blue Network.

The pattern of the show is simple. Each week three University of Chicago professors, in informal discussion, talk over the subject selected for the next broadcast. They distribute the items among each other, determine how much territory they shall cover, and generally, in what order the various aspects of the question shall be dealt with. Beyond this they have nothing else in their heads except a great deal of information. The subjects change each week, and so do the professors.

At the actual moment of broadcast, the participants sit down at a three-cornered table (so that they can all face each other) and talk extemporaneously for thirty minutes. To avert the danger of a long speech by any individual, a system of warning lights has been rigged into the table, a green flash meaning that the speaker has been going steadily for one minute and that it is time to give way to someone else. This system keeps the show moving and maintains its conversational flavor.

Every imaginable subject has been discussed by the Round Table, and in each case the university radio department has brought to the programs the university's experts on the matters discussed. "Can America Live Alone and Like It?" will be talked over one week, followed by something as different as "The President's 'Purge'" the next. All the broadcasts are reprinted by the university and, in addition to containing a complete transcript of the program, include suggested readings, an interesting department of listener reaction, future schedules, and short "profiles" of the participants in each show.

"Crisis in Coal," which is reprinted, is in one way not representative of the customary procedure of the Round Table, for in this program there were two remote pickups. During most of its course, however, the show is close to its normal self, and variations are of incidental interest only. "Crisis in Coal" illustrates not only the essential flexibility of the show but something of the enterprise of the organization that puts on the series.

Thursday afternoon, May 18, 1939, the Harlan County coal crisis was being headlined in every major American newspaper. The governor of Kentucky had ordered out troops "to preserve order." The C. I. O. was pledged to resist this "invasion of workers' rights." The Federal government was preparing to intervene "in the interests of the people." Sherman Dryer, the University of Chicago's radio director, sensing the tremendous social implications of the Kentucky coal snarl, canceled the scheduled program for May 21 and by telephone secured both Governor Albert B. Chandler and Mr. Lee Pressman, general Counsel of the C. I. O., for a special program on the Harlan County trouble. The governor "welcomed the opportunity to state his position." Mr. Pressman was "happy to give the C. I. O. position." Their remarks (the governor's from Frankfort, Kentucky, and Mr. Pressman's from Washington) were followed by a general discussion in the Round Table manner, with the usual trio of professors participating. In this program they were Maynard C. Kreuger, Professor of Economics; William H. Spencer, Dean of the School of Business and Professor of Business Law; and Raleigh W. Stone, experienced labor arbitrator and Professor of Industrial Relations. The broadcast scooped

American radio, which overlooked, that week, one of the great stories of 1939. For timely interest and honesty of expression and for the clarification of vexed and complicated issues, it was one of the most successful public discussions of the year. It was heard on the afternoon of May 21, 1939.

Crisis in Coal*

MR. LEE PRESSMAN.—The contract between the United Mine
Workers of America and the bituminous coal operators of the
country expired on April 1, 1939. Negotiations between the
United Mine Workers and the Appalachian coal operators,
who mine approximately 70 per cent of the coal tonnage of
the country, commenced in the early part of March.

The coal miners, prior to the expiration date, offered, on four
different occasions, to continue work under the existing
agreement after April, pending further negotiations on the
demands that were being presented by both sides. On each
such occasion the representatives of the coal operators
refused to accept this proposal. The coal shortage which
therefore followed was entirely due to the arbitrary and
unyielding attitude of the coal operators.

Propaganda in the press during the lockout attempted to
make the issue one of a demand by the United Mine Workers
for a closed shop, an attempted interference with the rights
of management. The real issue, however, in this struggle
was the fight undertaken by Bethlehem Steel Corporation,
Republic Steel Corporation, and utilities in an attempt to
strike a blow at the United Mine Workers of America and
the entire C.I.O. Through their economic power of being
large consumers of coal, they were able to force a deadlock
between the coal operators and United Mine Workers of
America.

The proposal of the United Mine Workers was a request for
a union shop provision in the contract. The actual language
proposed, and which was finally accepted, reads as follows:
"It is agreed that the United Mine Workers of America is
recognized herein as the exclusive bargaining agency representing the employees of the parties of the first part, namely
the operators. It is agreed that as a condition of employment, all employees shall be members of the United Mine

Workers of America, except those exempted classifications of employment as provided in the contract."

It should be carefully noted that this proposal did not involve any demand for a closed shop. There was no request that the coal operators in hiring their employees need do so through union hiring halls, or need request the union to furnish any employees. The proposal merely required that as a condition of employment, the employees shall be members of the United Mine Workers of America. The rights of management as to personnel were not infringed in the slightest respect.

Furthermore, under the proposal of the coal miners, several classifications of employees, representing supervisory persons, foremen, and office workers, were completely exempt from the provisions of the contract.

This provision is not a novel one. It is used extensively in union contracts throughout the country. For years this proposal has been incorporated in collective bargaining agreements in the men's and women's clothing industries, which have probably the most stabilized industrial relations.

The proposal is not unique to the C.I.O. To the contrary it is an extremely frequent provision found in the contracts of A.F. of L. unions. For instance, in pulp and paper, brewery, and building trades industries.

The union shop affords protection to unions against attempts of employers to destroy them, through subtle preference to nonmembers as against members; but of even greater importance, the union shop assures harmonious and peaceful industrial relations.

Under a collective bargaining contract, a union undertakes to administer the terms and assure compliance on the part of the employees. The union shop permits the union to enforce discipline among its members and to compel observance of the terms of the contract. A union, through collective bargaining, obtains benefits for all the employees in a particular plant or mine. It is, therefore, only fair that all the employees receiving such benefits should be obligated to bear their small proportionate share of the expenses necessary in the conduct of a union.

The situation in Harlan County deserves specific mention. All the bituminous coal-producing areas throughout the country, with the exception of bloody Harlan County, have executed the 2-year union shop contract with the United Mine Workers. The legality of this union shop provision is unquestioned. The National Labor Relations Act specifically provides that a collective bargaining agreement between an employer and representatives of employees may provide that it shall be a condition of employment for the employees to be members of the particular union.

The net results of Chandler's efforts in sending the National Guard to Harlan County, instead of attempting to arrive at a peaceful conference, have been that out of 12,000 coal miners in Harlan County, 1,200 armed, tin-hat troops have succeeded, at the points of bayonets, in driving approximately 1,400 men back to work.

General Carter, who is Happy's puppet, and in charge of the National Guard, very succinctly expressed his instructions as to shoot to kill.

The United Mine Workers of America have won a signal and outstanding victory, not only against the coal operators who attempted to cause a national shutdown and lockout but also against the most reactionary and antilabor interests of the country, who very foolishly believed they could stop the onward march of the United Mine Workers and the C.I.O.

MR. ALBERT CHANDLER.—My fellow countrymen: The people of Kentucky and the nation are very gravely concerned over the controversy in the coal industry. The dispute has been between the coal operators on one side and John L. Lewis and the United Mine Workers of America, affiliated with the C.I.O., on the other side.

The whole controversy has been occasioned by the demand of Lewis and the union for a closed shop and for the elimination of the penalty clause which prohibits illegal strikes, both of which are aimed at keeping American Federation of Labor miners from the mines and both provisions having been insisted upon by Lewis and the C.I.O. for the purpose of establishing his union as the sole bargaining agency in the coal field; and for the additional purpose of requiring every miner in America to join his union and pay dues to him in order to work.

In his controversy there has been no dispute between the representatives of the mine union and the operators with respect to wages, working hours, or working conditions. The controversy, therefore, did not raise an issue in which the people of the country were vitally interested, but it did raise a selfish demand on the part of Lewis and his associates.

On May 5, after the disputants had wrangled in New York for more than 35 days, the following letter came to the office of the governor of Kentucky, from the county judge of Harlan County:

"Conditions in Harlan County in connection with the labor situation have gradually grown worse during the past few weeks and have now become serious enough to warrant a request for protection from you. I have discussed this situation with many of our leading business and professional men and it is out combined judgment that the situation is beyond the control of the county officials.

"It is the consensus of opinion that 75 per cent of our people want to work if given protection. Their families are facing starvation and they need to work. The coal operators advise me that they are ready and expect to start operating their mines on Monday or Tuesday of next week, and I feel certain that would mean trouble and bloodshed unless we have soldiers in sufficient numbers to keep order.

"I have delayed making this request for protection until it seemed to me a last resort, and I sincerely believe that the time has come when the request is in order."

(Signed) CAM BALL, Judge of Harlan County

Prior to my inauguration as governor of Kentucky in 1935, the union had never been able to organize in Harlan County, due to the opposition of the mine operators and many of the miners themselves. At my special instance and request, in 1936 the legislature passed a law which abolished the company-paid deputy sheriffs and permitted union organizers, for the first time, to go into Harlan County, peaceably and undertake to organize among the miners.

I am now, and always have been, for collective bargaining and for the right of every worker to join the union of his choice. As a public official of Kentucky continuously for more than 10 years, there are abundant evidences of my friendliness to organized labor to be found in that record of public service. I believe in the right of every Kentuckian and every American to work in order to support his family, under conditions acceptable to him and to his employer.

The position taken by Lewis in this controversy would force every coal miner in America to join his union and pay dues to him, or be refused work. The people of Kentucky are not in sympathy with this demand, and I do not believe that the people of the nation are in sympathy with it. It violates the American principle of freedom and the legal rights guaranteed to workers under the Federal law known as the Wagner Act.

This act gives to every working man the right to join the union of his choice.

As governor of this commonwealth, I have taken the position that any unemployed citizen of Kentucky or any citizen of America who needs and wants to work and has an offer to work at wages and under conditions acceptable to him shall have the right to work, without intimidation, and free from molestation from anyone.

I believe in the right of the union to strike and, during the strike, to picket peaceably. Failure of the C.I.O. leadership to order peaceful picketing has made it absolutely necessary that troops be placed in Harlan County, Kentucky. During the last few weeks, miners have been thrown into the river; miners and public officials have been beaten and bruised; and miners have been baptized in the name of John L. Lewis and the C. I. O.; and many workers have been intimidated by the representatives of the union. This is not peaceful picketing.

During the last few years, the Federal government has spent billions of dollars trying to find jobs for the men and women of America who have been without employment, and to this good hour, the unemployment problem remains unsolved, despite heroic efforts of the government. Many of the men and their families in Harlan County were in need, and many of them wished to return to work.

The right to work is, in my opinion, as important as the right of collective bargaining.

The troops were ordered to Harlan County not to break the strike of the United Mine Workers of America but to protect the right to work of the citizens of this state. There is a great deal of difference between using the police power of the state to enable men to return to work and using the police power of the state to break a strike. I have acted to protect the right to work, not to prohibit the right to organize. The militia is not in Harlan County for the purpose of forcing men to return to work, but the fact that during the last week approximately 3,000 men have returned to work in Harlan

County in the face of determined and violent opposition from the union organization and anything but peaceful picketing indicates that a large number of the miners there wish to return to their jobs in order to provide for their families with the necessities of life.

Government depends upon the consent of the governed, and labor leaders must learn to lead with the consent of their followers. The right to bargain collectively must not become a club with which the organized may subdue the unorganized and prevent them from working.

We announced in 1937 that the sit-down strike of Lewis and the C.I.O. would not be tolerated in Kentucky and thereby established protection for the property of the people of our state. In 1939 we announce that in Kentucky the fundamental right of every citizen to work when he has a job must not be molested by anyone. The troops will remain in Harlan County just so long as it is necessary to protect the lives and property of the people of Kentucky.

I join with my fellow citizens in expressing the earnest hope that there may soon come an amicable settlement of this controversy. The Commonwealth of Kentucky is responsible for the protection of the life, liberty, and property of its citizens; and it is prepared to carry out its obligation to each one of them. We are saying to the whole country that law and order, with the help of God, will continue to prevail in the Commonwealth of Kentucky and, I pray, in the nation.

MR. RALEIGH W. STONE.—I should say that when these two speeches are stripped of the excessive amount of verbiage and the defense language and we get down to fundamentals, they both agree as to what the specific issue was that has given rise to this difficulty down in Harlan County.

MR. WILLIAM H. SPENCER.—That is the controversy over the closed shop. Mr. Pressman himself has drawn a rather interesting distinction between a closed shop as such and a union shop.

MR. MAYNARD C. KRUEGER.—Whether there is a distinction to be made between the closed shop and the union shop may depend upon the National Labor Relations Board in the future. It is quite apparent that the issue today is whether all the miners in Harlan County are going to be members of the United Mine Workers Union or whether they are not; and it is equally apparent that the forces of law and order, so-called, in Kentucky are rather determined that they shall not.

STONE.—It seems to me rather interesting that the C.I.O. is not willing to trust the National Labor Relations Board to protect the right of workers to join or not join a union as they see fit; that here, even though we have had 50 years of experience, is the first time that the United Mine Workers has raised that issue of a union shop or closed shop, whichever you may call it.

SPENCER.—The governor spoke of the selfish interest of the organizers, commenting on the fact that there was no demand for wages or other changes in working conditions. Now, Justice Holmes once said that a closed shop was justified, even though there was no dispute as to wages, as a defensive measure for the final skirmish with respect to the fundamental wages and conditions. I could not agree with the governor that, after all, a fight for this defensive position of the union is a perfectly selfish measure.

KRUEGER.—Don't you think, Spencer, that the demand for the union shop in this case, after 50 years of not asking for it, as Stone has pointed out, is strictly a defensive measure? I think probably the United Mine Workers and the whole C.I.O. realize that they are up against the reaction against the organizing drive of recent years. We have seen it in legislation in Oregon, Wisconsin, and Minnesota and attempted legislation in a number of other places.

We have seen some A. F. of L. unions willing to step in and act as operators' pawns in situations of that sort. I think they have a real problem of defense.

SPENCER.—Well, I agree with you on that, Krueger. It seems to me that the position which the American Federation of Labor has taken has forced the C.I.O. into this as a defensive measure, too.

STONE.—It does not seem to me that the American Federation of Labor, with its Progressive Miners in competition with the United Mine Workers, is particularly important. I agree with Krueger that there is a "grass roots" movement, as I call it, a fundamental change in the attitude on the part of the population as a whole, that in part is a reversion to individualism and is antiunion; but I think that *in addition to that* . . . and I think that is very important . . . there is a fundamental conflict between the interests of the coal operators in the South and the coal operators in the North, and I think that came out pretty well in connection with their negotiations.

SPENCER.—It seems to me that is the fundamental issue. It centers around this demand for a closed shop, and I can see that C.I.O. regards it as an important step in protecting itself in connection with the actual competitive situation between the North and the South.

KRUEGER.—Isn't that why the operators used the Unanimity Rule in their negotiations with the miner unions?

SPENCER.—What do you mean by that Unanimity Rule?

KRUEGER.—An agreement that none of them would sign until all of them did, which meant that the Northern operators would not sign until the Southern operators did. I take it the point at which President Roosevelt had some hand in the negotiations was in persuading them to abandon the Unanimity Rule and proceed to operate the mines of those who were willing to cooperate with the union.

STONE.—Yes. There was probably no question in the North of willingness to sign this agreement. It was an unobjectionable form of the closed shop, and they have had it, for all practical purposes, in the North anyway. The Unanimity Rule was perhaps the only basis on which they could get the South in.

KRUEGER.—But they have not had it in Harlan County. Despite the agreement they have had down there for some months, partly as a result of that famous Federal conspiracy trial not so long ago, the operators in Harlan County appear still to be basically antiunion.

It is still apparently true that there is no distinction to be made between the operators and the courts in Harlan County. The letter that was read was from a judge who is a stockholder in two of the mines that are now attempting to operate under the protection of the governor's troops.

SPENCER.—Well, I would still come back to the fundamental issue as to why this thing has come about and why Harlan

County has been the last to sign up. It does seem to reflect, first, a traditional attitude in the South which is strongly antiunion; and second, a very strong feeling on the part of the South that they have to do something to save themselves industrially.

STONE.—Yes, I should think that would come out in this connection. Why has Governor Chandler taken quite a distinctly opposite position from President Roosevelt in this issue? Roosevelt used every bit of his power to force them to sign up; Chandler is protecting the right to operate under a nonunion agreement.

KRUEGER.—Chandler probably thinks he is taking the position most popular in Kentucky, and Roosevelt probably thinks he is taking the position most popular throughout the country . . . and it is quite likely they may both be right. I think we will probably agree that the problem of Harlan County is not the coal problem in the United States. You would not consider that the basic issue in the coal industry?

SPENCER.—No . . . by no means! I consider the basic issue in the coal industry that it is, in a sense, a very sick industry. It finds itself in competition with all sorts of fuels; the employment is diminishing, and the union naturally is doing all that it can to protect itself against the day when it may be up against very serious embarrassments.

STONE.—And we ought to note, too, that the Southern operators have been complaining for the last 3 or 4 years that they have had exceedingly great difficulty in operating under present union contracts, that the differential in wages which has been narrowed down greatly under the present union agreement puts them at a disadvantage in competition with the North. This is not the first time they have protested.

KRUEGER.—In the maintenance of that relatively small differential the miners' union has had the support of the Northern operators in keeping a little heavier pressure on the Southern operators.

SPENCER.—Another factor undoubtedly is the fact that the government's agricultural policy in the South has driven a lot of agricultural workers into the mining industry, which has further weakened the ranks of organized miners and has also tended, of course, to reduce the wages.

171

STONE.—I think that is a very important matter, from a national standpoint as well as from the standpoint of the South. The coal industry is one of the industries that has some considerable possibility of developing into a wider field of employment in the South, on the condition that it be given wage rates that are fair and reasonable as compared to wage rates in the South and on condition that it be given fair consideration with respect to freight rates. But the industry cannot proceed under present conditions, and we have had that kind of complaint for the last several years.

KRUEGER.—It is true that the South needs a field of employment, but it is also true that the Northern miners need more employment. Now, are you going to get the kind of flexibility that you need in order to permit a Southern mine industry to grow? Are you going to get it without being able to guarantee the Northern miners some kind of equivalence of employment? I am inclined to think that you are either going to have less control in the coal industry than we now have, or you are going to have more control and a different kind of control, perhaps in the nature of socialization, in the long run.

SPENCER.—When you speak of socialization in the coal industry, what, specifically, do you have in mind?

KRUEGER.—I mean some type of centralized control that makes it possible to permit the development of an industry in the South where they do need it and that also makes it possible to protect the interests of the people in the North, who would otherwise be opposed to it.

STONE.—What you really mean is a government board that has the power to decide who can mine coal and who cannot mine coal; where it will be mined, and where it will not be mined; how much will be mined, as well as the price that will be charged for it.

KRUEGER.—It would mean a complete rationalization of the whole coal industry, which I think is probably the only alternative to the open shop conditions which the miners are trying to fight.

SPENCER.—In other words, you think this is a sick industry and in the competitive situation in which it finds itself you either are going to open it up wide again or you are going to nationalize it and let the government ration out coal as it is needed.

STONE.—I, of course, am fundamentally opposed to any program of rationalization and regimentation, and I think it is entirely unnecessary. What we have been doing is fooling around with this industry with all kinds of half measures of control. I think we need just a little bit more freedom and flexibility of prices and wages.

What Caused the Depression?

From THE PEOPLE'S PLATFORM

eeeeeeeeeeeeeeeeeeeeeeeeeeeeeeeeeeeeeeeeeeeeeeeeeeee

THIS BROADCAST series, now in its second year of performance, is unique among network discussion programs. It is not only the only broadcast that is completely unrehearsed and ad libbed but the only one thus far in educational radio in which the participants do not know when they go on the air. This last feature brings to the broadcast great spontaneity of thought and expression.

Subjects for discussion are determined five or six weeks in advance of each show, and suitable representatives are chosen and invited to the executive dining room at Columbia's Madison Avenue studios in New York. It is over the dinner table that these radio conversations actually occur— usually toward the end of the meal. Much of the dinner hour has that same atmosphere of unself-conscious talk and conversational pleasantry that marks the successful dinner party in any social get-together. The guest speakers, usually four in number, have opportunity to get acquainted with each other and with their host, Mr. Lyman Bryson; and Mr. Bryson has opportunity to study the characteristics of attitude, responsiveness, and contributive value of those over whom he presides.

As the moment for the air show nears, Mr. Bryson, by taking the conversational direction momentarily into his own hands, quietly relinquishes his duties as host and symposiarch for those of moderator. The microphone that is to pick up the program is concealed in the floral centerpiece on the table. The announcer who introduces the broadcast to the radio audience is out of sight and hearing of those who are about to speak—or, rather who are already speaking.

174

To steal in upon the after-dinner talk in this way gives the radio audience a pleasurable feeling of eavesdropping. As the program continues, however, as the issues themselves begin to precipitate out of the vessel of general talk, as the speakers take sides, and as their answers and opinions and challenges grow sharper, the initial audience reaction of eavesdropping gives way to one of personal participation, and it is to this quality of sustained give-and-take that the series owes its success and its increasing audience.

None but the readiest and most versatile of platform men can handle such broadcast assignments. His responsibilities are vast and various; he must remember everything significant that has been said and remember who said it; he must rephrase and simplify all points not likely to be immediately clear to the audience; he must keep the discussion from wandering; he must see to it that no one violates the laws of good conversation by making long speeches; he must give each participant equal opportunity to be heard; and he must, through his manipulation of attack and counterattack, give to the broadcast an animus of its own and at the same time control this animus so that it never leaks over into open animosity. In a broadcast with the declared purpose of the People's Platform there is much room for high feeling. There is none for bad feeling.

Like all good broadcasts, this one is a combination of many elements, the merging and resolving of many ideas, the work of many people. Even with all factors working properly, it would still fail if the moderator failed. In the appointment of Lyman Bryson to this spot, Columbia's Department of Education has brought to radio one of the most resourceful and one of the most gracious presiding officers in contemporary broadcasting. He is not new to the industry, and he is widely known to educators. As Professor of Adult Education at Teachers College, Columbia University, as a lecturer to many thousands of audiences for more than twenty years, Mr. Bryson is a prudent selection for handling public discussion on the air and quite probably the perfect choice for proceedings that are entirely impromptu.

For the production and coordination of the series Columbia went far afield to find the right man and finally did so in securing the services of Leon Levine. For three years Mr. Levine had served in a similar capacity for America's Town Meeting, and he is known throughout the industry as the best authority on technique and policy of public discussions on the air. He is assistant to Sterling Fisher in Columbia's Division of Education.

Out of the fifty programs thus far produced the broadcast of July 27, 1938, has been chosen as the most successful and most revealing of this type. For clarity, movement, variety of point of view, timeliness, humanness, and defensibility of argument; for choice of subject, response, and informativeness, "What Caused the Depression?" is noteworthy among radio colloquies of the past 12 months. The four who participated in the broadcast here reprinted were: Spencer Miller, director of the Worker's Education Bureau of America; George E. Sokolsky, author, journalist, and labor consultant for many industries; Timothy O'Rourke, a carpenter; and Miss Evelyn Brenner, an unemployed schoolteacher.

The People's Platform*

MR. LYMAN BRYSON.—But we're not only dealing with machine tenders. We're dealing also with machine makers. A vast number of people now are the machine tenders. But the sort of man who in the old days might have been a carpenter or a copper worker or something of that sort . . . you meet that type of man today in the making of machines and in the making of dies, all of which involve a great deal of manipulative skill, a great deal of hand work, and a great deal of what might be called "technical thinking." But the skilled worker can't exist in large numbers, I suppose.

Certainly the general attitudes of workers have been changed by a number of social trends, by shifts in the kinds of occupations and by differences in training periods. That has complicated the labor problem a good deal. But suppose we take unemployed labor for a little while as a social problem. That is, we have a certain number of people out of work. . . . We're responsible as a nation for the welfare of those people.

Last week when we were talking around this dinner table, we were discussing the question of whether or not we had got into an era of prosperity; whether we were on the up curve in the business cycle, and we had just about got to a point of trying to decide whether or not the government had any real part to play in that business. I'm wondering if in this question of labor we couldn't take a look at the government's responsibility. . . . What about the government's relation to labor? Does the government have at the present time what you consider a proper policy toward labor, Mr. Sokolsky?

MR. GEORGE SOKOLSKY.—No, not at all.

BRYSON.—Why not?

SOKOLSKY.—Because you've got to consider, principally, the question of who is going to control the means of production.

If the means of production and distribution are to be controlled by private enterprise, then the government's program
should be oriented toward cooperating with private enterprise, so that private enterprise can absorb labor, so that
private enterprise can create new commodities; so that
private enterprise can expand and in that way re-employ
those who are unemployed . . . even create new jobs, as
private enterprise has created 18 new industries in this
country since 1900.

BRYSON.—The difficulty is that the government's present policy,
in your opinion, is slowing up that creation of new jobs?

SOKOLSKY.—The present policy of the government is to frighten
industry, to smear industry, to attack industry, to make it
impossible for an industrialist to conduct his plant and to
prevent him from expanding his production. That is the
principal reason for the new depression. There would never
have been a Roosevelt depression after the wonderful
progress of his re-employment last summer had it not been
for the attacks on industry by the Labor Board and by the
speeches of Ickes and Jackson and Wallace and all the
others. It became a political question . . . frightened
industry . . . and industry stopped functioning.

BRYSON.—Mr. O'Rourke, you're a carpenter, aren't you?

MR. TIMOTHY O'ROURKE.—I am, sir.

BRYSON.—How does this look from the standpoint of a man who
is an active union member and who has made his way by
skill all his life? Do you think that the government is
handling the labor problem well?

O'ROURKE.—I think the government is doing wonderfully today.
And but for the way the government has taken over the
labor situation in the country, we'd have had civil war 4 or
5 years ago. We were on the edge of civil war when the first
depression was knocked in the head.

BRYSON.—But, you see, Mr. Sokolsky says that the first movement may have been all right, but after a certain amount of
restoration of business there was a mistaken attitude toward
business that slowed things up again.

O'ROURKE.—No . . . I don't agree to that at all, because the
work was carried on perfectly and was going along fine. The

government certainly did not step in at the start. It stepped in when present industry come to a standstill. That was the trouble in the labor field. But for the government, as I said before, we'd have had a civil war in 1933.

BRYSON.—And you think that it's not because the government interfered but because industry fell down on its job?

O'ROURKE.—That's it exactly . . . and ruined standards today.

BRYSON.—I'd like to know what you think about that, Mr. Miller. You look at this work question from a slightly different point of view.

MR. SPENCER MILLER.—I suppose that the problem we have to consider when we think of the relationship of government to labor is, in the first place, what is the present predicament that labor finds itself in in this country. As I see it, the problem which the labor community experienced and the condition which they now face is the problem of how they're going to provide, or find, some kind of continuity of employment.

BRYSON.—It's not high wages?

MILLER.—Not primarily high wages, although high wages are very important. Continuity of employment is an indispensable necessity for the maintenance of any living standards which we frequently describe as the American standard of life. We have come to a situation in which, under our present system of control and direction, we're not getting either the substance of high wages or the continuity of employment. And the reason for governmental intervention, as I see it, into the whole economic process, was to assure some greater measure of continuity of employment than had existed formerly. The government, in my judgment, has, in their zeal to repair the lack of balance . . . they have on a number of occasions gone farther than was necessary, and, in the perspective of time, I think we are going to say that their extension into the economic situation was excessive. But I think it represents an eagerness on the part of those charged with the responsibility of the administration of government to assure a larger measure of continuity of employment than had been possible over the past years and to make the government, for the first time, a partner in this whole economic enterprise.

BRYSON.—Do you mean a partner in raising the general level of consuming power on the part of the people or a partner in the sense that they were going into business on their own?

MILLER.—They tried at the outset, through the NRA, to raise wages. They attempted a process of . . .

BRYSON.—They succeeded for a while, didn't they?

MILLER.—Yes, they succeeded for a while. It proved to be a notable experiment. It broke down, as everybody now realizes, because of maladministration. It broke down, in my judgment, and I think in the judgment of most competent students, long before the Supreme Court declared it unconstitutional.

BRYSON.—Could it have worked?

MILLER.—I think it could have worked for one year.

BRYSON.—Because it was an emergency measure?

MILLER.—Yes, and it caught the public temper. It brought out the kind of response that people make in a great emergency of war or peace. But, as I said at the time and I've frequently said since then, the genius of that whole concept was that it rallied the American people together and gave them a sense of unity of purpose and action.

BRYSON.—And that's something that only the government can do?

MILLER.—Only the government can do.

BRYSON.—Miss Brenner, do you consider yourself unemployed?

MISS EVELYN BRENNER.—I do.

BRYSON.—You're young. You've got your life ahead of you. What do you think about having the government do something for the unemployed?

BRENNER.—Well, I feel that they should do all that they have done and do a great deal more. I agree with Mr. O'Rourke. I think that the government has stepped in at a time when it was necessary for them to step in. I believe that they will do more to restore the so-called confidence on the part of business by creating the buying power which is necessary for business to go on, because there is no real sense in producing if the people of America cannot buy back what they have produced. And I believe that only through increased government spending, increase of the buying power of a great mass of the American people, can we put back this wealth into more production and so finally give business a chance to go further and to re-employ all of these people who are now unemployed or partially employed.

BRYSON.—Well, if you've got a shortage of about 40 billion dollars in national income and the government spends 5 billion dollars out of that in taxes, which in a way reduces the buying power of the taxpayer, because instead of buying. . . .

SOKOLSKY.—Miss Brenner, you're paying taxes too . . . but we can ignore that phase of it. How are you going to create the other 35 billion dollars that is necessary to bring national income up to the figure that it was in 1929?

BRENNER.—Do I understand you, Mr. Sokolsky, to mean that you're worried about where the taxes are going to come from?

SOKOLSKY.—No, No! National income produced . . . in 1929 was about 90 billion dollars. We're down today to about 50 billion, roughly . . . maybe a little more . . . 51, 52. We need 40 billion dollars more of national income to have the kind of prosperity which we had in 1929 and which, I, personally, regard as insufficient for the United States. How do we get that 90 billion dollars of national income produced when we only have 50 and the government spends 5 billion dollars? You indicated that spending 5 billion dollars was going to do something.

BRYSON.—Perhaps Miss Brenner means . . . that the government ought to spend still more.

SOKOLSKY.—You'd have them spend the whole 40 billion dollars?

BRENNER.—Well, I'd have them spend enough to be able to put back as many people to work as is humanly possible, those who are not being put to work by business.

SOKOLSKY.—That would be 40 billion dollars. . . . Where do we get it?

BRENNER.—Well, they certainly cannot tax the little man, who hasn't very much right now. . . . I would suggest taxing the people who have it.

SOKOLSKY.—Suppose we took away . . . not in taxes . . . suppose we had a capital levy . . . and took away from those who have, let us say, over a million dollars . . . all that they have . . . how would that solve the problem?

BRENNER.—You mean just take a man's money and give it to somebody else?

SOKOLSKY.—No! Use it as the 5 billion is being used . . . to subsidize an election, or something.

BRENNER.—All wealth isn't money that we can count in our pockets. And I certainly believe there is still a great deal to be done in the United States which we could consider as wealth for the country. There are a great many roads to be built and a great many houses to be built and many bridges and schools and other things. We'll have to get the businessmen of this country who have sufficient money and who have been holding back on us to put up the money. . . . That's all there is to it.

BRYSON.—The difficulty between you may be something like this: You believe, Mr. Sokolsky, that if the businessman spent his money to expand his business, to increase his productive power, he would be paying it to the very same people that the government is now paying it to. . . .

SOKOLSKY.—Right!

BRYSON.—And he would be paying it out in production business, and you think that would increase our total income.

SOKOLSKY.—Right! And that might bring our total income up to 100 billion dollars.

BRYSON.—You see, it's Miss Brenner's opinion, and it's Mr. O'Rourke's opinion . . . Mr. Miller isn't committing himself on this yet . . . that the businessmen had a chance to do that but failed. What did you mean by that Mr. O'Rourke? Let's go back.

O'ROURKE.—We'll go back. . . . You spoke about 1929. You claim that we had boom days in 1929. Where did the boom come from?

BRYSON.—That's a fair question. . . . Where did the boom come from?

BRENNER.—From the purchasing power of the American people.

O'ROURKE.—Well, who is the purchasing power? Isn't it the working people?

SOKOLSKY.—Farmers, laborers, wage earners, and teachers and middle class people. The worker isn't the only purchasing power in the United States.

O'ROURKE.—He has to have work to get money to purchase, I believe.

SOKOLSKY.—He was one element in the total population, yes, and he had to have money.

O'ROURKE.—And he was in the majority.

SOKOLSKY.—No, he wasn't. Never in American history. You haven't got your statistics right.

O'ROURKE.—The unemployed in the few years after the depression were the majority, weren't they?

SOKOLSKY.—No, sir. Never in the history of the United States were the unemployed the majority. We had 40 million wage earners in the depth of the depression in 1931, and we had 12 million unemployed out of 130 million people. Twelve million unemployed was never the majority of 130 million people.

O'ROURKE.—How many capitalists were in that total?

SOKOLSKY.—I don't know what you call a capitalist.

O'ROURKE.—The man that employs labor . . . at low wages.

SOKOLSKY.—How about the man who employs them at high wages? Is he a capitalist?

O'ROURKE.—The capitalist is the man that makes the money.

SOKOLSKY.—Isn't everybody more or less a capitalist in the United States? Don't you own capital? Do you own an automobile?

O'ROURKE.—No.

SOKOLSKY.—Do you own an electrical refrigerator?

O'ROURKE.—I'm thankful I do.

SOKOLSKY.—Then you're a capitalist!

O'ROURKE.—Oh, but it belongs to the landlord.

BRYSON.—I don't believe we'll get anywhere discussing what a capitalist is. Nobody will admit that he is one.

SOKOLSKY.—I do. I'm not only a capitalist, I'm an advocate of capitalism. I fight for it.

O'ROURKE.—I should think you ought to . . . a man that holds down 10 jobs . . . I wouldn't be here at all if I had *two* jobs.

BRYSON.—The point of our discussion is . . .

O'ROURKE.—The question is, what happened from 1929 to 1932?

BRYSON.—Well, what did happen? Were you going to say something on that, Mr. Miller?

MILLER.—I was merely going to make this observation. It seems to me that the point of our discussion amounts substantially to this: that you can't distribute wealth unless you create it; that functionally and essentially the job of government is not to create wealth as private industry does. But the government does distribute wealth.

BRYSON.—But somebody else has to make it?

MILLER.—Yes. The government has an opportunity to be an instrumentality in the modern scene for equalizing the access of people to the sources of wealth of the country. Now, the thing which people are asking themselves and this is a proper question that everybody ought to be asking . . . if we're going to build up an economy of abundance in this country, are we going to do the thing under the direction of government or are we going to do it under the direction of private enterprise?

BRYSON.—Wait a minute, Mr. Miller. When you say, "Are we going to do it under the direction of government?" do you mean, are we going to put the production of wealth under the control of the government directly? Is that what you mean?

MILLER.—Yes, that's the sum and substance of it. But the American way, I think, is to assume that it is the job of industry not only to produce wealth but to produce jobs.

And increasingly as we insist that it is the job of industry to produce employment we insist also that it is the part of the task of government to assist industry in providing employment for people who are in need. Then we have related those agencies in a more healthy and organic way than they are at the present time.

BRYSON.—That is a point we could probably all agree on. I don't know about you, Miss Brenner. Do you agree?

BRENNER.—Well, I would say . . . you see, I feel that industry has fallen down. I believe that industry has had its chance to provide jobs. And I believe until the time comes when industry can be forced . . . and I believe it will be necessary to force industry to do this . . . I believe it will be the job of the United States government, which not only represents industry but represents the working man and the middle class and the doctor and the lawyer and the school-teacher, too, to provide means of existence at the so-called American standard of living.

SOKOLSKY.—That's something else again.

BRYSON.—When you say that the business of government is to provide a living at a reasonable American standard, do you mean that this should be done because it is a social duty of the government to the people, or do you mean that such action in itself would be the means by which government would assist business to create jobs?

BRENNER.—I think it's both. I think that the government has a social responsibility.

BRYSON.—We are questioning that. But it's a question of whether or not . . . well, now, let's, for instance, take the WPA. The WPA is a work project, isn't it? "W" means "work." Do you think, Miss Brenner, that the WPA serves its purpose by providing people who otherwise would have no means of living at all with at least a minimum? Or is it this thing that Mr. Miller is talking about . . . the instrument by which the government is going to assist business to get back to normal production growth?

BRENNER.—I think it's both.

BRYSON.—Both?

BRENNER.—I do.

BRYSON.—How does it help business?

BRENNER.—By creating a purchasing power without which . . .

BRYSON.—Do you want to use the word "create"? It doesn't create, does it?

BRENNER.—No, it just puts it in the right hand.

BRYSON.—It puts it there. The theory would be that it stimulates purchasing power.

SOKOLSKY.—But couldn't we just for a moment go back to what Mr. Miller said? I think it's very important.

BRYSON.—What was that, Mr. Sokolsky?

SOKOLSKY.—We've got a conflict between two essential theories of government and economics. Shall production and distribution of goods and services be controlled, managed, owned by government? Or shall production of goods and services be owned by private enterprise but regulated by government?

BRYSON.—Now, do you think, Mr. Sokol . . .

SOKOLSKY.—I would suggest . . . no, no, go ahead. . . .

BRYSON.—I just wanted to interrupt you with this question. Do you think the WPA is intervention in business by the government?

SOKOLSKY.—It's a confusing factor.

BRYSON.—How?

SOKOLSKY.—From the standpoint of industry. It creates standards and also peaks of employment, and it creates vested interests in continued unemployment which make it very difficult for big industry to adjust to conditions.

BRYSON.—Suppose we consider the government's action in various types of legislation, like the National Labor Relations Board and the Wages and Hours Bill, and so on. Are they an attempt on the part of the government to control business?

SOKOLSKY.—Oh, yes.

BRYSON.—What do you think about that, Mr. O'Rourke?

O'ROURKE.—I don't agree with Mr. Sokolsky on that at all.

BRYSON.—Well, let's define control and regulation.

SOKOLSKY.—All right, I'll say what I mean by control and let Mr. O'Rourke say what he means by control. Let me define regulation first. Regulation means that the government passes laws, of any kind: laws against murder, laws against theft, laws against anything; but they pass laws, and if you disobey the law and you're guilty, you're punished. That's regulation and was the system in which we functioned here for a long time. Control is altogether different. Control . . . the government sets up standards in advance and determines in advance what cannot be done and prevents anyone from taking free action in any direction at his own risk. When you have control, you naturally tend in the direction of the type of Fascism which exists in Germany and Italy. When there is regulation you don't go in that direction. The industrialists' objection to control is that it so binds him that he cannot use his own initiative at all.

BRYSON.—Control is not simply a question of more regulation, then? They're actually different?

SOKOLSKY.—They're different methods.

BRYSON.—What do you think about that, Mr. O'Rourke? Is the government trying to control industry?

O'ROURKE.—As far as I see it, private industry, as Miss Brenner has said, has had its chance before the WPA was ever established or the NRA was ever introduced. They had the chance to go out and do this work for the government and distribute the work. They fell down on the job. Industry was at a standstill for 3 years. Everybody knows that. The government had so many men and women on their relief rolls they had to do something. Then the NRA, the WPA, and the PWA followed up. That's why men are working today . . . not through private industry.

SOKOLSKY.—Then why are there 12 million unemployed?

O'ROURKE.—If private industry wanted to help this work, they have all the opportunities in their power to go to the government and figure the government work and do it the same as the government is doing it just now.

SOKOLSKY.—Here's the point: First of all, the amount of government work in the total of our national industry is trivial. Secondly, we still have 12 million unemployed . . . after 9 years. Would you say 12 million, Mr. Miller?

MILLER.—I don't think so many.

SOKOLSKY.—Would 11 be a conservative number?

MILLER.—The American Federation of Labor indicates about 11 million.

SOKOLSKY.—All right, 11 million. We had only that number in the worst period of the depression. . . .

MILLER.—A little more at that time.

SOKOLSKY.—And we've spent how many billion dollars since 1933?

MILLER.—Twenty billion dollars.

SOKOLSKY.—Twenty billion dollars! And we come out at the end of 6 years exactly where we were, except that we're 20 billion dollars poorer. That comes out of your pocket, Miss Brenner, and mine.

MILLER.—We're not exactly where we were, Mr. Sokolsky. . . .

O'ROURKE.—What would you have done with all the men that would be out of work that were employed on that 20 billions of dollars? What would they be doing during that period?

BRENNER.—Don't you think that something to restore business would be a better occupation for the industrialists than just trying to discredit the attempts of the President?

SOKOLSKY.—Any businessman is in business to make money, and if he can make money he'll make it. If Roosevelt could make money for industry, he'd be the most popular man in the country with industry, and they'd contribute to his campaign fund. As it is, they buy insurance policies.

BRENNER.—Well, I think Roosevelt has contributed a great deal . . . (*Discussion fades off the air*)

ANNOUNCER.—(*Closing announcement*)

How Can Government and Business Work Together?

From AMERICA'S TOWN MEETING OF THE AIR

IT WAS on May 30, 1935, that the Town Crier's voice and bell first resounded from the loud-speakers of the nation, announcing an uncensored, spontaneous discussion, based on the New England town meeting idea. Thus Town Hall, New York, which had been carrying forward a program of public enlightenment since its founding in 1894 as the League for Political Education, had lengthened its shadow till it stretched to the Pacific Coast. All the more remarkable was this growth when it is realized that this institution grew out of the efforts of six women who wished to prove their right to the ballot by improving their political equipment.

The man who conceived the idea for America's Town Meeting of the Air and who subsequently piloted the new program to its remarkable success is George V. Denny, Jr., moderator of the program and president of Town Hall, New York. Shocked by examples of political intolerance on every side, Denny, at that time associate director of the League for Political Education, sensed the possibilities of a radio program that would make it essential for a man to listen to all sides in order to hear his own. Thus Town Hall could do nationally, over the air, what it had been doing locally in New York for over forty years.

Town Hall's Radio Forum Division, directed by Marian S. Carter, plans and schedules individual programs, obtains the speakers, arranges preliminary open forums, coordinates Town Hall's efforts with those of the Educational Department of the National Broadcasting Company.

The program has developed a technique that, under most conditions, challenges and sustains the interest of the listener throughout its duration and, most important of all, leaves him in a state of mind that urges him to do something about what he has just heard.

The program is based on three principles; conflict, suspense, and fair play. Conflict is achieved by placing two basic affirmative contentions in direct opposition to each other. This deliberate avoidance of the old-fashioned debate technique (affirmative and negative) makes possible the most constructive sort of presentation for both sides, and it is precisely here that the great intellectual value of the broadcast lies. Because the emphasis is a constructive one (two opposed affirmatives) the listener is himself encouraged to think constructively about the problem at issue rather than to dismiss those views inhospitable to his prejudices or to applaud those that are naturally congenial to him. It is not the purpose of America's Town Meeting to influence public opinion in one direction or another but to stimulate the nation to think for itself.

The second principle, although of less intellectual respectability than the conflict factor just noted, is a dramatic indispensability to all programs of this type. It is the item of suspense. Anything at all is likely to happen, and at one time or another almost everything has.

The audiences are keyed up and partisan, and because they know they are to have the privilege of questioning the guest speakers at the conclusion of their formal statements, they have a feeling of direct personal participation in the program. Often they don't like what they hear, and their tussles with the speakers frequently burst into the microphones in condemnatory challenge and spontaneous rebuttal. The Town Hall series has always had the cycloramic advantage of a lively audience, and the scattered but recurrent percentage of irresponsibles, drunks, and crackpots. Most of the questions are, of course, sincerely and seriously put, and they are answered in kind, to the applause or hisses of the visible house. The sober extemporaneous questions have a definite dramatic contribution of their own, but the chance for the unexpected and the sometimes sensational sits over the atmosphere of these programs like a detonator on a stick of dynamite. It is this quality of suspense that turns a good broadcast into a good show.

The final ingredient is fair play. This is perhaps the most necessary of all, although not the most conspicuous. Everything possible is done to ensure a hearing for all constructive points of view on public questions. The very name, Town Hall, is becoming increasingly associated with the democratic tradition.

This excellent series has been renewed by contract for another three years. Its most effective follow-up service is the publication of printed copies of the season's twenty-six broadcasts. In the 1938–39 period the Columbia University Press sold a quarter of a million of these to listeners eager to have a permanent record of what had been said. A thousand listening groups throughout the country use the Town Meeting program as a basis for their own discussions following the broadcasts. An average of 4,000 letters come in after every show.

Almost every important public name in America today has been identified with one or another of the Town Hall broadcasts. The program selected for this volume of *Best Broadcasts* occurred on January 6, 1938, and still stands as one of the most effective public discussions ever broadcast in this country. For timeliness, for clarity of thought and expression, for audience appeal, it has had few equals in radio's long service to the advancement of an informed public opinion in America. "How Can Government and Business Work Together?" was the evening's question. The speakers were Robert Jackson, Assistant Attorney General of the United States, and Wendell L. Willkie, president of the Commonwealth and Southern Corporation.

America's Town Meeting
of the Air*

ϱ

MR. HOWARD CLANEY, ANNOUNCER.—As we bring you our first Town Meeting of the new year, it is my privilege to make an important announcement about the institution under whose auspices these programs are presented in cooperation with the National Broadcasting Company. Until yesterday the name of that institution was the League for Political Education, a nonpartisan, nonsectarian educational organization founded in 1894, which built and owns New York's Town Hall on West 43rd Street, where these meetings are held each week. Today the name of that institution is The Town Hall, Incorporated, and it ranks as one of the foremost institutions in the field of adult education. The title of the chief executive, who is our presiding officer, has been changed from that of director to president. And now I take pleasure in presenting the president of The Town Hall, Incorporated, and our moderator, Mr. George V. Denny, Jr.

CHAIRMAN GEORGE V. DENNY.—Good evening, neighbors! I would like to try to answer briefly a question that has been asked many times during the fall as to how this program is financed or, in the words of one of our correspondents, "How such a program came to happen."

About 3 years ago, The Town Hall, Incorporated, formerly the League for Political Education, presented the National Broadcasting Company with the plan for this program and explained at the same time that we had no funds with which to undertake it. Very courageously, I think, Mr. John Royal, the vice-president of NBC in charge of program, agreed to try an experimental series of six programs and

---

* Reprinted by special permission of The Town Hall, Inc., and copyright, 1939. The reprinted transcript is from the Town Hall bulletin, "Town Meeting," Vol. 3, No. 10, published by Columbia University Press, 2960 Broadway, New York.

pay all expenses. Your enthusiastic reception and continuing response to our efforts have encouraged the National Broadcasting Company to continue giving us this very excellent hour every Thursday evening. While cooperating with us fully in arranging these programs, there has never been the slightest attempt on the part of NBC at anything savoring of censorship. Due to the fair play and good sportsmanship on the part of both speakers and audience, we have continued to give you constructively useful programs. Only responsible qualified speakers are asked to participate in these discussions: and about half of the audience is composed of members of The Town Hall, Incorporated; the others have been given tickets upon written request.

Tonight we bring you a program that is a typical example of the kind of thing America's Town Meeting of the Air was founded to present. This is not a debate. It is not our purpose to widen cleavages but rather to find common ground upon which all classes and all groups of American citizens may work toward our general welfare. How can government and business work together? That is our subject. I know of none more interesting or important for this nation. We have been extremely fortunate in securing as our speakers the Hon. Robert H. Jackson, Assistant Attorney General of the United States, and Mr. Wendell L. Willkie, president of the Commonwealth and Southern Corporation. At the close of their addresses we will have the usual question period from the audience. It is now my very great pleasure to introduce our first speaker, Mr. Robert H. Jackson, Assistant Attorney General of the United States.

MR. ROBERT H. JACKSON.—Probably no two men who personally respect each other enough to appear in public together could look at the relations of government to business through more differently colored glasses than Mr. Willkie and myself. I have admired his consistent willingness to stand up man-fashion and submit his views to the test of dispassionate but frank discussion. This is the only process by which a democratic people can reach decisions on conflicting policies. I have recently paid my respects to that small but loud section of business which has been "ganging up" on democracy. So tonight I can address myself to that larger number who submit their case to the sound judgment of democracy.

193

Business means one thing to Mr. Willkie and another to me. In professional life I was a lawyer chiefly for what we would call small business. My stake in that is far more permanent and important to me than any stake in politics. And in government my particular job is to try to use the archaic antitrust laws to preserve this same kind of small and independent business. Mr. Willkie, on the other hand, has become not only one of the outstanding lawyers for big business but his mastery of finance and administration has carried him to the presidency of one of the largest public utility holding corporations in the nation.

Small business, of course, has its problems with government, one of the chief of which is the correction of inequities in the tax structure. But it is chiefly big business that is at war on many fronts with government. The most constructive thing we can do tonight is to analyze the reasons why they do not get along.

First of all, there is one thing which the people expect business as a whole somehow to do. That is to furnish steady jobs for all who want to work and to furnish enough goods to make up that standard of living which we have come to regard as American. The public is convinced that a proper economic arrangement, in a nation of such unlimited resources, can give that, and so am I. First we look to business for it. But if industry will not provide it, the people are determined to provide it for themselves through their government. This nation has repudiated for all time what Senator Wagner has so well called "the outmoded dogma that the helpless must help themselves." A man off the pay roll is a man on the tax roll. And whether or not business likes this as a philosophy, it must face it as a fact.

There are those who answer that private enterprise can take care of itself . . . that all government needs do is "let business alone." Let's see about that. It is important, if true . . . and it isn't true.

This circle of American private enterprise has never been continuously self-sustaining. It has always operated under concealed subsidies. Until the end of the last century we operated a WPA by which the unemployed could get a quarter section of public land just for occupying it. Then came the second WPA . . . government borrowing and spending for the World War. After the war came the third WPA. We went into a foreign boondoggling program.

American investors furnished funds . . . which they lost
. . . which ran a WPA, building schools and highways and
housing in Europe and South America.

We no longer have these costly but concealed subsidies
to take up the slack in employment. Private enterprise in
America today is in a situation where chiefly its own workers
are its customers, and its customers are its own workers.
Unless it can keep the circle of goods and wages moving
then the government directly and brazenly must fill the
gap in employment on one hand and the need for goods on
the other. We are right out in the open with sheer naked
taxes on private enterprise for cash relief. That system can
grow to Heaven knows what!

Government last year tried to cooperate with the business
demand to get out of government spending, and the problem
has come back with increased intensity. What, then, can
we do?

There is, to my mind, an essential first step. That is for
big business deliberately and speedily to go to a policy of
high volume production, low price, and the highest wage
scale possible. As one industry has put the philosophy, we
must have more goods for more people at less cost. Steel
prices cannot be geared to produce profits at 45 per cent
of capacity. Building materials must be priced so that building may go on from year to year, as needed. Building industries cannot prosper if we can afford to build only in the
years when we can afford to be extravagant.

In business that is really competitive, prices adjust themselves. But today a few companies in each industry have
grown so powerful that they can, by various devices not
reached by present laws, hold prices up for a long time even
if they lose customers. They have a short-sighted philosophy
that it is better policy in the long run to sell less goods at
high prices than more goods at lower prices. Steel has
declined in production from near 90 per cent of capacity
to near 30 per cent without dropping the price a cent. It is
interesting to know that even the government cannot get
really competitive bids for steel. For example, bids for
reinforcement bars for Fort Peck dam were filed by 10 companies, but each bid was exactly $253,633.80 . . . identical
to a penny. That could not happen in a truly competitive
industry. Indeed, there are reputable economists who

believe it would not happen even in a wisely managed monopoly.

Steel is not alone in this policy. Important basic industries, notably those supplying building materials, have followed the same policy and have simply priced us out of a housing program.

The other day when General Motors laid off 30,000 men Mr. Knudsen, their president, stated as one of the reasons, "I think the price level rose too fast in the spring of 1937, and we just could not get adjusted to it."

This dramatizes the fact that there is a silent economic conflict in this country between two kinds of industry. On the one hand we have high price, low volume industries, largely in the monopoly or semimonopoly class. On the other hand we have competitive industry, large and small. Competitive industry is much dependent on noncompetitive industry for its raw materials. The automobile industry as a whole has been competitive and has followed a high volume, low price policy. The unprecedented growth of this industry has been due to the fact that it did not shut down its plant and wait for the people to get rich enough to buy cars. It tried to make cars that people could buy without waiting to become rich.

I hope to see antimonopoly laws enacted that will be adequate to throw the power of organized government back of those businesses which are pursuing a policy of serving the public with an abundance of goods at prices it can afford to pay.

This brings us to another problem that faces both business and government. Mr. Knudsen gave another and very illuminating reason for laying off those 30,000 men. One reason was, he said, that new cars could not be sold, and the reason for that was that used cars could not be sold. In other words, one reason why those men are out of work tonight is that there is not enough buying power in the particular kind of people who certainly would buy used cars if they could.

But it has been the underlying policy of this New Deal administration to raise the incomes of just this sort of people. The administration has tried to keep the used car market open. On June 2, 1937, I opened the Congressional hearings on behalf of the President's proposal for a minimum wage bill to put a floor under depressed wages and to keep up purchasing power. The Wagner Labor Relations Act, to give labor the right to collectively bargain so that it could intelligently and effectively protect its own purchasing power, was an administration measure. Farm bills and relief measures have been advanced with the very purpose of helping purchasing power . . . purchasing power of this very low income group who are the people who are willing to take on the used car.

I do not need to point out the opposition; it announces itself. Big business opposition, in my opinion, has been as short-sighted as suicide. A low wage policy is inconsistent with the standard of living which American business is organized to serve. Unless it is willing to pay wages which will sustain a high standard of American living, it cannot have a market for the commodities which only a high standard of living will call for.

From all these important things the people want business to do, I now turn to an all-important thing they want business to do.

They do not want all of the business of the country to be swallowed up by a few corporations. So long as the American spirit lives and democracy survives, so that its spirit can be expressed in law, the American Congress will be trying to break down the concentration of power just as fast as the imperialists of business pile it up. We are a proud people raised on the doctrines of equality found in the Declaration of Independence. We do not like to be bossed too much, not even by a boss whom we know we can change through the ballot box. We do not like to have any one man or corporation own the town.

Because we are a democratic people we are a friendly and sociable people. We know the corner grocer, the automobile dealer, the fellow who runs the factory, and the men who run the bank. We know that they are harassed by the pressures of bigger competitors and by the prices of big industries that control their supplies. We do not care if, and we do not believe it is true that, the big concerns that swallow up these local businessmen do any better job, on the whole, for our community.

This fear of concentration represented by an anti-big-business feeling is one of the strongest instincts in American politics. Through the centuries people have been afraid of anyone's getting control of too much land, the basic resource of an agricultural civilization. The same instinct bids us now to keep power companies from getting too much of the nation's electric energy, because this is a basic resource of the coming industrial civilization.

This is the point where Mr. Willkie has his difficulties with the government. Mr. Willkie is a good operator . . . especially with the TVA alongside of him to strengthen his resolve to be good. But Mr. Willkie represents control of utility systems in six states through one great holding company. It is the democratic instinct of our people that arises in the holding company law. People would feel more comfortable if Mr. Willkie could control only two or three states. That simple illustration is typical of many of the contests between concentrated controls of business and popular government.

We have no present substitute for a system of private enterprise motivated by private profit, whatever its defects. To my practical mind, our job is to make the system that is here work. It will take all the strength and intelligence of both business and government to make it work under existing foreign and domestic stresses.

But the businessman asks, "Are there not risks in departing from old policies?" Yes, risk is the condition of winning, and consider the risks you take in not changing. Count the cost of not doing it against the cost of doing it. Business needs protection from stagnation far more than from adventure. Remember, the tax collector has to be most busy when industry is idle, in order to complete the circle with tax funds. We must reform to conserve.

Mr. Willkie was one of the pioneers . . . stimulated no doubt by a little competition from TVA . . . in the adoption of a low price, high volume basis for his industry. He ventured and it paid.

Business should get over thinking about men in public life as being different from themselves. There are dumb plays in government, matched by some in business. There is waste and incompetence in government, but get any banker's opinion, privately expressed, of some of his debtor's operations. I have seen politics interfere with administrative efficiency in government. I have also seen personal and family and banker politics do some pretty weird things in business. I have charged off enough small investments so that I am not sure big businessmen are any more infallible than politicians. In fact, I don't know which brand of wisdom I distrust the most, that of the theorists who have studied a business but never run one or that of the executives who have run a business but never studied it.

The greatest difference between the man I meet in government and the man I meet in business is this: The man who is in government is brought in contact with the problems of all kinds and conditions of men. Everybody's business is his business. He looks at society, if he does his duty, as a whole mechanism rather than specializing his interest in a single business. The private businessman, on the other hand, up to now has been intensely preoccupied with a very narrow sector of the world. He has seldom looked about to see the effect which his acts may be having upon the lives of other people. It is this fundamental difference in viewpoint that occasions much of the conflict between business and government.

The difficulty in getting along with business is not so much that it has a bad philosophy of the functions of government as that it has no philosophy as to the broader functions of itself. It tends to make great strife over temporary irritations, and it passes unnoticed fundamental menaces to its long-range interest.

Our need now is to settle upon a common objective for business and government. My little contribution is to suggest this program of high volume, low price industrial economy, which will sustain a high wage scale, which in turn will support a high standard of living, which will demand and pay for the high volume production, at prices determined by its wages. The economic organization must find ways in its bargaining, its ownership and its management to provide for the play of our democratic instincts . . . the most fundamental force in American life.

Regardless of any consequences, I am ready to go down the line to cooperate with anyone to foster this kind of American life, and I am just as ready to go down the line against anyone who tries to destroy this kind of American life. (*Applause*)

DENNY.—Thank you, Mr. Jackson. Now, we are ready to hear a different point of view. Mr. Willkie, president of the Commonwealth and Southern Corporation, has asked me to state that he cannot and does not attempt to speak for all American industry. His statements and opinions are entirely his own, as I presume are Mr. Jackson's. I take great pleasure in presenting Mr. Wendell L. Willkie.

MR. WENDELL L. WILLKIE.—I wonder if it seems strange to any of you tonight that we should be discussing the question of whether or not the government should cooperate with American business. I have an idea that if, from the town meetings of the past, our forefathers should arise to attend this meeting, they would be a little puzzled by such a topic. They might ask, with some surprise, if it was not the function of American government to encourage the development of private enterprise. They would, of course, first be astonished that such a town meeting as this was possible at all . . . that several million people, from all over the land, should be gathered together by means of the mysterious network of the air. They would want to be told about this big business of radio manufacture which in 15 years by large-scale production has cut the price of its product by three-fourths and sold it to nearly 25,000,000 families. And after they had learned about these things, they would, I think, be even more puzzled as to why, over the facilities made possible by American business genius, we should be discussing whether or not American business, big or little, should be encouraged to proceed.

For several years now we have been listening to a bedtime story telling us that the men who hold office in Washington, are, by their very positions, endowed with a special virtue, that they are men of far vision and of exceptional ability and capacity. Businessmen, on the other hand, particularly so-called big businessmen, are pictured as the ruthless dictators of sprawling industrial empires with no real ability except the talent for collecting money for themselves.

Now, most of you who are listening to this broadcast tonight will remember Joe or Tim or Dick or someone else who left your town and went to the city and made a name for himself in business. Most business leaders today were just such small town boys. You will remember also other Toms and Dicks and Joes who went into local politics and then into Federal politics, perhaps into one of the many new administrative bureaus in Washington today. On the basis of your own experience, which of these, the businessman or the man in politics, wears the longer horns or sports the whiter wings? Would you, from what you know personally, consider the politician to have the greater ability and the more noble character? I tell you quite frankly that I find no halo on the head of either. I have known men in government who were excessively greedy for power, and I likewise have known men in business who were excessively greedy for money. But this is not typical of either group, and whatever other monopolies Mr. Jackson may claim to find, I know he has not found, even among government officials, a monopoly on virtue.

But there is another myth that has been handed out to us in recent years, and that is that big business and small business have different and opposing interests. My distinguished companion on the platform has made this a favorite theme of his many speeches. He has warned against government cooperation with big business, maintaining that, to quote his words, "the governmental cooperation which the small businessman wants is a different kind."

The fact of the matter is that small business and big business prosper under exactly the same conditions, and the conditions that are harmful to one are harmful to the other. In fact, small business suffers more acutely from such things as heavy taxation, government hostility, and timidity of investment, because it has no reserves with which to preserve itself in time of adversity. Big business supplies a market to small business not only by buying its products but by stimulating the general market; moreover, it furnishes small business with low cost materials and supplies. The two are dependent, one upon the other. When we say that American industry is prosperous, we mean that the small businesses of America, which comprise the larger part of our industry, are prosperous.

After all, a large corporation is simply a corporation in which as a rule the interest is divided among a great many small stockholders. If government succeeds in destroying a large corporation, more people, both stockholders and employees, suffer at one time, that is all. It is not the size that makes a corporation bad or good; it is the way it operates. For example, the government has been currently

investigating most of the major industries of the country,
such as the oil industry, automobiles, telephone and telegraph, utilities, and railroads. These are typical big business
industries. What have they achieved? Do they make a good
product? Is it sold at a fair price? Does labor receive a
a fair wage?

Well, every American workingman knows that the highest
wages and the best working conditions are found in the
large corporations. If the wage and hour bill is passed, the
effect on America's big business corporations will be negli-
gible, because their wage levels are already above the
minimum suggested in the bill. Also, it seems a little ironical
for government officials to be lecturing big business on the
desirability of low price and large volume, because this
was the technique which was developed and made possible
only by mass production and distribution under the leadership of big business.

The oil industry, for example, is one in which there are a
number of very large companies of the kind Mr. Jackson
dislikes. Yet anyone who has driven a car abroad knows
that the system of service stations which we take for granted
here is duplicated in very few places outside our borders.
Although nearly half of what we pay for gasoline represents
the government tax, we can still buy it for less than in
almost any other place in the world. And, of course, no
country pays refinery workers as high a wage as they receive
here. In fact, the average hourly wage rates in refineries
have increased more than 50 per cent in the past 15 years,
while the gasoline price, excluding the tax, has declined by
nearly the same amount.

More than 50 per cent of all telephones in the world are
in the United States, and they cost the consumer a smaller
part of his income than anywhere else.

During the 4 years ended in 1932, the American automobile
industry lost 80 per cent of its business. In 1 year the
industry's net loss was half the cost of the Panama Canal.
Yet during that 4-year period the industry made a low
priced car which was better than the highest priced car in
1926. The public got a better car for considerably less
money; and the reduction in price did not come out of the
pockets of labor, because automobile labor continued to be
among the highest paid of all manufacturing industries.
Here again, it was big business that made the achievement

possible. At a press conference in 1936, President Roosevelt quoted with approval a remark made by Walter P. Chrysler, stating that because of the efficient production methods made possible by the big automobile companies we could buy a car for $600 today which otherwise would cost $3,500. The President stated at that time that the same methods should be applied to the housing industry.

Of all the industries mentioned, the utility industry, with its enormous demand for additional construction and equipment, is the most important to our economic recovery. And how has it been operated? Since the prewar years the cost of living has gone up about 40 per cent, and the cost of electricity in this country has gone down by almost exactly the same per cent. *The American consumer pays a smaller part of his income for electricity than the consumers in any country in Europe.* On an average, the American pays 9 cents a day for electricity or less than the government tax on a package and a half of cigarettes.

Since Mr. Jackson has at times employed the usual government argument against the utility holding company, perhaps we should note here that electricity costs less when it is supplied by one of the great utility holding company systems. In every one of the 48 states of the United States, you will find in operation both the so-called independent utilities which are unaffected by the death sentence of the Utility Holding Company Act, and the utility companies affiliated with holding companies. In 44 of those 48 states the rates of companies in holding company systems are lower than the rates of the independent companies.

For example, Mr. Jackson lives in Washington, D. C. . . . at least temporarily . . . which gets its electricity from one of the companies in the great North American Holding Company system. A few miles away, operating under identical conditions, is one of those so-called independent companies. The average rate for electric service in the Washington home is 3 cents per kilowatt-hour. The average rate for this same service in the independent company's territory is 4 cents, or 33⅓ per cent higher. Because of the low rate of the holding company utility, the home owners of Washington save approximately 1½ million dollars per year in their electricity bill. Which is worth more to the people of that city, a saving of 1½ million dollars on the electricity they use or the acceptance of a political formula which decrees that mere size is wrong even though it saves money for the people?

I use Washington as an example because Mr. Jackson comes from there. Similar comparisons can be made in almost every state of the Union. Mr. Jackson is mistaken: the Commonwealth and Southern Corporation, of which I have the honor to be president, operates in 11 states, 5 of them in the North. These 5 Northern companies are wholly remote from the Tennessee Valley Authority. The average rate of these companies and our Southern companies is lower than that of any utility group in America.

No doubt there have been weaknesses and abuses in all the industries mentioned, and in others, too. Betrayals of trust have stained the record of public officials as well as of businessmen. In the period following the great war there was a breakdown in both government and private morals. For the first time in history a member of the Presidential Cabinet was sent to the penitentiary. Some of those who were in charge of the hospitals for America's war veterans were indicted and some convicted for stealing the very blankets and towels provided for the care of these men who were injured in their country's service.

Speaking of abuses in his relief program, President Roosevelt stated: "It should be remembered that in every big job there are some imperfections. There are chiselers in every walk of life, there are those in every industry who are guilty of unfair practices, every profession has its black sheep. . . . " If this quotation from President Roosevelt represents what our attitude should be toward the mistakes of the few in government . . . and I think it does . . . then that should also be our attitude toward industry. In view of the friendlier tone of the President's last speeches, I hope that at last we can have done with the epithets, the calling of names, the catchwords . . . catchwords which have been so glibly used, such as "economic royalists," "Bourbons," "moneyed aristocrats," "banker control," "holding companies," and the nonsense about "sixty ruling families."

"A good catchword," Justice Oliver Wendell Holmes said, "can obscure analysis for fifty years." Today we are very much in need of analysis without catchwords. The business decline has become so serious that government officials, who at first sought to minimize it, are now seeking frantically to make big business responsible. Some of these officials allege that the present slump was caused by a few business "strong men," who, like Samson, were willing to destroy themselves in order to pull down the house. They would have us believe that the automobile companies are deliberately trying not to sell cars. They would have us believe that the steel companies which were operating at 90 per cent of capacity are now purposely losing money and operating at 20 per cent of capacity and that they increased their prices for no reason, whereas, in fact, these prices increased less than wages and cost of materials.

However absurd this charge may be, I see no point in arguing it. I suggest that we have now reached the time when we should stop discussing what caused the depression and should direct our attention to how to cure it. The real cure consists in convincing the millions of small investors throughout America that the government does not intend to continue its attack on American industry, big or little, for it is these investors upon whom industry depends for its funds.

For instance, the utilities need to spend several hundred million dollars for new construction, but they can only raise the money by selling securities. The investor will buy securities only if he thinks that he will get a safe and fair return. He knows that the government is now competing with private industry in the Tennessee Valley by selling electricity at less than cost and charting the loss to the Federal Treasury. He knows that the government is giving money away to municipalities to duplicate existing distribution lines. And he will not invest his money in utilities merely because someone says that the government is competing in only 15 per cent of the country's area.

If there is a smallpox epidemic in a city you cannot convince a man he is in no danger because at the moment only 15 per cent of the city is affected. The investor knows that if the government can compete in 15 per cent of the United States it can compete with any industry anywhere, and he is not reassured by government efforts to belittle or conceal this competition.

Mr. Jackson has previously spoken of a "strike of capital" against the government. If there is any strike of capital it comes from these millions of small investors, not from the wealthy few. As a matter of fact, due to the income tax laws which take up to 83 per cent of a rich man's investment in private enterprise, most of the very rich have been investing more and more in the flood of tax-exempt government securities. It might be helpful to industry as well as to government revenues if the government should remove these tax exemptions; but this in and of itself would not be enough. The main problem is to restore the confidence of investors in American business, and to do this will require more than pleasant speaking on the part of government. For several years the government has taken definite action to show its hostility to business. It must now take definite action to demonstrate the sincerity of its desire to cooperate.

I don't think that such cooperation should be difficult. The chief reason why government officials and businessmen fail to understand each other is because one thinks and speaks the language of politics and emotionalism, while the other thinks and speaks the language of economics and realism. One thinks economic forces can be controlled by politics, while the other realizes that economic forces are more powerful than either government or business. But if we look behind this difference in theory, we can find much upon which we agree in practice.

For example, there seems to be no important disagreement today on the need for a reduction in the undistributed profits tax and the capital gains tax, both of which fall with particular severity upon small businesses and both of which restrict the expansion of industry.

Nor is there any general disagreement as to the principles of the social legislation which has been put upon the statute books in recent years. Time has revealed both the virtues and the weaknesses of these laws. The proposal now is simply one of eliminating the weaknesses; of modifying those restrictions upon the buying and selling of securities that hamper the investment of funds; of readjusting the Social Security Act to a pay-as-you-go basis, so that the money paid by the people for social security is used only for that purpose; of protecting the rights of both capital and labor in the promotion of collective bargaining; of getting rid of intermediate holding companies in the utility industry without declaring a "death sentence" upon all of them.

Six weeks ago I left with the President a memorandum suggesting a solution of the utility problem . . . a solution which did not ask for less Federal regulation of utilities but did ask for an end to unfair government competition and unfair government destruction of the property of American citizens. I am still hopeful that that memorandum will provide a basis upon which the utilities may be permitted to go ahead with their construction plans.

Now, is there anything in this outline of a possible relationship between government and business that is not in the interest of the ill-housed, the ill-fed, and the ill-clad? Is there anything here that is opposed to the social regulation of business? Does this attitude imply that business is "ganging up" on government or that a few corporations are attempting to swallow up all American industry?

In such a time as this when we see the relief rolls lengthening again and the price of farm products declining, when many of us are discouraged and when the road to recovery seems long, surely business and government should put an end to the bitterness of recent years and sit down in conference like reasonable men with mutual tolerance and respect. But the purpose of this conference must not only be to plan intelligently for the future but to review those laws which have been passed . . . to see whether they cannot be so modified as to stimulate business activity, without removing any of the appropriate social controls. And above all, while these conferences are proceeding, the American people should be spared the confusion of hearing what one government official says in friendship today denied by another in hostility tomorrow.

At this critical point in our nation's history, it would seem fitting that business and government should bear in mind the warning which Abraham Lincoln gave to the two factions into which this country was dividing at the time of his first inaugural address. "I am loath to close," he said. "We are not enemies, but friends. We must not be enemies." (*Applause*)

DENNY.—Mr. Willkie has taken a little more than his allotted time, and as the clock is our yardstick of fair play, Mr. Jackson is entitled to 6 minutes, which he tells me he would rather waive in favor of the questions. Now, please save your own time and don't take up time applauding and demonstrating. Let's have your questions. Questions, please!

MAN.—Mr. Jackson, you made reference to a statement made by Mr. Knudsen. I chanced to read his testimony before the Senate Committee today. He made a statement before the committee today that the reason the sale of automobiles had declined was not because the people were thrown out of work and had no money to buy but that even though they had the money they were afraid to buy because they might not have jobs in the future. In other words, there is a period of uncertainty ahead which has reduced purchasing power.

JACKSON.—Unfortunately, I have not read Mr. Knudsen's testimony, and I don't like to comment on testimony that I haven't heard. I did read his statement as quoted in *The New York Times* at the time that the 30,000 men were discharged, and I am not surprised if as a result of that there is a good deal of uncertainty in the hearts and minds of a good many workingmen as to whether their jobs will last. (*Applause*)

MAN.—I would like to ask Mr. Willkie whether big business or small business is more likely to hire labor spies? (*Applause*)

DENNY.—Mr. Willkie, do you want to comment on that?

WILLKIE.—Certainly. Being a member of big business who never hired a labor spy in my life, I don't know the motive that actuates either a big or little business, and I would repudiate the act by both big business and little business. (*Applause*)

MAN.—Mr. Jackson, how do you reconcile the New Deal program for farmers to cut production to raise prices with its plan of increasing industrial production to lower prices?

JACKSON.—Every person who has ever lived upon a farm knows that there is an essential difference in the method of production on a farm and the production in a factory. No farmer can control his production unless he can control the weather, and that is one of the things we haven't gotten around to regulate yet. (*Laughter and applause*) Factory production is controlled and can be controlled, which makes an entirely different matter.

MAN.—Mr. Jackson, don't we, the people, fear an undue concentration in government as much or more than we fear this concentration in business?

JACKSON.—Yes, sir, we do fear it. We do fear it. And the American people never would concentrate government if they didn't have to concentrate government to regulate the concentration of big business. (*Applause, cheers, and cries of "No"*) How can a single state regulate Mr. Willkie?

VOICE.—That might be in Italy or Germany, but it isn't that in the United States of America. (*Applause*)

Man.—Mr. Willkie, what accounts for the Canadian electric rates being so much less than the rates of the utility companies on this side of the Niagara?

WILLKIE.—I was just hoping somebody would ask me that question. (*Laughter and applause*) The difference is that the American utility companies are now paying up to 20 per cent of their gross revenue in taxes, while the public plants in Canada pay no taxes, except a minor amount of taxes on real estate. (*Applause*)

MAN.—Mr. Willkie, you mentioned in your address that the large corporations pay a higher wage scale and have better working conditions than smaller concerns. Is that not by reason of the fact of the large labor turnover in large corporations?

WILLKIE.—First, I disagree with you about the facts. In the utility business, there is practically no turnover in labor. Most of our employees have been with us for more than 10 years. I would say that the policy of American industry, as is well illustrated by the attitude of General Motors, has been to attempt to make the production regular so that men may be employed as much as possible throughout the year and reduce to a minimum the turnover in labor. (*Applause*)

MAN.—Mr. Willkie, what do you think the attitude of the government should be towards the cement industry which controls prices throughout the country?

WILLKIE.—There is on the statute books the antitrust statute. You have seen demonstrating tonight one of the ablest lawyers in the United States who is charged with the prosecution of any violation of that statute. I would suggest that Mr. Jackson go to work, if there is anything wrong in the cement industry or in any other industry with reference to monopolistic practices. (*Applause*)

MAN.—I should like to ask Mr. Jackson what he thinks of the undistributed profits surtax?

JACKSON.—The undistributed profits tax undoubtedly is in need of amendment in several particulars, particularly as affects small industry. (*Applause*) I want to say to you that I believe in the undistributed profits tax in the main. I know that the representations that have been made that corporate surpluses are a cushion against depression are not true, because General Motors when it laid off 30,000 men had over $400,000,000 of corporate surplus. (*Applause*)

WOMAN.—Mr. Jackson said that farm production could not be controlled. Why did the government attempt it in the case of cotton?

JACKSON.—The most the government attempted to do was to place a maximum of production and to avoid the creation of a surplus which could not be handled, since the foreign markets had fallen away, due to the fact that we had quit sending foreign money abroad with which they could buy our products. (*Cries of "No"*)

WOMAN.—Mr. Jackson, if the government continues its expansion program in the power field, what will happen to the billions of dollars invested in stocks and bonds now held by our insurance companies, investment trusts, estates, and the public?

JACKSON.—The government of the United States has never attempted to destroy the power industry. (*Cry of "Not much"*) The government of the United States wants the power industry to furnish power at rates that are fair to the public as well as to the utility companies. (*Applause*) Long before I was in politics I pointed out to the utility industry in an address to the American Bar Association utility lawyers that the trouble with the power industry was that it was issuing too many securities called "power securities" that had little relation to power and none to security. (*Cry of "Right" and applause*)

MAN.—Mr. Jackson, do you think the fair way to get lower electric rates is to subsidize municipal competition with 50 per cent grants and free taxation?

JACKSON.—I don't think the question of fairness enters into it. I don't know that it is necessarily fair for two policemen to arrest one crook. But, if the government of the United States is going to carry out its power policy by competitive methods, because we have seen the methods of regulation due to the big holding companies' control break down, it must use ordinary competitive methods. (*Boos and applause*)

WOMAN.—Mr. Willkie, is it not true that the rates of Commonwealth and Southern are the lowest because of pressure from TVA.? (*Applause*)

WILLKIE.—As I said, we operate in 11 states, 5 in the North and 6 in the South. Our rate schedules in our major Northern companies are almost identical with the rate schedules in our Southern companies; only those in the North are slightly lower. The Tennessee Valley Authority is building competitive lines, and the Federal government is giving 45 per cent absolutely free with which to duplicate existing utility systems in Tennessee. The average rate of the Tennessee Electric Power Company is less than 3 cents, which is 25 to 30 per cent below the national average, and those properties will be destroyed and the investors will lose their money if this policy, which Mr. Jackson recognizes has no element of fairness in it, is not discontinued. (*Applause*)

MAN.—Mr. Jackson, is the aim of the New Deal ultimately to nationalize all the public utilities?

JACKSON.—I should say, no. I haven't heard of its nationalizing any public utilities. (*Applause*)

MAN.—Has it occurred to Mr. Jackson that the price government power operations quote does not include the interest on the capital invested in the form of the taxpayer's money nor for provision for amortization of the debt? In other words, an incomplete balance sheet is presented to the American public and endorsed as bona fide by the government. What is the difference between this procedure and Mr. Insull's? (*Laughter and applause*)

JACKSON.—I am not an accountant, and if I were, I wouldn't attempt to give an answer to that question in the time that is allowed here. I don't know the details of the accounting of TVA, and I don't know the details of the accounting of private utilities.

DENNY.—Thank you, Mr. Jackson, we must close now. I hope that all who are listening in as groups will continue their discussions as profitably as I know we are going to continue it here among ourselves. (*Applause*)

BEST COMEDY SHOW

Town Hall Tonight

by FRED ALLEN

ƐƐƐ

JOHN FLORENCE SULLIVAN, better known to radio millions as Fred Allen, started his professional life in the Boston Public Library. Here he found a book on juggling, and before long the staid atmosphere of the library was enlivened by the incongruous sight of a lost but earnest young man throwing all manner of things into the air and catching some of them again on their way down; inkwells and variorum editions, paper knives and date stamps, mucilage bottles, clipping shears, and packages of thumbtacks, all had their daily whirl. Even the furniture was violated. His employers, good Boston bibliophiles, did not get the idea, and he was fired before the full flowering of his legerdemain. He went into vaudeville, billed as "The World's Worst Juggler," which he no doubt was.

Bad as it was, audiences liked the act, especially liked the patter that went with it. This was a discursive and nasal monologue that was funnier than anything in vaudeville at the time and unique in that each new performance was refreshed with new material. This habit of output was to be of great use to him ten years later in radio.

Fred Allen first appeared on Broadway in the "Passing Show of 1922," and although he ascribes the decline of the theatre to this circumstance, he turned up again in many other shows . . . notably "Three's a Crowd," and "The Little Show." His take-off of Admiral Byrd's polar expedition (in "The Little Show") still lingers in the memory of the public as one of the great burlesques of the decade.

His radio work began in 1932 with a short-lived program called The Bath Club. This was followed shortly by his Town Hall Tonight series with The Mighty Allen Art Players, The Town Hall Quartet, Portland Hoffa (Mrs.

Allen), Peter Van Steeden and his orchestra, and others. It has been a top-ranking show ever since.

Fred Allen writes almost all the show himself. He works nearly all night and sleeps till early afternoon each day. At the conclusion of the Wednesday night repeat show (1:00 A.M.) he has a final huddle with the production crew and his two researchers, then goes home to bed. On Thursday he starts work on The Mighty Allen Art Players sketch and gets this done usually about dawn on Friday. Friday night he writes the Man You Didn't Expect to Meet routine. Saturday, with his floor littered with New York dailies, he prepares the newsreels. On Sunday he does the Portland spot. Monday is the preliminary rehearsal, after which Fred tears apart and rewrites the entire show. This keeps him up all Monday night and through most of Tuesday. Dress rehearsal takes place Wednesday noon, and from then on until air time the show is cut to fit its time limits. The broadcast at nine, the repeat show at midnight, and Fred Allen is ready to start another week.

Town Hall Tonight has every right to the headline position it occupies. The conscientious quest for good material, the tryouts and throw-outs and rewrites, the pace and variety of its sketches, and the drawling buffoonery of its central figure bring to it a sustained quality of high-grade entertainment that has no equal in radio shows of its type. Most one-hour shows—Vallee, Ameche, Kate Smith, Bing Crosby—are variety shows in the strictest sense, composed of a series of acts and spots in which no single personality is predominant. Fred Allen's show, although it is a variety program in a looser sense, is carried by Fred Allen. One can conceive the Vallee hour being presented without Vallee, but there would be no Town Hall without Allen.

For fertility of invention, for good-natured nonsense, for universality of appeal, for wholesomeness, I have selected Fred Allen's as the best comedy program of the year and his broadcast of December 7, 1938, as representative in structure and superior in material. Here is the "as broadcast" version of his show for that date.

Town Hall Tonight*

SOUND.—*Gavel sounds.*

ANNOUNCER.—Now let's come to order, folks. It's Town Hall Tonight!

MUSIC.—"*Smile Darn Yer, Smile.*"

VON ZELL.—An hour of smiles in Town Hall Tonight, folks. Sixty minutes of fun and music brought to you by Ipana Toothpaste and Sal Hepatica. Ipana for the smile of beauty. Sal Hepatica for the smile of health. Fun with our star comedian, Fred Allen. Music with Peter Van Steeden. New songs! New laughs. . . . It's Town Hall Tonight! (*Cheers*)

MUSIC.—"*Smile Darn Yer, Smile.*" . . . *up to finish.*

VON ZELL.—The roll has been called, folks. We're all here. The overture's "This Can't Be Love." So what are we waiting for, Peter!

MUSIC.—"*This Can't Be Love.*" (*Orchestra and singers*).

VON ZELL.—And now we present a man, ladies and gentlemen. He wasn't picked for the All-American. He isn't number one on Your Hit Parade. He hasn't been called back from a foreign country to be here tonight. How he got in nobody knows. What's your name again, Buddy?

ALLEN.—Fred Allen.

VON ZELL.—Oh, yes. It's Fred Allen, in person! (*Applause*)

ALLEN.—Thank you. Thank you. And good evening, ladies and gentlemen. Once again, through the courtesy of Mr. Marconi, we are enabled to convene for the next 60 minutes. Yes,

* Permission to reprint the broadcast text of the Fred Allen program for December 7, 1938, has been granted by Walter Batchelor, president of the Walter Batchelor Enterprises, Inc., sole copyright owner. Permission to use all or any part of this material for any purpose can be had only through negotiation with the copyright owner.

214

radio is a wonderful invention. Don't you think **radio is** wonderful, Harry?

Von Zell.—It sure is, Fred.

Allen.—Here I am. One man standing in Radio City. The minute I open my mouth people all over the country will be rushing out into the streets.

Von Zell.—Yes, it's wonderful, Fred. */Von Zell.*

Allen.—Radio is improving every day. Have you seen **one of** those new remote control sets?

Allen.—With the . . . ?

Von Zell.—Yes.

Allen.—No. I haven't, Harry.

Von Zell.—Say. They're wonderful. No aerial. No ground.

Allen.—No entertainment.

Von Zell.—No. No kidding, **Fred**. I'll explain how they work. You just have a little portable dial. You can turn the dial on. You can be anywhere you like . . .

Allen.—While Harry is explaining the remote control sets, we turn to the latest news of the week. May we have one of your tin catcalls, Mr. Van Steeden?

Music.—*Fanfare.*

Allen.—The Town Hall News. . . . Sees nothing . . . shows it in technicolor.

Music.—*Fanfare.*

Allen.—New York City, New York. After 60 years of continuous service, the Sixth Avenue Elevated Lines ceased operations at midnight, Sunday. Title of entire elevated structure passes to the city for $3,500,000, and work of demolition will begin at once. Town Hall News interviews native New Yorkers, young and old, to get opinions on the passing of this historic landmark. First, Mr. Bismark Tort, attorney for the stockholders. What caused the El's downfall, Mr. Tort?

Von Zell.—The trend has been down. When the trend is down the subways get the business.

ALLEN.—I see. Are you taking any legal action for the elevated, Mr. Tort?

VON ZELL.—We're taking the Sixth Avenue El into court.

ALLEN.—It will be quite a job, won't it?

VON ZELL.—Yes. But I think we can get it in in sections.

ALLEN.—You feel you have grounds for a suit, Mr. Tort?

VON ZELL.—Unquestionably. In 1903 we signed a lease for 999 years.

ALLEN.—Hasn't the city made you an offer to settle?

VON ZELL.—Yes. They want to give us the World's Fair when they're through with it.

ALLEN.—Well . . . I hope everything will come out all right, Mr. Tort.

VON ZELL.—It will. All's El that Ends El . . . That's Shakespeare.

ALLEN.—Oh . . . I thought the mayor was taking it down.

VON ZELL.—He is. He got the idea from Shakespeare. That is *sub rosa*.

ALLEN.—I have heard nothing, Mr. Tort.

VON ZELL.—Too bad. You should have told me. I'd have raised my voice.

ALLEN.—If I don't see you, again . . . Merry Christmas, Mr. Tort.

VON ZELL.—On Sixth Avenue its Happy No-El.

ALLEN.—A Sixth Avenue housewife who doesn't know what she'll do is Mrs. Elaine O'Gatty.

MIN.—I'm sure gonna miss the old El all right.

ALLEN.—Have you been living on Sixth Avenue long, Mrs. O'Gatty?

MIN.—Thoity years. I spent me honeymoon on the Staten Island Ferry. After that we was "at home" on Sixth Avenue.

ALLEN.—You've been there a long time.

216

MIN.—Thoity years, mornin', noon, and night . . . I been hearin' them stratosphere gondolas go by.

ALLEN.—Has stopping the trains bothered you and Mr. O'Gatty any?

MIN.—Yeah. The lack o' noise is somethin' brutal. Every midnight a train's been goin' by fer 30 years.

ALLEN.—Yes.

MIN.—Monday midnight nothin' went by. My old man jumps up in bed and says, "What's that?"

ALLEN.—I guess losing the El is going to take the romance out of your life, Mrs. O'Gatty.

MIN.—I got a lump here, mister.

ALLEN.—That bulge in your throat.

MIN.—No. That's me Adam's apple. I got a lump yer can't see. I guess it's sediment.

ALLEN.—You're going to miss those old trains passing your flat.

MIN.—Yeah. Thoity years seein' people's profiles. Wise guys throwin' cigarette butts in me window. Wavin' at the motorman. Stickin' me tongue out at dames dressed up.

ALLEN.—Yes. It must be an awful blow.

MIN.—Yeah. I wouldn't be surprised if it broke up me home.

ALLEN.—Why?

MIN.—Well, me old man woiks down at the Fulton Fish Market. He's the conjunction man.

ALLEN.—Conjunction man in a fish market.

MIN.—Yeah. His foim makes nothin' but finn and haddie signs. He puts in the conjunction.

ALLEN.—But the Sixth Avenue El . . . ?

MIN.—I'm comin' to that. Every Saturday night me old man gets plastered downtown. The bartender lugs him over to the Sixth Avenue El.

ALLEN.—And puts him on a train.

Min.—Carries him on, mister. He's stiff.

Allen.—What happens?

Min.—When the train pulls in to Twenty-thoid Street, the conductor rolls him down the stairs into me arms. . . . He's home.

Allen.—What will you do next Saturday night?

Min.—The subway guard can't roll him up the stairs. I'll be waitin' there to carry him home.

Allen.—Are you strong enough to lift that load?

Min.—I'll just carry me husband. He'll be carrying the load.

Allen.—Thank you. New York's oldest inhabitant has his say about the El. Grandpa Creep.

Announcer.—(*As old man*) I said, "She won't last." When I seen the El goin' up in '78 . . . I said, "She won't last." Well, it only goes to show . . .

Allen.—To show what, Gramp?

Announcer.—If ye live long enough, nothin' won't last.

Allen.—Have you lived in New York all your life?

Announcer.—Not yet, no. I been here 90 years.

Allen.—I guess you've seen many changes in the city.

Announcer.—Lord, yes. I remember Al Smith way back before his derby faded.

Allen.—You don't say.

Announcer.—I can remember the Aquarium when it was nothin' but a room full of bait.

Allen.—That's going back.

Announcer.—I can remember Tammany Hall when 'twarn't nothin' but a Democrat hidin' in a doorway.

Allen.—And you . . .

Announcer.—I says, "They won't last." And they ain't, have they?

Allen.—No.

ANNOUNCER.—It's like I say. Ef ye live long enough, nothin' won't last.

ALLEN.—Isn't there anything in New York that will last, Gramp?

ANNOUNCER.—Just one thing, son.

ALLEN.—What?

ANNOUNCER.—That show, "Tobacco Road."

ALLEN.—Why do you think "Tobacco Road" will last forever?

ANNOUNCER.—Tobacco's habit formin'.

ALLEN.—What are you going to use now that the Sixth Avenue El is down, Gramp?

ANNOUNCER.—Nothin', son. I ain't goin' no place.

ALLEN.—Aren't we all . . . and thank you, Grampa Creep. And now the Town Hall News brings you the dramatic speech that sealed the Sixth Avenue Elevated's doom. The scene . . . the recent Board of Estimate meeting. A delegate is pleading.

JOHN.—Gentlemen of the Board of Estimate, I beg you not to remove this structure. What is your answer, gentlemen?

VON ZELL.—Get the El out of New York!

MUSIC.—*Fanfare.*

ALLEN.—And now the Merry Macs reach into their musical oven to bring out a little hot confection for you. It's called "Patty Cake."

MERRY MACS.—*"Patty Cake."* (*Applause*)

ALLEN.—(*Ad lib thank you's*) Tonight, ladies and gentlemen . . . we inaugurate our Something-Must-Be-Done-about-Some-of-the-People-Who-Go-to-the-Movies Department in charge of our own Mr. Tater. Mr. Tater sounds off with several specific complaints. Complaint number one . . .

JOHN.—Feathers! The high feathers on women's hats! The other night I saw Marie Antoinette in technicolor, and with all those feathers I thought it was an Indian picture!

ALLEN.—(*Helpfully*) Why not take along a pair of scissors and snip your way *out* of that feathered shrubbery? What else?

219

JOHN.—*Knee* bumpers! Those lame brains who keep bumping the back of your chair with their nervous knees. *There ought to be a law!*

ALLEN.—Definitely. Meanwhile a hot foot will keep them on the inactive list. Anything else?

JOHN.—Yes . . . coughers and sneezers! Just at the ka-roo-shul part of the picture . . . whango! . . . Somebody starts to cough or sneeze, and the love scene sounds like an air raid!

FRED.—I know. . . . It's very trying. But that particular group needs sympathy rather than censure. After all, nobody can help catching cold.

JOHN.—Well, they ought to *do* something about their colds. I'd certainly like to tell them a thing or two.

VON ZELL.—Well, the best thing you could tell them would be to get after their colds immediately. . . . Tell them how to fight a cold two ways at once with sparkling Sal Hepatica. For, as so many physicians will tell you . . .

HOUSE.—You can often throw off a cold more quickly if, at its very beginning, you do two fundamental things . . . remove accumulated wastes . . . and help Nature counteract the acidity that so frequently accompanies a cold.

VON ZELL.—And ladies and gentlemen, *Sal Hepatica* was especially made to do those very things and to do them promptly. As a laxative, it brings quick yet gentle relief . . . and at the same time . . . it *also* helps Nature counteract acidity. So do the *wise* thing. . . . Get a bottle of Sal Hepatica at any drugstore tomorrow . . . and show your family this modern way to fight a cold . . . with Sal Hepatica.

MUSIC.—"*The Skaters' Waltz.*" (*Applause*)

ALLEN.—That was "The Skaters' Waltz," played by the Sonja Henie of icestros, Peter Van Steeden and his Ipana Whatcha Macallits. And now, ladies and gentlemen, tonight I know you didn't expect to meet . . .

VON ZELL.—Well, what are we in for this evening, Fred?

ALLEN.—Do you believe in mental telepathy.

VON ZELL.—Mental telepathy? What brought that up, Fred?

ALLEN.—It may surprise you to know, Mr. Von Zell, that during the past few weeks I have been taking a course in mental telepathy through the mail.

VON ZELL.—Fred . . . you can't . . .

ALLEN.—You are talking to a man, Mr. Von Zell, who is skilled in thought transference. At this very moment I can communicate impressions from *my* mind to the mind of any person in this studio without recourse to physical channels.

VON ZELL.—You're not kidding me, Fred.

ALLEN.—All right. I'll prove it to you, Harry. I'm not looking at Peter Van Steeden, am I?

VON ZELL.—No.

ALLEN.—He can't hear me right now, can he?

VON ZELL.—No.

ALLEN.—I'm going to send Peter a thought. Watch him.

MUSIC.—*"Says My Heart"* . . . *first three notes* . . . *stops short.*

ALLEN.—How was that?

VON ZELL.—Oh, there's something screwy around here. I saw it, and I still don't believe it.

ALLEN.—All right. Watch the Merry Macs. I'll send them a thought.

MERRY MACS.—*"A Tisket, a Tasket."*

ALLEN.—Well, my skeptical belittler, are you convinced now?

VON ZELL.—You'll never convince me, Fred, until you send me a thought message.

ALLEN.—All right, Mr. Von Zell. Here is your thought.

VON ZELL.—I get it. So long, Fred.

SOUND.—*Door slam.*

ALLEN.—You have just seen this wonderful demonstration, ladies and gentlemen. But our guest tonight makes me look like a novice. We are going to interview a young man who can transfer his thought impressions to the mind of a dog. The dog doesn't actually talk, but any stranger can ask him a question and through a process of thought transference between the trainer and the animal an answer is given in barks.

And so, ladies and gentlemen, tonight I know you didn't expect to meet this human canine . . . King. And his best friend and trainer, Mr. Lew Miller. Good evening, Mr. Miller.

LEW.—Good evening, Fred.

ALLEN.—Do you mind if I shake hands with King?

LEW.—No. Go right ahead.

ALLEN.—Say . . . that's mighty democratic of him. A lot of dogs are high-hat these days.

LEW.—King's a regular guy, Fred.

ALLEN.—What breed of dog is he, Mr. Miller?

LEW.—He's a German shepherd.

ALLEN.—Uncle Jim tells me that any stranger can ask King a question. And that, after you have conveyed the thought to him, without speaking, the dog will answer correctly.

LEW.—That is true, Fred.

ALLEN.—Do you mind if I try him out?

LEW.—No. Go right ahead, Fred.

ALLEN.—Fine. I'll start him on something easy. King, how many letters are there in the word "Ipana"? Tell me, King. (*Dog barks five times*) That is correct! Absolutely correct! King is probably the first dog to ever bark a commercial from coast to coast.

LEW.—Ask him something else, Fred.

ALLEN.—All right. King, what time did this program go on the air tonight, Eastern Standard Time? (*Dog barks nine times*) Nine is right. And beautifully barked, too. Nice pear-shaped tones. Tell me, Mr. Miller, will King bark "Yes" or "No" to a question?

LEW.—If I explain it to him first, he'll be glad to oblige.

ALLEN.—Fine. Will you tell the old boy?

LEW.—King! Three barks mean "Yes." Two barks, "No." Have you got that? (*Dog barks three times*)

ALLEN.—Yes! We're all set. Three barks for "Yes," two for "No." O.K., King. Have you ever been on the air before? (*Dog barks twice*) No! I see. Would you like to have a nice sustaining program of your own? (*Dog barks twice*)

ALLEN.—You wouldn't, eh? How about one with a thin, bony sponsor? (*Dog barks three times*) King is not only smart, Mr. Miller. He's a good businessman, too.

LEW.—Yes, King is no fool, Fred.

ALLEN.—I wouldn't be surprised if he did get a program of his own. I might end up working for King.

LEW.—I don't think so, Fred.

ALLEN.—Say . . . I worked for Katz one time in Chicago. Balaban and Katz. If I can work for Katz I can work for dogs. Tell me, Mr. Miller, how long have you had this four-footed intellectual? This caninestein?

LEW.—Since he was three months old. He's a little over six now.

ALLEN.—How were you able to establish this psychic bond between you two?

LEW.—Well, it was a long process, Fred. When King was a pup I started training him to respond to the various intonations of my voice.

ALLEN.—And now he will react to your commands without signals of any sort.

LEW.—Exactly.

ALLEN.—Have you introduced King to the public yet?

LEW.—Yes. We've been at the Roxy, the Brooklyn Strand, and the Midnight Sun Night Club.

ALLEN.—And King's I.Q. hasn't faltered under the strain.

LEW.—No, Fred. He does four or five shows a day and never makes a mistake.

ALLEN.—When I was in vaudeville all of the dogs in dog acts knew me. I was always billed so low that dogs kept bumping their noses into my name as they passed the front of the theatre. Is King planning to do any stage work in the near future?

LEW.—Why yes, Fred, King is opening tonight.

ALLEN.—Where?

LEW.—At the Rainbow Room, upstairs.

ALLEN.—A dog at the Rainbow Room? Is he wearing a white leash?

LEW.—No. They're letting King dress informal.

ALLEN.—His breath will come in Tuxedo pants, of course. Have you another dog to succeed King, if he shows up some day with a nervous breakdown?

LEW.—No, Fred. I'm training his son to succeed him now.

ALLEN.—What is King's son's name . . . Prince?

LEW.—No. It's Silver.

ALLEN.—Silver, eh? Why, you may be the Lone Ranger of tomorrow, Mr. Miller. But King is dozing off. . . . How about a couple of more questions?

LEW.—Go right ahead, Fred. Get ready, King.

ALLEN.—Fine. I think I'll try him out on politics this time. King, how many states voted Republican in the last presidential election? (*Dog barks twice*) Right. I don't want to ask him how many voted Democratic, Mr. Miller. He'll be here barking for the rest of the night.

LEW.—It's all right, Fred. When there are two digits in the answer he'll bark the first digit and stop. Then bark the second.

ALLEN.—A lightning calculator, eh? All right, King. . . . How many states voted Democratic in 1936? (*Dog barks four times . . . then six*) Forty-six. Mr. Farley himself couldn't have done any better.

LEW.—King is always right, Fred.

ALLEN.—Well . . . election questions would be easy. Every dog is an authority on polls. I'll see if I can double-cross him this time. King, how many men are here at the microphone? (*Dog barks twice*) Correct. How many good-looking men? (*Dog barks once*) I wonder which one of us he meant, Mr. Miller?

LEW.—King never tells a lie, Fred.

ALLEN.—I get it. . . . I lose again, eh? Even the dogs are wise to me. Now, just one more question, Mr. Miller. I'll make it a killer-diller. King, how many new jokes have you heard on the program tonight? (*Pause*) Come on, boy. How many new jokes? Give us the digits. (*Pause*) I think he's giving me the digit . . . Mr. Miller.

LEW.—That's his answer, Fred.

ALLEN.—He's too smart for me. Well, thank you a lot for this doggy little chat, Mr. Miller . . . and thanks a million, King.

LEW.—Good night, Fred. Say good night, King. (*Dog barks . . . applause*)

ALLEN.—The Town Hall Singers, under the direction of Lyn Murray, sing "Joshua Fit the Battle of Jericho."

MUSIC.—"*Joshua Fit the Battle of Jericho*" (*Town Hall Quartet*). (*Applause*)

ALLEN.—(*Ad lib thank you's*) And now, ladies and gentlemen, a little item left over from the Town Hall News. A little fanfare, Peter. . . (*Town Hall fanfare . . . one cornet*) A new restaurant is soon to be opened where your order for dinner is conveyed direct to the kitchen by means of a microphone. How's that for scientific progress?

VON ZELL.—You mean a mike at every table, Fred?

ALLEN.—Exactly.

VON ZELL.—No waiter to breathe down your neck while you're trying to decide whether to order something you want or something you know the French for?

ALLEN.—No, Harry . . . just a microphone. You pitch your voice in a melodious key, speak into the microphone, and order like this. . . . Calling all chefs . . . calling all chefs . . . you over there by the gas range . . . creamed chicken . . . mashed potatoes . . . and rice pudding. . . . That is all.

MAN.—(*On filter* . . . *same tone*) Very good, sir . . . but, of course, you realize those are all soft, creamy foods . . . so don't forget . . . Ipana Toothpaste and massage . . . that is all.

ALLEN.—Say . . . what's the big idea?

VON ZELL.—Why, it's a *grand* idea, Fred, to help anyone to have a winning smile . . . Ipana and massage. Maybe, ladies and gentlemen . . . you haven't stopped to realize how important *massage is* to sound teeth and healthy gums. Our gums certainly don't get the stimulation they need from the soft, well-cooked *foods* we eat. So they are naturally apt to become tender and, consequently, more susceptible to gum trouble. That's why, like so many dentists, we earnestly suggest this easy, modern routine. . . .

HOUSE.—Every time you brush your teeth with Ipana Toothpaste . . . put a little extra *Ipana* on your finger tip or your toothbrush . . . and massage it on your gums.

VON ZELL.—For Ipana is especially designed, when used with massage, to help stimulate and strengthen your gums . . . as well as to clean and brighten your teeth. And since healthier gums and sparkling teeth always add up to a far more attractive smile . . . you can readily understand why more and more people every day are depending on Ipana and massage. So stop at any drugstore tomorrow for an economical tube of Ipana Toothpaste.

MUSIC.—"*Could You Pass in Love.*"
(*Fade*)

VON ZELL.—Town Hall Tonight resumes immediately after a short pause for your station announcement.
(*Station break*)

MUSIC.—*Up to finish.*

PETE.—And now while your local announcer sits down for another half hour, ladies and gentlemen, we return you to the Old Town Hall. On Friday night . . .

PORTLAND.—Hello.

PETE.—Well. If it isn't Portland. (*Applause*)

PORTLAND.—Peter! What are you doing here?

226

PETE.—Clowning as usual. Ha! Ha! You know me, Porty.

PORTLAND.—But where's Mr. Allen?

PETE.—Who cares? Come on, Porty. How about a couple of quick gags. Did you hear the one about the two Irishmen . . .

PORTLAND.—Harry! Oh, Harry!

VON ZELL.—Yes, Porty. What's the matter? Is something wrong?

PORTLAND.—Mr. Allen isn't here, Harry.

VON ZELL.—He isn't?

PETE.—Who needs him? I can take care of the comedy. Did you hear the one about the two Irishmen . . .

VON ZELL.—Say! Where *is* Fred, Peter?

PETE.—I locked him out.

VON ZELL.—You what?

PETE.—Yes. He stepped out to take a smoke, and I locked the door. He'll see who's the comedian tonight. Two Irishmen . . .

SOUND.—*Door rattles.*

ALLEN.—(*Muffled*) Hey, let me in. It's Allen!

SOUND.—*Door rattles.*

PORTLAND.—You'd better let Mr. Allen in, Peter.

PETE.—Never mind, Allen. . . . Get this gag. . . . Two Irishmen met on the street. One Irishman said, "My sister married a man from Dublin." The second Irishman said, "Oh, really." And the first Irishman said, "No, O'Reilly."

SOUND.—*Knocks on door.*

ALLEN.—Hey! Quit telling those corny gags. . . . Let me in!

SOUND.—*Knocks on door.*

ANNOUNCER.—Here! Here! What's going on in this studio?

PORTLAND.—Mr. Allen is locked out.

ANNOUNCER.—I'll let him in.

SOUND.—*Door opens.*

ANNOUNCER.—There, it's open. Come in, Mr. Allen.

ALLEN.—Thanks.

ANNOUNCER.—If you get locked out again, just call on me.

ALLEN.—You work here at NBC?

ANNOUNCER.—Yes. I'm vice-president in charge of keyholes.

ALLEN.—If I have trouble with a keyhole . . .

ANNOUNCER.—Just call me. I'll look into it.

SOUND.—*Door closes.*

ALLEN.—Now, who locked that door? Who locked me out? Don't look so innocent, you three.

PORTLAND.—Don't look at me, Mr. Allen.

ALLEN.—No. You couldn't have done it, Portland. If you had locked the door you'd have locked yourself out. What about you, Mr. Von Zell?

VON ZELL.—Not me, Fred.

ALLEN.—That's all I wanted to know. Van Steeden, you are so low I can't even call you down.

PETE.—Watch those cracks, Allen. I wouldn't take that kind of talk from a relative.

ALLEN.—You and that hair do. Your head looks like a ferret's hip in a high wind.

PORTLAND.—Peter was only fooling, Mr. Allen.

VON ZELL.—Yes. Pete didn't mean any harm, Fred.

ALLEN.—He locked me out, didn't he? Where did he get the key? He couldn't get the right key from that orchestra of his.

PETE.—Why, I ought to pull your nose down and hook it under your chin.

ALLEN.—Why, you walking faux pas.

PETE.—Speak English, Allen.

ALLEN.—All right . . . I will speak English. You four-bar rest in the World of Music. You're through, Van Steeden.

228

PETE.—Says you! Sam!

JOHN.—Yeah, maestro.

ALLEN.—Just a minute . . . who are you? The trombone player?

JOHN.—And accidentally, on the side, I'm the union delegate.

PETE.—He says I'm fired, Sam.

JOHN.—Quit kiddin', Allen. You know what that means.

ALLEN.—What?

JOHN.—You fire Van Steeden, the Musician's Union pulls every musician out, from Toscanini to Borrah Minnevitch.

ANNOUNCER.—Fred Allen's unfair to organized . . .

JOHN.—Not yet, Joe.

ANNOUNCER.—O.K., Sam. I'll stand by.

ALLEN.—Union or no union. You can't strong-arm me.

JOHN.—You can't fire Van Steeden, Allen. The union says you gotta give him 4 years' notice.

ALLEN.—Four years? The President only gets 4 years' notice.

JOHN.—You ain't firin' the President, Allen. You're firin' Van Steeden.

ALLEN.—All right, I'm not firing him. But I'm through with him socially.

JOHN.—O.K., Joe, let's get back to our instruments.

ANNOUNCER.—O.K., Sam.

PORTLAND.—Gosh, I'm glad that's settled, Mr. Allen.

VON ZELL.—Yes, Fred. Now we're all one big happy family again.

ALLEN.—Why, I go through this every Wednesday. I turned down a job in Hollywood this week. . . . The Hardy Family wants to adopt a boy. I could have had it.

PORTLAND.—You wouldn't leave radio, would you, Mr. Allen?

ALLEN.—Why wouldn't I? My own band picketing me . . . Benny picking on me last Sunday . . . after I invited him to dinner. . . .

PORTLAND.—Do you really have laundry hanging up in your dining room, Mr. Allen?

ALLEN.—Laundry? I had a moving picture sheet hanging back of the table.

VON ZELL.—What for, Fred?

ALLEN.—I was going to show Benny his new picture. I knew he'd lose his appetite. For dinner I'd only serve coffee. . . .

PORTLAND.—Did you ever have dinner at Jack's house, Mr. Allen?

ALLEN.—And what a dinner! It looked like something he took away from a Boy Scout. When the flies saw how little was on the table, they started wiping their feet on the plates to help out.

VON ZELL.—What did Jack serve, Fred?

ALLEN.—The appetizer was filet of anchovy.

VON ZELL.—Filet of anchovy. They're pretty small, aren't they, Fred?

ALLEN.—Small? They look like damp hyphens. Benny served them with a magnifying glass and tweezers.

PORTLAND.—Did Jack have soup?

ALLEN.—Clam chowder, but the clam was out on location. It had a stand-in that night. The meat course was roast beef sliced so thin it looked like a wet glow on the plate.

VON ZELL.—What was dessert, Fred?

ALLEN.—A Good Humor man running through the house if you could catch him.

PORTLAND.—I guess Jack has changed a lot since he went to Hollywood.

ALLEN.—I'll say he's changed . . . sitting on the front steps of the Sherry-Netherlands . . . whittling all day. . . .

PORTLAND.—Is Jack really a Beverly Hill billy, Mr. Allen?

ALLEN.—I won't say he looks like a rube, but I will say that walking up Broadway he got pulled into three auctions and two dance halls.

VON ZELL.—Gosh, Jack is certainly slipping.

ALLEN.—He's holding his own financially. And how he's holding his own.

PORTLAND.—You're cheaper than Jack, aren't you, Mr. Allen?

ALLEN.—Compared to Benny I'm a conservative philanthropist. He's so tight his tongue looks like a bookmark. You didn't hear Rochester on his program Sunday night, did you?

VON ZELL.—Say, that's right, Fred. Rochester was missing.

ALLEN.—And you know why?

PORTLAND.—Why, Mr. Allen?

ALLEN.—To save one fare from Hollywood, Benny made Rochester work his way East as a porter.

VON ZELL.—What happened?

ALLEN.—Rochester found out he could make more money in tips than he could make on the program. He signed with the Pullman Company.

JOHN.—Say. Just a minute, Allen.

ALLEN.—Oh. Are you back from the Musicians' Union?

JOHN.—Yeah. Van Steeden just registered another complaint.

PORTLAND.—Did you, Peter?

PETE.—You bet. Jack Benny's a violin player. Nobody can pan a brother musician in front of me.

JOHN.—You better lay off, Allen, or the union's pullin' out every musician from Toscanini to Ben Bernie.

ALLEN.—What became of Borrah Minnevitch?

JOHN.—He pulled himself out to make room for Bernie.

PETE.—I've a good mind to pull the band out anyway.

ALLEN.—If they follow you it'll be the first time since you've been on the program.

231

PETE.—Oh, yeah? Sam!

JOHN.—O.K. And another thing, Allen. From now on Van Steeden's tellin' half the jokes on this program.

ALLEN.—And if he doesn't . . .

JOHN.—Joe . . .

ANNOUNCER.—Fred Allen's unfair. . . .

ALLEN.—That's the last straw. There's only one thing I can do. In self-defense I always resort to mental telepathy.

VON ZELL.—Not that, Fred.

ALLEN.—You saw me work with King, Harry. Van Steeden and those guys have caused me enough trouble tonight. I'm sending out some thought waves pronto. Get ready, all three of you.

PETE.—(*Barks*).

ALLEN.—Music, Portland.

PORTLAND.—One, two, boys. . . . (*Applause*)

ALLEN.—And now the Merry Macs revive an old favorite that was popular when swing was something only a hammock did. The song, "Ta Ra Ra Boom Te Ay!

MERRY MACS.—"*Ta Ra Boom.* (*Applause*)

ALLEN.—(*Ad lib thank you's*) Ladies and gentlemen . . . as we thumb our way through life, we seem to meet up with a lot of *signs* nowadays . . . the street sign, the traffic sign, and the Indian sign. There's even the *high sign* . . . and right now, I'm giving *that* to Harry Von Zell. Speak up, Harry. . . .

VON ZELL.—Well . . . I *would* like to speak up, ladies and gentlemen, about one sign that should never be neglected . . . the first sign of a cold. It's wise to get after that cold immediately with Sal Hepatica . . . because Sal Hepatica is an ideal laxative for fighting colds. But very often there are things that go along with a cold that are mighty uncomfortable. . . . You know, that stuffed-up feeling in your nose and throat . . . or a tightness in your chest muscles. Well . . . that's the time to use *Minit-Rub* . . . a new and better way to help bring quick relief. You

spell it this way . . . M-I-N-I-T-R-U-B. . . . You *use* it
this way. . . .

HOUSE.—Just squeeze a little Minit-Rub from the tube into the
palm of your hand and rub it briskly on your chest. And
right away Minit-Rub's counterirritant and pain-relieving
actions start soothing those aching muscles. At the same
time, Minit-Rub gives off effective vapors that help clear
away that aggravating, stuffed-up feeling in your nose and
throat.

So get a tube of greaseless, stainless Minit-Rub from
any druggist tomorrow. It's very inexpensive. Show your
family two modern ways to fight their colds . . . *internally*
with Sal Hepatica . . . *externally* with Minit-Rub.

MUSIC.—"*Night before Christmas.*" (*Singers and orchestra*).
(*Applause*)

ALLEN.—And now, ladies and gentlemen, the termitey Allen Art
Players. Tonight they bring you another rural court session.
It's called "Hillbilly Justice" . . . or . . . "The Judge
Refused to Open the Case until Somebody Brought Him a
Chaser." Overture, Peter!

MUSIC.—"*She'll be Comin' Round the Mountain.*" (*Hum of
voices*)

ANNOUNCER.—Rise, rubes! His Honor, Jedge Allen!

ALLEN.—Hi, rubes!

ALL.—Hi, Jedge.

SOUND.—*Gavel.*

ALLEN.—Order in the court. Put yer shoes on, ladies! Pike's
Puddle County Court is hereby open and in session. Fust
case!

ANNOUNCER.—Rubes of . . .

ALLEN.—Hold on, clerk. There's a draft in court. Whar is it?

ANNOUNCER.—There's a big hole in back of yer robe, Jedge.

ALLEN.—Ayar?

ANNOUNCER.—Ayar.

ALLEN.—Ayar is right, and it's assumin' the proportions of a lumber zephyr. I was sittin' on that sawmill case yestiddy. Musta tore my robe.

ALL.—(*Laugh*)

SOUND.—*Gavel.*

ALLEN.—Order in the court. Fust case. Taunton Caudle!

ANNOUNCER.—(*Drunk*) Right on deck, Jedge, old boy.

ALLEN.—Drunk again, hey, Taunton?

ANNOUNCER.—No. Thish is the same old bun, Jedge.

ALLEN.—And I'm a-givin' yer the same old sentence, Taunton. Thirty days.

SOUND.—*Gavel.*

ALLEN.—Next case. Happy Times Trio!

THREE BOYS.—Here, Your Honor.

ALLEN.—Charge says ye've been singin' in back yards. Disturbin' the peace.

VON ZELL.—We're workin' our way to New York, Judge.

ALLEN.—How come yer minstrelin' in alleys?

JOHN.—We're all that's left of Unit Number One, Judge.

ALLEN.—And yer singin' in back yards.

VON ZELL.—Yeah. We run outta theatres and church basements.

JOHN.—Our singin' don't disturb the peace, Judge. Honest.

ALLEN.—Court's ready to hear yer evidence. What's yer song?

VON ZELL.—"Ireland Must Be Heaven."

JOHN.—Let's go, fellers.

THREE BOYS.—(*Sing*) Ireland must be heaven, 'cause my mother came from there.

SOUND.—*Gavel.*

ALLEN.—Thirty days, boys, and don't appeal the chorus. Next case!

234

ANNOUNCER.—People of Pike's Puddle versus Titus Prouty. Charge is murder.

ALLEN.—Murder? Hot ziggetty!

ANNOUNCER.—Yep. Charge says Titus killed a vaudeville actor at Sloppy Mary's Boardin'house.

ALLEN.—Guilty, or did everythin' go black, Titus?

JOHN.—He stole my girl. Then tried to kill me, Jedge.

ALLEN.—Who was this small time Casanova?

JOHN.—Professor Snake, Jedge. Called hisself a snake charmer. I was his mongoose. . . . I'd do it all over again.

ALLEN.—Court'll hear yer say later, Titus. Stand down.

JOHN.—I'd do it all over again.

ALLEN.—It's too late fer retakes, Titus. Stand down. Fust witness.

ANNOUNCER.—Sloppy Mary.

DOUG.—Present, Jedge.

ALLEN.—Yer operatin' the boardin' house where the habeas was corpused.

DOUG.—I'm hostess and owner of Sloppy Mary's Bide a Wee Inn. Special rates to actors.

ALLEN.—What happened?

DOUG.—Well, Sunday night this dude checks in single.

ALLEN.—How'd ye sense he was a dude!

DOUG.—He was wearin' red velvet spats and a wampum watch fob.

ALLEN.—Ascot tie?

DOUG.—And a horseshoe pin. Down his vest it was rainin' Elks' teeth.

ALLEN.—He tuk yer best room, I reckin'.

DOUG.—Yep. Number seven. One bowl and two pitchers.

ALLEN.—Did he let on he was a snake manipulator?

235

DOUG.—Ayer. Said he had 20 trained snakes in the bag.

ALLEN.—Snakes alive!

DOUG.—Yep. Twenty of 'em.

ALLEN.—Lord! Twenty of 'em. . . . A man could save a lotta drinkin' jest openin' that little bag and lookin' in.

DOUG.—'Tain't fer me to say, Jedge.

ALLEN.—No, 'tain't. Now, what about the murder?

DOUG.—It was jealousy, Jedge. Emmy Suggs, the schoolmarm, is my prize boarder. She was Titus' intended.

ALLEN.—The dude started pitchin' woo at Emmy, eh?

DOUG.—He was pitchin', and Emmy was catchin'. Titus seen he was losin' his patootie, so he plugged the dude.

ALLEN.—That's all ye know?

DOUG.—All I know is I'm stuck with a body, a bill, and 20 trained snakes.

ALLEN.—Snakes still at yer boardinghouse, eh?

DOUG.—Yep. I'm holdin' 'em till their bill is paid. I got 'em all knotted into a reptile daisy chain.

ALLEN.—Mighty slick.

DOUG.—Ef ye need any venom, gimme a call, Jedge.

ALLEN.—Sure will. Stand down, Mary. (*Gavel.*) Next witness, Sheriff.

ANNOUNCER.—Emmy Suggs, the schoolmarm!

JOHN.—I'd do it all over agin, Jedge.

SOUND.—*Gavel.*

ALLEN.—Order in the court. We don't want no double feature killin' Titus. Next thing we know court'll be havin' Blackstone Bingo . . . (*laughs*) . . . Blackstone Bingo. I'll have to pull that on the Ozark Bar Association. Ha! Ha! (*Gavel*) Order in the court. And that goes fer me, too, Emmy Suggs.

MIN.—Present.

ALLEN.—What do you know about the prisoner at the bar?

MIN.—At the bar he kin hold his licker better'n you kin, Jedge.

ALLEN.—Court ain't here to brag, Trull.

MIN.—I seen you so full yer false teeth was treadin' licker to stay in.

ALLEN.—The court ain't on trial, Emmy. It's Titus. You and him was weldin' jowls on occasion.

MIN.—Yep. Titus has been sweet-talkin' me 15 years, Jedge. I gave him the best years of my life.

ALLEN.—What's he give you?

MIN.—A receipt.

ALLEN.—Wal, when did the demised dude rear his pretty head?

MIN.—I fell in love with him fust night at the dinner table, Jedge.

ALLEN.—His fancy manners catched yer eye, eh?

MIN.—Yep. We was both reachin' for the potatoes. His hand closed over mine on the same potato.

ALLEN.—What follered?

MIN.—I reddened. And he withdrew.

ALLEN.—Mighty polite.

MIN.—He was polite all through dinner. Always tippin' his hat 'fore passin' anuthin'.

ALLEN.—Jest like Emily Post says.

MIN.—He was jest reekin' with manners, Jedge. Hidin' his prune stones in the gravy. Puttin' his peas in his celery and rollin' them down into his mouth.

ALLEN.—That's ring-tail eatin', sure enough.

MIN.—When the coffee come, he didn't blow on it, Jedge.

ALLEN.—No?

MIN.—Not him. He whipped a little fan out of his pocket and waved it over the coffee. He carried a fan jest fer his coffee. That's savoy fairy, Jedge.

ALLEN.—Watch yer pixy talk, Emmy. When did you two start talkin'?

MIN.—He borrowed my toothpick after dinner. That broke the ice.

ALLEN.—And he took yer to the show.

MIN.—Every evenin' I was down to the Bijou watchin' his snake act.

ALLEN.—Professor Snake reciprocate this affection?

MIN.—He sure did. Friday night, after the show, six snakes come a-wigglin' into my room to spell out, "I love you." Them snakes never thought of that. It was him.

ALLEN.—Weren't yer boy friend, Titus, jealous?

MIN.—Titus was in a swivet, Jedge.

ALLEN.—When did the fighting start?

MIN.—Saturday night. I was in the sink bathin'. Titus and the Dude had words at the dinner table. Next thing I know, Titus had shot the dude.

JOHN.—(*Off*) I'd do it all over again, Jedge.

SOUND.—*Gavel.*

ALLEN.—Order in the court, Titus. Quit that repeatin', Lord! You musta been weaned on bicarbonate. Who broke the news to ye 'bout the killin', Emmy?

MIN.—Old Lucius Bilk. Lucius is Sloppy Mary's star boarder. Sits to the head of the table.

ALLEN.—Lucius Bilk here in court?

ANNOUNCER.—(*As old man*) I seen the whole thing, Jedge.

ALLEN.—How did it start, Lucius?

ANNOUNCER.—Wal, Saturday night all us boarders was eating dinner. The Saturday special.

ALLEN.—What's that?

ANNOUNCER.—Ozark squab.

ALLEN.—Ozark squab?

ANNOUNCER.—It's roast owl, Jedge. Dessert was April tapioca.

ALLEN.—What's April tapioca?

ANNOUNCER.—It's hailstones cooked into a puddin'.

ALLEN.—Jelled rain's mighty temptin'. But what about the murder?

ANNOUNCER.—Wal. The dude comes walkin' in late. Titus looks up and says, nastylike, "Wal, effen it ain't the Major Bowes of Snakes."

ALLEN.—The dude come back?

ANNOUNCER.—Quick's a flash. He says, "Snakes ain't as low as some folks."

ALLEN.—That teched off the fracas, eh?

ANNOUNCER.—Titus up and crowned the dude with the roast owl. Dressin' and all. Lord, his dickey front looked like it broke out with gravy measles.

ALLEN.—Then . . .

ANNOUNCER.—The dude picks up the lettuce and gives Titus a mayonnaise facial. Titus crowns the dude with a stewed tomater beret. Then the dude picks up the tureen and bean soups Titus from head to foot.

ALLEN.—Then what happened?

ANNOUNCER.—Then they started fightin'.

ALLEN.—Up to this time it was talkin'.

ANNOUNCER.—Lord! The air was so thick with calories I inhaled and gained 2 pounds.

ALLEN.—You try to break up this menu mayhem, Lucius?

ANNOUNCER.—No, Jedge. I was under the table gummin' the roast owl.

ALLEN.—And during the fracas the fatal shot was fired?

ANNOUNCER.—Yessuh. I got short arms, Jedge. 'Twas the fust time in 20 years I got white meat at the table.

JOHN.—(*Off*) I'd do it all over again, Jedge.

SOUND.—*Gavel.*

ALLEN.—Order in the court, Titus. You kin stand down, Lucius.

ANNOUNCER.—Thank ye, Jedge. (*Hiccups*) Lord, that owl's hootin' agin.

SOUND.—*Gavel.*

ALLEN.—The defendant, Titus Prouty, take the stand.

JOHN.—I'd do it all over again, Jedge.

ALLEN.—I know, Titus. Ye can't make a serial outta this murder, Titus. Yer here to tell why ye done it the fust time.

JOHN.—Wal, after me and the dude run outta food, the rowin' died down.

ALLEN.—Ye shake hands.

JOHN.—No. I went upstairs to clean up.

ALLEN.—You musta looked like a walkin' table dotey.

JOHN.—I was a mess, Jedge. My face looked like a blue plate special with a nose.

ALLEN.—When'd ye see the dude again?

JOHN.—Sloppy Mary, the hostess, comes up and says, "Professor Snake wants to see ye in his room, Titus."

ALLEN.—Ye suspicioned a trap, eh?

JOHN.—That's jest what it was, Jedge. Lucky I took my shotgun with me.

ALLEN.—Ye went to the dude's room?

JOHN.—I opened the door and says, "Come on, Dude, ef yer a buzzard I'm yer carrion."

ALLEN.—What'd he say to that?

JOHN.—He jest stood there fondlin' one of his snakes. It musta been a black rattler.

ALLEN.—It was rattlin', eh?

JOHN.—Like all git out. The dude says, "Titus, let's let bygones be bygones." "Fust," I says, "put down that rattlesnake."

ALLEN.—What'd he say to that?

JOHN.—He says, "This won't hurt ye, Titus."

ALLEN.—Ayar.

JOHN.—With that he jabs that rattlin' viper smack-dab into my face, Jedge.

ALLEN.—And that's when ye blazed away.

JOHN.—It was him or me, Jedge. He was aimin' to have that rattler poison me.

ALLEN.—The defunct rattler here in court, clerk?

ANNOUNCER.—Yep. Laid out in this long box, Jedge. Exhibit A.

ALLEN.—Lord! He's deader'n a shad.

ANNOUNCER.—Don't tech it, Jedge.

ALLEN.—Orneriest lookin' rattler. . . . All head and skinniest body' I ever seed.

JOHN.—Might be some northern snake, Jedge.

SOUND.—*Gavel.*

ALLEN.—Anybody here in court from up North Little Rock way? Any stranger in court?

VON ZELL.—(*Off*) I'm from New York, Jedge.

ALLEN.—Step to the bar, stranger. Can you identify this snake?

VON ZELL.—I'll take a look.

ALLEN.—Don't tech the viper. Ef rigor memphis sets in he'll coil yer to death.

VON ZELL.—(*Laughs*) Well, if this isn't rich.

ALLEN.—Ain't nothin' funny bout a rattlesnake.

VON ZELL.—A rattlesnake. Ha. Ha.

ALLEN.—Watcha laffin' about, stranger?

VON ZELL.—This isn't a snake.

ALLEN.—No.?

ANNOUNCER.—It's an electric razor on a cord.

ALLEN.—Well, fig dig ma pig. . . . Electric razor. What's that?

VON ZELL.—It's for shaving. Cutting your whiskers.

ALLEN.—Ain't nothin' sprouts on a man's face ye can't git off with a sickle, dude.

VON ZELL.—This is a new invention, Judge. If I can find a socket I'll show you how it works. Here's one on your desk here.

ALLEN.—Them two little holes. I thought them was termite footprints.

VON ZELL.—Watch. I'll plug the razor in. There!

SOUND.—*Electric razor buzzes.*

ALLEN.—Hold on! Git that sarpint away!

JOHN.—She's come to life again. I'll mow her down.

SOUND.—*Two shots . . . razor stops.*

ALLEN.—Nice goin', Titus. The gol-dane viper nearly had me.

JOHN.—Plugged him right atween the teeth.

ALLEN.—Ye finally got to do it all over agin?

JOHN.—It was self-defense agin, Jedge.

ALLEN.—Sure was. And the court's dismissing yer murder charge, Titus. It was justifiable hamicide.

JOHN.—It's homocide, ain't it, Jedge?

ALLEN.—Professor Snake was an actor, Titus. And killin' an actor is hamicide every time. (*Gavel*) Court's adjourned! (*Applause*)

MUSIC.—"*Broadway Rhythm.*"

ALLEN.—Ladies and gentlemen . . . before we salute a few snickers from next week's cavalcade of comedy . . . we hope . . . I would like to thank everyone whose medicine cabinet holds our famous products. Because *you* are making all of our Wednesdays together possible by your friendly and faithful *use* of

VON ZELL.—Ipana Toothpaste . . . for the smile of beauty . . . Sal Hepatica . . . for the smile of health . . . Ipana . . . Sal Hepatica.

ALLEN.—Thank you, Harry. And don't forget, ladies and gentlemen, next Wednesday evening Town Hall Tonight brings you more quiz questions.

MIN.—Fred Allen's teeth. True or false?

JOHN.—Get the low-down on Allen's set on your set next Wednesday.

MUSIC.—*Chord.*

ALLEN.—Songs from your Flop Parade!

ANNOUNCER.—(*Sings*) Till We Beet Again.

ALLEN.—Beet? It's meet again, isn't it?

ANNOUNCER.—I'm a vegetarian.

ALLEN.—Oh.

MUSIC.—*Chord.*

ALLEN.—People you didn't expect to meet!

VON ZELL.—A professional Santa Claus. Hang your stockings up on your radio, folks. If you want to put your foot in it, tune in next Wednesday.

MUSIC.—*Chord.*

ALLEN.—And music!

MUSIC.—"*Smile Darn Yer, Smile.*"

BEST HORROR SHOW

The Lighthouse Keepers

by PAUL CLOQUEMIN

~~~~~~

A LL FORMS of entertainment, not excluding opera and the dance, will always have room for the shivery, the macabre, the horrible. Radio has at one time or another exploited most of the accepted libraries of good horror and has brought to its audiences a considerable number of not very literary offerings of its own creation. Some of these have been trash, and some have been very exciting fun indeed. The hardy perennial of these thrillers is the NBC series called Lights Out. After five years it is still plucking out eyes, reviving corpses, twisting old ladies' heads off, and branding beautiful coeds every Wednesday night at 12:30. Its themes range from cannibalism to necrophilia and to subjects even less roly-poly than these. In its first two years of production it delivered many outstanding shows, but with the passing of its two best authors—one (Willis Cooper) to Hollywood, and the other (Arch Oboler) to radio free-lance writing—the series has not been able to recapture the thumbscrew fancy of its earlier work. It is still a good show, and it commands a tremendous audience; but it is not so horrible as it used to be.

At CBS, competitive interest in NBC's stranglehold on the horror market took shape in a series called Terror by Night. This failed and was withdrawn from the air after twenty-six weeks. But during this period the unique Grand Guignol library of horror plays was carefully explored. One hundred and seventy of the original French versions of these plays were purchased and translated. The great majority of them turned out to be unsuitable for air performance because of their themes, but three or four— classics in their stage versions—were highly workable. One of these, "The Lighthouse Keepers," was adapted for radio

244

by the continuity staff and performed by the Columbia Workshop on September 12, 1938. It is remembered as one of the Workshop's most intense and gripping thrillers of their three years of production. It was Columbia's first experience with the half-hour two-character drama and perhaps the only example in the history of the industry thus far.

With only two characters to work with, the play would seem to have every chance to go flat before its dramatic finish. But the three major ingredients of good horror—pacing, suspense, and atmosphere—appear in "The Lighthouse Keepers" to a degree unrivaled by anything produced in this division.

The Lighthouse Keepers*

SETTING.—The living quarters of the Maudit Lighthouse, 6 miles off the west coast of Brittany. The room is circular and is located just below the lantern floor of the lighthouse. It is 150 feet above the sea. It is roughly furnished. The walls are hung with rope coils, life preservers, signal flags, and lanterns. On stage are two couches, two chairs, a small oil stove, and a stool. Stage right is a control box . . . the electric switches for turning on and off the mechanism by which the light is revolved. The light itself burns oil, but its revolutions are driven by electric motors, and its flame is ignited by electric spark. It is late afternoon in March.

CAST.—Brehan, aged fifty-five, the keeper. Yvon, aged twenty-five, his son and his assistant.

SOUND.—*Off mike, sound of high wind, muffled, as if being heard from inside . . . door opens . . . wind comes up strong . . . door slams hard and wind down again as before.*

BREHAN.—Well, Yvon, you all finished down below?

VYON.—Yes, all finished. I filled both the reservoirs. Pumped 500 gallons into the reserve tank, too.

BREHAN.—You were quick. You must have hurried a bit.

YVON.—I wanted to get through.

BREHAN.—You never get through work on a lighthouse.

YVON.—I don't mind working around the tanks or even around the lenses . . . but, Mon Dieu, going from one place to another I could hardly get up the staircase. It's 200 steps, you know.

BREHAN.—Two hundred and six, mon fils. I've only kept this light for 20 years. You ought to be glad they didn't build the thing any higher.

YVON.—A 150 feet in the air is high enough for me. The wind outside is so strong it nearly blew me off the outside stairs.

BREHAN.—That's nothing. Nowadays it isn't so bad . . . keeping a light. Nowadays electricity does most of the work. When I first came out here I had to pump the oil up here with a hand pump.

YVON.—There's still plenty of work all the same.

BREHAN.—There's enough. But it's easier. I've trimmed all the wicks and polished the reflectors, and all I have to do is push the electric button . . . so . . .

SOUND.—*Electric motor hum . . . metallic grind of turntable as light revolves.*

BREHAN.—She's on. One little click of a switch and every wick burning and the whole mechanism running easy as a clock.

VYON.—Yes, it's simple enough. But it takes a lot of tending. . . . Isn't it too early to put the light on?

BREHAN.—Yes. I was just giving it a test. That new bearing. I always give her a test half an hour before lighting time . . . if there's been any change in the equipment. I'll turn it off now.

SOUND.—*Switch clicks . . . motor out.*

BREHAN.—You can never take a chance . . . not when other people depend on you.

YVON.—What's that? Oh, yes, I suppose so.

SOUND.—*Wind up slightly . . . then down.*

BREHAN.—What a night. And more wind to come, too, if I know anything.

YVON.—You're right. It'll probably be a long night. (*Yawns*) I'm tired. I'm awfully tired.

BREHAN.—Already? But we haven't been out here more than 6 hours. . . . But then . . . a whole month ashore . . . it goes by in a hurry. Makes one a little soft, too, n'est-ce pas?

YVON.—(*Not hearing*). What? What did you say?

BREHAN.—I say life ashore . . . well, one has a good time, and the hard thing about coming back to the Maudit is getting used to seeing no one, being alone, climbing stairs, and being alone, absolutely alone.

YVON.—Yes, that's it. We're so terribly alone. Cut off from civilization by 6 miles of open sea. If we only had a telephone even, or . . .

SOUND.—*Wind up with sudden violence, obliterating last line of Yvon's . . . wind down.*

BREHAN.—Listen to that. Screaming like a woman. Sometimes it sounds almost musical, too. Have you noticed that?

YVON.—Musical. I'd give it another word. I don't like it.

BREHAN.—Well, one has to call it something. One . . . one has to talk. Sometimes when there isn't anything to do, I talk to the sea gulls, or I talk to the water. One must talk. In a lighthouse one talks to oneself or to the rope on the flag-staff or maybe to the barometer. But that's all right. . . . You are beginning to do it. It makes the loneliness . . . it makes it less lonely.

YVON.—I don't talk to myself.

BREHAN.—Of course you do. I hear your conversations . . . the pictures in your head that come out in words. . . .

YVON.—(*Grudging*) Well, maybe . . . but it's silly . . . like women in an old ladies' home somewhere.

BREHAN.—It isn't silly. You mustn't think about it as silly.

SOUND.—*Wind up . . . short screaming gust . . . then down as before.*

BREHAN.—High wind and heavy rain.

YVON.—It's getting worse . . . seems to emphasize the loneli-ness.

BREHAN.—That's because you've just been ashore. By and by your philosophies will grow to accommodate these little . . . these phases.

YVON.—I . . . I suppose they will. But it's so *wild*, it's so ugly here. Maudit is on a cruel crag all right.

BREHAN.—Of course it's a cruel crag. That's why there's a light on it.

YVON.—And that's why we're on it.

BREHAN.—Well, maybe. Maudit is on the wildest piece of rock on the coast of Brittany. That's what one of the inspectors told me, and when those fellows say wild, they mean it.

SOUND.—*Wind up and down suddenly.*

BREHAN.—More wind. . . . (*Pause*)

YVON.—Father . . .

BREHAN.—H'm?

YVON.—Father, you said it took about 5 years to be a good lighthouse keeper. I . . . I suppose that in 5 years you see about everything that could possibly happen in a place like this.

BREHAN.—Oui. I have seen it. I've seen it all.

YVON.—Everything?

BREHAN.—Everything but the lighthouse topple into the sea. I've seen wrecks and drownings and men swimming in the surf. I've seen the lights fail; seen a time when I had to burn blankets and mattresses soaked in oil. Yes, I've seen a good deal, mon enfant.

YVON.—Have you ever been in a lighthouse when your partner . . . when your assistant keeper . . . when he . . . I mean . . .

BREHAN.—When he what?

YVON.—When he died?

BREHAN.—Yvon. Don't say such a thing.

YVON.—I . . . I didn't mean anything by it. I just wondered if . . .

BREHAN.—That's a frightful thing to think. To die without a priest. It's unthinkable. That's no way for poor Christians to go (*rebuke*), and it is not anything to be talking about either.

YVON.—Well, I . . . I just said it. It just seemed to . . . sort of . . . occur to me.

BREHAN.—Non, non, mon fils. Don't ever say such a thing. Those things don't happen. God knows we are here to protect others. Surely we can expect that much protection in return.

YVON.—Yes . . . I hope . . . I mean (*voice down . . . significant*). . . . But wouldn't it be a dreadful thing?

BREHAN.—(*Impatiently*) What's the matter with you anyhow? I haven't seen you like this since we lost Pierre. . . .

YVON.—It doesn't seem like 3 years. If only he could have lived.

BREHAN.—Yes. If only. That's the way with life. Things happen that hurt us, and the rest of us sit around and say, if only they hadn't happened. But they *do* happen. . . .

YVON.—Mother could never console herself over the loss of Pierre. Just the other day I found her rereading the letter she got from the master of Pierre's ship.

BREHAN.—Yes, that letter. I practically know it by heart. It went like this: "During a severe southeast blow, I ordered a change in our course and a reefing of the fore-tops'l. Your son was the first to spring into the rigging. Halfway up the ratlines his foot slipped, and he fell, immediately disappearing in the sea."

YVON.—Oh, well, maybe my lot would have been no better. . . . Even so, Pierre's life was a free life . . . a life packed with excitement, with limitless horizons, bright days, and sudden dangers. Nothing like it is here . . . all caged up in a stone tower.

BREHAN.—Danger, mon fils, is possibly a good thing. But duty . . . duty is the finest thing in the world. Don't ever forget that.

YVON.—All the same, it's hard to be locked up this way. (*Sharply*) A man's nerves aren't supposed to stand anything like this.

BREHAN.—Nonsense. For 30 days out here we can be proud of ourselves . . . what we do for commerce, what we do for France . . . and what we are making out of ourselves.

YVON.—I've felt that sense of pride . . . many times. But since our return to duty this time . . . I don't know what's happened to me. (*In and out of mike as if Yvon were moving about*)

BREHAN.—That's nothing. ça passe. It will go away soon.

YVON.—Yes, it will pass. Maybe tomorrow, maybe next week. . . .

SOUND.—*Wind up strong . . . hold . . . then take down.*

YVON.—Blowing harder than ever. It's going to get real ugly.

BREHAN.—It has to be ugly some nights.

YVON.—Why does it?

BREHAN.—So we'll know how beautiful it is other nights.

YVON.—I can't accept that. It's too grim to suit me.

BREHAN.—Some day you'll accept it and be more of a man for doing so.

YVON.—That's only an opinion.

BREHAN.—Everything is only an opinion . . . or state of mind.

YVON.—No. Some things are actual.

BREHAN.—Perhaps.

SOUND.—*Off mike . . . shrill crying of sea gulls.*

BREHAN.—Listen to those sea gulls. What a racket they make.

YVON.—Yes. They feel the bad weather coming.

BREHAN.—Don't worry about the weather. And do stop walking around so. Take it easy. Take it easy.

YVON.—I can't. I have to keep moving around like this.

BREHAN.—It's from being ashore . . . all those acres of open country. You got a little case of nerves . . . a crazy sort of thing for a lighthouse keeper.

YVON.—But I can't help it, I tell you. I'm all on edge.

BREHAN.—Maybe I could guess your trouble.

YVON.—I doubt it.

BREHAN.—You don't think so? Well, how does this sound. . . . Maybe you're in love with Marie?

YVON.—Yes. How did you know that? Marie and I are going to get married. Did she say anything?

BREHAN.—(*Laughs*) Pardieu. Of course not. You told me yourself . . . with everything you didn't say. I am very glad, mon fils. A splendid girl she is, and a wise girl, too.

YVON.—Wise?

BREHAN.—Wise to marry a lighthouse keeper. She'll always know where you are nights. (*Laughs*)

YVON.—Don't joke about it, father. We are very, very much in love.

BREHAN.—I'm not joking, mon petit. I congratulate you. I am very happy. Let me give you a kiss (*kisses him twice*). There now, good luck and God bless you.

YVON.—Thank you, father.

BREHAN.—(*Pleased*) Ah, yes. A fine thing to have an honest wife. I hope you will have some strong sons, too. Some day he will come out here and keep the Maudit light like his father and grandfather, eh, Yvon? (*Laughs*)

SOUND.—*Sea gulls cry . . . and fly against glass of light tower, striking it with beaks.*

BREHAN.—Listen to those gulls again. If they don't stop banging into the glass, they'll break right through it. It wouldn't be the first time. It's probably so thick outside, they don't know where they're going. (*Going off*) Guess I'll take a little look around outside myself.

YVON.—Father.

BREHAN.—(*Off mike*) What is it?

YVON.—I wish you'd . . .

BREHAN.—(*Off*) What did you say?

YVON.—I said I wished . . . nothing . . . never mind.

BREHAN.—Well, I'll be back in a jiffy. Au 'voir.

SOUND.—*Door open . . . powerful wind up strong . . . take down as door slams.*

YVON.—(*Shouts after*) Father, father. Don't leave me alone in here. Father! Oh, my God, what has gone wrong with me. My head is whirling around like a wheel. (*Breaks off and begins to sob . . . chokes this off*) Come out of this, Yvon. Get hold of yourself. He'll be coming back any minute.

SOUND.—*Doorknob rattles, and door opens as if with difficulty . . . wind up strong and door forced shut against wind . . . wind down.*

BREHAN.—Mon Dieu. What horrible weather. I'm soaking wet. It's been 4 years since we had a blow like this. Good thing we're on a pile of rocks. (*Off*) Guess I'll get out of these oilskins . . . and maybe polish up a couple of lanterns.

SOUND.—*Rasp of heavy oilskin material as he climbs out of coat.*

BREHAN.—(*Off*) I'll begin with this one, I guess. It seems to need it most.

SOUND.—*Sound of lantern being moved off hook, its bail banging against the chimney . . . then sound of chimney being lifted by lever . . . removal of chimney . . . then sound of polishing the glass with paper . . . real kerosene lantern necessary for this effect.*

BREHAN.—(*Continuing . . . not quite so far off mike . . . lighter vein*) No, it's not so bad, really, Yvon. Makes me proud, too, in weather like this . . . to think that but for you and me . . . nobody would be safe on the coast of Brittany. (*Sounds of polishing continue and tinkle of lantern and occasional banging of handle*) And the worse the night, the more important we are. Maudit will be there. Maudit will always be there, shooting her long beam for 14 miles into the darkness. Duty, mon fils. Duty, the first thing and the last thing in every man's life, n'est-ce pas?

YVON.—(*Not hearing*) I suppose so. (*Pause*)

SOUND.—*Polishing sounds continue quietly . . . no talk for 5 seconds.*

YVON.—Father, what are you doing there anyhow?

BREHAN.—What am I doing? Why, you can see for yourself. I'm just polishing these lanterns. A good sailor is always polishing something.

YVON.—I wish you'd leave it alone.

BREHAN.—What do you mean? What for?

YVON.—I don't want to see it. It shines so much it hurts my eyes. It seems to be burning a hole into me.

BREHAN.—What the devil are you talking about?

YVON.—(*Voice rising . . . and bring Brehan into same perspective as if they were standing together*) . . . Gimme that lantern, I tell you.

BREHAN.—(*Surprised and annoyed*) Pardieu! What are you trying to do? Qu'avez-vous?

YVON.—Give it to me, I tell you!

SOUND.—*Lantern snatched from Brehan . . . bail banging against chimney . . . lantern flung . . . and it crashes, the chimney splintering . . . off mike.*

YVON.—There . . . now leave the others alone, too!

BREHAN.—You fool! What's the matter with you? Have you gone out of your head?

YVON.—(*Frightened at the absurdity of his own act*) I . . . I don't know. I don't know. I just couldn't stand . . . oh, I'm so terribly afraid of something . . . I can't tell . . .

BREHAN.—(*Scornful and angry*) Afraid!

YVON.—(*Almost going to pieces*) I'm afraid. I'm afraid. Something is stifling me. I can't stand being alone this way any more. I've had 3 years of it. I won't stand any more of it. I've got to get ashore, I tell you. I've got to get ashore *right away!*

BREHAN.—(*Trying to comprehend . . . easier*) Yvon, please try to be sensible. You're tired. You're letting this thing excite you. It's nerves. We all get them now and then. Tell you what, I'll take the first watch tonight. A good sleep will set you up.

YVON.—Sleep! If I could only sleep. If I could sleep and then wake up and see it was all just a dream I was having. . . .

BREHAN.—Don't talk that way, mon petit. Of course you'll be able to sleep. You can't afford to carry on like this, Yvon. Supposing we both went to pieces like this and a ship broke up on the rocks below. No, no, Yvon. We can't afford to have these . . . these excesses. They lead to negligence. I know. I've seen it.

YVON.—(*Faint*) I know. I'm sorry. I should control myself . . . no matter what. I think I'll go out on the tower step. Maybe if I got a little air . . .

BREHAN.—Good. That's more like it. Hang on to the rail now. The wind . . . it's hurricane velocity by now.

YVON.—(*Going off*) Yes. I will. I'll hang on.

SOUND.—*Door open . . . sudden wind squall . . . door closes against wind . . . wind screams and fades down as door shuts.*

BREHAN.—Poor boy, poor boy. Now I'll have to get a broom and sweep up this mess.

SOUND.—*Sound of broom sweeping up glass. During next monologue, speech is broken by sound of sweeping, banging of dustpan, picking up lantern, and occasional grunts, as if Brehan were leaning over from time to time and picking up things.*

BREHAN.—What a thing for him to do. And him 3 years with the light. Three for him. But 20 years for me. Twenty years. I'm almost an old man now . . . old Brehan. (*Chuckles*) Just an old man who talks to himself when he's alone. Well, old folks can talk to themselves if they want to. It's better than not talking at all.

SOUND.—*Off-mike shout, barely audible.*

BREHAN.—Eh? What was that?

SOUND.—*Wind up slightly.*

BREHAN.—I thought that was somebody calling. I guess old Brehan is beginning to stoop a little in his mind as well as his back. Hearing things that don't happen . . .

SOUND.—*Off-mike shout, more audible.*

BREHAN.—No. That was a shout. Am I getting the creeps like Yvon? Mon Dieu! (*Going off*) What could that have been?

SOUND.—*Door opens, wind up.*

BREHAN.—(*Shouting over noise of wind*) Yvon! Yvon! Are you calling? (*Voice down*) Oh, here you are. I thought I heard you shouting. Come in out of the wet.

YVON.—Yes, I shouted. I guess I did, anyhow. I don't know why. I don't seem to be . . . Oh . . .

SOUND.—*Door closes . . . wind down again.*

BREHAN.—Well, never mind that now. Here, come inside and take off your oilskin.

SOUND.—*Rasp of heavy material of oilskin as it is removed.*

BREHAN.—Why, you're trembling all over.

YVON.—Am I? I feel so hot. I feel like I was going to fall down.

BREHAN.—Maybe you've caught yourself a cold since we came out.

YVON.—Perhaps. I feel burning up . . . as if my lungs were on fire. Every breath . . . I need a drink of water, father, I'm terribly thirsty.

BREHAN.—Let me feel your head. (*Pause*) Hum, I thought so. Got a bit of fever. No, you'd better leave water alone. It'll just raise your temperature.

YVON.—But I'm dying with thirst, I tell you. Give me some water. Just a little water.

BREHAN.—*No.*

YVON.—Please do. I beg you. Only the littlest bit.

BREHAN.—Don't be a fool.

YVON.—I'm sorry. I'm afraid . . . I'm afraid there's something awful the matter with me I . . . I'm not at all myself. I feel like I was someone else, someone I didn't know. Some force seems to be moving my arms and legs, and I can hardly hear what I'm saying. . . . Please, please let me have just a bit of water. I feel I'll faint. . . .

256

BREHAN.—All right, then. Just a little, and drink it very slowly. Just sip it.

SOUND.—*Water poured out of pitcher.*

BREHAN.—Here.

YVON.—Oh, thank you . . . I . . . I . . . (*Sudden alarm*) Father, father. . . .

BREHAN.—*Comment?*

YVON.—What can it be? I'm so thirsty, but I . . . I can't drink. The sight of it, of the water in this cannister . . . horrifies me.

BREHAN.—Better leave it alone then. It's fever. You'll be able to drink later on.

YVON.—Yes, perhaps. Later on. But the sight of it makes me sick. Take it away.

BREHAN.—That's your fever. . . . Here, Yvon, come over on the couch and lie down awhile. And let me cover you up.

YVON.—No, I don't want to be covered. I'm too hot.

BREHAN.—You do what I say. There now. That's better. (*Pause*) Yvon. Why are you staring at me so?

YVON.—Listen, father . . . I have to tell you something . . . I can't keep it to myself.

BREHAN.—You tell me. Tell your father, mon enfant. What is it?

YVON.—It's about what we . . . what I . . .

BREHAN.—Go on. Don't be afraid to tell me.

YVON.—The other day . . . over at Cousin Santec's . . .

BREHAN.—Yes, at Cousin Santec's. I remember. What about it?

YVON.—Santec's dog . . . that big hunter . . .

BREHAN.—Yes, I know. A fine animal. It was too bad they had to kill him.

YVON.—(*Starts*) Had to kill. So . . . they *did* have to kill him. Had to kill him because he was mad!

BREHAN.—But that was no fault of Santec's. He was always very kind to him.

YVON.—(*Earnest . . . voice down*) Father, that dog . . . that dog bit me. That's what's the matter. (*Voice rising*) That's why I'm dying with thirst. That's why my head is whirling. I'm mad. I'm mad! I'm turning into a mad dog like the hunter! (*Sobs*)

BREHAN.—(*Terrified and incredulous*) Lie down. Lie down. It can't be . . . mon fils . . . it's impossible!

YVON.—(*Voice dead*) It has already happened. Remember Guirec, the butcher? When he died? He had this fever and a thirst he couldn't bear. He couldn't drink either . . . not a drop. (*Voice beginning to rise*) I was there. I saw him. That means . . . it means that it's all over . . . when you can't drink. I'm mad. I feel the madness growing in my mouth . . . my eyes staring . . . (*Voice up suddenly*) I'm going to die like Guirec . . . howling and snarling like a mad dog. (*Sobs*)

BREHAN.—No, no, for God's sake!

YVON.—Yes, I am. It can't be anything else. It's been coming on for 2 days. I've been too terrified to say anything. . . .

BREHAN.—Yvon, Yvon, mon petit, mon cher.

YVON.—Oh, father, I can't die like this. Not alone. Not here. I've got to get ashore. (*Screams*) I tell you I've got to get ashore!

BREHAN.—Yes, yes! I'll save you. Yvon, mon cher, mon cher!

YVON.—Oh, I want to live! More than anything! I *must* live! I've *got* to live!

BREHAN.—Yes, yes, Yvon! You're going to live. You'll be all right. This will pass. It's . . . it's your fever climbing.

YVON.—Do you think so?

BREHAN.—Yes, yes, I think so. Mon Dieu. Of course I think so.

YVON.—(*Voice down*) Father, what would it be like. . . . What would you do (*quick*) if I *did* die? Would you throw me into the sea?

BREHAN.—(*Startled*) Yvon, you mustn't say that. It isn't true. It isn't going to be true. . . . You . . .

YVON.—(*Breaking in over*) That's why I ran out on the tower step. That's why you heard me screaming! I . . . I wanted to throw myself into the sea. I wanted to so you wouldn't have to.

BREHAN.—My God, my God! Yvon. Have pity. You can't know what you're saying.

YVON.—(*Dead voice*) I know what I'm saying.

BREHAN.—Yvon, I'll take care of you. I promise. (*Idea suddenly*) I'll launch the dory and row ashore and come back here with a doctor!

YVON.—You know you can't do that. . . . You can't row 6 miles in this weather. You could never get the boat in the water!

BREHAN.—(*Going off mike*) All the same I'm going. It's the only thing.

YVON.—No, no, no! Don't do that! You'll never come back! Don't leave me alone.

BREHAN.—(*Coming back in slow*) All right. I'll stay with you then. (*Trying to be soothing*) Yvon, soyez tranquille. You must be quiet now. (*Going off mike again*) I just want you to be calm . . . just calm for a little while . . . while I . . . I know what I will do. . . .

SOUND.—*Short pause here . . . 2 seconds . . . then sound of rope being hauled through pulley . . . pulley squeak way off mike.*

YVON.—What are you doing?

BREHAN.—(*Sound continues*) I'm hoisting the distress flag. They'll see it the first thing in the morning. They'll send out . . .

YVON.—In this weather! No sailor alive could reach us. And no boat either.

BREHAN.—Perhaps the bad weather won't hold. Perhaps God will perform some miracle.

YVON.—(*Sarcastic*) God.

BREHAN.—Don't blaspheme that way, Yvon. God is a just God.

SOUND.—*Sound of pulley wheel out.*

BREHAN.—There. It's flying now. . . . No, no, Yvon . . . God is good. (*Feeling that he has to remind God of this*) He *must* be! The 10 years I spent in the Coast Guard! Risking my life a thousand times! He owes me this much that you may live in exchange for the risks I have taken for others! He must! He must! He will! I know he will! . . . You wait and see . . . in the morning . . . yes, the first thing in the morning.

YVON.—(*Not impressed*) Yes, perhaps. . . . How my head swims! How hot I feel! Oh, God, I'm sick . . . I'm sick. . . . I'm sick. . . . I feel something terrible . . . something coming . . . coming soon. (*Delirium*) Maman! . . . Maman!

BREHAN.—Mon pauvre . . . mon pauvre . . . Yvon, please, lie still.

YVON.—(*Menacing*) Keep away from me. Get away. I'm going out of my head. I'm going mad! Going mad! (*Inhales sharply through his teeth*)

BREHAN.—(*Frightened*) Mon Dieu! There's foam on your face.

YVON.—Get away, I tell ya. Get away. I can't bear you near me. If you don't get away . . . I'll . . . I'll . . . (*Threat rises*) Keep away! Keep away from me!

BREHAN.—Yvon! Yvon!

YVON.—(*Beginning to scream at him*) I tell you to get away! (*Yvon begins to snarl . . . bring this in close . . . Brehan screams . . . sound of struggle*)

BREHAN.—What are you doing! Yvon! Let go of me! Let me go! (*Snarls continue*) I'll . . . I'll have to choke you, Yvon! (*Snarling suddenly gives way to choking and gasping sound . . . strangulation continues but grows weaker and weaker . . . Brehan pants with exertion . . . choking sounds out entirely . . . nothing is heard but Brehan's breathing . . . then sound of body fall*)

BREHAN.—My son! I've killed him! I'VE KILLED HIM! (*Brehan bursts into sobs. He weeps steadily for several seconds*

. . . over the sound of his weeping is gradually superimposed sound of wind rising . . . this comes up strong and obliterates weeping . . . wind rises to sudden shriek . . . then down slightly) Curse you! Curse your weather and your wind. Curse every black wave in your ocean's body! You've done this! You've taken my last son! Because I am here to snatch away your victims, *that's* why you've taken revenge! I curse the pitch-black spittle in your evil mouth. I hate you! I loathe you! I DESPISE YOU! (*Breaks off quickly and falls into convulsive sobs . . . these recede slowly*)

SOUND.—*Far off mike the whistle of a ship is almost indistinguishable against the storm . . . sobbing continues quietly . . . whistle is heard again . . . more distinctly.*

BREHAN.—(*Rousing . . . only half comprehending . . . in a whisper*) What's that! A ship! My light. I haven't put my light on!

SOUND.—*Ship's whistle closer.*

BREHAN.—She'll break up! She'll strike and break up. (*The full significance of this begins to take hold of him . . . begins to laugh slightly*) Let 'er smash. Let 'er rip 'er bottoms out. (*Laughs hysterically*) I'll never put this light on. Never! Never! Never! Nobody ever came to help me. (*Laughs again*)

SOUND.—*Whistle closer.*

BREHAN.—(*Suddenly stops laughing . . . voice goes down very tender*) NO . . . nobody ever came. I'm going to stay with Yvon. My little Yvon. Mon pauvre cher . . . (*His tenderness becomes the enfeebled whimpering of an old man*) Yes, Yvon . . . I'm going to stay with you, mon petit. Old Brehan is going to stay with you. . . .

SOUND.—*Whistle again . . . close by.*

BREHAN.—(*Startled*) Mon Dieu! She's almost on us! (*Hesitant . . . beginning to take courage*) I . . . I can't do this! I'm a lighthouse keeper!

SOUND.—*Whistle very close in.*

BREHAN.—(*The active man again*) All right! All right! I'm coming! Where's the switch now! Where is it, where is it? Here! Come on now! Light!

SOUND.—*Click of switch . . . sound of mechanism . . . metallic grind of turntable.*

BREHAN.—There it is! That did it! Yes, she sees it already. She's veering away.

SOUND.—*Three short quick blasts of whistle . . . not quite so close as before.*

BREHAN.—So . . . you salute me, eh? You say thank you. All right. All right. Old Behan says you're welcome. (*Sighs*) I've done everything I could. . . . (*Pause*) Now . . . I wonder what I should do about Yvon. . . . (*Pause . . . suddenly startled*) Mon Dieu . . . my arm! It's bleeding! I wonder . . . I wonder if Yvon has bitten *me!*

SOUND.—*Slow rise of wind . . . up to peak of sound load . . . sea gulls cry . . . slow fade . . . down and out on wind.*

The Story of John Milton

by HELEN WALPOLE *and* MARGARET LEAF

From ADVENTURE IN READING

NEW DISCOVERIES are the delight of any editor. This one was the privilege of Lewis Titterton, Script Editor for NBC. One day Welbourn Kelley, one of the senior writers of the Script Division at NBC, came in with a manuscript that he said had been written by a young and talented actress, Helen Walpole, in collaboration with Margaret Leaf, the wife of the creator of Ferdinand the Bull; that he had read it and thought it unusually good. Others promptly read the manuscript, which bore the general title, "Adventure in Reading," and were so impressed that it seemed that an approach to the wealth of interest latent in literature based less upon talks about authors and books or dramatization of scenes from books and rather upon an interpretation of a book through showing how it sprang from the events of an author's life might prove both entertaining and informing.

Lewis Titterton, manager of NBC's Script Division, started the series for a preliminary trial on April 18, 1938, with a study of Mark Twain. By complete contrast the second broadcast dealt with Raymond Ditmars, the curator of mammals and reptiles of the New York Zoological Park. Six broadcasts were given that season. So successful was the series that it was started again on October 17, and when its autumn and spring season was drawing to a close it was selected unanimously by the staff of the Educational Department as one of the two programs that should by all means be continued through the summer and into the next academic year.

This summer a variation was made from the pattern of the program as it was developed during its first year. The works and lives of contemporary authors are being used during certain weeks with the definite intention of showing that literature with a capital L does not necessarily wear the long white beard of the past but can be and is created before our very eyes by those whom we might meet on the street. An example of this is Elsie Singmaster's "Rifles for Washington," which illustrates sound but exciting writing on an historical subject by a contemporary author. The piece on John Milton has been chosen for this anthology for the reason that it is invariably this sort of subject upon which educators commit their greatest violence.

For the past hundred and fifty years the usual conception of John Milton in the imagination of America's school children has been a misty mezzotint of a blind man sitting in a dark room dictating "Paradise Lost" to his bored but dutiful daughters. That Milton was one of the most fearless and most revolutionary thinkers of his century few youngsters have ever been permitted to know. The script reprinted here is neither comprehensive nor literary. It should not be. Its value lies entirely in its approach and treatment. It gives the listener a flavor of the man and his times and in so doing replaces the usual stuffiness of biographical investigation by lively curiosities rarely encountered in the classroom.

The broadcast was heard over NBC's Blue Network on the afternoon of January 23, 1939.

The Story of John Milton*

NARRATOR.—The National Broadcasting Company brings you Adventure in Reading, by Helen Walpole and Margaret Leaf. This is another in the series of dramatized episodes in the lives of the men and women who . . . in their books . . . told some of the world's most thrilling and exciting stories.

MUSIC.

John Milton, called the great voice of England, was born in London, December the ninth, 1608, 5 years after Queen Elizabeth's death. From childhood he was destined for the study of literature. His father engaged the best tutors for his early training. At the age of sixteen he entered Christ's College, Cambridge, and spent 7 years there. It was an eventful period . . . that through which he lived . . . the merry England of good Queen Bess was passing . . . but changes in people and manners seldom come easily, and the Stuart kings felt so little the temperature of their times that they themselves finally became the target of the disorder and discontent. But when our story opens . . . Charles the First is still feasting in Whitehall. . . . Two young men are in the garden of the Milton home in Horton, Buckinghamshire . . . talking. One is Charles Diodati, Milton's closest friend, and the other . . .

CHARLES.—Ay, John Milton, you've argued me down on every point.

MILTON.—(*Laughs*) I have been talking at length this afternoon. We "tired the sun with talking and sent him down the sky." . . . Look.

CHARLES.—Yes. (*Pause*) How long, John, can your restless spirit spend itself in this quiet countryside?

MILTON.—I've had days here of the only perfect contentment I've ever known. I'm a hermit at heart. I could live in a cell with my books and my music.

* Copyright, 1939, by the National Broadcasting Company, Inc.

CHARLES.—Yes, you could . . . but you shan't if your friends have any influence with you.

MILTON.—Now that we're finished with the university . . . I feel that I can begin my real work. I want to absorb all the learning of all the ages!

CHARLES.—(*With friendly amusement*) Well, as you can read Greek, Latin, Hebrew, and Italian . . . I should think you'll be able to do that.

MILTON.—I know at school they said I had no sense of humor. . . .

CHARLES.—But why are you saying all this?

MILTON.—Oh, probably because you are my greatest friend, I want . . . what . . . not self-justification . . . no, not that. . . .

CHARLES.—What then?

MILTON.—To talk myself out . . . to say aloud some of the things I believe . . . to a trusted friend. . . .

CHARLES.—I can tell you that one reason you were . . . well . . . laughed at . . . if you *will* have it so . . . is because you . . . in school . . . made your star one of learning. . . . It's . . . well . . . it's more than our healthy, unambitious contemporaries can endure.

MILTON.—It's hard to understand . . . if I have a star, as you call it . . . and I do believe I have . . . it's not necessarily a *serious* star. I love gaiety . . .

CHARLES.—Your "L'Allegro" is proof of that. "L'Allegro" and "Il Penseroso." The two sides of your nature, John.

MILTON.—I believe so firmly in my own destiny that I know I must walk alone . . . work alone.

CHARLES.—What do you think your destiny to be?

MILTON.—I would like to know . . . the heartbeats of all nations. I would like to be in a high place and yet never leave a humility of spirit. . . . It's hard to speak of what's deepest inside us . . . isn't it?

CHARLES.—Yes.

MILTON.—I would like to dedicate myself . . . to England . . . to God . . . and to the truth in myself. That's all.

CHARLES.—You can do . . . all that.

MILTON.—But now . . . let's leave this seriousness. . . . There're only a few times in one's life when one talks as we have today. The moment has passed. Tell me, what must I do with Harry Lawes' suggestion for the masque?

CHARLES.—Lawes is a splendid musician. I'm glad you're doing another masque with him.

MILTON.—Yes, the success of "The Arcadians" spurs us to another one. You see, the difficulties with my Comus idea are that it's to be written for the Earl of Bridgewater. You remember when his daughter, the Lady Alice, was lost in Heywood forest . . .

CHARLES.—Are you going to use that?

MILTON.—I was thinking of it. I'm limited, as is usually the case in these things. I can only use so many characters. There must be parts in it for the Earl's children. . . . In other words, I'm facing a playwright's problem . . . of writing to order for a set company of actors.

CHARLES.—Will it be an elaborate production?

MILTON.—Not so elaborate, as masques go. . . . Think of the ones in the Queen's day.

CHARLES.—Scandals to the treasury!

MILTON.—Yes.

CHARLES.—Well, I'm glad you are doing it. . . . It's *active.* I was becoming worried about your living in the country and meditating on the past. This will prove better for you than working on the legends of King Arthur.

MILTON.—Oh, I haven't given up any of my plans. . . . My notebook is filled to overflowing. . . . I would like to have the lives of ten men. Then . . . then I might . . .

CHARLES.—John . . . John . . .

MILTON.—You're right. I've talked enough. It's now quite dark. . . . Shall we go in?

MUSIC.—*Bridge.*

MILTON.—Ludlow Castle! Well, whatever the reception of Comus and his crew this evening, Harry . . . we have had a pleasant stay here.

LAWES.—It's almost time, isn't it? Is not being a musician enough, John? I'm beginning to quaver at the thought of acting in "Comus."

MILTON.—Courage, Harry, courage! There's no one else who could play the attendant Spirit. It's most important for you to begin the masque and end it . . . the first words must set the pace of the whole.

LAWES.—"Before the starry threshold of Jove's court
My mansion is, where those immortal shapes
Of bright aerial spirits live insphered
In regions of . . . " (*Laughs nervously*)
'Tis there. Ah, I'm getting the nerves of play actors.

MILTON.—I'm hoping that the children of the Earl are getting the nerves of play actors and going over their lines.

LAWES.—Lady Alice is admirable as the "the Lady."

MILTON.—She has an ear for verse . . . the lads would fare better if I had written their parts in rhymed couplets. The scene between the brothers is the only one I fear.

LAWES.—Lord John will be pleased. All the kindred will be pleased . . . even if the Viscount Brackley forgets every other line.

MILTON.—Ay. . . . What say you, Harry . . . when it's done . . . do you think the Earl of Bridgewater will get aught from it?

LAWES.—He will say, "Beautiful! Delightful! my dear Mr. Milton."

MILTON.—Perhaps that's what I want to be said . . . my few lines written directly to the Earl . . . "He that hath light within his own clear breast . . . " and
                    "Love virtue, she alone is free,
                    She can teach ye how to climb
                    Higher than the spearing chime . . .

LAWES.—I speak those lines. I might look at his lordship as I say them . . . look at him as if I know he loves virtue and expect him to continue loving her.

MILTON.—Well, do that, then. Oh, the music, Lady Alice's dress to take away from any weightiness and lack of drama . . .

SOUND.—*Crowd record and other voices.*

LAWES.—Listen . . .

MILTON.—Yes . . .

LAWES.—Across . . . see . . . the Lady Alice . . . how lovely she looks . . . and such self-confidence . . . a great deal more than I have.

MILTON.—Harry, Harry! And you one of the greatest musicians in England! (*Crowd up*) Lord Bridgewater is bidding them welcome. . . . Now they're quieting down. . . . (*Crowd down*) It's time. . . . (*Light applause and conversation, off mike*) Walk forward now . . . and then enter swiftly. My sympathies and blessing!

LAWES.—(*Off mike*) I need them. (*Applause dies down. A second's pause . . . then . . . off mike*
"Before the starry threshold of Jove's court
My mansion is, where those immortal shapes . . .
(*Fades into-*)

MUSIC.—*Bridge.*

CHARLES.—It's good to have you here in London. Three years since the presentation of "Comus." . . . That's been the last masque performed, hasn't it, John?

MILTON.—(*Throwing line away*) They were near their end. It's a form of writing that belongs to a different day than ours. What are you doing? . . . Going through all my books?

CHARLES.—Oh, I was only glancing at these on the table. I'm glad the masque is published.

MILTON.—Thank Harry Lawes for that. He attended to it. Thank you for your letter about "Lycidas."

CHARLES.—I found it very difficult to express myself. I was . . . shocked at Edward King's death. I grieved, too, of course.

All of us did who knew him . . . but . . . it was the first time . . . I'd realized that . . .

MILTON.—That youth *can* die. Yes . . . it's only personal sorrow that can reach us . . . touch us.

CHARLES.—But "Lycidas" . . . in that you said everything. You made him universal . . . and immortal.

MILTON.—I attempted more than that. Oh, you remember the long hours of talk we had at the university . . . about religion . . . about bigotry and intolerance. . . . I felt it was part of Edward, part of you . . . part of those eventful years to write of that . . . too.

CHARLES.—As I've said, there are . . . no words . . . to express my feelings about the elegy.

MILTON.—Oh, and for truth's sake . . . I wrote of those things for myself . . . too.

CHARLES.—Of course, you did.

MILTON.—Well, soon I shall begin my travels . . . the journey I've planned for months.

CHARLES.—France first . . .

MILTON.—Yes . . . France . . . but then . . . Italy . . . Dante . . . Leonardo . . . Giotto. . . . All young Englishmen want to go to Italy. They want to use Italy as a polishing stone for their education, for their manners . . . but I . . . I want to see something of the essential differences between Italy today and our country.

MUSIC.—*Bridge.*

L'ALLEGRO.—(*Off mike or echo*) You! In your black cape . . . you on whom sorrow sits eternally and cannot leave . . . who are you? Why are you here?

IL PENSEROSO.—You know who I am. You found me out . . . you, in your golden garments, your train of sunlight borne by winds of Spring. . . .

L'ALLEGRO.—I did not expect you so soon.

IL PENSEROSO.—The boy Milton is growing older. His youth was part of England's sleeping happy time . . . but now . . .

L'ALLEGRO.—Do not look ahead. See . . . even now he's traveling toward Italy. He is young. Let him be young a few years longer.

IL PENSEROSO.—There is no potion for everlasting youth. I can do nothing.

L'ALLEGRO.—Mortals grow older through feeling, through suffering . . . not through thinking . . . not through building thoughts on thoughts high toward the star of reason.

IL PENSEROSO.—Can you not see in the distance the death of a friend? Charles Diodati will die before he returns to England. . . . You know that.

L'ALLEGRO.—I know that in Italy he will visit Galileo Galilei. He will learn from Galileo. . . . Do not speak of suffering. . . . It cannot touch him yet.

IL PENSEROSO.—Can you not see in the distance bloodstains on the clouds . . . bloodstains of civil war?

L'ALLEGRO.—I shall not forsake him. If shadows fall from your darkness . . . I shall be there. . . . I shall be there. . . .

MUSIC.—*Bridge.*

MILTON.—(*Off mike*) I was told I would find you here, Signor Galileo.

GALILEO.—You are . . .

MILTON.—(*Off mike*) John Milton.

GALILEO.—I am blind . . . you have been told that. . . . Come forward . . . come forward . . . I . . .

MILTON.—No, no, signor . . . please . . . don't rise. . . . Forgive me (*fading in*) for standing there staring. This is an honor . . . a greater honor than I can tell you.

GALILEO.—Don't talk of honor, young Milton. I'm glad you came. Ay, let me have your hand. . . . I can tell something of the manner of man you are. There. Now, you must sit down. . . . There's a stool . . . around somewhere. . . .

MILTON.—(*A little off mike*) Here . . . this is it.

GALILEO.—This is my workroom. . . . I like order. . . . I endeavor to keep order . . . but somehow . . .

271

MILTON.—Don't think of me, signor. . . . I can make myself comfortable, and your table seems in beautiful order to me.

GALILEO.—I finished dusting it myself before you came . . . a plague upon my maidservant. Try as I will, I cannot get her . . .

MILTON.—Signor Galileo.

GALILEO.—I can feel you looking at me. . . . You have curious eyes, have you not . . . young man?

MILTON.—I . . .

GALILEO.—I can even read your thoughts. "He is old," you are thinking . . . "older than I imagined" . . . and you're pitying me, thinking of my strength . . . strength overtaken by age and blindness. . . . *Don't* pity me.

MILTON.—I'm not, signor. I would never presume to pity you. One doesn't pity a stream of fire that has become blocked. . . . One cannot pity greatness.

GALILEO.—(*Suddenly*) Why did you come to Italy?

MILTON.—To enjoy the greater freedom you have here in art . . . in literature . . .

GALILEO.—You . . . too . . . then, are searching for freedom.

MILTON.—I am. There's something I want to ask you, signor . . . and if it's too personal . . . you must tell me you forgive me.

GALILEO.—Being a prisoner of the Inquisition hardens the soul. You can ask me what you will. I've always spoken my mind.

MILTON.—You were taken for astronomical heresies, were you not?

GALILEO.—I was taken by those who can't see beyond their own noses. I look for truth, and they call it heresy.

MILTON.—This is my question. Are you sorry? Are you sorry you've followed the god of Science . . . that you didn't scan the heavens unknowingly?

GALILEO.—You are young. That is youth attempting to see with the eyes of age. I don't think you believe in your own question.

MILTON.—I do believe in it. I want to know. Here in Italy I've seen the glories of Florence . . . the shining imprint all over your country of the clarity of the Renaissance. . . . Ideas are beating in my head to take home with me . . . and before I go I want you, Galileo Galilei, to tell me whether you consider your life worth while.

GALILEO.—I see, you, too, are a seeker of fact. . . .

MILTON.—We have spoken of truth. Truth is greater than fact.

GALILEO.—You ask me . . . old and beaten . . . and blind . . . whether I'm glad I lived as I did . . . when living in another way . . . might have spared me this end.

MILTON.—It's important to me.

GALILEO.—But what else could I do but live my life as it came? Worth while? Do you expect a saintly fanaticism from me . . . medieval banners blowing? No, there are no banners blowing. No, there are no banners in my soul . . . but I shall die at peace. We are all of us . . . all human beings . . . powerless. . . . Some of us are vessels of ideas. . . . If the vessel is caught in man-made stupidity and torment . . . the vessel may be destroyed . . . but the idea remains.

MILTON.—The idea remains. We as human beings are unimportant. Yes. And I have my answer. Thank you, signor.

GALILEO.—You're a strange young man. How much longer are you staying with us?

MILTON.—There are signs of war, of struggle at home. . . . I must go home. The will of our King is not the will or the good of our people. . . . Only a few of the people know it. . . . They will fight for their rights. I must be there.

GALILEO.—I wish you well. I wish I could live to see what you will do with your life. . . .

MILTON.—I shall never forget you. I would have walked across half the world to see you. . . . Perhaps I can carry back to England something of you in my heart, Signor Galileo. . . . I shall always remember . . . I promise you.

MUSIC.—*Few bars.*

L'ALLEGRO.—And now?

IL PENSEROSO.—Before he returns to his country he will learn of Charles Diodati's death. The curtain rises on the second act. Do you not see a king's crowned head fall?

L'ALLEGRO.—Yes.

IL PENSEROSO.—The boy Milton has been taught your way. The man Milton will be taught mine.

L'ALLEGRO.—In the end may he learn both our ways.

IL PENSEROSO.—But the end is not yet. King Charles the First of England is dead. . . .

MUSIC.

LAWES.—John, you're working too steadily.

MILTON.—Don't say that to me. Tell me . . . what are the people doing?

LAWES.—Weeping. They are in crowds all over the city.

MILTON.—Oh, can't you see? By beheading Charles they've made him a martyr.

LAWES.—He is a martyr, in a sense.

MILTON.—Harry . . . Harry . . . forget that you are primarily a musician and a Royalist.

LAWES.—If I hadn't forgotten my sympathies for the Royalists I wouldn't be here with you, John.

MILTON.—No, of course you wouldn't. When do you think I can venture out?

LAWES.—Not now . . . not till the city is calmer.

MILTON.—Oh, he died as an actor might. Trust the Stuarts to play their parts well . . . even to the end. And now nothing can be done for the people until that delusion of heroism is gone.

LAWES.—(*Off mike*) John . . . come to the window.

MILTON.—What is it?

LAWES.—A carriage has stopped. . . . A man has gotten out. He's coming here. I'd better go.

MILTON.—No . . . don't.

LAWES.—I can't stay here. If it's a Roundhead you . . . he'd best not see you in my company!

MILTON.—Ay . . . well, go . . . my friend. Thank you for coming. Go quickly. Walk by him on the stairs and say nothing.

LAWES.—Good-by. . . . (*A short pause*)

VANE.—(*Off mike*) Mr. Milton. You *are* Milton.

MILTON.—Come in. I'm sorry I don't see very well . . . I . . .

VANE.—I come on a hurried mission.

MILTON.—Who are you?

VANE.—(*Moving slightly*) I'm in the light now. . . .

MILTON.—Sir Harry Vane!

VANE.—Can we be heard here?

MILTON.—No.

VANE.—I come from him . . . who was Lord Lieutenant of Ireland. . . .

MILTON.—Cromwell.

VANE.—Cromwell . . . who is now Lord Protector of England.

MILTON.—Go on.

VANE.—You wrote the pamphlet, "Areopagitica" . . . about freedom of the press, about many things. You urged the Parliament on and showed them what to do. It made you many enemies.

MILTON.—What does Cromwell want of me?

VANE.—Even since Charles' death . . . the Royalists have pamphlets on the street that are doing irreparable damage to our cause.

MILTON.—You mean the published prayers of King Charles of England.

VANE.—They claim that they are the real prayers. . . . They claim that! Words have been changed, meanings have been diluted. . . . The people are now reading sentimental phrases which don't represent the bigotry and selfishness of the dead king. Those pamphlets must be counteracted.

275

MILTON.—I have been working on one called "The Tenure of Kings and Magistrates."

VANE.—We know that. We want you to publish it immediately. This will lead to a political appointment for you . . . so that you will be in a still better position to fight for what we all believe in. You will be made secretary for the "Foreign Tongues" and you and your family will move to Whitehall.

MILTON.—I want to do anything to serve the state.

VANE.—There is one other thing. . . . Your wife and her family are Royalists, are they not?

MILTON.—Yes. But . . . in these days of divided families . . . that can be no problem.

VANE.—We feel that it won't be in your case. Your apartments at Whitehall will be beautifully furnished. . . . You will use the King's furniture . . . the King's tapestries. . . . That should please your wife. . . .

MILTON.—Sir Harry Vane . . . it is your duty to tell me what I must do. It's my duty to obey Cromwell if I see fit. Your duty ends there. In these days the country comes first. My pamphlet on the death of tyrants is at your command.

MUSIC.—*Bridge.*

VANE.—Here from your apartment in Whitehall, you can see where the scaffold was on which the King was put to death. You are now to help lay even the ghost of his memory.

MILTON.—Sir Harry, you don't have to point out to me actualities to make my blood flame. I'm not one of the herd to be pulled by the nose by relics . . . ghostly or otherwise. I don't even approve of all that Cromwell is doing, but I do believe in the Commonwealth. . . . That's why I'm here.

VANE.—I beg your pardon.

MILTON.—Now about this Claude de Saumaise . . . or Salmasius . . . and his printed defense of King Charles.

VANE.—What shall you write?

MILTON.—I shall write a defense of the people of England.

VANE.—The tenor of your other writings, I presume . . . is
sufficient . . . to . . . er . . .

MILTON.—Prophesy the manner in which this will be written?
Yes.

VANE.—The state is greatly pleased with your performance of
your duties as secretary. You are invaluable. Mr. Milton,
I came today to discuss Salmasius with you . . . but
there's another thing. . . .

MILTON.—What?

VANE.—Your health. You don't look as well as you might . . .
and we hear that you are troubled by headaches . . . and
your eyes. . . . You . . .

MILTON.—It's nothing. Nothing. I've had headaches from over-
work since I can remember. . . . A little eyestrain . . .
that's all.

VANE.—A little!

MILTON.—Yes. It's nothing, I tell you. I don't want to speak
of it! On my answer to Salmasius I shall spend all the
strength I have. Oh, I shall make him laughed at, scorned
and hated. . . . If the young Charles who hopes to be the
Second is giving him gold for his writings . . . I shall make
him feel that the gold is dearly spent. Because I have a
great wealth of knowledge, Sir Harry, and it shall all be
used to destroy false images and false gods!

MUSIC.—*Bridge.*

L'ALLEGRO.—But he cannot spend the rest of his life used by
others . . . his pen an instrument of man's hatred.

IL PENSEROSO.—He will serve the state about 12 years before
he is done. . . .

L'ALLEGRO.—But he has his own work to do . . . work planned
in a garden at Horton . . . work thought of in his earliest
youth.

IL PENSEROSO.—He cannot do it now. The world of verse and
singing beauty has no place . . . in politics.

L'ALLEGRO.—Ah, but . . . about 12 years, you say . . . then
more is to come?

IL PENSEROSO.—What he's spending his health in preventing will come to pass. . . . Charles the Second will rule in England.

L'ALLEGRO.—The Restoration. Yes. I know of that. But there is a power, I tell you, that shapes even our misfortunes. . . . You will see.

IL PENSEROSO.—The restored King will feel little kindness toward his enemies. . . . You will see. The curtain rises on the third act. . . . Listen. . . .

MILTON.—You aren't writing, Mary, you aren't writing!

MARY.—How can I, father? How can I do anything . . . while we're waiting for the coming of Sir Harry!

MILTON.—Write. Take down what I say.

> "Wolves shall succeed for teachers, grievous Wolves,
> Who all the sacred mysteries of Heav'n
> To their own vile advantage shall turn . . .

MARY.—I cannot. I cannot. "Paradise Lost" may never be finished.

MILTON.—"Paradise Lost" shall be finished. I'm not a human being any longer, Mary. I'm an instrument . . . a vessel . . . you don't understand that . . . but no matter . . . I may seem hard on you and your sister . . . but that's not important either. . . .

MARY.—I shall try to write. . . . Dictate it again, father.

MILTON.—"Wolves shall succeed for teachers, . . . "

VANE.—(*Off mike*) I've news of the Attorney General's order.

MILTON.—Leave us, Mary.

MARY.—Yes, father.

MILTON.—What is it? What has Charles the Second decreed?

VANE.—(*Fading in*) There are seven names on the death list for high treason.

MILTON.—Well?

VANE.—Yours is not among them . . . nor is mine . . . yet.

MILTON.—Well?

VANE.—You are accused of treason, though. You advocated the killing of a king. That cannot be forgotten.

MILTON.—What is the verdict . . . ?

VANE.—Underlings who've quoted from your books are to be put to death.

MILTON.—Oh.

VANE.—There is to be a burning of your books. The King has issued a proclamation. All copies of your "Defense of the English People" and "Eikonoklastes" are called in and are to be burned by the common hangman.

MILTON.—Why did he spare me?

VANE.—Oh, Charles' vengeance has reason in it. You are a public figure . . . and hated. If you were put to death . . . well, the public is fickle. . . . Who knows . . . your importance might turn you into too interesting a personage.

MILTON.—Yes, I understand. This then may be the end. . . .

VANE.—What's that?

MILTON.—Nothing . . . nothing. Thank you for coming. God go with you. (*Board fade*) Thank you. . . .

MUSIC.

SOUND.—*Voices off mike or on echo.*

MILTON.—I am lost. I am lost.

IL PENSEROSO.—Lost!

L'ALLEGRO.—Lost!

MILTON.—These gray holes that were my eyes have yielded to total blackness. Oh, blind Galileo, forgive me! Forgive me for not stretching forth my hand and blessing the darkness on your face . . . for not letting my tears fall that you might feel the human sympathy that lessens pain.

IL PENSEROSO.—Are you finding divinity in your blindness, Milton?

MILTON.—(*Not answering him*) There is no divinity in my blindness. To lose the world, to lose the sight of color, of dear faces . . . streets, the Thames, of all near, familiar things . . . to sleep in darkness . . . to wake in darkness. I am a human being, and I've lost the light.

IL PENSEROSO.—Lost the light . . .

MILTON.—How is there virtue, valour or wisdom in human suffering? How can man profit by torment, O God? O fortune, is life, then, a riddle which we spend our span in solving . . . and never solve . . . and die? There can be no grandeur in life . . . no grandeur in death. . . .

IL PENSEROSO.—No grandeur . . . no glory. . . .

MILTON.—Blind among my enemies. . . . How can I fight?

L'ALLEGRO.—Fight!

MILTON.—Is my existence, then, separate from God's . . . and yet . . . I've been told that I was destined for high things. I've known all my life that my work must be done. I have walked in the presence of my enemies and known no fear. . . .

L'ALLEGRO.—John Milton . . . England has need of you!

MILTON.—What of my dreams? What of my dreams . . . that men . . . free-born, might find a lasting right to speak their wills and speaking be heard by all . . . a commonwealth whose only creed is freedom and only ruler . . . God?

IL PENSEROSO.—You have received a mortal wound, Milton. You have been pierced by the sword of mortality. . . . Your blindness can cut off the vision of your soul and make you as other men.

L'ALLEGRO.—The soul can see by its own light.

MILTON.—I cannot be as other men.

IL PENSEROSO.—Your one talent is lodged within you . . . useless.

MILTON.—I must have patience.

IL PENSEROSO.—Paradise was lost. . . .

L'ALLEGRO.—Ay, but Paradise . . .

MILTON.—Even Paradise was regained through a man's suffering. Am I so little . . . am I so weak and unhappy that I let myself be caught in a mesh of small suffering compared to the way Paradise was regained . . . ?

L'ALLEGRO.—Milton . . . England has need of you!

MILTON.—"God of our fathers, what is man!" Heaven works with a various hand that tempers our fortune. So at the height of noon may we who aspire to too much be struck down. But an eagle is still an eagle. From the ashes of despair the soul can rise new-armed. Ay, can rise from the ashes as that ancient bird, the Phoenix. If, by my own toil, I have fanned the flame that burned out my eyes . . . then from that darkness will be born new eyes. All natural objects shut away . . . I can see clearer into life itself. . . . My vision will not be blurred or turned aside! And so, O, Highest Wisdom, I submit. I am John Milton, whose sight was taken away that he might be given new eyes.

MUSIC.—*Bridge.*

NARRATOR.—John Milton was one of the greatest men the world has ever produced. His poems are a monument to England. In his lyric period, his prose period and his epic period he wrote under the wings of genius. His was the first great voice raised for freedom of the press. He is comparable only to Shakespeare in greatness. There is no writing in the world that can surpass the beauty and grandeur of "Paradise Lost," "Paradise Regained," and "Samson Agonistes." And "L'Allegro," "Il Penseroso," "Lycidas," "Comus," and all his earlier writings are the ones in which we first catch something of the clarity of his mind, the precision of his words, and the music of his spirit.

MUSIC.

ANNOUNCER.—You have just listened to an NBC educational presentation, "Adventure in Reading," by Helen Walpole and Margaret Leaf, bringing you dramatized episodes from the lives of the men and women who have written the world's most exciting stories.

This program was produced and directed by James Church. This is the National Broadcasting Company.

The Nuremberg Stove

by NILA MACK

From LET'S PRETEND

THIS CHARMING fairy tale, familiar to millions of children all over the world, has become an annual event on the venerable Let's Pretend program. Year after year it appears as a sort of command performance, insisted upon by children and parents alike. The original story presents two major problems in radio adaptation, both of which have been expertly resolved in this script. The first is a practical problem: to establish the child's adoration of the stove. The second is a didactic problem: to teach the importance of genuineness and to make clear the value of true art.

Nila Mack has handled this difficulty by a legitimate expansion of the scene in the antique shop. The magic hour of midnight plus the atmosphere of the shop itself make possible and feasible the animation of all the voiceless bric-a-brac in the scene; music boxes, the Cremona, the Dresden Shepherd and Shepherdess, and old Hirschvogel himself. The script at no time leaves the mental age limit for which it was written, and the integrity of the original, although elaborated upon, has been in no way harmed. The physical problem of moving the stove (with its voluntary prisoner) from place to place has been taken care of by proper use of sound (sleighbells, trains, boats, etc.), and the writing throughout is natural and human, an important point in this series, since the casts are made up of children.

"Let's Pretend" has been on the air each week for nine years. Under Miss Mack's direction many child actors of prominence have been developed, among them the famous Mauch twins, Kingsley Colton, and Billy Halop of the "Dead End Kids." The series has received awards and citations during every year of its production, and in the present year has already accumulated four, including that of the Women's National Radio Committee, as the best children's program on the air. Its great success as an educational feature is explained by its being constantly entertaining.

The Nuremberg Stove*

SOUND.—*Scene fades in with children laughing and talking.*

DOROTHEA.—Christof! Ermingilda! Albrecht! Please. I can't hear myself think.

SOUND.—*All laugh.*

ALBRECHT.—You're too busy getting supper to stop to think.

GILDA.—Supper, Dorothea . . . supper. Gilda is hungry.

DOROTHEA.—Of course you are, little Eyes-like-forget-me-nots. Dorothea will have your supper ready soon.

CHRISTOF.—What are we having, Dorothea?

SOUND.—*Dishes rattle.*

DOROTHEA.—Guess!

ALBRECHT.—Potato dumplings.

DOROTHEA.—No.

CHRISTOF.—Pigtails and cabbage.

SOUND.—*Stove lid clatters mildly.*

ALBRECHT.—Stuffed goose.

DOROTHEA.—(*Laughs*) Albrecht. Stuffed goose, indeed! Why, that is for the rich people.

GILDA.—Thoup! Thoup!

DOROTHEA.—(*Laughs*) Oh, boys . . . Gilda . . . the littlest . . . guesses it. You're right, Ermingilda. Sister has steaming hot onion soup with a great big slice of fresh baked bread for each bowl.

CHRISTOF.—Good! When can we eat?

* Copyright, 1938, by the Columbia Broadcasting System, Inc.

DOROTHEA.—Patience, brotherkins. Papa Karl is not back from the salt furnaces yet . . . or August either.

SOUND.—*Dishes rattle.*

GILDA.—August come soon?

DOROTHEA.—Yes, little one . . . soon. . . . (*Door opens . . . wind whistles and stops with closing of door*) August . . . there you are.

AUGUST.—Hello, Dorothea. (*Children shout welcome greetings*) Hello. . . . Oh, I'm so cold. My hands are numb. Albrecht, help me with my coat. Christof, please take my mittens. Hello, little Eyes-like-forget-me-nots. Been a good girl today?

GILDA.—Very good.

AUGUST.—Oh, Hirschvogel . . . beloved. Oh, how warm you are. And how good it feels to be near you, blessed Hirschvogel.

DOROTHEA.—August Strehla! How can you kiss the feet of an old enameled stove?

AUGUST.—Hirschvogel *isn't* an old enameled stove. Hirschvogel is my friend . . . our friend. He brings the summer to us in winter, and all through the icy days and nights he never wavers in his care of us. I adore Hirschvogel!

DOROTHEA.—All right, all right, little brother. I should have known better than to speak against Hirschvogel.

ALBRECHT.—Dorothea, I'm starving! Must we wait for papa Karl?

DOROTHEA.—No, Albrecht. . . . After all, papa Karl may be late, and so we will have our soup now and keep his hot for him, when he comes.

ALL.—(*Welcome this with ad lib, "Good. I'm hungry," etc.*)

GILDA.—Thoup. Thoup. Please, Dor'the . . . thoup.

DOROTHEA.—All right, little Gilda. Come along and I'll put you in your high chair. And after supper let's ask August to tell us a story.

GILDA.—Will August write a cow for Gilda?

ALL.—(*Laugh*)

DOROTHEA.—Yes, Gilda, dear . . . August will write a cow for you. Now then . . . wait a minute, baby . . . Dorothea will put you in your chair. Come along, youngsters. (*Chairs are pushed up to the table*) Watch the soup, Albrecht. . . . Don't spill it. Christof . . . are your hands clean?

CHRISTOF.—Clean as Kirschvogel's, Dorothea.

ALL.—(*Laugh*)

DOROTHEA.—Just a minute. Wait, baby. Bow your little head. That's right. (*Very reverently*) Give us, first, God, love for Thee. And fill our hearts with gratitude for Thy loving care. Amen. (*Dishes rattle*) All right, Gilda. . . . Here's your soup.

ALBRECHT.—Oh, this soup is good.

CHRISTOF.—And hot!

ALL.—(*Laugh*)

AUGUST.—And fresh baked bread (*start to fade*). It tastes good, too. I didn't know I was so hungry.
(*Board fade . . . completely out. Fade in*)

DOROTHEA.—Have we finished? Just a minute, Gilda. No, no . . . you must sit very still for just one second. Bow the little head.

GILDA.—It's bowed, Dorothea.

DOROTHEA.—That's right. Heavenly Father, we thank Thee for the Good Thou has bestowed upon us. Amen. . . . All right.

SOUND.—*Chairs push back.*

CHRISTOF.—Come on, August. . . . Tell us a story.

ALBRECHT.—Tell us about Hirschvogel.

AUGUST.—All right. . . . Let's all sit around Hirschvogel's golden feet, and I will tell you a story.

DOROTHEA.—First, you'd better feed Hirschvogel, August. He's probably hungry.

AUGUST.—Of course I'll feed you, blessed friend. (*Stove door opens. Wood is lifted and dropped in.*) There you are. (*Stove door shuts*) Look, Albrecht . . . Christof . . . look how he smiles and thanks me by glowing.

GILDA.—Here, August . . . here . . . charcoal stick.

AUGUST.—(*Laughs*) All right, I'll draw your pictures and tell a story at the same time. How's that?

ALBRECHT.—Sit with us, Dorothea.

DOROTHEA.—I can't Albrecht. I must put papa Karl's soup on the back of the stove and then straighten the table.

CHRISTOF.—All right, August. Tell us about Hirschvogel.

AUGUST.—What do you want to know first?

CHRISTOF.—First . . . how the stove got his name.

DOROTHEA.—(*Laughs*) He's told you a million times, Christof.

CHRISTOF.—But I want to hear it again.

AUGUST.—And I love to tell it. All right, Christof. Hirschvogel was a famous potter and painter who lived in Nuremberg, and he was known all over the world for the beautiful stoves he made. You see his initials on the stove . . . right there. . . .

CHRISTOF.—I see them . . . H.R.H. . . . 1532.

AUGUST.—Yes, he marked all his stoves like that. And if Hirschvogel, here, could talk he could tell us of all the millions of people he has warmed.

ALBRECHT.—Kings and princesses, do you think?

AUGUST.—Of course.

CHRISTOF.—The crimson stockings of cardinals, maybe?

AUGUST.—And gold-broidered shoes of duchesses too?

GILDA.—(*Yawns*) And brownies and fairies, August?

AUGUST.—Who should say no, Forget-me-not-eyes? After all, there must be fairies, or how else could grandfather Strehla ever had the luck to find Hirschvogel?

287

GILDA.—August! (*Yawns*) Write Gilda . . . a . . . a . . . (*Goes to sleep*)

AUGUST.—(*Laughs*) Write Gilda a lullaby. Dorothea, she's fast asleep.

DOROTHEA.—I'll take her, August. Those blue eyes are fast shut. Come along to your cradle, baby.

SOUND.—*Door opens . . . shuts.*

ALBRECHT.—Go on, August. Who are the four golden kings on each corner?

AUGUST.—Well, let me see. . . . That one was probably Charlemagne. And facing him there with the golden shield . . . that's the good King Wencelaus. At the far corner . . . let me see . . . that's John the Good. And the last one . . . that is Richard the Lionheart.

ALBRECHT.—And where is his lionheart?

AUGUST.—(*Laughs*) Albrecht, that means because he was so brave and fearless.

CHRISTOF.—I love the panels of enamel with their holly and roses and laurel. What do they mean, August?

AUGUST.—The panels represent the Ages of Man. There's the Child . . . see . . . and next is the Young Man. . . . Then comes the Father . . . and last . . . this one with the laurel wreath and mottoes . . . that's the Old Man.

ALBRECHT.—And the golden crown, away, *way* up on the top with the jewels . . . who did that belong to?

AUGUST.—Well, let's say tonight that it's August Hirschvogel's own crown that some great and good king gave him for making such handsome stoves. Oh, dear Hirschvogel! You deserve a crown, for you are so steadfast. Why, you are as great as the sun . . . better, I think, sometimes, because he leaves us for many long cold hours, but you . . . you make summer for us the whole winter through.

SOUND.—*Door opens and shuts.*

DOROTHEA.—Albrecht . . . Christof . . . time for bed.

ALBRECHT.—Oh, no, Dorothea . . . we want to hear more about Hirschvogel.

DOROTHEA.—But not tonight, Albrecht. Your bed is waiting for you.

CHRISTOF.—We'll talk about it tomorrow, August?

AUGUST.—Indeed we will. Good night.

ALBRECHT AND CHRISTOF.—(*Ad lib good night*)

SOUND.—*Door opens and shuts.*

DOROTHEA.—I wonder what keeps papa Karl. He is very late tonight.

SOUND.—*Door opens . . . wind blows . . . door shuts . . . wind stops.*

DOROTHEA.—Oh, there you are, papa.

AUGUST.—I'll help you with your coat, papa. Oh, you are cold.

KARL.—It's bitter out tonight. And the hearts of men are as cold as the snows of the Tyrol.

DOROTHEA.—Why, what's the matter, papa? Has anything happened?

KARL.—Besides the butcher, the grocer, the miller . . . hounding me for money? Yes . . . much has happened.

AUGUST.—Sit here by Hirschvogel, papa, and we will bring your nice hot soup to you.

KARL.—I don't want the soup.

DOROTHEA.—Oh, but you must eat, dear papa Karl. Really you must.

AUGUST.—What has happened, papa?

KARL.—(*Pause*) I have sold Hirschvogel! (*A slight pause*)

AUGUST.—Sold Hirschvogel!

DOROTHEA.—Oh, father . . . the children! And in midwinter!

AUGUST.—(*Absolutely stunned*) It isn't true! It *can't* be true

KARL.—It is true. And would you like to know something else that is true? The bread you eat . . . the meat in the stew . . . the roof over your heads . . . none of them is paid for. Two hundred florins won't take care of all of it . . . but it will help . . . and Hirschvogel will be carted off tomorrow morning.

DOROTHEA.—August . . . darling . . . don't look like that!

AUGUST.—(*In tears*) Oh, papa . . . you cannot mean it. You cannot sell our comfort . . . our very life! Oh, papa, listen. Tomorrow I will go out and get work . . . will go to the people you owe and explain to them. They will understand. But to sell Hirschvogel! Never, never, never! Oh, papa, give them back the 200 florins. . . . I beg you, on my knees! (*Sobs*)

KARL.—You are a fool. Get up! The stove is sold and goes to Munich tomorrow at daylight.

SOUND.—*Door opens and shuts.*

AUGUST.—(*Sobbing*) He can't! He can't sell you, Hirschvogel. He can't tear the sun out of the heavens like that. He can't.

DOROTHEA.—Oh, darling August. Don't! You'll burn your lips if you kiss the stove. Get up, darling. Come to bed. You'll be calmer tomorrow. . . .

AUGUST.—Leave me alone. I shall stay with Hirschvogel. Go away.

DOROTHEA.—But the room is getting cold, dear. We mustn't use any more wood tonight.

AUGUST.—It will never be warm again. Never. (*Sobs fade out*)

SOUND.—*Clock fades in, ticking. Let ticking run a moment pretty loudly. Clock strikes four . . . door opens and shuts . . . rooster crows faintly. This is followed immediately by the sound of the creaking well chain at the public watering place.*

OLD LADY.—Well, little neighbor August, you're up early. 'Tis scarcely light enough for me to see to draw the water from the well.

AUGUST.—I have not slept all night.

LADY.—Little fellows need sleep if they're to grow into fine big men.

AUGUST.—I do not wish to grow. I do not wish to live.

LADY.—Now, that's no way for a youngster to talk, What ails thee, neighbor?

AUGUST.—My father has sold Hirschvogel, and today . . . within the hour . . . they will come to take my friend away. Oh, I wish I were dead. (*Sobs*)

LADY.—Sold Hirschvogel? Then he must have gotten a fine sum for it. 'Tis a magnificent stove, that.

AUGUST.—He has sold my whole world . . . for 200 florins.

LADY.—Faith, now, and the man's a fool to let a masterpiece like a genuine Hirschvogel go for that. Why didn't he trade with an honest dealer if he *must* sell it?

AUGUST.—One shouldn't sell a living thing for money. (*Sobs*)

LADY.—If I were you I'd do better than cry. . . . I'd go with it.

AUGUST.—(*Brightening*) Go with it. . . . Do you think I'd dare?

LADY.—(*Laughs*) If I loved something and had been done out of it I'd stand by until I got at least a fair price.

AUGUST.—But how can I go with it?

LADY.—Well, 'tis not for me to say . . . but there is plenty of room inside the stove for a tiny lad like you.

AUGUST.—And perhaps I could find a way to buy it back.

LADY.—Who knows! Look . . . here is a loaf of bread and a sausage I was taking home. I'll give them to you, August. And I'll leave the rest to you.

AUGUST.—Oh, thank you, Madam Otho . . . (*fades*) thank you.

MUSIC.—*Sleigh bells and horses' hoofs on snow fade in and stop.*

STEINER.—Whoa! (*Calls*) Karl Strehla! Strehla!

KARL.—(*Off mike*) Aye! Come in, Steiner. We're expecting you. Come along.

STEINER.—We have come for the old stove. It is ready? Come on, Fritz.

DOROTHEA.—Oh, papa Karl . . . must they take it now?

KARL.—Aye . . . and go along. 'Tis better to get it out quickly.

DOROTHEA.—Papa, where is August?

KARL.—I can't be bothered with a lad who cries all the time.

DOROTHEA.—But, papa . . . all night long he lay on the floor by Hirschvogel sobbing his heart out.

KARL.—Oh! (*weakening*) Steiner! Would you . . . I mean . . . would you take back the 200 florins and let the stove stay?

DOROTHEA.—Papa!

ALBRECHT.—Oh, papa Karl.

CHRISTOF.—Oh, mister, please say you will.

STEINER.—(*Laughs*) Oh, now, what foolishness. A bargain's a bargain . . . and you got more than a fair price. Come on, Fritz . . . we've wasted plenty of time. Lift 'er up there.

FRITZ.—Hold it a minute. (*Stove scraping and bumping as they pick it up*) All right.

STEINER.—Open the door, will you, Strehla?

FRITZ.—Easy, there . . . take 'er over a little . . . little more.

STEINER.—Watch these steps, Fritz.

SOUND.—*Stove scrapes.*

FRITZ.—Easy now!

STEINER.—(*Fading*) Better back 'er up a little.

FRITZ.—Turn your end around for the sleigh.

ALBRECHT.—(*Off mike*) Good-by, Hirschvogel.

CHRISTOF.—(*Crying*) We'll never see him again.

GILDA.—Bye, bye, "Kirtsvokle."

DOROTHEA.—Farewell, kind friend.

STEINER.—(*Off mike*) Get up! Get up!

SOUND.—*Sleigh bells and horses' hoofs start and fade out. A slight pause. Bring in incoming train and pull it up to a stop.*

VOICE.—Get a move on there, men. This train can't wait all night. What y' got?

STEINER.—Give us a hand, will you? This stove is heavy.

FRITZ.—Careful there, fellow. Load her on easy.

HARRY.—A stove, eh? No wonder you had to wait for the freight goods train. All right . . . hoist 'er . . . easy . . . (*Other men grunt*) All right.

STEINER.—That check all right?

HARRY.—Yeah. Headed for Bavaria, eh?

STEINER.—By way of Marrienplatz. *We* go by express and meet it there.

HARRY.—Watch it . . . there's the signal.

SOUND.—*Start train record here.*

STEINER.—Auf wiedersehen, Herr Hirschvogel. We'll meet in Marrienplatz.

SOUND.—*Anticipate record of train leaving station so that this can run 15 seconds.*
(*Fade out. Fade in*)

MUSIC.—*Sleigh bells and horses' hoofs.*

STEINER.—(*Off mike*) Whoa! (*Horses stop*) Thank heaven, we're home!

FRITZ.—(*Off mike*) I never saw the old curiosity shop look so good.

STEINER.—(*Off mike*) Unlock the door. . . . One more minute and our job will be through.

FRITZ.—(*Nearer mike*) All right. (*Unlocks door. It opens next speech in mike*)

STEINER.—(*Off mike*) Come on. . . . Give me a lift with old Hirschvogel.

FRITZ.—(*Off mike*) All right. Got 'er?

STEINER.—Yep. Go ahead! (*Feet are heard and bumping of stove*) Easy there!

FRITZ.—(*Off mike*) Where shall we put it? (*Feet hit wooden floor of shop*)

STEINER.—Put him over there between the old Dutch clock and the Chinese idols. Careful! Don't stumble over those Turkish rugs. (*Stove bumps as it settles*) There!

FRITZ.—(*Relieved*) I'll say, "There." Shall I unwrap it?

STEINER.—Just take off that front covering. (*Paper rattles, and cloth rips*) Oh, Fritz! We have something precious here.

FRITZ.—Herr Steiner . . . is it such a fine stove?

STEINER.—Fine? Wunderschön! Fritz, my boy. . . . Now that it's really here in the old curiosity shop, I'll tell you we have a fortune. Here . . . here is the finest thing of its kind in the world. (*Laughs*) And *wait* until the king sees it!

FRITZ.—It goes to the king, then?

STEINER.—Aye, my lad . . . and for a fabulous sum, too. But come . . . it's nearly 12 o'clock. Tomorrow we sail at dawn for Bavaria. Come on. Let's get home and get some sleep. Lock the door of the shop.

SOUND.—*In order named, door opens and shuts and locks . . . clock strikes* 12 . . . *whiz bang.*

SHEPHERD.—At last! Twelve o'clock. Now the old curiosity shop belongs to us. Good evening, Dresden Shepherdess.

SHEPHERD.—Good evening, Dresden Shepherd! That's a fine old Hirschvogel that came in tonight.

MUSIC.—*Music box starts.*

DUTCH JUG.—Oh, good! The Nuremberg music box has come to life. . . . Come on, goblets . . . let's have a dance.

SOUND.—*Crystal goblets clinking in time to the music.*

SHEPHERDESS.—(*Laughs*) Look . . . Dutch Jug . . . the Venetian goblets are already dancing.

DUTCH JUG.—So they are.

JADE DRAGON.—(*In very deep voice*) Dutch Jug, will you dance with me?

DUTCH JUG.—Gladly, Mr. Jade Dragon.

SHEPHERDESS.—Dutch Jug and Jade Dragon dance very well, don't they?

SHEPHERD.—But so do you, Dresden Shepherdess. Let's jump down from the mantel and join them.

SHEPHERDESS.—Certainly, Dresden Shepherd. (*Music box and goblets stop*) Oh, the music box has stopped. Shall we ask the old Cremona to play a minuet for us?

SHEPHERD.—Not even our precious Cremona could refuse *you*, Dresden china lady.

ALBERT.—(*Deep voice*) The violins of Cremona have played before the royalty of Dresden for years, my lady. I shall be happy to play while you dance.

MUSIC.—*Boccherrini minuet starts. At this point stove door rattles pretty loudly. Music stops on cue. Stove rattles.*

AUGUST.—(*Timidly*) Hello!

SHEPHERDESS.—Why, what in the world?

SHEPHERD.—It's a boy . . . a little boy in the old Hirschvogel stove.

PRINCESS.—Why, fancy that!

AUGUST.—Oh, please, may I come out? You sound so friendly . . . and I'm so thirsty I can't stand it much longer.

SHEPHERDESS.—Of course you may come out. Poor little tot . . . he's faint from thirst.

SHEPHERD.—You, Japanese Bronze Dragon, help me open this window. . . . We can get snow from the window sill. (*Window opens*) There you are. Clean, sparkling snow.

AUGUST.—Thank you . . . oh, thank you, little Shepherd.

SHEPHERD.—You must have been in that stove for days. We heard them talk about the trip.

PRINCESS.—Are you hungry, little fellow? (*Window shuts*)

AUGUST.—Not so very, thank you. You see, I had some bread and sausage . . . but I couldn't get out to get any water. Oh, this tastes good.

PRINCESS.—Have some more.

AUGUST.—Thank you. Where am I, please?

SHEPHERD.—You're in the famous old curiosity shop of Marrien-platz. This lady is the Copenhagen Porcelain Princess of Saxe-Royale.

PRINCESS.—How do you do?

SHEPHERD.—This Dresden china Shepherdess and I have stood side by side for years on the mantelpiece of a king.

AUGUST.—What *beautiful* things you all are. But tell me, how is it that you people can speak?

PRINCESS.—My dear child, is it possible that you don't know?

AUGUST.—I'm sorry, I don't.

ALBERT.—It is because we are real.

SHEPHERDESS.—Those other stupid things are *imitation*.

PRINCESS.—They never wake up.

DUTCH JUG.—You see, after midnight all the genuine antiques in the shop come to life.

AUGUST.—Oh. . . . Then if that is true, why can't my beloved Hirschvogel speak to me?

HIRSCHVOGEL.—(*Deep majestic voice*) I *can* . . . while we are here, my little friend.

AUGUST.—Hirschvogel! My friend! Oh . . . how wonderful to hear your voice! Tell me more.

HIRSCHVOGEL.—We were made by artists of integrity, of faith, and high ideals. They put their hearts in their work, and their love of God shows in the perfection of their creations. You, little friend, love me because, in your childish way, you love art. You, like the masters of old, scorn sham and haste and imitation. All your life, my son, you must remember this night. You were named for August Hirschvogel. He led a wise and blameless life. He wrought in loyalty and love. He taught the value of genuine worth. Be like him always, my little friend.

AUGUST.—Oh, dear Hirshvogel, I love you so.

HIRSCHVOGEL.—And I love *you*. I have been honored by emperors; but my greatest happiness was in your humble dwelling, where little children gathered at my feet to sing and laugh.

AUGUST.—And must I leave you, Hirschvogel?

HIRSCHVOGEL.—I think not. Tomorrow we go to a famous person with an understanding heart.

AUGUST.—Oh. . . . Then may I go with you?

HIRSCHVOGEL.—Since you came this far. Then we shall see. Now, the witching hour is nearly ended. The time for speech is short, Dresden Shepherdess . . . lull my little friend to slumberland with your song.

MUSIC.—*Music box.*

SHEPHERD.—(*After song*) Our little friend nods. He's very tired.

PRINCESS.—Little lullaby lady, rock your melody cradle for him.

MUSIC.—*Brahms' "Lullaby" . . . music box. Princess softly sings to its melody.*
(*Fade out*)

SOUND.—*Sleigh bells fade in horses' hoofs.*

COUNCILOR.—Your Majesty! Your Majesty!

KING.—Yes, Councilor. What is it?

COUNCILOR.—It's here, sire. The Nuremberg stove. They're bringing it up the palace steps now.

KING.—Excellent! Page, open the doors.

COUNCILOR.—But the draft, sire . . .

KING.—I care not for drafts. (*Door opens*) I want to see Hirschvogel's masterpiece.

STEINER.—(*Fading in*) Easy there.

SOUND.—*Footsteps and bumping as they carry the stove.*

FRITZ.—I got 'er. Lift the end around.

STEINER.—(*Grunting*) Where shall we put it, please?

KING.—Here. Put it in the corridor. (*Stove bumps and settles*) Ah! Councilor . . . quickly . . . unwrap it. Help him, men.

SOUND.—*Paper rattles . . . cloth rips.*

COUNCILOR.—There you are, Majesty.

KING.—Ah, wunderschön . . . wunderschön . . . it is perfect! H.R.H., 1532. And look, Councilor . . . the gold figures . . . the crown at the top . . . the ages of man here on the enamel panels . . . and the door itself . . . how beautifully . . .

SOUND.—*Of iron stove door being rattled and opened.*

AUGUST.—*(Frightened but determined)* How do you do!

SOUND.—*General hubbub of excitement.*

KING.—Well, upon my word! A child . . . a little boy in the stove.

COUNCILOR.—The little ruffian! Men. Take this ragged knave away.

STEINER.—He's not mine.

FRITZ.—Nor mine.

STEINER.—Hey, you! How dare you . . .

KING.—A moment! Well, youngster! What are you doing here?

AUGUST.—Oh, please, meinheer, let me stay. I've come all the way with Hirschvogel. Please don't take me away now.

COUNCILOR.—Such impudence!

KING.—Silence, Councilor. My child, come here. How came you here, hidden in this stove? Don't be afraid, but tell me the truth. I am the King.

AUGUST.—Oh, dear sire! Hirschvogel belonged to us. I can't bear to part with him. Please let me stay and take care of him! Hirschvogel loves me. . . . He does indeed!

KING.—*(Very gently)* What is your name?

AUGUST.—August Strehla, sir.

KING.—How much did your father get for the stove, August?

AUGUST.—For 200 florins, sir, he sold my life.

KING.—I see. You . . . you merchant who sold me the stove . . .

STEINER.—*(Frightened)* Yes, Your Majesty.

KING.—You bought the stove for 200 florins?

STEINER.—Y-yes, sire. In a way . . .

KING.—*And then you asked me 2,000 ducats!*

STEINER.—Well, you see, it was this way . . .

KING.—I see! The first thing we do is this. Councilor, see that this merchant returns to the Tyrol, pays Herr Strehla 2,000 ducats, less the 200 florins he received!

STEINER.—(*Moaning*) Ay! Ay!

KING.—And also that he takes him a stove to replace this one.

STEINER.—But, Your Majesty, I wouldn't . . .

KING.—One more word from you . . . and you get what you *really* deserve. . . . Now go!

STEINER.—I'm going. Er . . . come on, Fritz.

SOUND.—*Footsteps heard . . . door opens and shuts.*

AUGUST.—Two thousand ducats! My father will never have to work again.

KING.—Does that please you?

AUGUST.—Yes, Your Majesty. But . . . would you please let me stay here, with Hirschvogel? I beg you to, my King!

KING.—Rise up, little man. Kneel only to your God. What do you want to be when you grow up?

AUGUST.—A painter, dear King. I wish to be like the master, Hirschvogel.

KING.—Very well, August. You may stay. You will take lessons from the greatest painters we can find. And if, when you have come of age, you have done well and bravely, then I will give you Hirschvogel for your very own.

AUGUST.—(*Delighted*) Oh, dear King! Hirschvogel told me that night in the old curiosity shop we were going to a famous person with an understanding heart.

KING.—Hirschvogel . . . *told you* that?

AUGUST.—Yes sire. . . . Truly he told me that.

KING.—(*Laughs very gently*) And who shall say, then, that he did not? For what is the gift of truly great artists if it is not to see visions, to feel rhythms, to hear sounds that we others cannot hear!

MUSIC.—*Up to finish.*

ANNOUNCER.—So ends the story of the Nuremberg Stove, and another story wish has come true. Was this your favorite? If not, write to Let's Pretend in care of this station, and we will try to make your favorite come true.

BEST CHILDREN'S EDUCATIONAL PROGRAM

New Horizons

by HANS CHRISTIAN ADAMSON

From the AMERICAN SCHOOL OF THE AIR

ℓℓ

THE MOST sustained, thoroughgoing educational effort in contemporary radio is without question Columbia's American School of the Air. For a half hour each day during the school year it broadcasts to millions of classrooms in every state in the country dramatizations, talks, discussions, and musical programs of considerable value. A pronounced effort is made to play these programs so that they will appear on the air at a time when they can be of definite supplementary use to the existing syllabuses throughout the country.

William C. Bagley, recently retired as Professor of Education, Teachers College, Columbia University, is and has been for some time chairman of the Board of Consultants of the Educational Division at CBS. His statement regarding the American School will serve as well as anything that I could write to make clear to the reader the objectives of this vast educational project, and I should like to quote him briefly.

The American School of the Air enters its tenth year of broadcasting with the second semester of the 1938–39 season. The increasing favor with which its programs have been received warrants the belief that it is meeting a real need.

From the outset the American School of the Air has recognized that a radio program is truly educational only as it elicits a response on the part of those who listen, only as it gives rise to a desirable change in thought or feeling or action, only as it contributes in a positive and constructive way to clarity of understanding, to discrimination in judgment, to an enhanced appreciation of worthy values. The topics and materials of the programs are selected on the basis of their probable influence in evoking such responses. To this end, the American School of the Air from the outset published and distributed a Manual for teachers which includes suggestions for discussions, readings, projects, and activities which, it is hoped, will be of substantial aid in making dynamic whatever values may inhere in the programs. To this end, too, those in charge of the broadcasts greatly desire and warmly welcome suggestions and criticisms from teachers, from pupils, and from other listeners-in who are interested in the educational possibilities of this relatively new agency of communication.

In the preparation of its programs the American School of the Air has been fortunate in enlisting the cooperation of recognized, important, and responsible educational institutions and organizations. This policy insures for the materials of the broadcasts an authenticity which it would be difficult if not impossible otherwise to provide. Among the programs scheduled in the present Manual, "This Living World" is produced in cooperation with the National Education Association. The Progressive Education Association has similarly cooperated in the preparation of "Frontiers of Democracy." "Tales from Far and Near" is presented in conjunction with the association for Arts in Childhood, the American Library Association and the National Council of Teachers of English. The National Education Association and the American Museum of Natural History are jointly collaborating in the production of the series "New Horizons."

The piece that I have chosen for this anthology is not new in technique, nor startling in content, and it is without literary value. It is, however, of tremendous educational value. It has carefully avoided dramatizing a subject that would appeal to most novices as being highly dramatizable. Instead the subject has been handled in the only way by which it can be properly done: by the use of the simplest of conversational structures. This treatment has two very important factors: a true quality of informality and a feeling in the listeners (school children) that they are over-hearing that most exciting of all things, adult conversation on events that are happening in a grown-up world. I do not need to point out the psychological advantage here.

Of hardly less importance is the function in the script of Helen Lyon. To the reader her presence might at first appear superfluous, even irritating. To the child listener, however, she has great value, for she represents the average inquisitive intelligent person and spends her time asking Dr. Andrews and his guests the questions the listener himself might wish to ask if he or she had the chance. In other words, it is through Miss Lyon that the audience has participant access to the show.

"New Horizons" is the Friday series of the American School of the Air, and it deals with adventures, exploration in research, and progress in natural science. The programs originate from the various exhibit halls in the American Museum of Natural History in New York City. Dr. Roy Chapman Andrews, world-famous explorer and author, is host and commentator for the program and in these capacities has been enormously efficient and likable; he is a natural radio personality.

The scripts for the series are written by Hans Christian Adamson, assistant to the President of the American Museum and the director of its Public Relations. Adamson, a Dane by birth, began his activities as a newspaperman and is well known to American readers as the author of any number of books and magazine articles on aviation and exploration. His great skill as a writer for programs directed to juvenile audiences is explained by the simplicity of his writing and his capacity for the visual phrase or sentence. Here is the broadcast of April 26, 1939.

New Horizons*

ℓℓℓ

SOUND.—*Trumpet call.*

ANNOUNCER.—Columbia's American School of the Air, with the cooperation of the American Museum of Natural History and the National Education Association presents New Horizons, a program of adventure, discovery, and exploration which comes to you from the director's room in the American Museum, with Dr. Roy Chapman Andrews, famous explorer, as your host and commentator. . . . Today we sail for the South Pacific, to those fabled islands of spice and pearls of the South Seas . . . where the rolling swells of the Pacific throw their sprays on sunlit shores and where strange and interesting forms of animal life are found on land and in the sea. . . . So . . . all aboard. . . . Pull the whistle cord. . . .

SOUND.—*One long blast of steamship whistle, followed by three short blasts.*

ANNOUNCER.—Let go aft. . . . Let go forward. . . . Start the engines. . . .

SOUND.—*Engine room telegraph bell rings, followed by pulsation of ship's engines, followed by three sharp blasts of whistle. Continue engine.*

ANNOUNCER.—Our first port of call as we leave Columbia's downtown studios is the American Museum of Natural History, where we will pick up Dr. Andrews and his guests. . . . Ahoy there, Dr. Andrews! . . . Are you ready to come aboard and take command?

(*Switch to museum*)

DR. ROY CHAPMAN ANDREWS.—Yes, Mr. King. Here we are all set for our South Sea journey. And as we get under way, I want to introduce my fellow travelers. . . . I know you will be glad to meet Mrs. Mary Sheridan Fahnestock, who

304

spent a whole year exploring the South Seas with her two sons, Bruce and Sheridan Fahnestock, aboard a sturdy little 65-foot schooner. . . . That must have been an exciting adventure, Mrs. Fahnestock.

MRS. MARY SHERIDAN FAHNESTOCK.—Of course it was, Dr. Andrews. Here I am . . . old enough to be a grandmother. . . . As a matter of fact, I *am a* grandmother . . . and yet I ran away to sea at the age of fifty. But of course . . . my adventures in the South Seas were nothing compared to those of Dr. Miner.

DR. ROY W. MINER.—Well, I don't know about that, Mrs. Fahnestock. From what I hear, you had some rather interesting experiences.

ANDREWS.—Yes . . . and we are all looking forward to hearing about them. But before we go on, let me present Dr. Roy W. Miner, who is also with us today. As an explorer, Dr. Miner is in a class by himself, for during the past 25 years he has gone to the bottom of the sea in quest of new horizons for science, including the pearl lagoons in the South Sea Islands. . . . Another member of our party is Miss Helen Lyon, a frequent shipmate on our radio journeys for New Horizons. . . . And now that everything is shipshape and Bristol fashion, let us set our course for the Island of Tongareva, famous throughout the world for its pearl fisheries. . . . Full speed ahead!

SOUND.—*Ringing of engine telegraph, followed by three sharp blasts on whistle. Bring up engines to full volume and fade out.*

MISS HELEN LYON.—(*On cue*) I hope we have smooth sailing, Mrs. Fahnestock, and that we don't run into any storms.

MRS. FAHNESTOCK.—Oh, there are worse things than storms on the Pacific, Miss Lyon. When we were on our way to Tongareva, we ran into doldrums.

ANDREWS.—You mean dead calm weather, with not a breeze stirring?

MRS. FAHNESTOCK.—That's right, Dr. Andrews. . . . For seven solid days there wasn't enough wind to make a candle flicker.

ANDREWS.—But didn't you have an engine . . . some sort of a motor aboard the ship?

MRS. FAHNESTOCK.—Oh, yes . . . we had a brand new Diesel engine. We started it when the wind died down. For a few hours it ran like a watch, and we rushed through the water at fine speed. Then the engine began to throw oil, and finally it gave a queer snapping sound and stopped dead.

LYON.—My . . . right in mid-ocean!

MRS. FAHNESTOCK.—Yes . . . and the ocean was as smooth as a mirror . . . not a ripple on it anywhere. Our sails were useless in a case like that. Our motor wouldn't tick. There was only one thing to do . . . and that was to sit down and wait.

LYON.—But weren't you worried, Mrs. Fahnestock?

MRS. FAHNESTOCK.—No. . . . There wasn't anything to be worried about. It was just a case of watchful waiting for the wind.

ANDREWS.—But the heat . . . you must have been very uncomfortable.

MRS. FAHNESTOCK.—Yes, Dr. Andrews, . . . the days were unbearable. The sun shone from six to six . . . twelve solid hours of blazing sun and never a cloud in the sky. . . . Day after day for seven solid days. . . .

MINER.—I've heard about ships and sailors being becalmed at sea by doldrums for so long that they ran out of water.

MRS. FAHNESTOCK.—True, Dr. Miner, but nothing like that happened to us. We had plenty of water. It was nice and warm too . . . 85 degrees . . . and the water in the ocean was 85 degrees.

LYON.—You could have taken a nice warm bath!

MRS. FAHNESTOCK.—Oh, we doused ourselves with sea water, but we didn't go swimming.

ANDREWS.—Too many sharks, I presume.

MRS. FAHNESTOCK.—Exactly. They were cruising all around us. . . . The only ripples on the sea were caused by their fins cutting through the water.

MINER.—But time must have been hanging heavily on your hands, Mrs. Fahnestock.

306

MRS. FAHNESTOCK.—No, Dr. Miner, we didn't have a dull moment. Sure, our backs were blistered . . . our lips were swollen . . . and our faces were parched by the sun. But when we weren't thinking of the heat and talking about the lack of wind, we would discuss the thrills that awaited us at Tongareva, where my two sons were planning to dive for pearls.

ANDREWS.—And when the wind finally did come, you headed straight for the pearl lagoons.

MRS. FAHNESTOCK.—Yes, on a good spanking breeze.

LYON.—Did you go diving for pearls yourself, Mrs. Fahnestock?

MRS. FAHNESTOCK.—No . . . I wanted to, but somehow I didn't work up enough courage to do it. I spent most of each day sitting on the deck of the *Director* . . . that's the name of the schooner . . . opening oysters. I opened enough oysters to start a string of oyster bars from New York to San Francisco.

MINER.—And opening those pearl oysters is no easy job, Miss Lyon.

LYON.—Why not, Dr. Miner?

MINER.—Because pearl oysters are much heavier and much larger than the oysters we have here at home. Some of them weigh 8 pounds.

LYON.—Goodness, you wouldn't need many of those for oyster stew! But tell me, Mrs. Fahnestock, did you find any pearls in them?

MRS. FAHNESTOCK.—Yes . . . we found a great many. . . . None perfect or very large, but they were all beautiful to me. All day long the native divers and my sons would dump big piles of oysters in front of me.

ANDREWS.—It must have been hard work, Mrs. Fahnestock.

LYON.—And hard on the hands. . . .

MRS. FAHNESTOCK.—It was all of that . . . but at the same time, it was a great thrill to slip in the knife, open the shell . . .

ANDREWS.—And peek for a pearl.

MRS. FAHNESTOCK.—Yes . . . and every time I found one, I just . . . I just . . . well, I just gloated with joy. What broke my heart, though, was that every night the oysters I hadn't been able to open were thrown back into the sea, and I would lie awake nights telling myself that the pride of all pearls might have been among them!

LYON.—But why did you throw the oysters back into the sea unopened?

MRS. FAHNESTOCK.—Because oysters spoil very fast, Miss Lyon, and they have a very unpleasant odor.

LYON.—Oh . . . of course! But what about sharks? . . . Are there no sharks in those waters?

MINER.—Yes, Miss Lyon. There are plenty of sharks there.

MRS. FAHNESTOCK.—And they made me cold with terror. But my sons weren't afraid of the sharks, and the native divers paid hardly any attention to them. Before we began diving for pearls, Sheridan, one of my sons, asked a native diver, "What do you do about sharks?" And the native replied, "Take rag, shake rag, small shark he go. Big shark, you go top quick."

LYON.—I'd go "top quick" for even a small shark!

MRS. FAHNESTOCK.—I'm afraid I feel the same way about it.

ANDREWS.—But Dr. Miner here has met sharks face to face on the bottom of the sea.

LYON.—Really, Dr. Miner? Big sharks?

MINER.—Well . . . on one occasion, four sharks paid me a visit while I was taking motion pictures under the water.

LYON.—Goodness . . . did you "shaky rag" or "go top quick"?

MINER.—(*Laughing*) No . . . I just shooed them off.

LYON.—Shooed them off! . . . But how do you shoo a shark?

MINER.—It was fairly simple that time. This is what happened. I was taking motion pictures of coral formations at the bottom of a submarine gorge shaped like a horseshoe. Midway at the opening of the horseshoe there stood a column of coral that almost reached the surface.

Mrs. Fahnestock.—I think I remember that particular place, and it certainly presents a beautiful picture, Dr. Miner . . . almost like a stage setting.

Miner.—Right, Mrs. Fahnestock. And suddenly four actors who were not in the cast made their entrance on that stage. Four large sharks came in from the left and began to edge toward me.

Andrews.—And you were standing at the bottom of the horse-shoe. . . . Seems to me those sharks had you trapped.

Miner.—That's what it looked like to me, Dr. Andrews. I waited for them to leave, but they didn't.

Andrews.—And you couldn't get out.

Lyon.—I should think you were petrified.

Miner.—Yes . . . I began to get a little nervous.

Mrs. Fahnestock.—But why didn't you go up, Dr. Miner?

Miner.—I thought of that. But then it occurred to me that if I started to climb up the ladder I would sway back and forth like bait on a line. . . .

Andrews.—(*Laughing*) And you didn't want to look like a piece of shark bait. . . .

Miner.—No, indeed. Meanwhile, the sharks were edging closer, so I decided to do what the natives do . . . namely . . . shoo them off.

Lyon.—And how did you do that?

Miner.—Well, Miss Lyon, I plunged toward the four sharks and at the same time waved my arms in a threatening manner . . . and lo and behold . . . the trick worked! The four sharks turned about quickly and swam out of sight.

Andrews.—I should mark that down as a very thrilling experience, Dr. Miner. But . . . suppose you tell us just how you conduct your diving operations.

Lyon.—Yes, how does it feel to go exploring on the bottom of the sea?

Miner.—Well . . . to start with, you get all wet.

LYON.—You mean your diving suit gets wet.

MINER.—No, I mean my bathing suit. For in tropical waters, where the water is warm, you don't need a diving suit.

ANDREWS.—Just how deep do you go below the surface, Dr. Miner?

MINER.—Oh, usually from 25 to 30 feet.

ANDREWS.—And the pressure of the water is not too great for comfort?

MINER.—No, you get quite used to it.

ANDREWS.—But tell us something about your equipment.

MINER.—Well, as you know, it is fairly simple. It consists of a brass diving helmet with an air hose and windows. This helmet fits over your head and rests on your shoulders.

LYON.—How much does the helmet weigh?

MINER.—Oh . . . about 65 pounds . . . just enough to help you stay on the bottom.

LYON.—But that's a lot of weight to carry around.

MINER.—No, on the bottom of the ocean that copper helmet feels as light as a straw hat. Roaming around on the bottom of the sea is really more like floating than walking . . . a very pleasant sensation . . . and thrilling, too.

LYON.—Thrilling in what way, Dr. Miner? Because it is dangerous?

MINER.—Dangerous? No, Miss Lyon, because it is beautiful.

ANDREWS.—You see, Helen, unless you have seen it with your own eyes you can't imagine the fragile, almost dreamlike beauty of a coral reef. But say, Dr. Miner, why not take us on a make-believe diving trip to the bottom of a pearl lagoon and show us what we would see?

MINER.—Well, first of all, the water is just as clear as crystal. And it melts into the distance like a pearly blue fog. Rising all around us are strange coral skyscrapers. Some steepled, some terraced, some domelike, some jagged. . . .

ANDREWS.—It looks almost like the fantastic sky line of a magic city from a book of fairy tales.

MINER.—And it is a world of many colors ranging from soft rose to light blue, from rich purple to pale green, and in the clifflike walls are deep, mysterious caverns. And in the depths of those caverns we see wavering light beams dancing down from concealed openings in shafts of weird, luminous blue.

LYON.—No wonder you compare a coral reef with a fairyland! You almost have me looking for Little Red Riding Hood!

MRS. FAHNESTOCK.—Or Mr. Shark . . . the Big Bad Wolf!

MINER.—(*Laughing*) Well, some sharks are sheep in wolves' clothing.

MRS. FAHNESTOCK.—Not always, Dr. Miner. I saw two native boys in Tongareva who had been attacked by sharks. One had a crippled leg, and the other had a badly maimed arm.

MINER.—That is quite true. Many sharks are dangerous, but there are other dangerous inhabitants of the pearl reefs to be reckoned with.

LYON.—But what could be more dangerous than a shark, Dr. Miner?

MINER.—Well, Miss Lyon, there are such things as octopuses, poisonous sea stars, moray eels, and mantrap clams.

LYON.—Mantrap clams? . . . Dr. Andrews, I think Dr. Miner must be joking!

ANDREWS.—No, he isn't, Helen. The mantrap clam can be a very bad customer.

LYON.—The only bad clams I ever met were on the half shell!

MINER.—Quite so, Miss Lyon, but the mantrap clam is no ordinary clam.

ANDREWS.—No, indeed, I knew the mantrap clam would be dragged into the conversation, so I brought a copy of *Natural History* magazine along with some pictures of the mantrap clam. Here . . . look. . . . Here it is. . . .

LYON.—You mean to say that that big thing is a clam?

ANDREWS.—Exactly, Helen.

LYON.—My, my! I wish I had a picture of that!

ANDREWS.—You *can* have one.

LYON.—Fine. . . . Say, I think a lot of those who listen to this story would like to have a picture, too.

ANDREWS.—All right, we can arrange that. It would be a nice souvenir.

LYON.—But how would they get it?

ANDREWS.—Oh, just send us their names and addresses, and we'll see that they get one. And after the broadcast, I'll show you a mantrap clam right here in the Museum, Helen. It comes from Australia, and it's 3½ feet long, 2 feet wide, and weighs over 500 pounds.

MINER.—Of course, those at Tongareva are not quite as large, but even then they are dangerous enough to pearl divers.

MRS. FAHNESTOCK.—Yes. As a matter of fact, the mantrap clam is a deadly menace, and the pearl divers are very much afraid of it.

LYON.—But I don't understand, Dr. Andrews. How can a clam be dangerous?

ANDREWS.—Well, you see, Helen, these clams lie partly buried in the ocean floor, with their two shells apart. But if a diver should be unlucky enough to stick a hand or foot between their shells, they close with the speed of a trap. There is no way of prying those shells apart. The only road to safety lies in cutting off the hand or the foot of the diver who is held in their viselike grip. It's either that or drowning.

LYON.—Why . . . how horrible! But what about octopuses? They are dangerous too, aren't they, Dr. Miner?

MINER.—There are plenty of reports to that effect, but none of them ever tackled me. My most interesting encounter was absolutely negative. One day I was working near a coral cavern when suddenly a tapering, serpentlike tentacle shot out . . . then another . . . and another . . all advancing in coils that became thicker and more formidable. Presently the bulb-shaped body and baleful eyes of an octopus came into view.

LYON.—And what did you do?

312

MINER.—To tell the truth, I didn't do anything. I was so spell-bound by interest that I couldn't move. I just watched the octopus as it hung half-suspended from the edge of its cave. Then, without effort, it darted out into the water right past me and settled down in another crevice, from which it kept watching me with cold malice.

ANDREWS.—And it didn't bother you at all?

MINER.—No . . . not beyond giving me a wave or two of goose flesh.

LYON.—Well, Dr. Miner, you can keep your fairyland at the bottom of the sea so far as I'm concerned. . . . I don't blame you for not going pearl diving, Mrs. Fahnestock.

MRS. FAHNESTOCK.—Well, that's the way I looked at it.

LYON.—But, say, Dr. Miner, what kind of diving equipment do the native pearl divers use?

MINER.—Oh, all a native pearl diver needs is a boat, a 30-pound stone, 50 feet of water, and an oyster bed with pearls.

LYON.—But wait a minute . . . a 30-pound stone . . . what's the stone for?

MINER.—There's a good reason for that. The weight of the stone helps to pull the diver toward the bottom. Not only that, but if you go down carefully and quickly, without waving your arms, the oysters keep their shells open, and in that way you get a peek at your pearl before you pick it.

ANDREWS.—But, Helen, don't think for a moment that pearls come easily.

MRS. FAHNESTOCK.—I should say not. We opened shells for one whole week before we got a single pearl.

ANDREWS.—But hold on there! Pearl diving isn't just done for pearls alone.

LYON.—But what, then?

ANDREWS.—Well, let's see. Look at these little pearl buttons on my shirt sleeves. They look very unromantic . . . but if you could see where they started you'd be tied up in knots of excitement, because the shells of pearl oysters become pearl buttons and other things. And those shells have a yearly market almost as big as that of pearls. Isn't that true, Dr. Miner?

MINER.—Right you are. And while pearl diving is a shell game, it is a game that is being played for very high stakes. If you strike it rich, you can live on the fat of the land.

ANDREWS.—But if you run into trouble, you are apt to find a swift and painful exit.

LYON.—Say, Dr. Miner. . . . Did you do any fishing on your expedition to the South Seas?

MINER.—Yes, plenty. We caught fish on hooks, with nets, and with dynamite.

LYON.—Dynamite! That's a new one! How did you do it?

MINER.—Oh, we had a gadget we called a bang-bang. It is a long bamboo pole with two dynamite caps attached to the end. We would probe around on the bottom of the sea with these poles, and when we saw a fish we wanted we would bring the pole within a foot of it, explode the dynamite, and stun the fish.

ANDREWS.—(*Laughing*) That's quite an idea. And speaking about dynamiting fish, that reminds me of an experience I had some years ago in the South Seas when I was a member of the *Albatross* expedition sent out by the United States Bureau of Fisheries to investigate the small islands of the East Indies.

MINER.—Yes, I remember the *Albatross* very well. She was the most famous deep-sea exploring ship of her time.

ANDREWS.—Right you are. And, among other things, we dynamited fish on coral reefs. And, by Jove, that was always exciting! It was there I found the most absent-minded man in the world . . . at least, so far as I know.

MRS. FAHNESTOCK.—Absent-minded? How?

ANDREWS.—Well, Mrs. Fahnestock, let me tell you what happened. When we dynamited for fish, one of the members of the crew was in the habit of tying two or three sticks of dynamite together. Then he would light the fuse and throw the dynamite 40 or 50 feet away into the sea. One day he was in a boat with two other sailors. He tied some sticks of dynamite together, lit the fuse, and what do you think he did?

MRS. FAHNESTOCK.—I have no idea, Dr. Andrews.

ANDREWS.—Well, he blew out the match and threw it in the water, and then, by golly, he dropped the dynamite with the sizzling fuse in the bottom of the boat.

LYON.—My goodness, he certainly *was* absent-minded!

ANDREWS.—I shouted at him from my boat: "Hey . . . pick up that dynamite or jump!" He looked at me, and I shall never forget his expression. His first impulse was to jump over the side from the spitting fuse, but in another second he leaned over, grabbed the dynamite, and threw it as far as he could . . . and he was just in time. The dynamite exploded in mid-air, but it didn't do any damage.

MINER.—I should think the men in that boat must have felt pretty sick.

ANDREWS.—Sick? They were so wobbly they could hardly row back to the ship and climb up the sea ladder! They were actually scared out of their wits.

LYON.—Whew! That certainly was a narrow escape. But say, Dr. Miner, before we get away from pearls, I would like to know how pearls are made.

ANDREWS.—That's a good question, Helen, and I'm glad you brought it up. Tell us how pearls are made, Dr. Miner.

MINER.—Well, Miss Lyon, it all starts when a grain of sand or a tiny parasite slips inside an oyster's shell. Now, oysters are very finicky about their shells. They want to keep them smooth, and when something irritating gets between the oyster and his shell, the oyster is very, very annoyed.

LYON.—Yes, I can understand that!

MINER.—Well, the oyster can't clean house by sweeping the sand out, and since it can't get rid of the invader, it covers it up by secreting a pearly substance over it. This substance is hard and glossy, and it is covered by another layer and another layer, and so on, until a pearl is formed.

LYON.—That's very interesting, Dr. Miner. Then pearls really come into existence by annoying the oysters.

ANDREWS.—It's rather odd to realize that pearls are created that way.

MRS. FAHNESTOCK.—All I can say is that it is a shame that more oysters aren't annoyed!

MINER.—(*Laughing*) Maybe so. After all, only about one oyster in a thousand produces a pearl.

LYON.—I heard a rhyme in Honolulu about pearls that went like this:

> "A little pearl may please a girl,
> But it sure annoys an oyster."

ALL.—(*Laugh*)

MINER.—But, Dr. Andrews . . . so far you have been mainly on the listening end of this discussion, and it seems to me that you ought to tell us something about your experiences and observations in the South Sea Islands during the cruise of the *Albatross*.

MRS. FAHNESTOCK.—That's a good idea, Dr. Miner.

LYON.—I should say so. Let's hear more about it, Dr. Andrews.

ANDREWS.—It certainly looks like you folks are ganging up on me. Well, anyway, I can truthfully state that some of my happiest memories and most wonderful experiences date back to the cruise of the *Albatross*. I learned many things on that expedition. But I think I can say that my most valuable acquisition was the lesson in patience I was taught in the jungles of Borneo.

LYON.—A lesson in patience?

ANDREWS.—Yes, I learned that it doesn't pay to lose your temper.

LYON.—And you learned that lesson in the silence of the jungle.

ANDREWS.—Silence of the jungle! . . . Say, my first impression of the jungle was one of sound rather than one of sight. Millions of insects and thousands of birds and monkeys filled the air with such a medley of noise that my eardrums ached. The jungle was a thick wall of giant trees stretching up and up almost to the clouds. The king tree dominates the Borneo jungle. It grows to a height of more than 200 feet.

All of these trees are hung with a tangled network of vines and creepers, and it was impossible to move except by cutting a path with a machete.

MINER.—I know, Dr. Andrews, and that's mighty slow going.

ANDREWS.—Well, one day I lost my patience. I tried to break through an opening because I wanted to make time. But in two minutes I was caught in a web of vines and thorns. Then I lost my temper. I tried to rush forward. That didn't work. Next I tried to back out. That didn't work either. The more I pulled, the deeper went the thorns into my skin and the tighter held the vines.

MRS. FAHNESTOCK.—But how did you finally get out, Dr. Andrews?

ANDREWS.—Oh, when my native boy caught up with me, he cut me loose. My clothes were in rags, and I was streaming with blood from wounds inflicted by the thorns. I was as mad as a hornet, and I didn't feel any better when my boy howled with glee. Finally he said, "Master better learn not get angry. Go slow . . . make time fast and use machete." He was right.

MINER.—Yes, the jungle is no place for an impatient man.

ANDREWS.—I found that out, Dr. Miner. But I must admit that I came doggone near losing my temper a short time later aboard the ship.

LYON.—Why?

ANDREWS.—Oh, among other things, after a lot of trouble, I had collected a number of birds, all new to my collection. I took them aboard the *Albatross* and spent the whole evening . . . until long after midnight . . . skinning the birds. It was hard, hot, and dull work. As I skinned each bird, I tossed it into a box that stood behind my chair. At last they were all done. I was half asleep and turned around to cover the box when . . . much to my amazement . . . the box was empty! Not a bird in it! Even the last one I had skinned was gone.

LYON.—All the birds were gone?

MRS. FAHNESTOCK.—But what happened to them, Dr. Andrews?

ANDREWS.—I'm just coming to that. In the open doorway of my cabin stood Admiral Dewey, the ship's mascot, a big, handsome goat . . . and that goat had eaten every one of my bird skins!

MINER.—(*Laughing*) That's when the goat got *your* goat!

ANDREWS.—Oh, I was furious! For two cents I could have wrung that goat's neck. But I didn't dare touch him, because he was the pet of everyone aboard, and Admiral Dewey could do no wrong.

MRS. FAHNESTOCK.—That was a disheartening experience. But tell me, Dr. Andrews, did you ever have any trouble with natives?

ANDREWS.—Only once, Mrs. Fahnestock. And that was on the island of Buru. It is a large, heavily wooded island which, up to then, had been only partially explored. Together with a member of the crew, I went ashore to take a look-see. As we made our way inland, we found three or four Malay villages but not a soul in them. Fires were left smoking and food half eaten.

MINER.—I should say that was a very bad sign.

ANDREWS.—Right you are. We couldn't see a single native, and still we had the uncomfortable feeling that hostile eyes were watching us from the blackness of the jungle which closed in all around us. Frankly, we expected to feel an arrow or a spear in our backs at any moment. We had our guns ready and were prepared to shoot on sight. I knew enough about Malay habits to be very cautious on the way back. We watched the trail very carefully, and it produced just what we had expected.

LYON.—What, Dr. Andrews?

ANDREWS.—Oh, poison bamboo sticks with needle-sharp points very cleverly concealed in the undergrowth along the path.

MINER.—Yes, that's an old Malay custom.

LYON.—Is that poison very deadly?

ANDREWS.—Very deadly, Helen. One deep gash would have doomed us to pushing clouds for all eternity.

318

Mrs. Fahnestock.—But, Dr. Andrews, with the path all blocked with poison barbs, how did you get out?

Andrews.—We broke away from the path, Mrs. Fahnestock. Cut through the jungle to a stream some distance on our left and waded down the stream until we reached the safety of the open beach.

Lyon.—But, Dr. Andrews, some time ago you told me about an experience you had with bats.

Andrews.—Oh yes. One day, in the late afternoon, we dropped anchor off a tiny coral island. I went ashore, and from the edge of the jungle I saw half a dozen low trees which seemed to bear a strange, black fruit. This fruit hung in masses from every branch. It moved. It was alive!

Mrs. Fahnestock.—But I don't understand. . . . How can fruit be alive, Dr. Andrews?

Andrews.—I thought I had the heebie-jeebies until I went up to the nearest tree and saw that they were bats, not fruit. Further back in the shadow the jungle was alive with them. Thousands upon thousands hung from the branches, head down, like big black pears. Suddenly a breeze swept out from the depths of the jungle, and it brought a sweetish, musty odor that was almost overpowering.

Lyon.—That must have been a creepy sort of an island! An island of bats.

Andrews.—Yes, Helen, and I called it Devil's Island. I had a shotgun with me. Just to see what would happen, I fired both barrels over the trees, and I certainly got action. Up to that moment the island had been hushed in a dead silence, with no living thing stirring. But no sooner had I fired the two shots than the picture changed. Bats . . . thousands of them . . . 50,000 . . . 100,000 . . . maybe a million, for all I know . . . came swarming out of the jungle. The sky was black with them.

Miner.—Those bats, Dr. Andrews, were they large or small?

Andrews.—I should call them large. Each had a wing spread of more than 2 feet. I had a very squeamish feeling as they soared all around me, not alone because there were so many of them but because of the utter absence of noise.

It was a weird sight. There was something ghastly and unhealthy about it that made me shiver.

MINER.—Isn't it strange that bats should affect us that way?

LYON.—Dr. Miner, I don't see anything strange about that.

MINER.—But Orientals consider bats to be omens of good fortune.

ANDREWS.—Yes, Helen, with the Chinese a bat is a good luck sign. But say . . . I think it is time for us to return the School of the Air to the Columbia Studios . . . and, as we say good-by on this, the last broadcast of New Horizons of the American School of the Air for this year, I want to tell all of you who listen in how much we have enjoyed being with you since this series started last fall. Good-by, good luck, and here's hoping our trails may cross again!

(Switch to studio)

ANNOUNCER.—Thank you, Dr. Andrews . . . and thank you, too, for your friendly offer to give our listeners a picture of the mantrap clam. I'm certainly going to get one of those for myself . . . a 500-pound clam . . . boy! Is that something! To get this interesting picture, send your name and address to New Horizons, Columbia Broadcasting System, New York City. A postal card will do. I repeat, send your name and address to New Horizons, Columbia Broadcasting System, New York City. This brings to the close the twenty-fourth presentation of New Horizons of Columbia's American School of the Air, with Dr. Roy Chapman Andrews as your host and commentator. Guests of Dr. Andrews today were Mrs. Mary Sheridan Fahnestock, Dr. Roy W. Miner, and Miss Helen Lyon. The script was written by Mr. Hans Christian Adamson and directed by Mr. George Allen. This is John Reed King speaking for New Horizons of the American School of the Air. This is the Columbia Broadcasting System.

BEST CHILDREN'S SHOW
(SCRIPT AND MUSIC)

Alice in Wonderland

From IREENE WICKER'S MUSIC PLAYS

by IREENE WICKER

IREENE WICKER has been a professional performer for nearly twenty years. She was on the stage at the age of twelve, and since 1930 her name has been conspicuous in radio. Her long series, The Singing Lady, established for her an authentic reputation as one of radio's most inventive and resourceful artists. It won for her program the largest daily audience of children in the history of radio; won for her the prestige of a biographical account of her achievements in *Who's Who;* and for her company (NBC), the prestige of more awards than any other network program ever offered to the American public.

The end of 1938 saw the end of The Singing Lady but by no means the end of Ireene Wicker. Early in 1939 she was back on the air (after her first vacation in eight years) with a half-hour weekly show musically and dramatically more ambitious than anything she had undertaken heretofore.

The current series of Ireene Wicker's Music Plays is one of the great educational delights of our day. In structure these productions more or less follow the proved pattern created by Nila Mack in her Let's Pretend series, but there is a sharp difference in the programs. Whereas in Let's Pretend, all music is incidental, in the Music Plays, the musical contributions are essential furnishings to each half hour and consume a large proportion of the air time. This music is original and is composed by Miss Wicker in collaboration with Milton Rettenberg, her pianist and musical director. The show is sumptuously produced—with orchestra, children's chorus, and a large cast of professionals.

Miss Wicker sings all the solos and plays leading roles as well. Her present series is unrestricted in its choice of themes. It has explored the lives of many famous people and has been equally successful in the realm of fancy and fairy tale. Within the past two years Ireene Wicker's work has been cited by the National Federation of Press Women, Radio Guide, the Women's National Radio Committee, the National Parent-Teacher Association, and has won two national polls for outstanding work in children's programs: the World-Telegram radio editors' poll and that of the Hearst newspapers radio editors.

Her program of January 1, 1939, is an excellent example of the type of thing she is currently doing. The story of Alice has, of course, been done on the air many hundreds of times, but Miss Wicker's treatment of these now familiar experiences is packed with ingenuity. She has demonstrated that she is a very able constructionist, and the following half-hour broadcast may well be studied by those interested in improving their own skills.

Alice in Wonderland[*]

MUSIC.

ANNOUNCER.—Alice . . . a little girl of long ago . . . is playing
on a peaceful country hillside in England. Her big sister is
reading from a large grown-up-looking book. The air is
warm and drowsy, and Alice is sleepily peering over her
sister's shoulder . . . but she yawns in spite of herself . . .
for the book has no pictures . . . and no conversation. . . .

MUSIC.—*Dainty . . . fun-poking at a lullaby . . . with yawns.*

ALICE.—(*Yawns*) And what is the use of a book without pictures
or conversation? It should have at least one or the other . . .
and this book has neither. . . . Oh . . . I am sleepy. . . .
Shall I make a daisy chain, or shall I take a nap? (*Yawns*)

MUSIC.—*Takes funny steps, flutelike.*

CHORUS.—

Of pictures and conversation the book had none.
And so to herself thought Alice, "Ho-ho-hum . . .
Of pictures or conversation there should be one."
Or, to herself thought Alice, "It's not much fun."

ALICE.—(*Sings*)

So I might make a chain of daisies
Or sleep for awhile in the sun.
Since of pictures and conversation
The book has none. . . .

CHORUS.—And so to herself, thought Alice, "Ho-ho-hum."

ALICE.—Oooh . . . my goodness me! There goes a white rabbit.
. . . (*White rabbit starts talking here*) Why . . . I do believe
. . . that . . . yes . . . he is . . . he is talking!

RABBIT.—(*Fading in*) Oh, dear, I shall be too late! Oh, dear, I
shall be too late!

[*] Copyright, 1938, by Ireene Wicker.

323

ALICE.—(*Whispers*) Oh, my goodness me! . . . He's all dressed up like a gentleman! And he's carrying a watch! And a walking stick . . . and he is really talking!

RABBIT.—(*On mike*) Oh dear, oh dear! I shall be too late. . . . I shall be too late. . . . (*Fading*) I shall be too late!

ALICE.—(*Close to mike*) Too late for what, I wonder. I must find out! I know what! . . . I'll follow him. Wherever can he be going? Oh . . . down a rabbit hole! Well, it's big enough for me. . . . I'll go down, too. Ooooh . . . I'm falling. . . . I'm falling . . . or . . . am I falling . . . ? (*Sings, with chorus humming*)

I'm falling . . . not falling . . . or am I? Dear me . . .
I'm surely not falling, for I easily see
There are cupboards and bookshelves, maps, pictures, and jam.
Oh, I'm surely not falling . . . but . . . oh, yes . . . I am!

MUSIC.—*Kerplunk.*

ALICE.—Oh, my! It's all over, and I'm not hurt . . . not a bit! How dark it is here . . . just like a tunnel. Ah . . . there goes the White Rabbit. I must hurry.

RABBIT.—Oh, dear . . . I shall be too late . . . I shall be too late indeed. Oh, my ears and *whiskers*, how late I shall be.

ALICE.—(*Laughing softly*) What a funny thing to say . . . "Oh, my ears and whiskers!" There he goes around a corner. Well, I shall go 'round it too. . . . Why . . . he's gone! . . . And what a strange place I'm in now. It's like a long hall, and there are doors on both sides. . . . I'll try them.

SOUND.—*Turns door knobs . . . shakes one door after another.*

ALICE.—Oh, dear . . . they're all locked. But here's something new! A three-legged table all made of glass and a tiny golden key on top. But of course it won't fit those big doors. Well, I'll sit down for a moment and try to think what to do. Oooh . . . here's a tiny door . . . the key must be for this one. I'll try it and see. . . . Oh . . . it is . . . it is (*Music . . . arpeggios up the piano, etc.*) . . . Oh . . . what a beautiful, beautiful garden! (*Sings as chorus hums*)

Such a beautiful garden I never did see.
If I could get in there how happy I'd be.

I'd dance, and I'd sing, and I'd run and explore.
I never saw any place nicer before!

Now if I could fold up like a telescope, I might get small
enough to crawl through this tiny door. I wonder if there
might be a book of rules on the glass table . . . rules for
folding up like a telescope. No . . . but . . . here is
something! It's a . . . a bottle . . . with a label on it,
like a medicine bottle. It says, "Drink me." Hmmmmmmm.
. . . (*Sings as chorus hums*)

Now I've always been told to be careful and think
And know what's in a bottle or else not to drink.
'Cause if it's marked "poison" you never must touch,
For it makes you quite ill . . . oh, yes . . . I know that
 much!

But this is not marked "Poison." So . . . I think I'll have
a little sip. Mmmmmm . . . it's *good!* But . . . ah . . .
how . . . curious it does make me feel. . . . How curious
and surprised and strange. . . . (*sings*)

> Oh, I feel so surprised and so strange. . . . Oh,
> dear me. . . .

CHORUS.—(*Sing*) Now why in the world do you think that can
 be?

ALICE.—(*Sings*) I feel like a telescope folding up tight.
  Can it be that I'm shrinking? If so, it's all right.

CHORUS.—(*Sing*) Can it be that she's shrinking? If so, it's all
 right.

SOUND.—*Descending whistle.*

ALICE.—If I *am* shrinking, I can take the tiny key off the table
 and open the tiny door. . . . Oh, dear! I did shrink, and
 now I can't *reach* the key way up on top of the table. But
 here's something underneath . . . a little glass box . . .
 and, oh . . . a little cake inside! At any rate, I shan't have
 to go hungry! Mmmmm . . . *this* is good, too!

SOUND.—*Ascending whistle. Music synchronizes with whistle,
 reaching height at soft thud following.*

ALICE.—Oh . . . oh . . . I feel curiouser and curiouser. . . .
 Whatever can be happening to me now . . . ?

SOUND.—*Soft thud.*

ALICE.—Ouch! Oh . . . ah . . . I've grown so tall I've hit the ceiling . . . the ceiling! Why, I must be 9 feet high! But here comes the White Rabbit again. Maybe he can help me. . . .

RABBIT.—(*Fades in*) Oh, the Duchess . . . the Duchess. Won't she be furious if I've kept her waiting? Oh, my ears and whiskers! But I did have to get my white kid gloves and my shining fan! Oh, my ears and whiskers . . . and I *do* want to go to the Mad Tea Party!

ALICE.—(*Whispering, close to mike*) Now I wonder what a Mad Tea Party can be. . . . I'd like to go to it, too. But I can't go any place this size. My head would keep bumping the ceiling. I must be at least four times as big as myself. Maybe Mister White Rabbit will help me. He didn't even see me. Ahem (*loudly*). Please, Mr. White Rabbit . . . if you please, sir!

RABBIT.—(*Jumping up and howling with fright*) Oh! Oh, my ears and whiskers (*fading*). Oh, my ears and whiskers!

ALICE.—Oh, dear . . . the White Rabbit was afraid of me. He ran off like a streak! He even left his white kid gloves and his shining fan. How cunning they are. . . . Why . . . if the White Rabbit was afraid of me . . . I . . . I must have changed into a different person. I wonder if I can remember things I used to know. If I can, then I *am* I. . . . If I cannot, then I am *not* I. Let me see. . . . Ah. . . . Four times five equals twelve. . . . Ah. . . . New York is the capital of London . . . and I used to know a song. . . . "How doth the little busy bee." . . . No. . . . "The crocodile . . ." Oh, dear . . . now, let me see. . . . (*Sings while chorus hums*)

> How doth the little crocodile
> Improve his shining tail
> And pour the waters of the Nile
> On every golden scale.
>
> How cheerfully he seems to grin
> How neatly spreads his claws
> And welcomes little fishes in
> With gently smiling jaws.

N-no . . . I do believe those words are wrong. Oh, look. . . . I've put on the White Rabbit's glove. (*Through this speech, sound effect of whistle going slowly down . . . then stops and goes up a little*) Then I must be getting small again! Oh . . . I'm getting smaller and smaller, and pretty soon I may disappear altogether. But I haven't eaten anything. Then it must be from holding the fan and the gloves. I must drop them! There, now . . . goodness me . . . I got rid of them just in time! I'm small enough now to go into the tiny door . . . and perhaps I'll find the mad tea party, too! Goodness . . . I *am* small. . . . Why, I can hardly reach the top of this big mushroom. Oh . . . my . . . a . . . a caterpillar!

CATERPILLAR.—(*Grumbling comically . . . low, thick voice. He is very superior*) Well . . . well . . . who are you? Who are you?

ALICE.—I . . . I hardly know, sir . . . just at present.

CATERPILLAR.—Humph!

ALICE.—At least . . . I know who I was when I got up this morning . . . but . . . I've changed.

CATERPILLAR.—What do you mean, you've changed?

ALICE.—Well . . . for one thing, I don't keep the same size for 10 minutes together . . . and I can't remember things as I used to.

CATERPILLAR.—Can't remember what things?

ALICE.—Songs I used to know, for one thing. They all come out quite different.

CATERPILLAR.—Humph! Repeat "You Are Old, Father William."

ALICE.—I'll try. . . . Ahem. . . . (*Sings*)
    "You are old, Father William," the young man said,
      "And your hair has become very white.
    And yet you incessantly stand on your head.
      Do you think, at your age, it is right?"

    "In my youth," Father William replied to his son,
      "I feared it might injure the brain.
    But now that I'm perfectly sure I *have* none
      Why, I do it again and again."

CATERPILLAR.—Humph! That is not right.

ALICE.—Not quite right, I'm afraid. . . . Some of the words have got altered.

CATERPILLAR.—It is all wrong from beginning to end. (*Pause*) Humph. . . . You say you keep changing size. What size do you want to be?

ALICE.—Well, I should like to be a *little* larger, sir, if you wouldn't mind. Three inches is such a wretched height to be!

CATERPILLAR.—(*Indignant*) Humph . . . it is a very good height, indeed. *I* am exactly 3 inches high.

ALICE.—(*Hastily apologizing*) But I'm not used to it. You see, though, I would like to be small enough to go through the garden door. . . . Then, too . . . I'd kind of like to be myself. . . . I . . . I really don't know. . . .

CATERPILLAR.—Humph. . . . I must be off. Try the mushroom. (*Going off, shouting*) One side will make you grow taller, and the other side will make you grow shorter!

ALICE.—The mushroom . . . try the mushroom. . . . Ummm. . . . Why . . . he's right. I keep changing sizes with each bite. Well . . . I think now I must be just the right height to go through the tiny door. . . . I wonder which way I ought to go. . . .

CHESHIRE CAT.—(*Speaks in rhythm to the music*) Meow. Meow. Meow.

ALICE.—Oh . . . Oh, Mr. Cheshire Cat!

CAT.—Meow?

ALICE.—Please . . . could you tell me which way I ought to go from here?

CAT.—Meow. . . . In that direction lives the famous Mad Hatter.

ALICE.—Oh . . . thank you.

CAT.—Meow. . . . And in *that* direction lives the Mad March Hare.

ALICE.—Oh . . . thank you. . . .

CAT.—(*In rhythm*) Visit wherever you like. . . . Meow. . . . Visit wherever you like!

ALICE.—Thank you. I shall go toward the house of the Mad March Hare. Maybe that is where the Mad Tea Party is. Oh . . . what a funny house . . . with a roof of thatched fur and a chimney like ears! Well . . . the tea party seems to have begun. That must be the Hatter wearing the big hat . . . and there's a little Dormouse. . . . The one at the end must be the March Hare. Goodness, what a lot of places at the table. I . . .

MARCH HARE, HATTER, AND DORMOUSE.—(*Together*) No room. No room. No room.

ALICE.—There's plenty of room. I shall sit right here at the head of the table in this big armchair.

MARCH HARE.—Have some milk.

ALICE.—I don't see any . . . not anything but tea.

MARCH HARE.—There isn't any.

ALICE.—Then it wasn't very polite of you to offer it.

MARCH HARE.—It wasn't very polite of you to sit down without being invited.

ALICE.—I didn't know it was *your* table. It's laid for a great many more than three.

HATTER.—I'm the Hatter. Your hair needs cutting, little girl.

ALICE.—Now, Mr. Hatter . . . you shouldn't make personal remarks. It's very rude.

HATTER.—I see. . . . Tell me, why is a raven like a writing desk?

ALICE.—Oh, good! Riddles! We shall have fun now. . . . I like riddles. I believe I can guess that one.

MARCH HARE.—Do you mean you think you can find the answer to it?

ALICE.—Exactly so, March Hare.

MARCH HARE.—Then you should say what you mean.

ALICE.—I do. . . . At least, I mean what I say. That's the same thing, you know.

MAD HATTER.—Not the same thing a bit. You might just as well say that "I see what I eat" is the same thing as "I eat what I see."

MARCH HARE.—Quite right, Hatter . . . and you might just as well say that "I like what I get" is the same thing as "I get what I like."

DORMOUSE.—Squeak, squeak, yes . . . and you might just as well say that "I breathe when I sleep" is the same thing as "I sleep when I breathe."

HATTER.—It *is* the same thing with you, Dormouse.

ALICE.—Ahem . . . eh . . . couldn't we have a . . . song, Mr. Hatter?

HATTER.—Of course we could. . . . I shall sing the song I sang at the great concert given by the Queen of Hearts. Ahem! (*Sings slightly off key, in comical voice*)

> Twinkle twinkle, little bat,
> How I wonder what you're at.
> Up above the world you fly,
> Like a tea tray in the sky.
> Twinkle twinkle, little bat,
> How I wonder what you're at.

You know the song, perhaps?

ALICE.—I . . . I know one something like it . . . (*Sings as nicely as possible*)

> Twinkle, twinkle, little star
> How I wonder what you are.

DORMOUSE.—
> Twinkle, twinkle, twinkle,
> Twinkle, twinkle, twinkle, twinkle.

HARE AND HATTER.—Wake up, Dormouse. . . . Wake up!

DORMOUSE.—Squeak, squeak. . . . I wasn't asleep. . . . I heard every word you fellows were saying.

MARCH HARE.—Tell us a story.

ALICE.—Oh, yes, Dormouse . . . please do.

HATTER.—And be quick about it, too, or you'll be asleep again before it's done.

DORMOUSE.—Squeak, squeak. . . . Once upon a time there were three little sisters, and their names were Elsie, Lacey, and Tillie; and they lived at the bottom of a well.

ALICE.—What did they live on?

330

DORMOUSE.—They lived on treacle.

ALICE.—They couldn't have done that, Dormouse. Treacle is rich, sweet syrup. They'd have been ill.

DORMOUSE.—So they were . . . *very* ill.

ALICE.—But why did they live at the bottom of a well?

DORMOUSE.—It was a treacle well.

ALICE.—Oh. . . .

DORMOUSE.—And so these three little sisters were learning to draw. . . .

ALICE.—What did they draw?

DORMOUSE.—Treacle.

ALICE.—But I don't understand. Where did they draw the treacle from?

HATTER.—You can draw water out of a water well . . . so I should think you could draw treacle out of a treacle well . . . eh, stupid?

ALICE.—But they were *in* the well, Mr. Hatter. Weren't they, Dormouse?

DORMOUSE.—Of course they were . . . *well* in. Ho-hum. (*Snores*)

ALICE.—Oh, dear . . . he's fallen asleep. This is the stupidest tea party I ever saw in all my life. . . . Why, this is curious. . . . Here's a door, leading right into this tree. I think I may as well go in at once. . . . Why, here I am in the long hall again. . . . Ah . . . oh. . . . And here's the door leading into the beautiful garden.

QUEEN.—(*Coming up*) Off with their heads! Off with their heads!

ALICE.—Ooh . . . there's . . . a Queen . . . a Red Queen. . . .

RED QUEEN.—(*Shouting in ridiculous caricature kind of voice*) Alice! Oh, Alice! I've been looking for you! Come along! Hurry! Come now. . . . I want you to go with the Gryphon to visit the Mock Turtle. Here's the crazy thing now. Here, Gryphon.

ALICE.—What . . . what is he?

RED QUEEN.—Can't you see? He's an animal . . . part lion . . . part eagle . . . and all Gryphon. Here he is asleep in the sun as usual. He must take you to visit the Mock Turtle.

ALICE.—And what . . . what is the Mock Turtle?

RED QUEEN.—A Mock Turtle is a make-believe Turtle . . . of course. Here's the Gryphon now. Gryphon! Gryphon! Wake up. . . . Take this young lady to see the Mock Turtle and hear his history. . . . I must go back and see after some executionings I have to make. (*Fading*) Off with their heads! Off with their heads. . . .

GRYPHON.—What fun! Oh, I say . . . what fun!

ALICE.—What is fun?

GRYPHON.—Why . . . she . . . the Red Queen . . . always talking about executions all the time. It's all make believe. They *never* execute anybody. Come on.

ALICE.—Everybody in this place says, "Come on." I never was so ordered about before in all my life . . . never!

MOCK TURTLE.—(*Starts fading in*) Boo hoo! Hoo!

ALICE.—What's that?

GRYPHON.—The Mock Turtle, of course.

MOCK TURTLE.—Boo . . . hoo . . . hoo! Boo! Hoo!

ALICE.—Oh, dear. . . . What is his terrible sorrow, Gryphon?

GRYPHON.—It's all make believe. He hasn't any sorrow. Come on!

ALICE.—Oh, my!

TURTLE.—Boo! Hoo! Oh . . . oh, oh. . . .

GRYPHON.—This young lady, she wants to know your history, she does.

TURTLE.—I'll tell it to her. Sit down . . . both of you . . . and don't speak a word till I've finished. (*Pause*)

ALICE.—Goodness . . . I don't see how he can ever finish . . . if he doesn't begin.

GRYPHON.—Shhhh. . . . He's beginning.

TURTLE.—Once upon a time I was a Real Turtle. When I was little, I went to school with the other little turtles . . . to school in the sea. The schoolmaster was an old Turtle, but we used to call him Tortoise.

ALICE.—But why? Why did you call him Tortoise if he wasn't one?

MOCK TURTLE.—We called him Tortoise because he taught us. Really, you ought to be ashamed of yourself for asking such a simple question. Well, as I said, we went to school, and we learned reeling and writhing . . . also mystery and drawling. Also laughing and grief.

ALICE.—How strange. I go to school, too, but I learn reading and writing . . . also history and drawing . . . but I'm too young to learn Latin and Greek.

TURTLE.—This is not *your* story. . . . It's mine . . . and we learned just what I said we did. We had games, too. The most popular was the Lobster Quadrule . . . a dance.

ALICE.—Lobster Quadrule! Oh, my! What kind of dance is that?

TURTLE.—I shall tell you. First . . . form a line along the seashore. Of course, each dancer must have a lobster for a partner. Take two steps forward. Change lobsters and go two steps back. Then throw the lobster out to sea!

ALICE.—Ah . . . I see. . . . It must be a very pretty dance.

TURTLE.—It is. We'll show it to you now, and I'll sing, if our sea friends will join in. Ready . . . together . . . go. . . .

MUSIC.—*Song.*

"Will you walk a little faster?" said a whiting to a snail.
"There's a porpoise close behind us, and he's treading on
my tail.
See how eagerly the lobsters and the turtles all advance.
They are waiting on the shingle (shingle means shore).
Will you come and join the dance?
Will you, won't you, will you, won't you, will you, won't you
join the dance?

ALICE.—Oh, thank you. . . . That is a very interesting dance to watch. And I like the song about the whiting. But if *I'd* been the whiting, I'd have said to the porpoise, "Keep back, please! We don't want you with us!"

333

TURTLE.—(*Hollow laugh*) Ha . . . ha. . . . No wise fish would ever go anywhere without a porpoise. Why, if a fish came to me and told me he was going on a journey, I should say, "With what porpoise?"

ALICE.—Ah . . . don't you mean . . . purpose?

TURTLE.—I mean what I say! Now . . . it's your turn to entertain. Stand up and repeat, "'Tis the Voice of the Sluggard."

ALICE.—I'll try . . . but I get so mixed up in this strange country. Well . . . at any rate, I'll try. Ahem. (*Sings*)

'Tis the voice of the Lobster; I heard him declare,
"You have baked me too brown, I must sugar my hair."
As the duck with his eyelids, so he with his nose
Trims his belt with his buttons and turns out his toes.

TURTLE.—(*Interrupts*) Wait! What is the use of repeating all that stuff if you don't explain it as you go along? It's the most confusing thing I ever heard. . . . Isn't it, Gryphon?

GRYPHON.—Yes . . . I think you'd better leave off.

ALICE.—I . . . I'm only too glad to. And now, I should like to find the White Rabbit and see the beautiful garden again . . . and then I'm going home . . . so good-by. . . .

GRYPHON.—Wait! Come back! You can't leave the Mock Turtle until you hear his song. It's a law. Sing her "Turtle Soup," will you, old fellow?

TURTLE.—"Turtle Soup"! Ah, yes . . . to be sure . . . to be sure! (*Groans and mournfully agrees and sings*)

Beautiful soup, so rich and green,
Waiting in the hot tureen!
Who for such dainties would not stoop. . . .
Soup of the evening, beautiful soup!
Soup of the evening, beautiful soup!
  Beau-oo-tiful soo-oop!
  Beau-oo-tiful soo---oop!
  Soo-------oop of the evening,
  Beautiful, beautiful soup!

ALICE.—Ah . . . that is beautiful . . . really! Why! I'm glad I came, Mock Turtle. It's the nicest thing I've seen in Wonderland. . . . I mean, heard . . . eh . . . found . . .

except the White Rabbit and the beautiful garden. Oh . . . where is the garden . . . ?

GRYPHON.—(*Running*) Come on! Come on, Alice!

ALICE.—(*Running*) I'm coming. . . . I'm coming. . . . Oh, there is the garden! We've found it . . . again.

GRYPHON.—Come on. . . . Come on. . . .

VOICES.—Come on. . . . Come along. . . .

CHORUS.—The trial's beginning, the trial's beginning.
I wonder who's winning, I wonder who's winning.
At any rate let's all be going,
And pretty soon we'll all be knowing.

GRYPHON.—Come on, Alice . . . come on . . . the trial's beginning. Let's be going. . . . Come on! Come on! The trial's beginning.

ALICE.—So I hear . . . but what trial is it? And where?

GRYPHON.—(*Running*) Come on, come on.

ALICE.—I'm coming. . . . Ah . . . is this it! Why, there's the White Rabbit . . . the Hatter . . . the Dormouse . . . and . . . and a pack of cards, come to life, sort of.

GRYPHON.—Yes . . . and there are the King and Queen of Hearts, sitting on a great throne in the center of them all.

ALICE.—Oh, look. . . . The White Rabbit has a scroll of paper in one hand and a trumpet in the other. He's only pretending to blow the trumpet, though. . . . He's really kind of singing with all the other Heralds. Listen. . . .

RABBIT.—   Ta-ta-ta-ta-ta-ta-ta-taaaa
                  Ta-ta-ta-ta-ta-ta. . . .

ALICE.—Oh, yummy, look at the tray of tarts beside the Queen. I wish they'd get the trial done and hand around the refreshments.

QUEEN.—Silence! Silence!

ALICE.—Why did the jurors write on their slates, Gryphon? They can't have anything to put down yet, before the trial's begun.

GRYPHON.—They're putting down their names for fear they should forget them before the end of the trial.

ALICE.—Stupid things.

KING.—Silence! White Rabbit, call for silence.

RABBIT.—(*Sings*) Silence in the court, silence in the court,
We want silence—silence of a sort.
And we think we ort—yes, we know we ort,
Reall-ly have silence in the court.

KING.—Herald! Herald! Read the accusation! Herald! Herald! Read the accusation! (*In rhythm*)

RABBIT.—Your Majesty, I am the Herald, so I shall read the accusation with all the other Heralds of the Court. Heralds . . . let us read . . . I mean sing. . . .

CHORUS.— The Queen of Hearts, she made some tarts
All on a summer's day.
The Knave of Hearts, he stole those tarts
And took them quite away.

KING.—Ahem. Call the first witness . . . all Heralds of the Court.

CHORUS.— Ta-ta-ta-ta-ta-taaaa
Ta-ta-ta-ta-ta-ta.
First witness, come up to the stand
And raise your good right hand.

ALICE.—(*Whispering*) There goes the Mad Hatter. He must be the first witness. Look . . . he has a teacup in one hand and bread and butter in the other. He does look frightened.

KING.—Well, Mad Hatter.

GRYPHON.—Shhh . . . the King speaks.

KING.—Take off your hat. Give your evidence. And don't be nervous.

ALICE.—(*Whispering*) He's more nervous than ever. Oh, look. . . . He's trying to drink his bread and butter and eat his tea. Goodness . . . I do believe I'm growing again!

DORMOUSE.—Squeak, squeak. . . . I know you are. . . . (*Sings*)

I wish you wouldn't squeeze so.
Why, I can hardly breathe!

Don't push me, Alice. Please, oh,
I'm crushed, I do believe.

ALICE.—I can't help it, Dormouse. I'm growing.

DORMOUSE.—Squeak, squeak. . . . You've no right to grow
here.

ALICE.—Don't talk nonsense. You know you're growing, too.

DORMOUSE.—Squeak, yes . . . but I grow at a reasonable pace
. . . not in that ridiculous fashion.

KING.—Silence!

GRYPHON.—Shhhh . . . the King will hear you. . . .

KING.—(*Sings*)   Silence, silence, silence in the court,
                     We want silence . . . silence of a sort.

Now, Mad Hatter . . . give your evidence. . . . What do
you have to say?

MAD HATTER.—I'm a poor man, Your Majesty. . . . I'm a very
poor man.

KING.—You're a very poor speaker, and if that's all you know
about the case, stand down.

MAD HATTER.—I can't go down no lower, Your Majesty. . . .
I'm on the floor as it is.

KING.—Then you may sit down. No, you may go. Call the next
witness.

RABBIT.—Next witness . . . next witness. Alice . . . Alice!

ALICE.—Here I am. . . . Oh!

SOUND.—*Clatter*.

ALL.—Ah . . . why, the very idea.

ALICE.—I beg your pardon. I've knocked over all the jurymen! I
didn't mean to. Truly I didn't, Your Majesty. . . .

KING.—The trial cannot proceed until all the jurymen are back
in their places. Well, Alice . . . what do you know about
this business?

MUSIC.—*Song.*

> "Nothing," said Alice. "Nothing."
> "Nothing whatever?" asked the King.
> "Nothing whatever," said Alice.
> "That," said the King, "Is very important.
> Very important, says I."

RABBIT.—Important. Oh, my ears and whiskers. . . . To me it seems most unimportant. . . .

KING.—Silence! And witness by the name of Alice . . . listen to Rule 42. *All persons more than a mile high to leave the court.*

ALICE.—Why . . . I'm not a mile high.

KING.—You are so. Nearly *two* miles.

ALICE.—Well, I shan't go at any rate. Besides, that isn't a regular rule. You invented it just now.

KING.—It's the oldest rule in the book.

ALICE.—If it is, then it ought to be Rule Number 1 instead of Number 42.

KING.—*Consider your verdict*, jury. . . . Consider your verdict. Sentence first . . . verdict afterwards.

ALICE.—Stuff and nonsense . . . the idea of having the sentence first.

QUEEN.—Hold your tongue.

ALICE.—I won't. I've done nothing wrong.

QUEEN.—Yes . . . off with her head . . . off with her head!

ALICE.—I'm not afraid. Who cares for you! You're nothing but a pack of cards!

SOUND.—*Whistle and wind effect up and fade to silence.*

ALICE.—Oh. Oh, my. Oh, me, oh, my. Why . . . why, I'm back again, sister. . . .

SISTER.—Wake up, Alice dear. It's supper time. You've been dreaming.

ALICE.—Dreaming. Oh, no . . . I'm sure it couldn't have been all a dream. It was so very real . . . adventures I had . . . in a kind of Wonderland.

CHORUS.—And so with a brightness that shines and gleams
    When mem'ries are sweet and happy are dreams,
    Alice kept with her always the adventures so grand,
    The adventures she had in that strange Wonderland.

ANNOUNCER.—And so the curtain falls on our music play for today, "Alice In Wonderland," as dramatized for radio by Ireene Wicker. You have heard Ireene Wicker herself in the part of Alice; James Meighan as the White Rabbit; Alfred Shirley and Eustace Wyatt as the March Hare and the Mock Turtle; Agnes Moorehead in the part of the Queen of Hearts; Florence Malone as the Red Queen; and John Brewster as the King. Junius Matthews was heard as the Caterpillar. Milton Rettenberg, our music director, arranged the music and the Children's Chorus sang the songs. And now, Ireene Wicker . . . will you tell us about the music play for next week?

IREENE.—Yes, Mr. Cross. Next Sunday we are going to present "The Boy, Verdi," a music play based on the childhood of the great composer, Giuseppe Verdi, and featuring some of Verdi's best loved music.

ANNOUNCER.—That will be beautiful, I know. We hope you will all be with us again next Sunday at this same time. This is the National Broadcasting Company.

BEST ORIGINAL SKETCH

The Twilight Shore

by MILTON GEIGER

MORE THAN thirty important weekly radio series include
as a feature of each show a dramatic sketch of short
duration, usually a spot of from eight to twelve minutes.
Such shows are of the variety type, and the included
sketches draw on every conceivable theme; humorous or
near-humorous domestic mix-ups, murder, revenge, war,
character study, impressionistic montages, historical and
biographical playlets, and old-fashioned vaudeville black-
outs. Frequently they are written for specific stage or
screen stars, and in these cases are written "close," that is
to say, fashioned in both line and structure to afford the
star the best possible piece in which to demonstrate his
particular brand of virtuosity. More often, however, they
are the spontaneous creations of radio's myriad free lances
and are written, as most things are, because the author
felt like it. These are more likely to have freedom of
individual thought and expression and, in consequence,
greater integrity of authorship.

From a mass of over five hundred I have selected the
sketch called "The Twilight Shore," by Milton Geiger.
It has positive and uncommon distinctions, not least of
which is its adroit handling of a dramatic problem usually
botched by radio writers: the problem of bringing reality
and movement to a property that is in every sense an
allegory.

The lumbering, unlubricated progress of the allegory; the
generally stilted and impersonal treatment of its characters; the moralizing mustiness of its metaphor—these are
features not likely to attract the dramatist. But Mr.
Geiger has escaped these dangers neatly and has done so in
ways that deserve brief mention. First, he has written cold
realism into his opening narration. This has great psycho-

logical value in that the listener instinctively knows that the resolution of the play will return him to the same situation; in other words, that the play will end, as it began, on a realistic note. Geiger's second device has been to include in his cast of allegorical figures a character (the Woman) who is an ordinary person. Her presence, her speech, and her response to her situation are all natural and reasonable, which eases the burden of our belief in the other two characters. His third device is his use of contemporary reference on the part of one of his shadow characters (the Idiot) and the very effective use of the sound effects naturally associated with those references. The Idiot speaks of poison gas, airplanes, bombs, etc., and in so doing injects these moments of the play with the starkest sort of realism, realism that is intensified by sound.

In performance this short sketch was powerful and convincing. It is to the credit of Rudy Vallee's showmanship that he accepted the play as it stood and then undertook the problem of its proper casting. Fay Bainter and Judith Anderson appeared in the major roles and delivered memorable pieces of work. The performance took place on the evening of March 17, 1938. The Texaco Star Theatre also gave this sketch an excellent production (December 14, 1938), with Olivia De Haviland and Nana Bryant in the leading roles.

The Rudy Vallee program was the first to make commercial use of Mr. Geiger's talents, and during the past three years twenty-three original sketches by him have been heard on this program alone. He was not discovered by the discerning Vallee, however, his first play having been produced by the Columbia Workshop in 1935.

As a radio writer Milton Geiger has greater versatility than any other professional in the industry today, moving with equal facility from the crepuscular to the grisly, from character study to gags. Despite his variety of theme and treatment, there is in most of his work a fine undercurrent of optimism, humor, and companionship. "The Twilight Shore," somber in mood during most of its action, returns the listener to a healthy and encouraging cheerfulness with its quick conclusion.

341

The Twilight Shore[*]

ANNOUNCER.—For crucial minutes a taxi has been threading its way through city traffic. In the back seat, a tense, anxious-eyed young man comforts a woman beside him. The woman's face is drawn, but pale and lovely in the half light. At last broken points of light appear on a distant hill . . . the maternity hospital! The taxi's engine drones louder as the driver puts on greater speed. . . . Then, curiously, the roar of the motor changes to the roar of an ocean surf; our scene changes. The woman of the taxi is standing on the dim shore of a great pounding sea. Her dark hair is loose, falling to her waist. She wears a flowing white gown. Her face, beautiful and transfixed, is turned to the fog-shrouded sea. But for the dull glow of the setting sun, the sea and sky are void and lonely. Far, far out in the mist, a bell buoy tolls in sad and muffled accents. Suddenly the woman on the beach is not alone. Another woman, tall and stately in the gathering gloom, stands beside her . . . speaks. . . .

ERDA.—(THE OTHER WOMAN) Welcome. I bid you welcome, Woman.

WOMAN.—I . . . I am lost! I do not know this place, or you.

ERDA.—My name is Erda.

WOMAN.—Erda?

ERDA.—I am called by many names in many tongues, since all men worship the fertile earth as it turns toward the sun.

WOMAN.—I am afraid! I do not know this misty sea. I hear the beating surf and a bell at sea, and it is strange, all strange!

ERDA.—These sands are strange indeed to you. Yet countless other footprints have long ago washed out to sea, with millions yet to come . . . and every woman born of woman walks these lonely shores . . . alone.

[*] Copyright, 1938, by Milton E. M. Geiger.

WOMAN.—But you . . . ?

ERDA.—You are alone. Will you take my hand and come with me, Woman?

WOMAN.—(*Dazed*) I am alone and lost. I *must* come.

ERDA.—Then take my hand and come. . . . Come with me. . . . Come. . . .

SOUND.—*Fade her voice, music, and the tolling of the bell. Fade in slowly the howl and whistling of a shrill, high wind.*

WOMAN.—(*Gasping*) This wind! . . . I . . . I cannot stand!

ERDA.—I will support you. Look where I point.

WOMAN.—I . . . I see a boy . . . a little boy . . . and a girl. . . . The boy is hurt! His knee is scraped and bleeding . . . but he does not weep.

ERDA.—Though it hurts him cruelly, he does not cry out.

WOMAN.—The little girl bends over him. . . .

ERDA.—Yes. Tears glisten in her eyes.

WOMAN.—(*Pleading*) Let me go! I must go to him!

ERDA.—Why?

WOMAN.—(*Perplexed*) Why . . . because . . . because . . . I *must!* Because . . . the boy is *mine!*

ERDA.—He *will* be yours, if you choose. Come. The little tragedies of childhood are soon over. Leave them to their precious anguish!

WOMAN.—Leave them?

ERDA.—Come. . . . Come with me. . . . Come. . . .

SOUND.—*Her voice fades momentarily. . . . The wind rises to an even fiercer pitch, supported this time by music.*

WOMAN.—I can go no further! This is mad! The wind and the sea and all this land . . . mad! Why am I here?

ERDA.—(*Gently*) Rest, Woman. You will need strength and courage and compassion. Look . . . look again where I point. . . .

WOMAN.—(*A pause . . . then dreamily*) I see a young man and a young woman. . . . They are building. What are they building?

ERDA.—It only matters that they *do* build. Watch!

WOMAN.—See how they struggle against the roaring gale . . . !

ERDA.—The wind is great, but they are greater.

WOMAN.—No! The framework bends. . . . It yields. . . . It cracks!

SOUND.—*A crackling sound as of timbers crunching and splintering.*

WOMAN.—It's going to fall!

SOUND.—*Terrific grinding crash . . . music out . . . wind down low.*

WOMAN.—Gone! All their labor spent for dust and ruin!

ERDA.—As it was, and is, and shall be. And yet I tell you . . . they are greater than the wind!

WOMAN.—(*Compassionately*) See how the woman tries to comfort him, tears in her gentle eyes. (*Suddenly*) Why . . . it's the same little girl, grown older . . . !

ERDA.—The same little boy, grown up . . . with eyes like the eyes you know so well and love so well. . . .

WOMAN.—But this is cruel. . . . This is heartless!

ERDA.—*This is life*, Woman. Look. . . . See how he grasps his hammer again and squares his shoulders. Come. . . . Let us leave them to their building and their splendor. . . . Come. . . . Come with me. . . . Come. . . .

SOUND.—*Fade the wind and Erda's voice. Then fade in loud, boisterous laughter that sounds brutal and a bit imbecilic.*

WOMAN.—(*Frightened*) Who is this?
(*This amuses the man. He laughs the louder*)

ERDA.—Courage, Woman! (*Raising her voice imperiously*) Stay your laughter! What amuses you, now that the black rocks split with your mirth?

MAN.—Ah, you must see, and the Woman, too. Look. . . . I turn this little valve on this pretty metal cylinder, and behold . . . !

344

ERDA.—(*Whispering*) Courage, Woman. . . .

SOUND.—*There is a hissing sound from the cylinder.*

MAN.—(*In idiot triumph*) See! Lovely purple gas . . . purple gas to *kill* the little people. *He chuckles in high satisfaction.*

WOMAN.—(*Choking*) It . . . it chokes me . . . ! Let us go from here . . . ! I . . . I fear . . . this . . . creature . . . !

SOUND.—*Hissing stops suddenly.*

MAN.—Wait. There is more. Look! *Airplane! Zum! Zum! Zum! Zum! Zum! Zum! Zum! Zum! Zum!*

SOUND.—*As he imitates, vocally, like a child, the drone of a heavy bombing plane, his voice is gradually seconded by deep, booming drone of a bomber.*

WOMAN.—(*In terror*) Stop. . . . Stop. . . . Stop . . . !

MAN.—See! The bomber has a great cathedral under his sights, and *presto* . . . !

SOUND.—*He whistles long and piercingly to imitate the hoarse whistle of a descending bomb. At the same time, his whistle is seconded again by the hoarse, tapering whistle of a bomb's descent. As the man exclaims "Boom," a mechanical effect creates a deep, resonant boom.*

WOMAN.—Take me away . . . ! I hate him! I hate him!

MAN.—(*Suddenly, sharply*) No! Stay, Woman! Stand before my altar!

WOMAN.—(*Moaning*) No, no, no, no, no, no, no . . . ! I dare not . . . !

MAN.—Woman, you will have a child. I must have his name for my record.

WOMAN.—(*In suddenly crystallizing determination*) I will not say!

MAN.—His name! The name of your man child! Quickly!

WOMAN.—There will be . . . no . . . son!

MAN.—What! (*Calming down*) Well, no matter. Your daughter will have sons, then. Give me *her* name!

WOMAN.—(*Firmly*) There will be no daughter.

MAN.—What? Erda . . . must we tolerate such insolence from this . . . this . . . mortal! No!

ERDA.—If *she* wills it, there will be no child. Come, Woman. We will go. . . .

MAN.—(*Shouting after them in fury*) Wait! Come back! Stop, I say! Do you know who I am? I am powerful! I am WAR! Come back! Come back. . . . Come back . . . !

SOUND.—*Fade his frenzied voice. The woman sobs brokenly.*

WOMAN.—It was terrible . . . terrible. . . .

ERDA.—(*Sadly*) Forgive him. He is an idiot.

SOUND.—*There is a pause. The woman's sobs cease gradually. Fade in slowly then, as before, the roar of the sea, the tolling of the bell buoy, with music.*

WOMAN.—(*Questioningly*) This is the sea again! It is here we started!

ERDA.—Aye, Woman. The sea.

WOMAN.—It is dark, and yet I see that there are countless sails upon the water. . . . Why are they so still and silent? The wind is fresh and blows upon us from the sea. Why are they still?

ERDA.—(*Oddly*) Forever silent and becalmed upon a wind-swept sea, those ships. The wind is fresh indeed, and yet those sails are limp and lifeless in the gale. So are they now . . . so shall they be while time exists.

WOMAN.—(*Frightened*) I do not understand.

ERDA.—You must not be afraid, Woman . . . now.

WOMAN.—The wind is cold and piercing.

ERDA.—Aye, cold and black, but do not fear. . . .

WOMAN.—I *am* afraid! I fear that bell and all those silent ships! This place is cruel . . . and strange. Where is my home . . . ?

ERDA.—Soon you will go back . . . though some do not.

WOMAN.—Some . . . do . . . not . . . ?

ERDA.—They are brave; they dip into the dark and surging tides of death to bring forth life. But those who lose their footing on the glazed wet rocks . . . *they* do not return. The Little Ones go back . . . alone.

WOMAN.—The . . . the Little Ones . . . ? (*Suddenly*) Wait! I remember. . . . (*Build music*) I . . . (*struggling for memory*) remember . . . in another place than this . . . a taxi . . . pain . . . a taxi . . . racing dimly through the streets. A taxi . . . pain . . . my husband . . . a taxi, racing . . . racing . . . racing . . . ! (*Music out*) Racing (*Suddenly dazed . . . bewildered*). . . . Racing . . . *where* . . . ?

ERDA.—To meet a ship, Woman. Look . . . look out to sea.

WOMAN.—Why . . . I see one ship that moves. I see a vessel with all sails spread. The water boils and hisses at her prow. What . . . what ship is *that*?

ERDA.—The ship you came to meet. See. . . . A shrouded figure poises in the bows. . . .

WOMAN.—She holds something in her arms, as if for me to take!

ERDA.—Yes. She holds a little child, yet unborn. *Your* child.

WOMAN.—Mine? Mine . . . ?

ERDA.—Your child.

WOMAN.—(*In sudden determination*) I . . . I will not have him!

ERDA.—(*Resignedly*) It is for you to choose, Woman.

WOMAN.—Then I *have* chosen. I . . . will . . . not . . . have . . . him!

ERDA.—(*Persuasive and gentle*) A helpless little child. A son, blue-eyed and gentle; caressing, to be caressed. . . .

WOMAN.—No!

ERDA.—Life would be sweet to him as to all things living.

WOMAN.—No. Life is bitter and tragic! It is cruel, pitiless! You have shown me!

ERDA.—It was my duty. Life is divine . . . a gift. . . .

347

WOMAN.—Life is meaningless! A grim and savage trick! I'll have no part of it! I understand everything now! I saw torment and pain for him; I saw disaster and futility; I saw the Idiot reaching for my son . . . and I will not have him!

ERDA.—(*Sighs*) It is a pity. Others have had greater courage. The countless others whose footprints long ago went out to sea.

WOMAN.—(*Steadfastly*) No. . . . No!

ERDA.—(*Angrily*) Be selfish, then, and, for yourself, think of the empty years! Think of the lonely years, when childless twilight comes for you, with none to light the darkening way . . . none to mourn your passing or to rejoice your having been!

WOMAN.—(*Struck*) No . . . no . . . no . . . !

SOUND.—*Music in.*

ERDA.—The ship draws near. Soon you may hold your child in your arms; and soon he may smile and laugh and curl his fingers round your own. . . .

WOMAN.—(*Whispering*) No. . . . No. . . .

ERDA.—The ship is beached. (*Pause*) Woman, your little son. Choose . . . or the boat returns to join that sorry fleet out on the murky waters . . . the fleet of unwanted souls . . . small souls drifting down eternity. . . . Look! The sea begins to moan; the sea is rising, and the wind grows bleak and rough. The sun is gone, and the scudding clouds close in like Final Judgment. . . . (*The wind begins to whistle mournfully*) Choose, Woman, e'er the restless ocean and the night take back your boy. For the last time, Woman . . . will you take your son . . . ? (*Fading*) *Will* you take your son . . . ? *Will* you take your son?

SOUND.—*Erda's voice is towering and deep with finality. The wind rises mournfully. . . . The tolling of the distant bell grows louder and louder and is the last to fade. The baby begins to cry in muffled, choked tones, gaspingly, after the manner of infants, leaving only the gasping, growing crying of the infant, alone in the silence. Then, a door opens and closes. Pause.*

NURSE.—(*Genially*) Hello? (*Tentatively*) Awake?

WOMAN.—Yes . . . I . . . I'm awake. . . .

SOUND.—*The baby is still crying, throughout.*

NURSE.—Well, then! It's a boy! A blue-eyed, bouncing baby boy! But, then, they *all* bounce. He's a gem.

WOMAN.—A . . . a . . . little . . . boy?

NURSE.—Yes! With extra-capacity lungs. Listen to him! (*She pauses a moment for the baby's energetic yowling to register*) Do you feel strong enough now? I mean . . . will you take your son, now . . . .?

WOMAN.—(*There is a kind of triumph and exaltation in her voice*) Yes . . . yes. . . . *Yes!* Give me my son!

MUSIC.—*Swell theme to finish.*

Peter Stuyvesant

by WILL McMORROW

From THE CAVALCADE OF AMERICA

IN SEEKING the historical drama that was to be considered the best of its kind, a small mountain of material was examined, but the questions for assaying values were simple: Was it history? Was it drama? A great many of the specimens tested showed a high content of historical accuracy; a great many assayed high in dramatic value; a few, including the one finally chosen, showed a proper and balanced content of both.

In "Peter Stuyvesant" the writer has not overstepped the barriers of historical truth. At the same time he has given depth and breadth and meaning to a character who, at first glance, would have seemed to most of us to be as unyielding as one of his own statues. It is obvious that the writer of the drama has met the obstinate and cantankerous old Dutchman, has heard the tap of the wooden peg echoing on the wharves of New Amsterdam, has listened in, across the centuries, to the dialogue that ends the piece. We feel that the writer fully enjoyed meeting Peter Stuyvesant, sympathized with the gruff old empire builder, saw something more there than a roaring tyrant and a swearing martinet; and in this sympathetic understanding of the man behind the one-dimensional picture lies the value of the piece.

Cavalcade of America, the series from which this drama was chosen, has uniformly maintained a high standard of workmanship in accordance with the formula we have given above. In view of the research entailed, the variety of subjects and historical incidents involved, no one writer can hope to maintain such standards alone, through constant weeks of output. Consequently, the work of writing the half-hour dramas is given to free-lance writers who devote as much time to their chosen subjects as the research and writing require. Since each writer is especially interested in the incidents or personages of some particular historical field, his approach to a subject is more sympathetic than if the subject had been arbitrarily assigned. That this working policy has proved successful is evidenced by the high rating and immense interest in the program. Cavalcade of America is now in its fifth year on the air.

Will McMorrow, the author of "Peter Stuyvesant," is a former fiction writer, the author of some hundreds of short stories, novelettes, and novels in the magazine field. His work illustrates once more that inescapable truth about radio: the best broadcast, whatever its field, is the creation of the best writer in that field. Here is Cavalcade's (and Mr. McMorrow's) Dutchman.

Peter Stuyvesant*

ᒫᒫᒫ

MUSIC.—*Theme music in and down.*

JEWETT.—The DuPont Company presents . . .

WEIST.—The Cavalcade of America!

MUSIC.—*Up and down.*

JEWETT.—With radio's distinguished commentator speaking for the DuPont Company . . . Gabriel Heatter! (*Applause*)

HEATTER.—Mention a figure in history to ten people . . . and nine, you will find, will be quick to classify him. One will say, "Why, he was a tyrant." And one will say, "No, he was a patriot." . . . A division of opinion which makes turning back pages in a book of time a fascinating adventure. And more. Because, by turning back to read of days gone down a corridor of time, we learn to measure our own times . . . and even to see what future years may hold. Best of all, turning back makes it possible to recapture colorful and compelling figures. . . .

Say a man like Peter Stuyvesant. To many of us I suppose Peter Stuyvesant was a cranky old gentleman who hobbled around on a wooden leg . . . quarrelsome, meddlesome, trying to run old New Amsterdam according to his own ideas.

But before we tell you his story let's hear Don Voorhees and the DuPont Cavalcade orchestra play "This Can't Be Love" from the musical success, "The Boys from Syracuse." (*Orchestra . . . overture . . . applause . . . music*)

Ladies and gentlemen! The narrator and chronicler of the Cavalcade of America . . . Tom Chalmers!

CHALMERS.—Thank you, Gabriel Heatter. Tonight we go back to the year 1647. A straggling village on the tip end of

---

* Reprinted by special permission of Batten, Barton, Durstine and Osborn, Inc., authorized agents for The Cavalcade of America on behalf of the E. I. DuPont de Nemours and Company, Inc., sole copyright owner.

Manhattan Island. A disorderly settlement of Dutch fur traders, trappers in mangy fur caps, Indians smelling of wood smoke, sailors, town loafers, English adventurers, soldiers in tarnished gold lace, women and children. A cluster of houses around a fort that looked about ready to fall down. Miles of forest in back and just this toe hold that the Dutch West India Company had on the edge of a continent. A troublesome little colony, this New Netherland, and the home government in Holland had been looking around for a man to handle the situation.

MUSIC.—*Up and down.*

FIRST MAN.—We're a free colony, and Peter Stuyvesant's got to know it. No one's going to order me around. Man or devil (*fade*) or wooden-legged tyrant. . . .

MUSIC.—*Up and down.*

SECOND MAN.—They say he's going to make you close your tavern on time, now. No more sellin' rotgut to the redskins with old (*fade*) Peg-leg Peter watching. . . .

MUSIC.—*Up and down.*

MOTHER.—He has a big beak of a nose like a buzzard. And a wooden stump of a leg. And do you know what he does to bad little boys who tease their sisters? He carries them off at night to his dark dungeon (*fade*) and eats them alive. . . .

MUSIC.—*Up and down.*

THIRD MAN.—Peg-leg Peter, eh? He's not going to march me around like he did those soldiers when he was fighting (*fade*) the Portugee. . . .

MUSIC.—*Up and down.*

FOURTH MAN.—He'll find we have minds of our own, here. We'll tell that to Peg-leg Stuyvesant (*fade*) when he comes. . . .

MUSIC.—*Up into roll of drums . . . peg-leg stomps on wharf.*

STUYVESANT.—I am Peter Stuyvesant, your new Director General. Who are these people?

KIEFT.—I'm Kieft, Your Excellency, former governor. We are here to welcome you in behalf of the citizens of this colony of New Netherland . . . in behalf of the great and glorious

353

free Dutch Republic, the noble West India Company, and Their High Mightinesses, the Estates General of Holland, whom we . . .

STUYVESANT.—Yes . . . yes. A long way off those Estates General and Their High Mightinesses. We will talk of it another time. Why is that cannon being fired?

KIEFT.—In your honor, Excellency. It was deemed proper . . .

STUYVESANT.—A waste of good gunpowder, my friend. We will save it for our enemies. That soldier there! Stand straight, man! You are a soldier not a civilian peddler!

SOLDIER.—Yeah. That's right.

STUYVESANT.—"Excellency," to me!

SOLDIER.—Y-yes, Excellency.

STUYVESANT.—That's better. We will make something of you yet. (*Loudly*) Master Kieft, I have not come for speeches and cannon firing. I find many things wrong with your colony. I see here disorder . . . laziness . . . everything in ruins . . . every man a master. We shall clean up all this, go to work, and hold this spot for God and the Company. I shall govern as a father governs his children. But there shall be but one master here. (*Crowd murmurs up*) Too much dirt, too much talk, too many taverns. We cannot work and drink schnapps, too. That we shall see to first.

SOUND.—*Crowd up threateningly.*

JOCHEM.—Yah! Who is this slave driver who's gonna make us close our taverns?

STUYVESANT.—Arrest that man!

KIEFT.—Careful, Excellency. He has a knife. . . .

JOCHEM.—Who is this wooden leg to tell free citizens . . .

SOUND.—*Scuffle and thud on planks.*

STUYVESANT.—Pick him up. Just a touch of my sword hilt to his thick head. You, there, soldier! And you! Lay hold and put that trouble maker in the stocks. Now we have had enough talk. Tomorrow we start rebuilding that fort . . . clean up this place. Here, you soldiers! Form up! Clear these good people off the wharf. March!

MUSIC.

HANS.—Are you a fool, man? It only takes a few bottles of firewater! The redskins'll meet us up the river. We give 'em the grog, and we get their pelts. Then we sell the pelts, no?

JOHANN.—No. If old Peg-leg Peter catches us . . . he'll put us in the stocks!

MUSIC.—*Up and down.*

JACOB.—Don't go in. Not yet, kleinchen. We can go over to the Green and . . .

TINA.—We can't. No one may stay out after dark.

JACOB.—I know. We can hide behind the big tree.

TINA.—No! Peter Stuyvesant has ordered it so. Quick . . . unlatch the gate! The warder's coming.

MUSIC.—*Up and down.*

SOUND.—*Tavern murmurs.*

HENDRICK.—One more . . . give us all another tankard of schnapps.

JOCHEM.—No. No, that's all tonight.

WILLEM.—Come on. . . . We're still thirsty.

SOUND.—*Banging of tankards.*

JOCHEM.—No. I said no. I close the tavern. Peter Stuyvesant's orders.

MUSIC.—*Up and down.*

CHALMERS.—You can picture him stumping around the old town with a silver-headed stick ready to crack down on any lazy worker and putting his shoulder to the wheel himself when he had to. They laughed at old Peg-leg, some of them . . . behind his back . . . and he was cordially hated by others. But somehow he got things done. A bit headstrong and arbitrary, but beneath that tough old hide was a fighting spirit and a firm belief in the future of New Netherland. He fought with his council for what he considered his right to run things his own way, but he was just as ready to fight the Indians or the English or anyone else that threatened this colony that, in the depths of his fighting heart, he had grown to love.

At the age of sixty-three, rheumatics, wooden leg, and all, he led an expedition against the Swedish colony on the Delaware. The Indian tribes threatened New Amsterdam. Alarms sounded through the town. The villagers ran to Bowling Green. But old Peter was away. (*Church bell . . . crowd*) Panic on Bowling Green. Terrified colonists crowd into town, mingling with the villagers.

SOUND.—*Crowd . . . church bell . . . women's hysterical voices . . . shots off.*

JAN.—They're in the woods . . . north of the wall . . . thousands of 'em. Thick as blackberries. They've killed Van Dyck. . . . Werckendam's farm is gone . . . all his family . . .

KIEFT.—Yes . . . we saw the smoke . . . and over there . . .

VAN TIENHOVEN.—A boat just drifted by . . . on the river. A man and a woman . . . scalped. . . .

FIRST WOMAN.—What can we do? What can we do? Oh, my babies! My babies!

SOLDIER.—Make way! Out of the way! Help me swing this blasted cannon. . . .

JAN.—What for, you fool? You can't do any good. . . .

KIEFT.—The powder! Where is the powder? Someone said we should hold the fort! Get la Montaigne, somebody! He would know where the powder . . .

SOUND.—*Crowd up . . . splintering of wood.*

JAN.—This way! Keep that crowd back!

SOLDIER.—Help here, one of you! Get this cannon . . .

KIEFT.—Where's Van Tienhoven? He knows where the key is.

SECOND WOMAN.—My man is at the palisades. Can't anyone tell me where to go? Willem . . . Willem . . .

KIEFT.—If only we had Stuyvesant here!

JAN.—They sent a messenger yesterday . . . if he got through the redskins. Look! Master Kieft! That cloud of dust on High Street . . . coming from the Water Gate!

VAN TIENHOVEN.—God help us if they've taken the palisades! Into the fort, you people!

SOUND.—*Above crowd in background, a rolling of drums.*

JOCHEM.—Our men are falling back! The palisade is taken! They're coming . . . thousands of 'em! We'll be burned! We'll be tortured!

JAN.—Stop it! Get into the fort, then.

KIEFT.—If we had the ships now . . . we could escape to the ships. . . .

FIRST WOMAN.—They're coming! They're coming!

SOLDIER.—Out of the way there! Out of the way before I ride this horse over you!

SOUND.—*Crowd up . . . trampling . . . woman's screams.*

KIEFT.—Hurry! Hurry! They're coming. . . . Can't anyone control this mob? Somebody . . . back that cart out of the way!

SECOND WOMAN.—Willem! Where are you, Willem?

JAN.—(*Shouting*) Wait! Everybody! Stop that noise! Can't you hear it? Listen, everybody! (*Crowd down . . . woman's sobs . . . rolling of drums off*) The drums! Don't you hear them? It isn't the Indians coming through! They're our drums! Look . . . behind the dust cloud there!

KIEFT.—(*Joyful*) He's back! He's come back! See!

VAN TIENHOVEN.—Yes, it is he. There . . . in front. . . .

JAN.—Stuyvesant! Old Peg-leg . . . he's back!

FIRST WOMAN.—He's back! (*Sobbing happily*) He's come back again!

SOUND.—(*Drums fading in . . . crowd cheering . . . cries of "Stuyvesant!" "Old Peter" . . . crowd and drums up and out.*

STUYVESANT.—So! You are glad to see Stubborn Peter, eh? You need the old tyrant again?

KIEFT.—Your Excellency, in the present danger that the colony faces . . .

STUYVESANT.—Master Kieft, you gave me a speech before. They are not good speeches. I am not satisfied with what I find here . . . disorder and an Indian attack when my back is turned. Doctor La Montaigne, you will take one troop and clear those woods to the north. Master Killean, you march at once to protect the river settlements. Seize what boats you need, and send the sailors ashore for arms. Master Cornelius! Those two Indians in the stocks! Release them for messengers to the tribes. I shall meet the sachems outside the palisade tomorrow at sunup. Let them tell their masters that Wooden Leg wants peace and (*menacingly*) . . . if he doesn't get it quickly he will hang every zotscap savage to the highest trees in New Netherland! March! Now get these women into the fort, and every able man report here in 10 minutes, ready to march and fight!

MUSIC.

CHALMERS.—So, between bullying and cajoling . . . for the old fellow was a diplomat when he wanted to be . . . Stuyvesant made peace and avoided what might have been a ghastly Indian war and the ruin of the colony. In his treatment of the Indians he was quick to punish, quick to reward, and honest. Never was an Indian brave allowed inside the smaller villages, and he outlawed any man who sold an Indian liquor.

But in his dealings with his fellow burghers, the veteran soldier never could get it through his head that people did not always want to be ruled as a father rules his children and get smacked with a silver-headed cane every so often.

MUSIC.—*Up and down.*

FIRST VOICE.—By order of the Director General: Henceforth regulations and decrees issued by us regarding the maintenance of our Colonial defenses, the promotion of our commerce and territorial interests, the preservation of our internal welfare shall be unalterably obeyed and take immediate and unquestioned effect in full force and virtue. (*Fade*) Peter Stuyvesant. Director General.

MUSIC.—*Up and down.*

SECOND VOICE.—By order of the Director General: A series of fortifications are hereby decreed and by our command will be constructed according to our purposes and plans without further delay. (*Fade*) Peter Stuyvesant. Director General.

358

MUSIC.—*Up and finish.*

SOUND.—*Crowd.*

BURGOMASTER.—And so, Your Excellency, we come to the matter of these new fortifications to protect the colony. With this insurrection that the English have started on Long Island . . .

STUYVESANT.—Yes . . . yes, burgomaster. We know all about that, my friend. Let us get to the point. We must have this new palisade built. Now! We waste time talking about it.

BURGOMASTER.—But, Your Excellency, the money for this work! We must have money. . . .

STUYVESANT.—Money! Money! That is all I hear. Find the money. Raise the taxes. Do what you like . . . but we must strengthen our defense.

SOUND.—*Crowd murmur up.*

BURGOMASTER.—But the taxes must come from the people, Your Excellency, and already they complain that their money is being spent without their consent.

STUYVESANT.—(*Thumping table*) *Their* consent! A thousand thundering *duyvils!* I must ask leave of every drunken beggar in town to build a wall around us!

BURGOMASTER.—The people have a voice, Your Excellency. . . .

STUYVESANT.—Bah! Tell me nothing of that, burgomaster. Rule by the people . . . rule by the fools and talkers . . . the clowns and bear skinners! Freedom! Freedom to be as dirty and lazy and helpless as when I first came to New Netherland! I am the law here for the Company . . . not the tavern loafers! I am the voice here! I . . . Peter Stuyvesant . . . Director General of this colony!

SOUND.—*Crowd up angrily.*

BURGOMASTER.—We shall try to raise the money, of course, if it is needed . . .

STUYVESANT.—Needed! You sit there like hens clucking on a roost waiting for the English fox, and you talk about fortifications being needed! Lawyers! *Zotscaps!* All of you!

Mark my words . . . if we don't hold this spot for Holland and the Company, someone else will! We are alone . . . enemies on every side! England ready to gobble us up!

BURGOMASTER.—As to that, Your Excellency, whether this be the King of England's colony or we hold it for the Netherlands . . . one rule is like another. . . . (*Crowd approving*) But if the English were to destroy our farms and take our cattle . . .

STUYVESANT.—Your cattle . . . you dunce-head civilians! You would put your herds of cows above your flag?

BURGOMASTER.—There are many of us here of that mind, Your Excellency. (*Crowd up approvingly*) The Dutch West India Company does nothing for our protection. They send us no powder, no shot, no ships, no soldiers but the handful we have to face these English. Why should we defend the Company who will do nothing for us?

SOUND.—*Crowd warmer.*

STUYVESANT.—Enough! You are a traitor! You are all traitors! I have listened to your idle talk. . . . Now you will listen to me. I know my duty here. We shall defend this colony with what we have! I will raise the taxes and build a defense if I have to put every burgher in New Amsterdam in irons! (*Crowd . . . angry protests*) Enough of this! Sergeant! March your men in and clear this hencoop out! I am still the ruler of this colony!

SOUND.—*Tramp of soldiers . . . scuffle . . . crowd up.*

MESSENGER.—(*Off*) A message for His Excellency! The Director General! Let me through here! (*Fading in*) Excellency!

STUYVESANT.—Yes. Yes. What is it? Let him speak.

MESSENGER.—They've come! Four ships. . . . They were sighted from the church steeple . . . in the lower bay . . . four ships crowded to . . . the gunwales. . . .

STUYVESANT.—Who, man? Speak up!

MESSENGER.—The English, Your Excellency! They're sending a boat . . . a flag of truce. . . .

STUYVESANT.—Hah! At last they come! Now it is swords . . . not words! You hear that, burgomasters? The English are in the harbor!

SOUND.—*Crowd.*

BURGOMASTER.—Excellency! What do you plan to do?

STUYVESANT.—You ask me that? I plan to fight! Jan Jans, get the drummers here. Run out the cannon!

BURGOMASTER.—But can we not wait? They have not told us what they want. . . .

STUYVESANT.—I know what they want . . . New Netherland. Four ships . . . you heard that. A thousand men at least. Do you think they come to play bowls on the green?

BURGOMASTER.—Excellency, we cannot face such odds. They will ruin us . . . crush us . . . take away our farms!

STUYVESANT.—And so . . . you will not fight them?

BURGOMASTER.—The odds are too great. We are not ready. The people will not face trained troops. . . .

STUYVESANT.—What of it if the odds were twice as great? Bah! You are not soldiers. What are you? Shopkeepers! Traders! Talkers!

BURGOMASTER.—Our families, Excellency. Our wives and children . . .

STUYVESANT.—Stand aside, cowards! This I have made here . . . this New Amsterdam. You could not have made it. And you will not fight for it. But I . . . I, Peter Stuyvesant . . . old as I am . . . I will fight for it . . . if I fight alone! Stand out of my way!

MUSIC.

CHALMERS.—Looking at it from any angle, there wasn't much hope of saving the colony. But old Stubborn Peter wasn't giving up without a fight. Once before he had bluffed his way out of a tight spot with the English, and he hoped to do it again.

But this time it was different. The envoy that Stuyvesant sent to the English commander, Colonel Nicholls, to stall for time, came back with an ultimatum. New Amsterdam was to be handed over to the Duke of York, and, if there was any delay, the town would be destroyed. Stuyvesant tore up the ultimatum so the panicky burghers wouldn't know about it and lined up his handful of soldiers.

STUYVESANT.—You are ready, Jan?

FIRST GUARD.—Yes, Excellency.

STUYVESANT.—Stand aside, so that I may see. Look, Jan! Your eyes are younger than mine. Do you see any boats on the river yet?

JAN.—No, Excellency. There are no boats coming. Only the English ones.

STUYVESANT.—They should be here from Rensselaerwyck if my messenger reached them. Perhaps they come by land. (*Crowd off*) What is that I hear, Jan?

SECOND GUARD.—(*Coming in*) The people that are massed in High Street, Excellency. They are shouting for you to surrender.

STUYVESANT.—*Zotscaps!* We will attend to them when we have beaten the English. Ready!

FIRST GUARD.—Ready, Excellency.

(*Fade in crowd*)

STUYVESANT.—Hold your fire! Who is this? Ah, my brave burghers! Well, my friends, have you come to perform your duty?

BURGOMASTER.—(*Coming in*) Your Excellency . . . we must not open fire on them. It is hopeless. The people are crowding below. . . . They are getting out of hand . . . threaten to burn the fort. . . .

STUYVESANT.—They dare do that!

BURGOMASTER.—They want to accept the English terms . . . save their homes. They are getting ready a white flag now. . . .

STUYVESANT.—Traitors! Cowards! It is the English among us!

BURGOMASTER.—Not so, Excellency. English and Dutch, they say the same. Our homes are at stake. The men from New England are at the palisades . . . ready to burn the town. Our people will not fight for the Company. . . .

STUYVESANT.—For the flag there . . .

BURGOMASTER.—Heed me, Your Excellency. You are alone . . . a handful of soldiers. Not a man in the colony will raise a hand to help you.

STUYVESANT.—Bah! There is help coming. The men from Rensselaerwyck . . . the river colonies.

BURGOMASTER.—They are not coming, Your Excellency. They have sent word. Here is Doctor La Montaigne. You will believe him.

LA MONTAIGNE.—It is as the burgomaster says, Director General. Rensselaerwyck is not coming to your aid. The English offer fair terms. If you resist you will bring destruction on the town.

STUYVESANT.—So. They also have . . . betrayed us.

FIRST GUARD.—(*Off*) Excellency! The English are coming. . . . We are ready to fire!

BURGOMASTER —All these helpless people . . . our women . . . our children. Look, Your Excellency! They are in the streets. Only a madman would resist. . . .

STUYVESANT.—Peace! Hold your peace! Yes, it is so. Let be, then. Go! Tell your Englishmen we will treat for surrender and . . . choose among you the greatest coward to haul down the colors!

SOUND.—*Of peg leg.*

MUSIC.

CHALMERS.—An end . . . and a beginning, too . . . for the town and the colony that Peter Stuyvesant ruled with an iron fist kept growing and remained under the English flag up to the Revolution. Old Stubborn Peter retired to his farm on the east side of Manhattan and raised fruit trees. . . . You can imagine he made them stand pretty straight in their rows, too, and no nonsense about them. He kept on friendly terms with Colonel Nicholls . . . now Governor Nicholls of New York Province . . . as between one soldier and another.

We catch a last glimpse of old Peg-leg Peter before the shadows close in. He is calling on Governor Nicholls in his mansion. The English governor is having some trouble with the people about quartering soldiers in their homes.

SOUND.—*Spinet in background softly.*

NICHOLLS.—The town council seems to be at the bottom of it. All this talk about the rights of the people!

STUYVESANT.—So. You are finding it, too, eh? It is in the air, my friend. The new world . . . new ideas, new words. Freedom, the rights of the people. It was so in my day, too. It will always be so.

NICHOLLS.—But you managed , , , somehow . . . to keep it down.

STUYVESANT.—There was no time for it then. So much work to be done. One cannot work and talk, too. They were sheep . . . huddled here . . . and no shepherd dog to bark at their heels. I made them work.

NICHOLLS.—And you succeeded. At least you overcame these mad notions of freedom . . . democracy . . . people's rights.

STUYVESANT.—No. Those things I did not overcome, Your Excellency. One does not overcome a tide. These things they speak of . . . freedom and the rights of the people . . . like a tide coming in. No man can stop it. (*Pause . . . spinet in background*) I was too old, perhaps, to see. Too old to learn new things. A worker. A trudger. Those fanciful things . . . they are like the music that your lady plays there . . . strange and not for me. I tried to fight that tide, push back something in men's minds. I failed. As you will fail. (*Pause*) Maybe it is better that I failed. The world is changing, and my work here is finished. Maybe they will not forget old Stubborn Peter. I found here nothing . . . a few lazy men, frightened men, traders, tavern keepers, loafers . . . a place to rob for beaver skins and drink *schnapps*. The others that came before me . . . Van Twiller, Kieft . . . did not see, looking only for their beaver skins. But I saw.

NICHOLLS.—A future colony, yes.

STUYVESANT.—Something more than a colony, Your Excellency. An empire. Maybe they will not forget. Good night. . . .

NICHOLLS.—Your Excellency is leaving? It is early. . . .

364

STUYVESANT.—Yes, I sleep now. It gets late, and my work is done. I leave you your empire . . . for England. But England will not hold that empire. You cannot fight the tide. Good night!

(*Fade wooden stump*)

MUSIC.

CHALMERS.—Yes, Peter Stuyvesant's work was done . . . well done. And if, as they say, his ghost with plumed hat and silver-headed stick stumps through lower New York in the wee hours of the morning, he has the satisfaction of knowing that his visions came true. And in any man's life that's what really makes it all worth while.

MUSIC.—*Up and finish.*

CHALMERS.—Last week radio listeners everywhere were glad to hear that Gabriel Heatter . . . popular news commentator . . . is now a regular feature of this program. Every week at this time, he'll bring you news of the wonders of chemistry. I am going to ask him now to tell you about one triumph of chemistry. Mr. Heatter . . .

HEATTER.—Thank you, Tom Chalmers. Good evening, everyone. A new day. A new week. And for me a new headline of better living for millions. A headline about Cellophane. Like many of us, I had always taken Cellophane transparent wrapping for granted until my visit to the wonder world of chemistry . . . and I realized here indeed is a chemical marvel of our day and age.

For me Cellophane had always been just a wrapper for cigarettes, bread, candy, and cigars . . . but today I found lightning wrapped in Cellophane. When I say lightning, I mean it in the Benjamin Franklin manner . . . electricity. Yes, wrapped in Cellophane. Let me give it to you as a man in a wonder world of chemistry explained it to me in a few words. He talked of modern electrical motors . . . compact; miraclelike; and built in a way to save every possible inch of space inside.

For every inch of space which is saved inside means more room for wire; more wire means more power; more power means better living. The old way was to use a bulky insulation which required a great deal of space . . . and one day a man decided to try transparent cellulose film. Offhand you would say, "Fantastic." But men who work in a wonder world of chemistry have seen many wonders come to pass . . . and here was one who decided to try Cellophane for a use to which it had never been put before.

And it worked. And today, a thin winding of this material on copper wire does noble service on electric motors . . . stepping up power . . . and thousands of miles of ribbon Cellophane . . . as narrow as $\frac{1}{64}$ of an inch . . . are now made each year for insulating electric wire.

I am so fascinated by what I found it's almost difficult to describe it in language quiet and restrained. Those DuPont men work wonders which tame all fabled miracles. Picture Cellophane used as bandages in hospitals. It's true. And the reason, simple. Surgeons find it important to keep certain kinds of wounds in plain sight. Cellophane bandages make it possible.

I could call a roll of hundreds of uses for Cellophane. But tonight my mind turns to Christmas morning . . . 2 weeks away. We have come out of a dark and weary strain, and everyone needs Christmas now as never before. And I am certain of all wonders DuPont chemists have brought . . . they share with me tonight a vision of sparkle and gaiety and color which Cellophane will bring to Christmas gift wrappings.

Well, today I was given a new little book that tells how to dress up Christmas gifts in these glorified wrappings . . . yes, makes it easy for anyone. And I'm told that DuPont will send this same book to you if you drop a postal card to them at Wilmington, Delaware. It will help you make Christmas a sparkling example of . . . better things for better living . . . through chemistry.

MUSIC.

HEATTER.—And now a word from Tom Chalmers about next week's show.

CHALMERS.—We're going to tell you about a man who lived during our own times. A man whose kindly ways and home-spun philosophy made him one of America's great characters . . . Will Rogers. So until next week at this same time, good night and best wishes from DuPont.

MUSIC.—*Up.*

JEWETT.—This is the Columbia Broadcasting System.

The Eddie Doll Case

From GANG BUSTERS

PHILLIPS H. LORD's Gang Busters, dramatizing the never-ending war on crime by law enforcement agencies throughout the United States, has become one of radio's leading dramatic programs. Created in July, 1935, and known as G Men, the program confined its scope to the interesting story of the agents of the Federal Bureau of Investigation and their fight on the underworld.

After thirteen weeks of broadcasting, Mr. Lord decided to expand the subject matter of the program and to include the work of all law enforcement agencies in America. The program was renamed Gang Busters at this time.

Since its inception, Gang Busters has broadcast the true story of over two hundred famous criminal cases, including the depredations of such unpleasant people as Dillinger, Pretty Boy Floyd, Karpis, Machine-gun Kelly, and others. Material for the Gang Busters program is obtained from police officials and the files of law enforcement agencies throughout the United States. This information is checked and double-checked for accuracy by the research department of Phillips H. Lord, Inc., before being turned over to a script writer for dramatization.

Gang Busters is unusual among radio programs because of its fast-moving and, at times, stark writing technique. Inasmuch as each script is a true case history, the manner of writing these scripts differs considerably from that of most other programs on the air. Great attention is paid to brevity of speech, to simulation of the actual characters involved, and to colorful atmosphere, descriptive of the environment of those characters. The result is that the listener has an impression of having heard true facts dramatized as they happened without any of the usual embroidery that characterizes most melodramatic programs on the air.

Gang Busters today is recognized by police officials as an active civic agency in crime prevention work and receives the cooperation and assistance of police chiefs throughout the nation. Each week Gang Busters broadcasts over a nationwide CBS network clues furnished by police officials for criminals wanted by various police officials. Through these clues over a hundred and thirty-five criminals have been apprehended by police officers, a fact not generally known to the public.

Gang Busters, with its dramatic slogan, "Crime Does Not Pay," has been endorsed by prominent educators, criminologists, and penologists as an effective aid in crime prevention work.

One of the most effective and elaborate sound-effects setups in radio is used in this program. Three modern turntables with the latest gadgets, plus all kinds of manual equipment, keep two or three sound engineers busy during rehearsals and air shows. Gang Busters is considered a pioneer program in the use of new and startling sound technique, and many of the devices and effects that are now commonplace were developed by this series.

Studio productions are handled personally by Phillips H. Lord, nimble creator of Seth Parker, We the People, Mr. District Attorney, and other hits. Most of the scripts are compact, well knit, and spunky, filled with plausible action, understandable plotting, and the properly acrid aroma of professional police work. In a dramatic series dedicated solely to the pursuit and conviction of public enemies, it is remarkable that the temptation to go overboard in a splash of histrionic bathos has been so well resisted. "The Eddie Doll Case," which has been selected for this book, is a fine example of the series. It is not, and should not be, literature. It is straight, compressed dialogue, and for its type, the show performs its function with economy and direction and a commendable absence of hokum. Its chief virtue is that, although it is muscular throughout, it is nowhere muscle-bound.

"The Eddie Doll Case" was heard over the CBS Network January 18, 1939.

The Eddie Doll Case*

COLONEL.†—Dr. Simon, I understand that tonight's case concerns Eddie Doll, alias Eddie Larue, alias Burlington Eddie, alias Edward Foley.

SIMON.—Yes, Colonel Schwarzkopf. The case starts on September 16, 1930. Late at night, in the gang's hide-out at Lincoln, Nebraska, a barren room in the back part of a dilapidated apartment house. The shades were drawn, the windows sealed. The room was stuffy . . . blue with smoke . . . a tenseness was in the air. The gang was waiting nervously.

SOUND.—*Sneak in footsteps walking back and forth.*

ROGERS.—Sit down, Buck, and take a load off yer feet!

TIM.—Yeah. You gimme the willies walking around!

BUCK.—We may have ter bump the two guards off. . . .

ROGERS.—Forget it. Wait until Eddie Doll gets here. He's got all the low-down.

TIM.—I'm glad Doll has joined up with the gang. He's got a cool head. . . . He's slick. . . . He ain't one of these guys that goes off half cocked.

BUCK.—This is going ter be the smoothest bank job ever pulled in this country!

SOUND.—*Three knocks . . . two knocks.*

BUCK.—There's Doll now. . . .

(*Half fade*)

TIM.—Make sure before you unbolt that door.

SOUND.—*Footsteps under Tim's line.*

---

* Reprinted by special permission of Colgate-Palmolive-Peet Company, sole copyright owners; sponsors of Gang Busters and makers of Palmolive Shave Cream and Palmolive Brushless Shave Cream. Copyright, 1939.
† Script written by Brice Disque, Jr.

ROGERS.—Who is it?

DOLL.—A guy.

SOUND.—*Slip bolt . . . door opens and closes . . . footsteps.*

DOLL.—Hi. . . .

SOUND.—*Subdued gang greets Doll.*

TIM.—Hi, Doll.

DOLL.—(*Moving chair*) Everybody here?

BUCK.—Yeah. . . . When we going ter crack the job?

DOLL.—We're going ter crack it in the morning, boys.

SOUND.—*Slight reaction.*

ROGERS.—What's the dope?

DOLL.—This is going ter be the most perfect bank cracking ever pulled in this country . . . and the biggest. One million dollars.

BUCK.—Everything's set.

DOLL.—We're going to rehearse this thing inch by inch right now. I've got every emergency covered. . . .

BUCK.—We been working on it 3 months.

DOLL.—Buck, you're responsible for the getaway. If anything slips we'll all get lead poisoning. . . . Give the boys the setup.

BUCK.—Here's the map of our getaway. (*Sound of paper*) The car will do 70. You guys jumps in. . . . We heads north, take the turn into Elm Street. . . . They're working on the road, so only one car can pass. I'm giving a taxicab driver 100 bucks. After we pass, he starts to drive through . . . stalls his car . . . so anybody chasing us will be stuck.

ROGERS.—Does he know what we're up to?

BUCK.—Of course not. . . . I told him it was a wedding party trying to get away. . . . We keeps going . . . on the state highway over the railroad track. We turns off the highway, here, and heads for the hangout. I've drove over that route three times a day for the past 2 weeks. I could drive it blindfolded.

Tɪᴍ.—How about license plates?

Buck.—I got that fixed, too. . . . While we're driving we can drop off the license plates . . . and swing new ones on. O.K., Doll?

Doʟʟ.—All right. Now . . . fer weeks I've had all you guys going in the bank . . . having money changed. . . . I hired a vault terday . . . got a good look through the cellar. (*Rustle of paper*) Here's a picture of the inside of the bank. There'll be four guns in the bank . . . one in this drawer here . . . one in that drawer there. . . . and the two guards are always standing right here in front of this cage. Frank . . .

Fʀᴀɴᴋ.—Yeah!

Doʟʟ.—You stands to the right of *this* guard, and Tim stands to the right of *this* one. . . .

Tɪᴍ.—O.K.

Doʟʟ.—At the signal . . . you crack them guards . . . snatch their guns. I'll get the two guns from the drawers. Ten seconds later, Sweeney comes in the bank with a machine gun. He covers the customers. (*Ad lib agreement*) We touch nothing in the bank but money. . . . *We leave no finger-prints.* Remember that!

Buck.—Suppose the two guards puts up a fight.

Doʟʟ.—Frank and Tim bumps 'em off. Now . . . let's study the layout. We'll spend the rest of the night *memorizing every detail.*

(*Fade in*)

Souɴᴅ.—*Slight bank commotion . . . adding light background.*

(*Fade in*)

Mᴀɴ.—Good morning, Mr. Smith. . . . I'd like to cash this check.

Tᴇʟʟᴇʀ.—Certainly, Mr. Brown.

Doʟʟ.—Stick 'em up. . . . This is a holdup!

(*Quiet*)

DOLL.—Number three . . . keep 'em covered with that machine gun. If anybody makes a move, mow the whole bunch down.

ROGERS.—Right.

DOLL.—Number one . . .

BUCK.—(*Half off*) Yes, sir . . .

DOLL.—Scoop all the loose cash into those laundry bags. Hey, you . . . you bank guy! Come here. Come with me and swing back the door of that vault.

BANK GUY.—Yes, sir.

SOUND.—*Footsteps.*

DOLL.—Swing it back.

SOUND.—*Several bolts.*

DOLL.—One false move and you'll get lead poisoning. . . Scoop all those bank notes into that bag.

SOUND.—*Much change being poured into bags . . . many packages of bills being tossed in . . . continues under* (*Fade in*)

ROGERS.—There's a lot of loose money in these drawers, boss.

DOLL.—Take yer time, Pal. . . . This ain't no peanut robbery. Keep cool. . . . Use yer heads. This is going to be a million dollar haul. . . . Lug the full bags of money as far as the front door.

SOUND.—*Change going into bags out.* (*Fade in*)

BUCK.—There's a crowd collecting in front of the bank.

DOLL.—Let them collect. . . . We're collecting in here.

ROGERS.—(*Coming on*) We got everything, boss.

DOLL.—You guys carry those bags. (*Projected*) Don't one of you people take one step to follow us . . . or *we'll* shoot holes in you. Come on. . . . (*footsteps*)

DOLL.—Number three . . . you stand at the door with the machine gun. As soon as we're all in the car, we'll give you the signal.

372

ROGERS.—Check.

DOLL.—Come on. (*Footsteps . . . crowd gets louder . . . sound of motor idling*) Throw the bags of money in the back. (*Several thuds*) Sound the signal. . . . Everybody get in. (*Horn two long blasts*) Here come the rest of the gang. . . . (*Car door slams*) Step on it, Buck.

SOUND.—*Roar of motor up strong and fade out.*

COLONEL.—As I recall, Dr. Simon, that million dollar robbery was the biggest bank robbery ever staged in this country. Please tell our Palmolive Shave Cream listeners what happened next.

SIMON.—At that time, Colonel, bank robbery was not under the jurisdiction of the Federal Bureau of Investigation, but the Lincoln, Nebraska, authorities asked the F.B.I. to furnish them with what information it could. On September 19, 1930, Inspector Haynes of the Federal Bureau of Investigation was in his private office in Washington, and I want you to see how a large organization operates in gathering complete information about a criminal. . . .

SOUND.—*Door opens and closes.*
(*Fade in*)

DENNISON.—You sent for me, Inspector Haynes.

HAYNES.—Dennison. This bank robbery in Lincoln, Nebraska, is the cleanest bank job ever done in this country.

DENNISON.—There isn't a clue. . . .

HAYNES.—Not one . . . *but* . . . we've *got* to *find* one. Now I've got here a complete report of how the robbery was executed. I want to check the *modus operandi* of this gang.

DENNISON.—Every musician has a definite individual musical touch. . . . Every painter has his own style. . . . Every criminal has his own individual approach to a crime.

HAYNES.—Yes, Dennison. We know there are some dozen gangs of bank robbers in the Middle West. . . . We know some recent gangs have been broken up. . . .

DENNISON.—You mean this robbery may have been committed by a leader who had his schooling from some gang that's already been caught?

HAYNES.—That's it. And if we can find a Middle Western gang, which operates similar to the procedure used in this robbery, it'll be a nail to hang our hat on.

SOUND.—*Buzzer . . . click.*

HAYNES.—Yes?

FILTER 1.—Mr. Frank is here, Inspector.

HAYNES.—Send him in at once.

FILTER 1.—Yes, sir.

SOUND.—*Click.*

HAYNES.—(*To Dennison*) I've asked several of the men to get reports on some of these Midwestern gangs, Dennison. . . .

SOUND.—*Door opens . . . closes.*

FRANK.—Frank reporting, Inspector.

HAYNES.—Get a report on that Salta gang?

FRANK.—Yes, sir. . . . They pulled four bank robberies. In each case, they shot the guards, and in each case they were careless about fingerprints . . . and they didn't bother to take along loose silver.

SOUND.—*Buzzer . . . click.*

HAYNES.—Yes?

FILTER 1.—O'Brien is waiting, Inspector.

HAYNES.—Tell him to come in.

FILTER 1.—Yes, sir. . . . That's all, Frank.

FRANK.—Yes, sir.

SOUND.—*Door opens . . . closes.*

HAYNES.—(*To Dennison*) Dennison . . . the Salta gang had no part in this bank robbery. This gang we're looking for *scooped up the loose silver.* . . . They left no *fingerprints.* . . .

SOUND.—*Door opens and closes.*

DENNISON.—And the leader of the gang we're chasing had *brains.*

O'BRIEN.—(*Coming in*) O'Brien reporting, sir.

HAYNES.—What about that Hoosier gang, O'Brien?

O'BRIEN.—There are six robberies laid to them, Inspector. In all six cases they entered the bank, bound their prisoners, took all money . . . *including loose silver.* Only in one case was there *shooting of a guard.* The gang wore gloves in all cases, and only in one instance did they desert their car.

HAYNES.—Thanks, O'Brien. . . . Is Smith waiting outside?

O'BRIEN.—Yes, sir.

HAYNES.—Ask him to come in.

O'BRIEN.—(*Fading*) Yes, sir.

SOUND.—*Door opens and closes.*

HAYNES.—Dennison . . . this gang sounds more like the one we're after. . . . their not shooting guards agrees. . . . Not deserting their car agrees. . . . Taking all loose silver agrees. . . .

DENNISON.—But the tying up of all those in the banks. . . .

SOUND.—*Door opens and closes.*

HAYNES.—That's where the Hoosier method differs from the gang that pulled this job. Hello, Smith. . . .

SMITH.—(*Comes on*) I got reports on the Five-finger Mob and on the Yates gang.

HAYNES.—Let's have them.

SMITH.—Three bank robberies during the past year have been laid to the Five-finger Mob. In every case they've been scared off.

DENNISON.—Isn't that the gang that always leaves a girl in the car out front as a blind?

SMITH.—Yes, sir.

HAYNES.—Um . . . they're just a rattlebrained mob. But there was a *super thinking mind* in back of this Lincoln, Nebraska, job. What about the Yates gang?

375

SMITH.—Broken up about two years ago. Three of them caught . . . one shot. . . . *Yates and two others escaped.* Nothing has been laid to this gang during the past 2 years.

HAYNES.—What was their procedure?

SMITH.—(*Rattle of papers*) I have it here. They entered the bank . . . made a thorough sweep of money . . . held employees at machine gun point. . . . In four cases they got reserve money from vaults, had a car waiting to make escape. In no case did they ever desert the car.

HAYNES.—Thanks, Smith. That's all.

SMITH.—Yes, sir.

SOUND.—*Steps . . . door opens and closes*

DENNISON.—Inspector, that's the same *modus operandi* used in the Lincoln, Nebraska, robbery.

HAYNES.—Yes, Dennison. (*Rustle of paper*) This report says that back in February our St. Louis field office was notified that a sheriff in Macomb, Illinois, picked up an Edward Doll for stealing a car. Doll was arrested, placed under $3,500 bail . . . skipped bail. A car thief doesn't usually have $3,500 to put up as bail . . . or to throw away by not appearing.

SOUND.—*Dictograph.*

HAYNES.—Fingerprint Department?

FILTER 1.—Yes, sir.

HAYNES.—Look up the record of Edward Doll. . . . See who he's been connected with in the past.

FILTER 1.—Yes, sir.

SOUND.—*Dictograph click.*

DENNISON.—Are you figuring that Doll may have joined up with the *Yates gang?*

HAYNES.—Let's think now. The Yates gang always makes a thorough cleaning of the bank. That tallies. They don't tie the customers and employees. That tallies.

DENNISON.—And their general plan of procedure was similar to the procedure just used in this bank robbery.

HAYNES.—All right. . . . Yates and two of his pals are still at large. . . . Edward Doll skipped his bail 4 months ago. . . . It's taken several months to plan this bank robbery. . . . Why do all of these facts fit so perfectly?

SOUND.—*Dictograph buzz . . . click of receiver.*

HAYNES.—Inspector Haynes speaking.

FILTER 1.—Report on Edward Doll . . . arrested several times on minor offences . . . known to be exceptionally clever. . . . It is possible that he is one of the leaders reorganizing a Western bank robbery gang. That's all.

HAYNES.—O.K. . . .

SOUND.—*Dictograph click.*

DENNISON.—So Doll *does* know Yates?

HAYNES.—Of course some of this is hypothetical, but Doll may have learned his bank robbing from Yates and now is even more clever. See that a picture of Doll, his history, and all of these facts are sent to the Nebraska authorities. It may be a good lead.

SIMON.—A number of months went by, Colonel . . . Doll completely disappeared. Then suddenly . . .

FILTER 2.—Kidnaping . . . South Bend, Indiana. Kidnaping corresponds to description of Edward Doll, recently distributed by the Federal Bureau of Investigation.

FILTER. 1.—Local bank in Tupelo, Mississippi, just robbed by Machine-gun Kelly. Description of his companion fits Edward Doll. Wanted . . . all information on Machine-gun Kelly and Edward Doll.

FILTER 3.—Attention . . . attention. . . . United States mail robbery at Effingham, Illinois. . . . Believe leader of gang was Edward Doll.

CHIEF.—Well, Colonel, orders came from headquarters to the G men to redouble their efforts to get Edward Doll. Inspector Haynes again called Dennison into his office in Washington.

HAYNES.—Dennison, all we know up to now is Edward Doll is somewhere in this country . . . and we've got to find him. I've just received some additional information.

DENNISON.—Something I haven't heard?

HAYNES.—Yes. Reports from all over the country. Doll's weakness is pretty girls. Has been known to visit Alice Kahn of New Orleans, Mildred Barling of San Francisco, Lucy Weber of Denver, Joan English of St. Louis. . . . There's a long list of them here, sir.

SOUND.—*Dictograph buzz . . . click.*

HAYNES.—Inspector Haynes.

FILTER 1.—Report on Doll, sir. Used to pal around with Kathryn and Machine-gun Kelly. We have his fingerprints . . . specimens of his handwriting, and a good picture of him.

HAYNES.—Send it all in immediately.

SOUND.—*Click of dictograph.*

HAYNES.—Well, Dennison, we're not very far ahead.

DENNISON.—Wait, Inspector, here's information I've dug up. Doll is fond of motion pictures . . . especially gangster pictures. And get this. . . . He has *tattoo marks on both his right and left forearms.* A heart and an anchor and figure of a girl on his right forearm . . . a cow girl and pierced heart on his left forearm. And he's quoted as having said that eventually he's going to retire to a chicken farm.

HAYNES.—Well, now we're getting somewhere! (*Dictograph buzz . . . click*) Inspector Haynes.

SMITH.—(*Filter*) Men at one of our Western field offices have just been to the jail and talked with Machine-gun Kelly. They didn't let Kelly know they wanted information on Doll . . . but they asked a lot of questions about other things, and Kelly intimated that about 9 months ago Doll married a girl by the name of *Janet Galaton* in New York.

HAYNES.—Thanks, Smith.

SOUND.—*Click.*

DENNISON.—Doll's *already* married, Inspector.

HAYNES.—That wouldn't stop *him* from marrying again. Um . . . that's the best tip we've had yet.

DENNISON.—It's going to be a big job to examine all the marriage licenses in New York. They probably got married under fictitious names, too.

HAYNES.—(*Thinking*) Let's see. . . . Doll meets a girl . . . wants to marry her. Is he going to let her know who he *really is?* If she were the type of girl that he could take in as one of the gang . . . he wouldn't care if she knew his identity. Right, Dennison?

DENNISON.—Yes.

HAYNES.—*But* . . . if Doll *doesn't want her to suspect anything,* then he can't ask *her* to sign a fictitious name to the marriage license. He'd change *his* name . . . but that marriage license is going to contain *her real* name. We've got to find a license made out to *Janet Galaton.*

COLONEL.—Dr. Simon, I know the most interesting part of the case will be the police search for Janet Galaton, but before you tell us about that, Frank Gallop has a few words for our listeners.

(*Commercial*)

COLONEL.—Dr. Simon, you were telling us that Inspector Haynes and Dennison went to New York to check the marriage license records.

SIMON.—Yes, Colonel Schwarzkopf, for over a month, Inspector Haynes and Dennison worked in the marriage bureau of New York, carefully going over every marriage license. It was a tedious job. (*Fade*) Then, late one afternoon . . .

SOUND.—*Typewriters and office hum in background.*

DENNISON.—(*Tense*) What is it, Inspector Haynes?

HAYNES.—This is worth our weeks of tiresome checking, Dennison. A marriage license made out to Miss Janet Gabrielle Galaton and Mr. Leonard E. Foley.

DENNISON.—Janet and Galaton are fairly common names.

HAYNES.—Married to Leonard E. Foley. . . . Give me that sample of Doll's handwriting.

DENNISON.—Sure, here it is.

SOUND.—*Rustle of paper.*

HAYNES.—Let's see. . . . Leonard E. Foley. . . . Um . . . Edward Doll. Those two E's are written exactly the same way.

DENNISON.—Yes . . . the ends on those two D's are the same too . . . and notice the R's?

HAYNES.—Dennison, it's our first clue!

DENNISON.—Foley gives his address there as the Nemo Hotel, Dallas, Texas. . . . That's probably fictitious.

HAYNES.—But Janet Galaton gives *her* address as Danville, Vermont. That's probably correct. Come on, Dennison. We're going to Danville, Vermont.

SIMON.—Several hours later, Colonel, Inspector Haynes, and special agent Dennison, posing as traveling salesmen, arrived at Danville, Vermont. They rented a car and drove up to the local post office.

SOUND.—*Car stopping.*

DENNISON.—But why come to the post office, Inspector? Let's go up to her home.

SOUND.—*Turn motor off.*

HAYNES.—This is safer.

DENNISON.—Why?

HAYNES.—Janet Galaton doesn't know she's married to a man like Doll, does she?

DENNISON.—No.

HAYNES.—If she doesn't know, *her parents* don't know.

DENNISON.—Um . . .

HAYNES.—It's natural for parents to communicate with their daughter. If they don't realize there is any need for secrecy the *most natural* communications would be through the mails.

DENNISON.—I get you.

HAYNES.—The safest way to close down on a criminal is not to let anybody in the world know you're looking for him. Come on . . . in the post office.

SOUND.—*Door of car . . . footsteps on cement . . . change footsteps to wood.*

HAYNES.—*(Fade in)* How do you do.

POSTMASTER.—How do you do, sir.

HAYNES.—I'd like five 3-cent stamps.

POSTMASTER.—Yes, sir.

SOUND.—*Money on counter.*

HAYNES.—Say . . . by the way. . . . Would you direct me to the home of Janet Galaton?

POSTMASTER.—Yes, sir. You turn right . . . a mile up the road . . . a green house on the right-hand side.

SOUND.—*Sealing letters.*

HAYNES.—Thanks. Thought I'd drop in and surprise her.

POSTMASTER.—She's not at home now, you know.

HAYNES.—*(Disappointed)* Doesn't she live here any more?

POSTMASTER.—*(Laugh)* Hasn't for a year. Married now . . . married some out-of-town fellow.

HAYNES.—I'm awfully disappointed. Say . . . I guess I'll drop her a postal card from here, though. You don't happen to know her address offhand, do you?

POSTMASTER.—Yes. . . . Her folks sent her a package yesterday and insured it. . . . The slip . . . here it is. The package was sent to Mrs. Janet G. Foley, Box 270A, Route No. 2, St. Petersburg, Florida.

HAYNES.—Thanks. I'll drop her a card. *(Slight pause)*

COLONEL.—That was a clever piece of work, Dr. Simon. Please tell our Palmolive Shave Cream audience how Inspector Haynes followed it up.

SIMON.—Well, Colonel, 4 days later, Inspector Haynes and special agent Dennison arrived in St. Petersburg and talked with the local post office officials.

(Fade in)

HAYNES.—But I tell you there *must* be a Leonard E. Foley listed somewhere here in St. Petersburg.

POST OFFICER.—(*Florida accent*) No Leonard E. Foley in the city directory.

HAYNES.—Is the postman who delivers over Route No. 2 around?

POST OFFICER.—He may be in the other room. (*Fade*) I'll see.

HAYNES.—(*Lower voice*) What do you think, Dennison?

DENNISON.—Funny there isn't a Leonard Foley in the directory. (*Fade in*)

POST OFFICER.—Mr. Jenkins was just going out delivering mail. He has Rural Route No. 2. These two gentlemen are Federal officers, so answer anything they ask you.

POSTMAN 2.—(*Florida accent*) Yes, sir.

HAYNES.—We have the address of a Leonard E. Foley, Box 270A, Route No. 2. Know anything about him?

POSTMAN 2.—Why . . . about 2 weeks ago he wrote out an order that all mail addressed to Foley should be delivered . . . Wait a minute. . . . I've got that order here in my book.

HAYNES.—Good. . . . Did he write the instructions himself?

POSTMAN 2.—Yes, sir.

HAYNES.—Dennison . . . let me have that sample of Doll's handwriting.

DENNISON.—Just a minute.

SOUND.—*Shuffle of cards.*

POSTMAN 2.—Here's the note he wrote out. Says to deliver any mail addressed to Janet or Leonard Foley to 5190 38th Avenue North.

HAYNES.—Let me see the paper. . . . Um . . . Dennison . . . notice this E. . . . See this R. . . .

DENNISON.—That's his handwriting!

HAYNES.—He and his wife have a house out there?

POSTMAN 2.—Yes, sir. Farm about 35 acres. They raise *chickens.*

382

HAYNES.—When's the last time you saw him?

POSTMAN 2.—He come out to the postbox about 2 days ago.

HAYNES.—Thank you, gentlemen, very much. Come on, Dennison, we'll go out and see this Mr. Foley!

SOUND.—*Slight pause . . . motor fading in.*

HAYNES.—That looks like the house, Dennison, ahead on the right.

DENNISON.—Think there'll be shooting, Inspector?

HAYNES.—There will be if he can get his hands on his gun . . . but first we've got to make *sure* he's the *right* man.

DENNISON.—Remember the tattoos. He should have a heart and anchor and a girl tattooed on his right forearm. . . .

HAYNES.—But on his forearm . . . if we try to force him to roll up his sleeves there may be shooting.

DENNISON.—That would be a sure way to identify him, though.

SOUND.—*Car slows up.*

DENNISON.—There's a man around back of the house.

SOUND.—*Car stops.*

HAYNES.—(*Low*) Change your gun into your outside pocket.

DENNISON.—(*Low*) Right.

SOUND.—*Car door opens . . . feet in straw walking.*

HAYNES.—(*Calling*) Hello, there. Mind if we come out back and see you?

DOLL.—(*Distance*) Come on.

SOUND.—*More walking.*
(*Fade in*)

HAYNES.—We're interested in buying some chickens. . . .

DOLL.—(*A little surprised*) You ain't *farmers*. . . .

HAYNES.—No . . . we've just moved to St. Petersburg. Thought we might arrange to get fresh chickens from you.

DOLL.—I ain't selling any. Wait a minute till I close that gate. (*Fade*) All the chickens will be out.

DENNISON.—(*Whisper*) Think it's Doll? He's about the right size . . . heavier, though.

HAYNES.—(*Whisper*) We got to get a look at his *forearm*. (*Fade in*)

DOLL.—What did you two fellers stop for, anyhow?

HAYNES.—I told you. . . . We'd like to have you kill us a fresh chicken every Sunday. You've got a nice place here. . . . This big hogshead makes a good watering trough.

DOLL.—Yeah. . . . It's always full of water, too. . . . This hose runs from that spring over there and keeps the hogshead full.

HAYNES.—Look here, Bill. . . . Lean over and look in it. . . Isn't that water clean?

DENNISON.—Mighty clear.

SOUND.—*Drop watch in water.*

HAYNES.—Oh! I dropped my watch into the water! You've got your coat off, sir. . . . would you roll up your sleeves and get it out before the water gets into the works?

DOLL.—All right. . . . Wait a minute. . . . (*Bending over and grunt . . . swish of water*) There. . . .

HAYNES.—Thanks. . . . It was awfully careless of me.

DENNISON.—Got a tattoo mark on your arm, haven't you? An anchor and a girl. . . . You must have been a sailor.

DOLL.—No. . . . I did it for the fun of it.

DENNISON.—This is interesting. . . . Tattoo always fascinated me. . . . Let me see it. . . .

DOLL.—Sure.

HAYNES.—That's beautiful work.

DENNISON.—Best I've ever seen!

DOLL.—You fellas think *this* is good? Wait til you see my *other* arm!

HAYNES.—(*Leading him on*) Oh, you've got *another* tattoo?

DOLL.—(*Proudly*) Look at *this!*

DENNISON.—A cow girl and a pierced heart.

HAYNES.—Hold your arms out together so I can compare the two designs.

DOLL.—Sure. What do ya think of 'em?

SOUND.—*Sudden click of handcuffs.*

DOLL.—(*Astonished*) Hey. . . . What's the idea . . . ? Take these handcuffs off me!

HAYNES.—Edward Doll, you're wanted for the million dollar bank robbery in Lincoln, Nebraska; the South Bend kidnaping and too many other crimes to mention.

DOLL.—So you *know* me? How'd you find me? . . . I didn't make *one* false move.

HAYNES.—That's one of the things that *helped* us find you, Doll.

SIMON.—And that, Colonel, was the end of Eddie Doll, master mind of the biggest bank robbery ever committed in this country.

COLONEL.—What happened to Doll, Dr. Simon?

SIMON.—He was sentenced to a long term in a Federal penitentiary.

COLONEL.—Thank you, Dr. Carleton Simon, for telling us this gripping case. You and I know that no matter how cunning a criminal may be, no matter how cleverly he may cover his tracks, sooner or later he is bound to be uncovered and suffer the full penalty of the law. Tonight's case has brought out vividly our oft-repeated statement . . . THE CRIMINAL CANNOT WIN.

The Steel Worker

by ARCH OBOLER

ϙϙ

THE DRAMATIC monologue is a radio rarity, and it is a great misfortune that this is so. Henry Hull has appeared in one or two; Sheila Barrett and Cornelia Otis Skinner have been heard many times in humorous bits of monologue. A year ago Barbara Weeks gave Dorothy Parker's famous piece, "The Telephone," a splendid reading; Ruth Draper, greatest monologist of this generation, made her first and only radio appearance over four years ago. But the total does not add up to a trend or to anything sufficiently regular to be looked forward to as an established feature in radio as we know it today.

This situation may seem uninteresting and unimportant to many people, and I am not concerned with an argument for the case. I have said only that it is a misfortune, and I believe this not so much for the sake of the monologue itself as for the shift in conditions that explains its virtual disappearance. I do not wish to suggest a return of the bird imitator. Rather it is my feeling that America's habits of entertainment have sustained a dislocation that nothing is going to change much very soon. Radio and movies and automobiles have done it. There are no more Chautauqua, no vaudeville, few popular lecture series, and no itinerant wits. Even circuses are having a bad time.

Although the public is still responsible for the type of entertainment it is currently receiving, it appears that the public no longer has much to do with it directly. America is being entertained by professionals; she has ceased to entertain herself. All one needs to do to determine how true this is is to compare an average Tuesday evening (after Information Please has signed off) with a Tuesday evening of twenty-five years ago. Nobody can recite any more, no one can declaim, and the business of elocution has passed into wheezing senescence. This may be all right; I do not know. I only know that if the testimony of my grandfather is reliable, those of us who never heard Artemus Ward missed a considerable something. Today we do not make our fun; it is made for us.

Now, although it is perfectly true that what we can buy is better than what we can make; although it is true that, despite the passing of the annual county pumpkin show, America is better entertained and more entertaining than ever before, it is equally true that spontaneous artistic diversions of even the most rudimentary intention have left the American scene, perhaps forever. Today we are critics and appreciators; we have ceased to be participants.

The humble monologue, simplest of dramatic forms, hangs upon the upright body of modern entertainment as a sort of vestigial tail. But, like many other enduring institutions, it is as respectable as it is humble, for it is the oldest entertainment known to man. It is the only genuine primitive in the entire gallery of dramatics. Radio, by reason of its peculiar character, can (if it will) express this known but neglected truth more forcefully than any other medium except the stage. I have heard bad monologues on the air, but I have heard surprisingly few. This is because as an art form in drama it is the most natural. It was common in pre-Christian times; it is common in all Oriental countries today; it occurs throughout the Bible and Shakespeare, and I believe it is something that radio will embrace increasingly.

A well-written, pointed monologue is a challenge to any actor. He is obliged to turn himself into a one-man show. Because so few actors can meet this challenge, the standard set by the good monologue is as animating as it is healthy. The piece that I have selected reveals many of the inherent opportunities afforded by this type of dramatic writing; opportunities to the writer and performer alike. Arch Oboler, whose monologue is reprinted, has used this medium for its commentary advantages. Oboler, who was mentioned in the prefatory statement to "The Lighthouse Keepers," is one of radio's best-known and most prolific writers.

The Steel Worker*

ANNOUNCER.—The scene . . . a hill overlooking Steel Town. Far below, the furnaces roar with flame. . . . The great chimneys pour smoke up to the cold blue sky.

Alone, one Giorgio Maslarovic, steel worker, sits looking down into the valley of steel. He lifts his face, a face lined deep with sorrow, and speaks.

GIORGIO.—(*Quietly . . . reminiscingly*) I tell you 'bout it . . . sure. . . . Me . . . I used like go to de mill, yah! I come up de street. . . . De air, she's cold. . . . De sky she's black like inside empty furnace. . . . I laugh. . . . (*Laughingly*) I say, "Hey, you old sun! You sleep late! Ah, dot's all right for you, but me, Giorgio Maslarovic, I got go mill. . . . I got go make steel! . . .

(*Chuckles*) Yah, dot's what I say. . . . (*Chuckles*) I keep walkin' to de mill. . . . I see my frien's. . . . Dey go work, too. Joe, Steve, Nick, Hasan . . . frien's from ole country. . . . Good, strong Croatian hands dey got, like me . . . strong hands for to make strong steel. . . .

Dey walk along. Dey say . . . (*back . . . calling*) "Kako si ti?" . . . How's everytin', George?

I say . . . (*up*) "Dobro! Dobro! Everytin', she's fine! She's goin' be good day for make good steel!" (*Chuckle*) Dey laugh! Dey say goin' be good day make mona buy more shoe, and pants, and bread, and meat for kids. . . . (*Sighs*) Ah, t'ings for kids. . . . Yah, I t'ink dot's good, too, make mona for buy t'ings for wife and kids . . . mona for send to old moder back in old country so she has eat. Yah, make mona for dot . . . dot be very good t'ing.

(*In close, fervently*) But first I like make steel! *Good* steel! Steel what run out white wit' blue flame 'round on top! Steel what cool slow red like the sun when she falls down from sky! Steel what run slow t'rough rollin' mill, blue-black steel like night when stars shine out real sharp an' cold! Yah . . . *good* steel! Dot my life, I tell you!

MUSIC.—*Mossolov's "The Steel Foundry" begins, continuing behind*

I go in mill. . . . Right away I hear music. Yah, music I tell ya! Every mornin' when I come to mill, I hear it! Out of furnace . . . out of smokin' pits . . . out of forges and de rollin' mills! A burnin' music . . . a hammerin' music . . . singin' out of de blowers . . . out of de machines draggin' de ingots . . . out of de furnace and hot pits! Every mornin' when I come in de mill I can hear it! I listen. . . . I feel good. . . . I like it. . . . It sing over and over again . . . de song of de steel . . . a good song for de good steel! And den . . . yah, I no fool you . . . de steel, she talk right out to *me!* Yah, to me, Giorgio Maslarovic! She talk to me strong and straight like a good woman talk! She say, "Hello, Giorgio! To work! To work, my frien'! (*Laughs*) Make me strong . . . yah, make me strong! I got be strong, Giorgio . . . strong for to hold big buildings on my back! Strong for to cross deep river! Strong for to hold train! Strong for to make house for peoples! Ah, I got hard work to do, Giorgio, so make me strong, my frien'!"

I laugh. I say, "Sure! Sure, I make you strong for such good t'ings! Sure, my frien', de steel, I make hard work for to make you strong steel!" Yah, me . . . Giorgio Maslarovic, I do it! (*Chuckles*) And den de machines . . . de big cranes and de rollin' mills and de hammers, dey laugh with me! Dey laugh and say, "Sure Giorgio! We help you! We help you make steel strong!" And de wheels go faster, faster over and over the whole mill I hear dem talkin', talkin', sayin', "Yah we help Giorgio! We help Giorgio! We help make strong steel! Strong steel for building what go up to de sky! Strong steel for trains what go fast! Strong steel for tool what make good t'ing for people to live better! Faster! Faster! Work! Work! Steel! Steel! Make steel strong! Make steel good! Good steel! (*Up*) Good steel!

MUSIC.—*Out.*

GIORGIO.—(*Voice dead . . . hopelessly*) And den for long time is no work. Layoff. . . . No more smoke from mill chimney. No more song from furnace. Everytin', she's cold and quiet. No work, no work. I sit by home. . . . I wait. . . . I know the world need for de steel. Yah, the mill, she start again. . . . She's got to! The peoples need good house, good tool, good everytin' de steel can make. . . . Yah, so I wait. . . . I wait. . . . Some day . . . (*In growing excitement*) And den one day de whistle blow! I run to door! My frien's call, "Giorgio, come on! De mill, she's open! The work, she start!" I grab my wife, my kids! I laugh! I jump! Right! I was right to wait! De time, she's come! De world wants steel again! Good steel! I run to de mill! "It's me!" I say. "I come for work! . . . Me, Giorgio Maslarovic!" Dey say, "Sure, Giorgio! We got work for you . . . plenty of work!" Ha ha . . . it's good . . . it's good! I run into de mill! I no can wait! My frien', de steel . . . I want to hear her! I *got to hear her!*

MUSIC.—*Begins again . . . final measures of composition.*

GIORGIO.—(*Aghast*) But no . . . de song, she's no de same. I know it right away! Is not de same! But why? What happen? Why she's not de same? Why? . . . And den de steel, she talk. And dis time her talk is no so sweet! Is hard talk like woman talk in street! She say (*harshly*), "To work, Giorgio Maslarovic! Get to work! I am airplane now what drop bomb from sky! I am gun now what shoot to kill! I am t'ing called "tank" now what crush out little people! To work, Giorgio Maslarovic—to work! Got no time for t'ings like building! Got no time for plow, and bridge, and train, and houses! Gun and airplanes . . . bomb and bullet! Make me fast now, Maslarovic! Make me fast for kill de people! Work, Giorgio Maslarovic! Work!"

MUSIC.—*Reaches climax and out.*

GIORGIO.—(*Up*) No! Not me! I don't make steel for dat! Not for guns! Not for killin'! No, not me! Let me eat de dirt from fields first! Let my kids starve in de streets first! But not for guns! (*Up madly*) *I hate de steel!*

BEST ORIGINAL PLAY (COMMERCIAL)

Expert Opinion

by TRUE BOARDMAN

From THE SILVER THEATRE

THE INITIAL broadcast of the Silver Theatre was presented on Sunday, October 3, 1937. The story, "First Love," an original written for Silver Theatre by Grover Jones and adapted by True Boardman, was a four-episode vehicle in which Rosalind Russell and James Stewart appeared for four successive Sunday afternoons. This was a definite departure in commercial radio programing. Half-hour dramatic broadcasts had, until then, either told one complete story in each thirty-minute period or projected one major story line throughout a series of at least thirteen weeks' duration. It was felt that the Silver Theatre should allot to the telling of each story as much time as was needed to tell that story well. In other words, a complicated plot that could not be satisfactorily condensed into the half-hour format was presented instead as a continued story in two, three, or four parts. As a result of this thinking, Silver Theatre has been able to offer its listeners material of greater depth and scope than might otherwise have been possible, the additional time allowing for clearer characterization as well as for more detailed development of situation. Many stories, however, are ideally suited to the half-hour period, and more than fifty per cent of the scripts used on Silver Theatre are concluded in a single episode.

With the exception of an occasional magazine story, Silver Theatre presents original material specifically written for the program. Story ideas are purchased from both motion picture and radio writers and then adapted for the show by True Boardman, its staff writer. Mr. Boardman has also contributed a number of his own originals to Silver

Theatre, one of which, "Expert Opinion," is published here.

There is a scene in "Expert Opinion" in which Gerald Conway is being questioned by alienists. The reader will note that in this sequence the device of the *montage* is employed to progress the action to a point that would have otherwise required at least six full scenes. While the use of the *montage* was not entirely new to radio when Silver Theatre first went on the air, it has probably been used with more regularity as a legitimate radio device on this commercial series than on any other. In scoring the music for the *montages*, Conductor Felix Mills thinks in the terms of a dramatist, subordinating the melody to the mood of the scene. Appropriate harmonies and rhythms add to the effectiveness of the *montage* without ever making the listener conscious of a musical accompaniment.

Silver Theatre, believing that listeners are prepared to welcome more mature radio drama, frequently presents actors and actresses who are of the same opinion. In these instances, star, writer, and producer spend many hours together in an effort to achieve the production they're seeking. "Expert Opinion" is a case in point. In discussing with Robert Montgomery the policies of Silver Theatre and his own story preferences, Mr. Montgomery pointed out that although he had had ample opportunity to display his versatility in the motion picture "Night Must Fall," an equal opportunity had never been afforded him in radio appearances. When True Boardman learned that Danny, in "Night Must Fall," was one of Mr. Montgomery's favorite characters, he conceived the story of the manic depressive, Gerald Conway.

Expert Opinion*

MUSIC.—*Opening signature.*

CONTE.—International Silver Company presents the Silver Theatre!

MUSIC.—*Musical progression.*

CONTE.—Starring Robert Montgomery in "Expert Opinion." . . . Directed by Conrad Nagel.

MUSIC.—*Musical Progression.*

CONTE.—Brought to you in behalf of two of the greatest names in silverware . . . International sterling, world-famous solid silver . . . and 1847 Rogers Brothers, America's finest silver plate!

MUSIC.—*Theme . . . fade to background.*

NAGEL.—Good afternoon, ladies and gentlemen. . . . This is Conrad Nagel, greeting you from the stage of the Silver Theatre in Hollywood and bringing you the twenty-ninth in our new series of dramatic productions. Among the many brilliant personalities whose names grace our guest book for future dates are Melvyn Douglas, Constance Bennett, Joan Crawford, Douglas Fairbanks, Jr., and Helen Hayes. . . .

And now a word about today's story. There are, as I am sure you all know, really two Bob Montgomery's in one. There is the debonair Bob of such pictures as Metro-Goldwyn-Mayer's currently popular "Fast and Loose." Then there is that other Bob . . . sinister and menacing . . . who brought us the unforgettable characterization of Danny in "Night Must Fall." In debating which of these such Messrs. Montgomery should bring you in Silver Theatre, we

* Copyright, 1939, by True Boardman, and reprinted by special permission of the author and Young and Rubicam, authorized agents. Permission to perform this play can be had only through arrangement with True Boardman or with his agent.

hit upon the novel idea of presenting both of them . . . in successive weeks. So while next week, in an entirely different play, you will meet Montgomery, the scholar and gentleman, tonight you will meet the other Montgomery . . . also a scholar . . . but certainly no gentleman. For Bob is going to play the role of Gerald Conway . . . in "Expert Opinion" . . . a psychological drama by True Boardman.

MUSIC.—*Curtain raiser.*

NAGEL.—The house lights dim. The Silver Curtain rises. The scene . . . an office in a metropolitan building, a strange office, large, yet somehow dark and somber. Heavy curtains drape the walls and windows . . . all save where a single shaft of light breaks through and casts its beam across the massive desk. This, the sanctum sanctorum . . . the private inner office of Gerald Conway . . . president and general manager of Conway Investment Company. As we meet him first he is standing before a combination radio-phonograph, listening intently. In the chair before the large desk sits his secretary, Evelyn Spear.

MUSIC.—*Over above . . . has segued to "Conway Melody" . . . to be selected . . . perhaps Sibelius's "Valse Triste" . . . record continues in background.*

EVELYN.—*(Tersely)* If you're going to keep on playing that record, I'll leave. I thought you sent for me to take dictation.

GERALD.—*(His normal manner of speech is quiet . . . incisive, with just a suggestion of scorn. We have the feeling that he is nearly always smiling . . . a smile which, were we to see it, we would probably dislike without knowing exactly why)* I did. You're nervous today, Evelyn. Whenever this music upsets you, I know you're not yourself.

EVELYN.—And suppose the music *does* upset me? Who wouldn't it upset? That one melody a dozen times a day . . . week in week out . . . month on end. . . . Why?

GERALD.—Suppose we just call it my eccentric taste in music. But . . . if you will. . . . *(Music out . . . laughs deprecatingly)* We'll get to work. Take a letter. To all stockholders in Conway, Inc. My good friends, all. As president and general manager of our great corporation, it is with sincere

394

pleasure that I inform you of a further expansion of our great company. And I . . .

EVELYN.—(*Dryly*) There's no need for you to dictate this, you know. I can write it from memory. You're doing now what you've done before with all your other promotions. Conway Incorporated is broke . . . so you're pyramiding. . . . Floating a new subsidiary to keep it going. But of course your dear, faithful stockholders musn't know that. Oh, no . . . we must make them think it's a privilege to pour more of their sand down this particular rat hole.

GERALD.—So charmingly graphic, Evelyn. Charming. . . . Where were we? Oh, yes. And I am offering to each stockholder . . . an opportunity to . . . (*Breaks off as*)

SOUND.—*Door opens. Outside the door we hear a sudden commotion . . . subsequent speeches of Markham and Lewis are simultaneous off.*
(*Fade in*)

MARKHAM.—I *will* see Conway . . . and there's no one going to stop me. I'm going to see him!
(*Fade in*)

LEWIS.—You can't go in there. If you make an appointment . . .

LEWIS.—Mr. Conway, I tried to . . .

GERALD.—(*Calmly*) It's all right, Mr. Lewis. The gentleman wishes to see me . . . ?

MARKHAM.—(*He is near hysteria . . . low . . . tense*) You! You don't even remember me, do you? You could take my money. That was easy . . . but now you don't even know my name. (*Slight pause*)

GERALD.—But of course I do. You're Markham . . . Edgar Markham of West Avenue. Sit down, Mr. Markham. Er, Mr. Lewis . . . Miss Spear . . . we can continue later.

EVELYN.—Yes, sir.

SOUND.—*Door closes.*

GERALD.—And now, Mr. Markham . . . I . . . (*Remembering*) Oh, may I offer you a drink?

MARKHAM.—(*Tersely*) No.

GERALD.—Smoke?

MARKHAM.—(*He rushes on* . . . *almost incoherent in his anxiety*) No! You know why I'm here. My stock. . . . Two thousand dollars' worth. I saved 5 years to get that money . . . and you were sure you'd double it. You told me so! And it's no good! It's no good! Do you hear?

GERALD.—(*Quietly*) Don't you suppose we could talk this matter over quietly?

MARKHAM.—(*A different tone*) Quietly? You want it quietly. All right. . . . I want my money . . . all of it . . . and I want it now. Every dollar I invested in this swindle of yours. Do you understand that, Mr. Conway? *You're going to give me back that money!*

GERALD.—(*Coolly* . . . *after slight pause*) Oh, am I?

MARKHAM.—What do you sit there grinning for?

GERALD.—Mr. Markham . . . this concern of yours astonishes me. I was sure I had the confidence of *all* our stockholders.

MARKHAM.—Our confidence? You formed three companies down South 5 years ago! They all went bankrupt. And now *this* company is going to the wall, too!

GERALD.—It is? And who says so?

MARKHAM.—Everybody! I heard it at my bank! And on the street.

GERALD.—(*Starts to laugh*)

MARKHAM.—What are you laughing at?

GERALD.—At you, Mr. Markham. A sober, intelligent business-man . . . allowing yourself to be upset by foolish sidewalk rumors.

SOUND.—*Door opens* . . . *off.*

GERALD.—Oh, Miss Spear. . . . Please ask Mr. Lewis (*seeing him*) . . . Oh, Lewis . . .

LEWIS.—(*Approaching*) Yes, Mr. Conway.

396

GERALD.—Somehow Mr. Markham has gotten some false information about our financial status. Take him and set him right, will you, Lewis? Even show him the company books if he desires.

MARKHAM.—I may see the company books?

LEWIS.—I'd be glad to. Come along, sir.

GERALD.—Glad you dropped in, Markham.

MARKHAM.—(*He's been railroaded . . . and senses it*) Yeah . . . yeah . . . thanks. . . . I . .

GERALD.—(*Going right on*) You'll get a letter in a day or so . . . about a new subsidiary. You want to give it some thought. It's a splendid proposition. Good day. Come in, Miss Spear.

EVELYN.—Yes, sir.

SOUND.—*Door closes . . . slight pause.*

GERALD.—(*With a sigh of relief*) You heard?

EVELYN.—Who could help it?

GERALD.—(*That smile again*) He had a gun.

EVELYN.—(*Startled*) A gun!

GERALD.—In his right-hand pocket. . . . So little imagination these fools have. What about some music?

MUSIC.—*Starting record . . . anticipate above orchestra . . . plays melody again.*

EVELYN.—Gerald! How can you go on like this? You talked that man out of here today. But he'll be back. Because you and I both know Conway Incorporated *is* going to collapse. And that will mean a government investigation. Then what are you going to do?

GERALD.—What would you suggest?

EVELYN.—(*Slight pause . . . then impulsively*) Gerald! Get out! Now! A plane! Out of the country. You have more money already than you'll ever need! Please . . . please go before it breaks on top of you. You've got to, Gerald. (*Slight pause . . . different tone*) For my sake!

GERALD.—For *your* sake. And what will you do?

EVELYN.—I'll . . . I'll go with you! Take me, Gerald. I don't care where. Just so you're safe . . . and we're together.

GERALD.—(*Very slight pause*) "Just so we're together."

EVELYN.—(*Not wanting to go on*) Gerald. . . . (*Slight pause*) You're going to make me say it, aren't you? You've known for months. . . . You must have known. But you've been waiting for me to put it into words. All right. I don't care now. I love you!

GERALD.—Well! This intrigues me. (*Laughs softly*) It's taken longer than I expected.

EVELYN.—Stop laughing! Gerald!

GERALD.—(*Sighs*) You women can never keep business separate from emotion, can you? So you had to fall in love with me. Why, Evelyn? Tell me. I'm interested. Because, you see, I know that you don't like me. You never have. There's a part of you that's hated me from the first, yet now you'd run away with me. It's very funny. Don't you agree? (*He laughs*)

EVELYN.—(*After a pause . . . slowly . . . with rising fury*) So it's funny is it? Well, laugh then! I can laugh, too! Because you're right! I do hate you. I had an idea that somewhere . . . far inside of you there was the shadow of a man . . . a man that I could love and respect, but I was wrong. Because you're *not* a man at all. You're . . . you're . . . a kind of devil.

GERALD.—And you would be my good angel, is that it? I'm afraid you're not the type, Evelyn. And if you were . . . (*Sound of slap in face . . . he laughs*) Yes, that *would* be next. A woman impotent of speech will turn to violence. It never fails. You'd better go now, Evelyn. At this point a woman in your position either becomes hysterical or wildly violent. And neither alternative appeals to me. So, suppose you just leave . . . quietly. And believe me . . . I'm sorry for you.

EVELYN.—(*An almost inaudible gasp of powerlessness*) Oh!

GERALD.—(*Tauntingly*) Well . . . ?

EVELYN.—(*Almost a whisper*) I wish I could kill you!

398

GERALD.—(*In the same tone*) Who knows? Perhaps you will. (*Then he laughs*) Good-by, Evelyn.

SOUND.—*Door opens . . . slams . . . slightly off.*

MUSIC.—*Transition.*

(*Fade in*)

GERALD.—(*Yawning*) What is this, Lewis. What's the idea of waking me at this hour? And you, too, Thomas? You're supposed . . .

LEWIS.—We had to, Gerald. It's happened! This is it.

GERALD.—What are you talking about?

THOMAS.—The stockholders. They held a secret meeting tonight.

LEWIS.—Evelyn Spear was behind the whole thing. She told the stockholders that the whole setup of the corporation was crooked from the start.

GERALD.—Evelyn said that, did she? (*Laughs*) "No fury like a woman scorned." I might have expected this. In fact, I think I did.

THOMAS.—You expected it? Well, then, you must realize that you've got to leave the state. Now . . . before they can swear out a warrant.

GERALD.—You're my lawyer, and you ask that, Thomas? Think of the fee you will lose if I don't stand trial.

THOMAS.—I'm not a fool, Conway. I've gotten you out of jams before, but on this one there's no chance. When they start digging up the other promotions that have failed, they'll compound felonies against you till they have enough to send you up for life.

LEWIS.—He's right, Gerald. You've slipped up this time.

GERALD.—You should know by now that I never slip up, Lewis. You say they'd send me up for life. They won't.

LEWIS.—Now, look, Gerald . . . I've . . .

GERALD.—No . . . *you* look. Both of you. I think this is a part of my library you've never seen.

SOUND.—*Small doors open.*

LEWIS.—(*Wonderingly*) Hey . . . ?

GERALD.—Read some of those titles. . . .

LEWIS.—*Textbook of Psychiatry* . . . *The Criminal Psychote* . . . *Psychology of Criminal Behavior.* (*Breaks off*) I don't get it.

GERALD.—It's quite simple. You're looking at perhaps the most complete library in this country on criminal insanity.

THOMAS.—Yeah, but what's it all about?

GERALD.—About? About the insane, Thomas . . . the insane . . . how they got that way . . . and how they act when they are. You see . . . as it happens . . . I've been planning for just this moment.

LEWIS.—But, look. . . . What has your knowing how insane people act got to do with . . . ?

GERALD.—It's got everything to do with it, Lewis. You see . . . Thomas here will bear me out that there's a law in this state which says that insane persons are not liable to imprisonment for crime. They *are* liable to be sent to a state institution for a minimum period of a year . . . to be released when they can prove themselves sane again. . . . And what's a year . . . if there's plenty of money waiting at the end of it? (*Slight pause . . . that smile again*) I wonder now . . . if you understand.

THOMAS.—(*Unbelieving*) You . . . you're going to plead not guilty . . . by reason of insanity?

GERALD.—Exactly, Thomas, exactly. . . . Because you see . . . a certain Gerald Conway made up his mind just 5 minutes ago . . . that he is hopelessly and positively . . . insane.

MUSIC.—*First act curtain.*

SOUND.—*Applause.*

NAGEL.—This is Conrad Nagel, ladies and gentlemen, turning the spotlight . . . during this brief moment of intermission . . . on the familiar figure of our Silver Theatre spokesman . . . John Conte!

CONTE.—I think most of you will agree, ladies and gentlemen, that background *does* count! And women who surround themselves with beautiful, genuine possessions *show* it! Realizing this, more and more modern young couples are choosing *sterling* silver for their new homes . . . solid silver of lifelong service and enduring beauty, bearing the fine old name International Sterling! You, too, will be lavish in your praise of International sterling silver . . . particularly their thrilling new pattern, "Prelude"! For "Prelude" possesses heirloom standards of craftsmanship. Its lines are incredibly graceful and tapering . . . its rose ornament richly, handsomely carved! An inspired pattern of solid silver through and through that's perfectly at home with fine crystal, new damasks, and the traditional elegance of fine china. And though you may think that silver so exquisite must necessarily be far beyond your means, it actually is not. For under International Sterling's budget payment plan you can buy a complete service of "Prelude" sterling *out of income*! . . . Or you can *build* a solid silver service by purchasing *single* place settings of "Prelude" . . . one or two at a time . . . as low as $16.75! Your silverware dealer will be delighted to explain the complete details if you'll visit him tomorrow . . . Monday. So be sure to see him and discover for yourself that *solid* silver . . . International *sterling* silver . . . is easier than you thought to *buy* . . . *more thrilling than you dreamed to own!*

Music.—*Second act curtain raiser.*

Nagel.—Once again the lights are being dimmed, and the Silver Curtain rises on the second act of "Expert Opinion," starring Robert Montgomery as Gerald Conway. The collapse of the Conway Investment Corporation, Gerald's arrest . . . and subsequent surprise plea of "Not guilty" by reason of insanity has been headline news for weeks. And the prosecution has assured the hundreds of enraged investors that Conway's obvious attempt to evade justice will not succeed; that he *will* be proved sane and sent to the penitentiary. Meanwhile, Gerald Conway himself, released on bail, is at his home. . . .

(*Fade in*)

Sound.—*Voices . . . question and response coming rapidly.*

Lewis.—Table!

Gerald.—Chair!

LEWIS.—Sickness!

GERALD.—Doctor.

LEWIS.—Mountain.

GERALD.—Trees.

LEWIS.—Cold.

GERALD.—Ice cream.

LEWIS.—Sweet.

GERALD.—Bitter.

LEWIS.—Lamp.

GERALD.—Light.

LEWIS.—Hungry.

GERALD.—Food. . . . (*Eagerly*) Faster, Lewis . . . read them faster.

LEWIS.—(*Concerned*) But wait a minute, Gerald. You're giving the right answers for these words.

GERALD.—(*Smilingly*) Exactly, Lewis. That's just the point. You see, this kind of test is one they always use if they suspect a person is feigning his insanity. Association of ideas. What other word does a given word suggest?

LEWIS.—But you've been saying things these words *do* suggest!

GERALD.—Ah, but so does an insane person, Lewis . . . at least the *kind* of insane person I have decided to be. Namely, a manic depressive.

LEWIS.—A manic depressive . . .

GERALD.—One of the subtler forms of mental derangement, Lewis. What a pity you don't know about these things. Here . . . (*Fading slightly*) Here, let me show you. (*Sound of book being taken from shelf*) I think it's best described in this book of Altman's. (*Riffles through pages*) Here . . . read this. . . .

LEWIS.—"The manic-depressive type. Here the individual is subject to violently alternating moods. In the low or depressive mood, he is frequently uncommunicative and monosyllabic. Reaction time is slow. He believes himself persecuted by friends and relatives. Often cries in self-pity . . . even contemplates suicide." (*Stops*)

GERALD.—(*Eagerly*) Go on! The manic state. Read about that.

LEWIS.—"In the opposing manic or elated state he has exaggerated ideas of his importance. A frequent symptom is extravagant dreams and nightmares. There is a record of the patient who boasted that he dreamt of owning all the money in the world . . . and then scattering it broadside to the poor. And in another case . . . "

GERALD.—You see, it's quite simple, Lewis. When I can learn from books like these how other insane men have acted, what's to prevent me from imitating their insanity to the last detail?

LEWIS.—But these men who'll examine you . . . they'll all be experts.

GERALD.—And they'll be dealing with an expert. Remember that. (*Laughing a little*) I wouldn't worry if I were you. Another week of studying the cases in these books . . . and I'll be ready for them. In fact . . . I've an idea I'm going to enjoy my little venture into madness. I'm sure of it.

MUSIC.—*Transition segue into mechanistic montage behind flashes of question.*

FIRST DOCTOR.—Black.

GERALD.—White.

FIRST DOCTOR.—Girl.

GERALD.—Boy.

FIRST DOCTOR.—Flower.

GERALD.—Beautiful.

FIRST DOCTOR.—Sane.

GERALD.—Insane.

FIRST DOCTOR.—Laugh. . . . Faster

GERALD.—Cry.

FIRST DOCTOR.—Hope.

GERALD.—Fear.

FIRST DOCTOR.—Faster. . . . Sleep.

GERALD.—Dream.

MUSIC.—*Up over above to wipe out fade.*

DOCTOR SAMPSON.—What makes you think these friends have tried to poison you? Answer me.

GERALD.—(*Apathetic*) I'm trying to. I . . . I *can't* think. They just are.

SECOND DOCTOR.—How long have you had this idea? Where did it come from?

GERALD.—Don't know. Leave me alone. I'm tired.

SECOND DOCTOR.—You've got to answer. And these depressions . . . how often do you have them?

GERALD.—Leave me alone. Leave me alone.

MUSIC.—*Up to cover.*

GERALD.—(*Eager . . . excited*) No one understands, that's all. But you do, don't you, Doctor? Those times when I'm depressed . . . well, everybody's like that sometimes. You know that, Doctor. You know that, don't you?

SECOND DOCTOR.—But times like now it's different. Is that it?

GERALD.—Now I'm myself. And I'm a genius when I feel myself. You can tell that. You're a great doctor. I am. I can make money faster than any man in this country. And not only that. . . . It's what I'm going to do with it. Listen to me, doctor. You'll understand . . . I . . .

MUSIC.—*Up to cover . . . this quickly now as whole montage picks up tempo.*

FIRST DOCTOR.—Deep.

GERALD.—Shallow.

FIRST DOCTOR.—Slow.

GERALD.—Slower . . . er fast.

FIRST DOCTOR.—Running.

GERALD.—Painting . . . I mean walking. (*Music up briefly . . . then down*) No . . . don't ask me now. Just let me be. Why can't you leave me alone? (*Music up . . . fade*) Of course (*up*) I'll tell you. You want to know about me. I'm Gerald Conway. . . . I'm *the* Gerald Conway! Of course I'll tell you. I'm Gerald Conway. . . .

MUSIC.—*Up full to cover in crescendo . . . the whole perspective of this court scene is as though the mike were at the counsel table where Gerald and Thomas are seated. Other proceedings are hears from relative distances.*

SOUND.—*Gavel.*

JUDGE.—(*Off*) The court will be in order. You may continue the cross-examination, Mr. Thomas.

THOMAS.—Thank you, Your Honor. . . . Dr. Sampson . . . during the course of this trial you have heard the testimony of the other alienists who examined my client. Alienists for both defense and prosecution!

SAMPSON.—I have.

THOMAS.—*They* testified that my client *was* definitely a manic depressive, did they not?

SAMPSON.—Yes.

THOMAS.—But you have as yet made no definite statement as to *your* opinion. Now . . . would you . . . speaking as a recognized expert, swear that the defendant, Gerald Conway, is sane?

SAMPSON.—I wouldn't swear that my own mother is sane.

SOUND.—*Laughter in court . . . gavel.*

THOMAS.—Please answer my question.

SAMPSON.—I wouldn't swear that he is sane. . . . No . . . I agree with the others. Conway's reactions are typical of those of a manic-depressive psychote.

THOMAS.—That's all.

PROSECUTOR.—No more questions.

JUDGE.—Next witness.

PROSECUTOR.—I'll call Miss Evelyn Spear.

405

CLERK.—Raise your right hand. Do you solemnly swear the testimony you are about to give to be the truth? The whole truth, so help you God?

EVELYN.—I do.

CLERK.—Take the stand.

PROSECUTOR.—Your name and occupation.

EVELYN.—(*Low . . . tense*) I'm Evelyn Spear. For the past 4 years I have been private secretary to Gerald Conway.

PROSECUTOR.—And naturally . . . in the course of business seen a great deal of the defendant?

EVELYN.—(*Very low*) I have.

JUROR.—(*Off . . . elderly*) We can't hear in the jury box.

EVELYN.—(*Louder*) I have.

PROSECUTOR.—During that 4 years, Miss Spear, have you seen any action on the part of the defendant which would lead you to believe he was insane?

EVELYN.—(*Letting go*) No. Of course I haven't! And he's not insane. Oh, don't you all see the thing he's done? He's played a part . . . for this court and for the doctors who examined him. You don't know Gerald Conway, any of you. He can make anyone believe anything he wants. Of course he's not insane! He's lying now just as he's lied about everything he's ever done. You've got to find him sane and then convict him! You've got to, do you hear!!

SOUND.—*Ad lib in courtroom . . . gavel.*

THOMAS.—Your Honor. I move the statement of Miss Spear be stricken. . . . Conclusion of the witness irrelevant, immaterial, and . . .

JUDGE.—Motion granted. Let it be stricken.

PROSECUTOR.—Miss Spear . . . please just answer this by "Yes" or "No." Did you ever see in Mr. Conway any signs of what appeared to you as insanity?

EVELYN.—No.

PROSECUTOR.—Your witness.

THOMAS.—Now, Miss Spear.

GERALD.—(*Low*) Thomas.

THOMAS.—(*Low*) Yes?

GERALD.—Just ask her two questions. If she was ever in love with me . . . and what I told her when she admitted it. Nothing more.

THOMAS.—But . . .

GERALD.—Do as I say!

THOMAS.—All right. (*Full voice . . . approaching stand*) Miss Spear . . . are you or were you ever in love with the defendant? (*Pause*)

EVELYN.—I refuse to answer that question.

THOMAS.—Could you tell us, then, just what the defendant said when you *confessed* your love for him?

SOUND.—*Murmur in court.*

PROSECUTOR.—I object. Improper cross-examination. Leading the witness. Assuming a fact not in evidence.

THOMAS.—(*Smiling*) I'll withdraw the question. That's all.

SOUND.—*Murmur in court ad lib.*

JUDGE.—Have you further witnesses, Mr. Prosecutor?

PROSECUTOR.—No, Your Honor. . . . That concludes the case for the . . . (*Breaks off as*)

VOICE.—(*Off*) Mac . . . wait a minute. . . .

PROSECUTOR.—Just a moment if the court please. Yes, Joe?

SOUND.—*A moment's whispered conversation.*

PROSECUTOR.—Your Honor. I have just been informed that Doctor Kurt Altman, one of the world's leading specialists in criminal psychology, has arrived in the city. The state asks an adjournment of this trial while the defendant is examined by Dr. Altman.

SOUND.—*Ad lib in court.*

THOMAS.—And I protest, Your Honor! We've had experts here already. Plenty of them. And all of them have agreed that . . .

GERALD.—(*Low*) Thomas. Don't argue. Let him examine me.

THOMAS.—(*Low*) But you can't. Why take a chance? Altman's that fellow from Vienna. He'll see through you in 5 minutes.

GERALD.—(*Smilingly*) Really? I don't think so! Tell the court that we agree. (*Slight pause*)

THOMAS.—(*Reluctantly*) Your Honor . . . the defense agrees to examination by Dr. Altman.

MUSIC.—*Transition.*

GERALD.—(*Very disconsolate . . . self-pitying*) But you don't understand, Dr. Altman. I . . .

ALTMAN.—(*Kindly . . . elderly . . . slight Viennese accent*) Yah . . . I know you feel unhappy . . . but still you must talk to me. Old Altman can help you, maybe. In Europe he has helped many who were depressed like you are now.

GERALD.—There's no one can help me. I have no friends, only enemies.

ALTMAN.—Ah . . . too bad. You feel like this often. . . . Yah. You sometimes think life is not worth living, maybe?

GERALD.—(*Almost wonderingly*) How did you know that?

ALTMAN.—I know many things. I am sorry for you, my son.

GERALD.—Oh, doctor, you don't know what it's like. (*He's almost crying*) With everyone against you. Alone and afraid, I never told the others this. But I am afraid. You won't let them hurt me, will you? You'll make them leave me alone. Please . . . doctor, please.

ALTMAN.—Yah . . . my son . . . yah. I think we talk enough for today. (*Door opens*) Guard . . . you will take him back.

GUARD.—Yes, doctor.

ALTMAN.—(*Low*) Oh . . . and guard. Watch him carefully. In such a case like this there should soon be a definite change of attitude. He will become elated . . . confident . . . and very talkative. When that has happened he must be brought to me again. At once.

GUARD.—Yes, doctor. Come along, Conway.

SOUND.—*Door closes . . . phone lifted . . . one number dialed.*

ALTMAN.—Stevens? . . . Altman speaking. . . . Yes . . . I have just sent him back. A peculiar case, Stevens. I need your help. . . . I want you to get for me all the records of this trial. And . . . the books of the company. . . . Don't ask me why. . . . Just get them. I told you this was a very peculiar case. (*Hangs up*)

MUSIC.—*Transition.*

GUARD.—And it's like you said the other day, doctor. Conway did change just overnight. He thinks he owns the joint this morning.

ALTMAN.—Good, good. . . . Send him in here. And leave us alone.

GUARD.—(*Fading*) Yes, sir.

SOUND.—*Door opens.*

GUARD.—All right, Conway. In here.

GERALD.—(*He's really high this time*) Thank you, thank you, guard.

SOUND.—*Door closes.*

GERALD.—Doctor Altman! You see, I remembered. Doctor Altman . . . you're from Vienna, aren't you?

ALTMAN.—Yah. I . . .

GERALD.—(*Heedless*) I'm sorry about the other day. I remember I was upset in a way. Just down . . . the blues, that's all it is. Everybody gets them once in a while. Didn't mean a thing. In fact, I . . .

ALTMAN.—(*Quietly but firmly stopping him*) Mister Conway! I want to talk to you. Please sit down here.

GERALD.—(*Anxious to keep going*) Of course . . . I'm glad to talk to you. It isn't very often that I meet a person on my own level of intelligence . . . You see, being a genius, I naturally . . .

ALTMAN.—(*In his same quiet, insistent tone*) I'll draw the curtain. So!

409

SOUND.—*Drawing curtains.*

GERALD.—(*Laughingly, protestingly*) But it's too bad to shut out the daylight. It's a glorious day outside. You know that, don't you. . . .

ALTMAN.—We will have music. The phonograph.

SOUND.—*Phonograph starts.*

GERALD.—Yes! Yes, do! I like music. I compose it sometimes. Melodies of . . . (*He breaks off as he recognizes melody. Over above record orchestra has begun to play "Conway's Theme," which we have heard in his office*) That music . . . (*forgetting his act just for a moment*) How did you know?

ALTMAN.—I told you before that I know many things, my son. (*Slight pause*) Now. Now that you feel better today, tell me about yourself.

GERALD.—That music. Do you know what it is? It's the theme song of my victory. It always has been. I heard it first when I was just a child. I'd licked another boy in a fight . . . and as I was going home I heard that melody.

ALTMAN.—You have said that you are a genius. How do you know?

GERALD.—The things I do. Money. I've always had it. More than I could spend. I even dream about money. Do you know that?

ALTMAN.—You dream about it? Yah! Tell me. That sounds interesting.

GERALD.—Why, I dreamed once that I owned all the money in the world, and I was scattering it broadside to the poor.

ALTMAN.—(*In a sudden, startling change of tone and manner*) So!

SOUND.—*Record stops.*

ALTMAN.—So . . . now it is out!

GERALD.—(*Astonished*) Doctor Altman. Don't you want me to . . .

ALTMAN.—I want you to stop pretending . . . acting that you are insane.

GERALD.—Acting . . . ?

ALTMAN.—(*Rapid*) Yes, my friend. From the first I am suspicious. Your reactions are those of a manic depressive. Yes. But they are too quick . . . too positive. But now I am sure. (*Slight pause*) Your dream . . . "I own all the money in the world and scatter it broadside to the poor." In the future, remember this, my friend. When you quote the actual words from a book . . . remember who was its author.

GERALD.—(*Slight pause*) You wrote that book.

ALTMAN.—I did.

GERALD.—(*His old smile again*) Well, this rather complicates the matter. You see, Doctor Altman, I am determined not to go to the penitentiary.

ALTMAN.—You prefer an asylum? I can understand it. (*Pause*) Well . . .

GERALD.—How much, Doctor?

ALTMAN.—How much?

GERALD.—For you to forget the last 5 minutes and report to the court. . . .

ALTMAN.—That you *are* insane? Hmm. How much would you say it was worth?

GERALD.—Fifty thousand.

ALTMAN.—(*Smiling*) So little from the man who has dreamed of owning all the money in the world?

GERALD.—A hundred.

ALTMAN.—No. Two hundred thousand. (*As Gerald starts to object*) And you can pay it. You see I have seen the books of your company.

GERALD.—You win. One hour after you swear that I am insane in that courtroom, the money will be delivered to you wherever you say. Is it agreed?

ALTMAN.—Let us just say, "I shall think it over."

MUSIC.—*Transition.*

(*Fade in on courtroom*)

CLERK.— . . . solemnly swear that the testimony you are about to give in this courtroom shall be the truth, the whole truth, and nothing but the truth, so help you God?

ALTMAN.—I do.

PROSECUTOR.—Your name, occupation?

ALTMAN.—Dr. Kurt Altman. I am a psychiatrist.

PROSECUTOR.—Inasmuch as defense has already stipulated as to your qualifications as an expert . . . will you tell us the findings of your examination of the defendant?

ALTMAN.—Yes.

PROSECUTOR.—Dr. Altman, is the defendant, Gerald Conway, sane or insane?

ALTMAN.—There is not the slightest doubt upon that point. Gerald Conway is . . . insane.

MUSIC.—*Quick wipe-out transition.*

SOUND.—*Footsteps along corridor . . . footsteps stop . . . key in . . . door opens.*

GUARD.—He's in here. Go right on in, Doc. I'll wait outside.

ALTMAN.—Thank you.

SOUND.—*Door closes.*

GERALD.—(*Smiling*) Hello, Doctor Altman.

ALTMAN.—Well, my son?

GERALD.—I asked them to let me see you before they took me away tomorrow. Wanted to check up. The money was delivered?

ALTMAN.—Yes, and in the correct amount.

GERALD.—(*Smilingly*) I doubt that psychiatry has ever been so profitable before, Doctor.

ALTMAN.—I do not know. You see . . . I did not have that money very long. I have already transferred it to the referee in bankruptcy of your company. Your investors will get back at least a portion of their money.

GERALD.—But that doesn't make sense, Doctor. If you weren't going to keep the money . . . why did you lie on the witness stand?

ALTMAN.—Why did I lie? You wonder about that?

GERALD.—Yes.

ALTMAN.—My dear young man . . . the testimony that I gave in court was under oath. I did not lie. (*Slight pause*) You *are* insane!

MUSIC.—*Sharp minor chord . . . low . . . sustaining into*

GERALD.—(*Pause . . . then, to make himself believe it*) You're . . . joking. (*He laughs*)

ALTMAN.—I do not joke about such things. There are other types of insanity besides the one you feigned. On some of them an expert is never fooled. You are insane.

MUSIC.—*Another chord . . . slightly higher in key.*

GERALD.—(*With rising fear*) You're lying to frighten me. You're lying and trying to frighten me! I know! I know!

ALTMAN.—(*Never raising his voice*) I did not lie. . . . You are insane.

MUSIC.—*Another chord.*

GERALD.—Stop saying that! Stop saying that. It's wrong! Wrong! do you hear? I planned all this. You've just been taken in like all the rest!

ALTMAN.—I was not taken in. The very way in which you planned it was part of what convinced me. You are insane.

MUSIC.—*Another chord . . . higher . . . menacing . . . maniacal.*

GERALD.—(*With rising hysteria*) I'm not insane. I'm not insane. You're going to tell me that I'm not.

ALTMAN.—Incurably and hopelessly . . . insane.

MUSIC.—*Another chord.*

GERALD.—(*Wildly*) Stop it! Stop it! (*Slight pause . . . then he has changed . . . he is low, tense . . . almost fiendish*) You're going to stop it . . . or I'll kill you! (*Almost screaming*) I'll kill you, do you hear! I'll . . .

413

SOUND.—*Blow . . . body fall.*

MUSIC.—*Up in crescendo . . . out suddenly.*

GERALD.—(*Moans hysterically . . . slightly off*)

SOUND.—*Door opens quickly slightly off.*

GUARD.—(*Rushing in*) Doctor . . . are you all right?

ALTMAN.—Yes, but I suggest you bring a strait jacket for that poor fellow on the floor.

GUARD.—Yeah. (*Wonderingly*) He's really pretty far gone, ain't he?

ALTMAN.—(*Quietly smiling*) Pretty far. You know, did you ever wonder at the eternal justice of such things? I have.

MUSIC.—*Curtain.*

NAGEL.—You have just heard Robert Montgomery in "Expert Opinion." In a moment we'll tell you about next week's show, but right now we think you'll be interested in hearing from a young man with a brief but special word for *you*, the hostess. . . . All right, John Conte.

CONTE.—Many of you women have probably said to yourselves time and again as you set the table for dinner, "I'm beginning to be ashamed of this silver. One of these fine days I'm going to buy some really *good* silverware instead." And you meant to keep that promise . . . but what with this and that and the other necessity constantly cropping up, you've felt you couldn't *afford* to buy new silverware! . . . Well, may I say that *now* is a very excellent time to *fulfill* your promise? Because now you can get the most famous silver plate in America . . . 1847 Rogers Brothers silver plate . . . at substantial savings! A service for 8 . . . 62 pieces of gleaming silver plate, beautifully wrought in 1847 Rogers Brothers "Lovelace" pattern . . . can now be yours at a saving of more than $14 over open stock price! And *believe* me, "Lovelace" is one of the finest creations of this distinguished house! A pierced pattern with sterlinglike detail . . . and ornament exquisite as old lace . . . "Lovelace" is a design of radiant loveliness executed in lifetime *plate! See* it tomorrow . . . Monday . . . wherever fine silverware is sold . . . and learn upon what easy, convenient terms you can own silver plate from the proudest house in America . . . silver plate that bears the design prestige of America's first great craftsmen . . . 1847 Rogers Brothers!

MUSIC.—*Theme sneak in and tag.*

CONTE.—And now back to Conrad Nagel.

NAGEL.—Ladies and gentlemen . . . next Sunday Robert Montgomery does a dramatic turnabout to play the starring role in a gay comedy drama. Be sure to listen. In the meantime, if you want *solid* silver, you want International sterling . . . if you want silver *plate*, you want 1847 Rogers Brothers, both proudly created by International Silver Company. . . . "Expert Opinion" was written for Silver Theatre by True Boardman. Original music heard on this program was composed and conducted by Felix Mills.

MUSIC.—*Theme if needed.*

CONTE.—All names and designations of persons and of business organizations used in the course of this broadcast are entirely fictitious, and no actual business organization and no living person is thereby actually referred to or designated. Silver Theatre originates at Columbia Square in Hollywood. John Conte speaking. This is the Columbia Broadcasting System.

MUSIC.—*Theme to fill.*

BEST INTERMISSION TALK

by DEEMS TAYLOR

Philharmonic Symphony Society of New York

THE INTERMISSION talk has become an accepted radio feature in many of the regular series of symphonic broadcasts, and eight or nine of America's best-known music men have been heard during the winter seasons as commentators or critics. The past few years have seen a shift from the formalism and austerity that characterized so many of these talks when they first began. Pedagogical stiffness, mechanical vocabulary, emphasis on the architecture of music . . . these have yielded to a more natural discourse and a more informal and friendly style.

This change has had a tremendous influence upon the public in increasing the size of audiences that have learned to enjoy fine music. Adherence to the strict form of speech familiar to listeners in the early 1930's did not make a great deal of sense in broadcasting for the reason that the musically informed knew the subject matter generally, and the musically uninformed did not want to hear about it; they just wanted to hear the music.

For four years Mr. Deems Taylor has been heard on the Sunday afternoon Philharmonic Symphony programs as intermission commentator, and in that time he has (with the possible exception of Walter Damrosch) created more friends of music than any other individual in America today. His talks are simple, amusing, direct, and personal. All of them are spattered with his own opinions, and his opinions are as various as they are attractive. He is incapable of anything stuffy, and it is so evident that he is having a good time listening to music and a good time talking about it that many who had previously lived on the border line of true appreciation have been waylaid and captured by this cheerful incognito crusader. He brings them everything to enjoy, much to understand, nothing to fear.

Deems Taylor's natural equipment for the type of commentary he does springs from the many unusual resources that make up the man himself. He is among the best of contemporary composers; he was for many years (on the old *New York World*) one of America's most penetrating music critics; he was the editor of *Musical America* for two years; he has been a foreign correspondent, a translator, a cabinetmaker, a vaudeville performer, a pianist, and a poet. The variety of his activities—and he has excelled in them all—not only marks him as one of this generation's examples of true versatility—but has had much to do with bringing to his work that flavor of agreeable cosmopolitanism that makes him understandable and acceptable to all.

He loves music, but he burns no joss sticks; he understands music but never pokes at it with the long rod of instruction; and he interprets it, but never by reference to thematic blueprints. He sees musicians as a specialized genus of fun makers. They delight him, but they don't bedazzle him, and he is as completely at home with Telemann as he is with Joe Venuti.

Such instinctive comprehension brings to Mr. Taylor's speech and writing a natural candor and spontaneity unequaled among present-day commentators. His frame of reference is so vast that one automatically accepts the thoroughness of his knowledge; his selection of reference is so discriminating that one accepts also the sincerity of his appraisals. Without any of the pinguid pomposity of the self-important critic, without any of the genuflection of the sentimentalist, his expressions and opinions tumble out of him with a youthful enthusiasm that proves his enjoyment in what he is doing and invites others to share in it. He can write the felicitous sentence with an almost Anacreontic grace and follow it with another that embalms some passing nonsense. But he never offends, because he is everywhere good-natured.

A few months before these pages were written, the New York press gave an enormous amount of publicity to the amusing fight then waging between the classicists and the musical roughnecks over the latter's right to "swing" Bach. The classicists claimed it was a slander and a shame and an outrage. The "cats" claimed it was nobody's business but their own and that they would swing Bach or anybody else who had written anything worth swinging. Most commentators would have ignored the issue, especially if they had happened to be identified with a program as dignified as the Philharmonic. But Deems Taylor considered the controversy to have both interest and significance, and his statement is one of the most sensible summaries of musical fad and fashion ever heard on the air. The talk was given on Sunday afternoon, December 11, 1938.

Best Intermission Talk*

MR. DEEMS TAYLOR.—Good afternoon, ladies and gentlemen.
The suite by Johann Sebastian Bach that opened today's
program reminded me of an incident that occurred not
long ago, that came in for a good deal of newspaper comment
here in the East. I don't know how far West the accounts
of it went. Not very far, I imagine, as it was purely a local
flurry. Assuming that a good many of you haven't heard
of it, I thought it might amuse you to tell you about it.
Briefly, then, the president of the Bach Society of New
Jersey sent a letter to the Federal Communications Commission, complaining of the practice of playing the music
of the classic masters, particularly Bach, in swing time. He
said, specifically, that on two recent occasions he had heard
a jazz orchestra giving its own rendition of Bach's Toccata
in D minor. "All the beautiful fugue effects," he wrote,
"were destroyed by the savage slurring of the saxophone
and the jungled discords of the clarinet." What started the
discussion was his proposed remedy, which was—I quote
from his letter—"that any station that violates the canon
of decency by permitting the syncopating of the classics,
particularly Bach's music, be penalized by having its license
suspended for the first offense. A second offense could be
punished by revocation of the license."

Now, I hadn't intended to discuss the incident at all, as it
didn't seem very important. It still doesn't. But I've had a
surprising quantity of mail from correspondents who have
opinions about it, pro and con, and seem to think that I
ought to have some. So, having a few, I suppose I might
as well air them.

In the first place, of course, the proposed remedy for the
offense seems to be a little out of proportion to the enormity
of the crime. If you're going to suspend the license of a
broadcasting station for permitting Bach to be played in
swing time, what are you going to do to a station for permitting swing music to be played at all? You might offer
the owner of the station his choice of either listening to

419

nothing *but* swing for, say, twelve hours, or a month in jail. No; you can't legislate against bad taste. The minute you start regulating people's likes and dislikes in music or books or whatnot, you're confronted by the question of who is to decide what is good and what is bad. And you soon discover that there's no Emily Post of the arts.

In the second place, I'm not so sure that Bach himself would fall on the floor in a fit if he heard a swing version of his Toccata in D minor. If there's one thing I'm pretty sure of, it is that the so-called classic masters were not aware that they were classic masters. As Gilbert Seldes once wrote, "The Japanese are not Oriental to themselves." The casual way in which Bach and Handel and Haydn and Mozart turned out suites and fugues and symphonies seems to me to indicate that they didn't take themselves with quite the deadly seriousness with which some of us take them. They wrote good music, and I think they knew it. But I don't for a minute think that they looked upon every note that they composed as a direct message from Heaven, never to be touched or altered. Take the structure of the suite that you heard today. Of what does it consist? First, an overture, in the style that a then ultramodern French-Italian composer named Lulli had made popular. Next an air. This particular one happens to be one of the greatest melodies ever written. But it happened to be written because, in the suite of Bach's time, a slow melody was usually the second number. Then follow two gavottes, a *bourrée*, and a *gigue*—or, if you want to spell it in modern English, a jig. Now, much as I hate to point it out, those last four pieces were equivalent, in Bach's era, to swing music. They were popular dances of the day. They may sound very slow and dignified to us, but the fact remains that when Bach wrote them he was thinking, not in terms of immortal music, but in terms of dance tunes. If there had been such a thing as a rumba or a tango when Bach was living, you may be sure that a Bach suite would have included a rumba and a tango.

I wonder if the so-called jitterbugs, to whom swing music comes as an utterly new and stunning discovery, realize just how old it is. As the result of considerable philological research, I find that one must draw a sharp line between jazz and swing. Jazz, as it is known today, is a term that is applied indiscriminately to almost every form of popular vocal and dance music except, possibly, the waltz. Swing music, on the other hand, is music that doesn't exist in any permanent form whatsoever. When they speak of a trumpeter or a clarinetist "swinging" a tune, they mean that he undertakes to execute a series of impromptu variations on a given air. These variations are never written down and are never twice alike, and the players who invent them are very scornful of what they call "paper men," that is, players who perform from written or printed notes.

Well, that practice, of course, is as old as the hills. In the Neapolitan school of opera, about the middle of the eighteenth century, it was accepted as a matter of course that opera singers should make up their own trills and ornamental passages and cadenzas as they went along. In eighteenth century concertos for piano and violin, the cadenzas were seldom written out. Usually the composer simply came to a stop at some point in the work, wrote "cadenza" in the score, and tacitly invited the player to make up his own cadenza, based on the main theme—in other words, to "swing" it.

Even great composers and virtuosi like Mozart and Beethoven did it as a matter of routine. In the closing years of the eighteenth century, Beethoven's great rival as a pianist was a virtuoso named Woelffl—W-o-e-l-f-f-l. The two used to meet at soirees given at the castle of Baron Raymond von Wetzlar. Let me quote you a line or two from Thayer's monumental biography of Beethoven, as to what used to go on.

"There," writes Thayer, "the interesting combats of the two athletes not infrequently offered an indescribable artistic treat to the numerous and thoroughly select gathering. . . . Now one, and anon the other, gave free rein to his glowing fancy; sometimes they would seat themselves at two great pianos and improvise alternately on themes which they gave each other, and thus created many a four-hand capriccio which, if it could have been put upon paper at the moment, would surely have bidden defiance to time." In other words, Beethoven and Woelffl sat down and had what, at the Onyx Club in New York, would be called a jam session.

Don't misunderstand me. I'm not saying that it's a laudable thing to play swing versions of the classics or that anyone ought to try not to be revolted by hearing a piece of familiar and beautiful music distorted. But the distortion itself, while it may be a nuisance, is hardly a crime.

Besides, if you're going to be completely consistent about this question of altering a composer's original work, where are you going to stop? After all, a so-called "swing" version of a piece of music is merely a debased form of a set of variations. And if it's wrong for a jazz band arranger to write his particular variations on a theme by Bach, why is it right for Brahms to write his particular variations on a theme by Haydn? Now there's a very obvious answer to that, of course, which is that the Brahms variations are great music and the jazz band's variations are trash. But while you and I may believe that, we can't prove it. We can only say, in the last analysis, "That's what *I* think." Most people would agree that we were right in an extreme case such as I have chosen. But cases are not always extreme. There is, for instance, a swing version of a Bach prelude and fugue that Paul Whiteman frequently plays, called "Thank You, Mr. Bach." To me, it's a delightful and witty piece of music and does Bach no harm. As a matter of fact, I'm sure that Bach would have been enchanted with it. But I've no doubt that a vast number of persons whose opinions are just as good as mine would find that particular piece a horrible desecration.

Do you know, I'm afraid I think it's a good thing that we do hear so much cheap humor and bad sentiment and bad music on the radio. Mind you, I think it would be an even better thing if we heard nothing but good stuff on the radio— *if* everybody wanted to hear it. But as long as there are people who want to hear bad stuff, they should be allowed to listen to it if it isn't obscene or criminal. Because if they're *not* allowed, they won't listen to anything else. Now I know that in some other countries, broadcasting is in the hands of certain persons who are so confident of the infallibility of their own taste that they undertake to decide what is or is not good for the public to hear on the radio. They allow the public to hear only such music as is, in their opinion, "good" music. It's my guess that large portions of the population simply turn their radios off when some of that "good" music is being played. It's one thing to offer a listener something, and it's another thing to get him to listen. So long as his receiving set is working, no matter how low his tastes are, you always have the chance of luring him into hearing and learning to like something better than what he thought he liked; in other words, of elevating his taste. But you can't elevate a man's taste through a dead radio.

I believe in letting people hear these swing monstrosities because I believe that it's the best method of getting rid of them. Occasionally, out of morbid curiosity, I, in common with the president of the Bach Society of New Jersey, have listened to some of those arrangements; and what strikes me about them is their spectacular dullness. There's one in particular that you've probably heard—the one that goes, "Martha, Martha, dum-de-dum-dum"—you know the one. Well, you don't have to *know* that;that's a distortion of "M'appari," from Flotow's "Marta," to know that it's bad. The most harm it can accomplish is to give a few innocent people the impression that "M'appari" is equally dull; but that impression will last only until they hear the real "M'appari." Meanwhile, the swing arrangement will long have been one with Nineveh and Tyre.

A great deal of this hatred and denunciation of swing arrangements rises, I'm sure, from a fear that they will do lasting damage to the music upon which they are based. I don't think there are any grounds for that fear. A real work of art is a good deal tougher than we assume that it is. Great music, like great painting and sculpture and literature, can stand an incredible amount of mauling. In fact, I'd go so far as to venture the opinion that one test of the greatness and vitality of a work of art is whether or not it can stand being burlesqued. One of the big musical comedy hits in New York at the moment is the new Rodgers and Hart show, "The Boys from Syracuse." That, in case you happen not to know it, is nothing more or less than Shakespeare's "The Comedy of Errors," adopted for the musical stage. And the title will give you a pretty clear idea of just how respectful that adaptation is. Yet nobody, up to now, has claimed or will claim, I think, that "The Boys from Syracuse" is ruining Shakespeare.

The same is true of music. You can't spoil anything really great. If you could, think of what the motion pictures have been doing to the music of the masters ever since the first silent films. In putting together scores for the pictures, the arrangers long ago discovered that Bach and Beethoven and Tchaikovsky and Wagner and the rest had written much more graphic and colorful and dramatic *action* music than they could hope to contrive. So they used their music without scruple—and still do—to go with any and all kinds of films. And what has happened to the masters? The answer is summed up very well, I think, in a letter from one of my correspondents, a college student. He writes: "What if Cab Calloway did, for a change, decide to arrange the B minor Mass as he arranges the Hi De Ho Miracle Man? Has any permanent or temporary harm come to Bach? I, for one, would hate to admit it. I am quite confident that the B minor Mass will last longer than Mr. Calloway. And so with the movies. What matter if they do use the second movement of the Beethoven Seventh and make "hurry music" out of it? How long is the life of a film? If Beethoven can't stand such competition, I'll take Hollywood. But I'm sure that will not be necessary. I, for one, will still climb to the top shelf of Carnegie Hall and feel lucky to have a seat."

Yes, but, as we all say, "It isn't that *I* mind so much. I can hear that stuff without harm, because my taste in music is already formed. It can't be corrupted. But think of the others. Think of the thousands of children whose taste is being ruined by that jazz stuff. Think of the thousands of men and women who are eager to hear music but don't yet know the good from the bad. It's the damage to *their* taste that worries me." Well, as far as the children are concerned, if you don't want your child to be corrupted by listening to jazz and swing arrangements, I might point out that the average parent is physically stronger than the average child; and whether or not he is to listen to any given program is partly *your* problem. As for the grownups, nine times out of ten, while you are busy worrying about what's happening to somebody else's taste, you would discover, if you could meet him, that he was engaged in worrying about what's happening to *your* taste. So don't waste too much energy worrying about other people or becoming indignant over cheap music. If your radio set insults your ears with a swing arrangement of Bach, don't get red in the face and roar and write to the *Times*. Just exercise the right of individual censorship that is the glorious privilege of every American radio listener. In other words, just grasp that little knob marked "Station Selector," and start turning it. And sooner or later, I guarantee you, you will discover that after all, that was not the only program your radio had to offer.

Squalus Disaster

by JACK KNELL

INTENSE public interest in the *Squalus* disaster of May 23, 1939, kept America's radio transmitters open for over seventy hours without interruption. Every development, day or night, was broadcast as it happened, and the catastrophe accounted for a new American record in sustained short-wave communication. The physical problem involved was a considerable one, and the demands on the personnel were little short of inhuman. Two CBS engineers, for example, "marooned" in a launch and ignored by every power craft at the scene of the sinking, were obliged to go without water for over forty hours. It wasn't much easier on the announcers. Because of the utter unpredictableness of the situation, they couldn't afford to sleep nor even to cat-nap sitting up in their chairs at the Portsmouth submarine base. The "breaks" could not be foretold; they could only be waited for.

Adverse conditions of this sort, maddening hours of uncertainty, and scenes of confusion, rush, and hysteria are, of course, not new to newspaper reporters. But few people realize that they are also not new to radio men— not any longer. A capacity to broadcast accurately and intelligibly in a circumstance of extreme nervous tension and suspense is requisite in any radio station news department, and most stations have men who can do this. All good sports announcers can do it, Bill Stearn and Ted Husing particularly, and radio news reporters of the type of Hans Kaltenborn and Bob Trout could talk imperturbably through a deluge without muffing a single word. In fact, both of them have done it.

The reporting of the climax of the *Squalus* tragedy did not, as it happened, fall to any of radio's nationally known veterans but to a young man who had had practically no network experience at all. He had worked for four years at Boston's independent outlet, WHDH, and for two more at WEEI, Columbia's most powerful New England transmitter. He was essentially a local station man.

At the moment when the diving bell was being reeled to the surface, Jack Knell was bobbing about in a thirty-foot cruiser as close to the *Falcon* as the Coast Guard would allow. He had had no sleep for sixty hours, but at the instant the "air" was thrown in his lap he accepted the assignment with the immediate response to the job that is the basic equipment of all ad lib reporters.

What he said is not exciting in cold type. I find this unhappily true of many of the pieces in this book. It cannot be otherwise, for much of radio depends upon the moment or upon inflection or upon some other intangible that cannot be recorded on a page of print.

The virtue of Mr. Knell's report is, primarily, its clarity. It told the audience where he was, what was about to happen, and graphically and simply described the procedure as it did happen. In his stark recital of the facts there is an almost photographic sharpness of truth. The episode was sufficiently colorful in itself, and Knell, realizing this, made no effort to make it more so. He told radio listeners that the first survivors had been rescued, and this was what they wanted to hear. And he described the process vividly and quickly as the United States Navy executed it before him.

His presence of mind, his control, and his accuracy in this spectacular emergency won for him the National Headliner's Club Award for the best radio reporting of a news event during 1938-39. As an editor and as one of the radio listeners lucky enough to catch the spot when it was on the air, I am happy to concur in the unanimous opinion of the journalists that it was the best thing of its sort during the past year. Here is what he said.

Squalus Disaster*

JACK KNELL.—This is Jack Knell speaking to you through short-wave transmitter WAAU operating on 2,190 kilocycles. We are at the present time in a small boat, riding at anchor at a spot approximately 50 yards from the scene of rescue operations of the sunken submarine *Squalus*, 16 miles due north from the Portsmouth Navy Yard. We have seen and are seeing one of the most thrilling sights of our lives today. We are seeing history in the making.

About 1 hour ago, that huge 10-ton diving bell disappeared from view as it sank to the bottom of the sea. We spent anxious minutes awaiting its return to the surface, and just a few moments ago, before we came on the air, that immense bell broke the surface of the water. Its huge, pear-shaped bulk is now bobbing around in the water close to the side of the rescue ship, *Falcon*. The men aboard the *Falcon* are maneuvering the bell toward the stern of the ship by means of long poles. They seem to have it in the desired position now, and two men are astride the bell working on the hatch cover in an attempt to unscrew the bolts which keep the cover tightly closed against the sea and the tremendous pressure down there, 250 feet below the surface.

One of the men is rising from his crouched position now, and the men aboard the rescue ship are leaning tensely over the side. . . . I think they're about to open the cover now . . . yes . . . the hatch cover of the diving bell is open! They're reaching down inside the bell now . . . and. . . . There's a man's head. . . . They're helping someone out of the bell now. . . . He's climbing out of the bell under his own steam. . . . He's stepping across the top of the bell and is boarding the *Falcon*. . . . The first survivor rescued from the sunken submarine *Squalus* is out and safely aboard the rescue ship . . . and now here's another man coming out of the bell. He's being helped aboard the *Falcon*, although he seems to be able to make it without

assistance . . . and here's another . . . and another. . . .
These men seem to be in remarkably good condition despite
the tremendous strain they've been under. . . . Another
man is out now, and they're reaching inside to aid another.
. . . We may have lost count during the excitement of
seeing these men emerge from that bell alive and well,
but I think that's the sixth man to come out of the bell . . .
and here . . . here's the seventh.

Seven men have come out of that big, white, pear-shaped
diving bell. We don't know if they have all been brought
out of the sunken submarine or if some of them went down
with the bell to control it. But there you are. . . . We've
seen and have attempted to describe to you the actual
rescue of the first seven survivors from the ill-fated submarine *Squalus*, which is lying at the bottom of the sea in
approximately 250 feet of water. Undoubtedly the bell will
immediately be sent down again in an attempt to bring up
more of the men trapped down there, but it's a long job, taking at least an hour for the round trip, so we're going to
sign off from this point for the time being, but we'll be on
hand to bring you the eye-witness account of the rescue
as the bell comes up again. Keep tuned to this network
for further developments. This is Jack Knell, speaking to
you through short-wave transmitter WAAU, operating on
2,190 kilocycles. . . . This is the Columbia Broadcasting
System.

Sandhogs

From AMERICANS AT WORK

by MARGARET LEWERTH

A MERICANS at Work is a series of adult education programs presented by the Columbia Broadcasting System and designed to give the radio audience a glimpse into
the lives and the work of the men and women whose every-
day jobs make up American life. The railroad engineer, the
bus driver, the girl at the telephone switchboard, the policeman on the corner, the artist in the studio, the executive
at his desk—in each job is a human story, and Americans
at Work tells it. The program tells something, too, of the
problems, the satisfaction, the dignity in every job—and a
little of the tradition behind it. Through these half hour
broadcasts, each devoted to one occupation, the program
aims to give the radio listener a better knowledge of his
country and a keener understanding of the men and women
around him, a quicker sympathy with those who do
America's jobs.

Since its start in April, 1938, Americans at Work has
covered jobs in every walk of life. The series has presented
such a diversity of occupations as those of the fireman, the
dynamiter, the nurse, the submarine man, the tugboat
captain, the secretary, the steel riveter, the glass blower,
and others too numerous to mention. The program has
taken the microphone down into coal mines, up in skyscrapers, out with the ice patrol, into settlement houses—
wherever there is a story of men and women at work. And
in this lies the program's distinguishing feature—and one
of the reasons for its outstanding success. In each half hour
broadcast the time is divided between an authentic studio
dramatization of the particular job and its background—

and an actual on-the-scene interview with the workers. Such a program, of course, requires a great deal of advance work and research. A regular research staff supplies factual information, and the writer of the program makes a trip each week to talk with the workers on the job for true stories, color, and human interest. The script is written for the first part of the broadcast, and an announcer and an engineering staff are sent to the mine or the factory for the first-hand interview in the second half.

Americans at Work is unique among educational programs on the air in giving not only a comprehensive dramatized picture of America's many jobs but in presenting a personal interview with the workers actually at the scene of those jobs. All of the broadcasts are published in pamphlet form by the Columbia University Press.

Americans at Work has won two awards for its contribution to adult education and for its general excellence—from the Women's National Radio Committee and from the Tenth Institute for Radio in Education in its convention at Ohio State University in May, 1939. The program printed in the following pages is typical of a long series of successful broadcasts, in which dramatization, narration, and interview are combined to present an authentic picture of Americans at work.

The following script is the story of the men who build tunnels—the sandhogs. It was written by Margaret Lewerth, CBS staff writer, who has been responsible for the whole series.

Sandhogs*

SOUND.—*Open with real factory whistle . . . up . . . sustain . . . out . . . no background for following.*

NARRATOR.—*(Forcefully, yet simply)* Across 3,000 miles of cities, plains, rivers, mountains, a nation goes to work . . . a nation young and strong, turning its resources into power . . . a nation of men and women at their daily tasks . . . building, digging, harvesting, exploring, planning . . . making the world you and I live in . . . weaving the solid fabric of life today.

Who are these builders of a nation? Who are these men aloft on swinging girders . . . in the cabs of giant locomotives . . . at desks covered with blueprints? Who are these women at humming switchboards, behind busy counters, in laboratories filled with test tubes? Who are these workers carrying on the nation's business . . . proud of the skill that is their contribution to the vast web of American life? Tonight the Columbia Network brings you another in the series, Americans at Work, to take you into the lives and hearts of those millions of men and women who are making America.

SOUND.—*Street noises . . . traffic . . . horns . . . background of voices.*

JIM.—All right, Helen . . . here comes our bus.

HELEN.—Wait a minute, Jim . . . that man there. . . . Look, he's ill.

JIM.—He's staggering blind. . . . I think he's . . .

HELEN.—*(Cutting in)* Oh, he's fallen. . . . Look . . . how awful!

OFFICER.—*(Fading in)* What's the trouble here . . . what's the trouble?

JIM.—This man has just collapsed, officer. . . . He needs a doctor.

OFFICER.—(*Up*) Stand back, everybody. . . . Stand back. Joe . . . call the ambulance. (*In . . . lower. Man moans once faintly*) all right, Buddy . . . take it easy. (*To Jim*) What happened?

JIM.—He just staggered . . . and fell . . . right on the sidewalk.

OFFICER.—(*Skeptical*) Staggered, eh? . . . Let's open his coat. What? (*Suddenly serious and excited*) Hey, Joe . . . never mind the ambulance. . . . Get the emergency wagon . . . *quick!*

JIM.—What is it, officer?

OFFICER.—(*Short*) The bends!

JIM.—The bends?

OFFICER.—(*Businesslike, very serious*) Yeah . . . this guy's a sandhog . . . a tunnel worker. The tag on his vest here tells you to take him to the compression clinic instead of a hospital. I had one case like this before. They get this way from air pressure. (*Low*) O.K., buddy . . . we'll get you straightened out.

JIM.—That's terrible. . . . What can they do for him?

OFFICER.—Put him back in the air lock under pressure and revive him slowly. They get the bends when they come out of the air pressure too fast. . . . It gives 'em nitrogen bubbles in the blood stream . . . and when they burst it cripples 'em or kills 'em. . . .

JIM.—Do sandhogs have to wear these tags?

OFFICER.—Yeah . . . otherwise we wouldn't know . . . might put 'em in jail for being drunk or take 'em to a hospital. The air chamber is the only thing that fixes 'em. . . .

JIM.—(*Impressed*) You mean . . all tunnel workers get the bends?

OFFICER.—No . . . nowadays very few of 'em get it . . . but they all got a *chance* of getting it while they work in air pressure. (*Siren, clanging bell coming in, speaking over it*) There's the wagon now . . . gimme a hand, will you?

432

JIM.—Sure. . . . (*Man groans once . . . faintly*) O.K., Buddy
. . . we'll get you to the air lock. . . .
(*Fade noises and scene out complete*)

NARRATOR.—Air pressure! Air pressure to keep the water out
of a tunnel under construction. . . . Air pressure is only
one of the many dangers in the lives of America's tunnel
makers . . . that courageous and determined body of men
who spend every day in close, compact chambers far below
the surface of the earth . . . wearing hip boots, fiber
helmets, stripped to the waist because of heat and damp-
ness . . . men in the prime of health, who can get no life
insurance because of the dangers they face. They are the
tunnel makers of America who make it possible for *you* to
drive with comfort under cities and through mountains . . .
to turn a tap and draw water.

ANNOUNCER.—But let us turn back to America of a half century
ago . . . a different America . . . growing, pushing, wrest-
ing new wealth from untouched resources . . . an America
where it took more than a week to travel by steam train
from New York to San Francisco . . . an America of gas
lights and horse cars, where industry was crowding the
East, and the West was still opening up its vast treasures.

It is Milwaukee of 1891 . . . a lusty, sprawling city in
the heart of the wheat country . . . a Milwaukee that
needed water to run its mills . . . to supply its fast-growing
population.

One day outside a shack on the shore of Lake Michigan a
group of men in rough work clothes gathered. . . .

SOUND.—*Crowd of voices up . . . calling . . . laughing . . .
greeting . . . talking . . . ad libs off.*

FIRST.—Hullo, Pete . . . glad to see you.

SECOND.—So we're doing a water job, eh?

THIRD.—So I tells him I'm a sandhog, see.

VOICE.—Hey, fellas . . . here comes Tom, the foreman!

SOUND.—*In greetings . . . "Hello, Tom . . . Hello, boss," etc.*

FOREMAN.—Well, boys . . . I'm certainly glad to see so many
of the old bunch here. We got a tough job on our hands.
(*Voices in assent*) The toughest we ever tackled. We got to

433

build this water tunnel under Lake Michigan. . . . That means compressed air . . . and it means you guys will have to watch your step . . . and take enough time in the air locks. . . . You know what the bends can do. . . .

SOUND.—*Voices in assent.*

VOICE.—We're going through sand, ain't we, boss?

FOREMAN.—Soapstone mostly . . . with clay and gravel and sand in it. It's solid stuff . . . and we'll be 140 feet under the surface of the lake.

SECOND.—It's gonna mean a lot to the city, ain't it?

FOREMAN.—Yes . . . it'll be a great thing . . . 3,200 feet long. . . .

VOICE.—And it'll take us — years to finish it.

VOICE.—Say, chief . . . I got a kid along with me. Think you can take him on as a mucker?

FOREMAN.—I guess so . . . if he doesn't mind shovelin' mud all day.

MUCKER.—My dad was a sandhog, Mr. Johnson. . . . I ain't afraid of work.

SOUND.—*Voices up . . . good-naturedly.*

FOREMAN.—(*Chuckle*) All right . . . we'll see. . . . Report here tomorrow morning at 8. . . . We start on the shaft first thing.

SOUND.—*Voices up . . . out.*

NARRATOR.—So Milwaukee's great water tunnel was started . . . a dangerous task in that old-fashioned wooden tunnel . . . dimly lit with incandescent lamps . . . with the menace of the lake always pressing over their heads.

SOUND.—*Voices in . . . sound of drilling . . . scraping.*

FIRST.—This stuff is hard, all right. . . . Look at that soapstone.

SECOND.—Yeah. Well, we can be glad it is. . . . It keeps the lake up where it belongs.

FIRST.—Shoot another car down, mucker. We're drilling through this fast.

MUCKER.—Yep . . . here she comes.

SECOND.—Well, kid . . . how's it going? You're new at this, ain't you?

MUCKER.—Yeah . . . but I'm getting on. I didn't know it was so dark in a tunnel.

SECOND.—Oh, it's not so bad when you get used to it . . . but that's why we carry candles. . . . You can't trust these new-fangled electric bulbs.

MUCKER.—I never saw candles burn so long either. . . . The flames must be a foot long.

SECOND.—Air pressure does that to 'em, kid.

MUCKER.—It makes your ears hurt, too, doesn't it?,

SECOND.—When you're first in it . . . but you get used to that, too.

MUCKER.—Say, boss, look at the water coming through that drill there.

FIRST.—Aw, that's nothing. . . . That's been dripping in for an hour now. . . . Just lake water. . . . We're 1,600 feet from shore now . . . and we're apt to get a little seepage.

FOREMAN.—(*Coming in*) All right, men . . . we gotta blast again. . . . Look's like we're far enough into the stone. . . . It's too tough for the drills.

FIRST.—We're ready. . . . We gotta couple holes drilled for dynamite, if you want to go.

FOREMAN.—All right, load 'em up . . . and give it plenty of fuse. Come on men, out of the heading. . . . We're going to blast.

SOUND.—*Drills stop . . . men's voices in background.*

SECOND.—Close the shield openings, Joe . . . and clear away everybody. . . . We're lighting the fuse.

FIRST.—All right . . . let 'er go!

SOUND.—*Splutter of match and fuse.*

SECOND.—This is a quick fuse . . . so look out. . . . (*Two dull explosions off mike*) There she goes!

435

FOREMAN.—Open the shield, Pete . . . and watch the smoke as she comes out. . . .

SECOND.—Right. . . . (*Clang of iron*) . . . Better stand back until the smoke clears. . . . (*Excited*) Hey, boss . . . look! it's water. . . . It's coming through the heading! (*Men all start to talk*) It's rushing in!

SOUND.—*Of water.*

FOREMAN.—(*Puzzled*) *Water! Water?* (*Tense and excited*) Man the pumps, men . . . quick!

SOUND.—*Water pouring in . . . men's voices getting excited.*

FIRST.—It's coming in stronger, Mr. Johnson. . . .

FOREMAN.—Pull on the pumps. . . . (*Half aside*) I don't understand. . . . We have plenty of roof. . . . .

SOUND.—*Men's voices up . . . sound of sloshing in water . . . deepening . . . men sloshing in it.*

SECOND.—It's gaining on us, chief! . . . the pumps can't handle it!

FOREMAN.—(*Shouts*) O.K., men . . . leave the pumps. (*Voices up in protest*) Clear the tunnel. . . . We gotta get out!

SOUND.—*Voices . . . sound of men sloshing in water . . . voices . . . clank of metal . . . etc. . . . up and out.*

ANNOUNCER.—By next morning the entire tunnel and the shaft were completely filled with water that bubbled up and spilled over the ground at the tunnel's mouth. . . . A few days later the men gathered at the foreman's shack waiting for word to carry on with the half-built tunnel.

FIRST.—You know, I don't understand that flood. . . . The engineer's chart shows we have plenty of ceiling. You could blast the tunnel all the way with a roof like that.

SECOND.—Yeah . . . it's funny. . . . Nobody expected the lake on our heads like that . . . 1,600 feet of tunnel washed up . . . and still running in. . . . Hey, chief . . . what's the news?

FOREMAN.—(*Fading in*) Well, men . . . it looks like we gotta job on our hands now for sure.

SOUND.—*Men's voices up.*

FIRST.—We don't mind that, Mr. Johnson. . . . A little lake water won't hurt us.

SOUND.—*Men laugh with him.*

FOREMAN.—That's just it. . . . A little lake water won't hurt us . . . but this isn't lake water.

SECOND.—Isn't lake water! . . . What d'ya mean?

FOREMAN.—The report just came back from the laboratory. . . . This water isn't lake water. . . . It's water from a subterranean river running right under Lake Michigan. Something the engineers didn't know about.

FIRST.—Subterranean river? . . . Holy smoke!

SECOND.—Gee, we must have blown the whole bed out. . . . What do we do now, boss?

FOREMAN.—We go back and start again . . . with a new set of plans to detour the river. . . . It means a delay of 3 years.

FIRST.—Three years!

FOREMAN.—Yes . . . it means Milwaukee won't get its water tunnel for a while yet. But we gotta see it through, boys. . . .

SOUND.—*Voices up . . . sure . . . you bet.*

SECOND.—We'll see it through, boss. . . . No subterranean river's gonna lick this sandhog. . . .

SOUND.—*Men's voices up . . . laughing . . . enthusiastic . . . ready for the job.*

NARRATOR.—On . . . (May 12, 1895) . . . the tunnel was finished, bringing precious water to Milwaukee . . . its mills . . . its surrounding wheat fields. The sandhogs had won this battle, and millions were to benefit. While the West built tunnels for water . . . and for great railroads that were burrowing through the mountains . . . the East turned to tunnels to solve the ever-increasing transportation problem in its cities. New York had already experimented with subways. . . . In 1870 an amazing tunnel a little over a block long was built under lower Broadway . . . 21 feet below street

437

level. Through it ran a single car blown in one direction by air pressure . . . sucked back on the return trip. It failed to attract the public, however, and was soon bricked up and forgotten. In 1905 New York's first successful subway went into operation from Manhatten to Brooklyn . . . and the city entered a new era of expansion. In 1915 the tunnel for a subway at Montague Street in New York was started. Tunneling conditions were much improved by this time. Gone were the old wooden timbers. . . . Steel and concrete were taking their place. Gone too were the dim, dangerous candles. The men trusted electricity now, and hundreds of bulbs lit the long tube. But the danger of water and air was ever present . . . the danger of water coming through the tunnel roof . . . and the danger of air pressure blowing through a soft spot in the roof, with a current that took everything up with it . . . a current no man would withstand.

ANNOUNCER.—It was late one afternoon in the Montague Street Tube when an event occurred that made tunnel history. . . . The men were working in the huge shield, digging out mud. . . . (*Sounds up and fade to B.G.* . . . *Men talking . . . rattle of cars, etc.*) . . . and slowly pushing the great steel cylinder forward through the river bottom. (*Rush of air*) Three men . . . Frank Driver, Marshall Mabey, and Joe McCarthy . . . were up in the heading. . . .

FRANK.—Push another car along, will you, Joe. . . . That's got all the muck it'll take.

JOE.—Yep . . . here she goes. . . . Say, this is soft stuff, isn't it?

MARSHALL.—Yeah . . . and this is some pressure we're under. . . . Boy, I'll be glad to get off this shift.

FRANK.—Thirty-five pounds to the square inch . . . and you oughta be glad of it. . . . It's keeping the river out of our laps.

MARSHALL.—Yeah . . . it's funny to think of all that water over us . . . boats and all . . . and nobody realizes we're down here.

JOE.—They'll realize it when we get this tunnel built. Hey, Frank . . . look at that roof!

438

FRANK.—Whatsa matter . . . a soft spot?

JOE.—No . . . a tough one. . . . Look at this boulder!

FRANK.—Holy smoke . . . that *is* a rock . . . right in the roof too . . . and we don't dare blast. . . .

JOE.—One blast . . . and we'd be flooded. . . . Nope . . . we gotta pry it out. Let's try the crowbars.

MARSHALL.—O.K. . . . here they are. . . .

SOUND.—*Clatter of iron.*

JOE.—(*Grunts*) Boy . . . this *is* a tough one. . . . It'll leave some hole.

FRANK.—(*Also grunts . . . sounds of metal on iron*) Golly, I hope there's plenty of ceiling left. . . . We'd go up through the roof with this air pressure like a cork off a bottle.

JOE.—It'll hold. . . . Here she comes.

MARSHALL.—She's moving!

FRANK.—Watch out below. . . . This rock's gonna fall!

SOUND.—*Men's voices . . . crash of rock . . . sudden rush of air.*

VOICE.—It's a blow! (*Rush increases to roar of air*) Look out, men!
(*Following lines quick but distinguishable*)

FRANK.—Help. . . . It's pulling me!

JOE.—Help . . . help. . . . I can't stand!

MARSHALL.—It's blowing me!

VOICE.—(*Off . . . horror in voice*) Men. . . . Quick . . . Grab their feet. . . . They're going off the roof. . . . Grab them!

SECOND.—They've gone . . . my God . . . right through the river bottom. . . .

SOUND.—*Rush of water.*

VOICE.—Here comes the water. . . . (*Rush of water*) Run for it, men—*run!!*

439

SOUND.—*Confusion of voices . . . rushing water . . . up . . . hold . . . out.*

ANNOUNCER.—Three men blown clear through the solid muck of river bottom . . . up through the river itself. Two of the men died instantly, but miraculously the third was blown through the hole made by the others and was picked up alive on the river surface.

A few weeks later, Marshall Mabey, the survivor, lay in the hospital recovering from an almost fatal case of the bends after being catapulted from 35 pounds of tunnel pressure to 14 pounds of normal air pressure. It was a recovery that was to take him a year.

FOREMAN.—*(Fading in)* Well, Marshall . . . I never thought I'd see you in a hospital bed. . . . You look almost as good as new.

MARSHALL.—Hello, chief. . . . I'm going to be all right. How's the tunnel going along?

FOREMAN.—All right. . . . It'll take us a couple of more years yet.

MARSHALL.—No more accidents?

FOREMAN.—Not after yours. . . . You know, Marshall, it's a miracle you're alive today after that blow.

MARSHALL.—I know it is. *(Voice low)* I'm sorry about Frank and Joe. . . . They went . . . a tough way. . . . They were real men. . . . I was proud to work with 'em.

FOREMAN.—*(Also low)* Yes . . . I know.

MARSHALL.—*(Trying to get back to normal conversation)* Well . . . how did you fix up the tunnel?

FOREMAN.—It was some job. . . . The tunnel flooded . . . and the hole was so bad the air pressure didn't keep the water out, so we had to tackle it from the river surface.

MARSHALL.—The surface.

FOREMAN.—Yes. To fill up the hole, we finally had to take a heavy canvas weighted with granite at each corner . . . sink it from a boat over the hole. . . . Then we dumped barge loads of yellow clay on top of that . . . and then turned on the air pressure inside the tunnel until it equaled the river pressure. Then we went back to work.

440

MARSHALL.—(*Admiringly*) Boy, chief . . . that was some stunt.

FOREMAN.—Yes . . . it was. Well, Marshall. . . . I suppose you'll give up sandhogging after this?

MARSHALL.—Give up sandhogging? . . . Listen, chief . . . I'm a sandhog . . . and if they ever let me out of here, I'm going right on being a sandhog. . . . Would *you* give it up?

FOREMAN.—No . . . I guess not.

MARSHALL.—Well, neither would I! This town's gonna need a lot more tunnels . . . and we're the guys that are gonna build 'em!

NARRATOR.—And they did build them! Through obstacles, through dangers, the tunnel men carried on . . . wherever tunnels were needed, wherever there was rock or sand or water to be conquered beneath the earth's surface, these men and their families went. One by one, they completed giant tasks. . . .

FIRST VOICE.—(*Forceful, brisk headline style*) A hundred and twenty-three miles of subway in New York City gave their passengers each day 1,237,000 hours . . . the equivalent each day of 18,000 full lifetimes for work, for play, for self-development.

SECOND.—Water tunnels across the nation contribute to the irrigation of 4 million acres of land . . . with annual crops worth 175 million dollars.

THIRD.—The 62-mile tunnel under Chicago carries the freight of the nation!

FOURTH.—The 6-mile Moffet tunnel carries transcontinental trains under the Rocky Mountain range in 10 minutes . . . trains formerly held up as much as 31 days in heavy snows.

FIFTH.—Fifty-nine miles of tunnels bring water from the Sierra Nevadas to San Francisco and the Pacific Coast!

ANNOUNCER.—The tunnels of America, made possible by the work of the tunnel men, the sandhogs: Americans at work!

[Program then switched to pick up an interview between Bob Trout and a sandhog actually conducted in a tunnel beneath the river. After an announcer had set the scene, Trout began his questioning as he was preparing to go into the lock which led to the chamber under pressure.]

TROUT.—Tell me, how great is the air pressure in the boring chamber ahead?

TALBOT.—Thirteen pounds per square inch.

TROUT.—That sounds like a lot of pressure to me. Do you vary it?

TALBOT.—Oh, yes, we vary it with the pressure above it.

TROUT.—Why do you vary it? Why do you have so great a pressure there?

TALBOT.—According to the depth that we're down and the water above us.

TROUT.—I see. You try to keep the water out by that air pressure.

TALBOT.—We do keep it out.

TROUT.—Do you vary your working hours with the pressure?

TALBOT.—Oh, yes, the men work according to the pressure. The higher the pressure, the lower the hours.

TROUT.—What sort of schedule do they work on, Mr. Talbot?

TALBOT.—On this job they're working on 6 hours. That's 3 in, 3 out, and 3 on. The greater the pressure, the shorter the hours and the higher the pay.

TROUT.—I see. Well, there's an awful lot of noise from that exhaust pipe. That's the exhaust from the chamber ahead where the men are under pressure. Well, let's just go into this lock and go forward. I'll take the microphone right with me. I have to stoop a bit to get into this lock and carry the portable microphone along. Perhaps you can hear the echoes of my heels hitting on the cement here. A lot of people point the way for me to go. It's sort of like a revolving barrel in an amusement park, Mr. Talbot. I have to kind of stoop to get in, but it doesn't revolve. . . . I hope it doesn't. Now, wait a minute, take it a little bit easy here now. This is all new to me, you know.

TALBOT.—All right, Mr. Trout.

TROUT.—What do I do?

TALBOT.—Just hold your nose and keep blowing to equalize the pressure when your eardrums become tight.

TROUT.—I've got a piece of chewing gum in my mouth; that's right, isn't it?

TALBOT.—Yes. You keep chewing.

TROUT.—I'll keep chewing, and I have to explain to the radio audience that I'll have to stop talking, too, when you turn that air on, right?

TALBOT.—Yes, that's right. There'll be so much noise.

TROUT.—Who's going to lock that door, that big metal door down there?

TALBOT.—Mr. Wheeler will take care of that, and the lock tender will open the valves.

TROUT.—I wouldn't have you think that I'm nervous at all, but don't men ever get nervous in here the first time?

TALBOT.—Yes, a little bit.

TROUT.—Have you ever had any interesting experiences?

TALBOT.—Yes, I had a gang run back at the door after it was closed in Belgium. I had them: they couldn't get out.

TROUT.—Why?

TALBOT.—Because the air pressure was holding the door closed.

TROUT.—The pressure holds it closed? I mean, I couldn't open it if I tried?

TALBOT.—You try it, Mr. Trout.

TROUT.—Well, go ahead and put the air on. I'm ready.

TALBOT.—There's 30 tons pressure going on now.

TROUT.—Let's have it. I'll hold my nose right now.

SOUND.—*Air pressure.*

TROUT.—Is that all?

TALBOT.—Not all yet.

SOUND.—*Air pressure.*

TALBOT.—Is everyone all right? Now, just a moment. We have one man back.

443

TROUT.—Oh, really? Do you think you can let the air out a little bit?

TALBOT.—All right now. Let it go a little further.

SOUND.—*Air pressure.*

TROUT.—I certainly will tell them how hot it is. It's like a Turkish bath. What happened to the temperature? Everyone's quite all right. I wouldn't want to have any accidents while we're on the air, naturally. It is a bit difficult to talk. As a matter of fact, it was a bit harder getting through here than you led me to believe, Mr. Talbot.

TALBOT.—Oh, yes. Well, after you've been through once, Mr. Trout, you'll be an old veteran.

TROUT.—Yes, I'm an old veteran. What happened to the crease in my trousers?

TALBOT.—It's the heat in here.

TROUT.—What makes it so hot? I'll have to take off my coat, I think, before we get through here.

TALBOT.—It's the air pressure.

TROUT.—Just air pressure alone? Well, I'll take the microphone in my hand, and now we'll actually step out of the man lock. We're through that metal barrel, and we're standing right out in the chamber under pressure. Once you get under pressure, there doesn't seem to be much to it. I don't notice any difference now, Mr. Talbot.

TALBOT.—Right where you stand now, Mr. Trout, is where you're entering the sand in the roof.

TROUT.—That's where the cast-iron lining is starting. There's nothing but sand up there on the top. The place is brilliantly lighted by some hundred electric globes, and I see about 30 men up there stripped to the waist and working furiously. They certainly don't shirk on that job, do they? What's that great big round thing like a door, like a vault on a bank door?

TALBOT.—That's not a vault, Mr. Trout, that's a shield.

TROUT.—What's a shield?

TALBOT.—That is a shield. It's like a big steel cylinder with 14 hydraulic jacks which force it forward and through; that is where the sandhogs work, in the front.

TROUT.—And that's the tunnel end. That shield moves forward as the tunnel advances, is that right? How fast does the tunnel advance?

TALBOT.—Oh, maybe about 10 feet a day.

TROUT.—Well, Mr. Talbot, let's stay back here out of the noise of those hydraulic drills fighting through that rock and the shovels going through the sand, and if you'd call Mr. Weaver over . . . I can see that he's one of your sandhogs who are working with you. He came through the lock with us. If you call Mr. Weaver over I'd like to ask you both a couple of questions. Mr. Weaver, you're not nervous, talking through the microphone, are you?

WEAVER.—No, no, no.

TROUT.—I must admit I was a little bit nervous with that air you had in there and what you did to me.

WEAVER.—I guess you're all right now, eh?

TROUT.—I think I'm all right. You've worked with Mr. Talbot a long time, Joe?

JOE.—Yes.

TROUT.—When did you start with him?

JOE.—In 1908.

TROUT.—Do you travel a lot in this job? You've been in other countries?

JOE.—Yes, Belgium, Canada, all over the world.

TROUT.—Don't you have a hard time when you're traveling? Being away from home so much . . . that sort of thing?

JOE.—We take our families with us, Mr. Trout.

TROUT.—Do you have families, both of you?

BOTH.—Yes.

TROUT.—Do you want your boys to become sandhogs?

445

Joe.—I guess they'll do the same as we did. We didn't have any choice. They'll have to follow in their fathers' footsteps, I guess.

Trout.—You don't think it's a bad job, do you?

Joe.—No, I don't.

Trout.—Tell me, Joe Weaver, don't you think it's sort of tiresome working here with the same men all the time, day in and day out 24 hours a day?

Joe.—No!

Trout.—You don't mind?

Joe.—I like 'em.

Trout.—How about you, Mr. Talbot? Does it get on your nerves working with the same men all the time?

Tablot.—Oh, no. No, no. I like 'em.

Trout.—You like them. That certainly is a good way to be as long as you work down in here. This is the most amazing sort of place I've ever been in, as a matter of fact. This is really dangerous sort of work, isn't it? Down here under this tremendous air pressure all the time. Are there many accidents?

Talbot.—Accidents are just part of the story. They build tunnels in spite of accidents. My father built them, his father built them, and I wouldn't do anything else. But, of course, you never can quite forget the air. It doesn't feel any different, once you're in it, except that you get tired out quickly. But you never can forget the tunnel either when you're in the tunnel or when you're at home. It does shorten your life, and you know a sandhog can't buy insurance.

Trout.—Why can't he, Mr. Talbot?

Talbot.—Because the premiums are so high.

Trout.—It's been pleasant indeed meeting both of you gentlemen here beneath Manhattan and talking to you while people above us on the surface go calmly about their daily routine, riding in streetcars, automobiles, elevators in skyscrapers. Most of them probably don't even know the sandhogs are burrowing beneath them down here, unless they were listening to their radios during this conversation. And now, fellows, I'll be getting decompressed. So long, Mr. Talbot; so long, Joe Weaver.

MEN.—So long, Mr. Trout.

TROUT.—Good-by, and next time I ride through a tunnel I'll remember you sandhogs down here, building tunnels to speed America on her way.

No Help Wanted

by WILLIAM N. ROBSON

O HELP Wanted" is one of a series of documentary broadcasts produced in New York for the British Broadcasting Corporation and broadcast from sound film over the BBC transmitters in England. It has never been heard in this country.

This series has included thus far "Crosstown Manhattan," a documentary inspection of a New York street; "G Men against Crime," an examination of the Federal Bureau of Investigation; and "No Help Wanted," a panorama of the nation's depression and the efforts of the Works Progress Administration to solve the nation's unemployment problem. The first of the American documentary broadcasts was "Ecce Homo," by Pare Lorentz. It was repeated in London in the summer of 1938, with British-American actors.

The BBC has for years been presenting documentary or "actuality" broadcasts, but "Ecce Homo," which presented a picture of American unemployment, was the first American experiment in this technique. To produce such a broadcast in London was perhaps an audacious attempt to carry coals to Newcastle, but the British press received the production with unanimous acclaim and editorially asked why their own radio producers did not give them such a picture of the British "distressed areas."

The British press acceptance of the American documentaries that followed has been increasingly generous and enthusiastic. Upon hearing "No Help Wanted," London newspapers insisted, "Nothing finer has yet come from America, including "Job To Be Done" [the British title for "Ecce Homo"].

As may readily be seen upon reading the script, the documentary technique differs greatly from the technique used in other forms of radio writing. First, the author must limit himself to fact. He must be able to prove what he says. He must make these facts interesting. He must (and here again is the persistent problem of all educational radio) entertain as he informs. For unless he does, he loses that vast section of his audience that are looking for escape rather than enlightenment in their radio listening. And usually it is of vital importance. that such people be reached with the message that the documentary broadcast carries.

For, it must be frankly admitted, the documentary broadcast is a form of propaganda. Impartial though the writer may be, he will find that in presenting a documented picture of any given subject, the facts presented will result in an over-all point of view. It has been said that there are three sides to a question, yours and mine and the facts. And the facts have a curious way of adding up to a point of view.

The student of radio scripts may be interested to note the unusual technique of "No Help Wanted." There are very few scenes. There is a preponderance of closely written narrative. This would be poor technique for radio plays of the standard type, but it is one way of presenting the documentary broadcast. Although such a presentation may seem dull to the reader, it should be remembered that from the printed script there are missing the color and emotional value, the dimension of the actor's voice, the musical background, and the sound effects. Without these, radio sometimes makes difficult closet drama.

"No Help Wanted" is included in this anthology because of the vigor of its expression, the effectiveness of its fast panoramic treatment, and particularly because the documentary show—still the nursling of the radio industry—now promises to cut its milk teeth. Some day when writers have more deeply explored this new horizon of broadcasting, this piece will have a purely museum interest. Today it stands as a challenge to the American writer to experiment with a new dimension.

No Help Wanted*

MUSIC.—*Theme . . . in . . . up . . . build . . . down for*

ANNOUNCER.—*No Help Wanted!*

MUSIC.—*Theme . . . up and under.*

NARRATOR.—This is a story of America. It is the story of the greatest suffering the people of the United States have ever known. It's a story of a people's improvidence and a nation's courage. It is the story of a greater collective experiment in human rehabilitation than any country in the world has ever before attempted. It is a story told in millions of men and billions of money . . . a story which may sound unbelievable but of which every word is true. Like all true stories, it is not perfect; like all human stories, it is not yet finished.

This is a story of America!

This was America 10 years ago.

MUSIC.—*Theme up and fade.*

VOICE.—(*Filter*) American Universal, consolidated, 185 . . . 185½ . . . 187 . . . 190 . . . 191. . . . (*This voice continues increasing stock quotes*)

SECOND VOICE.—Buy steel. . . .

THIRD VOICE.—Buy motors. . . .

FOURTH VOICE.—Buy Tel and Tel. . . .

SECOND VOICE.—Buy. . . .

THIRD.—Buy. . . .

FOURTH VOICE.—Buy. . . .

NARRATOR.—This was America 10 years ago, the America of the Coolidge boom, the America of Hoover prosperity, the fabulous America of country clubs and shiny automobiles, of electric refrigerators, modern plumbing, and six-tube heterodyne radio sets, the America of a new economy, an economy of perpetual prosperity ideally expressed by its President Hoover.

HOOVER.—Two cars in every garage and a chicken in every pot.

SECOND NARRATOR.—But in March, 10 years ago, in March of 1929 . . .

VOICE.—There are estimated to be 2,860,000 unemployed people in the United States.

NARRATOR.—What of it? What of a mere 2 or 3 million unemployed in a nation of a 125 million people?

VOICE.—A drop in the bucket.

SECOND VOICE.—There's always some people who won't work.

THIRD VOICE.—Seasonal unemployment, no doubt.

SECOND NARRATOR.—What of it? Listen to the music of that stock ticker. . . .

SOUND.—*Background ticker voice comes up.*

VOICE.—(*Fades to background, accelerating now*)

FIRST VOICE.—Buy steel. . . .

SECOND VOICE.—Buy motors. . . .

THIRD VOICE.—Buy copper. . . .

FOURTH VOICE.—Buy oil. . . .

FIRST VOICE.—Buy. . . .

SECOND VOICE.—Buy. . . .

THIRD VOICE.—Buy. . . .

FOURTH VOICE.—Buy. . . .
  (*Continues in order, accelerating*)

MUSIC.—*Sneaks under above and wipe out with crash!*

NARRATOR.—*This* was America in October of 1929. This was America after black Thursday.

451

VOICE OF TICKER.—(*Slow, monotonous*) United States Steel 21.
. . . American Tel. and Tel. 69. . . . General Motors
7. . . . Anaconda Copper 3. . . . (*Continues in background*)

MUSIC.

EMPLOYER.—Until things improve we have found it necessary
to dispense with your valued services. . . .

SECOND EMPLOYER.—Due to the present unstable conditions in
industry, we have been forced to shut down our Youngstown
plant and place the Aliquippa unit on half time. . . .

THIRD EMPLOYER.—I feel sure, men, that this depression will not
last long. Remember, our President has assured us that
prosperity is just around the corner. . . .

NARRATOR.—January, 1930. Four million unemployed, and
America sang a new song.

MUSIC.—"*Buddy Can You Spare a Dime?*" . . . *eight bars* . . .
(*Orchestra and chorus*).

SECOND NARRATOR.—Out from the great industrial centers, out
from New York, from Chicago, from Pittsburgh, from
Birmingham, surged the hopeless gray tide of panic, which
the nation preferred to call depression.

NARRATOR.—Westward, across the smoke-stained steel towns,
across the grimy mine towns, across the once busy ports
of the Great Lakes, westward across the vast flat plains, still
standing waist deep in waving yellow wheat and rustling
green corn, swept the waves of unemployment.
September, 1930, 5 million unemployed. . . .
January 1, 1931 . . . 6 million unemployed.

MUSIC.—*Last two bars, "Buddy Can You Spare a Dime?"*

NARRATOR.—And while bread lines formed on the snow-swept
streets of American cities, while gangster Al Capone opened
a soup kitchen in Chicago, Myron C. Taylor, president
of the United States Steel Corporation assured the nation by
radio . . .

TAYLOR.—(*Filter*) While the number of unemployed is considerable, the number in real distress is relatively few, because
the masses have been provident and are caring for themselves and each other.

MISTER MAN.—Turn it off, Mildred.

SOUND.—*Switch click.*

MISTER MAN.—The masses have been provident and are caring for themselves. Who's caring for us, I'd like to know?

MILDRED.—Now, Eddie, don't talk like that, we'll get along somehow.

MISTER MAN.—How? We're at the end of the rope, Mildred. Installment people have taken the car. They've taken the electric refrigerator, and they're coming for the radio tomorrow because I can't keep up the payments. Our last night with the radio, and I hear a stuffed shirt telling me we're taking care of ourselves.

MILDRED.—Well, John, he wasn't referring to us. . . .

MISTER MAN.—What do you mean?

MILDRED.—Well, after all, you're a salesman. . . . You aren't an ordinary day laborer. The masses are . . . well, oh, you know what I mean. . . . We don't belong to the masses. . . .

MISTER MAN.—I'm not so sure about that, Mildred. When you've been out of a job as long as I have, you get to thinking about a lot of things. When you see everything you've worked for go out from under you, your savings, your house, your car, your . . . your radio . . . you begin to wonder. . . . I guess we are the masses, Mildred. . . . I guess it's phony to have any ideas about being better than the next one any more. . . .

MILDRED.—Eddie, that's no way to talk.

MISTER MAN.—I dunno why it's happened. . . . All I know is that I can't get a job, and I can't borrow any more money on my life insurance . . . and the bank won't give me any . . . and everybody's as bad off as I am. . . . I guess we are the masses, all right, Mildred. . . . It's a cinch we're all in the same boat . . . and I guess that guy on the radio's screwy, because we haven't been provident, and we're not taking care of ourselves because we don't know how, and there isn't anyone to help us.

MUSIC.

NARRATOR.—September, 1931, 8 million unemployed. . . .

SECOND NARRATOR.—December, 10½ million. . . .

NARRATOR.—Another winter of soup kitchens and bread lines, of silent people on street corners selling apples, of hopelessness, of fear, of hunger and cold.

SECOND NARRATOR.—Local charities have exhausted their funds. State organizations have no money. From the Atlantic to the Pacific, from Canada to Mexico, from towns and farms and cities, there rises a rumble. . . .

VOICE.—The government must help.

SECOND VOICE.—The government must help. . . .

THIRD VOICE.—The government must help.

FOURTH VOICE.—The government must help. . . .

THIRD VOICE.—These people aren't hoboes, they're not tramps, they're Americans.

FOURTH VOICE.—They're our neighbors. . . .

FIFTH VOICE.—They're you and me. . . .

CHORUS.—This isn't a local matter or a state matter. . . .

SECOND VOICE.—It's a national matter. . . .

CHORUS.—The government *must* help.

MUSIC.—*Short chord or bridge.*

NARRATOR.—And from Washington comes the cool reply of the assistant director of the new and now frankly named Organization of Unemployment Relief. . . .

THORPE.—The proposition that the government should give aid to the unemployed is unwise, economically unsound, and fraught with public danger.

NARRATOR.—And in Pittsburgh, the sky was deep blue, and not a mill chimney belched smoke.

SECOND NARRATOR—And in Oklahoma, the dust buried the farms.

THIRD NARRATOR.—And in California, armed guards loaded starving Mexican families on to sealed trains bound south across the border.

FOURTH NARRATOR.—And in New York and Boston and Youngstown and Scranton, men shuffled along the streets, their freezing feet wrapped in rags. . . .

FIFTH NARRATOR.—And Chicago . . . the fourth largest city in the world, with half a million citizens on charity relief, cannot collect its taxes . . . cannot pay its schoolteachers, its firemen, its police . . . because there is no money. . . .

NARRATOR.—But at last a ray of hope . . . a bill providing for small loans to states for relief purposes is passed by Congress. . . .

SECOND NARRATOR.—And vetoed by President Hoover, who explains . . .

HOOVER.—It unbalances the budget . . .

NARRATOR.—Eight million unemployed. . . .

SECOND NARRATOR.—Ten million. . . .

THIRD NARRATOR.—Twelve million. . . .

NARRATOR.—And in small villages and towns all over the country is repeated the incident which occurred at Hazard, in the hills of Kentucky. . . .

CROWD.—(*Murmur comes in*)

LEADER.—Now, boys, there's the sheriff standin' in front of the warehouse. . . .

MAN.—He ain't gonna stop us. . . .

SECOND MAN.—Reckon he ain't. . . .

LEADER.—Don't get rough, boys. . . . I'll talk to him. . . . Howdy, sheriff. . . .

SHERIFF.—Howdy, boys. . . . Heard you was comin' to town. . . .

LEADER.—Yeah, reckon you did. . . .

SHERIFF.—Lookin' for trouble, boys?

LEADER.—No, we ain't aimin' for no trouble, sheriff. . . .

SHERIFF.—I didn't think you was . . . so better go along peaceablelike back to your farms. . . .

455

LEADER.—Shure, we figger to do that, sheriff, after we get us somethin' to eat. ....

SHERIFF.—Plenty to eat uptown. ...

LEADER.—Yeah, but we run outa credit. ...

SHERIFF.—I can't help that. ...

LEADER.—I know it, sheriff ... but you ain't gonna hinder us neither. ...

SHERIFF.—What do you boys want. ...

CROWD.—(*Murmurs several ad libs* ... *"something to eat"*)

LEADER.—Sheriff, you're standin' plumb in front of the door of a warehouse that's got vittles in it. .... We calculate to take them vittles home to our wives and kids.

SHERIFF.—It's unlawful.

LEADER.—I don't know much about the law, sheriff ... as you know it ... but I know about another law, and that law says when you're hungry you gotta eat. Well, my old lady's hungry, and my kids is whimperin' because their bellies is empty, and they can't eat no more grass and bark. Now, I don't know why that is. I don't know why I can't sell my crops or get credit at the bank. I don't understand any of them things ... but the boys and me know we're hungry. ...

CROWD.—(*Reaction*)

VOICE.—Come on, Lem, stop the jawin'. .... Let's get them vittles. ...

LEADER.—Well, sheriff, the boys is gettin' out of hand. Some of 'em is armed.

SHERIFF.—It's agin' the law. ...

LEADER.—I can't help that, sheriff. ...

SHERIFF.—You boys better go back home, and I'll see what I can do with the charity people. ...

VOICE.—The charity people ... them rats. ...

SOUND.—*Shot.*

LEADER.—Jake, I told you not to do that. ...

JAKE.—Aw, I jest knocked his hat off . . . to show him I ain't lost my touch. . . .

VOICES.—(*Laugh*)

LEADER.—Well, sheriff?

SHERIFF.—(*Wryly*) Guess you boys ain't in a talkin' mood. . . .

LEADER.—That's right, sheriff, so jest stand to one side. . . . Come on, boys. . . .

CROWD.—(*Low roar*)

SOUND.—*Heavy door opening.*

LEADER.—There y'are, boys, help yourself. . . . Flour, bacon, beans, molasses, the hull works. . . .

CROWD.—(*Ad libs rise*)

MUSIC.—*Tag.*

NARRATOR.—And the shelves groaned with goods that wouldn't move, and the warehouses burst with grain that no one could buy, and the wealthiest nation on earth suffered an embarrassment of riches which no one could explain.

SECOND NARRATOR.—Men fear what they do not understand. That inexplicable year of 1932, fear gripped America.

THIRD VOICE.—People who could afford it stocked their larders with staples and tinned foods.

FOURTH VOICE.—People who had any money changed it into gold and hid it.

FIFTH VOICE.—And people talked openly of revolution. . . .

VOICE.—The people in the upper income brackets.

NARRATOR.—The unemployed, the dispossessed, the hopeless talked of jobs, of work, of food and colonized the dumps and unsanitary vacant lots on the outskirts of the great cities . . . too dazed to think of revolution, too busy building communities of shanties which they grimly called "Hooverville."

MUSIC.

VOICE.—The richest land on earth.

MUSIC.

SECOND VOICE.—On February 14, 1932, the Union Guardian Bank in Detroit suspended business.

THIRD VOICE.—A week later, the Guaranty Trust Company of Atlantic City failed.

FOURTH VOICE.—In June, the Arcadia Trust Company of Newark closed its doors.

VOICE.—The richest land on earth.

SECOND VOICE.—And the money hidden, the gold hoarded, the currency out of circulation.

NARRATOR.—And the senseless horror of panic seized the nation.

VOICE.—In Michigan, in the winter of 1933, the governor closed all the banks. State after state followed his example. Commerce stood still. People bartered and traded, and in a little town in northern California, clamshells became the currency (*pause*) . . . and the nation held its breath.

NARRATOR.—Such was the situation on March 4, 1933, when the American people turned to their new leader, listened to the voice of their newly elected president, Franklin Delano Roosevelt, who, in his inaugural address said . . .

ROOSEVELT.—This is the time to speak the truth, frankly and boldly. A host of unemployed citizens face the grim problem of existence, and an equally great number toil with little return. Only a foolish optimism can deny the dark realities of the moment. This nation asks for action and action now. Our greatest primary task is to put people to work. I am prepared, under my constitutional duty, to recommend the measures that a stricken nation in the midst of a stricken world may require. I may ask the Congress for broad executive power to wage war against the emergency as great as the power that would be given me if we were in fact invaded by a foreign foe. We do not distrust the future of an essential democracy. The people of the United States have not failed.

MUSIC.—*Hail to the chief*.

VOICE.—And to save the nation from chaos, the President's first official act was to close all the banks in the land, to put a stop to senseless fear.

SECOND NARRATOR.—But 15 million people were still unemployed.

THIRD NARRATOR.—Thirty million hands idle . . . hands that once had run machinery, hands that had kept books, hands that had painted pictures and composed music and held test tubes, hands that had tilled the soil and run the engines and fished the seas of the nation. Hands skilled and unskilled hands that were now rusting and idle . . . hands through which no money passed. Thirty million idle hands, some of them 1, some 2, some 3, some 4 years idle. The wealth of the nation wasting away.

NARRATOR.—The only thing we have to fear is fear itself.

SECOND VOICE.—Backed by solidly Democratic Congress, backed by the confidence of a despairing nation, President Roosevelt begins a series of the most colossal experiments in social engineering in the history of the world.

VOICE.—Through Congress was rushed the Federal Emergency Relief Act, which authorized the spending of 500 million dollars for relief.

SECOND VOICE.—But this was direct relief. This was a dole.

VOICE.—And the American feels peculiar about such things. . . .

MAN.—I'll be darned if I'd take it if it weren't for Ella and the kids. I don't want a handout. I don't want charity. I want a job. . . .

VOICE.—Yes, a job and the radio and the refrigerator and an automobile . . . the symbols of the American way of life.

NARRATOR.—But most of all a job.

SECOND NARRATOR.—To put these millions of hands to work quickly, led to a new organization, the Civil Works Administration.

NARRATOR.—Through this administration, launched in October of 1933, the government put 4 million people to work in less than 90 days, put them to work at any jobs that could be found, leaf raking, snow shoveling, road building.

SECOND VOICE.—And for the first time in years, there were wages in 4 million pockets.

MUSIC.

459

CHILD.—Mama wants 2 quarts of milk today, please.

GROCER.—*Two* quarts?

CHILD.—Yes. Papa's got a job. He's workin' for the government.

MUSIC.—*Continues.*

GROCER.—Guess you can leave an extra two cases of milk today, Jim.

DRIVER.—Business lookin' up?

GROCER.—Well, there's more money in this neighborhood, since that government CWA started hirin' the men.

MUSIC.—*Continues.*

DRIVER.—Got orders for 10 more cases on my route today, boss.

BOSS.—That's fine.

MUSIC.—*Continues.*

BOSS.—Hello, Sunnyside Farms?

FARMER.—(*Filter*) Yes?

BOSS.—This is the Gilt Edge Dairy. Can you deliver us twice as much milk as you've been sending?

FARMER.—(*Filter*) Sure. Got so much I can't sell. I been dumpin' it.

BOSS.—O.K., we'll take it. Our orders are way up.

MUSIC.—*Continues.*

FARMER.—Well, mother, since we got that contract with the Gilt Edge, I'm thinkin' we might buy a new dress for you . . . and maybe a Sunday suit for me.

MUSIC.—*Continues . . . Builds and tags.*

NARRATOR.—Four million people with money in their pockets.

SECOND VOICE.—Four million people spending money for milk and bread and fuel and clothes.

THIRD VOICE.—Twenty million new dollars a week in circulation, changing hands, restoring confidence, moving goods.

460

FOURTH VOICE.—The corner was turned, the long-promised corner.

FIFTH VOICE.—To be sure, prosperity was not around that corner.

SIXTH VOICE.—But the road to recovery was.

NARRATOR.—The upswing began. The government maintained an average monthly employment of 2 million, making work for women as well as men, for professional, technical and other "white collar" workers as well as skilled and unskilled laborers.

SECOND NARRATOR.—And in the meantime, the many other ramifications of relief went on.

MUSIC.

NARRATOR.—In the hot and dry summer of 1934, the blasting, rainless winds again blew down across the high plains of middle America, scorching and shriveling the meager grass, blowing the topsoil into hideous unlivable dust storms, threatening the vast cattle herds of the West with starvation.

SECOND NARRATOR.—Into this emergency the government stepped.

VOICE.—The Agricultural Adjustment Administration is hereby authorized to buy 6 million head of cattle from the ranges in the drought area.

SECOND VOICE.—Why?

VOICE.—To help the farmer and to feed the unemployed.

NARRATOR.—And that summer, nearly 100 million pounds of fresh meat and over 200 million pounds of canned meat were distributed to unemployed American citizens.

MUSIC.—*Southern tune . . . quasi blues.*

NARRATOR.—Along the banks of the Mississippi River and East to the Appalachian Mountains and West into Texas lies the cotton belt of the American South.

Here, for generations, plantation owners and tenant farmers have sown and planted and picked only one crop . . . cotton.

461

Here the land is poor and tired. And so are the people. Here, for two decades, have existed a social and economic problem, an agricultural and a racial problem.

And here, in the midst of the depression no one dared call a panic, Nature played a grim joke. Nature smiled on the poor South and gave her a bumper cotton crop. Again the embarrassment of riches, again the confusion of plenty.

VOICE.—And again the government acted.

SECOND VOICE.—Buy up all the surplus cotton in the South. Stabilize the price. Don't let the price of cotton drop.

THIRD VOICE.—But what will the government do with all this cotton?

FOURTH VOICE.—Put the relief workers to work making mattresses and quilts, which can be distributed to the unemployed.

NARRATOR.—So the government was forced out of mattress making, but the cotton was used for the manufacture of quilts.

MUSIC.—*Bridge.*

BOY.—Well, I'm goin', ma.

MOTHER.—You're going? Where?

BOY.—I dunno, ma. Maybe I'll head out West. . . . Maybe I can get a job out there. . . .

MOTHER.—Bobbie, please don't leave.

BOY.—Listen, ma, I ain't doin' you any good here. A high school diploma doesn't help you get jobs when there aren't any.

MOTHER.—Yes, Bobbie, but maybe things will be different soon.

BOY.—Don't look much like it . . . dad on relief, and you and him without enough to eat half the time. I got a lot of stomach to fill, ma . . . so I'll go find me a job somewhere.

MOTHER.—Oh, Bobbie . . . you're all I have. . . .

BOY.—Now, ma, don't start that again. . . . I'll keep in touch with you . . . if I get to California, I'll send you a picture postcard of Hollywood Boulevard . . . California. . . . I'll bet it's warm there. . . .

NARRATOR.—Another recruit for the army of a million boys and young men aimlessly wandering from town to town, from city to city, looking for jobs.

VOICE.—But now the government steps in, and these transients disappear, first into the 250 temporary government camps and then into the CCC, the Civilian Conservation Corps, where they are fed, clothed, housed, and paid $30 a month.

SECOND NARRATOR.—Half a million young men in 15 hundred camps. . . . A volunteer army planting trees, building erosion dams, salvaging the soil that generations of Americans had allowed to run to ruin. An army of half a million young men . . . no longer standing idle at street corners or tramping the nation's highways; an army fit and strong, helping with their wages their families on relief at home.

MUSIC.—*Pastoral.*

VOICE.—What about unemployment insurance. . . . What about the sick, the disabled?

SECOND VOICE.—The Social Security Act was passed in May, 1935, establishing what other countries have had for years . . . unemployment insurance, old age benefits, pensions. But that is another story. It is the story of the acceptance by the American people of principles which they had long opposed. Unemployment insurance and benefits for the aged are now within the accepted pattern of American life.

NARRATOR.—Then in July, 1935, President Roosevelt defined the limits of Federal and local aid.

ROOSEVELT.—*Work* must be found for able-bodied but unemployed workers. The Federal government must and shall quit this business of giving relief without work.

SECOND NARRATOR.—Now the way was open for the program of the WPA, the Works Progress Administration, the gigantic plan to put Americans back to work.

VOICE.—Why should the government worry about the unemployed?

SECOND VOICE.—Because where there are millions of unemployed, it becomes a national and not a local problem. Because it is doubtful, in a highly industrialized country like America, even when industry returns to normal production levels, that all the able-bodied unemployed will be able to find work all the time.

VOICE.—What's to happen, then?

SECOND VOICE.—Possibly the permanent establishment of a Federal works program to function as a reserve labor pool for private industry.

VOICE.—Well, then, how does WPA work?

SECOND VOICE.—It works in 98 per cent of the projects in cooperation with the local or state and federal governments. Listen to this case of the little community of Crossroads, Ohio. . . .

SOUND.—*Gavel.*

MAYOR.—The Board of Selectmen of Crossroads will please come to order.

VOICES.—(*Ad libs subside*)

MAYOR.—Gentlemen, this special meeting was called to consider the Works Progress Administration, which has recently been established in Washington.

SELECTMAN.—What will it do for us?

MAYOR.—Well, as I understand it, the government pays for the labor for local projects, and the local community furnishes the supplies.

SECOND SELECTMAN.—I can think of plenty of public works that we need, but we can't afford them these days.

MAYOR.—That's just the point. We can't afford them, because we can't afford to hire men. Now the government will pay for the labor.

SELECTMAN.—What unemployed labor is available in our town?

MAYOR.—Well, let's look at the list. There are carpenters, bricklayers, painters, unskilled laborers, some stenographers, three real estate agents, a radio operator, a baker, a detective, a shirtmaker, and two teachers. . . .

SELECTMAN.—I can see where you can use those unskilled laborers, building roads, but what are you going to do with the shirtmaker and the radio operator?

VOICES.—(*Laughter*)

MAYOR.—We're going to ask advice from the WPA administrator, and somehow we're going to build that new junior high school we've needed for years. . . .

MUSIC.—*Bridge . . . indefinite.*

WPA ADMINISTRATOR.—Gentlemen, the WPA is pleased to approve your project for the construction of a new junior high school as well as the project for paving 12 blocks on Main Street.

SELECTMAN.—How much is it gonna cost?

WPA ADMINISTRATOR.—The labor cost will run around $20,000.

SECOND SELECTMAN.—Why, my soul alive, we haven't got that much in the city treasury.

WPA ADMINISTRATOR.—I said that was the labor cost. The government pays that. The cost to the city for the new school will represent building supplies.

VOICES.—(*Ad libs*)

SELECTMAN.—You mean we get a new junior high school for only $6,000?

WPA ADMINISTRATOR.—That's right.

SECOND SELECTMAN.—Well, it don't seem possible.

WPA ADMINISTRATOR.—Your street paving project will utilize 35 more of your unemployed and will cost approximately $27,000 in labor, but the cost to the city will be only $5,000 for supplies and material.

SELECTMAN.—Jehosophat . . . and that street's needed paving for 10 years. . . .

SECOND SELECTMAN.—Yeah, but look here, young feller, you can't put shirtmakers and that music teacher and these stenographers and other women to work paving streets.

WPA ADMINISTRATOR.—That's right, so we suggest a sewing project which will absorb most of them.

SELECTMAN.—What'll you do with the stuff they sew?

WPA ADMINISTRATOR.—Distribute it to the people on relief, to the very old and the very young.

SECOND SELECTMAN.—By golly, you fellers think of everything.
. . .

MUSIC.—*Indefinite.*

NARRATOR.—Thus, in nearly every community in America, local officials sat down with the WPA administrators and drafted a works program to suit the needs of the community and the aptitudes of the unemployed.

SECOND NARRATOR.—The entire plan of the WPA was unheard of, new, and revolutionary, and there were many who cried . . .

VOICE.—Un-American! Communistic!

NARRATOR.—Because for the first time in the history of the nation, the skill of the worker was being considered as part of the national wealth.
Yet, to protect private wage levels the WPA maintains established hourly minimum scales, but limits total monthly earnings to a family security income.

SECOND NARRATOR.—And does not compete with private industry. . . .

VOICE.—The WPA encourages its workers to return to private industry when the opportunity appears. . . .

SECOND VOICE.—The worker who refuses to accept a fair offer in private industry faces immediate dismissal from WPA.

THIRD VOICE.—Yet WPA re-employs any worker within 90 days of his employment in private industry, should his job end through no fault of his own.

NARRATOR.—Thus does the WPA work.

SECOND NARRATOR.—Good. But what has it accomplished?

VOICE.—This!

MUSIC.—*Chord.*

FOURTH VOICE.—Roads and bridges.

NARRATOR.—Over one-third of the entire WPA program is devoted to roads, streets, and bridges. The mileage of roads and streets newly built would reach ten times around the globe.

SECOND NARRATOR.—Including nearly 245,000 miles of rural road. No longer are farmers isolated in bad weather.

MUSIC.—*Chord.*

SECOND VOICE.—Parks and playgrounds.

NARRATOR.—A thousand playgrounds, 100 public golf courses, 4,000 public tennis courts, 1,000 parks, 1,000 swimming pools, 1,000 grandstands, 500 gymnasiums.

MUSIC.—*Chord.*

SECOND VOICE.—Public buildings!

NARRATOR.—Schools and libraries, stadiums, auditoriums, hospitals and jails, courthouses and city halls.

MUSIC.—*Chord.*

SECOND VOICE.—Water supply and sewage disposals.

NARRATOR.—Reservoirs, storage tanks, and cisterns, with a total capacity capable of supplying a city of 1 million people for a year without replenishment.

SECOND NARRATOR.—Four thousand miles of water mains and aqueducts; 6,000 miles of storm drains and sanitary sewers; 243 sewage disposal plants; 60 water plants, 250 pumping stations.

VOICE.—To many a small American town, these projects meant the first adequate sanitary water and sewage system the town had ever possessed.

MUSIC.—*Chord.*

SECOND VOICE.—Aviation.

NARRATOR.—One hundred and fifty landing fields with runways, landing light beacons; hangars and markers.

MUSIC.—*Chord.*

SECOND VOICE.—Education.

NARRATOR.—Thirty-four thousand jobless teachers heading a class of a million and a half adults and 50,000 young children . . . and leading 100,000 more in forums, lectures, and open meetings.

SECOND NARRATOR.—A million illiterate Americans have mastered a practical knowledge of reading and writing through WPA classes.

VOICE.—More than 200,000 aliens have, through WPA classes, become candidates for American citizenship.

MUSIC.—*Chord.*

THIRD VOICE.—Health.

NARRATOR.—Children's clinics; tuberculosis hospitals; bus service for crippled school children; therapeutic baths; malaria mosquito control; school children's lunches.

SECOND NARRATOR.—A million persons receiving free treatments at 2,000 medical and dental clinics; 3,000 nurses making 2½ million calls to the homes of the needy.

MUSIC.—*Chord.*

SECOND VOICE.—Libraries.

NARRATOR.—Thirty-five hundred new branch libraries and 4,000 reading rooms. More than 33 million books, reconditioned and repaired and returned to the use of the reading public.

MUSIC.—*Chord.*

SECOND VOICE.—Conservation.

NARRATOR.—Fish hatcheries in California, game farms in Massachusetts, wild fowl refuges in Louisiana.

SECOND NARRATOR.—Fire breaks in the parched mountains of the West, wells and water holes in the desert, miles of levees along the great river of the South.

MUSIC.

VOICE.—Food and clothes.

NARRATOR.—Ninety-five million shirts, dresses, and underwear made and distributed to the poor.

SECOND NARRATOR.—Thirty-six million pounds of foodstuffs canned or preserved.

THIRD NARRATOR.—Six hundred thousand pairs of shoes and 900,000 pieces of furniture repaired.

MUSIC.

VOICE.—Historical records. . . .

SECOND NARRATOR.—The WPA surveys America's historic structures, draws their plans, photographs them, and this record remains in the Fine Arts Division of the Library of Congress, a permanent record, available at all times to the public.

MUSIC.

SECOND NARRATOR.—Science and research!

THIRD NARRATOR.—Colorado wants to know the number and needs of the crippled children in the state.

FOURTH NARRATOR.—The University of Florida wants to study the location of tropical storms by static.

FIFTH NARRATOR.—Connecticut wants to survey its prison facilities.

SIXTH NARRATOR.—In 1924 a study was made in New York of a control group of subnormal children. New York now wants to know what sort of adults they have become.

NARRATOR.—In laboratories, WPA scientists study tuberculosis and silicosis. On street corners, they tabulate traffic. In museums, they build exhibits. On the tops of skyscrapers, they study the pollution of the air.

SECOND NARRATOR.—WPA scientists have completed nearly 2,000 surveys and studies since the government recognized their right to work and gave them back the opportunity.

MUSIC.

VOICE.—Recreation.

SECOND NARRATOR.—To meet the modern problem of leisure, WPA has trained 34,000 recreational leaders to supervise gymnasiums and playgrounds for children, to operate camps and conduct classes in handicraft, so that today the general public spends more than 16 million hours per week in WPA recreation activities.

MUSIC.—*Dvorak's Carnival Overture.*

SECOND VOICE.—The arts!

NARRATOR.—Across America, citizens are now hearing music who never before attended a concert, for 10,000 jobless musicians, organized into symphony orchestra, bands, and opera groups, are bringing great music to the people.

SECOND NARRATOR.—More than a million people each month attend the productions of the Federal Theatre, a WPA project, a national theatre on a vast scale which has given new life to the American stage, to men who would otherwise be jobless.

MUSIC.

NARRATOR.—Across America, the dingy walls of public buildings now are decorated with murals of the American scene. Bare public squares and gardens now are dignified with modern sculpture. Schools and institutions possess original American paints, the work of WPA artists.

NARRATOR.—WPA writers are performing a gigantic task in the American Guide series. The 3,000 writers, editors, and research men have produced more than 250 valuable and badly needed volumes of information about America. (*Pause*)

MUSIC.—*Tag background.*

SECOND NARRATOR.—There is still another service WPA provides for the nation. . . .

VOICE.—WPA workers are the shock troops to fight disaster. . .

SOUND.—*Thunder . . . rain . . . oscillator code.*

SECOND VOICE.—(*Filter*) Pittsburgh, Pennsylvania, river stage, 46 feet rising. . . .
(*Code fades*)

SOUND.—*Thunder.*

THIRD VOICE.—Cincinnatti, Ohio . . . 70 feet rising. . . .
(*Code fades*)

SOUND.—*Thunder.*

FOURTH VOICE.—Louisville, Kentucky, river 10 feet above flood stage, rising . . . river rising. . . .
(*Code fades*)

SOUND.—*Thunder.*

(*Fade in*)

VOICE.—Send a boat to 45 Breckinridge Street. . . . Fifty WPA workers needed at the emergency hospital in the Portland Street Library to evacuate patients. . . . Fifty WPA workers badly needed at the Portland Street Library (*fading*) to evacuate patients. . . .

SECOND VOICE.—(*Filter*) Hurricane warning . . . hurricane. . . .

NARRATOR.—WPA holds the levee against the angry flooded Mississippi. WPA fights the fires in the North woods. WPA cleans away the wreckage and the horror that follows the tropical hurricanes. WPA workers are indeed the shock troops of disaster.

MUSIC.

VOICE.—Such are the accomplishments of WPA.

SECOND VOICE.—And from an official survey, this report . . .

SOUTHERNER.—Little towns that once confused weeds with shrubbery now have no weeds. Little towns that once endured barbaric sanitary conditions are now clean and free of pest holes. Little towns whose people once swallowed all of the dust that did not accumulate on store stocks and household furnishings now have no dust. And they are equally free of mud. Little towns that had no community house where the cultural spirit might have an outlet now have one.

Little towns that had shabby city halls now have dignified city buildings. These are permanent gains. In the end it may be agreed that such gains offset the obvious losses of the worst depression that this republic has endured.

MUSIC.—*Tag . . . in and under.*

NARRATOR.—That is the story of the attempt of the American people to conquer unemployment, to find recovery from industrial disaster. Much has been done; much more remains. As conditions improve, the pendulum swings back. In Congress strong voices, powerful voices are beginning to cry "Economy; this spending must stop!" But the work goes on, and the achievements of the WPA will remain long after the depression which gave it birth becomes but a dim, sad memory.

MUSIC.

NARRATOR.—Never will America live again those thoughtless, careless years of illusionary prosperity, careless and callous to those who found themselves out of luck and out of work. The American people now know it is no longer a man's own fault if he can find no work; they have learnt that a nation must look after its people.

MUSIC.—*Up . . . resolve and out . . . 5 seconds pause . . . closing theme . . . in and under announcer.*

ANNOUNCER.—You have just heard "No Help Wanted," the story of American unemployment, directed and recorded by the New York office of the British Broadcasting Corporation in association with Federal Theatre Radio Division of the Works Progress Administration.

The players and the members of the orchestra were all WPA workers.

Leith Stevens composed the original score and conducted the Federal Music Project orchestra, and the entire production was written and produced by William N. Robson.

MUSIC.—*Theme . . . up to fill.*

We Become a Nation

From WHAT PRICE AMERICA

by BERNARD SCHOENFELD

THE PAST three years have seen a great change in the quality of broadcasting that the United States government has been doing. For years most of the programs consisted of interviews between an announcer and the head of one or another of the numerous government agencies, and, whereas these programs from time to time contained information that was of some benefit to the public, they also had the distinction to be the most inert bores on the air. There were no showmen in this branch of radio. There are some today, and what they have been able to do with the medium has been a very gratifying thing to watch.

Three men deserve most of the credit for this change: John W. Studebaker, Commissioner of Education; Shannon Allen, Director of the Radio Division of the Department of Interior; and Morse Salisbury, Chief of the Division of Information, Department of Agriculture. Among them, they have corrected the two fundamental blunders that mar the work of most radio amateurs; they have stopped dramatizing material that is not dramatizable, and they have employed dramatists (not research men) to write their dramatic programs.

This shift in policy occasioned an immediate reaction in performance. The broadcasts became shows, populated with believable people and sustained by emotional power, and many fine series resulted. Notable among these have been Let Freedom Ring, Treasures Next Door, The World Is Yours, Americans All—Immigrants All, Democracy in

473

Action, Brave New World, Education in the News, and What Price America. For its sustained dramatic interest, for its power to transport the listener to the scene, for proper subordination of informative content to entertainment value, and for accuracy of research, the series What Price America represented the outstanding radio effort of the United States government last year. The series was written by Bernard Schoenfeld under the able supervision of Shannon Allen. Research material was compiled by Hugh Russell Fraser. One of the most intelligent and complete publicity setups in radio history supplied the public not only with copies of the broadcasts but with supplementary information about the immediate territories the listeners lived in. An average of 25,000 communications were received and answered every week.

Reprinted is the broadcast of February 11, 1939. The series was carried by 102 stations of the Columbia Broadcasting System.

We Become a Nation*

eeeeeeeeeeeeeeeeeeeeeeeeeeeeeeeeeeeeeeeeeeeeeeeeeee

Music.—*Theme . . . up and diminuendo . . . "America the Beautiful."*

Voice.—(*Dramatically*) What Price America!

Music.—*Up . . . ominous and under.*

Second Voice.—(*Calling above music*) Plow up the soil! Plow up the soil!

Third Voice.—(*Calling above music*) Dig into the ground. . . . Silver! Gold! Coal! Copper! Dig up the ground!

Fourth Voice.—(*Calling above music*) Chop down the trees! Destroy the forests! Chop down the trees!

Music.—*Dissonant chord and out sharply . . . pause.*

Voice.—(*Dramatically*) This waste must stop!

Second Voice.—Waste must give way to conservation.

Third Voice.—(*Quietly, questioningly*) But what is . . . conservation?

Voice.—The Department of the Interior is your agency of government charged with protecting and safeguarding the majority of your natural resources.

Second Voice.—Harold L. Ickes, Secretary of that Department, has said, "Conservation is the wise use of those gifts of nature upon which we rely for support, comfort, and spiritual solace. Every natural resource must be made to serve mankind while preserving all that is possible for the needs of future generations!

Voice.—What is our obligation in this democracy to protect our heritage and the heritage of our children? Listen to the story of our past. . . . Hear of our triumphs and failures. . . . Listen, America!

* Copyright, 1939, by the Columbia Broadcasting System, Inc.

MUSIC.—*Up and under . . . "New World Symphony" . . . first movement.*

VOICE.—Ohio . . . Illinois . . . Indiana . . . Michigan . . . Wisconsin . . . Minnesota . . . 265,500 square miles of American earth! Here flow the Mississippi, the Wabash, the Ohio. . . . Here is a treasure land Nature has bestowed upon America! Today a land . . . civilized . . . productive . . . populated! Alive with the sound of the assembly line, the dynamo, the threshing machine! Today the cities of Chicago, Detroit, Milwaukee, Indianapolis, Cincinnati, St. Paul! Today . . . millions of farms, corn and wheat, hogs and cattle! This is the 265,500 square miles lying between the state of Minnesota and the state of Illinois!

SECOND VOICE.—But yesterday? Only silence . . . a wilderness . . . only the howl of a wolf deep in the forest. . . . This was the land known as the Northwest territory!

MUSIC.—*Up and under.*

VOICE.—It is a gray afternoon in the fall of the year 1787. In the little village of Danford, Massachusetts, in the tavern of the Widow Stone, a group of farmers, carpenters, blacksmiths and mill hands sit drinking their ale. . . .

MUSIC.—*Out.*

SOUND.—*Murmuring of men . . . clinking of glasses. . . .*

FIRST MAN.—Widder Stone, your ale is like the day . . . cloudy!

WIDOW.—When ye be able to pay me, ye kin complain!

SECOND MAN.—We kin give you a pile of Continental paper bills?

WIDOW.—Tush, I kindle my fire with Continentals!

THIRD MAN.—I can't even kindle a fire with 'em. They're too dirty. How 'bout yerself, Obediah? . . . Obediah Weeks, 'tis harmful to sit and brood.

WIDOW.—What's ailin' ye, Obediah?

SECOND MAN.—He's waitin'.

WIDOW.—Waitin' for what?

FOURTH.—The red flag hangs atop of his farm. The sheriff is comin' to take him any day now.

WIDOW.—Obediah's farm, too? Seems as how the whole blessed town is goin' ter jail for debt.

SOUND.—*Distant thundering.*

OBEDIAH.—(*Bitterly*) Liberty . . . freedom. . . .

WIDOW.—What ye say, Obediah?

OBEDIAH.—Liberty . . . freedom . . . fine soundin' words! When we git back from fightin' fer 'em, what do they do? Don't give us our back pay! Promises they made us! Fightin' fer 'em! Dyin' fer 'em! And all the while they send (*sneak in sound of rain*) their gold to England to buy fancy dresses fer their wimmen an' painted snuffboxes . . . an' I sit here . . . waitin' . . . waitin'. . . . (*Pause*)

WIDOW.—(*Quietly*) 'Tis raining hard. . . .

SOUND.—*Door opens . . . closes.*

JARED.—Hello, everybody. . . .

WIDOW.—Well, young Jared, you come from the mill early today!

JARED.—(*Young voice*) Hello, Widder Stone! Where's my brother! . . . Oh, there ye be, Obediah! Better come long home! It's begun to rain right smart.

OBEDIAH.—Hello, Jared. . . . Let it rain. Sit down, brother.

FIRST MAN.—(*Slowly*) Today it's Obediah's. Tomorrow it'll be *my* farm with a red flag flying.

JARED.—Some day the mills at Hampton will be closin' down, and I'll be out of work like you men. But then I'll do sompthin'! (*Angrily*) Yes, by the Lord God of Israel, all of ye men fought in the Revolution! Where's your spunk!

OBEDIAH.—Ye're a young 'un, Jared. Twenty-four. Wait till ye're forty.

JARED.—But why don't ye all go out in the new lands and begin again? Ain't none of ye got grants of land?

FIRST MAN.—*Poor men* sell their grants.

477

SECOND MAN.—Ye got to *buy* land, Jared. But Congress has a law that says no one kin buy less than 640 acres!

JARED.—That land in Ohio belongs to all of us! It's . . . called . . . called . . . Public . . .

THIRD MAN.—Yes, Public Domain, but you've got to hev enough money to buy 640 acres of it.

WIDOW.—The gentleman comin' 'crost the yard kin buy 640 acres. Look . . . see him skipping the puddles like an old granny!

MAN.—Jumping mackerel, it's Squire McCrae.

JARED.—Comin' here! In the rain?

WIDOW.—Any time the Squire comes a-visitin' my tavern, he's got a bee buzzin'!

SOUND.—*Door opens . . . closes.*

SQUIRE.—Good afternoon, Widow Stone!

WIDOW.—Dry yourself at the fire, sir. I'll fetch ye . . .

SQUIRE.—No, I thank you. They told me that I could find a man here called Obediah Weeks.

WIDOW.—That be Obediah Weeks, over there.

SQUIRE.—Farmer Weeks, I'm Squire McCrea.

FIRST MAN.—From the width across yer waistcoat and yer five chins, they ain't no need to introduce yerself.

VOICES.—(*Laughter*)

SQUIRE.—(*Sternly*) Keep still, man. I'm not addressing you. . . . (*Unctuously*) Weeks!

WEEKS.—Yes, sir?

SQUIRE.—The Deacon tells me you plow the straightest furrow in this section.

OBEDIAH.—The Deacon should know. He's got my farm mortgaged.

SQUIRE.—What is the extent of your debt to him?

OBEDIAH.—Eight pounds, five shillings, an' fourpence.

SQUIRE.—If I were to pay it for you, would you be willing to go out to Ohio?

VOICES.—(*Excitement*)

OBEDIAH.—I . . . I don't ketch yer drift, Squire.

SQUIRE.—I own two shares in the Ohio Land Company. Best investment in the world, these new lands out in the Northwest. I have 2,000 acres. The company is starting a settlement out there in Ohio. I want a man to go out with them and clear a few acres, plant and raise crops, and build cabins.

JARED.—Obediah kin do it, sir! I'm his brother, Jared, and I know he kin do it!

OBEDIAH.—*You* . . . you will pay off my debt! I'll be able to keep my farm here in Danford?

SQUIRE.—Yes. Of course. I will pay you nothing from then on in Ohio until you have repaid me in work.

OBEDIAH.—Yes, sir, of course not, sir . . . thank ye . . . thank ye . . . !

SQUIRE.—By the way, have all you men who were soldiers received your land grants from the Board of Treasury?

FIRST MAN.—We did. A hundred fine acres apiece. Had to sell 'em . . . to buzzards. . . .

SQUIRE.—Widow Stone, if you hear of any soldier wanting to sell his grant, I'll buy it.

WIDOW.—(*Craftily*) Aimin' to settle out there in th' wilderness, Squire?

SQUIRE.—Me? Certainly not.

WIDOW.—Jest sort of . . . *buyin'* up land?

SQUIRE.—Don't forget. If you hear of any other man who needs ready money and wishes to sell his grant, let me know. Weeks, come to my house at 8 tonight for final instructions. Good-by.

SOUND.—*Door opens . . . closes.*

VOICES.—*Ad lib excitement.*

OBEDIAH.—I jest can't believe it. . . . Now Martha and the children kin live on the farm with Jared. You'll watch over Martha while I'm out there, Widder Stone?

WIDOW.—Don't ye fret. . . . Ha, the Squire is a shrewd critter. Wantin' ter buy all the land grants that the soljers git! And he'll git 'em, too! For what man these days don't need money right quick? And the pity of it is that out there lies land for *all* of ye to buy!

MAN.—Yes . . . if ye kin buy 640 acres at a time. . . .

SOUND.—*Thunder . . . crash.* . . .

JARED.—(*Angrily*) Go on an' thunder! Thunder away! It's how all of us be feelin' right now!

MUSIC.—*Up and out.*

VOICE.—That night in the library of Squire McCrae the curtains have been drawn; the leather book bindings and the satin chairs reflect the soft candlelight. It is a few minutes before 8, and the Squire sits with a guest, Representative Bingham from Pennsylvania.

BINGHAM.—Beautiful furniture, Squire.

SQUIRE.—Sent from London, Representative Bingham.

BINGHAM.—You live in luxury.

SQUIRE.—Thanks to land companies like the Ohio Company. How many shares do *you* own?

BINGHAM.—None.

SQUIRE.—What! A man of vision like yourself!

BINGHAM.—(*Sardonically*) The Reverend Manassah Cutler called me the same when he tried to bribe me with a few shares in the company if I would vote in Congress to sell him the land in Ohio. I cast an opposite vote. I believe those lands in the Northwest should be settled by the small farmer.

SQUIRE.—You have been listening to Mr. Jefferson . . . too much.

BINGHAM.—Would that we all listened to Mr. Jefferson . . . too much. The United States will regret the day that Congress ruled no land less than 640 acres could be sold.

480

SQUIRE.—The treasury needs revenue. Why not limit sales to 640 acres . . . or more?

BINGHAM.—The poor cannot afford 640 acres. (*Ironically*) Have you forgotten, Squire, that this is a democracy?

SQUIRE.—(*Smoothly*) I was not even aware of that fact, sir. A democracy to me is a country where the crude farmer rubs elbows with the gentleman.

BINGHAM.—And the gentleman buys up the land that is rightfully due the farmer?

SQUIRE.—Sheer sentimentality, sir!

BINGHAM.—Perhaps. But I wanted a law passed to develop that Northwest territory of Ohio into small units so that poor people might have the chance to settle. But Mr. Cutler and the other lobbyists of the Ohio Company were clever. I lost.

SQUIRE.—But, sir . . . Reverend Cutler is an ordained minister. General Rufus Putnam, another officer of the company, is beyond reproach.

BINGHAM.—Then *they* have a broader concept than their . . . fellow shareholders?

SQUIRE.—*I* am a fellow shareholder.

BINGHAM.—Have you not bought your land for speculation?

SQUIRE.—Most certainly.

BINGHAM.—You answer honestly, and so I see you will not take offense at what I say.

SQUIRE.—I am thick-skinned.

BINGHAM.—Cutler and Putnam should not have sold you these lands.

SQUIRE.—I see I must defend those men. In a month, Putnam and 45 others will take a boat and sail down to the Musaqum River to their settlement in Ohio. They will organize counties and townships; they will spend time and patience and money in building up civilized communities where men may start new lives and worship God as they please. To do this the Ohio Company *had* to sell stock in their million and a half acres.

481

BINGHAM.—To speculators like yourself?

SQUIRE.—Men like myself are of as lasting importance to the future of America as is your rabble who cannot buy land on which to dwell!

BINGHAM.—No. You buy up land which you do not intend to use! You buy only to sell at an exorbitant price! You are setting a precedent! In years to come, unscrupulous men will continue to buy up huge areas of land from Congress, but will they wish to settle on it or help America grow? No! They will buy land to exploit! Land sharks, swindlers, wasteful and greedy men will be able to buy all the land they wish because you have set a precedent! The few will possess what the many should own!

SQUIRE.—The few should possess . . . *all!*

BINGHAM.—By heaven, sir, no!

SQUIRE.—(*A shrug in his voice*) Blame Congress, of which you are a member.

BINGHAM.—I do. Congress has adopted a dangerous land policy, and it will suffer the consequences, as I fear, all of us shall! (*Pause*)

SQUIRE.—(*Dryly*) Your pipe is out, sir. More tobacco?

BINGHAM.—Thank you.

SOUND.—*Door opens . . . closes.*

SERVANT.—(*Woman*) Squire McCrae, there is a person . . .

SQUIRE.—Oh, yes, Farmer Weeks. . . . Send him in.

SERVANT.—Yes, sir.

SOUND.—*Door opens . . . closes.*

SQUIRE.—A country bumpkin. . . . I have a task for him.

BINGHAM.—I see.

SQUIRE.—More Madeira?

BINGHAM.—No, thank you.

SOUND.—*Door opens . . . closes.*

SQUIRE.—Well, come in, come in. Are your shoes clean?

OBEDIAH.—Yes, sir. I brought my young brother, Jared, if you do not . . .

JARED.—May I stay, sir?

SQUIRE.—You may stay. Now, Farmer Weeks, you will leave in a fortnight for Trenton. You will see my land agent, who will hand you over to General Putnam, with whose party you will go to Ohio. Here in this envelope are my instructions. Can you read?

OBEDIAH.—(*With quiet anger*) Yes, sir!

SQUIRE.—Good. The General has hired three more men, who will assist you out there. You will be in charge. Clear about 100 acres. . . . Dig a well. . . . Clear the springs. . . . Plan the best acres for habitation. . . . Observe what the soil will grow. . . . I shall be out there in a few months. That is all.

OBEDIAH.—Yes, sir. Thank ye. I can't tell ye what it means to be free of debt . . . to hev my own place again in Danford fer Martha and . . .

SQUIRE.—Work hard. Good-by.

OBEDIAH.—Good-by.

JARED.—Good-by, Squire.

SOUND.—*Door opens . . . closes.*

SQUIRE.—The best farmer in these parts. I'm sending him with the party to clear my land and determine the agricultural value of the soil.

BINGHAM.—He looks bright.

SQUIRE.—As farmers go, yes.

BINGHAM.—He is made of the stuff our country will thrive on. . . .

SQUIRE.—What a man of sentiment you are, sir! Look, have you seen my miniatures? Remarkable paintings! I bought them from the Count de Vaudrac (*board fade*) of Paris. They cost me a pretty penny!

MUSIC.—*Up and out.*

VOICE.—The fall of 1788. A year later. In the small farmhouse of Obediah Weeks in Danford, three people listen to a letter being read by Obediah's wife, Martha. Around the table sit Aunt Sophie and Jared and Jared's young wife, Emily. Martha reads on.

MARTHA.—(*Reading*) . . . "Jineral Putnam won't let wimmin be out here yit . . . and even if they could come, I won't be hevin' ye come to this Godforsaken spot, Marthy. Onct the Injuns attacked us, but we chased them. There be 90 of us here now. We call the town Marietta. I got four men a-workin' on pertaters and corn, and the soil be real fine fer plantin'. I'm glad, Marthy, ye kin hold yer head above water and make the farm go so good, now that the Widder Stone is partners. Give a big kiss to Aunt Sophy. . . ."

SOPHIA.—Shucks!

MARTHA.—(*Reading*) . . . "And tell Emily, that young bride of Jared, I wish I could meet her. Tell my brother, Jared, I'm happy he's still workin' in the mill. God bless ye and keep ye. Your loving husband, Obediah Weeks." (*Sniffs*) I wish I could go out to him, Aunt Sophia.

SOPHIA.—Land sakes, look at Jared! What a funny look in yer face!

JARED.—I'm jest a-thinkin'.

MARTHA.—Wish I could help Obediah out there.

JARED.—No, yer place is here, Marthy, taking care of the farm. Yer husband will be coming back some day, and ye'll have a fine farm fer 'im. (*Pause*) You wimmin will have lots t'do . . . when I'm gone.

MARTHA.—You go?

SOPHIA.—Go where!

EMILY.—Jared . . . what do you mean?

JARED.—I s'pect I'm . . . kind o' restless. . . .

SOPHIA.—I'll put a cat-o'-nine-tails to yer, Jared Weeks, as old as ye be, if you don't speak up!

JARED.—The . . . the mill closed down today.

484

MARTHA.—Oh!

SOPHIA.—S'pected it right along.

EMILY.—Jared!

JARED.—I want to go west to Ohio and make a home to bring ye to, Emily.

EMILY.—No, Jared, no!

SOPHIA.—He's jest talkin'. Hasn't a penny and wants to buy land!

JARED.—I ain't reck'nin' on buy'n' land. I'm goin' out with 10 other men from Danford and squat.

EMILY.—What's he mean, Aunt Sophia!

SOPHIA.—Sum folk jest get a team of oxen an' their belongin's and git out to the Northwest an' pick a plot of ground an' start squatting. . . .

MARTHA.—The government won't let ye do that!

JARED.—Government! Will they let us buy a few acres of land to call our own? No! I'll jest go out and squat.

EMILY.—I won't let ye go, Jared!

MARTHA.—I need ye to help me with the farm, Jared!

JARED.—But, Marthy, ye got Widder Stone as partner. A good thing when she sold the tavern and bought half the farm. She's got a head, the widder. No, I want to go out there and try my luck!

EMILY.—Git work here!

JARED.—Half the town is starvin', and ye know it!

EMILY.—Then I'll go with you!

MARTHA.—No, Emily!

JARED.—I'll be sending fer you in a year or two.

EMILY.—I won't be having you go alone!

SOPHIA.—My mother come all the way from Wales in a 40-foot boat and then helped my father chop down th' trees that built half of Danford. Let Emily go if she wants.

JARED.—She can't take th' risk!

EMILY.—I love ye, Jared! I'm your wife! Where ye go, I go!

JARED.—True, there's other wimmen coming. Nathan Woodbridge's sister an' Ezra Hamlin's wife an . . .

EMILY.—Then I go!

SOPHIA.—(*Slowly*) Don't know what good I'm gonna be in Danford since people ain't got money to buy my cakes and tarts. Might jest as well go along and look ater you children.

MARTHA.—Aunt Sophia, don't ye git crazy notions.

SOPHIA.—Crazy, huh? I kin drive a team of oxen better'n Jared. You don't need me, Marthy. These youngen's need me.

JARED.—We kin git a wagon and oxen! Emily! Aunt Sophia! Start putting together what we need! You'll see! We'll git out there! I'm going to talk to Nathan Woodbridge right now!

MARTHA.—Squatters . . . jest squatters. . . . Don't like the word.

JARED.—What else kin a poor man do if he wants land? Emily, I'll be back in an hour!

SOUND.—*Door opens . . . closes.*

SOPHIA.—You got spunk, Emily, goin' with 'im now.

EMILY.—I'm glad you're comin' with us.

MARTHA.—Why . . . why won't you stay here, Aunt Sophia?

SOPHIA.—Well . . . er . . . you see, Marthy . . . Emily and me have a little secret. Even Jared don't know yit. I think I better go with 'em . . . 'cause . . . Emily's goin' ter have a baby. . . .

MUSIC.—*Up and over.*

VOICE.—In March, 1789, five women and fifteen men leave Danford, riding out in wagons and on horseback for Ohio. One night in May the party is high in the hills of Pennsylvania. A campfire is burning. Jared Weeks stands alone with Aunt Sophia.

SOUND.—*Camp sounds.*

JARED.—Aunt Sophia, are ye sure she's all right?

SOPHIA.—Shucks, 'tain't the first time and 'twon't be the last!

JARED.—(*Wildly*) If she dies!

SOPHIA.—Now, now Jared . . . (*Calling*) Nate Woodbridge!

WOODBRIDGE.—(*Off*) Yes, Auntie! (*On*) What is it?

SOPHIA.—Tell this young cub not to go on frettin'.

WOODBRIDGE.—Emily will be all right, Jared.

JARED.—But it's so dark here . . . so wild . . . and cold. . . .
She would have had attention back in Danford.

SOUND.—*Frightened whinny of horses.*

JARED.—What's that!

SOPHIA.—Shucks, it's only the horses. Mebbe they sniff a wolf.

JARED.—Why don't it happen?

WOODBRIDGE.—Here comes my sister, Betsy. . . . Well, Betsy?

BETSY.—Now don't ye worry, Jared, it will all be over soon.

JARED.—We should've stayed home! We shouldn't hev come.
. . . I should've waited till I saved some money and try to
buy land instead of comin' with ye all jest squattin' . . .
squattin' . . . where?

WOODBRIDGE.—We'll find a valley near a river, and we'll make
clearin's and build our cabins. Crops will grow. There'll be
a cool river bubblin' near by. . . .

SOPHIA.—It'll be dandy, Jared.

JARED.—And if the government won't let us stay there?

BETSY.—We'll fight to stay! We got rights like others, and if we
got spunk enough to go out there . . . we've got spunk
enough to *stay* there.

WOODBRIDGE.—Six months from now there'll be smoke pourin'
out of the chimneys, and others'll come from the East and
squat near by, and it'll be plumb neighborly.

JARED.—I'm skeered. Never was skeered before. . . .

SOUND.—*Murmuring of men drawing near. . . .*

BETSY.—I'll go see how she is.

SOPHIA.—Wait, Betsy. Here come the others. There's Mrs. Jamison comin' out of the wagon!

JARED.—Mrs. Jamison! Mrs. Jamison! How's my wife?

MRS. JAMISON.—(*Hesitantly*) The . . . the baby's fine. A . . . a fine boy!

JARED.—How's Emily! Tell me . . . how's Emily! (*Pause*) What's the matter? . . . What ye all turnin' yer heads away fer? (*With a scream*) No! No!

WOODBRIDGE.—Stiddy, Jared . . . stiddy!

SOPHIA.—Let him cry. It takes a real man to cry.

MRS. JAMISON.—We . . . we did all we could, Jared.

JARED.—(*Low . . . wearily*) Mebbe it was jest as well.

SOPHIA.—Jared!

JARED.—Well, mebbe it was! What are we! Jest squatters!

WOODBRIDGE.—Stop, son!

JARED.—The better she *is* dead. Havin' to live like this . . . like we was beggars! Ain't we willin' t' make homes out there, t' buy land, t' bring our families . . . our wives . . . our (*he breaks*) . . . Emily . . . Emily. . . .

SOPHIA.—All of ye . . . kneel. . . . (*Pause*) Dear God, you have taken from our midst a young girl we all loved, Emily, wife of young Jared. Thy will be done. . . .

MRS. JAMISON.—(*Low*) The Lord giveth and the Lord taketh away. . . .

SOPHIA.—But we thank you, dear God, for a fine boy child this night. (*Distant faint cry of a baby*) Watch over him. Watch over Jared, his father, and give him strength to start a new life. Some folks have the wherewithal to live comfortably all the days of their lives. Others like us ain't got a Continental. We pray to you to bring us into green pastures. Let your divine light shine down on us so that we kin be brave to face whatever hardships we got to. Make us spunky and wise so that our children's children kin be proud of what we're doin'. . . . Amen!

488

ALL.—Amen. . . .

MUSIC.—*Up and out.*

MARTHA.—(*Tearfully*) You finish readin' the letter from Aunt Sophia, Widder Stone. Me eyes . . . be kind o' blurred. What does Sophia say next?

WIDOW STONE.—Well, Marthy, she goes on to say. . . . Let's see (*reading*) . . . "It's been a year since we left Danford. Jest think of it . . . 1790 already! We're squattin' in Ohio near the Hocking River. . . . we've built us a fort and 20 cabins and planted our crops. . . . The corn is high as your head. . . . Jared is the leader of our little colony. . . . He works harder and later than any other man. . . . You wouldn't know him, he's so different since Emily passed on. . . . Onct or twice we've been pestered by Injuns, and two of our men most died but didn't. . . . Obediah, your husband, is comin' West to visit us. He lives at Marietta, about 90 miles away, on the Muskingum River. It's the Ohio Company's settlement and is fast turning into a real town with purty trees and a real livin'. All we got is cabins, but we do our best, and God (*board fade*) watches over us all.

MUSIC.—*Up and out.*

VOICE.—Six months later . . . the fall of the year 1790 . . . at the settlement of Marietta, Ohio. Arthur St. Clair, governor of the Northwest territory, sits at a desk in his simple frame house. He is writing. There is a knock on the door.

SOUND.—*Knock at door.*

ST. CLAIR.—Come in.

SOUND.—*Latch raised . . . door opened . . . closed.*

SQUIRE.—Governor St. Clair?

ST. CLAIR.—Yes, sir.

SQUIRE.—I am Squire McCrae, from Danford, Massachusetts.

ST. CLAIR.—How do you do, sir! . . . and . . . why, hello, Obediah Weeks! How are you?

OBEDIAH.—Fair to middlin', governor. The Squire come here 2 days ago to look over his land. . . .

St. Clair.—You intend to settle here now?

Squire.—Oh, no. I am not suited to pioneer life.

St. Clair.—(*Coldly*) I see.

McCrae.—I came to congratulate you on the astounding way in which you and General Putnam have turned a wilderness into a paradise of . . .

St. Clair.—(*Curtly*) Come, come, Squire, surely a log fortress and a row of houses does not constitute a paradise?

McCrae.—A figure of speech.

St. Clair.—Ill chosen, eh, Obediah? I trust you found your land thriving? Obediah has done well. He has cleared 200 acres, leveled much of the ground; plowed it; built cabins. Why, one might have thought that your property was Obediah's.

McCrae.—Yes . . . ah . . . Obediah is leaving today.

St. Clair.—What! But why?

Squire.—His work is done. The Deacon Halssop will have his men come out here and . . .

St. Clair.—Deacon . . . ?

McCrae.—A friend of mine. He is buying the property on my return to Massachusetts.

St. Clair.—And will he come out here to settle?

McCrae.—The Deacon? Heavens, no! He has his dry goods emporium to watch over in Boston.

St. Clair.—Then he . . . like yourself . . . buys for speculation!

McCrae.—The Deacon knows that my property will be worth five times as much within a few years. As it is, I make a neat profit. The only reason I sell is because I have bought so much land that I wish to be freed of some of it. . . . You frown, governor?

St. Clair.—(*Coldly*) I do not like the Deacon, sir, and, what is more, I do not like others of his ilk. Good day, Squire. (*Pause*)

Squire.—Good day. Come, Obediah.

490

OBEDIAH.—Yes, Squire.

ST. CLAIR.—Stay a moment, Obediah. I wish to speak to you.

SQUIRE.—(*Commandingly*) Come, Obediah.

ST. CLAIR.—(*Bristling*) There is no slavery, here, sir! Every man is his fellow's equal! Perhaps Obediah wishes to remain here for a moment? (*Pause*)

SQUIRE.—I will see you by the meeting house, Farmer Weeks.

OBEDIAH.—Yes, Squire.

SOUND.—*Door opens . . . closes.*

ST. CLAIR.—Thank heaven there are not too many shareholders in our Company like your good Squire! You have spent 2 years taking care of his land, and now he ships you off home! Did he pay you well?

OBEDIAH.—A few pounds and my horse to return to Danford.

ST. CLAIR.—We will miss you. You leave today?

OBEDIAH.—First I go to my young brother, Jared, and his baby. He is 90 miles from here . . . on the Hocking River.

ST. CLAIR.—What settlement is that? The military district?

OBEDIAH.—No, sir. He . . . he . . . and 40 others are . . . jest livin' there.

ST. CLAIR.—Squatters!

OBEDIAH.—Yes, sir.

ST. CLAIR.—Do they know that the government forbids such practices!

OBEDIAH.—Yes, sir.

ST. CLAIR.—You had better warn your brother, Obediah. The government has issued a decree that all squatters be commanded by force to move on. Only yesterday I spoke to Lieutenant Forbes, who has been sent here with 10 men to order squatters off our property. If he should learn that only 90 miles away . . . I do not tattle, Obediah. But others may learn of the settlement.

OBEDIAH.—Yes, sir.

St. Clair.—Good-by and good luck. You say your home is Danford?

Obediah.—Yes, sir.

St. Clair.—I shall recommend while you are gone that the government give you land here in Marietta for you and your family. Would you like that?

Obediah.—I've come to feel like this was my home. My wife, Marthy, would like it, too.

St. Clair.—By next year women can come out. You'll hear from me.

Obediah.—Thank you, governor.

St. Clair.—And warn your brother.

Obediah.—Yes, sir. . . . Good-by. . . .

Sound.—*Door opens . . . closes.*

Music.—*Up and out.*

Voice.—Two weeks later in the sunlit cabin of Jared Weeks. On the earth floor sit a group of settlers. Jared and Obediah stand by a crude table.

Men.—*(Ad libbing, discussing . . . low . . .)*

Jared.—Ye men heerd my brother Obediah's words. What ye think?

Man.—Congress won't listen to us!

Second Man.—What you propose to do is foolishness!

Sound.—*Baby crying.*

Sophia.—Yes, baby. . . . Yes . . . yes. . . .

Jared.—What do you say, Nate Woodbridge?

Woodbridge.—I think Obediah's right when he says we ought to petition Congress to change the land law.

Jared.—I s'pect so. Let's write it out, and when you git to Philadelphia, Obediah, you kin give it to the postmaster. He'll send it to Congress.

Sophia.—Here's fresh ink I jest made. Got the quill?

JARED.—Yes. . . . Now let's see. . . . (*To himself as he writes*) Members . . . of . . . Congress. . . . (*Board fade*) A petition . . . from . . . 48 . . . settlers. . . .

JARED.—(*Fading in*) Here's the last part! (*Reading*) "We assure you we don't like to criticize you gentlemen of Congress, but there ought t' be a land policy for rich and poor alike. We don't like t' be squatters, but we kin do nothin' else. We humbly ask that you pass a law lettin' folks like us be able to buy small parcels o' land so we kin hev the protections of the government agin Injuns. Some of us fought in the war fer freedom, an' we think Congress shouldn't be forgettin' so quick. The council of the settlement of Emily ask that this law be passed at the next session, and we herewith sign our names." . . . Well, men, how is it?

MEN.—(*Voices in agreement*)

OBEDIAH.—That's good, Jared. You sign yer name first.

JARED.—There! . . . Now you, Nate Woodbridge. . . .

MAN.—There's my name!

SECOND MAN.—And mine . . . you next, Aunt Sophia!

SOPHIA.—Good.

THIRD MAN.—There's mine!

SOUND.—*Horses galloping in distance.*

JARED.—All the councilmen signed? Good! Now let's . . .

SOUND.—*Door opened and slammed quickly.*

SOPHIA.—Land's sake, what's up!

FOURTH MAN.—(*Breathlessly*) Folks, there be sojers comin!

MEN.—(*Voices ad lib excitement*)

JARED.—Come, men, let's welcome them out in the clearin'!

SOUND.—*Door opened . . . men running out . . . galloping draws closer.*

SOPHIA.—Shucks, there's only five of 'em!

WOODBRIDGE.—They got guns!

SOPHIA.—Don't be addled! They ain't goin' t' shoot us!

493

SOUND.—*Galloping nearer.*

LIEUTENANT.—(*Shouting*) Halt!

SOUND.—*Horses come to stop.*

JARED.—Hallo!

LIEUTENANT.—Who is the leader of this settlement?

SOPHIA.—Speak yer piece, Jared.

JARED.—I be. I'm Jared Weeks.

LIEUTENANT.—This property belongs to the government. You can't settle here.

JARED.—We're here, ain't we?

OBEDIAH.—Ye be Lieutenant Forbes, ain't ye? Remember me from Marietta? I'm Obediah Weeks.

LIEUTENANT.—(*Pleasantly*) I do remember you, Farmer Weeks. What are you doing here?

OBEDIAH.—I come to see my brother.

LIEUTENANT.—Well, tell your brother that he had better be off this property in a month.

JARED.—We ain't gittin' off!

LIEUTENANT.—(*Politely*) I don't mean to argue with any of you. I only have my orders. I'll be back with my men in a month. If you're still here, I'll have to force you to leave.

MEN.—(*Ad lib angry voices*)

WOODBRIDGE.—(*Sarcastically*) Gonna burn us out or shoot us down?

LIEUTENANT.—Don't take that attitude, man. It's none of my doing.

SOPHIA.—Where kin we go?

LIEUTENANT.—Back where you came from. Or else save some money and buy land like decent people.

SOPHIA.—(*Angrily*) Decent! We're law-abidin', God-fearin' folks, every one of us! We got a little church we built and a meeting house, and we've made laws we stand by. That's more than kin be said fer most people!

LIEUTENANT.—I'm sorry, ma'am. I'll be back in a month. (*Calling*) All right, men! Back to Marietta!

SOUND.—*Horses galloping off—into distance.*

JARED.—(*Shouting*) Ye'll find us all here when ye come back!

SOPHIA.—Hush, Jared!

JARED.—(*Shouting*) Ye ain't turnin' us out!

OBEDIAH.—(*Quietly*) It's the law.

JARED.—Public domain fer us all! No! It's public domain for them who kin pay!

OBEDIAH.—You kin stay here no longer. That's final.

JARED.—(*Wearily*) We was comin' along so nice . . . gardens planted and a fort half built. . . .

OBEDIAH.—Forget it.

SOUND.—*Baby crying.*

SOPHIA.—Poor baby. . . .

JARED.—Mebbe by the time the youngen grows up, he kin buy some land . . . jest enuf t'live on out here and be happy. . . .

OBEDIAH.—I'll go back with you all to Danford.

JARED.—No! I'm not going back! I'm going to stay out here in the Northwest!

MAN.—No . . . I won't do the same thing again! Clear trees . . . build cabins . . . fight Injuns . . . freeze. . . . No!

SOPHIA.—I'm with ye, Jared!

VOICES.—(*Ad lib disagreement*)

JARED.—Wait for me, wait! (*Pause*) We wanted t' come out here to the new land and open it up. . . . Now if Aunt Sophia be willin' t' go out yonder still further . . . an' I'm willin' fer my baby to grow up out there where it's new and free and the ground be tender to livin' things . . . then ye should all be willin'. Mebbe they'll find us again and force us off. . . . Mebbe we'll just be wanderers on this land we can't buy . . . but I say, let's not go back. Are you with me!

MEN.—(*All cry agreement*)

JARED.—Good! We'll start with the wagons next week!

OBEDIAH.—I'll be starting off for Danford now, Jared.

JARED.—Wait a day more.

OBEDIAH.—The horse is saddled. . . . Nate, get my horse fer me, please.

SOPHIA.—Give our love to the folks in Danford. Tell 'em we wish them well.

OBEDIAH.—Give me the petition. I'll put it in my knapsack. . . . There. . . . Well, Jared . . .

JARED.—You'll be getting ground from Governor St. Clair. Ye'll be a real Ohio farmer in Marietta.

OBEDIAH.—Ye kin live with us in Marietta.

JARED.—No, thanks.

OBEDIAH.—Then good-by, Jared.

JARED.—Good-by, Obediah.

OBEDIAH.—Good-by, baby. . . . He looks kind o' like . . . Emily.

JARED.—Yes.

OBEDIAH.—Here's a kiss, Aunt Sophia.

SOPHIA.—(*Tearfully*) Good-by, Obediah! Bless you and Marthy!

SOUND.—*Off horse.*

WOODBRIDGE.—Here's your horse, Obediah! Up with you!

OBEDIAH.—Quiet, Flossy, quiet! We got a long way to go. . . . There! Good-by, all of you!

VOICES.—(*Ad lib good-bys*)

OBEDIAH.—Giddap!

SOUND.—*Horse galloping away . . . pause.*

JARED.—(*As sound grows faint*) Funny . . . how the land kin change the lives of folks . . . all of us likin' this Northwest . . . Squire McCrae scheming to git it ter speculate . . .

496

Obediah achin' ter hev a farm out here ter plant things on . . . and us wantin' land for a home. . . . Funny, the land out here is s'posed to belong to us all . . . but you certainly wouldn't know it. . . .

SOUND.—*Baby crying.*

SOPHIA.—Yes, baby . . . yes, don't cry. . . . Don't cry. . . .

JARED.—(*Assuredly*) This is *our* home now fer good.

MUSIC.—*Up and out.*

VOICE.—Thus did men like Jared and his comrades make possible the treasure land that is the state of Ohio today. They watched over the natural resources of Ohio carefully, but those who followed violated the law of nature! Down came the trees! Into the rivers ran the valuable topsoil! Greed and waste! No thought of conservation! Now . . . today . . . in the very same territory in which our story has taken place, Ohio citizens are wisely looking at the mistakes of the past and planning for the future! Conservation is a familiar word to the citizens of the Muskingum Valley. They have helped the Department of the Interior to fight those destructive forces . . . flood and erosion. The Muskingum Watershed Conservacy District, 8,000 square miles of land, is a gigantic Ohio Conservation project. Fourteen dams have been constructed on Ohio streams, and, even at this minute, as the Ohio River is sending its spring flood, these projects are proving of far-reaching benefits. The government and the Ohio farmers work hand in hand in this Muskingum program to reforest timberlands and rehabilitate eroded soil. Here is conservation! Here is the American spirit that brought Jared and his comrades through hardships and suffering to bring greatness to Ohio. Conservation must be the twentieth century American ideal! We must plan to use our natural resources for the good of all! Look to the future, America!

MUSIC.—*Up and out.*

VOICE.—Here is a special announcement. . . . Listen carefully. . . .

SECOND VOICE.—Every listener to this program may have a free publication packed full of interesting information about our country's natural wealth. It is a publication which every man, woman, and child in America should have. Send for your free copy *now*. Address What Price America, Washington, D.C., and this free publication will be sent to you at once. Let me .repeat, if you want this important booklet, just send your name and address . . . a postcard will do . . . to What Price America, Washington, D. C.

VOICE.—Next week at this same time, the Department of the Interior, in cooperation with the Columbia Network, presents the third program of the series, What Price America. Listen next week to What Price America.

MUSIC.—*Up and out.*

BEST VERSE EXPERIMENT

Seems Radio Is Here to Stay

by NORMAN CORWIN

RADIO's acquisition of Norman Corwin has brought to the industry one of the most surprising talents in the entire field of present-day broadcasting. In the space of fifteen months he has established himself as one of the truly creative directors in the business and has at the same time written and directed and adapted more first-class program material than anyone else in radio's history, that is to say, more than anyone else in an equal period of time. Although he is at present only twenty-eight years of age, he had had a considerable record of accomplishment prior to his entering radio. At one time or another he had been sports editor of the Greenfield (Mass.) *Recorder*, radio editor of the Springfield (Mass.) *Republican*, and director of the radio bureau of Twentieth Century Fox. In between times he had published two volumes of verse.

In the past year and a half he inaugurated a new series of programs (Words without Music) which has revolutionized the presentation of poetry on the air. He has given to poets a new flexibility of format so vigorous and so sensible that it is bound to attract many new writers to the business of broadcasting. His original verse drama, "They Fly through the Air with the Greatest of Ease," was considered by the Tenth Institute for Radio in Education to be the finest single broadcast of the year. His skillful adaptation of Stephen Vincent Benét's "John Brown's Body" was another superior contribution. The piece of his which I have selected to reprint became the inspirational source for a whole series of half hour originals that appeared under the title, "So This Is Radio." Two of his pieces have already appeared in book form, and negotiations to convert certain others into motion picture "shorts" are in progress.

He has written a short statement regarding the genesis and development of "Seems Radio Is Here to Stay." It should be of interest to the student and to any of those who are curious about an author's method of approach, his habits of work, and the attitudes authors have toward their own work. Here is what he said.

"Seems Radio Is Here to Stay" is an example of a script made to order on short notice. I would like to say that it was inspired by noble ideals and sentiments concerning radio which I carry around with me daily, but this would be somewhat of an exaggeration. Actually it was inspired by the campaign of the National Association of Broadcasters to enable the public "to know more intimately something of the energies and the values and the services that go into our daily schedule."

I was anxious, in writing this script, to make its opening arresting and to present all the facts and conceits in a way that would sustain interest. The hardest part of the job, as is usually the case in any script of this sort, was the opening. I finally hit upon the device of a great chord in the orchestra because I knew it would come after the regulation twenty seconds of silence following the previous program on the network and that if the chord were *followed* by seconds of silence the listener would wonder what this strange business was all about. Once the introductory narration was written the rest was quite simple, and I had little trouble with the script, even though I was backed right up against the deadline of the broadcast. The script was unfinished when we went into rehearsal and the apotheosis of radio which constitutes the ending of the show was written in a break between rehearsals.

I was conscious in writing this script of the necessity to cover the subject comprehensively and yet with care to avoid sounding like a tract on the subject. I have included within the compass of this piece the treatment of such diverse elements as the physical and spatial aspects of radio; its properties of speed; its penetrability and universality as the medium of entertainment; implication of the type of the finest thing done in radio (Shakespearean drama and symphonic music); the unsung but necessary contribution of the technical personnel; the importance of free speech and the role of radio in the democracy; the extra-mundane consideration of radio.

Technically this was a moderately complicated show, requiring a very careful balance between the component elements whenever used simultaneously. The music was very helpful in giving substance and spirit to the passages concerning Beethoven, and the flourishes which Bernard Hermann furnished me for the "Hamlet departure" cues were humorous indeed. The *montage* of code coming from twin oscillators and music from the "Marconi" suite made a very effective fanfare after the deliberately tardy opening announcement.

I placed my principal narrator in "dead booth" and put my whisperer ("Hello, Antipodes") on a filter microphone. I accented the speech concerning the freedom of the air with slow crescendo on a thunder drum, leading into a vigorous fanfare from the orchestra.

The show was not especially difficult to produce and was rehearsed in five hours. All of us seemed to get a lot of fun out of it, and I was pleased when the broadcast met with immediate and intelligent response, because a reception like this encourages further exploration in the direction of similar forms for radio.

(Presented by the Columbia Workshop, April 24, 1939.)

Seems Radio Is Here to Stay*

MUSIC.—*Single, brief chord, followed by silence.*

NARRATOR.—Do we come on you unaware,
  Your set untended?
  Do you put down your paper to lift up an ear,
  Suspend what you were just about to say,
  Or stay the fingertip that could snap shut
  The traps of night between us?

  Were you *expecting* us?
  Your dial deputized to let us in
  At thirty minutes after ten along the seaboard on
   the East,
  Nine-thirty inland by a thousand miles,
  A mountain's half-past-eight,
  And dinner dishes still uncleared on shores that
   face Japan?

  In either case, good evening or good afternoon,
   good morning or good night,
  Whichever best becomes the sector of the sky
  Arched over your antenna.

  We wish a thousand words with you
  Concerning magics that would make a Merlin turn
   pistachio with envy:
  The miracle, worn ordinary now, of just such busi-
   ness as this
  Between your ears and us, and ocean tides of ether.
  We mean the Genii of the Radio,
  Kowtowing to Aladdins everywhere,
  As flashy on the run as Light, and full of services to
   ships at sea and planes in air and people in their
   living rooms, resembling you.

All this by way of prologue, Listener;
And prologues should not be prolonged.
Let our announcer do what he's engaged to do:
Announce
What this is all about.
And let there be, when he is done, some interest
expressed
By brasses and by strings.
A little music, as they say,
To start an introspective program on its way.

ANNOUNCER.—The Columbia Workshop presents an original
verse brochure by Norman Corwin, entitled, "Seems Radio
Is Here to Stay."

SOUND.—*Fade in oscillator 1, with symbolic stream of code in
definite rhythmic pattern, bring in oscillator 2 at lower pitch
and with contrapuntal rhythmic pattern. Hold both until*

MUSIC.—*Orchestra picks up pitch and tempi of both oscillators and
develops material into heroic fanfare of salutation.*

NARRATOR.—That will take care of overtures and prologues for
tonight.
You'd think that we were warming up
To something slightly mighty in the way of
melodrama,
Magniloquent with love and hate, with sacrifice
and sin, repentance, and with sound effects;
Or else you'd think that we were mobilizing moods
To make way for an epic chronicling a war;
But no;
But neither;
As we said before,
We're here to talk of radio.

VOICE.—Say, mister.

NARRATOR.—Yes?

VOICE.—What do you mean by *we?*

NARRATOR.—You wonder at the pronoun *we?*
Well, radio's collective.
No one *in* it's indispensable.
The proof begins right here:
Just watch and see

How neatly your narrator is dispensed with.
Come, take it from me, you who stand near by;
Speak on, of us and radio. (*Pause*)

NARRATOR.—It's taken and we speak.

Let's start by setting forth
That it is good to take a swig of fancy every now
    and then,
A nip or two of wonderment,
To jag the mind.
It's good to send your thoughts excursioning
Beyond the paved and well-worn alleys of your life
If only as a form of exercise,
Especially in wanton days like these.
The fashion now's to wonder on such things
As whether London phrases will displease Berlin,
Or how the Romans will react
To the reaction of the French,
And who's the enemy of whom,
And has he guns enough to run a war for more than
    thirty days?

At times like these, when headlines blaze their
    blackest,
And the heavens crackle with short-waved details
Of Peace's latest coma,
There's little fitness for the luxury
Of contemplations on the majesty of man.
And yet it serves a momentary antidote for toxins
    of the soul
To think away from crises;
To think that even for man's monkeying with
    mania and murder,
He's still a noble article,
Bound round by marvels of all manner.

Do you remember what it was that Whitman said
About the miracles?
Come in, Walt Whitman, and refresh our memories.
   . . .
Come in, and bring with you a snatch of music of
    the spheres.

MUSIC.—*Passage similar in spirit to the eerie variation which concludes Holst's "Planets."*

WHITMAN.—(*On filter mike*)
> I believe a leaf of grass is no less than the journey-work of the stars,
> And the narrowest hinge in my hand puts to scorn all machinery,
> And the cow crunching with depress'd head surpasses any statue.
> And a mouse is miracle enough to stagger sextillions of infidels.

MUSIC.—*Up and out.*

NARRATOR.—You call these wonders, Whitman?
> Well, they are. And we'll agree
> They put to scorn *most* all machinery,
> And yet no field mouse in Vermont, by his own talents,
> Ever squeaked a squeak
> Heard with distinctness in Australia.
> Nor has a cow of any breed
> Devised a means of mooing in a three-way conversation
> With two other cows in distant pasture lands.
> Here is machinery for you, Walt,
> To tickle the imaginings of all the poets in the world.
> We speak now of the innards of this Radio;
> The dials, filaments, and microphones,
> The crystals, coils, and rheostats and rectifying tubes
> And towers that inject the sky
> With certain ectoplasms:
> And there where you sit listening,
> O Listener,
> The sentinels inside your set
> Selecting, sifting strands of ether, letting pass
> That only which it pleases you to hear.
>
> Let's see the gods do better.
> Dare they vie
> With engineers of radio?
> Ho ho. It is to laugh.
> The fulminating thunderclaps of Jove

> Sound beepish just a country's breadth away,
> Whereas the mildest microphonic whisperings,
> Like this . . .

FILTER VOICE.—(*Whispering*) HELLO, ANTIPODES!

NARRATOR.—. . . Go spinning round the globe
> Not once, but seven times
> Within the twinkling of a mouse's eye. . . .
> And on its way . . . mark well the point . . .
> Unswerved by all four winds,
> Dissolving in no mists,
> Unfrozen by contacts with glaciers,
> Undrowned in any deeps,
> And never tangled in a jungle's undergrowth.
> Nor can the frowning Himalayas, range on range,
> But even momentarily
> Intimidate our whispering.
> The Himalayas, did we say?
> Why, the planet proper! Yes, the earth itself,
> Its ingrown mountains and its scoriac seas
> Still hot and smoking from Creation!
> A solid-enough shape to penetrate,
> And yet . . .

FILTER VOICE.—*Hello, Antipodes.*

NARRATOR.—. . . Thrusts through the earth as clean
> As would a guillotine
> Through cheese cake.

> Indeed, the ground has ears!
> Perhaps, for all we know,
> This is telephony with *buried* listeners.
> If all a planet's denseness
> Cannot stop our whisperings,
> Will then mere coffin walls?

> We hardly think so.

> We will make our microphone directional
> And speak to whom we please:

> (*Calling*)
> O Beethoven!

O Ludwig!
Have you got your hearing back?
We call your hallowed bones!
We shout.
Do we disturb your dust?
How restful is your rest there in Vienna, anyway?
Death is too long a leisure, we suspect,
For one of such invention.
You must be out assembling harmonies somewhere.
But listen, Master: hear:

MUSIC.—*Sneak in.*

NARRATOR.—There are more ears attending you tonight
Then ever you imagined could perceive a note:
And all at once; this instant.
More by millions than you ever saw
In continents of concert halls.
Your music gets around these days.
On plains, on mountains and on shores you never
    heard of,
You are heard tonight.

Your music beats against a sounding board of stars;
It flows in raptures down spillways of space;
It sweeps, precisely in the pattern you set down,
Across immensity.

MUSIC.—*Up full to conclusion.*

NARRATOR.—You see, Beethoven?
You have not been changed
By so much as a hemidemisemiquaver.

Let's turn our microphone
And hail a hunk of loam in Stratford.

O Shakespeare!
William Shakespeare!
We are calling from a land you'd like to be ac-
    quainted with:
Four dozen federated states in North America
Not far from those Bermudas that you wrote about.
Here are new Venices and Elsinores
New Athenses and Troys,

507

> New Englands and New Londons and New Yorks
> Where you are better known than all the kings in
>   Britain's history.
> Your language trips upon the lips of schoolboys,
>   lovers, soldiers, justices,
> And lean and slippered pantaloons.
> You stand with Bibles on our shelves
> And are as often quoted as a savior.

FIRST MAN.—Aah, hanging is too good for him.

SECOND MAN.—Well, you have to give the devil his due.

FIRST WOMAN.—The course of true love never did run smooth.

THIRD MAN.—It was Greek to me.

SECOND WOMAN.—He eats me out of house and home!

THIRD WOMAN.—Why don't you send him packing?

FIRST MAN.—It's a wise father that knows his own son.

SECOND MAN.—(*Oratorical*) I pause for a reply.

THIRD MAN.—It smells to heaven.

FIRST MAN.—I'll tell the world.

SECOND MAN.—Sweets to the sweet.

THIRD WOMAN.—I am nothing if not critical.

FIRST MAN.—Dead as a doornail.

SECOND WOMAN.—Uneasy lies the head that wears the crown.

NARRATOR
Three-and-a-quarter centuries
  ago tomorrow afternoon
They put you in a tomb.
Since then, the world has
  cracked a little at the seams,

And nations have been crossed
  and double-crossed

FIRST MAN
What's in a name?
FIRST WOMAN
He loves to hear himself talk.
  . . .
SECOND MAN
Every mother's son . . .
SECOND WOMAN
Paint the lily. . . .
THIRD MAN
And thereby hangs a tale. . . .

And many generals have died
  in peace
And many peaceful people died
  in war
And arts and attitudes and
  sciences grown stale.

THIRD WOMAN
. . . Killed with kindness . . .
FIRST MAN
Tell truth and shame the devil.
FIRST WOMAN
Truth will out. . . .
SECOND MAN
Time out of mind.
SECOND WOMAN
Stand on ceremony.

And ancient gods turned gangrenous;
And yet, there's not a trace of mold about your poetry;
Your plays flash undiminished lightnings.
And more so now than ever, for the theatre has grown
To take in all the stages of the land:
All villages and hamlets,
Cabins hard to get to,
Houses high on hills, and islands where the ferry plies but once a
  week.
Lone trapper in the woods
And ranger on the range
And lighthouse keeper polishing his glass;
They all can hear you now within the compass of this voice.
Your audience has grown.
They hear you well in Louisville,
Orlando, Reno, Buffalo,
Toronto, San Antonio
And Wheeling and Duluth;
In Wichita and Washington
In Birmingham and Utica,
In Chattanooga, Baltimore, and Colorado Springs.

CHORUS.—(*Repeats refrain*)

NARRATOR.—Shakespeare, it may well flatter you to learn
     All modern actors want to play your Hamlet.
     These much-mingled Americans wish hotly to
       personify a royal Dane
     Created by an English butcher's son.

     Well, who are we to stand between
     Ambition and the act?
     One plays him now; forthwith:
     A fragment passionate and murderous

509

And fatal to Polonius.
Remember it?
Attend, for Hamlet enters now the closet of the
Queen.
Polonius is hid behind the arras:

HAMLET.—Now, mother, what's the matter?

QUEEN.—Hamlet, thou hast thy father much offended.

HAMLET.—Mother, you have my father much offended.

QUEEN.—Come, come, you answer with an idle tongue.

HAMLET.—Go, go, you question with a wicked tongue.

NARRATOR

This Hamlet was not advertised tonight, and yet a multitude is listening.

More than they seated at the Globe in London, incidentally.

And none sits in the balcony.

The seats of Radio are Row A Center,
And the tickets always complimentary.

QUEEN
Why, how now, Hamlet?
HAMLET
What's the matter now?
QUEEN
Have you forgot me?
HAMLET
No, by the rood, not so. You are the Queen, your husband's brother's wife;
And—would it were not so— you are my mother.
QUEEN
Nay, then, I'll set those to you that can speak.
HAMLET
Come, come and sit you down. You shall not budge.
You go not till I set you up a glass
Where you may see the inmost part of you.
QUEEN
What wilt thou do? thou wilt not murder me?
Help, help, ho!
POLONIUS (*Off*)
What ho! Help, help, help!
HAMLET (*Sound of drawing . . . off*)

How now! A rat! Dead, for a
ducat, dead!

POLONIUS

O! I am slain!

QUEEN

O me, what hast thou done?

HAMLET

Nay, I know not. Is it the king?

QUEEN

O! what a rash and bloody
deed is this!

HAMLET

A bloody deed! almost as bad,
good mother,
As kill a king and marry with
his brother.

QUEEN

As kill a king!

HAMLET

Ay, lady, 'Twas my word.

. . . .

Leave wringing of your hands:
peace! sit you down,
And let me wring your heart;
for so I shall
If it be made of penetrable
stuff,
If damned custom have not
brazed it so
That it is proof and bulwark
against sense.

QUEEN

What have I done that thou
dar'st wag thy tongue
In noise so rude against me?

HAMLET

Such an act
That blurs the grace and blush
of modesty,
Calls virtue hypocrite, takes
off the rose
From the fair forehead of an
innocent love

NARRATOR

You were an actor, Will.
You know a play does not
spring suddenly from floor
boards unrehearsed
Or drop full blown and edited
from heaven.
It must be written first, then
cast,
Directed, and produced;
And when it's done by radio
It must be engineered.
How else can Hamlet rant in
in Honolulu
As he rants right here?
This is a question for the engi-
neers.

511

Their language has a listenable
  cadence of its own;
To wit:

ENGINEER
I'm getting a low-frequency
tone. Will you check to see
where it's coming from?
SECOND ENGINEER
The S. E. filter is set for cutoff
at 200 cycles.

HASTINGS
Hastings reporting for Workshop. Studio 3. 10:30.
THIRD ENGINEER
Columbia Workshop going local, New York state, north
round robin except RR5;
Dixie; RR19; W2XE; and
pipe to Ed Strong.

FIRST ENGINEER
Say, what's the nemo point on
that late show?
SECOND ENGINEER
KNX.

And sets a blister there, makes
  marriage vows
As false as dicers' oaths; O!
  such a deed
As from the body of contrac-
  tion plucks
The very soul, and sweet religion makes
A rhapsody of words; Heaven's
  face doth glow,
Yes, this solidity and compound mass,
With tristful visage as against
  the doom,
Is thought-sick at the act.

QUEEN
Ay me! what act,
That roars so loud and thun-
  ders in the index?

HAMLET
Look here upon this picture,
  and on this;
The counterfeit presentment of
  two brothers.
See, what a grace was seated
  on this brow;
Hyperion's curls, the front of
  Jove himself,
An eye like Mars, to threaten
  and command,
A station like the herald Mer-
  cury
New lighted on a heaven-
  kissing hill,
A combination and a form
  indeed,
Where every god did seem to
  set his seal,

NARRATOR

Poor Hamlet, he has never been so interrupted.
He is making such a scene behind our engineers
It seems a pity to obtrude.
Obtrude?
Why, come to think of it, our Mr. Hastings has more venom at his finger tips
Than the assassin Laertes upon his sword.
The turning of a dial can efface our Hamlet quicker
Than a most incisive foil.
Stand by to hear a Dane evaporate.

(Hamlet is faded)

To give the world assurance of a man.
This was your husband: look you now what follows.
Here is your husband; like a mildew'd ear,
Blasting his wholesome brother. Have you eyes?
Could you on this fair mountain leave to feed,
And batten on this moor? Ha! have you eyes?
You cannot call it love, for at your age
The hey-day in the blood is tame, it's humble,
And waits upon the judgment: and what judgment
Would step from this to this? Sense, sure, you have,
Else could you not have motion: but, sure, that sense
Is apoplex'd; for madness would not err;
Nor sense to ecstasy was ne'er so thrall'd
But it reserved some quantity of choice,
To serve in such a difference.
. . .

NARRATOR.—Go, rest now, Hamlet.
    You've been around the world and back
    And in a million homes
    And in the tomb of him who gave you utterance.
    We've faded you and been discourteous, and that's enough.
    So thanks; so long; good-by;
    We meet again some day
    In some such pleasant studio as this.
    A little music, please
    For a departing royal gentleman.

MUSIC.—*"Hamlet" flourish.*

513

INTERRUPTER.—Say, mister.

NARRATOR.—Yes, sir?

INTERRUPTER.—What kind of a radio program is this without sound effects?

NARRATOR.—This is a verse brochure, sir.

INTERRUPTER.—(*Puzzled*) Well, what's a verse brochure?

NARRATOR.—Why, this is.

INTERRUPTER.—How very definite. I see I get no satisfaction.

NARRATOR.—But you do indeed. You wish some sound effects? Let this instruct your curiosity:

SOUND.—*In with hoofbeats.*

INTERRUPTER.—Now what is this?

NARRATOR.—A horseman of Apocalypse.

INTERRUPTER.—But only one? Where are the other three?

NARRATOR.—This one is Conquest, and he's riding harder than the other three right now. He has outdistanced them.

SOUND.—*Fade under narrator.*

NARRATOR.—Now would you hear the bravest bird in all the world?

INTERRUPTER.—How's that again?

NARRATOR.—Here is a bird who talks right back to thunder: Give an ear!

SOUND.—*Great clap of thunder. Bird box triumphant at the end of reverberation.*

NARRATOR.—Now would you hear Niagara's cataract, roaring with 100,000 lionpower? Come in, Niagara.

SOUND.—*Feeble stirring of water tank.*

NARRATOR.—Oh, shame!
Oh, shame,
Niagara trickles like three drops of rain
Which have joined forces down a windowpane!
What fell anemia is this?
What drouth has been at work on you?
Alas, alas, Niagara!

INTERRUPTER.—Now, now, I've heard enough. Which way did Hamlet exit?

NARRATOR.—Right through here.

INTERRUPTER.—I follow!

MUSIC.—*Repeat Hamlet departure cue.*

NARRATOR.—Good listeners,
  There is a delicacy in the fact
  That all things delicate were once exceeding crude.
  The orchid can be traced to low beginnings,
  And the sweetest scents to illnesses of whales;
  The raw material of men is dust;
  Of diamonds, lampblack.
  The vast mainsprings of Time
  Which keep the very stars to their appointments
  Were forged, no doubt, out of some coarse Galactic
    ore.
  But here's the point we're getting to:
  That radio itself, so delicately tuned and timed,
  Transmitted and received,
  Is, too, compounded of base clays and perspiration,
  Plans and graphs and conferences,
  Instruments and agencies whose labor is unheard,
    unseen, unsung.
  They serve the industry and you
  With intimacies equal to the service of the trunk
    unto the tree;
    the wrist unto the hand;
    the service of the letter to the word,
    the figure to the total.
  If you are skeptic,
  Here is testimony swarming from transmitter tips:
(The following cross-fade into each other on cue)

CABINETMAKER.—Now you take me, I'm a cabinetmaker working in that factory across the river. We make cabinets for radio sets. When the season's good . . .

SALES REPRESENTATIVE.—And naturally, since I am national sales representative of 16 of the country's biggest stations, I certainly have every reason to be consulted when the occasion calls, as this one obviously did . . .

SOUND.—*Phone buzzer.*

OPERATOR.—Columbia Broadcasting System, WEEI. Mr. Fellows? Just a moment, please. . . .

ACTOR.—And I was picked out of 50 in the audition. It's a contract for 52 weeks, and I play the lead. Of course, I will be permitted no conflicts, but considering the terms . . .

WORKER.—I am engaged in the manufacture of porcelain water coils and porcelain pipe for carrying water to radio tubes in transmitting stations. We turn out an average of . . .

ATTORNEY.—In my experience as a lawyer practicing before the Federal Communications Commission, I have many times represented applicants for a license to own and operate . . .

SOUND.—*Typing.*

GIRL.—Yes, sir. I will have this report typed up in about 5 minutes.

SALESMAN.—It really takes very little salesmanship in my line. We make the finest antenna impedance-measuring units and dielectric capacitators in the business. . . .

WIFE.—No, Bert, I'm sorry. I'm working late on the script tonight. You'd better try to exchange the tickets for Wednesday night. Yes. What? Well, the script's got to be ready for typing tomorrow morning, so's it can go into rehearsal by noon. . . .

AGENT.—I'll get an estimate on the program tomorrow. Talent costs, director, music, sound, scripts, and rights. . . . It sounds like a good show to buy. . . .

SCRUB WOMAN.—(*Slavic accent*) Sunday night I have off. I come in at 10 every night and wash the floors on the fifteenth and sixteenth floors. . . . Sometimes also on the seventeenth. . . .

DIRECTOR.—Sound, bring up the train effect behind the narrator, and don't start fading until after cue 118 on page 23. Mr. Carpenter, will you please work a little closer to the mike in your scene with Miss Kent. . . . All right, everybody. From the top of page 22. . . .

EDUCATOR.—And we are adding to the curriculum for the spring term a course in radio writing by the head of the script division of . . .

RECORDING.—Do you want that recorded on 78's or 33's. O.K., then, I'll start to cut on 'phone cue from you. . . .

MUSIC.—*Instrument sounding "A."*

CONDUCTOR.—All right, gentlemen, now, take it from "C," 10, 11, 12 measures; and I'd like a little more brass, please, and much heavier afterbeats. All right?

SOUND.—*Rapping of baton.*

MUSIC.—*Lively, popular dance tune . . . fade under.*

NARRATOR.—Here are the toils, the hopes, anxieties,
    The deals, the overtime put in,
    Wages and hours, clauses in the contract,
    Cornerstones laid down,
    Floors scrubbed and phone calls answered,
    Memoranda written, figures added up,
    Pay checks distributed,
    And inquiries and answers.

SECOND NARRATOR.—Here is the budget and the copyright
        release,
    The time clock and the elevator guard,
    The whistle in the factory proclaiming
        noon;
    The Yes and No and Sorry-try-again,
    The date for lunch,
    The swell idea,
    The new man coming in next Monday
    And the program ending on the nose.

THIRD NARRATOR.—Here is transmitter tone
    And resin for the bow
    And sales gone up by twenty-two per cent.
    Here is an industry
    Built out of air and cyclical vibrations,
    Primed high to entertain, instruct
    And serve the common weal.
    So much for our side, here, where studios
        surround.
    And now for you, who sit at home or ride in
        cars
    Or hear us, visiting a friend.

    You are the critic and the judge,
    The mighty ear,

The twister of the dial knob.
You rule the wave lengths
By selection.
Do you like it *this* way?
Thank you. This way it shall be.
You like it *that?*
Then that.

We broadcast not to cabbages and walruses.
We do not throw our signals at the moon
But aim for you, and watch to see if we have
made a hit.

FIRST LISTENER.—Say, mister.

NARRATOR.—Yes, sir?

FIRST LISTENER.—I rather like this kind of program, but my wife doesn't. She prefers drama and variety shows.

SECOND LISTENER.—Well, as for me, I don't care so much for variety shows, but I sure love the baseball games and the quiz programs.

WOMAN.—Myself, I never miss the symphony.

SECOND WOMAN.—For the last 6 months I've been following that grand serial that comes right after the news in the morning. My son likes to hear the baseball, but I never got around to learning what the game is all about. (*Laughs*)

THIRD LISTENER.—Give me swing anytime. Boy, that Artie Shaw is something. In the groove! Hey, hey!

FOURTH LISTENER.—Frankly, I don't like swing. Most of all I like to hear the news come over. Especially Mr. Kaltenborn's interpretations.

THIRD WOMAN.—My little boy always wants to hear that cowboy program at dinnertime, but my daughter Betty gets into a fight with him because she wants to hear that Let's Pretend program . . . the fairy tales. So I finally had to get two radios to keep peace in the family. Bill, that's my husband, he likes to hear the sports and politics. But not for me. Well, everybody's entitled to his opinion, I always say.

NARRATOR.—Thank all the heavens and the gods for diff'rences.
Let men's opinions be as varied and as free to come
and go as weather is. . . .

Like wind, spontaneous; like storm, forthright.
The saying is, that difference of opinion makes the
world go round.
And *that's* a platitude you tip your hat to when you
meet it on the street.
You'll find, wherever viewpoints must be such-and-
such . . . or *else*
And opinion is smuggled out like contraband,
In such a place the world *stops* short and goes
around no more.
The world stands still because it is *afraid* to move,
And liberty's convulsed for want of air.

SOUND.—*Thunder drum in ominously . . . build under*

NARRATOR.—The air we listen to must be as free as that we
breathe
Or there will rise such dissonance and such
cacophony
As will stave in the eardrum.
Damn the very thought and stab it through!
There'll be no muffing of the ear, no licking of the
boot
In this America.
Come, now, you men who make our music!
Beat that out in harmonies for all to hear!

MUSIC.—*Spirited, martial passage.*

NARRATOR.—Think hard upon these words which tumble toward
you through the night:
The race of man is shrewd and silly, brutal and
benign
And full of sudden starts and tardy reckonings.
One day, when all the menacing is done with
And a man can wish another well across a border-
line,
His speech will sweeten;
He will cast abroad such sentiments
And should be radiated in the skies.

Seems radio is here to stay,
And granting this, grant further
That these air lanes were marked out
By that same Architect who popped the stars in
place

519

And set afire the sun and froze the moon
And dug the furrows wherein oceans flow.
Do you grant radio is here to stay?
Then grant this further:
That the mystic ethers were established well before
    the first word passed between two men;
It's only latterly we've seen that speech is buoyant
    in these waves;
A puff or two of years, that's all it is.
There may this very moment be,
As close to us as one discoverer away,
Whole firmaments of stuffs awaiting comprehension.

That we'll see about.

Meanwhile some homage to the High Commissioner
Who first assigned these frequencies to earth,
Who marked these air lanes out.
He is the same who fixed the stars in place,
Who set afire the sun and froze the moon and dug
    the furrows wherein oceans flow.
Who put some molecules together in a way
To make a man.

He holds the formula for genesis and death.
His hand rests on a dial bigger than infinity.

This microphone is not an ordinary instrument,
For it looks out on vistas wide indeed:
My voice commingles now with northern lights and
    asteroids and Alexander's skeleton,
With dead volcanoes and with donkey's ears
It swims with minnows and it's in the Sphinx's
    jaw.
It drifts among whatever spirits pass across the
    night.

Here is a thought to fasten to your throat:
Who knows who may be listening? And where?

Music.—*Concluding passage . . . pyramid effect.*

BEST VERSE DRAMA

Air Raid

by ARCHIBALD MACLEISH

ᒪᒪ

DESPITE many handicaps, radio has managed to improve the quality of its own literature remarkably during the past three years. Many new writers have been discovered by the industry, and many established writers have been persuaded to work for it. The case of Archibald MacLeish is worth mentioning. CBS secured his first radio effort, "The Fall of the City," and the production carried a tremendous impact to listeners. It is one of the great broadcasts of all times. There are two interesting points to be made in this connection. The first is that that although MacLeish had no technical knowledge of radio, his first play required almost no revision whatever and furthermore was within forty seconds of being "on the nose" when it was first submitted. To me this means that those writers who look sideways at radio as an unfamiliar medium do not have so much to fear as they think. Any writer who can write a play can write a radio play.

MacLeish's great interest in radio as a medium for verse drama yielded in the course of time a second piece, "Air Raid," which is reprinted here. The creation of this single half hour property (and this is my second point) took MacLeish *seven months*. Its writing and its construction show the painstaking effort that went into it. It is not the sort of thing that could duplicate itself every week. That is the main reason why those efforts that must duplicate themselves every week can never compete in literary value with those that are written as all the world's best work is written—leisurely, soberly, reflectively, voluntarily.

Archibald MacLeish is sufficiently well known to the reading public and radio public alike not to require much biographical comment. By Presidential appointment he was made Librarian of Congress in June, 1939. Prior to that he had been Curator of the Nieman Foundation at Harvard University, one of the editors of *Fortune* magazine, Professor at Princeton University, a lawyer. Throughout his life he has been a poet, and as such he is today one of the great talents of this generation. He was awarded the Pulitzer Prize for poetry in 1935. If his new work in Washington prevents further output, it will be a disastrous loss to contemporary literature. His broadcast, "Air Raid," follows.

Air Raid*

ϙϙ

ANNOUNCER.—The Columbia Workshop presents "Air Raid,"
a play for women, by Archibald McLeish.

SOUND.—*Cut in transmission tone . . . fade under following.*

VOICE.—When you hear the gong sound . . .
  The time will be. . . .
  Ten seconds past 2 A.M. precisely. . . .

SOUND.—*Gong.*

VOICE.—WABC . . . New York. . . .

SOUND.—*Transmission tone cuts.*

ANNOUNCER.—(*In sub control*) Ladies and gentlemen!
  You have only one thought tonight, all of you . . .
  You who fish the fathoms of the night
  With poles on rooftops and long loops of wire . . .
  Those of you who, driving from some visit,
  Finger the button on the dashboard dial
  Until the metal trembles like a medium in a trance
  And tells you what is happening in France
  Or China or in Spain or some such country.
  You have one thought tonight and only one:
  Will there be war? Has war come?
  Is Europe burning from the Tiber to the Somme?
  You think you hear the sudden double thudding
   of the drum
  You don't, though. . . .
    Not now. . . .
  But what your ears will hear within the hour
  No one living in this world would try to tell you.
  We take you there to wait it for yourselves.
  Stand by: we'll try to take you through. . . .

SOUND.—*Transmission and static crackle surges . . . hold for* 30 *seconds.*

ANNOUNCER.—One moment now: we'll try to take you.

SOUND.—*Continues for* 15 *seconds . . . continues background.*

ANNOUNCER.—The ultimatum, you remember, was for sunrise
　　　　　by their clock:
　　　　　Midnight by ours! Now ours is long past midnight.
　　　　　The sun is up on the whole curve of that continent.

SOUND.—*Fades out.*

ANNOUNCER.—The weather is fair, with winds southwest going
　　　　　southerly:
　　　　　A few clouds at ten thousand . . . cumulus:
　　　　　Mists among the passes of the upper Julian Alps:
　　　　　Some fog on the east Baltic, but lifting:
　　　　　Otherwise sun: the Tyrrhenian Sea all sunshine:
　　　　　The Adriatic creased with curling light:
　　　　　The Atlantic tumbles forward into morning on
　　　　　those beaches:
　　　　　The whole continent lolls in summer sunlight:
　　　　　Spain is drifting eastward with the shapes of
　　　　　clouds:
　　　　　France is smooth with morning like a turf:
　　　　　Germany is checkered with the squares of green
　　　　　and grain:
　　　　　The visibility is perfect. . . .
　　　　　You think you hear the lonely droning danger of
　　　　　the planes. . . .
　　　　　You don't, though. . . .
　　　　　　　Not yet. . . .

SOUND.—*Transmission and static cuts in* 15 *seconds.*

ANNOUNCER.—One moment now: we'll take you through:

SOUND.—*Continues* 10 *seconds . . . then fade to background.*

ANNOUNCER.—We take you to a town behind the border . . .
　　　　　One of those old-time hill towns where the papers
　　　　　Come tomorrow morning and the wars
　　　　　Come years ago or in some other country:
　　　　　The planes will come, though . . . if they come
　　　　　at all:

The pass above the border is to eastward in those
    mountains.
Our men are on a roof above the houses of the
    town.

SOUND.—*Fades . . . pause.*

ANNOUNCER.—Strange and curious times these times we live in:

SOUND.—*Out.*

ANNOUNCER.—You watch from kitchens for the bloody signs:
    You watch for breaking war above the washing
        on the lines.
    In the old days they watched along the borders:
    They called their warfare in the old days wars
    And fought with men, and men who fought were
        killed.
    We call it peace and kill the women and the
        children.
    Our women die in peace beneath the lintels of
        their doors.
    We have learned much: civilization has gentled
        us:
    We have learned to take the dying and the wounds
        without the wars. . . .
    Stand by, please: we take you through now:

SOUND.—*Transmission tone and static cut in and established for
  15 seconds . . . becoming increasingly louder and fuller under
  following.*

ANNOUNCER.—We take you now across the traveler's sea,
    Across the trawler's coast . . .
        The parson's orchard. . . .
    Across the merchant's villa with the vine above
        the porch . . .
    Across the laborer's city with the flames above
        the forges . . .
    Across the drover's plain . . . the planter's
        valley . . .

    The poplar trees in alleys are the roads.
    The linden trees in couples are the doors.
    The willows are the wandering water flowing.
    The pines in double lines are where the north wind
        burns the orchards.

525

> Those are the mountains where no meadow is
> squared nor a
> Stream straight: nor a road: nor water quiet.
> The town is in those mountains: you are there!

SOUND.—*Cuts sharply on first word of announcer . . . fades out to meet next sound cue.*

ANNOUNCER.—*(Filter 500–4,000 . . . in isolation booth)* You are
twenty-eight miles from the eastern border.
You are up on top of a town on a kind of tenement:
You are out the other side the night. . . .
The sun dazzles you: not the light bulb.
You are staring out to eastward toward the sun.

SOUND.—*Blends imperceptibly into sounds of waking town. Dogs bark . . . horse and cart clatter over cobbles . . . women laugh and chatter.*

ANNOUNCER *(Continues after slight pause)*
We have seen nothing and heard nothing:
Before dawn we thought we heard them:
It was the wind we heard in the valley cedars.
Sounds rise to this roof . . .
Hoofs of stabled horses: leaves:
Even the speaking of sleepers rises.
Many sleep in the one house here:
They work in the fields: sleep in the village:
The men go out at dawn; return
To evening burning from the chimneys:
The women keep the town between.

SOUND.—*Laughter.*
FIRST GIRL
Maudie! Maudie!
SECOND GIRL
Where's the milk, Maudie?
THIRD GIRL
She's asleep! She's always asleep.
FIRST GIRL
She's dreaming of raspberries.
What was she doing at dusk in the raspberries!
Ask her!

SOUND.—*Laughter.*
OLD WOMAN
And the country trees and the sun handling them easily. . . .

SOUND.—*Laughter.*
THIRD WOMAN
You don't tell me!
FOURTH WOMAN
Don't I, though! I heard them. I heard them with my own ears. I can hear!

SOUND.—*Women's chatter continues to grow louder.*

ANNOUNCER

They keep it now: the tenement's full of them . . .
A four-story building of women:
They're filling the court with
their quick talk:
They call back and forth from
the windows:
They laugh behind the kitchen
doors:
They rinse the shirts in the first
real shine of the morning:
They talk . . . their arms to
elbows in the tubs. . . .

THIRD WOMAN
Whispering there on the stairs
on the second landing.
SOUND.—*Laughter.*
FIRST WOMAN
And a day's work to do . . .
a day's washing!
How can I go to the woods with
a day's washing!
SECOND WOMAN
The wash will keep: the wash
will keep forever.
Whoever heard of a wash
spoiling?
FOURTH WOMAN
He didn't.
He never spoke. Not a word.
It was her that was speaking.
THIRD WOMAN
What did they say?
SECOND WOMAN
What do you say she was
saying?

FIRST WOMAN.—Who did she say?

SECOND WOMAN.—   When did she say so? . . .

THIRD WOMAN.—   . . . Look at it!
Look at the cuff of his shirt! What's he been
into?
Black grease!

FOURTH WOMAN.—   What would you think he'd be into . . .
A man like yours with an eye like his for
wandering.

THIRD WOMAN.—And you to talk! . . . you with that redheaded
lollypop!
Hardly a day at dark but his head's in the
window:
He's wearing his elbows out on the stone sill
Looking us over from one floor to the next:
If it's only the eye with him that wanders, I
wonder. . . .

527

OLD WOMAN.—A fine day, I told him: a fine day:
   A fine willing day: he could trust it for certain.
   He could hay today and cock it tomorrow for certain.
   Ah, those Arctic stars, he said . . .

FIRST BOY.—(*Calling off*)   Harry!
   Harry! Be quick, Harry! Be quick! Quick!

OLD WOMAN.—Men are the fools: they have no trust in the world:
   To make a crop of hay you're bound to trust it:
   There's no sin but not to trust the world.

FIRST GIRL.—When will she marry?

SECOND GIRL.—   She won't marry:
   He's always planning for something or other.
   He's always fearing or hoping or something.

FIRST GIRL.—They never seem to know it's now . . .
   Men don't: women sometimes do.

SECOND GIRL.—They're always waiting for the time
   They've waited for.

THIRD GIRL.—   And when it comes
   They still wait.

SECOND GIRL.—   Don't they?

THIRD GIRL.—   But they do.
   They never take the clock for *now* . . .
   For *this* . . . for *here*. They never take the
   Risk that this was why they waited.

FIRST GIRL.—Men don't: women sometimes do. . . .

SECOND GIRL.—No: not sometimes: always do. . . .

THIRD GIRL.—Life's more like itself for us than them.
   They're always meddling with it . . .
   Always making life come true.

MUSIC.—*Singing woman begins scale . . . off . . . under preceding scene.*

ANNOUNCER.—We have seen nothing and heard nothing.
   If they left at dawn we should have heard them.
   It's two hours now since dawn.

They could make it in two: they could make it under
One and a half from their fields to the border:
Ten minutes more. . . .

FIRST WOMAN.—It's war again! Have you heard them talking?

SECOND WOMAN.— We've heard them:
How can we help but hear them . . . blab-
bing about:
Cocking their feet on the kitchen table and
talking.

THIRD WOMAN.—It's always war when they talk and it's always
talk.

FOURTH WOMAN.—It's always talk when they get to the beer and
tobacco.

FIRST WOMAN.—The beer comes out of the bottles; so does the
talk too.

SECOND WOMAN.—Yes, and the wars.

THIRD WOMAN.—Wasting their time on wars with the
Dishes to do and the children to chasten.

FOURTH WOMAN.—The wars!
As though to make the wars were something
wonderful!
Millions of men have made the wars and
talked!

FIRST WOMAN.—Talking of wars as though to die were something!

SECOND WOMAN.—Death's the one thing every creature does
And none does well I've ever seen . . . the
one thing
Weak and foolish every creature does.

THIRD WOMAN.—Only boys and men like boys believe in it.

FIRST WOMAN.—It's sticking to this giddy world that's hard . . .
Not turning limp and letting loose and tumbling.

MUSIC.—*Singing woman.*

FIRST BOY.—Harry! Harry! Harry! Be quick, Harry!

ANNOUNCER.— We have seen
Nothing at all. We have heard nothing.
The town is very quiet and orderly.
They are flushing the cobblestones with water.
The sidewalks are slippery with sun!
It smells of a summer morning anywhere:
It smells of seven o'clock in the morning in
Any town they water dust in:
Towns are all the same in summer.
A man can remember the name of his own in
Any city after the water carts.

FIRST GIRL.—Ah, the petticoat! Look at the petticoat, Maudie!
Look at the petticoat, will you! Isn't it hers?

SECOND GIRL.—Who would wear it but her? But who? . . . who?

THIRD GIRL.—Who but my mother!

FIRST GIRL.—Who but her mother!

SOUND.—*The girls' voices picked up a chanting beat which works
into a kind of tuneless tune.*

SECOND GIRL.—Who but her mother, and where will she wear it to?

THIRD GIRL.—Who will she show it to?

FIRST GIRL.—Where will she go in it?

SECOND GIRL.—Where will she go in the silk of her petticoat?

THIRD GIRL.—Who will she show the silk in her petticoat?

FIRST GIRL.—How would he know it was silk in her petticoat?

SECOND GIRL.—How would he know . . .

THIRD GIRL.—How would he know. . . .

SOUND.—*There is a shriek of laughter . . . the chant and the words
are repeated indistinguishably under the announcer's voice
. . . they fade out to a murmur of voices.*

ANNOUNCER.—We have seen; nothing and heard nothing.
If they left at dawn we should have heard them.
It's two hours now since dawn.

They could make it in two: they could make it
   under . . .
One and a half from their fields to the border:
Ten minutes more. . . .

MUSIC.—*A tinny piano begins far off . . . a few indistinguishable
phrases of summer morning music . . . "Summer Time" or
"Dead End Blues."*

ANNOUNCER.—   We have seen
Nothing at all. We have heard nothing.
The town is very quiet and orderly.
They are flushing the cobblestones with water.
The sidewalks are slippery with sun!
It smells of a summer morning anywhere:
It smells of seven o'clock in the morning in
Any town they water dust in:
Towns are all the same in summer.
A man can remember the name of his own in
Any city after the water carts.

MUSIC.—*The singing woman's voice rises again in the high, pure
scale.*

ANNOUNCER.—The last shutters are opening . . .
The rooms where no one hopes: the rooms
Where all the hope's been had and sleep
Covers it: folding it. Rooms where the old lie;
Rooms where the young lie late with their
   lovers. . . .

SICK WOMAN.—How much longer must I wait? They've told you.
(*Close . . . weak . . . wandering*)

SECOND BOY.—Wait for what mother? Wait to be well?

SICK WOMAN.—Wait to be . . . yes. Not long . . . a day is
            long. . . . It's always long the first time. . . .
            I remember someone saying it was always
            long. . . .
            Someone saying it will come: don't fear it. . . .

SECOND BOY.—Were you never afraid, mother?

SICK WOMAN.—Never: of anything.
            There's nothing comes by day or night to fear.

SECOND BOY.—Not even war? Not even if they came here?

SICK WOMAN.—They came when I was young once: I remember
them.
We smelled the smoke that morning in the
alders. . . .
They had their tents by the stream in the water
meadow. . . .
I'd never eat the sausages. . . . I was the dainty
one:
I used to rinse my things in seven waters . . .
Well water: brook water: rain. . . .
I dried them on the gravel by the river.
Even at night late they would smell of the sun
on them. . . .
I ate the water cress to make my mouth sweet.
. . .
They had blue capes on their coats with scarlet
linings.
They spoke together in another tongue:
They were slow and soft in their speech with
laughter and looking. . . .
Evenings come home across the evening:
Seeing the constellations of the stars:
They gave us milk to drink from jars of metal.
. . .
You sit in the dark and drink: you don't say
anything.

SECOND BOY.—They kill the children when they come. I've read
it.

SICK WOMAN.—Not "It's a pleasant night." Not even "Thank
you."
They seem to want you not to speak or move:
They seem to want you quiet like the heifers:
You sit in the dark and rest: you don't say
anything. . . .
You don't say "Thank you" even . . . not
"Good night."

SECOND BOY.—I've heard they kill the children, mother: I've
heard it.
I've heard at night in sleep they kill the children.

SOUND.—*Single plane fades in . . . barely audible.*

532

SICK WOMAN.—A day is longer. . . . I was very young!
    Everyone coming and looking, and isn't she
     young. . . .
    You sit in the dark and rest: you don't say
     anything. . . .

ANNOUNCER.—Listen! Motor throbbing!
    Probably one of their own.
    No one watching it anyway.

SICK WOMAN.—The water cress between the crusts of water. . . .
    The wild iris in the water meadows:
    The roses like the closing of desire. . . .
    And rest: you don't say anything. . . .

ANNOUNCER.—There he is: we've got him:
    One of the home ships:
    He's combing the hills in circles:
    Working heavily . . .
         laboring . . .
    Leveling now. He's high enough. . . .
    Spark in the sky when he hangs and the
    Sun angles the fuselage:
    Gone when the sunlight loses him:
    Sound coming down out of nowhere:
    Eddying: floating down.

    No one noticing anyway:
    No one looking or listening:
    Only that sleepers waken. . . .

YOUNG MAN.—(*Close, low*) O are you there? Are you still there?
        I dreamed you had gone. Never go!

GIRL.—(*Close, low*) Say we're happy. Tell me that we're happy.

YOUNG MAN.—Stay as you are: do not move:
     Do not ever move: stay there:
     Stay with this sunlight on your shoulders.

ANNOUNCER.—Still circling and wheeling,
    He's working the air as a hawk would . . .
    Stalking with height for cover:
    Hovering lost in sight.
    We see him and lose him and see him.

GIRL.—Tell me we're happy. No, but say we are.
    How can I know we are unless you tell me?

How can a woman know the world is good?
Which is the world and which is her and which is
Things she's known for sure that never happened?
She can't tell. She can't and be a woman.
Can a cupful of well water tell you the taste of the well
    water?

SOUND.—*Plane is fading.*

YOUNG MAN.—Stay with this sunlight on your shoulders:
    Stay with this sunlight on your hair.

MUSIC.—*Singing woman sneaks in.*

ANNOUNCER.—We've lost him this time.

SOUND.—*Plane very faint surges.*

ANNOUNCER.—   Wait!
    Wait! We've got him! He's doubled.
    He's doubling back into sun:
    He's running her east for the border.

    Orders from somewhere certainly!
    They've heard something or guessed it.

    He was west of the town when he banked:
    He yanked her round on a wing
    Like swinging a colt on a bridle:
    He's east of us now in the hills.

    They've found something . . . or feared it!

SOUND.—*Siren distant . . . runs scale in parody of woman's voice
    . . . repeats in background.*
    They've found it!
               Feared and found!
    There's the siren: the signal:
    They've picked them up at the border. . . .

FIRST BOY.—Harry! Where are you, Harry! Where are you!
    Where are you!

ANNOUNCER.—(*Dry and quick over the siren*) Ten minutes to
                    wait.
                    If they're cruising a
                    hundred and
                    eighty it's

Ten minutes: if less,
More: if more, less.
Ten we'd guess if we
   had to.
Depends how old
   they bring them.
The slow ones hobble
   the fast.

SOUND.—*Siren at crescendo.*

ANNOUNCER

Probably bringing the lot of
   them.
Strike at a hinge you must kill.
. . .
You strike in sleep at a king
When you strike by trick at a
   people.
The treacherous wars must be
   quick
Or the victims live for the vic-
   tory.

FIRST WOMAN

That's enough!

SECOND WOMAN

That's enough of it!

THIRD WOMAN

Stop it!
Stop it for heaven's sake!

FOURTH WOMAN

It's stopping! It's stopping!

SOUND.—*Siren dies rapidly away . . . voices of the women have
been rising under it.*

FIRST WOMAN.—Thank God that's over.

SECOND WOMAN.—Fit to deafen a woman.

THIRD WOMAN.—Fit to deafen the cattle for twenty miles.
            And what for? For a war. To say there's
            another.

FOURTH WOMAN.—What's a war to us. . . . There's always
            another.

FIRST WOMAN.—All that noise to tell us there's a war.

SECOND WOMAN.—Schoolboys banging the bells and blowing the
            bugles.

ANNOUNCER (*Women's voices
        under*)

Eight minutes more:

Town quiet: waiting:

THIRD WOMAN

They're worse than schoolboys
   . . . much worse.

FOURTH WOMAN

Noisier, too!

535

Women's skirts in the court:
Women's arms in the windows:
Women's talk on the stair. . . .

They lean there careless and talking:
Their shawls are bright in the doors:
The morning air's in their aprons:
They shape their hair with their hands:
They stand there softly and simply.
> (*Pause*)
> The women lean from the stairs.

THIRD WOMAN.—They're always waking us up for a war somewhere.
> Get up! They say. We're at war.

FOURTH WOMAN.—   It's no news
> Thousands of years they've been saying it.

FIRST WOMAN.—   Crazy government:
> Can't they run the country decent and quiet till
> Eight in the morning even? The rest of the day
> They can rule as loud as they like and as long
> as they mind to.
> They can do what they want with the country
> from eight on.
> Only till eight if they'd wait for the difficult
> sleepers . . .
> Those that count their heartbeats every hour.

SECOND WOMAN
A woman's got no time to watch the wars. . . .
Scrubbing the kitchen Tuesdays: marrying Mondays.
Bearing and burying . . . men to be born and to bury.
People dying never died before.
. . .

FIRST WOMAN
Sillier, too!
THIRD WOMAN
Stupider!
SECOND WOMAN
Lord, I was almost frightened, though!
THIRD WOMAN
Almost!
Almost, does she say!
SECOND WOMAN
The men! The men!
The great big babies that they are!
The children!

SOUND.—*Police whistle distant
. . . distant men's voices
. . . excited.*
FIRST MAN
Air raid.
SECOND MAN
Air raid.

536

SOUND.—*Whistle nearer.*

THIRD MAN

Air raid!

FOURTH MAN

Air raid!

FIFTH MAN

The bombers!

SECOND MAN

The bombers!

THIRD MAN

The bombers.

SERGEANT

The cellars.

SERGEANT

Take the cellars. . . .

ANNOUNCER

A police sergeant: he's shouting: He's marching down through the street. He's beating the shutters and shouting. He's calling them out:

SERGEANT.—   The cellars!

ANNOUNCER.—Listen.

SERGEANT.—   Take to the cellars!

WOMEN.—(*Laugh*)

SERGEANT.—Take to the church cellars.

ANNOUNCER.—They only laugh! They lean from the open windows and laugh at him.

FIRST WOMAN.—You take the cellars!

SECOND WOMAN.—   You can take them, Sergeant!

THIRD WOMAN.—Let the town policemen take the cellars!

FOURTH WOMAN.—They'll smell the mice in the cellars!

FIRST WOMAN.—Maybe they'll catch them!

SOUND.—*Police whistle.*

SERGEANT.—The alarm has been given. Five minutes have passed.
          In five minutes more they must be here.

537

They are coming in numbers: I do not know how
many.
The instructions are to occupy the vaults.
Those are the orders of persons of proper authority.
You will march to the church by twos and at suit-
able intervals.

FIRST WOMAN.—Will we? And who'll be watching the pot while
we're squatting there?
Counting the mother spiders? The police?

SECOND WOMAN.—There are frogs in the vaults.

THIRD WOMAN.— There are also people's relations . . .
Not the kind that care to gossip either.

FOURTH WOMAN.—And who will iron the underwear now that it's
sprinkled?

FIRST WOMAN.—Oh, the police will. . . .

OLD WOMAN.— Listen to me, policeman!
Perhaps it's true they're coming in their planes:
Perhaps it isn't true. But if it is
It's not for housewives in this town they're
coming.
They're after the generals: they're after the
cabinet ministers.
They're coming to capture the square in the
capital city.
They always have: they always capture the city.
A fine sight we'd be . . . a parcel of housewives
Spinning with the spiders in a hole
With soldiers that don't know the hole is there
Or we are there or anything is there . . .
Go running through the wonderful great sky
Hunting before and after for that city.
(*Continues behind announcer*)

ANNOUNCER	OLD WOMAN
Six minutes gone!	A fine sight! A fine sight for
Four more by the count.	our grandfathers!
They must be clear of the mountains:	Sitting there in darkness with the bones!
They must be here in the hills:	Cracking our knuckles in black dark in the bone yard!
They must be near. . . .	Fine fools we'd feel with the bones of our grandfathers.

538

OLD WOMAN
We're women. No one's making
war on women . . .
The nation with no land: with-
out history:
The nation whose dates are
Sunday and Monday: the
nation
Bounded by bread and sleep
. . . by giving birth:
By taking death to keep: the
ancient nation
Settled in the seasons of this
earth as
Leaves are and oblivious as
leaves:
Neutral as summer in the fierce
divisions. . . .

ANNOUNCER
If they picked them up to the
right
We'll sight them over the river:
Horizon flat to the flight:
Rising or seeming to rise
As geese do coming inland.
Blur of light on the fins.

FIRST WOMAN
They're always marching past
to capture something!
SECOND WOMAN
It's all one if they march or
they fly. They won't hurt us!
THIRD WOMAN
It's all one to us if they wing or
they walk!

FOURTH WOMAN.—They've never troubled us yet!

FIRST WOMAN.—   They've never harmed us!

OLD WOMAN.—They never will. You are a new policeman.
                  Less than ten years you have been in this district.
                  I do not mention this to shame you: only
                  You do not know the history of this neighborhood.
                  We have seen such people in this place before.
                  They come in uniforms carrying elegant banners.
                  They march up and down. They ruin roads.
                  They interfere with the cattle. They rob the
                      fruit trees.
                  They frighten calving cows. They trample clover.
                  No one would say they were likable people for
                      visitors . . .
                  Making history over the corn and the cabbage:

539

> Writing glorious pages in the beans:
> Disturbing serious men in haying season.
> Nevertheless it is true that few have suffered. . . .
> Maybe a girl would be rumpled a little. . . .

WOMEN.—(*Laugh boisterously*)   Not many.

SERGEANT.—I do not say the order was expedient.
> I say it was issued. I do not account for orders.
> It is not my duty to account for orders.
> Nevertheless it was issued by men of experience:
> Persons of sound sense. It may have been thought
> The wars have changed with the world and not for
> the better.

WOMEN.—(*Laugh*)
> It may have been thought: this enemy kills women!

SOUND.—*Laughter louder.*

SERGEANT.—It may have been thought: this enemy kills women,
> Meaning to kill them!

SOUND.—*Laughter rises to a shriek.*

SERGEANT.—I say it may be thought
> *He makes his wars on women!*

SOUND.—*Laughter drops sharply away but continues.*

SERGEANT.—   It may be thought
> This enemy is not the usual enemy!
> That this one is no general in a greatcoat
> Conquering countries for the pride and praise!
> That this one conquers other things than countries!
> (*There is dead silence*)
> It may be thought that this one conquers life!
> That life that won't be conquered can be killed!
> That women are most lifelike! That he kills them!
> It may be as I say. It may be thought he
> *Makes his wars on women.* It is possible.

SOUND.—*Women shriek laughter . . . singing woman begins under laughter . . . antiaircraft explosion under singing woman.*

FIRST WOMAN.—It's an ogre is coming!

SECOND WOMAN.—The devil is after us!

THIRD WOMAN.—Hide in the church from the devil!

FOURTH WOMAN.—I know him. . . .
>I've seen his face in the photographs. Oh, but he's fierce!

SOUND.—*Antiaircraft burst.*

ANNOUNCER.—(*Low and close*) Listen. . . .

SOUND.—*Antiaircraft.*

FIRST WOMAN.—He gets his photograph taken and sent around!

ANNOUNCER.—Antiaircraft.

SOUND.—*Burst.*

SECOND WOMAN.—He gets his photograph made in his belt and his buttons!

SOUND.—*Antiaircraft.*

ANNOUNCER.—We can't see it; we hear it.

SECOND WOMAN.—He gets his photograph made at the big parades!

SOUND.—*Antiaircraft.*

ANNOUNCER.—Wait. There's a burst.

SOUND.—*Antiaircraft.*

ANNOUNCER.—There's another.

FOURTH WOMAN.—He gets his photograph made with his fist stuck out.

ANNOUNCER.—The first was the farther: they're nearing.

FIRST WOMAN.—And his chin stuck out!

SOUND.—*Antiaircraft* (*closer*) *. . . ad lib.*

ANNOUNCER.—Another nearer. . . .

SOUND.—*Antiaircraft.*

ANNOUNCER.—Another. . . .

SOUND.—*Bursts in cadence . . . continue to police whistle.*

SECOND WOMAN.—And his chest stuck out!

541

ANNOUNCER.—They follow each other like footsteps.
The steel stamps on the sky; the
Heel hits.
They hang like
Quills driven in the sky:
The quarry invisible. . . .
nearer . . .

SOUND.—*Police whistle.*

SOUND.—*Fleet of bombers very low* . . . 16 *cycles.*

SERGEANT.—You can hear for yourselves! You will now follow
the orders
To occupy the vaults of village churches;
In any event to descend from upper floors and
Scatter in streets avoiding visible gatherings.

FIRST WOMAN.—They're coming.

SECOND WOMAN.—I hear them.

THIRD WOMAN.—They're nearer.

FIRST GIRL.—(*Frightened*) They're nearer: they're nearer.

FIRST WOMAN.—Ah, they'll go over. There's nothing to fear;
they'll go over.
They always do; they go over. Don't you fear.
Don't you fret. Don't you peer in the air. . . .
They'll go. They will. You'll forget they were
ever by Saturday.

OLD WOMAN.—Dukes; kings; emperors . . . now there's this
kind.
They're all fools . . . the lot of them; always
were;
Marching around with their drums; shooting
their guns off!
Let them step till they stop if it gives them
pleasure.
It's all one to us if they do or they don't.
We needn't crick our necks to watch it. . . .

SOUND.—*Roar of the planes increases in slow, oppressive crescendo
. . . the explosions are no longer heard.*

ANNOUNCER.—We hear them. . . . We can't see them.
We hear the shearing metal.
We hear the tearing air.

542

All we see is sun . . .
Sun: the hawk's ambush . . .
 Their flight is from the sun.
They might be low: they might be
Well down . . . three thousand.
They might be less. . . .
                    They are many:
Hard to guess how many. . . .
We've got them now: we see them:
They're out of the dazzle; they're flying
Fighting formation in column.
Squadron following squadron . . .
Ten . . . fifteen squadrons. . . .
Bombing models, mostly;
Big ones . . . three motors
Not so low as we figured them
Almost over.

SOUND.—*Planes climb into line . . . pitch falls.*

WOMEN'S VOICES.—Look! Look! Look!

ANNOUNCER	FIRST WOMAN
They're changing formation, they're banking.	Look! Look how it turns!
	SECOND WOMAN
The whole flight is banking.	Look how it wheels!
Front wheeling to flank.	THIRD WOMAN
Flank anchored and climbing.	Look at it!
Climbing bank into line . . .	Look at it!
The line swung like a lariat.	FOURTH WOMAN
	Turning and turning.

FIRST WOMAN.—Look! It's circling as a bird does!

SECOND WOMAN.—It circles as a hawk would circle hunting!

THIRD WOMAN.—It's hunting us under the roof: the room: the curtain.

ANNOUNCER	FIRST WOMAN
They're wheeling round for the town.	It won't hurt us!
	SECOND WOMAN
They're rounding in by the river.	It won't touch us!
	THIRD WOMAN
They're giving it throttle, they're climbing.	It won't if it knows!
	FOURTH WOMAN
The timing is perfect, they're flying with	It won't if it sees us!

543

Perfect precision of timing,
Perfect mechanical certainty.

FIRST WOMAN.—Show it our skirts!

SECOND WOMAN.—   Show it out shawls!

THIRD WOMAN.—All of us: into the street, all of us!

ANNOUNCER.—They turn like stones on a string:
They swing like steel in a groove:
They move like tools not men:
You'd say there were no men:
You'd say they had no will but the
Will of motor on metal. . . .

SOUND.—*The roar of the planes increases constantly.*

FIRST WOMAN.—Show it our skirts in the street; it won't hurt us!

SECOND WOMAN.—Show it our softness! Show it our weakness!

THIRD WOMAN.—Show it our womanhood!

FIRST WOMAN.—   Into the street!

SECOND WOMAN.—Into the street all of us!

THIRD WOMAN.—   All of us!

SOUND.—*The pitch of the roar rises sharply . . . vicious . . . sharp.*

ANNOUNCER.—They swing: the wing dips:
There's the signal: the dip; they'll
Dive. They're ready to dive:
They're steady: they're heading down:
They're dead on the town: they're nosing:
They're easing over: they're over.

SOUND.—*Plane dives.*

ANNOUNCER.—There they go: there they . . .

SOUND.—*Machine gun burst.*

FIRST WOMAN.—(*Shrieking*) It's us . . . do you see . . . ?

SOUND.—*Plane dives.*

SECOND WOMAN.—(*Shrieking*) It's us, don't you see us?

SOUND.—*Machine gun burst.*

WOMEN.—(*Shriek*)

SOUND.—*Ominous roar of bombers continues . . . plane dives . . . machine gun bursts . . . plane dives . . . machine gun burst . . . women's shrieks fade under burst . . . ominous roar of planes blends with*

MUSIC.—*Note low . . . throbbing . . . always diminishing.*

FIRST BOY.—(*Voice rises and breaks on each word*) Harry! Harry! Harry!

MUSIC.—*Note continues throbbing . . . fading.*

YOUNG MAN.—(*Close*) Stay as you are: do not move.
Do not ever move. . . .

MUSIC.—*Note continues throbbing. . . . fading . . . singing woman on slow, screaming scale of purest agony, broken in ghastly scream at the highest possible note. The long music note of the planes fades to silence . . . five seconds' silence.*

ANNOUNCER.—You have just heard "Air Raid," an original verse play for radio written by Archibald MacLeish and produced by the Columbia Workshop.

SOUND.—*Bombers . . . faint . . . steady.*

ANNOUNCER.—The Columbia Network, believing that this performance of "Air Raid" should not be lost with the last sounds of the broadcast, has arranged for a recording which will be available shortly in your local record shops. This is the Columbia Broadcasting System.

BEST CLASSIC PLAY ADAPTATION

The Trojan Women

by EURIPIDES

Translated from the original Greek by EDITH HAMILTON

Radio adaptation by HARRY MACFAYDEN

From GREAT PLAYS

GREAT PLAYS is the logical outgrowth of the time-honored Radio Guild of the National Broadcasting Company. For ten years, starting in 1928, this program offered every week a one-hour adaptation of a stage play. It started with the melodramas of the 1870's and 1880's. It approached Shakespeare and during the years gave over seventy one hour adaptations of Shakespearean plays. It dealt with the Greeks, and it came down to contemporary playwrights as its audience and its budget grew. There were one or two things lacking about the old program, however. One was a pattern or arrangement of the plays so that each successive week offered a work that had some special reason for being chosen for broadcasting in that week. Another was the crying need for informing that large but widely separated audience for plays of this nature that they were on the air and were available.

Mr. Blevins Davis, who came from the Yale School of Drama, has done yoeman work in preparing study manuals giving background material which were available in advance of the broadcasts of the second year. These manuals are prepared well before the broadcasts, and thousands of them have been purchased by colleges, schools, and libraries so that classes and listening groups may know in advance something about the play and its author and thereby enhance their listening pleasure when the broadcast is actually given.

The wide experience of those members of the program department who for years had been concerned with the choice and broadcasting of the old Radio Guild series was available to sift the suggestions of Mr. Davis for plays to be included in the Great Plays series, and, as a result, in the first season a wide sweep was made from the days of the Greek drama down through to a final play of the season by Maxwell Anderson that gave point to the studying of the theatre as a living force over two thousand years.

The response to the series was electric, and the number of stations carrying it in its second year was greatly increased in spite of the fact that the only available hour proved to be from 1:00 to 2:00 P.M. EST on Sundays, which meant that it was heard on the West coast at 10:00 A.M.

The temptation arose, of course, not to repeat any of the plays of the previous season, but the pitfall of putting in another play just for the sake of being different was warily avoided, and the second season did, as a matter of fact, include certain offerings that had been heard the year before, and this repetition turned out in no way to detract from the strength of the dramatic season.

The third season is already organized, and again plays heard in previous seasons will be broadcast, but whereas in the first year one Greek play, "The Birds," of Aristophanes, was offered and in the second, a single Greek play, "The Trojan Women," of Euripides, the third year will offer "The Antigone" and "The Alcestis," both in modern translations made by Fitts and Fitzgerald.

The particular play printed in this volume opened the second year. In it Miss Blanche Yurka gave a heartrendingly powerful performance as Hecuba, so much so that this, the greatest and oldest of plays on behalf of peace, reduced many members of the orchestra to tears and shook the conductor, members of the cast, and Mr. Burns Mantle, the veteran critic.

The function of the commentator in this series has been not so much to describe action or transition of scene but where possible to explain to the listening audience the social, economic, and political background of the times in which the play was written—not for stuffy, pedagogical reasons

547

but in order that the contemporary listening audience may identify themselves to some degree with those audiences of the past to whom these Great Plays first came in all their newly born power and beauty.

Mr. Harry MacFayden, who made the adaptation, is a veteran producer of the legitimate stage who has been in radio for many years. His wide practical familiarity with dramatic literature and the staging of plays that have survived the test of time made him peculiarly fitted to direct the production of "The Trojan Women."

The use of a chorus in the radio version of "The Trojan Women" raised peculiar problems. It was retained, and the result of the production seemed to justify its retention because, whereas the action and theme of the play is carried forward rapidly and unerringly by the characters partaking in it, there come times when the emotional tension would be too great were there not given to the audience a pause in which the generalizations of the chorus in its impersonal meditation on the power of the unfolding tragedy broke the rhythm and tempered the strength of the play to the capacity of the listener to bear it.

Edith Hamilton did the translation from which the radio adaptation was derived. She is known on three continents as one of the great educators and scholars of our day. She was the first woman ever admitted to the University of Munich. *Fortune* magazine, in an article on schools of today, referred to Miss Hamilton as an educational "comet." She is the author of "The Greek Way," "The Roman Way," and "The Prophets of Israel." Her translation of the Prometheus of Aeschylus was produced in New York in 1930. Her translation of the play we are now to read— "The Trojan Women"—was given by the American Actors' Association in New York in 1938 and by the Federal Theatre at the Golden Gate International Exposition in San Francisco in 1939.

The broadcast took place on October 16, 1938, and was carried by fifty-four stations of the Blue Network.

The Trojan Women[*]

ANNOUNCER.—Great Plays!

MUSIC.—*Fanfare of trumpets . . . majestic music in overture during following announcement.*

ANNOUNCER.—The National Broadcasting Company presents Great Plays—a series of famous plays selected to show the development of drama from the sunrise performances in ancient Athens down to the contemporary theatre. Mr. Burns Mantle, dean of American drama critics and known throughout the country for his yearly volume of Broadway's best plays, will act as commentator at today's production of "The Trojan Women," by Euripides. Mr. Burns Mantle.

MR. BURNS MANTLE.—The first production in the Great Plays series which the National Broadcasting Company will present is "The Trojan Women," by Euripides, translated into the modern idiom by Miss Edith Hamilton, who declares that even though this play was written 2,350 years ago it remains "the greatest piece of anti-war literature there is in the world. Nothing since, no description or denunciation of war's terrors and futilities, ranks with 'The Trojan Women,' which was put upon the Athenian stage by Euripides in 416 B.C." On this afternoon's broadcast you will hear Miss Blanche Yurka, distinguished for her portrayal of classic roles, who will appear as Hecuba in "The Trojan Women."

So we ask you to come with us to ancient Athens and attend a *première* of this great play. As quick as thought we eliminate the centuries and invite you to be seated in the Theatre of Dionysus, in Athens, 416 years before the birth of Christ.

MUSIC.—*A swift cadenza suggestive of flight through time and space. . . . effect of huge throngs of people in stadium . . . fade for noises of the time.*

MANTLE.—A holiday spirit has settled over Athens. It is late in the afternoon, and the warm March sunshine blends with the revelry of these pleasure-mad Athenians assembled here for the plays produced at the annual religious festival in honor of the wine god, Dionysus. . . . Whole families anticipate this afternoon's performance of "The Trojan Women." Business is suspended; the law decrees that debts may not be collected during the festival season when thousands of visitors are here in Athens. . . . Strange to relate, prisoners, released temporarily from jail, are seated here with their guards. The stone seats rise in a great semi-circle from the open space on the ground level, called the orchestra. In the center of the orchestra is an altar erected to the god, Dionysus. Every available seat is now occupied, and those who could not afford to pay the entrance fee have been admitted as guests of the state. At this moment the leading actors and members of the chorus are entering the orchestra level from the scene building which forms a background for the action of the play.

The scene is a space of waste ground, except for a few huts right and left where the captive Trojan women selected for the victorious Greek soldiers are housed. After a long war the Greeks have taken Troy by storm. The women are held captive, their husbands are dead, their children taken from them, and they are waiting to be shipped off to slavery. Far in the background Troy, the wall in ruins, is slowly burning. In front, near the audience, an aged woman, Hecuba, the Trojan Queen, lies prostrate on the ground, grieving for the King, her husband, who was cut down before her eyes in their home as he clung to the altar; her sons, too, are dead, and she, a queen, is to be a slave to the conquerors. The day begins to dawn. . . . Hecuba, Queen of the Trojans, makes a feeble attempt to rise. . . .

MUSIC.—*Up and fade.*

HECUBA.—Up from the ground . . . O weary head, O breaking neck,
This is no longer Troy. And we are not the lords of Troy.
Endure. The ways of fate are the ways of the wind.
Drift with the stream . . . drift with fate.
Sorrow, my sorrow.
What sorrow is there that is not mine,
grief to weep for?

550

Country lost and children and husband.
Glory of all my house brought low.

(*She begins to get up*)
Oh, this aching body . . . this bed. . . .
It is very hard. My back pressed to it . . .
Up! Quick, quick. I must move.
Oh, I'll rock myself this way, that way,
to the sound of weeping, the song of tears,
dropping down forever.

O ships, O prows, swift oars,
out from the fair Greek bays and harbors
over the dark, shining sea,
you found your way to our holy city,
and the fearful music of war was heard,
the war song sung to flute and pipe
as you cast on the shore your cables.
Who am I that I wait
here at a Greek king's door?
A slave that men drive on,
an old gray woman that has no home.
O wives of the bronze-armored men who fought,
and maidens, sorrowing maidens,
plighted to shame,
see . . . only smoke left where was Troy.
Let us weep for her.
As a mother bird cries to her feathered brood,
so will I cry.

MUSIC.

MANTLE.—The door of one of the huts opens, and a woman steals
out, then another, and another.

WOMAN 1.—Your cry, O Hecuba . . . oh, such a cry . . .
What does it mean? There in the tent
we heard you call so piteously,
and through our hearts flashed fear.
In the tent we were weeping, too,
for we are slaves.

HECUBA.—Look, child, there where the Greek ships lie. . . .

WOMAN 2.—They are moving. The men hold oars.

WOMAN 3.—O God, what will they do? Carry me off
over the sea in a ship far from home?

HECUBA.—You ask, and I know nothing,
    but I think that ruin is here.

WOMAN 4.—Oh, we are wretched. We shall hear the summons.
    Women of Troy, go forth from your home,
    for the Greeks set sail.

HECUBA.—But not Cassandra, oh, not her.
    She is mad. . . . She has been driven mad. Leave her within,
    O Troy, unhappy Troy, you are gone,
    and we, the unhappy, leave you,
    we who are living and we who are dead.
    (*More women now come out from a second hut*)

WOMAN 5.—(*Trembling*)
    Out of the Greek king's tent,
    trembling I come, O Queen,
    to hear my fate from you.
    Not death. . . . They would not think of death
    for a poor woman.

WOMAN 2.—The sailors . . . they are standing on the prow.
    Already they are running out the oars.

WOMAN 6.—(*She comes out of a third hut, and several follow her*)
    It is so early . . . but a terror woke me.
    My heart beats so.

WOMAN 7.—(*Inquisitive*)
    Has a herald come from the Greek camp?
    Whose slave shall I be?

HECUBA.—Wait for the lot drawing. It is near.

WOMAN 7.—(*Inquisitive*)
    Argos shall it be, or Phthia?
    or an island of the sea?

HECUBA.—I watch a master's door?
    I nurse his children?
    Once I was Queen in Troy.

WOMAN 4.—Poor thing. What are your tears
    to the shame before you?

WOMAN 2.—The shuttle will still pass through my hands,
    but the loom will not be in Troy.

WOMAN 8.—My dead sons. I would look at them once more.
Never again.

SOUND.—*Approaching soldiers marching . . . confusion of voices.*

WOMAN 2.—(*Strong*)
Oh, look. A man from the Greek army . . .
A herald. Something strange has happened,
he comes so fast. To tell us . . . what?
What will he say? Only Greek slaves are here,
Waiting for orders.

SOUND.—*Soldiers stopping. Enter Talthybius, with soldiers.*

TALTHYBIUS.—You know me, Hecuba, I have often come
with messages to Troy from the Greek camp.
I am Talthybius. . . . These many years you've
known me.
I bring you news.

HECUBA.—It has come, women of Troy. Once we only feared it.

TALTHYBIUS.—The lots are drawn, if that is what you feared.

HECUBA.—Who . . . where? Thessaly? Phthia? Thebes?

TALTHYBIUS.—A different man takes each. You're not to go
together.

HECUBA.—Then which takes which? Has anyone good fortune?

TALTHYBIUS.—I know, but ask about each one, not all at once.

HECUBA.—My daughter, Cassandra . . . who drew her? Tell
me. . . .

TALTHYBIUS.—King Agamemnon chose her out from all.

HECUBA.—Oh! but . . . of course . . . to serve his Spartan
wife.

TALTHYBIUS.—No, no . . . but for the king's own bed at night.

HECUBA.—Oh, never. She is God's, a virgin, always.
That was God's gift to her for all her life.

TALTHYBIUS.—He loved her for that same strange purity.

HECUBA.—My other child you took from me just now?

TALTHYBIUS.—(*Speaking with constraint*)
Polyxena, you mean? Or someone else?

HECUBA.—Yes, Polyxena. Who drew her?

TALTHYBIUS.—They told her off to watch Achilles' tomb.

HECUBA.—To watch a tomb? My daughter?
That a Greek custom?
What strange ritual is that, my friend?

TALTHYBIUS.—(*Speaking fast and trying to put her off*)
Just think of her as happy . . . all well with her.

HECUBA.—Those words . . . Why do you speak like that?
She is alive?

TALTHYBIUS.—(*Determined not to tell her*)
What happened was . . . well, she is free from
trouble.

HECUBA.—(*Wearily giving the riddle up*)
Then Hector's wife . . . Andromache . . .
Where does she go, poor thing?

TALTHYBIUS.—Achilles' son took her. He chose her out.

HECUBA.—And I, old gray head, whose slave am I,
creeping along with my crutch?

TALTHYBIUS.—Slave of the King of Ithaca, Odysseus.

HECUBA.—His slave . . . vile, lying man. I have come to
this. . . .
There is nothing good he does not hurt . . . a lawless
beast,
A double tongue, as false in hate as false in love.
Pity me, women of Troy,
I have gone. I am lost . . . oh, wretched.
An evil fate fell on me,
a lot the hardest of all.

WOMAN 7.—You know what lies before you, Queen, but I . . .
What man among the Greeks owns me?

TALTHYBIUS.—Soldiers, attention! Bring Cassandra here. Be
quick!

MUSIC.—*Of harp.*

TALTHYBIUS.—You, fellows. We must give her to the chief,
into his very hand. And then these women here
to all the other generals. But what's that . . .
that flash of light there?

(*Light shines through the crevices of one of the huts*)
>   Set fire to the huts . . . is that their plan,
>   these Trojan women? Burn themselves to death
>   rather than sail to Greece. Choosing to die instead.
>   Open there, open the door.

HECUBA.—No, no, there is nothing burning. It is my daughter,
Cassandra. She is mad.

MUSIC.—*Up.*

MANTLE.—Cassandra enters from the hut dressed like a priestess,
a wreath in her hair, a torch in her hand. She does not
seem to see anyone.

CASSANDRA.—Lift it high . . . in my hand . . . light to bring.
>   I praise him. I bear a flame.
>   With my torch I touch to fire
>   this holy place.
>   Hymen, O Hymen.
>   Blessed the bridegroom,
>   blessed am I. . . .
>   Hymen, O Hymen.
>   Mother, you weep
>   tears for my father dead,
>   mourning for the beloved
>   country lost.
>   I for my bridal here
>   lift up the fire's flame
>   to the dawn, to the splendor,
>   to you, O Hymen.
>   Fly, dancing feet.
>   Up with the dance.
>   Oh, joy, oh, joy!
>   Dance for my father dead.
>   Dance, mother, come.
>   Keep step with me.
>   Sing to the marriage god,
>   oh, joyful song.
(*She dances on*)

WOMAN 2.—Hold her fast, Queen, poor frenzied girl.
>   She might rush straight to the Greek camp.

HECUBA.—Daughter, give me your torch. You do not hold it
straight.

You move so wildly. Your sufferings, my child,
have never taught you wisdom.
You never change. Here! Someone take the torch
into the hut. This marriage needs no songs
but only tears.

CASSANDRA.—O mother, crown my triumph with a wreath.
    Be glad, for I am married to a king.
    Send me to him, and if I shrink away,
    drive me with violence. If Apollo lives,
    my marriage shall be bloodier than Helen's.
    Agamemnon, the great, the glorious lord of
    Greece . . .
    I shall kill him, mother, lay his house as low
    as he laid ours, make him pay for all
    he made my father suffer, brothers, and . . .
    All, all because he married me and so
    pulled his own house down.
    But I will show you. This town now, yes, mother,
    is happier than the Greeks. I know that I am mad,
    but, mother, dearest, now, for this one time
    I do not rave.
    One woman they came hunting, and one love,
    Helen, and men by tens of thousands died.
    No man had moved their landmarks
    or laid siege to their high-walled towns.
    But those whom war took never saw their children.
    No wife with gentle hands shrouded them for their
    grave.
    They lie in a strange land. And in their homes
    are sorrows, too, the very same.
    That was the glorious victory they won.
    Lonely women who died, old men who waited for
    sons that never came . . .
    But we . . . we Trojans died to save our people;
    no glory greater. All those the spear slew,
    friends bore them home and wrapped them in their
    shroud
    with dutiful hands. The earth of their own land
    covered them. The rest, through the long days they
    fought,
    had wife and child at hand, not like the Greeks,
    whose joys were far away.
    This truth stands firm: the wise will fly from war.

But if war comes, to die well is to win
the victor's crown.
The only shame is not to die like that.
So, mother, do not pity Troy,
or me upon my bridal bed.

TALTHYBIUS.—(*Has been held awe-struck through all this but can
bear no more*)
Now if Apollo had not made you mad
I would have paid you for those evil words.
(*Grumbles to himself*)
The great, who seem so wise, have no more sense
than those who rank as nothing.
Our king, the first in Greece, bows down
before this mad girl, loves her, chooses her
out of them all.
(*Turns to Cassandra*)
You know your mind is not quite right.
So all you said against Greece and for Troy
I never heard. . . . The wind blew it away.
Come with me to the ship now.
(*To Hecuba*) And you, do follow quietly
when Odysseus' soldiers come.

CASSANDRA.—(*Seeming to see Talthybius for the first time and look-
ing him over haughtily*)
A strange sort of a slave, surely. . . .
Come, let us hasten to my marriage.
Where is the ship? How do I go on board?
Spread the sail. . . . The wind comes swift.
Those who bring vengeance . . . three are they,
And one of them goes with you on the sea.
Mother, my mother, do not weep. Farewell,
dear city. Brothers, in Troy's earth laid, my father,
a little time and I am with you.
You dead, I shall come to you a victor.
Those ruined by my hand who ruined us.

MANTLE.—Cassandra goes out with Talthybius and the soldiers.
Hecuba, motionless for a moment, falls to the ground.

WOMAN 3.—The Queen! See . . . see . . . she is falling.
Oh, help! She cannot speak.
Miserable slaves, will you leave her on the ground,
old as she is? Up . . . lift her up.

HECUBA.—Let me be.
　　　　I cannot stand. Too much is on me.
　　　　O God . . . do I call to you? You did not help.
　　　　Yet there is something that cries out for God
　　　　when trouble comes.
　　　　Oh, I will think of good days gone,
　　　　days to make a song of,
　　　　crowning my sorrow by remembering.
　　　　We were kings, and a king I married.
　　　　Sons I bore him, many sons.
　　　　They were the best in all Troy.
　　　　No woman, Trojan, Greek, or stranger,
　　　　had sons like mine to be proud of.
　　　　I saw them fall beneath Greek spears.
　　　　Their father . . .
　　　　I, my own self, saw him fall murdered
　　　　upon the altar when his town was lost.
　　　　My daughters, maidens reared to marry kings,
　　　　are torn from me.
　　　　All gone . . . no hope that I shall look upon
　　　　their faces any more, or they on mine.
　　　　And now the end . . . no more can lie beyond . . .
　　　　an old, gray slave woman, I go to Greece. . . .
　　　　I who bore Hector . . .
　　　　on the ground lay this old body down that once
　　　　slept in a royal bed; torn rags around me,
　　　　torn flesh beneath.
　　　　No son, no daughter, left to help my need,
　　　　and I had many, many. . . .
　　　　Why lift me up? What hope is there to hold to?

MUSIC.—*Up.*

MANTLE.—The chorus now in measured step encircle the altar
　　　　and relate how the Greek soldiers hid inside a great
　　　　wooden horse; how the Trojans believed it was a gift
　　　　for the goddess, Athena, and opened the walls of
　　　　their city and drew the horse in triumph through the
　　　　streets; and how, when darkness fell, the Greek
　　　　soldiers, hiding in the huge wooden image, came forth
　　　　and captured the city.

MUSIC.—*Up and down and background with vocal . . . iambic
　　　　beat.*

CHORUS.—Sing me, O Muse, a song for Troy,
    a strange song sung to tears,
    a music for the grave.
    Oh, lips, sound forth a melody
    for Troy.

WOMAN 3.—A four-wheeled cart brought the horse to the gates,
    brought ruin to me,
    captured, enslaved me.

WOMAN 4.—Gold was the rein and the bridle,
    deadly the arms within,
    and they clashed loud to heaven as the threshold
    was passed.

WOMAN 5.—High on Troy's rock the people cried,
    "Rest at last, trouble ended.
    Bring the carven image in.
    Bear it to Athena,
    fit gift for the child of God."

WOMAN 6.—Who of the young but hurried forth?
    Who of the old would stay at home?
    With song and rejoicing they brought death in,
    treachery and destruction.

WOMAN 7.—All that were in Troy,
    hastening to the gate,
    drew that smooth-planed horse of wood
    carven from a mountain pine,
    where the Greeks were hiding,
    where was Troy's destruction,
    gave it to the goddess,
    gift for her, the virgin,
    driver of the steeds that never die.

WOMAN 8.—With ropes of twisted flax,
    as a ship's dark hull is drawn to land,
    they brought it to her temple of stone,
    to her floor that soon would run with blood,
    to Pallas Athena.

WOMAN 2.—On their toil and their joy
    the dark of evening fell,
    but the lutes of Egypt still rang out
    to the songs of Troy.

WOMAN 1.—And girls with feet light as air,
    dancing, sang happy songs.
    The houses blazed with light
    through the dark splendor,
    and sleep was not.

MUSIC.—*Iambic beat music ends.*

GIRL.—(*A dancer*)
    I was among the dancers
    I was singing to the maiden of Zeus,
    the goddess of the hills.
    A shout rang out in the town,
    a cry of blood through the houses.
    And a frightened child caught his mother's skirt
    And hid himself in her cloak.
    Then War came forth from his hiding place.
    Athena, the virgin, devised it.
    Around the altars they slaughtered us
    Within on their beds lay headless men,
    young men cut down in their prime.
    This was the triumph crown of Greece.
    We shall bear children for her to rear,
    grief and shame to our country.

SOUND.—*Chariot approaches and stops.*

MANTLE.—A chariot approaches, loaded with spoils. In it sits
    Andromache, widow of Hector. . . . She is holding
    her son Astyanax in her arms.

MUSIC.—*Somber, emotional music background.*

WOMAN 3.—Look, Hecuba, it is Andromache.
    See, in the Greek car yonder.
    Her breast heaves with her sobs, and yet
    the baby sleeps there, dear Astyanax,
    the son of Hector.

WOMAN 8.—Most sorrowful of women, where do you go?
    Beside you the bronze armor that was Hector's,
    the spoil of the Greek spear, stripped from the dead.
    Will Achilles' son use it to deck his temples?

ANDROMACHE.—I go where my Greek masters take me.

HECUBA.—Oh, our sorrow . . . our sorrow.

ANDROMACHE.—Why should you weep? This sorrow is mine.

HECUBA.—O God . . .

ANDROMACHE.—What has come to me is mine.

HECUBA.—My children . . .

ANDROMACHE.—Once we lived, not now.

HECUBA.—Gone . . . gone . . . happiness . . . Troy. . . .

ANDROMACHE.—And you bear it.

HECUBA.—Sons, noble sons, all lost.

ANDROMACHE.—Oh, sorrow is here.

HECUBA.—For me . . . for me.

ANDROMACHE.—For the city, in its shroud of smoke.
        Come to me, O my husband.

HECUBA.—What you cry to lies in the grave.
        My son, wretched woman, mine.
        O country, desolate, empty.

ANDROMACHE.—My tears fall for you.

HECUBA.—Look and see the end. . . .

ANDROMACHE.—Of the house where I bore my children.

HECUBA.—O children, your mother has lost her city,
        and you . . . you have left her alone.
        Only grief is mine and mourning.
        The dead . . . they have forgotten their pain.
        They weep no more.

ANDROMACHE.—Mother of him whose spear of old brought death
        to Greeks unnumbered, you see what is here.

HECUBA.—I see God's hand that casts the mighty down
        and sets on high the lowly.

ANDROMACHE.—Driven like cattle captured in a raid,
        my child and I . . . the free changed to a slave.
        Oh, changed indeed.

HECUBA.—It is fearful to be helpless. Men just now
        have taken Cassandra . . . forced her from me.

ANDROMACHE.—And still more for you . . . more than that.
    . . .

HECUBA.—Number my sorrows, will you? Measure them?
          One comes. . . . The next one rivals it.

ANDROMACHE.—Polyxena lies dead upon Achilles' tomb,
          a gift to a corpse, to a lifeless thing.

HECUBA.—My sorrow! That is what Talthybius meant. . . .
          I could not read his riddle. Oh, too plain.

ANDROMACHE.—I saw her there and left the chariot
          and covered her dead body with my cloak
          and beat my breast.

HECUBA.—Murdered . . . my child. Oh, wickedly!
          Again I cry to you. Oh, cruelly slain!

ANDROMACHE.—She has died her death, and happier by far
          dying than I alive.

HECUBA.—Life cannot be what death is, child.
          Death is empty. . . . Life has hope.

ANDROMACHE.—Mother, O mother, hear a truer word.
          Now let me bring joy to your heart.
          I say to die is only not to be,
          and rather death than life with bitter grief.
          They have no pain, they do not feel their wrongs.
          She is dead, your daughter. . . .
          She does not know the wickedness that killed her.
          While I shall be a slave to those who murdered
          . . .
          O Hector, my beloved, you were all to me,
          wise, noble, mighty, in wealth, in manhood, both.
          And you are dead, and I, with other plunder,
          am sent by sea to Greece. A slave's yoke there.
          Your dead Polyxena you weep for.
          What does she know of suffering like mine?

WOMAN 3.—We stand at the same point of pain. You mourn your
          ruin,
          and in your words I hear my own calamity.

HECUBA.—O dear child, now let Hector be,
          and let be what has come to him.
          Your tears will never call him back.

Give honor now to him who is your master.
Your sweet ways . . . use them to allure him.
So doing you will give cheer to your friends.
Perhaps this child, my own child's son,
you may rear to manhood and great aid for Troy,
and if ever you should have more children,
they might build her again. Troy once more be a city!
—But why again that servant of the Greeks?

SOUND.—*Approaching soldiers.*

HECUBA.—I see him coming. Some new plan is here.

TALTHYBIUS.—Wife of the noblest man that was in Troy,
O wife of Hector, do not hate me.
Against my will I come to tell you.
The people and the kings have all resolved . . .

ANDROMACHE.—What is it? Evil follows words like those.

TALTHYBIUS.—This child they order . . . Oh, how can I say it.
. . .

ANDROMACHE.—Not that he does not go with me to the same
master? . . .

TALTHYBIUS.—No man in Greece shall ever be his master.

ANDROMACHE.—But . . . leave him here . . . all that is left of
Troy?

TALTHYBIUS.—I don't know how to tell you. What is bad,
words can't make better. . . .

ANDROMACHE.—I feel you kind. But you have not good news.

TALTHYBIUS.—Your child must die. There, now you know
the whole, bad as it is.
It was Odysseus had his way. He spoke
to all the Greeks.

ANDROMACHE.—O God. There is no measure to my pain.

TALTHYBIUS.—He said a hero's son must not grow up . . .
but from the towering wall of Troy be thrown.
Now, now . . . let it be done. . . . That's wiser.
Don't cling so to him. Bear your pain
the way a brave woman suffers.

563

You have no strength. . . . Don't look to any
help.
There's no help for you anywhere. Think . . .
think.
The city gone . . . your husband too. And you,
a captive and alone, one woman. . . . How
can you do battle with us?
For your own good
I would not have you try, and draw
hatred down on you and be shamed.

ANDROMACHE.—Go die, my best beloved, my own, my treasure.
in cruel hands, leaving your mother comfortless.
Your father was too noble. That is why
they kill you. He could save others.
He could not save you for his nobleness.
Weeping, my little one? There, there.
You cannot know what waits for you.
Why hold me with your hands so fast, cling so
fast to me?
You little bird, flying to hide beneath my wings.
And Hector will not come . . . he will not
come
up from the tomb, great spear in hand, to save
you.
Not one of all his kin, of all the Trojan might.
You little thing
curled in my arms, you dearest to your mother,
how sweet the fragrance of you.
Kiss me. . . . Never again. Come closer, closer..
Your mother who bore you . . . put your arms
around my neck.
Now kiss me, lips to lips.
O Greeks, you have found out ways to torture
that are not Greek.
A little child, all innocent of wrong,
you wish to kill him.
Quick! take him . . . seize him . . . cast him
down . . .
if so you will. Feast on his flesh.
God has destroyed me, and I cannot,
I cannot save my child from death.
Oh, hide my head for shame and fling me
into the ship.

(*She falls, then struggles to her knees*)
      I am coming.
      Oh, I have lost my child, my own.

TALTHYBIUS.—(*Drawing the child away*)
      Come boy, let go. Unclasp those loving hands,
      poor mother.
      Come now, up, boy, up, to the very height,
      where the towers of your fathers crown the wall
      and where it is decreed that you must die.
(*To the soldier*)
      Take him away.
      A herald who must bring such orders
      should be a man who feels no pity,
      and no shame either, not like me.

HECUBA.—Child, son of my poor son, whose toil was all in vain,
      we are robbed, your mother and I, oh cruelly,
      robbed of your life.
      What can I do for you, poor piteous child?
      Troy lost, now you, all lost.
      My cup is full. Why wait? For what?
      Hasten on, swiftly on to death. . . .

MANTLE.—The soldiers, who have waited while Hecuba speaks,
      go out with the child and Talthybius. One of them
      takes Andromache to the chariot and drives off with
      her.

SOUND.—*Chariot drives off. The chorus again lament the fall of
Troy, calling to mind the glories of the city's past . . .
IAMBIC BEAT.*

CHORUS.—The shores of the sea are wailing for Troy.
      As a bird cries over her young,
      women weep for husbands, for children,
      for the old too who gave them birth.
      While Priam's land
      lies ruined by Greek spearmen.
      Hope was high once over our town,
      but the magic that brought her the love of the gods
      has gone from Troy. . . .

MANTLE.—The chorus ends, and Menelaus, husband of the
      beautiful Helen, enters with a bodyguard of soldiers.

SOUND.—*Fanfare and soldiers.*

MANTLE.—He bears vengeance in his heart because his wife
deserted his home in Greece and fled with the Trojan
prince, Paris.

MENELAUS.—How bright the sunlight is today . . .
this day, when I shall get into my power,
Helen, my wife. For I am Menelaus,
the man of many wrongs.
I came to Troy and brought with me my army,
not for that woman's sake, as people say,
but for the man who from my house,
and he a guest there, stole away my wife.
Ah, well, with God's help he has paid the price,
he and his country, fallen beneath Greek spears.
I am come to get her . . . wretch. I cannot
speak her name
who was my wife once.
In a hut here, where they house the captives,
she is numbered with the other Trojan women.
The men who fought and toiled to win her back
have given her to me, to kill, or else,
if it pleases me, to take her back to Argos.
And it has seemed to me her death in Troy
is not the way. I will take her overseas,
with swift oars speeding on the ship,
and there in Greece give her to those to kill
whose dearest died because of her.
(*To his men*)
Attention! Forward to the huts.
Seize her and drag her out by that long blood-
drenched hair. . . .
(*Stops suddenly and controls himself*)
And when fair winds come, home with her to Greece.

SOUND.—*Soldiers begin to force the door of one of the huts; confusion
among the women.*

HECUBA.—Kill her, Menelaus? You will? Oh, blessings on you!
But . . . shun her, do not look at her.
Desire for her will seize you, conquer you.
For through men's eyes she gets them in her power.
She ruins them and ruins cities, too.
A flame comes from her to set on fire homes,
magic for death. I know her, so do you
and all these who have suffered.

566

MUSIC.

HELEN.—(*Enters with sweet, injured dignity*)
  Menelaus, these things might well make a woman fear.
  Your men with violence have driven me from my room,
  have laid their hands upon me.
  Of course I know . . . almost I know . . . you hate me,
  but yet I ask you, what is your decision,
  yours and the Greeks? Am I to live or not?

MENELAUS.—Nothing more clear. Unanimous, in fact.
  Not one who did not vote you should be given me,
  whom you have wronged, to kill.

HELEN.—Am I allowed to speak against the charge?
  To show you if I die that I shall die
  most wronged and innocent?

MENELAUS.—I have come to kill you, not to argue with you.

HECUBA.—Oh, hear her. She must never die unheard.
  Then, Menelaus, let me answer her.
  The evil that she did in Troy you do not know.
  But I will tell the story. She will die.
  She never can escape.

MENELAUS.—That means delay. Still if she wants to speak,
  she can. I grant her this because of what you say,
  not for her sake. She can be sure of that.

HELEN.—And perhaps no matter if you think I speak
  the truth or not, you will not talk to me,
  since you believe I am your enemy.
  Still, I will try to answer what I think
  you would say if you spoke your mind,
  and my wrongs shall be heard as well as yours.
  Listen and learn.
  This Paris, he was made the judge for three,
  all yoked together in a quarrel, goddesses.
  Athena promised he should lead the Trojans
  to victory and lay all Greece in ruins.
  And Hera said if he thought her the fairest
  she would make him lord of Europe and of Asia.
  But Aphrodite . . . well, she praised my beauty . . .
  astonishing, she said, and promised Paris

that she would give me to him if he judged
that she was loveliest. Then, see what happened.
Aphrodite won, and so my bridal brought
all Greece great good. No strangers rule you,
no foreign spears, no tyrant.
Oh, it was well for Greece, but not for me,
sold for my beauty and reproached besides
when I deserved a crown.
But . . . to the point. Is that what you are thinking?
Why did I go, steal from your house in secret?
That man, Paris, or any name you like to call him,
Oh, when he came to me, she, Aphrodite,
the mighty goddess, walked beside him.
And you, poor fool, you spread your sails for Crete,
left Sparta, left him in your house.
Ah, well. . . . Not you but my own self I ask,
what was there in my heart that I went with him,
a strange man, and forgot my home and country?
Not I, but Aphrodite. Punish her.
She is my absolution. . . .
When Paris died and went down to the grave
I should have left his house . . . gone to the Greeks.
Just what I tried to do . . . oh, many times.
I have witnesses . . . the men who kept the gates,
the watchmen on the walls. Not once but often
they found me swinging from a parapet,
a rope around this body, stealthily
feeling my way down.
The Trojans then no longer wanted me,
but the next man who took me . . . and by force . . .
would never let me go.
My husband, must I die, and at your hands?
You think that right? Is that your justice?
I was forced . . . by violence. I lived a life
that had no joy, no triumph. In bitterness
I lived a slave.
Do you wish to set yourself above the gods?
Oh, stupid, senseless wish!

WOMAN 3.—O Queen, defend your children and your country.
    Her soft persuasive words are deadly.
    She speaks so fair and is so vile.
    A fearful thing.

HECUBA.—Her goddesses will fight on my side while
I show her for the liar that she is.
Never make gods out fools to whitewash your own
evil.
No one with sense will listen to you.
My son was beautiful exceedingly.
You saw him . . . your own desire was enough.
It was my son. You saw him in his Eastern dress
all bright with gold, and you were mad with love.
Your luxuries, your insolent excesses,
Menelaus' halls had grown too small for them.
Enough of that. By force you say he took you?
You cried out? Where? No one in Sparta heard you.
And when you came to Troy and on your track the
Greeks,
and death and agony in battle,
if they would tell you, "Greece has won today,"
you would praise this man here, Menelaus,
to vex my son, who feared him as a rival.
Then Troy had victories, and Menelaus
was nothing to you.
Looking to the successful side . . . oh, yes,
you always followed there.
There was no right or wrong side in your eyes.
And now you talk of ropes . . . letting your body
down
in secret from the wall, longing to go.
Who found you so?
Was there a noose around your neck?
A sharp knife in your hand? Such ways
as any honest woman would have found,
who loved the husband she had lost?
Often and often I would tell you, Go,
my daughter. My sons will find them other wives.
I will help you. I will send you past the lines
to the Greek ships. Oh, end this war
between our foes and us. But this was bitter to you.
In Paris' house you had your insolent way.
You liked to see the Eastern men fall at your feet.
These were great things to you.
Look at the dress you wear, your ornaments.
Is that the way to meet your husband?
You should not dare to breathe the same air with him.

569

Oh, men should spit upon you.
Humbly, in rags, trembling and shivering,
so you should come,
with shame at last, instead of shamelessness,
for all the wickedness you did.
King, one word more and I am done.
Give Greece a crown, be worthy of yourself.
Kill her. So shall the law stand for all women,
that she who plays false to her husband's bed
shall die.

WOMAN 2.—O son of an ancient house, O King, now show
that you are worthy of your fathers.
Be strong. Be noble. Punish her.

MENELAUS.—(*Impatiently*)
I see it all as you do. We agree.
She left my house because she wanted to.
Her talk of Aphrodite . . .
big words, no more.
(*Turns to Helen*)
Go! Death is near.
Men there are waiting for you. In their hands are
stones!
Die . . . A small price for the Greeks' long suffering
You shall not any more dishonor me.

HELEN.—(*Kneeling and clinging to him*)
No! No! Upon my knees . . . see, I am praying to you.
It was the gods, not me. Oh, do not kill me.
Forgive.

HECUBA.—The men she murdered. Think of those
Who fought beside you . . . of their children, too.
Never betray them. Hear that prayer.

MENELAUS.—(*Roughly*)
Enough, old woman. She is nothing to me.
Men, take her to the ships and keep her safe until
she sails.

HECUBA.—But not with you! She must not set foot on your ship.

MENELAUS.—(*Bitterly*)
And why? Her weight too heavy for it?

HECUBA.—A lover once, a lover always.

MENELAUS.—(*Pauses a moment to think*)
> Not so when what he loved has gone.
> But it shall be as you would have it.
> Not on the same ship with me. The advice is good.
> And when she gets to Argos she shall die,
> a death hard as her heart.
> So in the end she will become a teacher,
> teach women chastity . . . no easy thing,
> but yet her utter ruin will strike terror
> into their silly hearts,
> even women worse than she.

MUSIC.—*Bring in magic.*

CHORUS.—(*In unison*)
> The sacrifice is gone, and the glad call
> of dancers, and the prayers at evening to the gods
> that last the whole night long.
> My city is perishing,
> ending in fire and onrushing flame.

WOMAN 2.—O dear one, O my husband,
> you are dead, and you wander
> unburied, uncared for, while overseas
> the ships shall carry me.

WOMAN 8.—Children, our children,
> At the gate they are crying, crying,
> calling to us with tears,
> "Mother, I am all alone.
> They are driving me away
> to a black ship, and I cannot see you."

WOMAN 3.—Oh, if only, far out to sea,
> the crashing thunder of God
> would fall down, down on Menelaus' ship.

MUSIC.—*Stops . . . soldiers enter.*

MANTLE.—Talthybius approaches with a few soldiers. He is
> carrying the dead boy, Astyanax. . . . He gives the
> lifeless form to Hecuba.

WOMAN 8.—Look, unhappy wives of Troy,
> the dead Astyanax.
> They threw him from the tower as one might pitch a
> ball.

TALTHYBIUS.—One ship is waiting, Hecuba.
    The chief himself has sailed.
    He went, and with him went Andromache.
    She drew tears from me there upon the ship
    mourning her country, speaking to Hector's grave,
    begging a burial for her child, your Hector's son,
    who, thrown down from the tower, lost his life.
    And this bronze-fronted shield, the dread of many
    a Greek,
    which Hector used in battle,
    that it should never, so she prayed,
    hang in strange halls where she must be a wife,
    Andromache, this dead boy's mother.
    She begged that he might lie upon it in his grave.
    And in your arms she told me I must lay him,
    for you to cover the body, if you still
    have anything, a cloak left . . .
    And to put flowers on him if you could,
    since she has gone. Her master's haste
    kept her from burying her child.
    So now, whenever you have laid him out,
    we'll heap the earth above him, then
    up with the sails!
    Do all as quickly as you can. One trouble
    I saved you.
    I let the water run on him and washed his wounds.
    I am off to dig his grave now, break up the hard
    earth.
    Working together, you and I,
    will hurry to the goal, oars swift for home.

HECUBA.—Set the shield down . . . the great round shield of
    Hector.
    I wish I need not look at it.

SOUND.—*Soldiers march off.*

HECUBA.—You Greeks, your spears are sharp but not your wits.
    You feared a child. You murdered him.
    Strange murder. You were frightened, then? You
    thought
    he might build up our ruined Troy? and yet
    when Hector fought and thousands at his side,
    we fell beneath you. Now when all is lost,
    the city captured and the Trojans dead,
    a little child like this made you afraid.

MUSIC.—*Mother's lament.*

HECUBA.—Beloved, what a death has come to you.
    If you had fallen fighting for the city,
    if you had known strong youth and love
    and godlike power, if we could think
    you had known happiness . . . if there is
    happiness anywhere.
    Poor little one. How savagely our ancient walls,
    have torn away the curls
    your mother's fingers wound and where she pressed
    her kisses. . . .
    Dear hands, the same dear shape your father's had,
    how loosely now you fall. And dear proud lips
    forever closed. False words you spoke to me
    when you would jump into my bed, call me sweet
    names,
    and tell me, Grandmother, when you are dead,
    I'll cut off a great lock of hair and lead my soldiers all
    to ride out past your tomb.
    Not you, but I, old, homeless, childless,
    must lay you in your grave, so young
    so miserably dead.
    What could a poet carve upon your tomb?
    "A child lies here whom the Greeks feared and slew."
    Ah, Greece should boast of that.
    Child, they have taken all that was your father's,
    but one thing, for your burying, you shall have,
    the bronze-barred shield.
    It kept safe Hector's mighty arm, but now
    it has lost its master.
    Come, bring such covering for the pitiful dead body
    as we still have. God has not left us much
    to make a show with. Everything I have
    I give you, child.

WOMAN 6.—Here, for your hands, they bring you clothing for the
      dead,
      got from the spoils of Troy.

WOMAN 1.—Oh, my heart! As if you touched it . . . touched it.
      Oh, this was once our prince, great in the city.

HECUBA.—Now on your body I must lay the raiment,
      all that is left of the splendor that was Troy's.
      And the dear shield of Hector, glorious in battle,

mother of ten thousand triumphs won,
it too shall have its wreath of honor.
Undying it will lie beside the dead.

WOMAN 5.—You, O child, our bitter sorrow,
earth will now receive.
Mourn, O mother.

HECUBA.—Mourn, indeed.

MUSIC.—*Ends here.*

WOMAN 3.—Weeping for all the dead . . .

HECUBA.—Bitter tears.

WOMAN 4.—Your sorrows that can never be forgotten . . .

HECUBA.—I heal your wounds; with linen I bind them.
Ah, in words only, not in truth,
a poor physician.
But soon among the dead your father
will care for you.
Go: lay our dead in his poor grave
with these last gifts of death given to him.
I think those that are gone care little
how they are buried. It is we, the living,
our vanity.

WOMAN 4.—Poor mother . . . her high hopes were stayed on you,
and they are broken.
They called you happy at your birth,
a good man's son.
Your death was miserable exceedingly.

SOUND.—*Low rumble of fire . . . start fire music.*

WOMAN 2.—Oh, see, see . . .
On the crested height of Troy
fiery hands. They are flinging torches.
Can it be
some new evil?
Something still unknown?

SOUND.—*Shouts off stage.*

TALTHYBIUS.—Captains, attention. You have been given charge
to burn this city. Do not let your torches sleep.
Hurry the fire on.

574

When once the town is level with the ground,
then off for home and glad good-by to Troy.
(*To women*) And you, (*fading in*) you women . . .
I will arrange for you
as well, one speech for everything. . . .
Whenever a loud trumpet call is sounded,
go to the Greek ships, to embark.
Old woman, I am sorriest for you.
Follow. Odysseus' men are here to get you.
He drew you. . . . You must leave here as his
slave.

HECUBA.—The end, then. Well . . . the height of sorrow, I stand
there.
Troy is burning. . . . I am going.
But . . . hurry, old feet, if you can,
a little nearer, here, where I can see
my poor town, say good-by to her.
You were so proud a city, in all the East
the proudest. Soon your name the whole world knew
will be taken from you. They are burning you
and carrying us away, their slaves.

TALTHYBIUS.—Lead her away. Hold her; don't be too gentle.
She must be taken to Odysseus.
Give her into his hands. She is his . . .
his prize.

WOMAN 5.—Oh, terrible!
The fire lights the whole town up.
The inside rooms are burning.
The citadel . . . it is all flame now.

WOMAN 3.—Troy is vanishing. . . .
War first ruined her.
And what was left is rushing up in smoke,
the glorious houses fallen.
First the spear and then the fire.
(*Fade in wind*)

HECUBA.—O dwellings of the gods and O dear city,
the spear came first, and now
only the red flame lives there.

WOMAN 2.—The dust is rising, spreading out like a great wing of
smoke.
I cannot see my house.

575

WOMAN 3.—The name has vanished from the land,
and we are gone, one here, one there.

SOUND.—*A great crash is heard . . . falling walls of the city.*

HECUBA.—The fall of Troy.

WOMAN 1.—Earthquake and flood and the city's end . . .

MUSIC.—*Trumpet.*

HECUBA.—Farewell, dear city.
Farewell, my country, where once my children lived.
On to the ships. . . .
There below, the Greek ships wait.

MUSIC.—*The trumpet sounds again, and the women pass out . . . music swells to finale.*

ANNOUNCER.—You have been listening to the first production of the Great Plays series . . . "The Trojan Women," by Euripides, translated by Edith Hamilton, and starring Blanch Yurka in the role of Hecuba.

The commentator this afternoon was Mr. Burns Mantle, dean of American critics. "The Trojan Women" was adapted and directed by Harry MacFayden. The music was especially arranged for the play and conducted by Dr. Frank Black. The Great Plays series is an educational feature of the National Broadcasting Company and is under the supervision of Blevins Davis. Next week at this same hour "Everyman," a sixteenth century morality play, will be presented. A study manual giving complete background material for the Great Plays is available for our radio audience at the cost of 10 cents. Send stamps or money orders to the National Broadcasting Company, Radio City, New York.

Consult your local library for reading material on the remaining Great Plays of this series.

MUSIC.—*Swells to climax.*

ANNOUNCER.—"The Trojan Women" was a presentation of the National Broadcasting Company, Radio City.

576